Annals of Ulster, otherwise Annals of Senat

A chronicle of Irish Affairs from A.D. 431. To A.D. 1540

(Volume I)

Editor

William M. Hennessy

Alpha Editions

This edition published in 2019

ISBN : 9789353890599

Design and Setting By
Alpha Editions
email - alphaedis@gmail.com

annala uladh.

ANNALS OF ULSTER,

OTHERWISE,

annala senait,

ANNALS OF SENAT;

A CHRONICLE OF IRISH AFFAIRS

FROM A.D. 431, TO A.D. 1540.

EDITED, WITH A TRANSLATION AND NOTES,

BY

WILLIAM M. HENNESSY, M.R.I.A.,

THE ASSISTANT DEPUTY KEEPER OF THE RECORDS.

VOL. I.

A.D. 431—1056.

PUBLISHED BY THE AUTHORITY OF THE LORDS COMMISSIONERS OF HER MAJESTY'S TREASURY, UNDER THE DIRECTION OF THE COUNCIL OF THE ROYAL IRISH ACADEMY.

DUBLIN:
PRINTED FOR HER MAJESTY'S STATIONERY OFFICE,
BY ALEXANDER THOM & CO. (LIMITED), ABBEY STREET.

And to be purchased, either directly or through any Bookseller, from
HODGES, FIGGIS & Co., 104, GRAFTON STREET, DUBLIN; or
EYRE & SPOTTISWOODE, EAST HARDING STREET, FLEET STREET, E.C.; or
ADAM AND CHARLES BLACK, 6, NORTH BRIDGE, EDINBURGH.

1887.

Price 10s.

PREFATORY NOTE.

The Editor was desirous that the important publication of which this forms the first volume should be published in a complete form, and not in separate volumes, for the reason that, considering the great value of the Chronicle, the questions so often discussed regarding the compilers and the sources from which the work was compiled, and the relation to each other of the MSS. from which the text has been formed, it seemed necessary that these subjects should be dealt with in an Introductory Essay. But it would be obviously impossible to write an Introduction of the nature required before the whole work was in print. The Council of the Royal Academy, under whose direction the publication of the work has been placed by the Lords Commissioners of Her Majesty's Treasury, having ordered the immediate publication of this volume, the Editor submitted respectfully to their directions. The Introduction must therefore appear in the last volume of the work—in that, namely, containing the Appendices and Index.

W. M. H.

June, 1887.

Annala Uladh.

ANNALS OF ULSTER;

OTHERWISE,

Annala Senait.

ANNALS OF SENAT.

ANNALA ULADH.

IHC,

MEI EST INCIPERE, TUI EST FINIRE.

Fol. 16*aa*. Kt. Ienair. Anno ab incarnatione domini cccc.° xxx.° i.° Palladius ad Scotos a Celestino urbis Romae episcopo ordinatur episcopus, Aetio et Valerio consulibus primus mittitur in Hiberniam, ut Christum credere potuissent, anno Teodosi uiii°.

---

1 *Palladius.*—Prosper Aquitanus, in his *Chronicon*, Basso et Antiocho coss. (*i.e.* A.D. 431), after mention of the Council of Ephesus adds: "Ad Scotos in Christum credentes, ordinatus a papa Cœlestio Palladius, et primus episcopus mittitur" (*Opp.* p. 432). This cardinal record in Irish church history has been repeated by Beda, *Chron.*, p. 26, and *Hist. Eccl.* twice, i., 13, v., 24; where he assigns 430 as the year, *i.e.* of his mission, whereas 431 was the date of his arrival. See Pagi, *Critica*, t. ii., pp. 214*b*, 238*b*. Subsequent chroniclers, enumerated by Ussher, *Wks.* vi., 353, have adopted the same form of words, among them Marianus Scotus, who notices both Palladius and Patricius, under the 8th of Theodosius, junior. Palladius is styled by Muirchu, writing circ. 690, "Archidiaconus pape Caelestini" (Bk. Arm., fol. 2*aa*). So the Vit. Sec. in Colgan, *Trias Thaum.*, p. 13*b*; the Vit. Quarta, *ib.* p. 38*b*; Probus, *ib.* 48*b*; the Vit. Tripart. huasal dechon, which Colgan not very closely renders, "eximium Diaconum," *ib.* p. 123*a*.

2 *Celestinus.*—The writers in the Book of Armagh note him as "quadragensimus quintus a sancto Petro apostolo," fol. 2*aa*, 16*aa*. But Prosper, Idatius, and Marcellinus, whom these ann. profess to follow, have XLI. Sixtus, his successor, is set down next year as XLII.

3 *Etius and Valerius.*—Their consulship belongs to 432. Bassus and Antiochus were the consuls of this year.

4 *Might believe.*—Prosper's *in Christum credentes* has, from Ussher down, been generally understood as implying that there existed at the time in Ireland a number of acephalous Christians. Muirchu, who, writing about 690, says of Palladius that he had been ordained and sent "ad hanc insolam sub brumali rigore possitam convertendam" (Bk. Arm., fo. 2*aa*), or "ad doctrinam Scottorum" (*ib.*

ANNALS OF ULSTER.

JESUS,

Mine it is to Begin, Thine it is to Finish.

KALENDS of January. In the year 431 from the Incarnation of the Lord, Palladius,[1] ordained by Celestinus,[2] bishop of the City of Rome, is sent, in the consulship of Etius and Valerius,[3] into Ireland, first bishop to the Scots, that they might believe[4] in Christ; in the 8th year of Theodosius.[5] [431.]

16*aa*). Nennius comes next, about half a century after the Book of Armagh was written, and he, drawing as he says, "de historiis Scottorum licet inimicorum," expressly states "ad Scottos in Christum convertendos" (p. 41). Probus uses language similar to that of Muirchu (Tr. Th. 48*b*). The Tripart. Life, the substance of which can be proved to be older than 800, says, do praicept do Goidelaibh, 'to instruct the Gaeidhil'. So Vit. Sec. in Colgan, *Tr. Th.*, 13*b*; Vit. Tert. (*ib.* 23*a*); Vit. Quart. (*ib.* 38*b*); Jocelin (*ib.* 70*a*). Ussher's Irish Life had what his interpreter renders "ad prædicandum Hibernis"; while his Latin Tripart. Life had "ad Scotos convertendos ad Christum" (*Wks.*, vi. 368). Even for the wording of the present text, which is so rude, there is a counterpart in the Annals of Inisfallen at 431, "Palladius ad Scotos a Caelestino, urbis Romae episcopo, ordinatus, primus mittitur in Hiberniam, ut Christum credere potuissent." This and the text would seem to imply that the Irish had the offer of conversion, but refused it. Prosper closed his chronicle in 455, but in a work which is peculiarly important as having been written in 433, *i.e.* 2 years after Palladius' arrival, he says of Caelestine, "Ordinato Scotis episcopo, dum Romanam insulam (*i e.* Britanniam) studet servare Catholicam, fecit etiam barbaram Christianam" *Contra Cassianum*, c. 20 (Opp. 209*a*). Innes reconciles the two statements of Prosper to his own satisfaction (*Hist.*, p. 55); but Sir James Ware, more in accordance with Irish writers, says "Et ad Prosperi ipsa verba, *Scotos in Christum credentes*, quod attinet, ea fortasse referenda sunt ad tempus quo Prosper Chronicon suum scripsit, quando nempe longe maxima pars Hiberniæ ad Christi fidem, S. Patricii prædicatione et operâ suâ fuit conversa" (*S. Patr. Opusc.* p. 107).

[5] *Theodosius.*—See note on Theodosius the younger, in the year following.

Kl. Ienair (ui. f. lun). Anno domini cccc.° xxx.° ii.° (iiii. dc. xxxii. secundum Dionisium). Patricius peruenit ad Hiberniam nono anno regni Teodosii minoris, primo anno episcopatus Xisti, xl. ii. episcopi Romane eclesie. Sic enumerant Beda et Marcillius et Issiodorus in cronicis suis. [In xu (uel xiiii) anno regni Laegaire mic Neill. Ab initio mundi iuxta lxx. interpreter u. dccc. lxxxii; iuxta uero Ebreos iiii. dcxxxiii. Ab incarnatione uero iuxta Ebreos dclxxxii, secundum autem Dionisium cccc. xxx. ii.° anni sunt; secundum uero Bedam cccc. xxxi anni sunt.]

Kl. Ienair. Anno domini cccc. xxx. iii° (iiii. dc. xxxiii.)

Kl. Ienair. (ii. f. lu. u.) Anno domini cccc.° xxx.° iiii.° (iiii. dcxxxiiii.) Cetna brat Saxan di Ere [no ind Eirinn].

---

[1] *Friday.*—This was leap-year, and the Sunday letter CB, as the 1st of January fell on the sixth day of the week. It may be observed here, once for all, that the chronological notations, except the year of the Lord, whether at the beginning or close of the entries of each year, are not in *prima manu*, but added subsequently in paler ink.

[2] *Dionysius.*—See his system referred to at A.D. 531 *infra.*

[3] *Patrick arrived.*—See Ussher, *Wks.*, vi., 370, 371, 396-407, 443; Todd, *St. Patrick*, pp. 392-399.

[4] *Theodosius the younger.*—There are three dates for the commencement of the reign of Theodosius junior—1st, A.D. 402, when he was declared *Augustus* by his father, Arcadius; 2nd, A.D. 408, when Arcadius died, and he succeeded to the empire of the East; 3rd, A.D. 423, when, on August 15, his uncle Honorius, Emperor of the West, died, and thus left him supreme in the regions of Latin. The third era is that which these Annals adopt, as did Beda, in *Chron.*, and *H.E.*, i., 13. So also the Chron. Scot.; Ann. Inisf.; Leab. Brec.; Vit. Tripart., and Marianus Scotus. Tirechan states, "xiii. anno Teothosii," but 30+24 would be according to the earlier computations, so that his xiii. is evidently a clerical error for uiii. Baronius takes exception to the present date, and observes at A.C. 429, vii., "ex Prospero corrigendum esse Bedam"; upon which Smith well observes, "non ex Prospero Beda, sed ex Beda Baronius corrigendus est" (Baeda, i., 13, p. 51). See Pagi, *Critica*, ii., 214*b*, n., xi.

[5] *Xistus.*—Over this name is written, in another hand *Celestine*, which is an error. Celestine died 13 July, 432, and Sixtus iii. was consecrated eleven days afterwards. In the chronicles of Prosper, Idatius, and Marcellinus, Sixtus is set down as 42nd Bishop of Rome.

Chronicles.—This is a very slov-

Kal. Jan. (Friday,[1] m. . . .) A.D. 432 (4636, according [432.]
to Dionysius).[2] Patrick arrived[3] at Ireland, in the 9th year of the reign of Theodosius the younger,[4] in the first year of the episcopate of Xistus,[5] the 42nd bishop of the Church of Rome. So Beda, and Marcellinus, and Isidorus compute in their chronicles.[6] [In the 15th (or 14th) year of the reign of Laegaire, son of Niall.[7] From the beginning of the world,[8] according to the LXX. Interpreters, 5885 years; but according to the Hebrews, 4636. Also, from the Incarnation, according to the Hebrews, 685; but, according to Beda, there are 431 years.]

Kal. Jan. A.D. 433 (4637). [433.]

Kal. Jan. (Monday. m. 5.) A.D. 434 (4638.) The [434.]
first prey[9] by the Saxons[10] from Ireland [or, in Ireland].

---

enly entry; the chronological order of the writers is inverted, and Beda says nothing on the subject. Marcellinus has—"Valerio et Aetio coss. (*i.e.* 432), Romanæ ecclesiæ Xystus xlii. episcopus ordinatus, vixit annis viii."

[7] *Laegaire, son of Niall.*—O'Flaherty makes the 4th of Laeghaire to synchronize with 432; therefore 428 + 35, the length of his reign, makes 463, the correct date of his death. Ann. Inisfall., and the ancient authorities cited by Petrie from Leabhar Brec, place Patrick's arrival in the 4th of Laeghaire (*Tara*, 77, 79); so also the F. Mast. Nennius says, "In quinto anno Loygare regis exorsus est praedicare fidem Christi" (p. 44). But though Ann. Inisf. here assign the 4th, further on they have a stray sentence, which contradicts this—"Patricius vero xiii$_o$ vel ut alii dicunt xiiii°. anno ejusdem venit ad Scotos Patricius." And in the present entry xiiii. is written *al. man.* over xii. The addition therefore of 10 to the regnal year of Laeghaire brings us down to 443, the date at which Todd has arrived from independent considerations, *S. Patr.* 392–399

[8] *Beginning of the world.*—The whole of this chronological paragraph is added by another hand, which subsequently appears in similar additions.

[9] *Prey.*—The Irish brat or brad seems to be cognate to the Latin *praeda.* From brad comes the adject. bradach "thievish," the noun bradaig, a "thief," and the name mac bradaig, now Brady. At 820 *infra*, we find brad in the form praed.

[10] *Saxons.*—The Saxons first appear in history at A.D. 287, and then as marauders. At 364, according to Ammianus Marcellinus, "Picti Saxonesque, et Scotti et Attacotti Britannos ærumnis vexavere continuis" (xxvi. 5). They were associated with the Picts when defeated by the Britons in the Alleluiatic victory, which Ussher, on just grounds, places at the year 430, and which was certainly prior to the year 435, as St. Germanus the leader died that year. See his excellent obss., *Wks.* v. 385,

Kl. Ienair. Anno domini cccc.° xxx.° u.° (iiii. dc. xxxix.) Mors Bressail regis Laigen. [Orosius et Prosper et Cirillus in doctrina Christi floruerunt secundum quosdam].

Fol. 16ab. Kl. Ienair. (4 f. l. 27.) Anno domini cccc.° xxx. ui.° (iiii. dc. xl.) Uel hic mors Bresail. Orosius et Prosper et Cirillus in Christo floruerunt, [uel in doctrina Christi, secundum alios. Uel hoc anno Bresal mortuus est secundum alios].

Kl. Ienair. (6 f., l. 9, alias 8a.) Anno domini cccc.° xxx.° uii.° (iiii. dc. xli°.) Finnbarr mac hui Bardene.

Kl. Ienair. (7 f., 20 lunae.) Anno domini cccc.° xxx.° uiii.° (iiii. dc. xlii.°) Senchus mor do scribunn; [uel quod hic debet inseri Secundus cum sociis secundum alium librum].

Also Thorpe's Lappenberg, vol. i., 62, 63. The Irish invasion here recorded may have been a sequel to their defeat in Britain. These annals assign their permanent arrival in England to 464; and they add a second descent on Ireland at 471 *infra*. The authorities, followed by the Books of Lecan and Ballymote, represent the wife of Eochaidh Muighmedhoin, Cairenn Casdubh ("curly black"), mother of Niall ix. Host., as daughter of a king of the Saxons. Which is adopted by O'Flaherty, *Ogyg.* 376, 393. Indorb Find, also, wife of Eoghan, son of Niall, is said to have been daughter of a Saxon prince. Mac Firbis, however, *Geneal. MS.*, p. 108, contends that the first named woman was more likely to have been Pictish or North British. It is curious that the B. of Armagh, referring to the death of Munissa, a disciple of St. Patrick, whom some of his Lives style *Britonissa*, speaks "de morte Moneisen *Saxonissæ*" (fol. 20 *ab*).

[1] *Bressal.*—More fully in the F. Mast. (435), "Breasal Bealach, son of Fiacha Aiceadh, son of Cathair Mór (king of Leinster), died." The death of Cathair Mór is set down at A.D. 174, so that there must be a deficiency of several generations in the descent. See Keating, 308; *Ogyg.* 311; *B. of Rights*, 201–203.

[2] *According to some.*—This, from *Orosius*, added *al. manu.* See under next year.

[3] *Orosius—Cyril.*—Ororius, in A. by a clerical error. Paulus Orosius, a priest of Tarragona, flor. 416. In 413 he was sent by two Spanish bishops to St. Augustin; during his stay with whom, and at whose instance, he composed his *Historia.* St. Augustin characterizes him as "Vigil ingenio, promtus eloquio, flagrans studio," *Epist.* 166. Prosper, of Aquitaine, appeared before pope Cœlestine, in 431 (the year of Palladius' mission), to vindicate the memory of St. Augustin. In 433 he

Kal. Jan. A.D. 435 (4639). Death of Bressal,[1] King of Leinster. [Orosius, and Prosper, and Cyril flourished in the doctrine of Christ, according to some.][3] [435.]

Kal. Jan. (Wedn., m. 27). A.D. 436 (4640). Or, here the death of Bresal. Orosius, Prosper, and Cyril,[3] flourished in Christ [or, in the doctrine of Christ, according to others. Or, in this year Bresal died, according to others.] [436.]

Kal. Jan. (Frid., m. 9, or 8). A.D. 437 (4641). Finnbarr[4] son of Ua Bardene. [437.]

Kal. Jan. (Saturd., m. 20). A.D. 438 (4642). The Senchus Mor[5] was written. (Or, here should be inserted[6] Secundus with his companions, according to another book.) [438.]

---

published his *Collator*, and in 455 he completed his *Chronicon*, which is a very important record. Cyril, patriarch of Alexandria, presided at the third General Council, in 431, and died in 444. The mention of his name here was probably suggested by Isidore, who says, in his *Chronicon*, "Hoc tempore Cyrillus Alexandriæ episcopus, insignis est habitus." *Opp.* vii. 101. The best edition of his works is that by Jo. Aubertus, 6 tom. (in 7 voll.), fol. Paris, 1638. Gibbon accuses him of tyranny, murder, and a long list of crimes and infirmities. *Decline*, ch. 47. With such a wide margin as the *claruere* of these three writers it was absurd to repeat the entry the year following.

[4] *Finnbarr.*—The F. Mast. borrow this entry, changing the descent to mac Ua Ƅaıṗꝺene, and adding ꝺecc, 'died'; but they give no clue to his lineage or history. O'Donovan supposed that *Ua Baird*, which appears in St. Patrick's kindred, might be intended. It is more likely, however, that the reference is to some one maccu Ƅaıṗꝺene, 'of the sons of Bairdene,' such as the *Dal Bairdine* of Uladh, whom Tighern. notices at 628, these Annals at 627, and the F. Mast. at 623. Colgan's conjecture of Firtnanus, *Tr. Thaum.* 268*a*, is inadmissible.

[5] *Senchus Mor.*—"Chronicon Magnum scriptum est." O'Connor, *R. H. SS.* iv. 1. It was a body of laws, the first materials of which were compiled by St. Patrick and some of his disciples; and which grew by subsequent accretions till it attained its present voluminous dimensions. The Senchuſ Móṗ, occupying 4 vols. of the intended series of the *Ancient Laws of Ireland*, was published in the years 1865, 1869, 1873–79, edited by Professors Hancock, O'Mahony, and Richey, from the texts and translations of the late Dr. O'Donovan and Professor O'Curry. In the learned Prefaces to these important volumes full information is given of the code.

[6] *Inserted.*—*Inserti*, for *inseri*, A. See under next year.

.b. Kl. Ienair. (1. f., l. 1.) Anno domini cccc.° xxx.° ix.° (iiii. dc. xliii.) Secundus, Auxilius, et Serninus mittuntur et episcopi ipsi in Hiberniam in auxilium Patricii.

Kl. Ienair. (2 f., l. u.) Anno domini cccc.° xxxx.° (iiii. dc. xliiii.) Exitus Xisti episcopi Romane aeclesie, qui uixit uiii. annis in episcopatu Romane eclesie et xxuii. diebus, ut Beda narrat in cronico suo. Alii libri dicunt Maine filium Neill in isto anno perisse. [Augustin naem ar na gabail on Beathaigh so ansa seised bliadain dhec ar 3 xx.id a aise, episcopatus uero sui anno 40. Floruit Augustin circa annos domini cccc.tos.]

---

[1] *Secundus.* — *Recte* Secundinus. Called Sechnall by the Irish, and from him domnach Sechnaill, now Dunshaughlin, in the S.E. of Meath, derives its name. Born in 374, which is the alleged year of St. Patrick's birth, who was his uncle, and in honour of whom he composed the hymn *Audite omnes.* See Ussher, *Wks.* vi. 383, 384, 401, 518; Colgan, *Tr. Thaum.*, 226*b*; Todd, *Lib. Hymnor.* 7–42. His death is entered below at 447.

Auxilius.—Brother of Secundinus, sixth son of Restitut Ua mBaird, and, with Isserninus, ordained as a coadjutor of St. Patrick. In Irish his name assumes the form of Ausaille or Usaille. Cill-Ausaille, now Killashee, in co. Kildare is called from him, and he is also patron of Cill Ua mBaird, now Killymard, near Donegal, in the county of the same name. His death is entered at 459 *infra.*

[3] *Serninus.*—Generally written Isserninus; but sometimes Eserninus, *B. Arm.* fol. 15*bb*; Serenus, *Tr. Thaum.* p. 14*a*; Iserinus, Nennius, 43. In the B. of Armagh he is in three instances called epscop Fith, one of which is as a gloss upon his name, in the following passage "Patricius et Iserninus (.i. epscop Fith) cum Germano fuerunt in Olsiodra civitate. Germanus vero Isernino dixit ut praedicare in Hiberniam veniret, atque prumptus fuit oboedire, etiam in quamcumque partem mitteretur nisi in Hiberniam. Germanus dixit Patricio, et tu, an oboediens eris? Patricius dixit, Fiat sicut vis. Germanus dixit, Hoc inter nos erit; et non potuerit Iserninus in Hiberniam non transire. Patricius venit in Hiberniam. Iserninus vero missus est in aliam regionem: sed ventus contrarius detulit illum in dexteram [*i.e.* australem] partem Hiberniæ," (fol. 18 *aa*); probably Magh Itha, or the barony of Forth, on the south coast of the county of Wexford. *Ann. Inisfall.* at 440, say, "Secundinus et Auxiliarius, et Iserninus mittuntur in auxilium Patricii, nec tamen tenuerunt apostolatum, nisi Patricius solus." So also *Chron. Scot.* 438. This joint action appears in the titles of some collections of Irish Canons, and strikes the eye in the

Kal. Jan. (Sund., m. 1). A.D. 439 (4643). Secundus,[1] Auxilius,[2] and Serninus,[3] themselves also bishops, are sent to Ireland, in aid of Patrick.[4] [439.]

Kal. Jan. (Mond., m. 5). A.D. 440 (4644). The decease of Xistus,[5] bishop of the church of Rome, who lived 8 years and 27 days in the episcopate of the church of Rome, as Beda, in his chronicle, relates. Some books say that Maine son of Niall[6] perished in this year. [Saint Augustin[7] taken away from this life in the 76th year of his age, and the 40th year of his episcopate. Augustin flourished about the year of Our Lord 400.] [440.]

---

earliest synodicals which appear in Sir Henry Spelman's, and Wilkins' great collections of British Councils. For the entry of the death of Iserninus, see at 468 *infra*.

[4] *Patrick.*—In the margin of A. is an entry partly obliterated: no comaḋ air . . . . genemain brigoi, 'or, perhaps, on this [year] should be the birth of Brigid.' See under 456, *infra*.

[5] *Xistus.*—Sixtus iii. In the chronicles of Prosper, Idatius, and Marcellinus, he is reckoned 42nd Bishop of the church of Rome; as also in these annals, at 432. His tenure of 8 years and 19 days, as calculated by Anastasius, is the correct period. These annals add 8 days, and also err in citing Beda as the authority, for he makes no mention, in either his Chronicle or History, of the pontificate of this Sixtus.

[6] *Maine, son of Niall.*—Fourth son of Niall ix. Host. and one of the four brothers, whose posterity constituted the Southern Hy Neill. His descendants, who occupied Teathbha or Teffia, were represented by O'Caharny or Fox, Magawley, O'Breen, O'Daly, &c. in the present counties of Longford and Westmeath, see Keating, p. 372; *Ogyg.* p. 401. The *Tripart. Life* (ii. 26) states that Patrick, when he visited south Teffia, converted and baptized this Maine; after which he founded the church of Ardachadh (Ardagh); but that Maine, on account of a deception which he practised, incurred the saint's severe displeasure. Colgan, *Trias Thaum.*, 132*b*.

[7] *St. Augustin.*—Bishop of Hippo. Possidius, in his *Life*, says (cap. 31), "vixit annis LXXVI. in clericatu autem vel episcopatu annis ferme xl." Beda has the same words, *Chron.* p. 26; and Marianus Scotus, *Chron.* 431. He was ordained priest in 391, and bishop in December, 395. He died v. Kl. Sept. (Aug. 28), A.D 430. The insertion in the text is, therefore, ten years too late. See Tillemont, *Memoires*, tom. xiii. p. 943; and the Latin version of the substance of his admirable memoir, which was made by Dom Hugues Vaillant and Dom Jacques du Frische, members of the congregation of St. Maur, in the exhaustive *Vita* which forms the first portion of the last volume of the Benedictine St. Augustin, cols. 102, 141, 491.

Kl. Ienair. Anno domini cccc.° xl.° i.° Leo ordinatur xl. ii. Romane eclesie episcopus; et probatus est in fide catolica Patricius episcopus.

Kl. Ienair. Anno domini cccc.° xl.° ii.°

Fol. 16ba. .b. Kl. Ienair. Anno domini cccc.° xl.° iii.° Patricius episcopus ardore fidei et doctrina Christi florens in nostra prouincia.

Kl. Ienair. Anno domini cccc.° xl.° iiii.° Ard Maċa fundata est. Ab urbe condita usque ad hanc ciuitatem fundatam m. cxc. iiii.

Kl. Ienair. Anno domini cccc.° xl.° u.° Naṫi mac Fiacraċ ṁaiġe Tail, mic Eachach Muiġmedoin ag sleib Ealpa [no iar na ḃeim] do ṡoiġnen ṫeinntiġe og dol tar torainn obiit, et xx.a tribus annis regnauit in Hibernia.

---

[1] *Leo.*—Consecrated Sept. 22, 440. These annals, at 432, correctly reckoned Sixtus III, 42nd Bishop of Rome, so that 42 here is a mistake for 43, which is the number in Prosper, Idatius, and Marcellinus.

Catholic faith.—*Ann. Inisfal.* at 442, have "Probatio sancti Patricii in fide Catholica." *Ann. Clonmacnois*, at 427, say "Pope Leo was ordained the 46th or 47th to succeede; by whom St. Patrick was approved in the Catholique Religion, and by the rest of the Popes of Rome that succeeded in his time, and then after flourished in the heate of Christian Religion in this Land."

[3] *In our province.*—Todd understands this of Ulster, and couples it with the founding of Armagh mentioned under the next year. *St. Patrick*, 470. O'Conor's copy, however, reads *nostra Hibernia*, which gives the term *provincia* a wider application. At the council of Arles in 314 Britain was regarded as a *provincia*. In 592 Pope Gregory designates Italy a *provincia;* and half a century later John, pope-elect, writing to the Irish prelates speaks of Ireland as "provincia vestra" (Beda, H. E., ii. 19). The use of the term *provincia* at that date forbids the limitation of it to the Irish coiġeaḋ or province, as long subsequently adopted in ecclesiastical language. See Reeves, *Adamnan*, p. 451. Sicily was the first recipient of the designation *provincia*.

[4] *Ard-Macha was founded.*—In the Book of Armagh is the following curious notice concerning Trim: "ædificavit æclessiam cum illis xxv. anno antequam fundata esset æclessia Altimacbæ (fol. 16*ba*); which Ussher reads "vigesimo secundo" (*Wks.*, vi. 414). His *Tripart. Vit.* had xxv.; so also the Bodleian *Tripart. Life*, Colgan's copy (*Tr. Th.*, p. 129*a*); but the Brit. Mus. copy has xxii. See Colgan's note, p. 100 (*recte* 110) *b*, n. 57. The *F. Mast.* place the found-

Kal. Jan. A.D. 441. Leo[1] ordained 42nd bishop of the church of Rome: and Patrick, the bishop, was approved in the Catholic faith.[2] [441.]

Kal. Jan. A.D. 442. [442.]

Kal. Jan. A.D. 443. Patrick, the bishop, flourishing in the zeal of faith and the doctrine of Christ, in our Province.[3] [443.]

Kal. Jan. A.D. 444. Ard-Macha was founded.[4] From the building of Rome[5] to the founding of this city is 1194 years. [444.]

Kal. Jan. A.D. 445. Nathi,[6] son of Fiachra of Magh Tail,[7] son of Eochaidh Mughmedhoin,[8] was struck by lightning at the Alps mountain as he was passing the limits of the same, and died. He reigned 23 years in Ireland. [445.]

---

ing of Trim at 432, and of Armagh at 457. See Colgan, *Tr. Thaum.*, 290*b*; Ussher, *Wks.*, vi., 414, 570 (an. 445); Lanigan, i., 312, 315, 317; Todd, *St. Patrick*, 260, 268–480.

[5] *Building of Rome.*—Foundation of Rome (according to Polybius), 751, B.C., which + 444 = 1195. See Ussher, *Wks.*, vi., 414; Colgan, *Tr. Th.*, 110*b*, n. 57. Todd errs in saying, "The Dublin MS. of these Annals seems to read 1197" (p. 469); it is plainly 1194. Ussher, who owned the MS, so read it, and there can be no uncertainty about the reading, for a later hand has entered in the margin opposite, in Arabic numerals, 1194.

[6] *Nathi.*—The death of Nathi, or Dathi, occurred before the year at which these Annals commence, namely in 428; as he succeeded in 405, and reigned 23 years. Accordingly it is at 428 that his death is recorded by the *F. Mast.*, and O'Flaherty (*Ogyg.*, 159, 413). His name, however, occurs in the *Ann. Inisfal.* at 446, and it would seem that that chronicle, as well as this, borrowed from some authority which used a different computation. Supposing it to be correct, and that the arrival of Patrick occurred in the 15th of Laeghaire, it would almost coincide with the death of Sen Patrick, and would upset the chronology of these Annals. We must, therefore, conclude that the present entry is 18 years too late. Regarding Dathi's death, see Keating, 394; *Ogyg.*, 413; and above all O'Donov. in *Hy Fiachrach*, 17–27, 345, 346. The *F. Mast.*, at 449, enter, instead, the death of his brother Amhalgaidh.

[7] *Magh Tail.*—Seems to be a poetical name for Fiachra's inheritance. O'Huidhrin applies the term móp maġ Tail to the Dalcassian dominion of Brian Boru (*Topogr. Poems*, 98). O'Curry, *MS. Mater.*, p. 479.

[8] *Mughmeadhoin.*— "In English *Moist-middle*, because he was much troubled with ye flux of ye bellye."—*Ann. Clonmac.*

Kt. Ienair. (iii. f., l. 18.) Anno domini cccc.° xl.° vi. (iiii. dc. l.) Bellum Feimin in quo cecidit filius Coerthin filii Coelbot. Alii dicunt di Cruithnib fuisse.

.b. Kt. Ienair. (4. f., l. 29.) Anno domini cccc.° xl.° vii.° (iiii. dc. li.) Quies Secundini sancti lxx. v.° anno etatis sue.

Kt. Ienair. Anno domini cccc.° xl.° viii.° Ingenti terraemotu per loca varia imminente plurimi urbis auguste muri recenti adhuc re aedificatione constructi cum l. vii. turribus conruerunt.

Fol. 16bb. Kt. Ienair. Anno domini cccc.° xl.° ix.° Teodosius imperator iuvenis finem fecit sicut adfirmat Marcillinus. Locum Teodosii Marcianus imperator adeptus est, ut Marcillinus dicit.

Kt. Ienair. Anno domini cccc.° l.°

---

[1] *Femhin.*—Or Magh Feimhin, as in *Ann. Inisfal.*, 448. Keating gives the origin of the name at p. 142. It was a plain in the S.E. part of the present co. of Tipperary, comprising the barony of Iffa and Offa, and represented by the old rural deanery of Kilsbillan, in the diocese of Lismore. It was taken about this time from Ossory, in Leinster, by Aengus, son of Nadfraech, king of Munster, and transferred to the northern Deise in his province, for which he suffered at Cenn-Losnadh in 489. Another battle of Femhin is recorded at 472 *infra.*

[2] *Son of Coerthenn.*—*Ann. Inisfal.*, at 448, have Cath muighe Femin etir Munechu 7 Laighniu in quo cecidit Cartinn meic Coelbath qui iecit genus Laing. Coelbadh, son of Crunn Badhrai, king of Uladh, was slain in 358. He was great-grandson of Fiacha Araidhe, from whom the Dal-Araidhe, or Irish Picts, derived their descent and name. The grandson of Coelbadh, who fell in this battle, was probably the leader of Dalaradian auxiliaries in the service of the king of Munster, and mainly instrumental in the acquisition of Femhin. See note on *Cruithne* at an. 573 *infra.* Reeves, *Eccl. Antiqq.* 337, 349, 353, and *Adamnan*, 93, 94. The *Chron. Scot.* an. 445, makes Colboth son of Niall.

[3] *Secundinus.*—Or Sechnall, of whom an. 439 *supra.* His festival is Nov. 27, at which day, Aengus wrote in his *Felire*, circ. 800—

Sruaim ecnai conani
Sechnall mind ar flatha
Rogab ceol soer sodaid
Molad Patraic Macha.

A stream of wisdom with splendour,
Sechnall diadem of our realm,
Chanted a song, a noble solace,
A praise of Patrick of Macha.

The *Life of Declan* says: "de quo fertur quod ipse primus episcopus sub humo Hiberniæ exivit." See Ussher, *Wks.*, vi., 384; *Vit. Tripart.*, iii., 81; (*Trias Thaum.*, 165*b*.) The deaths of St. Patrick's three coadjutor

Kal. Jan. (Tuesd., m. 18.) A.D. 446 (4650). Battle of Femhin,[1] wherein fell the son of Coerthenn,[2] son of Coelboth. Some say that he was of the Cruithne. [446.]

Kal. Jan. (Wednesd., m. 29.) A.D. 447 (4651). Repose of Secundinus[3] the holy, in the 75th year of his age. [447.]

Kal. Jan. A.D. 448. By a violent earthquake,[4] which prevailed in various places, very many walls of the Imperial city[5] rebuilt of masonry still fresh, together with 57 towers, were thrown down. [448.]

Kal. Jan. A.D. 449. The Emperor Theodosius[6] closed his life, as Marcellinus affirms.[7] Marcianus succeeded as Emperor in room of Theodosius, as Marcellinus states. [449.]

Kal. Jan. A.D. 450. [450.]

---

bishops are entered in these annals at the years 447, 459, 468.

[4] *Earthquake.*—This account is borrowed word for word from the Chronicle of Marcellinus, where it is recorded under Indict. xv. *Ardabure et Callepio Coss.* (*i.e.*, A.D. 447). Beda also notices the event, *Chron.* p. 31, and *H.E.*, i., 13. The fullest account of it is in Evagrius, who explains the word *imminente* by ὅ δὲ πάθος καὶ ἐπὶ χρόνον τῆς γῆς ἐπεκράτησεν (Eccl. Hist., i. 17).

[5] *Imperial city.*—"Urbs Augusta" is ten times used by Marcellinus, and is borrowed by other writers, to denote Constantinople. The expression in Evagrius—ἀνὰ τὴν βασιλίδα was rendered *in palatio*, till Valesius gave the proper interpretation, *in urbe Regia.* We find *Regia urbs* of Marcellinus copied in these annals, at 526 *infra*.

[6] *Theodosius.*—Junior. In the top margin of A. there is this note on the name, in a different, but nearly coeval, hand, "Ab isto Theodossio Bononia habuit privilegia studii po: et regnare cepit anno Domini cccc. 25 . Et regnavit annis xxvii. De hoc vide gl. in Cle , *i.e.*, de *Magistris* in verbo *Bononiensi.*" The refereuce is to the Corpus Juris Canonici, in the Clementinæ, lib. v., tit. i. c. 5, where it is stated, "Hoc constat quod Bononia habuit privilegia studii a Theodosio: de minore tamen intelligo, qui regnare cepit (prout ex chronicis quas veriores puto, percipio) anno Domini ccccxxxv., et regnavit annis xxvii. (xxvi. in some copies). Quo tamen anno sui imperii hec concesserit, non percipio: currentibus autem ccccli. successit Martianus." Tom. iii., col. 286.

[7] *Marcellinus affirms.*—His words are: "Indict. iii. Valentiniano, vii., et Abieno Coss. (*i.e.*, A.D. 450). Theodosius Imperator vivendi finem fecit: regnavit post mortem Archadii patris sui annos xlii. Loco ejus Marcianus imperium adeptus est." Galland. *Bibl.* x., 348. He died, 28 July, 450. Pagi, ii., 317. Beda agrees with these annals in antedating Marcianus' accession one year. *H.E.* i., 15.

.b. Kl. Ienair. Anno domini cccc.° l.° i.° Pasca domini uiii.° Kalendas Maii celebratum est. [Vel uerius hic quieuit Teodosius minor.]

Kl. Ienair. Anno domini cccc.° l.° ii.° Hic alii dicunt natiuitatem sancte Brigite. Interfectio magna Lagenarum. [Vel uerius hoc anno Marcianus imperator successit Teodosio Minori.]

Kl. Ienair. (u. f., l. 5.) Anno domini cccc.° l.° iii.° (iiii. dc. luni.) Caṫroineaḋ ria Loeġaire mac Neill for Laiġniḃ.

Kl. Ienair. (6ª f., l. 16.) Anno domini cccc.° l.° iiii.° (iiii. dc. luiii.) Cena (alias feis) Teṁra apud (alias la) Loeġaire filium Neill.

---

[1] *The Lord's Passover.*—The Sunday letter of this year was G, and the 24th of April fell upon Tuesday; from which some might suppose that the Irish at this period were Quartodecimans, *i.e.*, observing Easter not on the Sunday which followed the 14th after the vernal equinox, but on the 14th itself, irrespectively of the day on which it fell. Both A and B mark this year in the margin as bissextile; but it is 452 that was really so; and its Sunday letter is FE, the 24th of April falling upon Sunday. But there can be little doubt that the present entry is misplaced, and properly belongs to 455, in which year Easter was kept on the 24th of April by the Church of Alexandria, but on the 17th by some of the Latins, who followed the computation of Victorius. Prosper, in the closing paragraph of his Chronicle, Valentiniano, viii. et Anthemio Coss. (*i.e.*, an. 455), writes: "Eodem anno Pascha Dominicum die viii. Kalendas Maii celebratum est, pertinaci intentione Alexandrini Episcopi, cui omnes Orientales consentiendum putaverunt: quamvis sanctus Papa Leo XV. Kalendas Maii potius observandum protestaretur." *Opp* p. 438. In this year Leo the Great wrote to the Emperor Marcian to state that "eundem diem venerabilis Festi omnibus Occidentalium partium sacerdotibus intimasse, quem Alexandrini Episcopi declaravit instructio, id est, ut anno præsenti viii. Kalendas Maii Pascha celebretur, omissis omnibus scrupulis propter studium unitatis et pacis." Leo referred the question in 451 to the best informed authorities, especially Paschasinus of Lilybæum, and further commissioned Julianus, when proceeding to the Council of Chalcedon, to consult the most eminent fathers present on the subject, in order to avoid all future uncertainty. Pagi, ii., an. 453. The *Ann. Clonmac.* give a curious turn: "The Resurrection of Our Lord was celebrated the Eight of Kalends of May by the Pelagian heresie"! See Labbé, *Concordia Chronol.*, Pt. i., pp. 105, 108. The *Ann. Inisfal.* are very exact in assigning to the year 455 "Pascha in viii. Kal. Maii." These annals, however, are four years behind. Marianus Scotus says "Hoc anno, *i.e.*, 455

Kal. Jan. A.D. 451. The Lord's Passover[1] was celebrated on the 8th of the Kalends of May. [Or, in this year, Theodosius Minor[2] rested.] [451.]

Kal. Jan. A.D. 452. Here some place the nativity of Saint Brigid.[3] A great slaughter of the Leinstermen.[4] [Or, truly, in this year the Emperor Marcianus[5] succeeded Theodosius Minor.] [452.]

Kal. Jan. (Thursd., m. 5.) A.D. 453 (4657). [Defeat in battle[6] of the Leinstermen by Loeghaire, son of Niall.] [453.]

Kal. Jan. (Friday, m. 16.) A.D. 454 (4658). The Cena (or Feast) of Temhair,[7] kept with (or by) Loeghaire, son of Niall. [454.]

---

incarnationis (iuxta Dionysium) Pascha Dominicum 8 die Calendis Maii recte celebratum est, ordinatione sancti Theophili: quod sanctus Leo Papa 15 Calend. Maii potius observandum protestatur."

[2] *Theodosius Minor.* -- A and B have this entry in *al. man.* After *minor* A adds: "ut patet ex glossa predicta in 1° anno in Clementinis, *i.e.*, de Magistris, in verbo Bononiensi, juncto eo quod habetur in 2° anno pagine precedentis."

[3] *St. Brigid.*—These annals record her death in her 70th year, at 523 and 525, which refers her birth to 453 or 455, the former being the date generally received. Ussher proposed 453 (*Wks.* vi., 445-447, 573), which Colgan, *Tr. Th.*, 620*a*, and Lanigan (i., p. 378) have accepted. A marginal note in A, at 438 *supra* suggests that year. *Ann. Inisf.* have 456, and *An. Clonmac.* 425.

[4] *Leinstermen.*—This seems to be taken from a Latin version of what is recorded in Irish under the year following.

[5] *Marcianus.*--In A and B, from *verius* to *minori* is in *al. man.* A adds, "ut patet in Clementinis, *i.e.*, de *Magistris*, in verbo *Bononiensi* predict. 1° anno."

[6] *Defeat in battle.*-Literally 'battle-breach.' See Hennessy, *Chron. Scot.*, p. 352*a*. *Interfectio* is the equivalent in the preceding year. The old English translation makes the word a proper name, "the battle called Cathroine," but the place is not recorded. The *F. Mast.*, at 453, add mór and it is properly rendered by O'Don. 'a great defeat.' *Ann Inisfal.*, at 456, curtly say fairdbe Lagen, 'cutting off of Leinstermen.' fairdbe = foirtbe the older form. The battle was probably fought in Leinster, and concerning the *Borumha* or 'Cow-tribute,' see at 458 *infra*.

[7] *Feast of Temhair.*--In A and B feis is given as the Irish word for *cena*, and is the only word employed in the entry at 461 *infra*. O'Flaherty calls it "Temorensis comitia" (*Ogyg.*, 213). Similar celebrations used to be held at Tailte (Teltown), and Uisnech (Ushnagh); but concerning this, which was the imperial one, see Keating, p. 414, and especially Petrie, *Tara*, 31, 32, 82–85, who asserts that

.b. Kl. Ienair. Anno domini cccc.° l.° u.° Uictorius astrologus f[lor]uit.

Kl. Ienair. (i. f. l. ix.) Anno domini cccc.° l.° ui.° (uii. dc. lx.) Mors Ennai mic Cathbotha, et natiuitas sancte Brigide, ut alii dicunt. Marcianus imperator uite spiritum amisit. Imperauit annis sex (alias
Fol. 17aa. quatuor) et mensibus ui, uel uti Marcillinus docet. Leo eidem successit [defuncto].

Kl. Ienair. Anno domini cccc.° l.° uii.° Calcedonensis senodus congregatus est. Quies senis Patricii ut alii libri dicunt.

---

this was the only convention of Tara held by Laeghaire during his reign (p. 82).

[1] *Victorius.*—Or Victorinus, a native of Limoges in Aquitaine, whom Gennadius, *Vir. Illustr.*, c. 88, styles "Calculator scripturarum," flourished in 457. In that year he composed a new Paschal Canon, at the instance of Pope Leo, who, to prevent a recurrence of the controversy which arose in 455, between the Eastern and Western Churches, about the proper Sunday for the celebration of Easter, commissioned Hilary, his Archdeacon, to employ a competent person for the purpose. He framed a cycle of 532 years, *i.e.*, 28 × 19, the product of the solar and lunar cycles, commencing from A.D. 28, the computed year of the Passion, or A.M. 5229. Cummian, in his Paschal epistle (A.D. 634) mentions this cycle. Ussher, *Wks.*, iv., 440. And the anonymous Irish writer of the tract *De Mirabilibus Sacr. Scripturæ* reckons by it. See Pagi, *Critica*, ii., 370*b*, 582*a*, 626*a*; O'Conor, *Rer. Hib. SS.*, ii., 112; Tillemont's *Memoires*, xv., 770. *Ann. Inisfal.*, in the parallel entry (an. 458) have "Victorius scripsit ciclum Pascha."

[2] *Enna, son of Cathboth.*—O'Conor conjectures that this was Enna of Aran (ii., pt. 1, p. 109), but unhappily, for that saint was son of Conall derg, and was alive in 530. The present entry is found in *An. Inisfal.* (an. 459); *An. Buell.* (an. 462); *Chron. Scot.* (an. 455); *F. Mast.* (an. 456); but none of them help to identify the subject of it. In the B. of Armagh mention is made of the seven sons of Cathbadh, a Leinster clan, who with Bishop Isserninus were expelled by Enna Cennsalach (fol. 18*aa*).

[3] *St. Brigid.*—See note at 452 *supra.*

[4] *Marcian.*—Accession, Aug. 20, 450; death, Jan 31, 457. B. reads *quievit*, which is technically incorrect, and not the expression of Marcellinus, from whom this entry is borrowed. His words are: "Indict. x. Constantino et Rufo Coss. (*i.e.*, A.D. 457), Marcianus Imp. bonis principibus comparandus vitæ spiritum amisit: imperavit annos vi. menses vi. Leo eidem defuncto successit, cujus voluntate Majorianus apud Ravennam Cæsar est ordinatus." *Galland*, x., 348*b*. Beda, less correct, says: "Septem annis tenuit," and with this entry, antedates by a year the acces-

Kal. Jan. A.D. 455. Victorius[1] the astronomer flourished. [455.]

Kal Jan. (Sund., m. 9.) A.D. 456 (4660). Death of Enna, son of Cathboth,[2] and birth of Saint Brigid,[3] as some say. The Emperor Marcian[4] resigned the vital breath. He reigned six (or four) years and six months, as Marcellinus states. Leo succeeded him [on his decease]. [456.]

Kal. Jan. A.D. 457. The synod of Chalcedon[5] was assembled. Repose of Old Patrick,[6] as some books state. [457.]

---

sion of Marcian. *An. Inisfal.* have 454; *Marian. Scot.*, 452. But 457 is the true date. See *L'Art de Vérif. les Dates*, p. 180. Instead of *annis sex* the *al. man.* in A. and B. have iiii.or which is a manifest error.

5 *Synod of Chalcedon.*—Six years too late. The fourth General Council, held at Chalcedon, to condemn the Eutychian heresy, sat from October 8th till November, 451. *Concilia*, t. iv., cols. 761–2074; *Baronius*, t. viii., p. 87; *L'Art de Vérifier les Dates*, p. 180; *Ann. Inisfal.*, 452.

6 *Old Patrick.*—Distinguished by the epithet Sen or 'Old,' from Patrick the Apostle of Ireland, who was somewhat his junior. The acts of the two are so interwoven that it is very difficult to resolve them. The present entry, however, affords some help. Nennius says: "A nativitate Domini usque ad adventum Patricii ad Scotos ccccv. anni sunt. A morte Patricii usque ad obitum sanctæ Brigidæ ix. anni," which numbers are utterly inapplicable to the Patrick of 432 and 493. Gir. Cambr. dates Patrick's death, "ab incarnatione Domini cccclviii."; this he learned in Ireland; but it cannot be strained to suit the Apostle. Allowing, however, for the slow year of these Annals, it is identical with the date in the text. Again, three of the Armagh lists (published by Todd, *St. Patrick*, 174, 181) make Sen Patraic *third* abbot, while these annals reckon Iarlath his successor once removed, the *third;* therefore they ignore the first two, namely Patrick and Sechnall, and leave to Sen Patraic, the *first* place. Ussher saw that two names should be expunged (*Wks.* vi., 437), but he erred in making Sen Patraic one of them. In two of these lists Sen Patraic is allowed an incumbency of ten years, which deducted from 457, gives 447 as his inception, within three years of the founding of Armagh, which event is most probably to be referred to him, not to the Apostle; and further it is equally probable that the encomiums bestowed upon Patrick the Bishop, at the years 441 and 443, belong to the earlier ecclesiastic. His successor, Bishop Benignus, died in 467, which allows the exact ten years assigned to Sen Patraic in the lists. So far the

Kt. Ienair. (iiii. f., l. i.) Anno domini cccc.° l.° uiii.° (iiii. dc. lxii.) Cath Atho dara for Laigaire re Laignibh [in quo et ipse captus est, sed tunc dimissus est iurans per solem et uentum se boues eis dimissurum].

.b. Kt. Ienair. (u. f., l. xii.) Anno domini cccc.° l.° ix.° (iiii. dc. lxiii.) Auxilius episcopus quieuit. No gumadh air an Kt. so cath Atha dara secundum alios.

Kt. Ienair. (6 f., l. 23.) Anno domini cccc.° lx.° (iiii. dc. lxiiii.) Leo papa mortuus est. Romane eclesie obtinuit sedem Petri xxi. (alias quatuor) annis et mense uno et diebus xiii., sicuti enumerat Beda in cronico suo.

Kt. Ienair. (i. f., l. 4.) Anno domini cccc.° lx.° i.° (iiii. dc. lxu.) Hilarius Romane aeclesie pontifex .xl. iiii.us factus, et uixit annis .ui. Hic alii quietem Patrici dicunt. Loegaire filius Neill post cenam Temro annis .uii. et mensibus .uii. et dies .uii. uixit. Cath Atha dara ria Laignibh for Laegaire, quibus Cremthann tunc preerat.

Apostle does not appear at all in official connexion with Armagh. Sen Patrick's death is commemorated in the *Felire* of Ængus, at the 24th of August, thus:—

> Sen Patraic cing catha,
> Coem-aite ar srotha.
>
> 'Old Patrick, champion of battle,
> Loveable tutor of our Sage.'

Upon which the Irish annotator writes "Old Patrick, of Ros Dela in Magh Locha: sed verius est that he may be in Glastonbury of the Gael, in the south of Saxonland (for Scoti formerly used to dwell there in pilgrimage). But his relics are in the tomb of Sen Patrick in Ard Macha." *Felire*, pp. cxxv., cxxxiii. At 461, *infra*, his death is again recorded, but simply as *Patricius*.

[1] *Ath-dara.*—'Ford of the oak,' on the river Barrow, in Magh Ailbhe (a plain in the co. Kildare). Shearman conjectures, and indeed states, that it was at Mageney Bridge (*Loc. Patric.*, 67, 101), which is in the parish of Dunmanoge in the extreme south of the county of Kildare, on W. side, O.S., s. 39. This battle is entered under next year, and again at 461. See next note.

[2] *Cow-tribute.*—Borama; which O'Flaherty renders *Boaria.*—*Ogyg.*, 305. Said to have been first imposed on the Leinstermen by Tuathal Teachtmar, circ. A.D. 130. After proving a source of violent contention for a long series of years between the chiefs of Ulster and of Leinster, it was abandoned by Finnachta Fledach, about the year 680. There is a full

Kal. Jan. (Wednesd., m. 1.) A.D. 458 (4662). Battle [458.]
of Ath-dara,[1] by the Leinstermen against Laeghaire, [in which he was made prisoner, but was presently liberated on his swearing by the Sun and Wind that he would remit to them the cow tribute].[2]

Kal. Jan. (Thursd., m. 12.) A.D. 459 (4663). Auxi- [459.]
lius,[3] the bishop, rested. Or, in this year, according to some, the battle of Ath-dara was fought.

Kal. Jan. (Frid., m. 23.) A.D. 460 (4664). Pope Leo [460.]
died. He occupied the chair of Peter in the Church of Rome 21 (or 24) years, 1 month, and 13 days, as Beda reckons in his chronicle.

Kal. Jan. (Sund., m. 4.) A.D. 461 (4665). Hilary[4] [461.]
was made 44th bishop[5] of the church of Rome, and lived 6 years.[6] Here some record the repose of Patrick. Laeghaire, son of Niall, lived after the Feast of Tara 7 years, and 7 months, and 7 days. The battle of Ath-dara *was gained* over Laeghaire, by the Leinstermen, of whom Crimthann[7] was then commander.

---

and most curious tract, in prose and verse, on the subject in the Books of Leinster and Lecan. See O'Curry's *Lect. on MS. Mat.*, 230–232; Keating, 303–306; O'Donovan, *Hy-Fiachr.*, 32, 33.

[3] *Auxilius.*—See under an. 439. His festival is August 27th, at which day his name occurs, in the *Mart. Taml.*, *Mar. Gorman*, and *Mart. Doneg.*, as Usaille son of Ua mBaird, bishop of Cill-Usaille in Leinster, now Killashee. He is not noticed by the *Felire*. Colgan has collected the little that is known of him at 19th March in *Actt. SS.*, pp. 657–659.

[4] *Hilary.*—Over the name Hilarius, there is written in a very old Irish hand in MS. A., Uel hoc anno Leo obiit, ("or in this year Leo died"). The death of Pope Leo (who died on Nov. 4, A.D. 461), is entered under the previous year.

[5] *Bishop.*—Pontifex, B.; om. in A.

[6] annos, A.

[7] *Crimthann.*—This entry is added in A., in a very old hand. In B. it appears in the hand of the transcriber of that MS. See under 458. The Crimthann here referred to was the son of Enna Ceinnselach, whom he succeeded as king of S.E. Leinster, about the year 444. His residence was at Rathvilly, in the N.E. of the present county of Carlow, which gives name to a parish and barony. In the Irish notes in the *Book of Armagh* (fol. 18aa), St. Patrick is stated to have visited Crimthann at Rathvilly: Luid iarsuidiu cu Crimthan mac n-Endi ceinnselich, et ipse credidit ucc raith bilich. "He (St.

Kl. Ienair. (2 f., l. 15.) Anno domini cccc.° lx.° ii.° (iiii. dc. lxii.) Mors Laeghaire filii Neill oc Greomaigh Daphil (alias oc Grellaigh Gaifil, for taebh Caisse, in campo Lifi) etir in da chnoc .i. Eriu 7 Albu a n-anmanda. Gumadh a ratha re Laighnibh grian 7 gaeth rosmarbsat.

.b. Kl. Ienair. (3[a] f., l. 26.[a]) Anno domini cccc.° lx.° iii.° (iiii. dc. lxiii). Inicium regni Ailella muilt mic Nathi.

Kl. Ienair. (4 f., l. 7.) Anno domini cccc.° lx.°
Fol. 17ab. iiii.° (iiii. dc. lxiiii.) Primum bellum Arrda corann ria Laignibh. Angli venerunt in Angliam.

Kl. Ienair. (6 f., l. 18.) Anno domini cccc.° lx.° u.° Hilarius episcopus Romane aeclesie mortuus est, qui resedit cathedram Petri .iii. annis et mensibus .iii. et diebus .x. Semplicius ordinatur, qui sedit annis .xii. mense .i. diebus . . Eogan mac Neill mortuus est.

Patrick) went after that to Crimthan son of Enda Ceinnselach, and he believed at Rath-bilich." Crimthan was a strenuous assertor of Lagenian independence, and won many battles in defence thereof, which are enumerated by Dubtach Ua Lugair, in his eulogistic poems on the triumphs of Crimthan, some of which have been published, from the *Book of Leinster*, by O'Curry (*Lectures, &c.*, pp. 484–494).

[1] *Alias.*—The alias reading in A., put here in parenthesis, and which is in an old hand, agrees substantially with the text of B. The name of the place where Laeghaire met his death is variously written in different authorities. But the oldest form of the name seems to be *Grellach Daphil*, as appears from the reference to Laeghaire's death in *Leb. na hUidre*, 118*b*. The Four Masters (458) say that the place of Laeghaire's death was in Ui-Faelain, *i.e.* the northern part of the co. Kildare. In the *Borama* Tract (*Book of Leinster*, 299*b*), it is stated that Laeghaire was killed by the elements (earth, sun, and wind), by which he had pledged himself two and a half years before (*supra*, 458), not again to exact the tribute called *bórama* (or "cow tribute"). But he came, and seized cows at Sidh-Nechtain (Carbury Hill, co. Kildare, at the foot of which is the source of the River Boyne), and met his fate on the side of Caiss, between the two hills called Eriu and Alba (supposed to be the present Hill of Dunmurry, and Hill of Allen).

[2] *Ailill Molt.* — The cognomen

Kal. Jan. (Mond., m. 15). A.D. 462 (4666). Death of Laeghaire, son of Niall, at Greomach-daphil (alias[1] at Greallach-gaifil, on the side of Caiss, in Magh-Lifè), between the two hills, viz., Eiriu and Alba their names. May be it was his guarantees to the Leinstermen, the Sun and Wind, that killed him. [462.]

Kal. Jan. (Tuesd., m. 26.) A.D. 463 (4667). Commencement of the reign of Ailill Molt,[2] son of Nathi. [463.]

Kal. Jan. (Wedn., m. 7.) A.D. 464 (4668). First battle of Ard-Corann[3] by Leinstermen. The Angles[3 (a)] came into England. [464.]

Kal. Jan. (Frid., m. 18.) A.D. 465. Hilary, bishop of the Church of Rome, died, who occupied the chair of Peter 6 years,[4] and 3 months, and 10 days. Simplicius was ordained, who sat 12 years,[5] 1 month and . . days. Eogan[6] son of Niall died. [465.]

---

molt, a "wether," is Latinized *vervecinus* by O'Flaherty. *Ogygia*, p. 429. He was son of Nathi (an. 445 *supra*), whom he succeeded as provincial king of Connaught. From his brother Fiachra descended the Ui-Fiachrach of Connaught. O'Flaherty gives 463 as the date of his accession, and 20 years as the length of his reign. See for Ailill's death ann 482, 483 *infra*. Dr. O'Conor absurdly renders *molt* by "laudabilis"; Tigh. 463.

[3] *Ard-Corann.*—This place is again mentioned as battle-ground at 506, 507, 510 and 626. In the Ann. Inisfallen the battle here recorded is mentioned under 467; but the Four Mast. omit all the foregoing entries except the last, having probably thought that Ard-Corann was a place in Scotland, and, as such, foreign to their scope. From the mention of Leinstermen in the foregoing entry, however, it must be presumed that the place of the battle was in Ireland.

[3] (*a*) *Angles.* — Marianus Scotus places their arrival at 450. In the Saxon chronicle the date is 449. Ussher assigns 450.

[4] *6 Years.*—B. reads, erroneously, "7." See an. 461 *supra*. Hilary's death is placed here three years too soon. He died Feb. 21, 468.

[5] *Years.* — The length of the pontificate of Simplicius is given in B. as "ten years, two months, and one day," which is also wrong, as the real duration was 15 years and 6 days, Simplicius having been ordained 25th Feb., 468. The beginning of the Pontificate of his successor, Felix, is entered *infra*, under the year 481.

[6] *Eogan, i.e*, Eogan son of Niall Nine-hostager, from whom the powerful sept of the Cinel-Eogain (or Cinel-Owen) derived their name and lineage.

Kl. Ienair. (7 f., l. 29.) Anno domini cccc.° lx.° iii.° Rauennam ciuitatem terremotus deterruit. Domangart mac Nisi quieuit.

.b. Kl. Ienair. (1. f., l. 10.) Anno domini cccc.° lx.° iii.° Quies Benigni episcopi (successoris Patricii). Cena Teṁra la hAilill molt (mac Daṫi mic Fiaċraċ mic Eaċaċ muiḋeṁoin). Sic in libro Cuanaċ inueni. Bas Uiter pendragen regis Anglie, cui successit filius suus .i. Cingh Airtur .i. do ordaig an bord cr[uind].

Kl. Ienair. (2 f., l. 21.) Anno domini cccc.° lx.° iiii.° Isserninus episcopus moritur. Bellum Dumai achir .i. for Oilill molt, sicut inueni in libro Cuanaċ.

Kl. Ienair. (4 f., l. 2.) Anno domini cccc.° lx.° ix.° No feis Teampa la hAilill molt hoc anno secundum alios.

Kl. Ienair. (5 f., l. 13.) Anno domini cccc.° lxx.° Feis Tempa la Ailill molt, ut alii dicunt.

.b. Kl. Ienair. (6^a f., l. 24.) Anno domini cccc.° lxx.° i.° Preda secunda Saxonum de hibernia, ut alii dicunt, in isto anno deducta est, ut Maucteus (.i. Moċtae) dicit. Sic in libro Cuanaċ inueni.

Fol. 17*ba* Kl. Ienair. Anno domini cccc.° lxx.° ii.°

Kl. Ienair. Anno domini cccc.° lxx.° iii.° Leo senior imperator, Leone iuniore a se iam cessare constituto morbo perit, tam sui imperii annis quam huius Leonis

---

[1] In A. the day of the week on which the 1st of January fell is omitted; and the age of the moon is given as 20, in place of 29, as in B., in which the 1st of January is stated to have fallen on a Saturday.

[2] *Domangart.*—This entry (from B.), not found in either the older and better copy (A.), nor in the so-called 'translation' in the MS. Clar. 49, (Brit. Museum), is probably the result of a great prolepsis, as there appears to have been no ecclesiastic of the name of Domangart Mac Nisi at such an early period. The term quieuit used by the Annalist, in recording the death of Domangart, indicates that he regarded the deceased as an ecclesiastic. The demise of a Domangart Mac Nisi is given by the Four M. under A.D. 462; in the Chron. Scotorum under A.D. 464 (=462), and in the Ann. Inisfall. at 495 in O'Conor's ed. (=464). The

Kal. Jan. (Saturd., m. 29.)[1] A.D. 466. An earthquake frightened the city of Ravenna. Domangart[2] Mac Nisi rested. [466.]

Kal. Jan. (Sund., m. 10.) A.D. 467. Rest of Benignus, the bishop, successor[3] of Patrick. The Feast of Tara *held* by Ailill Molt (son[4] of Dathi, son of Fiachra, son of Eochaid Muidhemhoin). So I find in the Book of Cuana. Death[5] of Uter Pendragon, King of England, to whom succeeded his son, *i.e.* King Arthur, *i.e.* who ordained the Round Table. [467.]

Kal. Jan. (Mond., m. 21.) A.D. 468. Iserninus, bishop, dies. The battle of Duma-achir, *i.e.* over Ailill Molt, as I find in the Book of Cuana. [468.]

Kal. Jan. (Wedn., m. 2.) A.D. 469. Or, the Feast of Tara by Ailill Molt this year, according to others. [469.]

Kal. Jan. (Thursd., m. 13.) A.D. 470. The Feast[6] of Tara *was held* by Ailill Molt, as others state. [470.]

Kal. Jan. (Frid., m. 24.) A.D. 471. The second prey[7] of the Saxons from Ireland, as some say, was carried off in this year, as Maucteus[8] (*i.e.* Mochtae) states. So I find in the Book of Cuana. [471.]

Kal. Jan. A.D. 472. [472.]

Kal. Jan. A.D. 473. The Emperor Leo the Elder was carried off by disease, Leo the Younger having been previously created Cæsar by him. Leo the Younger, who was [473.]

---

person intended may have been Domangart, 3rd king of Dalriada in Scotland, son of Fergus Mór. See Reeves's *Adamnan*, pp. 434, and the Genealogical Table accompanying. See also note at A.D. 506.

[3] *Successor of Patrick.*—This clause is only in B. A marg. note in A., in an old hand, adds that Benignus was bishop of Armagh.

[4] *Son of Dathi*, &c.—The geneal. particulars here given from A. are not in B.

[5] *Death*, &c.—The original of this entry is in B. only, and in a more recent hand.

[6] *Feast.*—The author of the so-called 'translation' of the Ann. Ult. in Clar. 49, renders ꝼeıꞅ by "another feast"!

[7] *Second prey.* — The first prey taken by the Saxons from (or in) Ireland, is recorded above under A.D. 434, where see note.

[8] *Maucteus.* — Mocteus, B. See note under A.D. 511, referring to the so-called "Book of the Monks."

regni mensibus computatis anno x.° uii.°, mense ui.° Zenonem Leo iunior idemque imperator filius principem constituit. Quies Docci episcopi sancti Britonum abbatis. Dorngal Bri Eile for Laighniu ria nAilill molt.

Kl. Ienair. Anno domini cccc.° lxx.° iiii.° Uel hic cath Dumai achir for Ailill molt ria Laignib.

.b. Kl. Ienair. (4 f., l. 9.) Anno domini cccc.° lxx.° u.° (iiii. dc. lxxix.) Bellum (alias dorndgal) bregh h-Eile re n-Ailill molt for Laighniu. Sic in libro Cuanach inueni.

Kl. (Ienair. 5 f., l. 20.) Anno domini cccc.° lxx.° ui.° (iiii. dc. lxxx.) Cath Dumhai Aichir for Ailill molt ria Laignib.

Kl. Ienair. Anno domini cccc.° lxx.° uii.° Mors Tocco mic Aedha regis Cualann.

Kl. Ienair. Anno domini cccc.° lxx.° uiii.° Bellum bregh h-Eile.

.b. Kl. Ianair. (3 f., l.) Anno domini cccc.° lxx.° ix.°

Kl. Ianair. Anno domini cccc.° lxxx.° Mors Conaill Cremthainne mic Neill.

Kl. Ianair. (5 f., l. 15.) Anno domini cccc.° lxxx.° i.°

---

[1] *17th year and 6th month.*—B. has anno x.° uiii.°, mense ui.°, although O'Conor prints anno x.° uiii.°, mense u.° (18th year and 5th month). But the date is not accurate in either MS. Leo I. was crowned February 7, 457. He died in January, 474; so that his reign wanted but a month of 17 years. His daughter, Ariadne, was married to Zeno, and their son Leo was born in 458. His grandfather, the year before his death, appointed him his successor. He died in November, 474, at 17, in the eleventh month of his sole reign. At the instance of his mother, and of his grandmother Verina, Leo II. associated with him in the throne his father, Zeno, whom his own father-in-law had passed over on account of his vices and deformity. This entry seems to have been borrowed from the Chronicle of Marcellinus, where the computation above given is "tam sui imperii annis quam Leonis Junioris regni mensibus computatis, anno xvii., mense v."

[2] *Doccus.*—The only individual of this name whom we meet with in British Ecclesiastical History is the Docus who is set down in an ancient authority, cited by Ussher, as the contemporary of David and Gildas, and a preceptor of the Second Order

also Emperor, and son to Zeno, creates him Prince in the 17th year and 6th month,[1] reckoning as well the years of the former, as the months of the latter, Leo's, reign. Rest of the holy bishop Doccus,[2] Abbot of the Britons. The 'fist-fight'[3] of Bri-Eile over the Leinstermen, by Ailill Molt.

Kal. Jan. A.D. 474. Or, in this year[4] the battle of Duma-Achir *was gained* over Ailill Molt by Leinstermen. [474.]

Kal. Jan. (Wedn., m. 9.) A.D. 475 (4679). The battle (otherwise 'fist-fight') of Bri-Eile *gained* by Ailill Molt over Leinstermen. So I find in the Book of Cuana. [475.]

Kal. (Jan. Thursd., m. 20). A.D. 476 (4680). The battle of Duma-Achir *gained* over Ailill Molt by Leinstermen. [476.]

Kal. Jan. A.D. 477. Death of Tocca, son of Aedh, King of Cualand. [477.]

Kal. Jan. A.D. 478. Battle of Bri-Eile. [478.]

Kal. Jan. (Tuesd., m.) A.D. 479. [479.]

Kal. Jan. A.D. 480. Death of Conall Cremthainn[5] son of Niall. [480.]

Kal. Jan. (Thursd., m. 15). A.D. 481 (4685). Rest of [481.]

---

of Irish Saints (*Brit. Eccl. Ant.*, c. 17; *Works* vi., p. 478), and who is mentioned in the Life of St. Cainnech as the abbot under whom he studied in Britain (*ib.*, p. 520). This Docus is commonly called Cadocus, and is known in Welsh hagiology as *Cuttwg Ddoeth*, "Cadoc the Wise." He was abbot of Llancarvan, and flourished about A.D. 500. The entry of his death, above given, would therefore be too late, and may be regarded as out of its place. But see Shearman's *Loca Patriciana* (Dublin, 1879), pp. 223-5, where the learned author states that Cadoc, the preceptor of St. Cainnech (or Canice) was the nephew of Doccus whose obit is given above.

[3] *Fist-fight.*—Dorngal. O'Donovan translates this "boxing-battle," and regards it as "nothing more than a boxing match between the pugilistic champions of Leinster and Meath." (*Four Mast.*, A.D. 468, note [u]). In the so-called Translation in Clar. 49, it is described as "the handie skirmish." It seems to be the same as the conflict designated by the term *bellum* in these Annals, under the years 475 and 478.

[4] *Or, in this year.*—Uel hic, B. Not in A.

[5] *Cremthainn.* — Cramthainne (in the genit. form), A. More usually written Crimthainne, in the genit. case; nom. Crimthainn; although it is Cremthainne in the *Book of Leinster* (p. 24*b*.)

(iiii. dc. lxxxii.) Quies Iarlaṫi mic Trena tertii episcopi Ardmaċai. Romane eclesie Felix xl.uiis episcopus ordinatur, uixit annis xii. uel xiii. Ab inicio mundi iuxta .lxx. interpretes u. dccc. lxxix. Secundum Hebreos autem iiii. dc. lxxxii. Ab incarnacione secundum Hebreos dcc. xxxiiii. Secundum Dyonisium uero cccc. lxxxi.

Kt. Ianair. Anno domini cccc.° lxxx.° ii.° Bellum Oche in quo cecidit Ailill Molt .i. la Lugaid mac Laegaire 7 la Muirchertach mac Erca. A Conċobro filio Nesae usque ad Cormac filium Airt anni ccc. iiii. A Cormac usque hoc bellum c. xiii., ut Cuana scripsit.

.b. Kt. Ianair. Anno domini cccc.° lxxx.° iii.° Iugulatio Chraumthain mic Enna Ceinnselaig mic Breasail belaiċ mic Fiaċa baicceaḋa mic Caṫair ṁoir, regis Lagen. (Uel in hoc anno caṫ Ocha secundum alios, la Luġaid 7 la Muirchertaċ mac Earca 7 la Ferġus Cerḃall mac Conaill cremṫainn, 7 la Fiaċra lon mac riġ ḋal Araiḋe).

---

[1] *Third.*—Iarlathi, son of Trian, is set down in the *Book of Leinster* List of St. Patrick's successors at Armagh (p. 42, col. 3), as the fourth in order; and is said to have been from Cluain-fiacla (Clonfeakle, co. Tyrone); but under the reigns of the "Kings after the Faith" in the same MS. (p. 24*b*), Iarlathi is described as "third Bishop."

[2] *Felix.*—Felix III., consecrated on Sunday, March 6, 483; died 24 February, 492. His Pontificate therefore lasted only 8 years, 11 months, and 18 days; and not 12 years, or 13, as in the text.

[3] *From the beginning*, &c.—The remaining entries for this year, which appear in an old hand in A, are not in B.

[4] *Ocha.*—The date above given for this battle (which was fought in Meath, as stated in the Life of St. Kieran, and near Tara, as Animosus asserts in his Life of St. Brigid (Colgan's *Trias Thaum.*, p. 551*b*, and notes 9 and 10, p. 565), seems to be a year too soon, the correct date being 483, under which it is also entered. The battle of Ocha forms an important era in Irish history, many events recorded in the Irish Chronicles being dated from it. See the *Annals of the Four Masters*, at A.D. 478, where the particulars of the battle are more fully detailed, and O'Donovan's notes on the subject.

[5] 116. This calculation must surely be wrong. The death of Cormac

Iarlathi, son of Trian, third[1] bishop of Armagh. Felix,[2] ordained 46th bishop of the church of Rome, lived twelve years, or thirteen. From[3] the beginning of the world, according to the Seventy Interpreters, 5879 *years*; but according to the Hebrews, 4685. From the Incarnation, according to the Hebrews, 734 *years*; but according to Dionysius, 481.

Kal. Jan. A.D. 482. The battle of Ocha,[4] in which Ailill Molt fell, *was gained* by Lugaid, son of Laegaire, and by Muirchertach Mac Erca. From Concobhar Mac Nesa to Cormac Mac Airt, 308 years. From Cormac to this battle, 116,[5] as Cuana has written. [482.]

Kal. Jan. A.D. 483. The killing of Crimthann,[6] son of Enna Cennselach, (son of Breasal Belach, son of Fiacha Baicceadha, son of Cathair-mór), King of Leinster. (Or in this year, according to others, the battle of Ocha *was gained* by Lugaid, and by Muirchertach Mac Erca, and by Fergus Cerbhall, son of Conall Crimthainn, and by Fiachra Lon,[7] son of the king of Dal-Araidhe.[8]) [483.]

Mac Airt is entered in the *Annals of the Four Masters* under A.D. 266. O'Flaherty, however (*Ogygia*, p. 341), places the accession of his son and successor, Cairbre Lifechair, in A.D. 279, the year, it is to be assumed, of King Cormac's death. The addition of 116 years to this number would, according to this calculation, give A.D. 395 as the date of the battle of Ocha, which is unquestionably wrong. The *Chronicon Scotorum*, which gives the battle of Ocha under A.D. 482, states that 207 years intervened between the time of Cormac Mac Airt and the said battle. The MS. Clar. 49, has "A Cormac usque ad hoc bellum 206, ut Cuana scripsit." This would be more near the mark.

[6] *Crimthann.* — Corruptly written *Chraumthain* in A., and *Chraeumthain* in B.

[7] *Fiachra Lon*, or "Fiachra the Fierce."—In O'Conor's ed. of these Annals the name is printed "Fiachra Aon." The *Four Mast.* (A.D. 478 erroneously call him son of Laeghaire, as he was really son of Caelbad. See Reeves's *Eccl. Antiq.*, pp. 330, 339.

[8] *Dal-Araidhe.*—A large district, including the southern half of the county of Antrim, and the northern half of Down. In O'Conor's ed. of these Annals, the name is inaccurately printed Dalriada. For a full account of Dal-Araidhe, see Reeves's *Eccl. Antiq.*, pp. 334–348.

Kl. Ianair. (f., l.) Anno domini cccc.° lxxx.° iiii.° Inicium regni Lugdech mic Laegaire hoc anno.

Kl. Ianair. (f., l.) Anno domini cccc.° lxxx.° u.° Bellum primum Granaerad; Coirpri mac Neill .ix. ġiallaiġ uictor erat, in quo cecidit Fincaṫ. Uel filius Erce uictor ut alii dicunt. Uel hic guin Cremṫaind mic Enna Cheinnselaiġ.

Kl. Ianair. (5 f., l. 21.) Anno domini cccc.° lxxx.° ui.° Uel hoc anno primum bellum Graine in quo Muircheartaċ mac Earca uictor erat.

.b. Kl. Ianair. (6 f., l. 2.) Anno domini cccc.° lxxx.° uii.° (iiii. dc. xcii.) Quies sancti Meil episcopi in Ardd aċuṫ.

Kl. Ianair. (1. f., l. 13.) Anno domini cccc.° lxxx.° uiii.° (iiii. dc. xciii). Quies sancti Ciannani cui sanctus Patricius euangelium largitur est.

Kl. Ianair. (2 f., l. 24.[a]) Anno domini cccc.° lxxx.° ix.° (iiii. dc. xciiii.) Quies Mic Caille episcopi. Bellum Cinn losnado (no Ceall losnaiġ i maiġ ḟea), ubi cecidit Oengus filius Nadfraiċ ri Muġan, ut Cuana scripsit.

Fol. 18aa. Kl. Ianair. (3 f., l. 5.) Anno domini cccc.° xc.° (iiii. dc. xcu.) Zeno Augustus uita decessit tam fui

---

[1] *Commencement.* — This entry is written in pale ink in A., in the hand of the person who has made most of the additional entries in that MS.

[2] *Granaerad.*—The name of this place is differently written in some Chronicles. The Four Masters give the name (in the genit. form) *Granaird*, which in the nom. would be 'Granard,' and would be somewhat like the form above given. But under the very next year (486) the name is written 'Graine,' as in the *Chron. Scotorum* (484), *Annals of Clonmacnoise* (at 497), and in Keating. The version of these Annals in Clar. 49 has 'Granard.' At 494 (*infra*) these Annals further vary the orthography by giving 'Granairet.' The place is now called Graney, and is situated in the south of the county of Kildare.

[3] *Or, in this year.*—Uel hic, B. Not in A.

[4] *Graine.*—The entry of this event is not fully given in B., which does not refer to the victory of Muirchertach Mac Erca.

[5] *Mel.*—First bishop of Ardagh, in the county of Longford; said to have been Patrick's nephew. Some call him a Briton. His foreign extraction

Kal. Jan. A.D. 484. The commencement[1] of the reign of Lugaidh son of Laeghaire, in this year. [484.]

Kal. Jan. A.D. 485. The first battle of Granaerad.[2] Coirpre, son of Niall-Noighiallach, was victor. In it fell Fincath. Or Mac Erca was victor, as others say. Or, in this year,[3] the killing of Crimthann son of Enna Ceinnselach. [485.]

Kal. Jan. (Thursd., m. 21.) A.D. 486. Or, in this year, the first battle of Graine,[4] wherein Muirchertach Mac Erca was victor. [486.]

Kal. Jan. (Frid., m. 2.) A.D. 487 (4692). Rest of Saint Mel,[5] the bishop, in Ardagh. [487.]

Kal. Jan. (Sund., m. 13.) A.D. 488 (4693). Rest of Saint Cianan,[6] to whom Saint Patrick presented the Gospel. [488.]

Kal. Jan. (Mond., m. 24.) A.D. 489 (4694). Rest of Mac Caille,[7] the bishop. Battle of Cenn-losnado (or Cell-losnaigh,[8] in Magh-Fea), in which fell Aengus son of Nadfraech, King of Munster, as Cuana has written. [489.]

Kal. Jan. (Tuesd., m. 5.) A.D. 490 (4695). Zeno[9] Augustus departed *this* life, in the 17th year and 6th [490.]

---

might account for the absence of his pedigree from the ancient lists.

[6] *Cianan.*—The founder of the church in East Meath which was called, *par excellence*, 'Daim-liag,' or the 'Stone-church.' Saint Cianan was tenth in descent from Cian, son of Oilill Oluim, King of Munster (ob. 234, *Four Mast.*), who gave name to the various tribes of *Cianachta*.

[7] *Mac Caille.*—After the name Mac Caille in B., and Clar. 49, the word "Mannensis" has been added. But this is an idle gloss, as it confounds two persons who were quite distinct. St. Patrick is stated to have converted an unbeliever in Magh-inis (or Lecale, co. Down), called Macal dus, Mac Cuil, or Mac Fail, who afterwards became bishop of Man. (See *Trias Thaum.*, p. 16; and *Book of Armagh*, fol. 6.) The Mac Caille whose obit. is above given was a totally different individual, being the saint commemorated in the Calendar, at April 25th, as the bishop who placed the veil on the head of St. Brigid, and whose church was at Cruachan-Brig-Eile, in Ui-Failge (*i.e.* near the well-known Hill of Croghan).

[8] *Or Cell-Losnaigh*, &c.—The alias reading is not in B. See note under A.D. 491.

[9] *Zeno.*—This entry is taken from Marcellinus; but a clause necessary to the sense is omitted here. The

imperii annis computatis anno xvii.° mense sexto. Hi sex menses et sex menses Marciani addunt annum quem non numerant cronica. Anastasius imperator creatus est. (Uel hic caṫ ċell osnaid, secundum alios. Mac Earca uictor, rex Cairil uictus).

.b. Kl. Ianair. (4ª f., l. 16.) Anno domini cccc.° xc.° i.° (iiii. dc. xcii). Dicunt scoiti hic patricium archiepiscopum defunctum (fore).

Kl. Ianair. (6ª f., l. 27.ª) Anno domini cccc.° xc.° ii.° (iiii. dc. xciii.) Bellum Sroṫa. Romane eclesiae xluiii^us Galasius episcopus ordinatus annis uixit iii. Bellum secundum Granairet. Patricius archiapostolus (uel archiepiscopus et apostolus) scotorum quieuit c.^mo xx.° anno etatis sue, 16 Kl. Aprilis, lx.° autem quo uenit ad Hiberniam anno ad baptizandos Scotos. Ab inicio mundi secundum .lxx. interpretes u. dcccc. xlui. Iuxta autem Hebreos iiii. dc. xciiii. Ab incarnacione iuxta Hebreos dcc. xlui. Ab incarnacione secundum Dionisium cccc [xcii].

Kl. Ianair. (7ª f., l. 9.ª) Anno domini cccc.° xc.° iii. Cath Taillten for Laiġniu ria Cairpri mac Neill.

Kl. Ianair. (1. f., l. 20.ª) Anno domini cccc.° xc.° iiii.° Bellum secundum Granairet in quo cecidit

---

original is "tam sui imperii annis quam Basilisci tyrannidis computatis, anno XVII., mense VI." He reigned from Feb., 474, to 9th April, 491. This includes the period of Basiliscus' usurpation, who, in the third year of Zeno, by Verina's instrumentality, drove the Emperor into Isauria, and took possession of the throne, creating his son Marcus Cæsar. But he was dethroned by Zeno in August, 477, after a 20 months' usurpation.

[1] *Anastasius*.—Crowned April 11, 491. These Annals are, therefore, only a year behind the common reckoning at this period.

[2] *Cell-osnaid*.—This is also the form of the name in Tigernach and Keating. The Annal. Inisfall., at 484, have Cend-losnai. In the entry above for last year (489) the place is called 'Cenn-losnada,' or 'Cell-losnaigh,' and is stated to have been in Magh-Fea. Keating says that Cell-osnaid was situated in the county of Carlow, four miles to the east of Leighlin. It is now called Kellistown, and gives name to a parish chiefly comprised in the barony of Carlow. Dr. O'Donovan states that 50 years ago the remains of an ancient church and Round Tower were

month, the years as well of his reign [as of the tyrant Basiliscus] being computed These 6 months, and 6 months of Marcian, add a year which the chronicles do not count. Anastasius[1] is created Emperor. (Or, in this year, the battle of Cell-osnaidh,[2] according to others; Mac Erca was victor; the King of Cashel vanquished.)

Kal. Jan. (Wedn., m. 16.) A.D. 491 (4696). The [491.]
Scoti say that Patrick, the Archbishop, died this year.[3]

Kal. Jan. (Frid., m. 27.) A.D. 492 (4697). Battle of [492.]
Sruth.[4] Gelasius having been ordained 47th bishop of the Church of Rome, lived 3 years. Second battle of Granairet.[5] Patrick, the arch-apostle[6] (or archbishop and apostle) of the Scoti, rested on the 16th of the Kalends of April, in the 120th year of his age, and also the 60th year after he had come to Ireland to baptize the Scoti. From[7] the beginning of the World, according to the LXX. Interpreters, 5946, but according to the Hebrews, 4697. From the Incarnation, according to the Hebrews, 746. From the Incarnation, according to Dionysius, cccc [xcii].

Kal. Jan. (Saturd., m. 9.) A.D. 493. The battle of Tailltiu [493.]
was gained over the Leinstermen, by Cairpri, son of Niall.

Kal. Jan. (Sund., m. 20.) A.D. 494. The second [494.]
battle of Granairet,[8] in which fell[9] Fraech, the son of

---

still existing, which are now all effaced. (*Four Mast.*, A.D. 489, note). The site of the Round Tower, however, is marked on Sheet 8, Ordnance Survey Maps, co. Carlow. The entry is added in a very coarse hand in A.

[3] *This year.*—This entry seems to be antedated by two years.

[4] *Sruth.*—Sroṫa, in the gen. case. Tigernach calls it "Srath;" but the *Annal. Inisfall.* (485) have the entry more fully, thus:—"The battle of *Srath-Conaill*, in which fell Fiacha, son of Finchad, King of Leinster, and Eochu, son of Cairpre, was victor."

[5] *Granairet.*—See note under A.D. 485, respecting this place.

[6] *Arch-apostle.*—Archipostolus. The altered reading uel archiepiscopus et apostolus is interlined in the old hand in A. Archiepiscopus in B., without the apostolus.

[7] *From.*—The remaining entries for this year are not in B.

[8] *Granairet.*—See above, under 485, note [2]. B. commences the entry with a "Vel hic."

[9] *Fell.*—Cecidit, B. Cecidid, A.

Fraeċ mac Finchada (mic Garrchon mic Foṫaiġ mic Eachach Laṁḋoid mic Ṁeisseancorb) ri Laigen. Eoċu filius Coirpri (.i. Eochu mac Cairpri mic Oilella mic Ḋunluing mic Enna niaḋ) uictor fuit.

.b. Kl. Ianair. (2 f., l. 1.) Anno domini cccc.° xc°. u°. Solis defectus apparuit. Quies Mic Cuilinn Episcopi Luscan. Expugnatio Duin Leṫglaissi. Uel hic caṫ Talten.

Kl. Ianair. (4a f., l. 12a.) Anno domini cccc°. xc°. ui°. Romane eclesie xl.uiiius Anastasius pontifex ordinatus uixit annis duobus. Moċoei n-Oendroma quieuit. Cormacci episcopi Ardmacha heredis Patricii quies. Uel hic bellum secundum Grane, in quo cecidit Fraech mac Finnchada riġ Laiġean desgaḃair. Eachu mac Cairpri uictor fuit.

fol. 18ab Kl. Ianair. (5 f., l. 23). Anno domini cccc°. xc°. uii°. Uel hic expugnatio Duin Leṫglaisse. Bellum Inni moer i criċ oa n-Gabla for Laigniu. Muircertaċ .i. filius Erce uictor erat. Hoc anno ingens terremotus ponticam concussit prouinciam. Quies Chuinneḋa mic Caṫṁoġa, .i. Mac Cuilinn epscop Lusga.

Kl. Ianair. (6a f., l 4.) Anno domini cccc°. xc°. uiii°. Romane eclesie xl. ixus Simaċus episcopus factus, uixit annis .xu. Bellum in quo mac Erce uictor erat. Bellum Sleṁna Miḋe ria Cairbre mac Neill for Laiġniu. Uel hic Moċoe nḋaendroma secundum librum alium.

---

[1] *Son.*—This parenthetic addn. is in an old hand in A. Om. in B.

[2] *Eochu.*—The orig. of the parenthesis here is om. in B.

[3] *Cormac.*—In the margin in A. he is called Epscop Cormac Criċ inna Ernaiḋe ("Bishop Cormac of Crich-in-Ernaidhe.") See O'Donov. *Four Mast.*, A.D., 496, note *k*.

[4] *Grane.*—Granaiiet, in B. See above, under 485, note [2]. The text from this to the end of the entries for this year is wanting in B.

[5] *Or, in this year.*—Uel hic, in B. only.

[6] *Dun-lethglaissi.* — Downpatrick. See under 495.

[7] *Crich-ua nGabla*—O'Conor's ed. has *Crich Congabhla.* But the version in Clar. 49 has "O'Gawla's Country" It was the name of a territory in the south of the present

Finchad (son[1] of Garrchu, son of Fothadh, son of Eochu Lamhdoid, son of Messincorb), King of Leinster. Eochu, son of Cairpri (*i.e.*, Eochu,[2] son of Cairpri, son of Ailill, son of Dunlang, son of Enna Niadh) was victor.

Kal. Jan. (Mond., m. 1.) A.D. 495. An eclipse of [495.]
the sun appeared. Rest of Mac Cuilinn, bishop of Lusk. The storming of Dun-lethglaissi. Or, in this year, the battle of Tailltiu.

Kal. Jan. (Wedn., m. 12.) A.D. 496. Anastasius [496.]
having been ordained 48th bishop of the Church of Rome, lived two years. Mochoe of Oendruim rested. The rest of Cormac,[3] bishop of Armagh, successor of Patrick. Or, in this year, the second battle of Grane,[4] in which fell Fraech, son of Finnchad, King of Laighen-desgabhair. Eochu, son of Cairpri, was victor.

Kal. Jan. Thursd., m. 23.) A.D. 497. Or, in this [497.]
year,[5] the storming of Dun-lethglaissi.[6] The battle of Inne-mor in Crich-ua-nGabla[7] *was gained* over the Leinstermen. Muirchertach, *i.e.*, Mac Erca, was victor. In this year a great earthquake shook[8] the province of Pontus. The rest of Cuinnidh (son of Cathmugh, *i.e.*, Mac Cuilinn,)[9] bishop of Lusk.

Kal. Jan. (Frid., m. 4.) A.D. 498. Simacus,[10] ordained [498.]
49th bishop of the Church of Rome, lived 15 years. A battle[11] in which the son of Erc was victor. The battle of Slemhain[12] of Meath *was gained* by Cairbre, son of Niall, over the Leinstermen. Or, in this year,[13] Mochoe of Aendruim [rested], according to another book.

---

county of Kildare. See O'Donovan's *Four Mast.*, A.D. 497, note *l*.

[8] *Shook.*—Conclurrit (for concurrit), A. B.

[9] *Mac Cuilinn.*—The origl. of this parenthesis is not in B.

[10] *Simacus.*—Symmachus, a Sardian, was ordained Pope on Sunday, Nov. 22, 498. He sat till July 19, 514, that is, for 15 years, 7 months, and 27 days. The length of his Pontificate is given as 12 years in B.

[11] *Battle.*—This entry is not in B. Neither is there any indication in A as to where the battle was fought.

[12] *Slemhain.* — Now divided into Slanebeg and Slanemore, two townlands in the parish of Dysart, co. Westmeath.

[13] *This year.*—This entry is not in

.b. Kl. Ianair. (7 f., l. 15.) Anno domini cccc.° xc.° ix.° Bellum. Quies Ibuir episcopi .ix. Kl. Mai.

Kl. Ianair. (2 f., l. 26ª.) Anno domini ccccc.mo Muircertaċ uictor fuit, et mors episcopi Ibair .ix. Kl. Mai. An Soisgel noċ do scriḃ Maṫa suiḃisgel da laṁaiḃ fein, 7 taise Barnabais, d'faġḃail hoc anno. Caṫ Ċind ailḃe for Laiġniu ria Cairbri mac Neill.

Kl. Ianair. (3ª f., l. 7ª.) Anno domini ccccc.mo i.° Bellum Segaisse in quo cecidit Daui (no Duaċ) tinga uṁai .i. ri Connacht. Muirċertaċ mac Earca uictor fuit.

Kl. Ianair. (4ª f., l. 18.) Anno domini ccccc.° ii.° Caṫ Ḋroma Lochṁuiḋe ria Laiġniu for huiḃ Neill.

.b. Kl. Ianair. (5 f., l. 29ª.) Anno domini ccccc.mo iii.° Cerban mortuus est, episcopus o Ferti Cherbain oc Temuir. Bellum Ṁanann la hAeḋan. Uel hic mors episcopi Iḃair.

Kl. Ianair. Anno domini ccccc.mo iiii.° [Mors Bruidi mic Mailċon.

Kl. Ianair. Anno domini ccccc.mo u.° Quies Espuic Mic Cairthinn Ċloċair.

B. The death of Mochoe of Aendruim (or Nendrum: Mahee Island, in Strangford Lough, co. Down), is entered before under the year 496, at which date his obit is also given by the Four Masters. See Reeves's *Antiq. of Down and Connor*, 187, *sq.*

[1] *Battle.*—This entry is left unfinished in A. and B.

[2] *Victor.*—It is to be feared that there is some confusion here, and that the battle mentioned in the last entry, the site of which is not there specified, was the one in which the victory was obtained, here credited to Muirchertach. But Clar. 49 says M. was victor "toto anno."

[3] *Found this year.*—Bede's Chronicon says:—"Corpus Barnabæ apostoli, et Evangelium Matthæi ejus stylo scriptum ipse revelante, reperitur." The entries for this year in B., though substantially the same as in A., differ slightly in arrangement.

[4] *Cend-Ailbhe.*—O'Conor's ed. of *Ann. Ult.* incorrectly has *Cnoc-Ailbhe.* O'Donovan (*Four Mast.*, 494, note *g*) conjectures that Cenn-Ailbhe was probably the name of a hill in Magh-Ailbhe, in the south of the co. Kildare.

[5] *Segais.*—Pronounced like *shayish.* It was the old name of the Curlieu Hills, near Boyle, county Roscommon.

[6] *Or Duach.*—Dani (or Dui seems to be the nomin. form of the name, gen., Duach. The epithet *tenga-umha*

Kal. Jan. (Saturd., m. 15.) A.D. 499. Battle.[1] Rest of Bishop Ibar on the 9th of the Kalends of May. [499.]

Kal. Jan. (Mond., m. 26.) A.D. 500. Muirchertach was victor,[2] and death of Bishop Ibar on the 9th of the Kalends of May. The Gospel which St. Matthew Evangelist wrote with his own hands, and the relics of Barnabas, were found this year.[3] The battle of Cend-Ailbhe[4] *was gained* over the Leinstermen by Cairbre, son of Niall. [500.]

Kal. Jan. (Tuesd., m. 7.) A.D. 501. The battle of Segais,[5] in which fell Daui (or Duach)[6] tenga-umha, *i.e.*, King of Connaught. Muirchertach Mac Erca was victor. [501.]

Kal. Jan. (Wed., m. 18.) A.D. 502. The battle of Druim-Lochmuidhe *was gained* by the Leinstermen[7] over the Ui-Neill. [502.]

Kal. Jan. (Thursd. m. 29.) A.D. 503. Cerpan died—a bishop from Fert-Cherpain[8] at Tara. The battle of Manann by Aedhan.[9] Or, in this year the death of Bishop Ibar. [503.]

Kal. Jan. A.D. 504. Death of Bruide, son of Maelchon.[10] [504.]

Kal. Jan. A.D. 505. Rest of Bishop Mac Cairthinn, of Clochar. [505.]

---

signifies "of the brazen tongue." O'Donovan (*Four Mast.*, A.D. 494, note *p*) says that he was otherwise called Duach Galach, *i.e.*, the Valorous, and was the son of Brian, who was brother of Niall Nine-hostager. But this is an error. Duach Galach succeeded Ailill Molt as King of Connaught about A.D. 463; and two Kings (Eogan Bél and his son Ailill Inbanda) intervened between Duach Galach and Duach Tenga-umai. See *Book of Leinster*, p. 41, col. 1.

[7] *By the Leinstermen.*—The transl. in Clar. 49 wrongly says, "against Leinstermen by O'Neales."

[8] *Fert-Cherpain.* — Or "Grave of Cerpan." In the Book of Armagh, Tirechan writes (fol. 10, *b. a.*), "Fundavit [Patricius] aecclesiam i Carric Dagri, et alteram aecclesiam immrnig Thuaithe, et scripsit elimenta *Cerpano.*" The site of Fert-Cherpain is marked on Petrie's plan of Tara (*Essay*, plan facing p. 129).

[9] *Aedhan.*—He was not yet born. This entry belongs to 581 or 582, as does the next to 583. This is a remarkable prolepsis, and the error must have existed in very ancient authorities, for it occurs in Tigernach at 504, 505, in anticipation of 582, 583.

[10] *Maelchon.*—See under 583.

Fol. 18ba. Kl. Ianair. Anno domini ccccc.° ui.° Bellum Arda corann, et mors Lugdach filii Loegaire, et ut alii dicunt, Domangart mac Nisse reti secessit anno xxxu.° Quies Mic Nisse Condaire episcopi.

.b. Kl. Ianair. Anno domini ccccc.° uii.° Uel hic mors Lugdach filii Laegaire, 7 cath Arda corrand.

Kl. Ianair. Anno domini ccccc.° uiii.°

Kl. Ianair. (6a f., l. 5.) Anno domini ccccc.° ix.° Bellum Fremonn for Fiachaig mac Neill. Failgi berraide uictor fuit.

Kl. Ianair. (7a f., l. 16.) Anno domini ccccc.° x.° Bellum secundum Arda corrann, ut alii dicunt.

b. Kl. Ianair. (1. f., l. 27a.) Anno domini ccccc.° x.° i.° Quies Bronii episcopi. Defectus solis contigit. Natiuitas sancti Ciarani filii artificis. Uel hic bas Lugdach mic Laegaire secundum librum monachorum.

Kl. Ianair. (3 f., l. 9a.) Anno domini ccccc.° x.° ii.° Quies Erci episcopi Slane. Dubthach (a Druim dearb), espuc aird Machai, obiit. Muirchertach mac Earca regnare incipit.

---

[1] *Ard-Corann.*—See under the year 464, *supra.*

[2] *Reti secessit.*—This expression is very obscure, and may be a blunder for 'vita secessit,' or for 'requiescit,' according as the transcriber took Domangart for a king or an ecclesiastic. This entry and the one which follows are fused into one in B., which has Domangart mac Nisse episcopus Connere hic quieuit. There was no Domangart bishop of Connor. But Mac Nisse, *i.e.*, Oengus, whose death is recorded under the year 513, *infra*, was the first bishop, and founder of Connor. The subject is further complicated by the marginal entry, Domangart episcopus, which occurs in A., in a very old hand. In the entry of his death in *Tigernach* (A.D. 505), Domangart is called "King of Alba." At A.D. 559 *infra*, the death of Gabran, son of Domangart, is given. This Domangart was the son of Fergus Mor Mac Nisse, and 3rd King of the Dalriadic Scots. Five years was the length of his reign, according to the best authorities. It was in the year 502, according to Tigernach, that the colony went over to Scotland; and, allowing three years for the joint reign of Lorn and Fergus, the date of Domangart's accession would be 505, and his obit (after a reign of five years) A.D. 510. It is worthy of observation that 35 years is

Kal. Jan. A.D. 506. The battle of Ard-Corann,[1] and the death of Lugaid son of Laegaire, and as others state, Domhangart Mac Nisse *reti secessit*[2] in the 35th year. Rest of Mac Nisse,[3] bishop of Connor. [506.]

Kal. Jan. A.D. 507. Or, in this year,[4] the death of Lugaid son of Laegaire, and the battle of Ard-Corann.[5] [507.]

Kal. Jan. A.D. 508. [508.]

Kal. Jan. (Frid., m. 5.) A.D. 509. The battle of Fremhonn *was gained* over Fiacha son of Niall. Failghi Berraide was victor. [509.]

Kal. Jan. (Sat., m. 16.) A.D. 510. The second battle of Ard-Corann, as others say. [510.]

Kal. Jan. (Sund., m. 27.) A.D. 511. The rest of Bishop Bron.[6] An eclipse of the sun happened. Birth of Saint Ciaran[7] son of the Carpenter. Or, in this year, the death of Lugaid son of Laegaire, according to the Book of the Monks.[8] [511.]

Kal. Jan. (Tuesd., m. 9.) A.D. 512. The rest of Erc, bishop of Slane. Dubthach from Druim-dearbh,[9] bishop of Armagh, died. Muirchertach Mac Erca begins to reign. [512.]

---

the length assigned to his son Comgall's reign by these Annals (*infra*, 537), from which date, if 35 years be deducted, we get the year of the migration. See Reeves's *Adamnan*, pp. 433–436.

[3] *Mac Nisse.*—See under A.D. 513.

[4] *Or, in this year.*—Uel hic, B. 7 (for et), A.

[5] *Ard-Corann.* — See under the year 464, *supra.*

[6] *Bishop Bron.*—Bishop of Cashel-Irra, now called Killaspugbrone ('church of Bishop Bron'), a little to the west of Sligo.

[7] *Ciaran.*—Founder of Clonmacnoise. His obit, in the 34th year of his age, is given *infra*, at 548, which would refer his birth to the year 514, the true year, and the year at which Tigernach has it.

[8] *Book of the Monks.*—Secundum librum monachorum, A. Not in B., nor in Clar. 49. The word monachorum is written in an abbrev. form in A.; but there can be no doubt as to the way in which it should be represented in full. There is no other reference to a "*liber monachorum*"; and the name here may possibly be a mistake for "*liber Mochod*," or "Book of Mochod," referred to *infra*, at 527.

[9] *From Druim-dearbh.*—Not in B., though Clar. 49 has "de Druimderb." The addition also occurs in the Ann. Four Mast. at this year.

Kl. Ianair. (4ª f., l. 20.) Anno domini ccccc.° x.° iii.° Cairpri daimairgit (mac Eaċaċ mic Crimthoind mic ḟeig mic Deaġa Ḋuirnn mic Reoċaḋa mic Colla da crich) ri Airgiall. Mac Nisi .i. Aengus epscop Coindere quieuit.

Kl. Ianair. (5 f.) Anno domini ccccc.° x.° iiii.° Romane eclesie l.us Hormisda episcopus ordinatur, uixit annis .ix.

Fol. 18bb. Kl. Ianair. (6 f., l.) Anno domini ccccc.° x.° u.° Bellum droma derge for Failgi. Fiaċa uictor erat. Deinde campus Miḋe a Lagenis sublatus est. Natiuitas Comgaill Beannċair.

Kl. Ianair. (1. f., l. 23.) Anno domini ccccc.° x.° ui.° Quies Darercae Cille sleibe Cuilinn .iii. nonas iulii. Uel secundum alium librum natiuitas Ciarain hoc anno. Caṫ Droma dergaiḋe ria Fiaċaiḃ mac Neill for Failġe m-berraiġe. Inde maġ Miġe a Lagenis sublatus est, ut Cennfaelad cecinit.

Digal dia seacht m-bliadan,
Ba si digde a ċriḋe;
Caṫ inn dromaiḃ dergaiġi,
Ba de dochear maġ Miḋe.

An ri aile aríḃeriḋ,
Fiaċa mac Neill ni ċelaid,
Ba fair tar cremla cili
Caṫ Fremon [Mide] meṁaid.

Kl. Ianair. (2 f., l. 4.ª) Anno domini ccccc.° x.° uii.° Anastasius imperator subita morte peruentus est, maior octogenario periit. Regnauit annos .xx. uii., mensibus duobus, diebus .xx. ix.

---

¹ *Eocha.*—The original of the parenthesis is not in B., nor in Clar. 49.

² *Mac Nisi.*—See under the year 506, *supra.*

³ *Failghi,* i.e., Failghi Berraide, whose victory over Fiacha son of Niall, in the battle of Fremonn (Frewin, co. Westmeath), is recorded at 509, *supra.* This battle is entered in the Ann. Four Mast. under 507. See O'Dono-

Kal. Jan. (Wed., m. 20.) A.D. 513. Cairpri Daimargit (son of Eocha,[1] son of Crimthand, son of Fiag, son of Deaga-duirn, son of Reochaid, son of Colla Daerich), king of Airghialla, [died]. Mac Nisi,[2] *i.e.* Aengus, bishop of Connor, rested. [513.]

Kal. Jan. (Thurs., . .) A.D. 514. Hormisda, having been ordained 50th bishop of the Church of Rome, lived nine years. [514.]

Kal. Jan. (Frid., m. . .) A.D. 515. The battle of Druim-derge *was gained* over Failghi.[3] Fiacha was victor. Thereupon the plain of Meath was taken from the Leinstermen. Birth of Comgall of Bangor. [515.]

Kal. Jan. (Sund., m. 23.) A.D. 516. The rest of Darerca of Cill-Sleibhe-Cuilinn, on the 5th of July. Or, according to another book, the birth of Ciaran in this year. The battle of Druim-dergaidhe *was gained* by Fiacha son of Niall, over Failghi Berraide; after which the plain of Meath was taken from the Leinstermen, as Cennfaelad sang:— [516.]

His seven years' vengeance
Was the wish of his heart.
The battle in Druim-dergaidhe—
By it the plain of Meath was lost.

The[4] other king they mention—
Fiacha son of Niall—hide it not—
Over him, contrary to a false promise,
The battle of Fremhon [of Meath] was won.

Kal. Jan. (Mond., m. 4.) A.D. 517. The Emperor Anastasius was overtaken by a sudden death. He died over eighty years old. He reigned 27 years, 2 months, and 29 days.[5] [517.]

---

van's notes under that year, respecting the extent of the lands lost to the Leinstermen, as the result of their defeat.

[4] This stanza, which is not in B., is added in the lower margin of fol. 18*b* in A.

[5] *Days.* — The numbers of the months and days are added in an old hand in A.

Kl. Ianair. (3 f., l. 15.) Anno domini ccccc.° x.° uiii.° Natiuitas Coluim Cille eodem die quo Bute mac Bronaigh dormiuit. Quies Darercae que Moninne nominata est.

.b. Kl. Ianair. (4 fa., luna 26.) Anno domini ccccc.° x.° ix.° Conlaedh espcop Cille daro mortuus est. Bellum Detnae i n-Drumbaidh Bregh, in quo cecidit Ardgal filius Conaill filii Neill. Colggu moo Cluaethi rex Orientalium, ocus Muirchertach mac Erca uictores erant. Comhgall Benncuir natus est secundum [alios].

Kl. Ianair. (6 f., l. 7.) Anno domini ccccc.° xx.° Cainneach Achaid bó natus est secundum quosdam.

Kl. Ianair. (7a f., l. 18.a) Anno domini ccccc.° xx.° i.°

Kl. Ianair. (i. f., l. 29.a) Anno domini ccccc.° xx.° ii.° Cath Dethna i n-Drommaibh Bregh in quo cecidit Ardgal mac Conuill crethmhainne mic Neill secundum alios. Buithi mac Bronaigh obiit. Colum cille natus est.

.b. Kl. Ianair. (2 f., l. x.) Anno domini ccccc.° xx.° iii.° (alias iiii.°) Bellum Cairpri filii Neill, 7 Beoigh (Espcop) Arda carna. Quies sancte Brigitae anno .lxx. aetatis sue.

Fol. 19aa. Kl. Ianair. (4 f.) Anno domini ccccc.° xx.° iiii.° Iohannis Romane eclesie papa l.i.us duobus annis in sede Petri uixit, Constantinopolim uenit, qui dum

[1] *Colum Cille.*—The birth of Colum Cille is also entered *infra*, at 522, which is the date adopted by Ussher. (*Index* Chron. ad an). Tigernach gives it at 520.

[2] *Darerca.*—The "rest" of Darerca is entered before, at 516.

[3] *Son of Cluaeth.*—In A. and B. the words "son of Cluaeth" are represented by moo cluaethi, which seems corrupt. The name in the corresponding entry in the Ann. Four Mast. is mac Loiti, "son of Loit." But the Chron. Scot. (518), has Mocloithe, altered by Rod. O'Flaherty to *Mac Cloithe*, or son of *Cloth*. See *Chron. Scot.*, p. 39, note [10].

[4] *Others.*—The corresponding Latin is not in A. or B. In fact, even the word secundum is neither in B., nor in Clar. 49. See 601 *infra*.

[5] *According to some.*—Secundum quosdam. Not in B. St. Cainnech's birth is again entered under 526.

Kal. Jan. (Tuesd., m. 15.) A.D. 518. The birth of Colum Cille,[1] on the same day in which Buite, son of Bronach, slept. The rest of Darerca,[2] who was called Moninne. [518.]

Kal. Jan. (Wed., m. 26). A.D. 519. Conlaedh, bishop of Cill-dara, died. The battle of Detna, in Droma-Bregh, in which fell Ardgal, son of Conall, son of Niall. Colgu, son of Cluaeth,[3] King of Airthera, and Muirchertach Mac Erca, were victors. Comgall of Bangor was born, according to [others[4]]. [519.]

Kal. Jan. (Frid., m. 7.) A.D. 520. Cainnech of Achadh-bó was born, according to some.[5] [520.]

Kal. Jan. (Sat., m. 18.) A.D. 521. [521.]

Kal. Jan. (Sund., m. 29.) A.D. 522. The battle of Detna,[6] in Droma-Bregh, in which fell Ardgal, son of Conall Cremthainne, son of Niall, according to others.[7] Buiti, son of Bronach, died. Colum Cille was born.[8] [522.]

Kal. Jan. (Mond., m. 10.) A.D. 523 (alias[9] 524). The battle of Cainri,[10] son of Niall, and [the rest] of Beoid, bishop of Ard-carna. Rest of Saint Brigit, in the 70th[11] year of her age. [523.]

Kal. Jan. (Wedn. .) A.D. 524. John,[12] the 51st Pope of the Church of Rome, having lived two years in the See of Peter, came to Constantinople; and when, on [524.]

---

[6] *Of Detna.*—Not in B.

[7] *Others.*—The orig. of this clause, which is not in B., is added in the marg. in A.

[8] *Born.*—The entry in B. is uel hic natiuitas Coluim Cille, "or here, the birth of Colum Cille." See under 518.

[9] *Alias.*—The suggested correction is in a very old hand in A. Not in B.

[10] *Battle of Cainri.*—There is some error in this entry, which it is very hard, if not impossible, to rectify. Niall had no son named Cainri. The name might have been so written, by mistake, for Cairbri.

[11] *In the 70th.*—The death of St. Brigit is recorded in these Annals, from different authorities, at 523, 525, and 527. Tigernach has it at 526. Early authorities state that she survived St. Patrick 30 years, in which case the year of her death would be 523. See *Chronicon Scotorum*, A.D. 523.

[12] *John.*—Iohannis, A.

rediens Rauennam uenisset, Teodoricus rex Arrianus eum cum comitibus carceris adflictione peremit, cuius corpus de Rauenna translatum in basilica beati Petri sepultum est, post duos annos 7 .ix. menses 7 dies xiii.

Kl. Ianair. (5 f.) Anno domini ccccc.° xx.° ii.° Dormitatio sancte Brigite anno .lxx. etatis sue. Ailill espcop Ard Macha quieuit.

Kl. Ianair. (6 f.) Anno domini ccccc.° xx.° iii.° Natiuitas Cainnigh Achaid bo. Mors Illaind mic Dunlainge mic Enna niadh mic Breasail belaigh. Anno regiae urbis .i. Constantinopolim conditae, c.xc.iiii., Iustinus imperator Iustinianum ex sorore sua nepotem, iamdudum a se nobilissimum designatum quoque regni sui successoremque creauit, Kl. Aprilis. Ipse uero quarto ab hoc mense uita decessit, anno imperii ix.° mense ii.° Pausatio sancti Ailbe.

.b. Kl. Ianair. (7 f., l. 24.) Anno domini ccccc.° xx.° iiii.° Felix Romane eclesie episcopus sedit annis .iiii. mensibus ix. diebus .xiiii. Iohannis et dies. xuii. et mensibus .ii. et diebus .xiii. Felix eficiunt quartum annum, et sepultus est in basilica Petri beati apostoli. Bellum Cinneich et bellum Aetha sighe for Laighniu. Muirchertach mac Ercae uictor fuit. Uel hic dormitacio Brigide secundum librum Mochod.

Kl. Ianair. (2 f., l. 5.) Anno domini ccccc.° xx.° u.° Natiuitas Coemain bricc. Benedictus monachus claruit.

---

[1] *St. Brigit.*—See under 523.

[2] *Ailill.*—A mutilated note in the marg. in A. suggests that he was of the Ui-Bresail. In the List of the Successors of St. Patrick, contained in the *Book of Leinster* (p. 42, col. 3), this Ailill, who is there called "primus," as well as his successor, Ailill "secundus," is stated to have been from Druimchád, in Ui-Bressail. The death of Ailill "the second" is entered under 535 *infra*.

[3] *Cainnech.*—St. Canice, Patron St. of Ossory. His birth is also entered *supra*, at 520. Tigernach places his birth at 517, which seems the true date, as his obit is given at 599 *infra* (=600), in his 84th year, according to Tigern.

[4] *Saint Ailbhe.*—Founder and Patron

his return, he had arrived at Ravenna, Theodoric, the Arian king, put him and his companions to death under the rigour of imprisonment. His body, removed from Ravenna, was buried in the church of St. Peter, after two years, and nine months, and seventeen days.

Kal. Jan. (Thursday.) A.D. 525. The repose of St. Brigit,[1] in the 70th year of her age. Ailill,[2] bishop of Armagh, rested. [525.]

Kal. Jan. (Friday.) A.D. 526. The birth of Cainnech,[3] of Achadh-bo. Death of Illand, son of Dunlaing, son of Enna Niadh, son of Bresal Belach. In the 197th year after the foundation of the regal city (*i.e.*, Constantinople), on the Kalends of April, the Emperor Justin appointed as his successor on the throne Justinian, his nephew by his sister, who had, long before, been designated "*Nobilissimus*" by him. He died in the fourth month following, in the 9th year and 2nd month of his reign. Rest of Saint Ailbhe.[4] [526.]

Kal. Jan. (Sat., m. 24.) A.D. 527. Felix, bishop of the Church of Rome, sat 4 years, and 9 months,[5] and 14 days (and the 17 days[6] of John, and the two months and 13 days of Felix, make the fourth year); and he was buried in the church of Saint Peter the Apostle. The battle of Cenn-eich, and the battle of Ath-sighe, *gained* over the Leinstermen. Muirchertach Mac Erca was victor. Or, in this year, the repose of Brigid,[7] according to the Book of Mochod.[8] [527.]

Kal. Jan. (Mond., m. 5.) A.D. 528. Birth of Coeman Brecc. Benedict, the monk, attained celebrity. [528.]

---

of Imlech-Ibhair (Emly, county Tipperary). His death is also entered under 533 and 541, *infra*.

[5] *Months.* — menṡibuṡ, B.; menṡe, A.

[6] *Days.*—The original of the parenthesis here, which in A. seems very corrupt, is not represented in the text of B.

[7] *Repose of Brigid.*—See note under 523, *supra*.

[8] *Book of Mochod.*—See note on the "Book of the Monks," under 511 *supra*. The clause ṡecunдum libꝛum Mochoд is only found in A. (*al. man.*) and Clar. 49.

Fol. 19ab. Kl. Ianair. (3 f.) Anno domini ccccc. xx.° ix.°

Kl. Ianair. (4 f.) Anno domini ccccc.° xxx.° Corpus sancti Antonii monachi diuina reuelatione repertum Alaxandriam perducitur, et in eclesia sancti Iohannis
.b. baptistae humatur.

Kl. Ianair. (5 f., l. 9.) Anno domini ccccc.° xxx.° i.° In hoc anno Dionisius pascales scripsit ciclos, incipiens ab anno dominicae incarnationis d.° xx.° qui est Diocliciani cc.us xl. ui.us

Kl. Ianair. (7 f., l. 20.) Anno domini ccccc.° xxx.° ii.° iii. bellum in hoc anno gesta uno, et possito ergense ecc leccam lias, Felix sepultus est in basilica beati Petri apostoli. Bellum Eblinne ria Muircertach mac Erce, 7 cath muighi Ailbe for Laigniu, 7 cath Aidhne for Conachta, 7 cath Almuine, 7 cat Cinneich for Laigniu, 7 orgain na Cliach in uno anno. Cath Atha sighe. Muircertach mac Earca uictor erat.

Kl. Ianair (1. f., l. 1.) Anno domini ccccc.° xxx.° iii.° Demersio Muircertaig filii Erce, .i. Muircertaig mic Muiredhaidh mic Eoghain mic Neill .ix. giallaigh, in dolio pleno uino, in arce Cletig supra Boinn. Quies Ailbe imlecha Ibuir. Bonifatius romanus episcopus sedit annis .ii. diebus xx.ui., sepultusque est in basilica beati Petri apostoli.

---

[1] *Year* 520.—This should be the year 532.

[2] *The* 246*th*.—Should be "248th," Dioclesian having been proclaimed Emperor in A.D. 284. The old hand adds "Dion. Exiguus," in the margin in A.

[3] *Three battles*.—In orig. (A.) .iii. bellum. The entry seems quite unintelligible, being, as it stands "tria bellum (sic) in hoc anno gesta uno et possito (corrected from possite, by old hand) ergense ecc leccam lias." For .iii. bellum, we might perhaps read ui. bella ("six battles"—this being the number mentioned in the latter part of the entry.) But the Editor cannot attempt to explain the meaning of *possito ergense ecc leccam lias*. The introduction also of the name of Pope Felix (ob. 530), whose death and burial are referred to at the year 527, seems to indicate that some great confusion has occurred in the transcription of the text. The entry, unfortunately, is not found in B., and is only represented in Clar. 49, by "3a Bella hoc anno." The so-called "translator" who composed that version of these Annals must have had the full

Kal. Jan. (Tuesd.) A.D. 529. [529.]

Kal. Jan. (Wedn.) A.D. 530. The body of St. Anthony, the monk, having been recovered by Divine revelation, is conveyed to Alexandria, and buried in the church of St. John the Baptist. [530.]

Kal. Jan. (Thursd., m. 9.) A.D. 531. In this year Dionysius wrote his Paschal Cycle, commencing from the year 520[1] of the Incarnation of our Lord, which is the 246th[2] of Dioclesian. [531.]

Kal. Jan. (Sat., m. 20.) A.D. 532. Three[3] battles were fought in this one year, et possito ergense ecc lecam lias, Felix was buried in the church of St. Peter the Apostle. The battle of Eblinne, *gained* by Muirchertach Mac Erca, and the battle of Magh-Ailbhe, *gained* over the Leinstermen, and the battle of Aidhne over the Connaughtmen, and the battle of Almhu, and the battle of Cenn-eich, over the Leinstermen, and the plunder of the Clius, in one year.[4] The battle of Athsighe. Muirchertach Mac Erca was victor. [532.]

Kal. Jan. (Sund., m. 1.) A.D. 533. The drowning of Muirchertach Mac Erca, *i.e.*, Muirchertach, son of Muiredach, son of Eoghan, son of Niall Nine-hostager, in a vat full of wine, in the fort[5] of Cletech, over the Boyne. The rest of Ailbhe[6] of Imlech-Ibhair. Boniface, bishop of Rome, having sat 2 years and 26 days, was buried in the church of St. Peter the Apostle. [533.]

---

entry before him, in some ancient copy, but was probably unable to understand it, and therefore passed it by.

[4] *In one year.*—In uno anno. Not in B.

[5] *In the fort.*—In axe, A. and B. But, of course, by mistake for arce. In an ancient account of the death of Muirchertach Mac Erca, contained in the *Yellow Book of Lecan*, it is stated that his destruction was contrived by a fairy woman named *Sin* (pron. Sheen), for whose society he had discarded his queen. But his relative St. Cairnech of Dulane (in Meath), having persuaded him to take back h's queen, and dismiss his fairy favourite, the latter, through her fairy machinations, successfully plotted the destruction of King Muirchertach. The tale is wild and imaginative, but contains much historical information. See the Ann. Four Mast., under A.D. 527, and *Chron. Scot.*, at 531.

[6] *Rest of Ailbhe.*—His "rest" is also entered under 526 and 541.

Kl. Ianair. (2 f., l. 12.) Anno domini ccccc.° xxx.° iiii.° Dormitatio Muchti discipuli Patricii xiii. Kl. Septembris; sic ipse scripsit in epistola sua, Mauchteus peccator presbiter, sancti Patricii discipulus, in Domino salutem. Bellum Lóchara móre etir da inber ria Tuathal maelgarb mac Cormaic chaeich mic Cairpre mic Neill .ix. giallaigh for Cianacht. Cath Aiblinne ria Muircheartach mac Earca for Laighniu ut alii uolunt.

.b. Kl. Ianair. (3 f., lu. 23.) Anno domini ccccc.° xxx.°
ol. 19ba. u.° Huc usque Marcellinus perduxit cronicon suum. Mercurius qui et Iohannis natione romanus romane ecclesiae episcopus sedit annis .ii. mensibus .iiii. diebus .iii., sepultus est in basilica beati Petri apostoli. Perditio panis. Ailill epscop Aird macha obiit. Uel hic bathadh Muircheartaigh mic Earca, secundum alios.

Kl. Ianair. (5 f., l. 4). Anno domini ccccc.° xxx.° ui.° Bellum Eiblinne montis. Tuathal maelgarb regnauit annis .xi. Uel hic dormitatio sancti Mochta discipuli Patricii.

Kl. Ianair. Anno domini ccccc.° xxx.° uii.° Agapitus natione romanus, Romane ecclesie episcopus sedit mensibus .xi. diebus .uiii., et in basilica beati Petri apostoli sepultus est: xxui dies Bonifatii, et .iiii. menses et .ui. dies Mercurii, et .xi. menses et dies .uiii. Agapiti, efficiunt annum et .iiii. menses

---

[1] *Mochta.*—(Mauchteus) A. The clause here quoted is not in B., but is in Clar. 49.

[2] *Luachair-mór.*—The Four Mast., who have the entry of this battle under A.D. 528, state that it was called the "battle of Ailbhe in Brega," and was gained over the "Cianachta of Meath." The place is now supposed to be represented by Clonalvy, bar. of Upper Duleek, co. Meath. It is entered again, under 538.

[3] *As some say.*—ut alii uolunt. Not in B.

[4] *Ailill.*—A marg. note in A. has do ib Bresail beos ("of the Ui-Bresail still.") See note under 525 *supra*, regarding another bishop of Armagh of the name.

[5] *Sliabh-Eibhlinne.*—Aibhlinne, at

Kal. Jan. (Mond., m. 12.) A.D. 534. The repose of [534.] lochta, disciple of Patrick, on the 13th of the Kalends f September. Thus he wrote in his epistle: "Mochta,[1] sinner, presbyter, disciple of Saint Patrick, sends greetng in the Lord." The battle of Luachair-mór[2] between wo 'invers,' *was gained* by Tuathal Maelgarbh, son of Cormac Caech, son of Cairbre, son of Niall Nine-hostager, ver Cianachta. The battle of Aibhlinne *was gained* y Muirchertach Mac Erca over the Leinstermen, as some ay.[3]

Kal. Jan. (Tues., m. 23.) A.D. 535. Thus far Marcel- [535.] inus brought down his Chronicle. Mercurius, who was lso called John, a Roman by birth, bishop of the Church f Rome, sat 2 years, 4 months, and 6 days; and was uried in the church of St. Peter the Apostle. Failure f bread. Ailill,[4] bishop of Armagh, died. Or, in this ear, the drowning of Muirchertach Mac Erca, according o others.

Kal. Jan. (Thursd., m. 4.) A.D. 536. Battle of [536.] Sliabh-Eibhlinne.[5] Tuathal Maelgarbh reigned eleven[6] ears. Or, in this year, the repose of Saint Mochta,[7] lisciple of Patrick.

Kal. Jan. A.D. 537. Agapitus, a Roman by birth, [537.] bishop of the Church of Rome, sat 11 months and 8 days. He was buried in the church of St. Peter the Apostle. Twenty-six days of Boniface, and 4 months and 6 days of Mercurius, and 11 months and 8 days of Agapitus, nake up a year, and 4 months, and 10 days. The battle

---

A.D. 534. Now known as the Sliabh-Phelim Mountains, on the confines of Tipperary and Limerick.

[6] *Eleven years.*—A. and B. have "annis xi". But Clar. 49 has ii. (for two' years), which is probably a mistake for 11. The murder of Tuathal Maelgarbh is recorded *infra*, at 543, and as the length of his reign was eleven years, the date of his accession must have been 532. Tuathal *Maelgarbh* was grandson of Cairbre, son of Niall, and the only sovereign of Ireland in this line. His surname is interpreted *calvo-asper* by O'Flaherty.

[7] *Mochta.*—His "dormitatio" is entered above, under the year 534.

et .x. dies. Bellum Cloenloċa ubi cecidit Mane mac Cerbaill. Mors Comgaill mic Domangairt, xxx.° u.° anno regni.

Kl. Ianair. Anno domini ccccc.° xxx.° iiii.° Perditio panis. Bellum Loċar. Tuaṫal maelgarb (mac Cormaic caiṫ mic Cairbri mic Neill .ix. ġiallaiġ) uictor erat, ut alii dicunt. Siluerius natione Romanus sedit anno .i. mensibus .ii. dies .xi., confesor obiit.

.b. Kl. Ianair. Anno domini ccccc.° xxx.° ix.° Natiuitas Grigorii Rome. Uigilius natione romanus episcopus romane ecclesie sedit annis .xuii. mensibus .ui. diebus .xxii. Saracussis defunctus est; Uia salaria sepultus est.

Kl. Ianair. Anno domini ccccc.° xl.°

l. 19bb. Kl. Ianair. Anno domini ccccc.° xl.° i.° Mors Comgaill mic Domangairt. Albeus pausat.

Kl. Ianair. Anno domini cccc[c].° xl.° ii.° Bellum Torten .i. fria Laignib, ubi cecidit mac Erce filius Ailella molt. Bellum Sliciġe ubi cecidit Eugen bel rex Connacht. Fergus 7 Domnall, duo filii mic Erce, uictores erant, 7 Ainmire mac Setna 7 Ninniḋ mac Setni.

.b. Kl. Ianair. Anno domini ccccc.° xl.° iii.° Tuaṫal maelgarb iugulatus est .i. a n-Greallaiġ allta, la Maelmorḋa, cui successit Diarmait mac Cerbaill.

Kl. Ianair. (i. f., l. 2.) Anno domini ccccc.° xl.° iiii.° Mortalitas prima que dicitur blefed, in qua

---

[1] *Cloenloch.*—The Four Mast., at 531, place it in Cinel-Aodha (or Kinalea), a district well known as O'Shaughnessy's country, and lying round the town of Gort, in the co. Galway.

[2] *Mane son of Cerbhall.*—He was of the "Ui-Maine" of Connaught, who derived their tribe-name from Maine, fifth in descent from Colla-da-crich.

[3] *Comgall.*—See note under A.D. 506, *supra.*

[4] *Luachair.*—See this battle entered above, at 534.

[5] *Son.*—The parenthetic matter is not in B.

[6] *Confessor.*—confesor̄, A. cf̄, B.

of Cloenloch,[1] in which fell Mane[2] son of Cerbhall. Death of Comgall[3] son of Domangart, in the 35th year of his reign.

Kal. Jan. A.D. 538. Failure of bread. The battle of Luachair.[4] Tuathal Maelgarbh, (son[5] of Cormac Caech, son of Cairbre, son of Niall Nine-hostager), was victor, as some say. Silverius, a Roman by birth, sat 1 year, 5 months, 11 days, and died a confessor.[6] [538.]

Kal. Jan. A.D. 539. Birth of Gregory[7] at Rome. Vigilius, a Roman by birth, bishop of the Church of Rome, sat 17 years, 6 months, and 22 days. He died at Syracuse, and was buried in the Via Salaria. [539.]

Kal. Jan. A.D. 540. [540.]

Kal. Jan. A.D. 541. Death of Comgall,[8] son of Domangart. Ailbhe[9] rested. [541.]

Kal. Jan. A.D. 542. The battle of Torten[10] *was gained* by the Leinstermen, in which fell Mac Erca,[11] son of Ailill Molt. The battle of Sligech, in which fell Eogan Bel, King of Connaught. Fergus and Domnall, two sons of Mac Erca, were victors, and Ainmire son of Setna, and Ninnidh son of Setna.[12] [542.]

Kal. Jan. A.D. 543. Tuathal Maelgarbh was slain by Maelmordha, *i.e.* at Greallach-allta, to whom Diarmait Mac Cerbhaill succeeded. [543.]

Kal. Jan. (Sund., m. 2.) A.D. 544. The first mortality, which is called 'blefed,'[13] in which Mobi Clarainech [544.]

---

[7] *Gregory.*—See under A.D. 544.

[8] *Comgall.*—His death is entered before under 537, which seems the proper date. See a note on the subject at 506, *supra.*

[9] *Ailbhe.*—The "quies" of Ailbhe is recorded above under the year 533.

[10] *Torten.*—So called from the Ui-Tortain, a small branch of the Airghialla, who settled near Ardbraccan in Meath. They derived their name from Tortan, fifth in descent from Colla-da-crich.

[11] *Mac Erca.*—Tigernach states that the "men of Cera" (or tribes inhabiting the barony of Carra, co. Mayo), descended from him. This battle is entered again under 547.

[12] *Setna.*—This should be "Duach," as in Tigernach and the Ann. Four Mast.

[13] *Blefed.*—See several references to this plague in the *Census of Ireland* for 1851, part V., vol. I., p. 46, where some curious information on the subject of this and other plagues is collected.

Mobi claraineċ obiit. Mors Comgaill mic Domangairt ut alii dicunt. Diarmait mac Fergusa Cerrbeoil mic Conaill cremthainne mic Neill .ix. ġiallaiġ regnare incipit, secundum librum Cuanach. Uel hic Natiuitas Gregorii secundum alios.

Kt. Ianair. (2 f., l. 13.) Anno domini ccccc.° xl.° u.° Daire Coluim cille fundata est.

Kt. Ianair. (3 f., l. 24.) Anno domini ccccc.° xl.° ui.° (alias 47.) Bellum Sligiḋe in quo ceciderunt Eugen bel (.i. rex Connacht), 7 Domnall 7 Fergus duo filii Muircertaig mic Erca, 7 Ainmire mac Setna mic Ferġusa mic Conaill gulban mic Neill .ix. giallaig, uictores erant.

.b. Kt. Ianair. (4 f., l. 5.) Anno domini ccccc.° xl.° uii.° Dubtaċ (no Duaċ, do ṡil Cholla uais) ab Ard maċa quieuit. Cluain mic Nois fundata est. Caṫ Tortan ria Laiġniu, in quo cecidit mac Erca mic Ailella muilt. Uel hic caṫ Sligiḋe.

Kt. Ianair. (6a f., l. 16.) Anno domini ccccc.° xl.° uiii.° Dormitacio filii artificis .i. Ciaraini, anno xxx. iiii. aetatis sue (uel anno 7° postquam Cluain mic Nois construere cepit). Tigernaċ Cluana eois. Mortalitas magna in qua isti pausant, Finnio macc
Fol. 20aa. u Telduib, Colaim nepos Craumṫainan, Mac tail Cille cuilind, Sinċeall mac Cenanndain abbas Cille achaid drumm[a] foto, 7 Columbae insae Celtrae. Uel hoc anno Tuaṫal maelgarḃ ri Teamrach in-

---

[1] *Gregory.*—Afterwards styled the "Great." See also under 539.

[2] *Alias* 47.—Added in old hand in A.

[3] *Sligech.*—The river which gives name to the town of Sligo. This battle is entered above at the year 542.

[4] *Domnall.*—The remainder of this entry is not in B.

[5] *Duach.*—This is the name in B., and also in the list of the *Comarbs* (or successors) of St. Patrick, in the *Book of Leinster*, p. 42, col. 3. The original of the parenthesis appears as a gloss in the original hand in A., and also in B.

[6] *Tortan.*—This battle is entered above at the year 542, where see note. The text of this and the entry which follows in A. is represented in B. by uel hic bellum tortan 7 bellum Sligiḋe.

[7] *Clonmacnoise.*—This clause is not in B., nor in Clar. 49.

[8] *Cluain-eois.*—Clones, co. Monaghan.

ed. The death of Comgall, son of Domangart, as some y. Diarmait, son of Fergus Cerrbeoil, son of Conall imthainne, son of Niall Nine-hostager, begins to reign, cording to the Book of Cuanu. Or, in this year, the rth of Gregory,[1] according to some.

Kal. Jan. (Mond., m. 13.) A.D. 545. Daire-Coluim- ille was founded. [545.]

Kal. Jan. (Tues., m. 24. A.D. 546 (alias 47).[2] The [546.] ttle of Sligech,[3] in which fell Eugen Bel (*i.e.*, King Connaught), and Domnall[4] and Fergus, the two sons Muirchertach Mac Erca, and Ainmire son of Setna on of Fergus, son of Conall Gulban, son of Niall Nine- ostager), were victors.

Kal. Jan. (Wedn., m. 5.) A.D. 547. Dubtach (or [547.] uach,[5] of the race of Colla Uais), abbot of Armagh, sted. Cluain-mic-Nois was founded. The battle of ortan[6] *was gained* by the Leinstermen, in which fell ac Erca, son of Ailill Molt. Or, in this year, the battle Sligech.

Kal. Jan. (Frid., m. 16.) A.D. 548. The falling asleep [548.] the son of the Carpenter, *i.e.*, Ciaran, in the 34th year his age, (or in the 7th year after he had commenced to uild Clonmacnoise.[7]) Tigernach of Cluain-eois[8] [died.] reat mortality, in which these persons rested: Finnio acc-U-Telduibh;[9] Colam descendant of Craumthanan;[10] ac-Tail of Cill-Cuilind; Sinchell son of Cenandan, bbot of Cill-achaidh of Druim-fota, and Colum of Inis- eltra. Or, in this year,[11] Tuathal Maelgarbh, King of

[9] *Macc U Telduibh.* — Corruptly ritten maccuċ duib in A. Not in The name is *Mac Creduib* in ar. 49. But this is more corrupt ill. Tigernach, at the parallel place, ves the name as printed above.

[10] *Descendant of Craumthanan.*— e Four Masters (A.D. 548) call him lum son of Crimthann. But he s really the son of Ninnidh, who was the fifth in descent from Crimthann.

[11] *This year.*—This entry is added at foot of fol. 19*bb.* in A., in an old hand. It is represented in B., in the text, after the name of *Columba of Inis-Celtra*, merely by uel hoc anno Tuaṫal maelġarb ingulatur fuit. The entry in Clar. 49 is nearly the same as in A.

ternt i n-grellaig eilte, iugulatur o Maelṁor hu mic hI, qui et ipse statim occisus est. Unde dicitur echt ṁaeilṁoir.

Kl. Ianair. (7 f., l. 27.) Anno domini ccccc.° xl.° ix.° Bellum cuile Conaire i Ceru, ubi ceciderunt Ailill inbanna (.i. ri Connacht), 7 Aeḋ fortobol .i. a braṫair. Fergus 7 Domnall (.i. da mac Muircertaig mic Erce) victores erant. Vel hoc anno quies Tigernaci.

Kl. Ianair. (1 f., l. 9.) Anno domini ccccc.° l.° Quies Dauidis Farannaini (filii Guaire i ḟaranain), episcopi Ard macha et legati totius Hibernie.

Kl. Ianair. (2 f.) Anno domini ccccc.° l.° i.° Bellum Cuilne in quo ceciderunt corcu Oche Muman orationibus Itae Cluano. Mors Foṫaiḋ filii Conaill.

Kl. Ianair. (4 f.) Anno domini ccccc.° l.° ii.° Mors Euċaċ mic Conleid .i. ri Ulad, a quo hu Eċaċ Ulad nati sunt, 7 mors Bic mic Deiċi. Mors Crauiṁtain mic Briuin. Sic in libro Cuanaċ inueni .i. Reilci Patraic do tabairt i scrin i cinn tri xx^it bliadan iar n-etsecht Patraic la Colum cille. Tri minna uaisle do faġbail isin aḋnucal .i. a ċoaċ 7 soiscela ind aingili, 7 clocc in aiḋeċta. IS amlaid so ro ḟoġail

---

[1] *Feat.*—echt.—Translated "great act," in Clar. 49.

[2] *Aedh Fortobol.*—More correctly called Aedh Fortamhail ("Aedh the Strong") by the Four Mast., at the year 544.

[3] *Tigernach.*—His death is among the entries for the previous year.

[4] *Son of.*—The parenthetic clause is added as a gloss in A., in a very old hand. There is no entry for this year in B., but Clar. 49 has the notice of David in exactly the same words as A. The name of David does not occur in any of the Lists of the Bishops of Armagh accessible to the Editor. See Ware's *Works* (Harris's ed.), vol. 1, p. 38, where reasons are adduced in disproof of the statement above given regarding David, and Colgan's *Trias Thaum.*, p. 293, col. 2, where it is stated that this David was the same person who was called Fiacher [or Fiachra] in the "Psalter of Cashel." The name "Fiachra," occurs in the *Book of Leinster* (p. 42, col. 3), and in other ancient lists, as the successor of Duach, bishop of Armagh, whose obit is given above under the year 547. The entry is written in a coarse hand in A.

Tara, perished in Grellach-cilte, being slain by Maelmor Ua-Mic-Hi, who himself was slain immediately after. Hence is said the 'feat[1] of Maelmor.'

Kal. Jan. (Sat., m. 27.) A.D. 549. The battle of Cul-Conaire in Cera, in which fell Ailill Inbanna (*i.e.*, King of Connaught), and Aedh Fortobol,[2] *i.e.*, his brother. Fergus and Domnall (*i.e.*, the two sons of Muirchertach Mac Erca) were victors. Or, in this year, the rest of Tigernach.[3] [549.]

Kal. Jan. (Sund., m. 9.) A.D. 550. The rest of David, descendant of Farannan, (son[4] of Guaire, descendant of Farannan), Bishop of Armagh, and Legate of all Ireland. [550.]

Kal. Jan. (Mond.) A.D. 551. The battle of Cuilen,[5] in which the Corco-Oche of Munster were slain, through the prayers of Ita of Cluain.[6] Death of Fothad, son of Conall. [551.]

Kal. Jan. (Wed.) A.D. 552. Death of Eacha, son of Conled, *i.e.*, King of Ulad, from whom the Ui-Echach of Ulad are descended; and death of Bec Mac Deiche.[7] Death of Craumthan, son of Brian. Thus I find in the Book of Cuanu, viz.:—The relics of Patrick were placed in a shrine, at the end of three score years after Patrick's death, by Colum-cille. Three splendid *minna*[8] were found in the tomb, to wit, his goblet, and the Angel's [552.]

---

[5] *Cuilen.*—Written Cuilne in Irish text. But Cuilne is the genit. form, the nom. of which may be Cuilen. (Compare *colinn*, "caro;" gen., *colno*, Ebel's Zuess, p. 41.) As the Corco-Oche of Munster were certainly located in what is the present county of Limerick, if this suggestion is correct, the site of the battle was probably the present village of Cullen, near the Limerick Junction, but situated within the limits of the county Tipperary. Keating (at reign of Diarmait mac Cerbhaill) calls the event the battle of *Cill-Cuile*.

[6] *Ita of Cluain.*—St. Ita of Cluain. The site of St. Ita's church, anciently called Cluain-Credail, is now known as Killeedy, in the parish of the same name, barony of Upper Connello, and county of Limerick.

[7] *Bec Mac Deiche.*—His death is entered at 557 *infra*, where the name is written Bec Mac De, the more usual form.

[8] *Minna*, plur. of *minn*, or *mind*, which signifies a crown, diadem, or precious thing. The term was also generally applied to reliquaries, on which oaths were sworn; and thus came to signify, in a secondary sense, an oath.

int aingel do Colum cille inna minna .i. in coach do dhun 7 cloc in aidechta do Ard macha 7 soiscela inn aingil do Colum cille fein. IS aire do gabar soiscela in aingil de, ar is a laim in aingil arroét Colum cille he. Uel hic quies Dauidis episcopi Ard macha et legati.

Kl. Ianair. Anno domini ccccc.° l.° iii.° Natiuitas Lugdag mic u Ochae. Pestis (.i. lepra) que uocata est in samthrosc.

Kl. Ianair. Anno domini ccccc.° l.° iiii.° Cathub mac Fergusa epscop Achid cinn obiit. Colman mar mac Diarmata deirg mic Fergusa cerrbeoil mic
Fol. 20ab. Conaill Cremthainne mic Neill .ix. giallaig, quem Dubsloit iugulauit. Ecclesia Benncuir fundata est.
.b. Kl. Ianair. (7 f., l. 4.) Anno domini ccccc.° l.° u.° Pelagius natione romanus sedit annis .xi. diebus .xuiii. sepultus est in basilica beati Petri apostoli. Mortalitas magna hoc anno .i. in chron chonaill .i. in buidhe chonaill.

Kl. Ianair. (2 f., l. 15.) Anno domini ccccc.° l.° ui.° Mors Fergna (uel Fiachach) nepotis Ibdaig, regis Uloth.

Kl. Ianair. (3 f., l. 26.) Anno domini ccccc.° l.° uii.° Iugulatio Colmain moir mic Diarmata quem Dubsloit iugulauit. Cena Temra la Diarmait mac Cerbaill, et fuga ante filium Maelchon, et mors Gabrain mic Domangairt. Brendinus ecclesiam i cluain ferta fundauit. Mors Eathach mic Conlaith righ Uladh. Mors Bigh mic Dhe prophetae.

---

[1] *The rest of David.*—Added in coarse hand in A. See the note under the year 550 in reference to the person called David, Bishop of Armagh and Legate of all Ireland. The foregoing entry is not in B., nor in Clar. 49.

[2] *Samthrosc.*—In the Cambridge Cod. Canon. Hibern. (p. 134) *trusci* is glossed by "scabiem;" which would prove, without the gloss *lepra* in the entry, that the "samthrosc" was a cutaneous disease.

[3] *Colman.*—This entry is faultily constructed. The death of Colman is again entered under 557, in more accurate terms. See under A.D. 599.

[4] *Founded.*—The foundation of the church of Bangor is again entered at the year 558.

[5] *Cron-Conaill.*—This is further ex-

Gospel, and the Bell of the Testament. This is how the Angel distributed the treasures for Colum-cille, viz.:—the goblet to Down, and the Bell of the Testament to Armagh, and the Angel's Gospel to Colum-cille himself. The reason it is called the Angel's Gospel is, because it is from the Angel's hand Colum-cille received it. Or, in this year, the rest of David,[1] Bishop of Armagh, and Legate.

Kal. Jan. A.D. 553. The birth of Lugaid Mac Ui Ochae. The distemper (*i.e.*, leprosy), which is called the Samthrosc.[2] [553.]

Kal. Jan. A.D. 554. Cathub, son of Fergus, bishop of Achad-cinn, died. Colman[3] the Great, son of Diarmait Derg, son of Fergus Cerrbeoil, son of Conall Cremthainne, son of Niall Nine-hostager, whom Dubsloit killed. The church of Bangor was founded.[4] [554.]

Kal. Jan. (Sat., m. 4.) A.D. 555. Pelagius, by birth a Roman, sat 11 years and 18 days. He was buried in the church of St. Peter the Apostle. A great mortality in this year, *i.e.*, the *cron-conaill*,[5] *i.e.*, the *buidhe-conaill*. [555.]

Kal. Jan. (Mond., m. 15.) A.D. 556. Death of Fergna (or Fiacha), descendant of Ibdach, King of Ulad. [556.]

Kal. Jan. (Tuesd., m. 26.) A.D. 557. The slaying of Colman[6] the Great, son of Diarmait, whom Dubsloit slew. The Feast of Tara by Diarmait Mac Cerbhaill; and the flight before the son of Maelchon, and the death of Gabran, son of Domangart. Brendan founded a church in Cluain-ferta. The death of Eacha,[7] son of Conlaedh, King of Uladh. The death of Bec Mac De, the prophet.[8] [557.]

---

plained by *buidhe-conaill*. *Crón* means 'saffron-colour,' and *buidhe* 'yellow.' The term is usually written *crom-conaill*. (See *Census of Ireland*, 1851, part 5, vol. 1, pp. 46–7.) But the form *cron-conaill* seems the more correct. The second member of the name, 'conall,' is evidently the same as the word *connall* (gl. stipulam: *Reliq. Celt.* 38). The disease was of the nature of jaundice. It seems to have been the same kind of disease as that which proved so fatal in 548. It was variously Latinized *flava pestis*, *flava icteritia*, and *icteritia*.

[6] *Colman.*—See under the year 554.

[7] *Eacha.*—The death of this person is also entered under the year 552 *supra*.

[8] *Prophet.*—The epithet prophetæ (or 'propetae,' as in A.), is not in B.

Kl. Ianair. Anno domini ccccc.° l.° iiii.° Ecclesia Benncair fundata est.

.b. Kl. Ianair. Anno domini ccccc.° l.° ix.° Feiss Temra la Diarmaid mac Cerbaill 7 mors Gabrain mic Domangairt secundum alios. Immirge re mac Maelchon (.i. Bruide rex). Cath Cuile dreimne.

Kl. Ianair. Anno domini ccccc.° lx.° Bellum Cuile dréimne for Diarmait mac Cerbaill, ubi .iii. milia ceciderunt. Ferggus 7 Domnall da mac mic Erce (.i. da mac Muirchertaig mic Muireadaig mic Eogain mic Neill), 7 Ainmire mac Setni, 7 Nainnid mac Duach (ri Connacht) uictores erant, 7 Aedh mac Echach tirmcharna ri Connacht. Per orationes Coluim cille uicerunt. Fraechan mac Temnan ise do rigne in n-erbe n-druad do Diarmait. Tuathan mac Dimain mic Sarain mic Cormaic mic Eogain ise rola in erbe n-druad tar cenn. Maglaine ro cing tarre qui solus occisus est. Bellum Cuile uinsen.

Kl. Ianair. Anno domini ccccc.° lx.° i.° Uel hic bellum chuile uinsen i Tebthai for Diarmait mac Cerbaill re n-Aedh mac Brenain. Diarmait fugit.

Fol. 20ba. Bellum Mona daire.

The death of Bec Mac De is entered above at the year 552, where the name is differently written.

[1] *Founded.*—See under 554, where the foundation of the Church of Bangor is also recorded. In Clar. 49, in the passage parallel to the present, the word 'finita' is used instead of 'fundata.' But Clar. 49 is a very poor authority.

[2] *According to others.*—Secundum alios. In B. only.

[3] *Expedition.*—This entry is not in B., nor in Clar. 49. The Irish word immirge means a hosting, expedition, or assembly. Skene (*Chron. of the Picts and Scots*, p. 344) understands immirge (or as he writes it *Inmirge*) to mean "expulsion." But this is wrong.

[4] *Battle of Cul-dreimne.*—The ostensible cause of this battle was the execution, by King Diarmait Mac Cerbhaill, of Curnan, son to the King of Connaught, who was forced from St. Columba's protection, to which he had fled, and the desire on the part of the Northern Hy-Neill to revenge the insult offered to their kinsman. The real cause would seem to have been the rivalry of the two great families. In the account of the battle in the *Ann. Four Mast.*, at 555, however, an additional cause is assigned, namely

Kal. Jan. A.D. 558. The church of Bangor was founded.[1] [558.]

Kal. Jan. A.D. 559. The Feast of Tara by Diarmait Mac Cerbhaill; and the death of Gabran, son of Domangart, (according to others[2]). An expedition[3] by the son of Maelchon (*i.e.*, King Bruide). The battle of Cul-dreimne. [559.]

Kal. Jan. A.D. 560. The battle of Cul-dreimne,[4] *gained* over Diarmait Mac Cerbhaill, in which 3,000 fell. Fergus and Domnall, two sons of Mac Erca (*i.e.*, two sons[5] of Muirchertach, son of Muiredach, son of Eogan, son of Niall), and Ainmire, son of Setna, and Nainnid, son of Duach, King of Connaught,[6] were victors, and Aedh, son of Echa Tirmcharna,[7] King of Connaught. Through the prayers of Colum-Cille they conquered. Fraechan, son of Temnan,[8] it was that made the Druids' *erbe*[9] for Diarmait. Tuatan, son of Diman, son of Saran, son of Cormac, son of Eogan, it was that threw over head the Druids' *erbe*.[9] Maglaine that passed over it, who alone was slain. The battle of Cul-Uinsen. [560.]

Kal. Jan. A.D. 561. Or, in this year, the battle of Cul-Uinsen, in Tebhtha, was gained over Diarmait Mac Cerbhaill, by Aedh son of Brenan. Diarmait fled. The battle of Moin-Daire. [561.]

---

a decision given by King Diarmait in a dispute between Colum Cille and St. Finnen. See O'Donovan's notes on the subject, *Four Mast.*, A.D. 555. That it was considered an era in the life of St. Colum Cille appears from Adamnan's words, who dates the arrival of St. Colum Cille in Britain as occurring in the 'second year after the battle of Cule-Drebene.' The name Cooledrevny is now obsolete, but Colgan states that the place was in the territory of Carbury, near Sligo, on the north. (*Trias Thaum.*, p. 452.) It must therefore have been in the neighbourhood of Drumcliff.

[5] *Two sons.*—The clause within brackets is interlined in original hand in A. It is not in B. The notice of this battle is more briefly given, under the year 559, in Clar. 49.

[6] *King of Connaught.*—Not represented in B.

[7] *Tirmcharna.*—Not in B.

[8] *Temnan.*—'Tenusan,' in the *Four Mast.*, *Chron. Scot.*, and other authorities. These particulars are not in B.

[9] *Druids' erbe.*—eրbe ոօրuaօ— The meaning of this 'Druids' *erbe*,' some kind of charmed invention, or obstacle, has not been yet explained.

Kl. Ianair. (2 f., l. 21.) Anno domini ccccc.° lx.° ii.° Bellum Mona daire Loṫair for Cruiṫniu re n-uib Neill in tuaisceirt. Baetan mac Cinn co n-dib Cruiṫnib nodfiċ fri Cruiṫniu. Genus Eugain 7 Conaill mercede conducti inna Lee 7 airde Eolargg.

Sinsit faebra sinsit fir
I moin moir Daire Loṫair,
Adbar comroma do cert,
Secht riġ Cruiṫne im Aed m-brec.

Fillset da mac [mic] Erca
Cummai in chetnai;
Fillis in ri Ainmere
Le selbaib Setnai.

Fiċtir caṫ Cruiṫne n-uile,
[Ocus] forloiscset Eilne;
Fiċtir caṫ n-Gabra Life
Ocus caṫ Cuile dreimne.

Bertair giallno iar congail
[Ass siar] im chnass nauch,
Forggus Domnall Ainmire
Ocus Nannid mac Duach.

Is alaind feras alluaḋ,
Gabair Baetain for in sluaġ.
Fo la Baetan fuilt buiḋe;
Berad a eren fuiri.

---

[1] The account of this battle in Clar. 49 is as follows:—"The battle of Moindoire Lothair upon the Cruhens, by the Nells of the North. Baedan mac Cin with two of Cruhens fought it against the rest of the Cruhens. The cattle and booty of the Eolargs were given to them of Tirconnell, and Tirowen, conductors, for their leading as wages."

[2] *Sharp weapons.*—These four stanzas are written in the lower margin, fol. 20*ab*, in A. They are not in B. A note in the top marg., fol. 20*b* in A., states that the stanzas above printed should be inserted where they are here introduced.

[3] *Seven.*—VII., A.

[4] *They bear.*—Bertair (lit. "are borne"). Berrait, *Four Mast.*, at

Kal. Jan. (Mond., m. 21.) A.D. 562. The battle of Moin-daire-lothair *was gained* over the Cruithni, by the Ui-Neill of the North. Baetan, son of Cenn, with two of the Cruithni, fought against the Cruithni. The Lee and Arda-Eolairg were given to the Cinel-Eogain and Cinel-Conaill, as a reward.[1] [562.]

Sharp weapons[2] stretch, men stretch,
In the great bog of Daire-lothair—
The cause of a contention for right—
Seven[3] Cruithnian Kings, including Aedh Brec.

The two sons [of Mac] Erca return
In the same manner.
The King Ainmire returns
With the possessions of Setna.

The battle of all the Cruithni is fought,
[And] they burn Eilne.
The battle of Gabhair-Lifè is fought,
And the battle of Cul-dreimne.

They bear[4] pledges after valour,
[Thence westwards] about . . . . ,
Ferggus, Domnall, Ainmire,
And Nandidh, son of Duach.

Splendidly[5] he bears his course—
Baetan's steed—upon the host.
Pleasing to Baetan of the yellow hair.
'Twill bear his burden upon it.

A.D. 557. ƀeɲraıτ, *Chron. Scot.*, at A.D. 563.

[5] *Splendidly.*—This stanza is written on the top margin of fol. 20*b*, in A. It is not in B. Although printed by O'Donovan in connexion with the battle of Cul-dreimne, *Four Mast.*, at 555, it seems to belong to the poem of which the foregoing is a fragment, relating to the battle of Moin-daire-lothair, in which the name of Baetan occurs.

Aedan mac Fiaċraċ moritur. Nauigatio Coluim Cille ad insolam Iae, anno etatis sue xl.° ii.° Iugulacio Colmain ṁoir mic Diarmoda.

.b. Kl. Ianair. (3 f., l. 2.) Anno domini ccccc.° lx.° iii.° Uentus magnus factus est. Mors Laisre o Daiminis. Uel hoc anno Brenaind fundauit ecclesiam Ċluana ferta.

Kl. Ianair. (5 f., l. 13.) Anno domini ccccc.° lx.° iiii.° Occissio Diarmato mic Cerbuill .i. la hAeḋ n-duḃ mac Suiḃne, cui successerunt duo filii mic Erce, Fergus 7 Domnall. Quies Brendain Biror ut alii dicunt. Bellum Gabrae Liphi 7 mors Daimin daim-airgit.

Kl. Ianair. (6 f., l. 24.) Anno domini ccccc.° lx°. u.° Bellum Gabrae Liḟi. Ferggus 7 Domnall uictores erant. Mors quoque Domnaill filii Muirchertaig mic Earca, cui successit Ainmire mac Setni. Iustinus minor annis .xi. ut Beda dicit regnauit.

Kl. Ianair. (7 f.) Anno domini ccccc.° lx.° ui.° Iohannes natione romanus sedit annis .xii. mensibus .xi. diebus .xxui., et in basilica beati Petri apostoli sepultus est. Fecht in Iardoman.

.b. Kl. Ianair. (1. f., l. 16.) Anno domini ccccc.° lx.° uii.° Feċt in Iardoman la Colman m-bec mac n-Diarmato 7 Conall mac Comgaill.

---

[1] *Island of Ia.*—Iona. B. has merely de hibernia, and does not refer to the age of Colum Cille at the time of leaving Ireland.

[2] *Laisre.*—There were three famous saints of this name, who generally appear in Irish hagiology, with the devotional prefix *Mo* ("my"), in the form *Molaisi*, namely, Molaisi, son of Cairill, abbot of Leithglinn; Molaisi, son of Declan, abbot of Inishmurray, and Molaisi, son of Nadfraech, abbot of Daimhinis, the one in question. He founded the church of Daimh-inis, 'Bovis insula,' in Loch-Erne, now called Devenish, near Enniskillen. The death of Molasse (above called Laisre) is entered again at the year 570.

[3] *Cluain-ferta.*—Omitted from the entry in B. The foundation of the church of Cluain-ferta (or Clonfert, co. Galway), by St. Brendan, is entered before under the year 557.

[4] *Diarmait MacCerbhaill.* — Properly, Diarmait son of Fergus Cerbhaill (or Cerbheoil). In the Ann. Four Masters, the Chron. Scotorum and other Chronicles, it is stated that

Aedan, son of Fiachra, dies. Voyage of Colum-Cille to the Island of Ia[1], in the 42nd year of his age. The slaying of Colman the Great, son of Diarmait.

Kal. Jan. (Tues., m. 2.) A.D. 563. A great storm occurred. The death of Laisre[2] of Daimhinis. Or, in this year, Brenaind founded the church of Cluain-ferta.[3] [563.]

Kal. Jan. (Thurs., m. 13.) A.D. 564. The murder of Diarmait MacCerbhaill,[4] *i.e.*, by Aedh Dubh[5] son of Suibhne, to whom succeeded the two sons of Mac Erca, Fergus and Domnall. The repose of Brendan of Birr, as others say. The battle of Gabair-Liphe; and the death of Daimin Daimairgit. [564.]

Kal. Jan. (Frid.) A.D. 565. The battle of Gabair-Liphe. Fergus and Domnall were victors. Also the death of Domnall, son Muirchertach Mac Erca, to whom succeeded Ainmire son of Setna. Justin the younger reigned, as Bede says, eleven years. [565.]

Kal. Jan. (Saturd.) A.D. 566. John, a Roman by birth, sat twelve years, eleven months, and twenty-six days, and was buried in the church of St. Peter[6] the apostle. An expedition into Iardoman.[7] [566.]

Kal. Jan. (Sund., m. 16.) A.D. 567. An expedition into Iardoman,[8] by Colman Bec, son of Diarmait, and Conall son of Comgall. [567.]

King Diarmait's head was buried in Clonmacnois, and his body in Connor.

[5] *Aedh Dubh.*—"Black Hugh." He was King of Dalaradia, whose father Suibhne Araidhe had been put to death by King Diarmait, and he had in early life been taken in fosterage by Diarmait. But Diarmait having been warned against Aedh, the latter was banished into Alba (Scotland), whence he returned to perpetrate the deed recorded in the above entry. Aedh afterwards fled back to Scotland, and took the clerical habit in one of the Columban Monasteries. But he returned to Ireland, and became King of Ulad in 581; and was himself slain in 587. Adamnan gives a very bad account of him. See Reeves's Eccl. Antiqq., p. 279.

[6] *Peter.*—peitri, A.

[7] *An expedition into Iardoman.*—This entry is not in B. See the next entry.

[8] *Iardoman.*—"The Western region." In the Ann. Four Mast., at A.D. 565, it is stated that Colman Beg, son of Fergus, son of Diarmait, and Conall son of Comgall, King of Dal-Riada, brought a sea fleet

Kl. Ianair. (3 f., l. 27.) Anno domini ccccc.° lx.° uiii.° Occisio Ainmirech mic Setna la Fergus mac Neilleni.

Fol. 20bb. Kl. Ianair. (4 f., l. 9.) Anno domini ccccc.° lx.° ix.° Iugulatio Fergusa mic Nelleni. Oena, abb cluana mic Nois, 7 Itae cluana credail, dormierunt. Gillas obiit. Aedan .h. Fiachrach obiit.

Kl. Ianair. (5 f., l. 20.) Anno domini ccccc.° lxx.° A morte Patricii c. anni. Uel hoc anno quies Molaisse daiminnse.

.b. Kl. Ianair. (6 f., l. 1.) Anno domini ccccc.° lxx.° i.° Occisio da aeu Muiredaig .i. Baetán mac Muirchertaig, 7 Echaid mac Domnaill .i. mic Muirchertaig mic Erca, tertio anno regni sui. Cronan mac Tigernaig rí Ciannachtae glenna géimin occisor eorum erat. Moenu epscop cluana ferta Brenaind quieuit. Mors Demain mic Cairill. Uel hoc anno occisio Diarmoda mic Cearbuill. In hoc anno capta est in muirgeilt. Quies Brenuinn Birra ut alii dicunt.

(murchoblach) to *Sol* and *Ile*, and carried away spoils therefrom. Here we have the *Sol* and *Ile* of the Four Mast. corresponding to the Iardoman of these Annals. In the Book of Leinster (p. 24*b*) the expedition to *Iardomon* is stated to have been i Sóil 7 in Ili ("to Sol and Ile"), agreeing with the Four Masters. The latter is Islay; and the former is either Seil or Colonsay—not Coll, which is too far off, although O'Donovan thought so (note ad an. 565, F. M.). Islay was at this time in the possession of the Scots, as appears from Adamnan's life of St. Columba (ii. 23), having been occupied by Muiredach, son of Aengus, who was first cousin of Conall's grandfather Domangart. Conall's territory lay in Cowall, and this expedition was probably against the rival house of Gabhran. But it is strange that Colman Beg, whose territory lay very near the centre of Ireland, was adventurous enough to engage in maritime warfare.

[1] *Ainmire.* — Called "Ainmorius filius Setni" by Adamnan. *Vit. Columb.* i., 7. See again under A.D. 575.

[2] *Fergus.*—Slain in the following year by Aedh son of Ainmire, in revenge of his father.

[3] *Fergus.* — The Four Mast. say (568) that Fergus was slain by Aedh, son of Ainmire, in revenge of his father. The entry is repeated under 576.

[4] *Ita of Cluain-credail.*—See note on *Cuilen*, under 551, *supra*. The death of St. Ita is repeated under the year 576, where the repose of Oena of Cluain-mic-Nois, and of Gildas, is also repeated.

Kal. Jan. (Tuesd., m. 27.) A.D. 568. Murder of Ainmire,[1] son of Setna, by Fergus[2] son of Nellen. [568.]

Kal. Jan. (Wed., m. 9.) A.D. 569. The slaying of Fergus[3] son of Nellen. Oena, abbot of Cluain-mic-Nois, and Ita of Cluain-credail,[4] fell asleep. Gildas died. Aedhan Ua Fiachrach[5] died. [569.]

Kal. Jan. (Thursd., m. 20.) A.D. 570. From the death of Patrick one hundred years.[6] Or, in this year, the repose of Molasse of Daiminis.[7] [570.]

Kal. Janair. (Frid., m. 1.) A.D. 571. The assassination of two grandsons of Muiredach, viz.:—Baetán son of Muirchertach, and Eochaid son of Domnall (*i.e.*, son of Muirchertach Mac Erca) in the third year of their reign. Cronan, son of Tigernach, King of Cianachta of Glenngeimin, was their slayer. Moenu, bishop of Cluain-ferta-Brenaind, rested. The death of Deman son of Cairill. Or, in this year, the killing of Diarmait Mac Cerbhaill. In this year the 'muirgeilt'[8] was captured. The repose of Brendan[9] of Birr, as others say. [571.]

---

[5] *Aedhan Ua Fiachrach.*—This may be the Aedan 'son' of Fiachra, whose obit is given above at the year 562.

[6] *One hundred years.*—The entry at 552 would refer the death of St. Patrick to the year 492, but this to 470. Tigernach indicates 571 as a hundred years after that event. Again, in these Annals, the year 663 (and in Tigernach 664) is set down as 203 years from the death of St. Patrick. See at the years 999, 1013, *infra.* According to these computations 471 is the latest date. The death of *Sen Patrick* is entered above under the year 461, which partly explains the confusion of dates.

[7] *Molasse of Daiminis.*—Called "Laisre," under A.D. 563, where see note.

[8] *Muirgeilt.*—"Sea Wanderer." Sometimes called *Murgein*, "sea-born," and *liban*, "sea-woman." The entry is fuller in Tigernach. "In this year was caught the *Muirgelt* on the shore of Ollarba, in the net of Beoan, son of Innli, fisherman of Comgall of Bangor;" to which the Four Mast. add "that is, Liban, daughter of Eochaid, son of Mairid." The legend concerning her (see *Lebor na hUidre*, p. 39, sq.) is, that she was daughter of Eochaid, King of the tract now covered by Lough Neagh, who was drowned by its eruption about the time of the Christian Era; that she was changed into a salmon, and traversed the sea until she allowed herself to be captured on this occasion. Under the names *Muirgen* and *Liban*, she appears mentioned in the Calendar at Jan. 27, and Dec. 18.

[9] *Brendan.*—See under A.D. 564. The death of St. Brendan, of Birr, is

Kl. Ianair. (1. f., l. 12.) Anno domini ccccc. lxx.° ii.° Bellum Feiṁin in quo uictus est Colman modicus filius Diarmato, et ipse euasit. Uel hic bellum Gabrae Liṗi for Laiġniu. Uel hoc anno bas Domnaill mic Muircheartaiġ mic Earca, cui successit Ainmire mac Setnai. Uel sic bellum Tola 7 Fortola .i. nomen camporum etir Eile 7 Osraiġe, 7 etir Cluain ferta Molua 7 Saiġer. Fiaċra mac Baetain uictor erat.

Kl. Ianair. (2 f., l. 23.a) Anno domini ccccc.° lxx.° iii.° Bellum Tola 7 Fortola in regionibus Cruitne. Mors Conaill mic Comġaill anno regni .xui. sui, qui obtulit insolam Iae Columbe cille.

Kl. Ianair. (3 f., l. 4.) Anno domini ccccc.° lxx.° iiii.° Magna conuentio Droma ceata in qua erant Colum cille ocus Aeḋ mac Ainmireċ.

.b. Kl. Ianair. (4 f., l. 15.) Anno domini ccccc.° lxx.° u.°

---

recorded in *Tigernach* under the year 573, which is probably the true date, although the *Mart. Donegal* and the *Four Mast.* have his obit under A.D. 571.

[1] *Femhin.*—Commonly called Magh-Feimhin, a plain comprised in the barony of Iffa and Offa, East, county Tipperary. The *Annals of Inisfallen*, which have the entry of this battle under 565, state that Colman Bec was slain therein by the men of Munster. But *Tigernach* (at 573) and the *Four Masters* (at 571) agree with this chronicle in recording the escape of Colman Bec, whose death is mentioned, *infra*, at A.D. 586, and again at 592.

[2] *Gabair-Liphe.*—'Gabair of the Liffey.' The situation of this place has not yet been fixed; but Father Shearman, a very good authority, states that it was the name of a district comprising "the hilly country bounded by the Dublin Mountains on the north; on the east by the River Liffey, from its source in Kippure to Ballymore-Eustace;" its western boundary including "the hills from Tipperkevin, by Rathmore, to Athgoe, towards Tallaght, and the hill of Lyons." *Loca Patriciana*, p. 28, note [2].

[3] *Tola and Fortola.*—This entry is in the margin in B, and also in A. (in which it is partly obliterated). The *Four Masters* (at 571) have but the name of Tola, which O'Donovan (*Loc. cit.*, note *i*,) identifies with Tulla, in the parish of Kinnitty, barony of Ballybritt, King's County.

[4] *Ele and Ossory.*—Ele, called from its occupants Ele-O'Carroll, comprised the present baronies of Ballybritt and

Kal. Jan. (Sund., m. 12.) A.D. 572. The battle of [572.]
emhin,[1] in which Colman Bec, son of Diarmait, was
anquished; but he escaped. Or, in this year, the battle
Gabair-Liphe[2] over the Leinstermen. Or, in this year,
e death of Domnall, son of Muirchertach Mac Erca,
whom succeeded Ainmire, son of Setna. Or thus, the
attle of Tola and Fortola,[3] viz., the names of plains
etween Ele and Ossory,[4] and between Cluain-ferta-Molua
d Saighir.[5] Fiachra, son of Baetan,[6] was victor.

Kal. Jan. (Mond., m. 23.) A.D. 573. The battle of [573.]
ola and Fortola, in the territory of the Cruithne.[7] The
eath of Conall, son of Comgall,[8] in the 16th year of his
ign, who granted the island of Ia to Colum-Cille.

Kal. Jan. (Tuesd., m. 4.) A.D. 574. The great Con- [574.]
ention of Druim-Ceta,[9] at which were Colum-Cille, and
edh son of Ainmire.

Kal. Jan. (Wed., m. 15.) A.D. 575. A spark of leprosy,[10] [575.]

---

onlisk, in the south of the King's unty; from which the territory of ssory, now partly represented by e baronies of Upperwoods and Clandnagh, in the Queen's County, is ided by the Slieve-Bloom Mounins.

[5] *Cluain-ferta-Molua and Saighir.* The former, commonly called Clontmulloe, is now known as Kyle, a rish in the barony of Clandonagh, een's County. Saighir, or Seiran, is a parish in the barony of llybritt, King's County.

[6] *Fiachra, son of Baetan.*—Otherse called Fiachra Lurgan, afterrds King of Ulidia. His death is orded under the year 625, *infra*, ere the name is Fiachna.

[7] *The Cruithne.*—The Picts. In the ry of the battle of Tola and Fora under the preceding year (572) site of the battle is fixed in the south of the present King's County, which was hardly Pictish territory; though Fiachra, son of Baetan, the victor, was an Ulster chieftain.

[8] *Conall, son of Comgall.*—See under A.D. 567, *supra*, where Conall is mentioned as leagued with Colman Bec, son of Diarmait, in a maritime expedition.

[9] *Great Convention of Druim-Ceta.*—Magna contio, for M. conuentio, A., B., and Clar. 49. The word mordail, 'great assembly,' is added as a gloss over contio in B., and in the margin in A. On the date and place of this famous Convention, see Reeves's *Adamnan*, page 37, note *b*.

[10] *Leprosy.*—This entry is misplaced in the MSS., being introduced into the middle of the record of the battle of Teloch, which should probably follow it, as in the printed text in the next page (66).

Scintilla leprae et habundantia nucum inaudita. Bellum Telocho[1] i ciunn tire, in quo cecidit Duncaṫ mac Conaill mic Comgaill et alii multi de sociis filiorum Gabrain ceciderunt. Mors Brendain mic Briuin.[2] Uel hic occisio Ainmireċ mic ḟetna, de quo dictum est:—

Femen[3] an tan robui ri,
Nir bo mennot naċ detlai;
Indiu is forḋerg a li
La hAinmire mac Setnai.

Kl. Ianair. (6 f., l. 26.) Anno domini ccccc.° lxx.°
Fol. 21aa. vi.° Bellum Teloċo.[4] Initium regni Tiberii Constantini qui regnauit annis .vii. Quies Brendain Clona ferta.[5] Iugulatio Aeḋa mic Echaċ Tirimcarna (alias Timrim, mic Ferġusa mic Muireḋaiġ ṁaeil mic Eoġan sreiḃ mic ḋuaċ ġalaiġ mic Briain mic Eathaċ muiġmeḋoin) la hui Briuin. Primum periculum Uloth in Eufania. Uel hic iugulatio Ferġusa mic Neilline, 7 Oena abb ċluana mic Nois, 7 Itae Cluana creḋail, 7 Gillas.

Kl. Ianair. (7 f., l. 7.) Anno domini ccccc.° lxx.° vii.° Quies episcopi Eitchen Cluana fota Baetan. Reuersio Uloth de Eumania. Feiḋlmiḋ finn abb Arḋ maċa quieuit.

Kl. Ianair. (1 f., l. 18.) Anno domini ccccc.° lxx.°

[1] *Of Teloch.*—Deloċo, A.; teloċo, B. Cenn-tire, in which Teloch was situated, and which signifies 'Head of the region,' was the territory of the Cinel-Gabrain.

[2] *Brendan, son of Brian.*—Chief of Teffia. He was brother of Cremthann, mentioned at the year 552, and father of Aedh, whose death is recorded at 588.

[3] *Femen.*—See under the year 572. This *rann*, which is written in *al. man.* in A., and in original hand in B., seems taken from a poem in praise of some king of Munster, after whose death Magh-Femhin was wasted by Ainmire, son of Setna. The death of Ainmire is recorded above under 568.

[4] *Teloch.*—Deloċo (gen. of Deloch), A. See under 575.

[5] *Brendan.*—He died, according to his Acts and the *Four Masters*, on the 16th of May, in the 94th year of his age, at Enach-duin, in the nunnery of his sister Briga, and was buried at Clonfert. Enach-duin, now Annadown, county Galway, had been granted to him by the King of Connaught; and it is probable that the nunnery there was founded by him, and placed under his sister's superintendence. See under the year 582

an unheard of abundance of nuts. The battle of)ch,[1] in Cenn-tire, in which fell Duncath, son of Conall, of Comgall, and many others of the allies of the sons Gabran. The death of Brendan, son of Brian.[2] Or, his year, the killing of Ainmire, son of Setna, of whom said :—

Femen,[3] when there was a King,
Was not a place without valour.
To-day, crimson is its aspect
By Ainmire, son of Setna.

:al. Jan. (Frid., m. 26.) A.D. 576. The battle of)ch.[4] The beginning of the reign of Tiberius stantinus, who reigned seven years. The repose of ndan,[5] of Cluain-ferta. Murder of Aedh, son of Eocha ncarna (alias[6] Timrim, son of Fergus, son of Muiredach ɜl, son of Eoghan Srebh, son of Duach Galach, son of ɩn, son of Eocha Muighmedhoin), by the Ui-Briuin. The ; adventure of the Ulidians in Eufania.[7] Or, in this r, the murder of Fergus, son of Nellin,[8] and [the repose Oena, abbot of Cluain-mic-Nois, and of Ita,[9] of Cluain-lail, and of Gildas.[9] [576.]

Kal. Jan. (Sat., m. 7.) A.D. 577. The rest of Bishop hen,[10] of Cluain-fota-Baetain.[11] The return of the dians from Eumania.[12] Feidilmidh Finn, abbot of nagh, rested. [577.]

Kal. Jan. (Sund., m. 18.) A.D. 578. The repose of [578.]

ı, where the entry of St. Brendan's h is repeated.

lias.—The clause within brackets, h is not in B., is interlined in A. very old hand.

Eufania.—Under next year the e is written 'Eumania.' *Tiger-* has 'Eamania.'

Fergus, son of Nellin.—See under 569.

Ita, Gildas.—The obits of these persons are not in B. under this year; but they occur therein, as in A., at 569.

[10] *Bishop Etchen.*—He is best known as the bishop at whose hands St. Columba received holy orders. See the curious legend concerning him in Colgan's AA. SS., p. 306, *b.*, *n.* 17, and the Introduction to the Obits of Christ Church, p. liv. See under 583.

[11] *Cluain-fota-Baetain.* — Clonfad, par. of Killucan, county Westmeath.

[12] *Eumania.*—See note [7].

viii.° Quies Uinniani episcopi, mac nepotis Fiataċ. Benedictus natione romanus sedit annis .iiii. mense .i. diebus xx. ix., sepultus est in basilica beati Petri apostoli. Occisio Aeḋa mic Geno, et mors Bruidiġi regis nepotum Failgi.

.b. Kl. Ianair. (2 f., l. 29.) Anno domini ccccc.° lxx.° ix.° Bellum Droma mic Erce, ubi Colggu filius Domnaill filii Muircertaiġ mic Muireaḋaiġ mic Eoġain cecidit. Aeḋ mac Ainmireċ victor extitit. Fecht Orc la h-Aeḋan mac Gabrain. Cennalaṫ rex Pictorum moritur.

Kl. Ianair. 4 f., l. .) Anno domini ccccc.° lxxx.° Vel hic bellum Droma mic Ercaae. Mors Baetain mic Cairill. Fecht Orc.

Kl. Ianair. (5 f.) Anno domini ccccc.° lxxx.° i.° Bellum Manonn in quo victor erat Aeḋan mac Gabrain mic Domangairt. Mors Fergna mic Caibleine.

Kl. Ianair. (6 f., l. 2.) Anno domini ccccc.° lxxx.°
Fol. 21ab. ii.° Mors Feraḋaiġ mic Duaċ regis Ossraiġi. Pelagius natione romanus sedit annis .x. mensibus .ii. diebus .x. Bellum manand fri Aeḋan. Mors Fergna mic Caibleine. Vel hoc anno quies Brenainn Ċluana ferta secundum alios.

---

[1] *Vinnian.*—Erroneously printed Umaniain by O'Conor. This was St. Finnian, of Magh-bile, or Movilla, the patron saint of the Ulidians.

[2] *Aedh, son of Geno.*—This entry is not found in any of the other Annals. At 587, *infra*, the entry 'Mors nepotum Geno' occurs.

[3] *Brudig.*—In the list of kings of Ui-Failgi, or Offaly, contained in the *Book of Leinster* (p. 40, col. 3,) the name of a 'Bruidgin, son of Cathair,' occurs immediately before that of Aedh Roin, whose death is entered within at the year 603. And in the Pedigree of the Ui-Failgi, in the same authority (p. 314, col. 2), a Bruidgi is set down as fourth in descent from Ros Failgi, the ancestor of the Ui-Failgi.

[4] *Druim-mic-Erca.*—This place has not been identified. Colgu's father, Muirchertach, bore the matronymic of *Mac-Erca*, and from him this place may perhaps have derived its name. See under 580 and 585.

[5] *Or, in this year.*—Vel hic, in B. only.

[6] *Baetan, son of Cairell.*—Entered again at 586, with a 'vel hic.'

nnian,[1] the bishop, son of Ua Fiatach. Benedict, a ›man by birth, sat four years, one month, twenty-nine ys; and was buried in the church of Saint Peter the ›ostle. The killing of Aedh, son of Geno,[2] and the ath of Brudig,[3] King of the Ui-Failgi.

Kal. Jan. (Mond., m. 29.) A.D. 579. The battle of [579.]
ruim-mic-Erca,[4] in which fell Colgu, son of Domnall, son Muirchertach, son of Muiredhach, son of Eogan. Aedh, n of Ainmire, remained victor. An expedition to the rkneys by Aedhan, son of Gabran. Cennalath, King of e Picts, dies.

Kal. Jan. (Wedn., m. .) A.D. 580. Or, in this year,[5] [580.]
e battle of Druim-mic-Erca. The death of Baetan, son Cairill.[6] The expedition to the Orkneys.[7]

Kal. Jan. (Thursd.) A.D. 581. The battle of Manonn,[8] [581.]
which Aedhan, son of Gabran, son of Domangart,[9] was ctor. The death of Fergna, son of Caiblein.

Kal. Jan. (Frid., m. 2.) A.D. 582. The death of [582.]
eradach, son of Duach, King of Ossory. Pelagius, a oman by birth, sat ten years, two months, and ten ys. The battle of Manand against[10] Aedhan. The ath of Fergna,[11] son of Caiblein. Or, in this year, the pose of Brenaind, of Cluain-ferta, according to others.[12]

---

[7] *Orkneys.*—This is, of course, a ›etition of the entry under the year 9. The Orkneys are also noticed the years 681 and 1013, *infra.*

[8] *Battle of Manonn.*—Dean Reeves inks that this was the name of he debateable ground on the con- es of the Scots, Picts, Britons, and xons, now represented in part by e parish of Slamannan (*Sliabh anann*, 'Moor of Manann'), on e south-east of Stirlingshire, iere it and the counties of umbarton, Lanark, and Linlithgow eet." *Adamnan*, p. 371, n. *d.* O'Donovan was surely wrong in thinking Manann the Isle of Man. (Frag. of Annals, 581.)

[9] *Son of Domangart.*—In A. only.

[10] *Against.*—ꝼꝛı, A., probably a mistake for ꝛı, "by" (*i.e.*, "won by"); in which case the entry would seem a repetition of that under 581. Not in B. Clar. 49 has 'per.'

[11] *Fergna.*—A repetition of the entry at 581.

[12] *According to others.*—ꝼecunꝺum alıoꝛ, in B. only. The death of St. Brendan is entered above at the year 576.

.b. Kl. Ianair. (7 f., l. 13.) Anno domini ccccc.° lxxx.° iii.° Quies Fergusso episcopi Duna Lethglaise qui fundauit Cill biein. Mauricius annis .xxi. regnauit ut Beda et Isiodorus dicunt. Mors Bruide mic Maelcon regis pictorum, et mors Feradaig mic Duach regis Osrige. Uel hoc anno quies Eitchen.

Kl. Ianair. (2 f., l. 24.) Anno domini ccccc.° lxxx.° iiii.° (alias 85.) Quies mic Nisse abb cluana mic u Nois, .xuii.° anno. Mors Aeda [mic] Suibne, regis Moenmaigi.

Kl. Ianair. (3 f., l. 5.) Anno domini ccccc.° lxxx.° u.° Occisio Baetain mic Ninnedo filii Duach (alias mic Fergusa ceannfada) filii Conaill gulban regis Temro, qui uno anno regnauit. Cummaene mac Colmain big mic Diarmata, 7 Cummaene mac Libraen filii Illannon mic Cerbaill occiderunt eum consilio Colmain .i. oc Leim ind eich. Uel hoc anno cath Droma mic Erce.

Kl. Ianair. (4 f., l. 16.) Anno domini ccccc.° lxxx.° ui.° Bellum Daethe in quo cecidit Colman bec mac

---

[1] *Of Dun-lethglaise.*—The name was originally written (in the genit. form) droma Lethglaise (of Druim-lethglaise) in A., as in B., but a rude attempt has been made in the former MS. to alter droma (droma) to Duna, to make the name Dun Lethglaise (Dun-lethglaise), the usual form. See Reeves's *Eccl. Antiq.*, pp. 41, 144, 224. At the year 589 *infra*, however, the name of the place is as originally written in the present entry.

[2] *Bruide, son of Maelcon.*—Tigernach, too, has the obit of Bruide at 583. But, by a strange prolepsis, the death of Bruide is entered above at 504, and in Tigernach at 505. For the *mors* of Bruide at 504, in his edition of the Ann. Ult., Dr. O'Conor proposes *nativitas*, an emendation which, as Dean Reeves observes (Adamnan, 148, note *l*), "harmonises very well with the true date of his death, as it allows a period of 78 years for the term of his life, but is open to the objection that in both authorities the 'Battle of Manann by Aedhan,' is entered under the preceding year (503), although Aedhan was not yet born, and the true date of that battle is 582: which creates a suspicion that these entries were taken from an earlier record whose chronological system was different, or that they were displaced through carelessness in the scribe."

[3] *Feradach.*—The death of Feradach is also recorded under the preceding year. The *Four Mast.* at 582, and *Tigernach* at 583, state that he was slain by his own people.

[4] *Bishop Etchen.*—See under 577,

Kal. Jan. (Sat., m. 13.) A.D. 583. The repose of [583.]
'ergus, bishop of Dun-lethglaise,[1] who founded Cill-Bien. Mauricius reigned twenty-one years, as Bede and Isidore tate. The death of Bruide, son of Maelcon,[2] King of he Picts; and the death of Feradach,[3] son of Duach, King of the Osraighe. Or, in this year, the repose of Etchen.[4]

Kal. Jan. (Mond., m. 24.) A.D. 584 (alias 85). The [584.]
epose of Mac Nisse, abbot of Cluain-mic-u-Nois, in the 7th year.[5] Death of Aedh [son of] Suibhne, King of Moenmagh.

Kal. Jan. (Tuesd., m. 5.) A.D. 585. The assassina- [585.]
ion of Baetan, son of Ninnidh, son of Duach (alias, son f Fergus Cennfada[6]), son of Conall Gulban, King of 'ara, who reigned one year. Cummaene, son of Colman Bec, son of Diarmait, and Cummaene, son of Libraen, son f Illannan, son of Cerbhall, killed him, at the instance f Colman—namely, at Leim-ind-eich. Or, in this year, he battle of Druim-mic-Erce.[7]

Kal. Jan. (Wed., m. 16.) A.D. 586. The battle of [586.]
Daethe,[8] in which fell Colman Bec, son of Diarmait;

here the death of this prelate is ntered also.

[5] *The 17th year*, *i.e.*, of Mac Nisse's abbacy.—The death of his redecessor, Oenu, is entered above nder the year 569, and again at 576. Mac Nisse's death is entered also nder 590 *infra*.

[6] *Fergus Cennfada.*—The orig. of his clause is interlined in an old hand A., and in the orig. hand in B. he death of Baetan is given by the *our Masters* at the year 567; but *igernach* has it at 586, agreeing ith these Annals. Fergus Cennfadda as otherwise called Duach. See eeves's *Adamnan*, Geneal. Table at 342.

[7] *Battle of Druim-mic-Erce.*—This battle is also referred to at the years 579 and 580.

[8] *Battle of Daethe.*—The name of this place is written ᴅaeṫe in A. and B., although O'Conor prints Dromaethe. O'Donovan, under an extraordinary misconception, states (*Ann. Four Mast.*, A.D., 572, note) that Cod. Clar. 49 has 'Bellum Droma-Ethe,' whereas it really reads 'Bellum Doothe.' See under 592, *infra*. The record of this battle under this year, in A., B., and Clar. 49, is somewhat confused, the notice of the death of Daigh, son of Cairill, being introduced into the middle of it. The Editor has taken the liberty of putting it in its proper place in the text.

Diarmato. Aeḋ mac Ainmireċ uictor erat; 7 in quo cecidit Libraen mac Illannon mic Cearḃaill. Daiġ mac Cairill obiit. Uel hic mors Baetain mic Cairill riġ Ulaḋ.

.b. Kl. Ianair. (5 f., l. 27.) Anno domini ccccc.° lxxx.° iii.° Quies Cairlaen episcoip Ard maċa. Quies Senaic episcoip Cluana Iraird. Mors nepotum Geno. Conuersio Constantini ad Dominum, 7 nix magna, 7 iugulatio Aeḋa nigri mic Suiḃni, i luing.

Kl. Ianair. (7^{a} f., l. 9.) Anno domini ccccc.°
Fol. 21ba. lxxx.° iiii.° Quies espuic Aeḋa filii Bricc. Aeḋ mac Brendain rex Teṫba mortuus est, (.i. asé ro eḋbair Dermaġ do ċolum cille.) Eodemque tempore aestas torrida et sicca contigit.

Kl. Ianair. (1 f., l. 20.) Anno domini ccccc.° lxxx.° ix.° Mors Feidelmṫie mic Tigernaig regis Muman. Bellum Leiṫreid la Aeḋan mac Gabrain. Bellum Maiġi oċtair re mBrannuḃ mac Echach for ui Neill. Uel hoc anno quies Fergusa episcopi Droma leaṫglaise qui fundauit Cill m-Biain.

Kl. Ianair. (2 f., l. i.) Anno domini ccccc.° xc.°

---

[1] *Baetan.*—See under 580.

[2] *Carlaen.*—A marg. note in A. gives his name as "Ciarlaech," and states that he was from *Crich ua Niallain*, "the territory of Ui-Niallain," now Oneilland West, in the county of Armagh. His day in the Calendar is the 24th of March. In the list of the *comarbs* of St. Patrick in the *Book of Leinster* (p. 42, col. 3), his name is written 'Caurlan'; and he is stated to have ruled 4 years, and to have been from *Domnach mic U Garba*, and of the Ui-Niallain. See Colgan's Acta SS., p. 744.

[3] *Grandsons of Geno*—nepotum Geno.—Clar. 49 has "nephewes of Geno." This Geno is not noticed in the other Annals. The assassination of his son Aedh is recorded under the year 578, *supra*.

[4] *Constantine.*—He had been King of Cornwall; but abandoned the throne, and became a monk under St. Carthach (otherwise called Mochuda), at Rahin, in the present King's county, whence he passed over to Scotland, and founded the church of Govan on the Clyde. He suffered martyrdom in Cantyre, where there is a church, Kilchonstand, called after his name. His festival, in the Calendars of both Scotland and Ireland, is March 11. See Reeves's *Adamnan*, p. 371, note c.

[5] *Aedh Dubh.*—"Black Hugh."

Aedh, son of Ainmire, being victor. And in which fell Libraen, son of Illannon, son of Cerbhall. Daigh, son of Cairill, died. Or, in this year, the death of Baetan,[1] son of Cairill, King of Uladh.

Kal. Jan. (Thurs., m. 27.) A.D. 587. The repose of Carlaen,[2] bishop of Armagh. The repose of Senach, bishop of Cluain-Iraird. The death of the grandsons of Geno.[3] The conversion of Constantine[4] to the Lord; and great snow; and the murder of Aedh Dubh,[5] son of Suibhne, in a ship. [587.]

Kal. Jan. (Sat., m. 9.) A.D. 588. The repose of Bishop Aedh, son of Brecc.[6] Aedh, son of Brendan, King of Tethba, died. (It was he that presented Dermhagh[7] to Colum-Cille.) And, in the same time, there was a scorching and droughty summer. [588.]

Kal. Jan. (Sund., m. 20.) A.D. 589. The death of Fedelmith, son of Tigernach, King of Munster. The battle of Lethreid *was gained* by Aedhan, son of Gabran. The battle of Magh-ochtair *was gained* by Brandubh, son of Echa, over the Ui-Neill. Or, in this year, the repose of Fergus, bishop of Druim-lethglaise,[8] who founded Cill-Bian. [589.]

Kal. Jan. (Mond., m. 1.) A.D. 590. An eclipse of the [590.]

Lord of Dalaradia, and afterwards King of Ulster. The murder by him of Dermot MacCerbhaill, King of Ireland, is recorded above under the year 564. Adamnan gives a bad character of him (*Vit. Columbae*, i. 36).

[6] *Aedh, son of Brec.*—Better known as Aedh Mac Bric. Founder of Killare, in Westmeath. Also venerated at Sliabh Liag (Slieveleague), in the Co. Donegal. He was also the founder and patron of Rathhugh, near Kilbeggan, in the Co. of Westmeath. His life has been published by Colgan (AA., SS.), at Feb. 28th. See under 594 *infra*.

[7] *Dermhagh.* — Durrow, in the barony of Ballycowan, King's County. Added as a gloss in A. Not in B. In the *Annals of the Four Masters*, at A.D. 585, Brenainn, the father of Aedh, is represented as the person who presented Durrow to St. Columba. But this is an error. The death of Aedh son of Brendan (or Brenann) is entered again under 594 *infra*.

[8] *Druim-lethglaise.*—See the entry under 583, where the name has been altered, so as to read Dun-lethglaise.

Difectio solis .i. mane tenebrosum. Uel hic quies Mic Nisi abbaiḋ Cluana mic Nois.

.b. Kl. Ianair. (3 f., l. 12.) Anno domini ccccc.° xc.° i.° Obitus Lugide Lis moer. Natiuitas Cummeni Longi. Matutina tenebrosa. Inicium regni Aeḋa mic Ainmireaċ.

Kl. Ianair. (5 f., l. 23.) Anno domini ccccc.° xc.° ii.° Mors Aengusa mic Amalngado. Gregorius natione romanus, ex patre Gordiano, sedit annis .xiii. mensibus .ui. diebus .x. Fuit tempore imperatoris Mauricii et Focatis; secundo anno regni eiusdem Foccatis seu Foce sepultus est in basilica beati Petri apostoli ante secratarium. Uel hoc anno caṫ Bealaiġ ḋaiṫe in quo cecidit Colman beag mac Diarmoda a quo clann Cholmain .i. .h. Maeileachlainn et ceteri. Aeḋ mac Ainmireach uictor erat.

Kl. Ianair. (6 f., l. 4.) Anno domini ccccc.° xc.° iii.° Bellum Geirtide ri Cianachtae; oc eudonn mor ro mebaid. Fiaċna mac Baetain uictor erat (.i. Fiaċna mac Baetain mic Cairill mic Muireaḋaiġ muinnderg.)

Kl. Ianair. (7 f., l. 15.) Anno domini ccccc.° xc.° iiii.° Quies Columm cille .u. idus iunii, anno aetatis

---

[1] *Mac Nissi.*—See under the year 584. This entry is added in a coarse hand in A. In text, in B.

[2] *Lismore.*—This is the Lismore of Scotland, whose founder, Molua (or Moluag, as the Scotch call him), was in after times the patron saint of the diocese of Argyle. See Reeves's *Adamnan*, p. 371, note *g*.

[3] *Gregory.*—St. Gregory the Great. Styled *belóir*, "of the golden mouth," by the *Four Mast.* (A.D. 590); a name given to him by the Irish so early as 634; for Cummian writes in his Paschal Epistle of that year—"Ad Gregorii papæ, urbis Romæ episcopi (a nobis in commune suscepti, et *oris aurei* appellatione donati) verba me converti." (Ussher, *Syllog.* xi; Wks. vol. iv., p. 439). Gregory the Great was consecrated on Sunday, the 3rd of Sept., 590, in the 9th year of the Emperor Mauricius. He was buried on the 12th of March, 604, in the 3rd year of the Emperor Phocas, having governed the See of Rome for 13 years, six months, and ten days. Gregory was son of Gordian, a wealthy senator, and Sylvia, a lady of rank and piety. O'Conor adds "Sed secundum Bedam, Gregorius quievit xiv. anno ab hoc loco infra." (*Rer. Hib.*

sun, that is, a dark morning. Or, in this year, the repose of Mac Nissi,[1] abbot of Cluain-mic-Nois.

Kal. Jan. (Tues., m. 12.) A.D. 591. The death of Lugaid of Lismore.[2] The birth of Cummen the Tall. A dark morning. The beginning of the reign of Aedh, son of Ainmire. [591.]

Kal. Jan. (Thurs., m. 23.) A.D. 592. The death of Aengus, son of Amalgaid. Gregory,[3] a Roman by birth, son of Gordian, sat 13 years, 6 months, and 10 days. He was [Pontiff] in the time of the Emperors Mauricius and Focas. In the second year of the reign of the same Foccas, or Foca, he was buried in the church of Saint Peter the Apostle, in front of the sacristy. Or, in this year, the battle of Bealach-Dhaithe,[4] in which fell Colman Bec, son of Diarmait, from whom [are descended] the Clann-Colmain,[5] viz., the Ui-Maelechlainn and others. Aedh, son of Ainmire, was victor. [592.]

Kal. Jan. (Frid., m. 4.) A.D. 593. A battle [against] Geirtide, King of Cianachta.[6] At Eudon-mor it was won. Fiachna, son of Baetan (*i.e.*, Fiachna,[7] son of Baetan, son of Cairill, son of Muiredhach Muinderg), was victor. [593.]

Kal. Jan. (Sat., m. 15.) A.D. 594. The repose of Colum-Cille,[8] on the 5th of the Ides of June, in the 76th [594.]

Script., vol. 4, p. 32). But this is not in any of the texts. See under 605 *infra*, and O'Donovan's note *x*, *Ann. Four Mast.*, A.D. 590.

[4] *Bealach-Dhaithe.* — O'Donovan states (*Four Mast.*, 572, note *n*) that the site of this battle was Ballaghanea, par. of Lurgan, co. Cavan. The name of the place is written (in the genitive case) *Daethe* (or *Doethe*) under 586 *supra*, where see note.

[5] *Clann-Colmain.*—This sept were really descended from Colman Mór (brother of Colman Bec), whose death is entered *supra*, at 554 and 557.

[6] *Cianachta.* — The Cianachta of Brega; a tribe occupying the S.E. portion of the county Meath, probably the barony of Duleek.

[7] *Fiachna.*—The parenthetic clause, which is in the marg. in A, occurs by way of gloss in B. Fiachna was lord of Dalaradia, king of Ulidia. The death of his father, Baetan, is entered at 580 *supra*, and his own death at 625 *infra*. See Reeves's *Eccl. Ant.*, pp. 202, 340, 353.

[8] *Repose of Colum-Cille.*—Regarding the date of St. Colum-Cille's death, see the learned note of Dean Reeves, *Adamnan*, p. 309, sq.

sue lxx. iii. Mors Eugain mic Gabrain. Uel hoc anno quies episcoip Aeḋa mic Bricc 7 Aeḋa mic Brenainn.

.b. Kl. Ianair. (1 f., l. 26.) Anno domini ccccc.° xc.°
Fol. 21bb. u.° Bellum Raṫo in druaḋ. Bellum Aird sendaim. Iugulatio filiorum Aedain .i. Brain 7 Domangairt. Bellum Corainn.

Kl. Ianair. (3 f., l. 7.) Anno domini ccccc.° xc.° ui.° Occisio Cumascaiġ mic Aeḋo la Brannuḃ mac n-Eċaċ i n-Dun Buċat. Bellum montis Cuae in regionibus Mumen, ubi Fiaċna mac Baetain uictor erat. Mors Tibraitti filii Calggaig.

Kl. Ianair. (4 f., l. 18.) Anno domini ccccc.° xc.° uii.° Quies Baeiṫeni abbatis Iae. Occisio (alias bellum) Duin bolg ubi cecidit Aeḋ mac Ainmireċ la Branduḃ mac Eċaċ, 7 Beacc mac Cuanaċ rex nepotum micc Uais. Eoċo abb Aird maċa quieuit. Augustinus uenit in Angliam. Inicium regni Colmain riġmeḋo 7 Aeḋa slaine simul.

Kl. Ianair. (5 f., l. 29.) Anno domini ccccc.° xc.°

---

[1] *Eugan.*—In the valuable "Genealogical Table of the Dalriadic Kings," compiled by Dean Reeves, facing p. 438, in his splendid edition of Adamnan's Life of St. Columba, the name is 'Eoghanan.' The Dean identifies him with 'Iogenanus,' the brother of Aedan (son of Gabran), whom St. Columba wished to inaugurate as King of the Scotch Dalriada, in the place of his brother Aedan (lib. iii., cap. v.)

[2] *Bishop Aedh.*—His obit is entered above, under 588.

[3] *Aedh, son of Brenann (or Brendan.)*—See above, under 588.

[4] *Rath-in-druadh.* — *Aed-Sendaim.* —The sites of these battles have not been satisfactorily identified.

[5] *Aedan.*—A marginal note in A. adds that he was the son of Gabran, son of Domangart.

[6] *Dun-Buchat.* — Dunhoyke, par. of Hollywood, co. Wicklow. See O'Donov. *Four Mast.*, A.D. 593, note *d*, and Shearman's *Loca Patriciana*, p.29

[7] *Sliabh-Cua.*—The ancient name of the range of mountains now known by the name of Knockmeldown, in the N.W. of the co. Waterford. This battle is again entered at 602.

[8] *Calggach.*—First written "Galggaig" (genit. of "Galggach") in A. But the copyist has written a C over the first G, by way of suggesting that the name should be "Calggaig" (nom. "Calgach.") This name has been rendered classical by Tacitus' account of the battle fought between

year of his age. The death of Eugan,[1] son of Gabran. Or, in this year, the repose of Bishop Aedh,[2] son of Brecc, and of Aedh, son of Brenann.[3]

Kal. Jan. (Mond., m. 26.) A.D. 595. The battle of Rath-in-druadh.[4] The battle of Ard-Sendaim. Murder of the sons of Aedan,[5] viz.:—Bran and Domangart. The battle of Corann. [595.]

Kal. Jan. (Tues., m. 7.) A.D. 596. The slaying of Cumascach, son of Aedh, by Brandubh, son of Eocha, in Dun-Buchat.[6] The battle of Sliabh-Cua,[7] in the regions of Munster; in which Fiachna, son of Baetan, was victor. The death of Tibraitte, son of Calggach.[8] [596.]

Kal. Jan. (Wed., m. 18.) A.D. 597. The repose of Baitheni,[9] abbot of Ia. The slaughter (or battle[10]) of Dun-bolg,[11] in which fell Aedh, son of Ainmire, by Brandubh, son of Echa, and Bec, son of Cuanu, King of Ui-mic-Uais.[12] Eocho,[13] abbot of Armagh, rested. Augustin came to England. The beginning of the joint reign of Colman Righmidh and Aedh Slaine. [597.]

Kal. Jan. (Thurs., m. 29.) A.D. 598. Ailither, abbot [598.]

Galgacus and Agricola, at the Grampian Hills. The ancient name of Derry was *Daire Calgaich*, which is Latinized by Adamnan *Roboretum Calgachi* (lib. i., cap. II.)

[9] *Baitheni.* — See, regarding this person, Reeves's *Adamnan*, p. 372.

[10] *Or battle.*—Added as a gloss in A. For 'occisio,' B. reads 'bellum.'

[11] *Dun-bolg.*—'Fort of Sacks.' For the situation of this place, and the causes which led to the battle, see O'Donov. *Four Mast.*, A.D. 594, note *h.*, where a full summary is given from the account of the battle of Dun-bolg contained in the *Bórama* Tract, *Book of Leinster*, p. 294, *b.*, *sq.*

[12] *Ui-mic-Uais.*—A name borne by a powerful sept of the Airghialla, who were settled in or near the present county of Armagh, a branch of which emigrated southwards, and gave name to the district now corruptly called the barony of *Moygoish*, county Westmeath. See Reeves's *Eccl. Ant.*, p. 387.

[13] *Eocho.*—In the List of the *Comarbs* of St. Patrick, *Book of Leinster*, p. 42, col. 3, he is called Eochaid son of Diarmait, and the length of his abbacy is limited to *three* years, which differs considerably from the period assigned in other ancient Lists published by Dr. Todd. (*St. Patrick*, pp. 177, 179).

uiii.° Ailiṫer ab Clono mic Nois pausat. Quies Cainniġ in Aċaiḋ bó ut Cuana docet.

.b Kl. Ianair. (6 f., l. 10.) Anno domini ccccc.° xc.° ix.° Quies Cainniġ sancti, 7 bellum Saxonum in quo uictus est Aedan. Iugulatio Suibne mic Colmaen moer (mic Diarmoda deirg mic Ferġusa cerrbeoil mic Conaill cremṫainne mic Neill .ix. giallaiġ), la hAeḋ slane, i m-Bri dam for Suaniu .i. riuulus.

Kl. Ianair. (1. f., l. 21.) Anno domini cccccc.° Terremotus i m-Bairchiu. Mors Brendain mic Coirpri [mic] Feiċeni. Sic inueni in libro Cuanaċ. Bellum Slemne, 7 bellum Cule coil, 7 pausa Comġaill, 7 mors Oddaċ mic Aeda in isto anno perfecta esse. Uel hoc anno quies Choluim ċille in nocte dominica.

Kl. Ianair. (2. f., l. 2.) Anno domini dc.° i.° Quies Comġaill Bennċair. Bellum Slennae in quo Colman rimiḋ rex generis Euġain uictor erat, 7 Conall cuu mac Aeḋo mic Ainmireċ fugitiuus euasit. Bellum
Fol. 22aa. Cule coil in quo Fiaċna mac Demain fugit. Fiaċna mac Baetain uictor erat. Mors hUataċ mic Aeḋo. Bellum Eċrois.

---

[1] *Repose of Cainnech.*—See under 526 *supra*, note 3.

[2] *Battle of the Saxons.*—This seems to be the battle recorded in the Saxon Chronicle at A.D. 603, as fought between Aegthan, King of the Scots, against [*recte* with] the Dalreods, against Æthelferth, King of the Northumbrians, at Dægsanstan (Dawston in Cumberland), where all his (Aegthan's, or Aedan's) army is said to have been slain. Bede also refers this battle to the year 603. (*Hist. Eccl.* i., 34.)

[3] *Son.*—The original of this clause is interlined in A. and B. in very old writing.

[4] *Suaniu.*—Supposed to be the ancient name of a river near Geshill, in the King's County. See O'Donov. *Four Mast.*, under 596, note *o*.

[5] *Coirpre* [*son of*] *Feichen.*—The name is Coirpri Feicheni in A., but 'Coirpri mic Feicheni' ('C. son of Feichen') in B., and in the *Four Mast.* Clar. 49 has 'Cairbre St. Feichin,' which is a blunder. In the Geneal. Table of the Hy-Maine, given by O'Donovan (facing p. 97, *Tribes &c. of Hy-Many*) Cairpri Mac Fechine is set down as the son of a Feradach, and 5th in the line of descent from Maine Mor, from whom the Hy-Many sept was named. See also the Work referred to, at p. 15.

[6] *Slemain, Cuil-coil, Comgall, Odda.*

f Cluain-mic-Nois, rested. The repose of Cainnech[1] in .chadh-bó, as Cuana states.

Kal. Jan. (Frid., m. 10.) A.D. 599. The repose of aint Cainnech;[1] and the battle of the Saxons,[2] in which .edan was vanquished. The killing of Suibhne, son of olman Mor (son[3] of Diarmaid Derg, son of Fergus Cerr-eoil, son of Conall Cremthainne, son of Niall Nine-hos-ager), by Aedh Slane, in Bri-dam on the Suaniu,[4] *i.e.* a ream. [599.]

Kal. Jan. (Sund., m. 21.) A.D. 600. An earthquake Bairche. The death of Brendan, son of Coirpre [son] Feichen.[5] Thus I have found in the Book of Cuanu: ie battle of Slemain,[6] and the battle of Cuil-coil,[6] and ie rest of Comgall,[6] and the death of Odda[6], son of edh, took place in this year. Or, in this year, the pose of Colum-cille, on Sunday night. [600.]

Kal. Jan. (Mond., m. 2.) A.D. 601. The repose of omgall[7] of Bangor. The battle of Slemain,[8] in which olman Rimidh, King of Cinel-Eogain,[9] was victor, and onall Cu, son of Aedh, son of Ainmire, escaped by flight.[10] he battle of Cul-coel, in which Fiachna, son of Deman, ed. Fiachna, son of Baetan, was victor. The death of 'ata,[11] son of Aedh. The battle of Echros.[12] [601.]

These entries are recorded under e next year, which is the correct te according to the enumeration of ese Annals.

[7] *Comgall.*—His birth is entered at 5, and again at 519, *supra.*

[8] *Of Slemain.*--Slenne, for Slemne, B. Supposed to be now repre-ited by Slanemore and Slanebeg, the parish of Dysart, near Mullin-r, county Westmeath.

[9] *King of Cinel-Eogain.*—But also nt-monarch of Ireland. See above der 597.

[10] *Escaped by flight.* — Fugitiuꝑ aꝑit, A. Fugitiuꝑ euaꝑꝑit, B. The death of Conall Cu is recorded *infra*, under 603.

[11] *Uata.*—Written Oddaċ, gen. of Odda, under last year. In the Chron. Scot., at A.D. 592, where he is called King of Connaught, the name is written *Uadu;* but *Uata* by the *Four Mast.*, 597. From him was derived the name *Clann-Uadach*, "descendants of Uadu," the tribe-name of the O'Fallons of Roscommon, whose patronymic was also derived from Fallomhan, the great-grandson of Uadu.

[12] *Echros.*—See under next year.

Kl. Ianair. (3 f., l. 13.) Anno domini dc.° ii.° Quies Finntain filii nepotis Eċdaċ. Bellum Eċrois imMuirisc inter genus Coirpri 7 nepotes Fiaċraċ Muirsce. Maelcothaig rex nepotum Fiaċraċ in fugam euersus est. Omnia que scripta sunt in anno subsequente inueni in libro Cuanaċ in isto esse perfecta. Sinell epscop campi Bili [quieuit.] Caṫ sleiḃe Cua imMuṁain.

.b. Kl. Ianair. (4 f., l. 24.) Anno domini dc.° iii.° Iugulatio Colmain rimeḋo (mic Baedain brigi mic Muircertaig mic Earca) a uiro de genere suo qui uocatus est Locan 'Diolmana :—

Cedu riġe cedu reċt,
Cedu nert for riġraḋa,
Inid Colmain rimid ri
Rombi Locan diṫnada.

Iugulatio Aeḋo slane (mic Diarmoda deirg mic Fearġusa Cerrḃeoil mic Conaill Creṁtainne mic Neill noigiallaiġ) o Chonall mac Suibne, qui regnauerunt Temoriam aequali potestate simul. Iugulatio Aeḋo roin rex nepotum Failgi i faeṫgi mic Meccnaen for bru loċa Seiṁdiḋe, eodem die quo iugulatus est Aeḋ sláne. (Aeḋ gustan comalta

---

[1] *Battle of Echros.* — O'Donovan identifies this place with Aughris, a townland in the parish of Templeboy, bar. of Tireragh, co. Sligo. *Hy-Fiachrach*, p. 138.

[2] *Muirisc, i.e.*, the "Sea Plain."— A district in the bar. of Tireragh, co. Sligo. For its exact situation, see O'Donovan's *Hy-Fiachrach*, p. 257, note *b*, and the Map prefixed to the same Work.

[3] *Magh-Bile.*—Now Movilla, near Newtownards, in the co. Down. See O'Donovan's important note on *Magh-Bile*, *Four Mast.*, 602, note *t*.

[4] *Sliabh-Cua.* — Already entered under 596.

[5] *In Munster.* — ImMuġain, A. More correctly imMuṁain, B.

[6] *Son of Baetan, &c.*—This clause is interlined in A. and B. by later hands.

[7] *Who was called.*—The equivalent of this clause, "qui dictus est Locan Diolmana," is interlined in *al. man.* in A.

[8] *Dithnada.*—A variation of the epithet Dilmana. These lines, which are not in B., are written in the lower margin of fol. 21*b* in A., with a mark

Kal. Jan. (Tues., m. 13.) A.D. 602. The repose of 'inntan son of Ua-Echdach. The battle of Echros[1] in Iuirisc,[2] between the Cinel-Coirpri and the Ui-Fiachrach f Muirisc.[3] Maelcothaig, King of the Ui-Fiachrach, was ut to flight. All things which are written in the folowing year, I find in the Book of Cuanu to have taken lace in this. Sinell, bishop of Magh-Bile,[3] [rested]. The attle of Sliabh-Cua[4] in Munster.[5] [602.]

Kal. Jan. (Wed., m. 24.) A.D. 603. Assassination of 'olman Rimidh ([6]son of Baetan Brigi, son of Muircherach Mac Erca), by a man of his kindred (who was called[7] ocan Dilmana). [603.]

Notwithstanding kingship, notwithstanding law,
Notwithstanding power over chieftains;
Behold! Colman Rimid, a king—
Locan Dithnada[8] slew him!

ssassination of Aedh Slane (son of Diarmaid[9] Derg, son f Fergus Cerrbheoil, son of Conall Cremthainne, son of 'iall Nine-hostager), by Conall, son of Suibne. They [*i.e.* 'olman Rimidh and Aedh Slaine] reigned[10] together at 'ara with equal power. The assassination of Aedh Roin, Cing of the Ui-Failgi, in Faethgi-mic-Meccnaen[11] (on the rink of Loch-Semdidhe), on the same day in which

reference to their proper place in e text.

[9] *Son of Diarmaid, &c.*— This ause is interlined in A. and B. 'Conor has created some confusion his edition of these Annals, by aking this clause a continuation of at above given (see note 6) in conexion with the name of Colman imidh; thus giving both kings the me pedigree, which is wrong.

[10] *Reigned.*—This entry is very osely constructed in both A. and B. he events are recorded by the *Four fast.*, under A.D. 600, in a much ore simple and intelligible way.

[11] *Faethgi-mic-Meccnaen.* — "The Fair-green of Mac Meccnaen." *Faithche-mic-Meccnain*, Chron. Scot. (604; *F. mic Menenain, Four M.* (600). The so-called Translator of Clar. 49 renders it by "the field of Macnaen." The parenthesis which follows (interlined in A. and B.) fixes the *faithche* as on the brink of Loch-Semdidhe, or Lough-Sewdy. The name is now obsolete, but there can be little doubt that the "green" occupied the site of the present village of Ballymore-Lough-Sewdy, barony of Rathconrath, co. Westmeath.

Conaill, 7 baeṫal bile, ronġonsadar), unde dictum est:—

Nir' bo airṁirt ind airle
Dona h-ogaib tuaiḋ tuirṁe;
Conall ro bi Aeḋ sláne;
Aeḋ slane ro bi Suibne.

Aeḋ búidi ri cenuil Maeni [occisus est]. Mors Chonaill Chuu mic Aeḋa mic Ainmireċ. Cuu cen maṫair mortui sunt.

Kt. Ianair. Anno domini dc.° iiii.° Bellum Slaeḃre in quo uictus est Branduḃ mac Eaṫaċ. Nepotes Neill uictores erant, .i. Aeḋ Uaredac, in quo tempore regnauit. Iugulatio Branduib regis Lagen a genere suo per dolum (mac Eathach mic Muireaḋaiġ mic Aeḋa mic Ḟeiḋlim mic Enna Ceinnsealaiġ mic Labrada mic Breasail belaiġ mic Fiaċa baicceaḋa mic Caṫair ṁoir.) Triginta annis regnauit in Laginia, 7 a caṫ na Damcluana ro marḃaḋ. No gomaḋ e Saran saeḃderg .i. oirċinneaċ Seanḃoiṫe sine rosṁairsseaḋ, ut poeta dixit .r.

Saran saebderg seol co se,
Oirċinneach Senboiṫe sine;
E ni dalḃ gan ḃranḋal braṫ,
Ro ṁarḃ Branduḃ mac Eachach.

Foccas annis .uii. regnauit. Obitus Laissren abbatis Iae.

---

[1] *Aedh.*—This clause is added in *al. man.* in A. Interlined in B.

[2] *Of which was said.*—Unde dictum est, A. Not in B. The verses which follow (and which also are not in B.) are in the top marg. of A., fol. 22*a*; another, but more corrupt, copy being written in the lower margin, fol. 21*b*.

[3] *Tuath-Tuirmhe.* — O'Donovan (*Four Mast.*, 600, note *g*) says that this was a Bardic name for Bregia, 'from Tuirbhe, or Turvey, near Swords, in the county of Dublin.'

[4] *Aedh Buidhe.*—He was king, or chieftain, of the Cinel-Maine (or descendants of Maine, son of Niall Nine-hostager), whose territory was in later times known as Tethbha, or Teffia, a district comprising the western part of the present county of

edh Slane was assassinated, (Aedh[1] Gustan, Conall's ster-brother, and Baethal Bile, that killed him); of which as said:[2]—

Not wise was the counsel
For the heroes of Tuath-Tuirmhe;[3]
Conall that slew Aedh Slánè;
Aedh Slanè that slew Suibne.

.ed Buidhe,[4] King of Cinel-Maini, [slain]. Death of Conall uu,[5] son of Aedh, son of Ainmire. Cu-cen-mathair[6] died.

Kal. Jan. A.D. 604. The battle of Slaebhre, in which randubh, son of Eacha, was vanquished. The Ui-'eill were victors, (*i.e.*, Aedh Uaridnach, who then reigned). he killing of Brandubh, King of Leinster, by his wn tribe, through treachery: (son of Eacha, son of [uiredach, son of Aedh, son of Fedhlim, son of Enna ennselach, son of Labraidh, son of Bresal Belach, son of iacha Baicceda, son of Cathair Mor). He reigned thirty ears in Leinster, and in the battle of Damcluain he as slain. Or it may have been Saran 'Saebhderg,' *i.e.*, ie 'Herenagh' of Senboth-sine, that killed him, as the)et said:— [604.]

False-eyed Saran, a guide hitherto,
'Herenagh' of Senboth-sine,
Was he, no falsehood, without bright judgment,
That killed Brandubh son of Eacha.

)ccas[7] reigned seven years. Death of Laisren abbot 'Ia.

---

estmeath, with adjacent parts of ngford and King's cos. See Donov. *Four Mast.*, at A.D. 1207, ;e *z*, and Ir. Topog. Poems, note 35.
e *Four Mast.* (A.D. 600) and the *ron. Scot.* (604) state that Aedh s slain by Conall son of Suibhne, the same day on which Aedh Slane s killed.
Conall Cuu.—Said to have been eated in the battle of Slemain, *ra*, 601. O'Conor thinks the name signifies 'Conallus placidus,' and not 'Conallus canis,' as O'Donovan suggests (*Four Mast.* 600, note *k*).

[6] *Cu-cen-mathair*, *i.e.*, "Canis sine matre." The record of his obit here is decidedly wrong, and for "mortui sunt", we should probably read "natus est," as his death is recorded *infra*, at 664.

[7] *Foccas.*—The Emperor Phocas. This and the following entry are not in B., nor in Clar. 49.

Kl. Ianair. Anno domini dc.° u.° Quies Beugnai abbatis Bennċoir. Mors Aeḋain mic Gabrain (mic Domangairt, riġ Alban). Iugulatio filiorum Baetain .i. mic Cairill. Secundo anno Foccae imperatoris, Gregorius papa secundum Bedam migrauit ad dominum. Bonifatio rogante statuit sedem romanae et apostolicae aecclesiae caput esse omnium ecclesiarum, quia ecclesia Constantinopolitana primum se omnium ecclesiarum scribebat.

Kl. Ianair. Anno domini dc.° ui.° Uel ut alii dicunt hic migrauit Gregorius ad Christum, scilicet hoc anno.

Fol 22ab .b. Kl. Ianair. (2 f., l. 9.) Anno domini dc.° uii.° Mors Fiachraċ caiċ mic Baetain la Cruiṫniu, 7 quies Aedaċ mic Daill. Sabunianus natione Tuscus sedem Petri tenuit anno .i. mensibus .u., diebus .ix., et sepultus est in basilica Petri.

Kl. Ianair. (4 f., l. 20.) Anno domini dc.° uiii.° Occisio Seċnusaiġ mic Garbain, 7 mors Conaill mic Daimeni, 7 quies Lugdaċ mic U Ochae.

---

[1] *Beogna.*—Written Beugnai (the gen. case) in A. and B. O'Conor has erroneously printed the name 'Bengnai,' and Latinized it *Benignus*, in his ed. of these Annals. His festival is given as 22 Aug., in the *Martyr. of Donegal*, where the name is Beoghna.

[2] *Aedhan.*—The *Chron. Scotorum*, in giving his obit at the year 606, adds that this was the 37th year of Aedhan's reign, and the 88th, or 86th, of his age. But Aedhan died in the 74th year of his age, according to Tigernach.

[3] *Sons of Baetan.*—The death of this Baetan is entered, *supra*, under the years 580 and 586. The *Chron. Scot.*, which records the murder of Baetan's sons at the year 606, adds that they were slain in 'Dun-Mogna,' *a filio matris suæ*. In the *Book of Leinster* (p. 330. col. 4), the slayer of the sons of Baetan is stated to have been his brother, Maelduin, and the place where they were slain is called *Dún-Mugnae*.

[4] *According to Bede.*—See Bede's *Eccl. Hist.*, Book II., chap. I.

[5] *He*, *i.e.*, the Emperor Phocas. Vid. Paul. Diacon., *de Gest. Reg. Longobard.*, lib. 4, cap. 37.

[6] *Fiachra Caech*, *i.e.*, 'Fiachra the one-eyed.' Craiċ (gen. of craeċ), A. Written Fiaċra craiṫ in B., and printed *Fiachrait* by O'Conor, who has fused the name and the epithet into one. Skene prints the

Kal. Jan. A.D. 605. The repose of Beogna,[1] abbot of Bangor. The death of Aedhan,[2] son of Gabran, son of Domangart, King of Alba. Assassination of the sons of Bactan,[3] son of Cairill. In the second year of the Emperor Phocas, Pope Gregory migrated to the Lord, according to Bede.[4] At the request of Boniface, he[5] had decreed the See of Rome and of the Apostolic Church to be the head of all Churches, for the Constantinopolitan Church used to describe itself the first of all Churches. [605.]

Kal. Jan. A.D. 606. Or, as others say, in this place Gregory migrated to Christ; to wit, in this year. [606.]

Kal. Jan. (Mond., m. 9.) A.D. 607. The death of Fiachra Caech,[6] son of Baetan, by Cruithni; and the repose of Aedh, son of Dall.[7] Sabinian, by birth a Tuscan, held[8] the See of Peter one year, five months, and ten days, and was buried in the Church of Peter. [607.]

Kal. Jan. (Wed., m. 20.) A.D. 608. The killing of Sechnasach,[9] son of Garban, and the death of Conall, son of Daimin, and the repose of Lugaid Mac-Ui-Oche.[10] [608.]

---

ntry of Fiachra Caech's death (*Chron. f the Picts and Scots*, p. 346,) as if e regarded Fiachra as a Scottish ersonage; but Fiachra was evidently he son of the Baetan above menoned (580, 586).

[7] *Son of Dall.*—Daill (gen. of all) A. and B. O'Conor prints *Domhnaill* ('of Domhnall'); and lar. 49 has 'Donill.' The word uier would imply that the person ferred to was an ecclesiastic. There no corresponding entry in the *Ann. our Mast.*

[8] *Held.*—The words petri tenuit, the original text, omitted in A., re supplied from B.

[9] *Sechnasach.*—In the *Ann. Four Mast.* (605), and *Chron. Scot.* (609), echnasach is stated to have been King of Cinel-Boghaine, a tribe located in the district corresponding to the present barony of Banagh, co. Donegal.

[10] *Lugaid Mac-Ui-Oche, i.e.*, 'Lugaid, son of the descendant of Oche.' His birth is entered under the year 553, *supra*. He is better known by his *alias* name Molua, which is the form used in *Tigernach*. His father was one Carthach, of the Munster tribe Corco-Oche, mentioned *supra*, at 551. Hence the description Mac-Ui-Oche. Lugaid, or Molua, founded the church of Cluain-ferta-Molua, or Clonfert-Mulloe, now known as Kyle, in the barony of Clandonagh, Queen's co. O'Conor erroneously prints the name *L. mac Cuochae.*

Kl. Ianair. (5 f., l. 1.) Anno domini dc.° ix.° Mors Aeḋo mic Colggen regis na n-Airṫer. Mors Sillani mic Cumminn abbatis Bennċoir, 7 mors Aedain anchoritae Bennċoir, 7 mors Maelehumai mic Baetain. Senaċ (o ċluain uAingriġi), abb Aird maċa, quieuit. Finis cronici Iusebii.

Kl. Ianair. (6 f., l. 12.) Anno domini dc.° x.° Fulminatus est exercitus Uloṫ im mBairċiu fulmine terribili. Mors Maeileduin mic Aleni regis Mogdornae, 7 mors Eugain mic Eċaċ Laiḃ. Quies Colmani Elo. Sic est in libro Cuanach, Aeḋ Roin 7 Aeḋ Laiġen.

.b. Kl. Ianair. (7 f., l. 23.) Anno domini dc.° xi.° Mors Aeḋo aldain filii Domnaill regis Temro. Bellum Odbae re n-Oengus mac Colmain, in quo cecidit Conall laeġbreġ filius Aeḋo sláne. Maelcoḃa regnare incipit hoc anno.

Kl. Ianair. (2 f., l. 4.) Anno domini dc.° xii.° Quies Finntain Oentraiḃ abbatis Benncoir. Mors Colmain uaċ[aig]. Bellum Caire legion ubi sancti occisi sunt, 7 cecidit Solon mac Conaen rex Britanorum. Eraclius annis .xxvi. regnat.

---

[1] *Aedan.*—This entry, which is not in B., is in Clar. 49.

[2] *Cluain-U-Aingrighi.*—In the List of Successors of St. Patrick, contained in the *Book of Leinster* (p. 42, cols. 3–4), Senach, who is called *garbh* ('rough') is stated to have been from *Cluain. h. mic Gricci* ('Plain of the descendant of Gricci's son'), and of the Ui-Niallain; and it is further added that Senach was 'a blacksmith in Orders, from Kilmore.' The Kilmore here referred to is probably Kilmore, in the bar. of O'Neilland West, co. Armagh. See Todd's *St. Patrick*, p. 180. The clause is not in B.

[3] *Chronicle of Eusebius.*—This cannot refer to the genuine chronicle of Eusebius, who died A.D. 340, but may possibly allude to some copy thereof, with additions, known to old Irish Annalists.

[4] *Echa Laibh.*—The *Echodius Laib* of Adamnan (*Vit. Columb.*, i., 7). See Reeves' *Adamnan*, p. 33, note *h.*

[5] *Aedh Roin—Aedh Laighen.*—The preceding statement, "Thus it is in the Book of Cuanu," seems to refer to the imperfect conclusion of the

Kal. Jan. (Thursd., m. 1.) A.D. 609. Death of edh, son of Colgu, King of the Airthera. Death of llan, son of Cummin, abbot of Bangor; and death of edan,[1] anchorite of Bangor; and death of Maeluma, son ' Baetan. Senach (from Cluain-U-Aingrighi[2]), abbot of rmagh, rested. End of the Chronicle of Eusebius.[3] [609.]

Kal. Jan. (Frid. m. 12.) A.D. 610. The army of ladh was struck by terrible thunder in Bairche. The ath of Maelduin son of Alen, King of Mogdorna; and e death of Eugan, son of Echa Laibh.[4] The repose of olman Elo. Thus it is in the Book of Cuanu. Aedh oin[5] and Aedh Laighen.[5] [610.]

Kal. Jan. (Sat., m. 23.) A.D. 611. Death of Aedh ldan,[6] son of Domnall, King of Tara. The battle of dba *was gained* by Oengus, son of Colman, in which ll Conall Laegh-bregh, son of Aedh Slánè. Maelcobha gins to reign in this year. [611.]

Kal. Jan. (Mond., m. 4.) A.D. 612. The repose of nntan of Oentraibh,[7] abbot of Bangor. The death of olman Uath[ach][8]. The battle of Caer-legion,[9] in which ly men[10] were slain, and Solon son of Conaen, King of e Britons, fell. Heraclius reigns 26 years. [612]

---

ry that follows, and not to the uies" of Colman Elo (St. Colman Lainn-Elo, or Lynally, in the ng's Co.), the date of whose death given in the Irish Annals generally 610. Of Aedh Roin and Aedh ighen, nothing is known, at least the Editor.

[6] *Aedh Aldan.*—An *alias* name for dh Uaridnach, King of Tara. See ler the year 604 *supra*. The ession to the throne of the real dh Aldan (or Aedh Allan) is entered he year 733 *infra*.

[7] *Oentraibh.*—The Irish form of the name of Antrim.

[8] *Uathach.*—"The hateful." Written uaϲh. in A. and B.; but uaϲhaıϩ (genit. of uaϲhach) in Chron. Scot. (613).

[9] *Caer-legion.*—Chester. The Anglo-Saxon Chron. records this battle under the year 606. See Thorpe's ed., London, 1861. See also Bede's account of it, *Eccl. Hist.*, Book 2, Chap. 2.

[10] *Holy men.*—ſcı, for *sancti*, A., B.

Fol. 22ba. Kl. Ianair. (3 f., l. 15.) Anno domini dc.° xiii.° Tolfa fota abb Cluana mic u Nois pausat. Stella uisa est hora uiiiª diei.

Kl. Ianair. (4 f., l. 26.) Anno domini dc.° xiiii.° Iugulatio Maelicoba mic Aeḋo in bello montis (bealgaḋain) Tueṫ (uel caṫ Sleiḃe truim). Suibni menn uictor erat et regnauit post eum. Quies Diarmato tertii abbatis Cluana iraird. Bellum Fidnaiġi ei legg in riaddai. Coeman brecc quieuit.

.b. Kl. Ianair. (5 f., l. 7.) Anno domini dc.° xu.° Mors Suibne mic Craeċeni regis Cianaċtae glinne gaimin, 7 mors Aeḋain mic Mongain regis Dalriata (no araide), 7 mors Petrain episcoip Luscan. Eo [anno] Aeḋ 7 Critan aréni obierunt. Combustio Benncoir.

Kl. Ianair. (7 f., l. 18.) Anno domini dc.° x.° u.° i.° Combustio martirum Ega. Combustio Donnain Ega hi xu. Kal. Mai cum .cl. martiribus, 7 occisio Torchae, 7 loscaḋ Condiri. Usque hunc annum scripsit Isidorus Cronicon suum, ita dicens, Eraclius dehinc quintum annum agit imperii, hoc est anno quinto

---

1 *Tolua.*—Tolfa, A., B., and Clar. 49. But "Tolua" in the *Ann. Four Mast.*, which have his obit under the year 609.

2 *Sliabh-Tueth.*—Originally written mon̄ tueth in A., over which a second hand has added tis bealgadain, as if to correct the name to *montis Bealgadhain*, or Sliabh-Belgadain (as in MS. B.) The alias reading which would fix the site of the battle at Sliabh-Truim (now known as "Bessy Bell" Mountain, in the bar. of Strabane) is added in the margin in A. and B. Clar. 49 has simply "in bello Montis Belgadhain." But the *Four Masters* write the name Sliabh-Toadh; and the Chron. Scot. has "in bello montis Toath (or Taeth)"; whilst in the *Book of Leinster* (p. 25*a*) Maelcobha is stated to have been slain in the battle of Sliabh-Toad. Keating writes "Sliabh-Bealgadain."

3 *At.*—ei (for ec, or ic) A., B. O'Conor prints *ic* ("at.") Clar. 49 has "at Legg-in-Riada." The name signifies "the stone of punishment." The place has not been identified.

4 *Coeman Brec.*—His birth is recorded *supra*, at the year 528; so that he lived to the age of 86.

5 *Dalriata or [Dal]araide.*—Over the name dalriata, in A., the copyist has written ɫ araide (or *araide*) rightly correcting the name to *Dala-*

Kal. Jan. (Tues., m. 15.) A.D. 613. Tolua[1] the Tall, ,bot of Cluain-mic-Nois, rests. A star was seen the ghth hour of the day. [613.]

Kal. Jan. (Wed., m. 26.) A.D. 614. The killing of aelcobha son of Aedh, in the battle of Sliabh-Tueth[2] Sliabh-Belgadain ; otherwise, the battle of Sliabh-uim.) Suibne Menn was victor, and reigned after him. he repose of Diarmait, third abbot of Cluain-Iraird. he battle of Fidnacha, at[3] Legg-in-riaddai. Coeman rec[4] rested. [614.]

Kal. Jan. (Thurs., m. 7.) A.D. 615. The death of uibne, son of Crachen, King of the Cianachta of Glenn-aimhin, and the death of Aedhan son of Mongan, King f Dalriata or [Dal]araide[5]; and the death of Petran, ishop of Lusca. In the same year[6] Aedh, and Critan ureni, died. Burning of Bangor. [615.]

Kal. Jan. (Sat., m. 18.) A.D. 616. The burning of he martyrs of Egg. The burning of Donnan[7] of Egg, n the 15th of the Kalends of May, with 150 martyrs; nd the devastation of Torach,[8] and the burning of Condere. Isidore wrote his Chronicle down to this year, hus saying :—Heraclius completed the fifth year of his eign from this time,[9] which is in the fifth year of the [616.]

---

aide, of which Aedhan was King. ee Reeves' *Eccl. Antiqq.*, p. 340.

[6] *In the same year.*—Eo in A. and B., the word anno being omitted in oth MSS. Clar. 49 has *eo an.* O'Conor, in his ed. of these Annals, as joined Eo to the following name Ceḋ, and formed from the conjunction the unusual form of name "Eacaedh."

[7] *Donnan.*—The original of this ntry is added over that of the preeding entry in A., and partly in B. Regarding St. Donnan of Egg (or Donnan Ega, as he is generally called), see Reeves' *Adamnan*, Additional Note K., p. 303, where much curious information on the subject is given.

[8] *Devastation of Torach.*—occiрio is the word used for "devastation," in A., B., and Clar. 49. The *Chron. Scot.* has uaрtatio. Torach is Tory Island, off the N.W. coast of Donegal. The devastation of Torach is mentioned under the year 612 by the *Four Mast.*, who have no notice of the massacre of Donnan's people above recorded.

[9] *From this time.*—dehinc, A., B., and Clar. 49.

imperii Eraclii et quarto religiosissimi principis Sisebuti; sunt ab exordio mundi anni usque ad Eraclii annum presentem, hoc est quintum, ū. dccc. xiiii.

Kl. Ianair. (1 f., l. 29.) Anno domini dc.° x.° uii.° Int immairecc in Eiluuin in die pasca. Iugulatio Colggen mic Suibni 7 mors Fiaċraċ mic Conaill, 7 iugulatio Fergusa filii Colmain magni .i. o Anfartaċ hU Mescain do muinntir Blatine:—

Mai dom isedsa com ṫech,
hUa Mescain Anfortach,
Uisque dorbach dombeuir do,
Fobiṫ gono Fergusso.

Ni tan doregat buidne
Cenuil Colmain sech ċuilne,
Iarmifoiset disuidiu
Sil Mescain im Blatiniu.

Coemgin glinne da loċa 7 Comġall epscop, 7 epscop Eogan Raṫa sithe, quieuerunt. Indraeḋ Maċa, et terremotus in Gallia.

Kl. Ianair. (2 f., l. 10.) Anno domini dc.° x.° uiii.° Liber abbas Achaid bo Cainniġ. Mors Sillani abbatis campi Bili. Mors Aeḋo Bennain 7 Fingin mic ḟiaċraċ.

---

[1] *Of the most religious.*—Relegiossimi, A. Sesihutus was King of the West Goths in Spain, A.D. 612–620.

[2] *Eiluuin.*—Eiluini, in B., which O'Conor inaccurately prints *Eili unn*, and he then translates the entry "*Disceptatio in Eili hoc anno in Die Pasche*," which is worse. The place alluded to was not any of the territories called Eile. Elphin, in the co. Roscommon, may possibly have been intended.

[3] *Colggu.*—The killing of this person, whose name is written *Colggen* in the genit. case in A. and B., is entered in *Ann. Four Mast.*, under the year 613.

[4] *Anfortach Ua Mescain.* — This name is written *Anfartech .h. Mescill* in the *Book of Leinster* (p. 42, col. 1), where it stated that he slew Fergus "in the battle of *Blatteine.*"

[5] *Blatini.*—See last note.

[6] *Coemgin of Glenn-da-locha.*—St. Kevin of Glendalough. The *Chron. Scot.*, and the *Martyr of Donegal* (at June 3), give his age as 120 years. This and the remaining entries for

ign of Heraclius, and the fourth of the most religious[1] ince Sesibutus. From the beginning of the World to ie present year, that is the fifth, of Heraclius, there are 314 years.

Kal. Jan. (Sund., m. 29.) A.D. 617. The conflict in iluuin[2] on Easter Day. The killing of Colggu,[3] son of aibne; and the death of Fiachra, son of Conall; and ie killing of Fergus, son of Colman Mór, by Anfartach a Mescain,[4] of Muintir-Blatini. [617.]

If to me, to my house, should come
Mescan's descendant, Anfartach,
Poisonous water I would give him,
Because of the slaying of Fergus.

When bands of the Cinel-Colman
Shall go past Cuilne,
They will question, therefor,
The Sil-Mescain in Blatini.[5]

)emgin of Glenn-da-locha,[6] and Bishop Comghall,[7] and ishop Eogan, of Rath-sithe,[8] rested. The devastation ' Macha ;[9] and an earthquake in Gallia.

Kal. Jan. (Mond., m. 10.) A.D. 618. Liber,[10] abbot Achad-bo-Cainnigh [rested]. The death of Sillan,)bot of Magh-bile. The death of Aedh Bennain,[11] and Fingin son of Fiachra. [618.]

---

s year, added in the margin in A., partly illegible. The text is refore taken from MS. B. See ler the year 621.

[7] *Comghall.*—In Clar. 49, Comghall called Bishop of Daire (Derry). t this must be an error.

[8] *Rath-sithe.*—Now Rashee, bar. of per Antrim, co. Antrim. O'Conor, his ed. of these Annals, prints this ry very inaccurately, and trans- es "Comgall Episcopus et Episco- ı Eogan Ecclesiæ Sancti collis ritum, seu lemurum, quieverunt *in edmacha.*" He seems to have taken the ınopaeð maċa ("devastation of Macha") of the following entry for the name of a place. See Reeves' *Eccl. Antiqq.*, p. 68, note *p.*

[9] *Devastation of Macha.* ınopaeð maċa. — See last note. Possibly *Macha* may be for *Ard-Macha* (Armagh).

[10] *Liber.*—Printed "Libren," with characteristic inaccuracy, by O'Conor.

[11] *Aedh Bennain.*— King of West Munster. His death is entered in *Ann. Four Mast.*, under the year 614, as is also that of Fingin son of Fiachra.

Fol. 22bb. .b. Kl. Ianair. (3 f., l. 21.) Anno domini dc.° x.° ix.° Occisio (.i. immaigh slecht i crich Conacht) generis Baetain .i. Ailealla mic Baetain, 7 Maeleduin mic Fergusa mic Baetain, 7 mors Fiachrach mic Ciarain filii Ainmerech mic Setni.

Kl. Ianair. (5 f., l. 2.) Anno domini dc.° xx.° Senach garbh abbas Cluana ferta moritur. Iugulatio Aengusa mic Colmain magni .i. regis nepotum Neill. Duncath mac Eugain, Nechtan mac Canonn, 7 Aedh obierunt.

Kl. Ianair. (6 f., l. 13.) Anno domini dc.° xx.° i.° Bellum Cind delgden. Conall mac Suibne uictor erat. Duo filii Librain mic Illandon mic Cerbaill ceciderunt. Conaing mac Aedhain dimersus est:—

Tonna mora mogalna,
Grian rodbatoigsetar,
Fri curach flesc fann
For Conaing coirsetar.

Mors Mailembracho mic Rimedho mic Colmain filii Cobthaigh 7 Ailello mic Cellaigh. Bellum Lindair. Quies Coemgin glinne da locha. Bellum Cenbuigi in quo cecidit Colman mac Cobthaigh. Iugulatio Ailello mic Cellaigh. Mors Colggen mic Ceallaigh.

Kl. Ianair. (7 f., l. 24.) Anno domini dc.° xx.° ii.° Obitus Fergnai abbatis Iae. Quies mic Lasre abba-

---

[1] *Magh-slecht.*—The ancient name of a plain in the present bar. of Tullyhaw, co. Cavan. This clause is added by way of gloss in A., over the word occisio.

[2] *Ui-Neill.*—The southern Ui-Neill. In the list of the Kings of Uisnech, contained in the *Book of Leinster* (p. 42, col. 1), Aengus is stated to have reigned 7 years, and to have been slain by one Domnall son of Mur-[chadh.]

[3] *Eugan.*—Apparently the Eugan (or Euganan), son of Gabran (King of Dalriada), whose death is entered at the year 594 *supra*.

[4] *Nechtan.*—A Pictish king.

[5] *Conaing son of Aedhan, i.e.*, son of Aedhan Mac Gabhrain, King of Alba, whose death is entered above at the year 605. The verses that follow, referring to the drowning of Conaing, and which are not in B., are so corrupt that they could scarcely be set right without the expenditure of more time and trouble than the subject is worth. They are much more correctly given in the *Chron.*

Kal. Jan. (Tues., m. 21.) A.D. 619. The murder (in [619.]
gh-slecht,[1] in the territory of Connaught) of the
aily of Baetan, viz., of Ailill, son of Baetan, and of
ielduin, son of Fergus, son of Baetan; and the death
Fiachra, son of Ciaran, son of Ainmire, son of Setna.

Kal. Jan. (Thursd., m. 2.) A.D. 620. Senach Garbh [620.]
bot of Cluain-ferta, dies. The killing of Aengus, son
Colman Mór, *i.e.*, King of the Ui-Neill.[2] Duncath son
Eugan,[3] Nechtan[4] son of Canonn, and Aedh, died.

Kal. Jan. (Frid., m. 13.) A.D. 621. The battle of [621.]
nn-delgden. Conall, son of Suibne, was victor. Two
ns of Libran, son of Illandan, son of Cerbhall, were
in. Conaing, son of Aedhan,[5] was drowned:—

Great bright sea waves,
[And] the sun, that killed him,
At his weak wicker skiff,
Arrayed themselves against Conaing.

he death of Maelbracha, son of Rimidh, son of Colman,
n of Cobthach, and of Ailill, son of Cellach. Battle
Lindair.[6] The rest of Coemgin,[7] of Glenn-da-locha.
attle of Cenbuigh,[8] in which Colman, son of Cobthach,
as slain. Murder of Ailill, son of Cellach. Death of
olggu, son of Cellach.

Kal. Jan. (Sat. m. 24.) A.D. 622. The death of [622.]
ergna,[9] abbot of Ia. The rest of Mac Laisre,[10] abbot of

---

ot., under the year 622. Skene
s published them as they appear in
igernach, with a translation; and
th text and translation are very
accurate. (*Chron. Picts* and *Scots*,
69.)

[6] *Lindair.*—Not. identified.

[7] *Rest of Coemgin.*—A marginal
ote in *al. man.* in A. adds "secun-
um alios." St. Kevin's death is
itered before under the year 617.

[8] *Battle of Cenbuigh.*—The *Four
Mast.*, who record this battle under
e year 617, write the name of the
place *Cenn-gubha* (*or* *Cenn bughbha*),
which O'Donovan identifies with
Cambo, in the co. Roscommon.

[9] *Fergna.*—Or, as he is sometimes
called Fergna Brit, fourth Abbot of
Ia. See Reeves' *Adamnan*, p. 372.

[10] *Mac Laisre.*—Some old annotator
wrote the alias name of MacLaisre in
the margin in A.; but only the letters
epr . . . .ı. ᴅaba . . . (Bishop .i.
Daba. . . .) can be read. Ware com-
plains that his "proper name is no
where mentioned." (Harris's *Ware*,
Vol. i., p. 39.)

tis Ard maċae, 7 Uinei abbatis neir. Expugnatio Raṫo guali la Fiaċna mac Baetain.

Rogab tene Raiṫ n-guaili,
Taiscid biucatan uaidi,
Is dian adranadat ind uilc
Tenid irrait Aeda builc.

.b. Kl. Ianair. (1 f., l. 5.) Anno domini dc.° xx.° iii.° Mors Ronain mic Colmani, 7 Colman stellaen obiit, 7 iugulatio ḋoir mic Aeḋo Aldain. Natiuitas Adomnani abbatis Iae.

Kl. Ianair. (3 f., l. 16.) Anno domini dc.° xx.° iiii.° Annus tenebrosus. Aeḋan mac Cumuscaiġ, 7 Colman mac Comgellain ad Dominum migrant, 7 Ronan mac Tuaṫail, rex na n-Airṫer, 7 Mongan mac Fiaċ[n]ae Lurgan moriuntur:—

Lann Cluana airṫir indiu,
Amra ceṫrar forsriaḋat,
Cormac [caem] fri imoċaiḋ
Ocus illann mac Fiaċach.

In dias aile
Forsgniat mor di tuathaib,
Mongan mac Fiaċnai Lurgan,
Ocus Ronan mac Tuaṫail.

Maeḋoicc Fearna quieuit.

Fol. 23aa Kl. Ianair. (4 f., l. 27.) Anno domini dc.° xx.° u.°

---

[1] *Rath-Guali.*—These lines, which are not in B., are written on the top marg. of fol. 22*b* in A.

[2] *Ronan.*—King of Leinster. In the *Book of Leinster* (p. 39, col. 2), Ronan son of Colman, King of L., is stated to have died *de rith fola*, "of the bloody flux."

[3] *Colman Stellain.* — Abbot of Terryglass, co. Tipperary.

[4] *Aedh Aldan.*—The same as Aedh Uaridnach, King of Tara, whose death is recorded at the year 611, *supra.*

[5] *Ia.*—I-Columcille. Not in B.

[6] *Colman, son of Comgellan.*—Clar. 49 has 'Comgellan mac Colmain,' which is an error. Regarding Colman, son of Comgellan, see Reeves' *Adamnan*, p. 92, note *c*.

[7] *Mongan, son of Fiachna Lurgan.*—In the List of Kings of Dal-Araide contained in the *Book of Leinster* (p.

·magh, and of Vineus, abbot of Neir. The destruction Rath-Guali by Fiachna, son of Baetan.

Fire seized Rath-Guali,[1]
Save ye a little from it.
Vehemently the wicked have ignited
Fire in the Rath of Aedh Bolc.

Kal. Jan. (Sund., m. 5.) A.D. 623. The death of ·nan,[2] son of Colman; and Colman Stellain[3] died; and e murder of Doir, son of Aedh Aldan.[4] The birth of ·lamnan, abbot of Ia.[5] [623.]

Kal. Jan. (Tues., m. 16.) A.D. 624. A year of dark-ss. Aedhan, son of Cumuscach, and Colman, son of ·mgellan,[6] pass to the Lord; and Ronan, son of Tuathal, ·ing of the Airthera, and Mongan, son of Fiachna ·ırgan,[7] die. [624.]

The church of Cluain-airthir[8] to-day—
Famous the four on whom 'twas closed—
Cormac [the mild], through suffering,
And Illann son of Fiacha.

And the other pair,
Whom many tribes obeyed—
Mongan, son of Fiachna Lurgan,[9]
And Ronan, son of Tuathal.

·aedhocc[10] of Ferns rested.

Kal. Jan. (Wed., m. 27.) A.D. 625. The battle of [625.]

· col. 5), the name of Fiacha Lurga · it is there written) occurs after ·t of Aedh Dubh, whose death is ·ered under the year 587, *supra*. ·chna is also in the List of Kings of ·d in the *Book of Leinster* (p. 41, . 3).

[8] *Cluain-airthir*. — Dean Reeves ·nks is the place now called ·gheracloone, in the co. Monaghan. ·eves' *Adamnan*, p. 373, note *k*. The Irish text of the first of the foregoing stanzas (neither of which is in B.) is written in the lower margin of fol. 23*a* in A., and the second in low. marg. 22*b*, in orig. hand.

[9] *Lurgan*.—Luɼgaɼ, A.

[10] *Maedhocc*.—St. Mogue, as the name is now usually written. See O'Donovan's *Ann. Four Mast.*, at A.D. 624, note *p*.

Bellum Leithet midind, in quo cecidit Fiaċna Lurgan. Fiaċna mac Demmain uictor erat. Obresio Boilg luaṫa a nepotibus Neill.

Kt. Ianair. (5 f. l. 9.) Anno domini dc.° xx.° ui.° Bellum ardda Corrand, Dalriatai uictores erant, in quo cecidit Fiaċna filius demain. Bellum Cairn Feraḋaiġ i Cliu, ubi Failḃe flann Féimin uictor erat. Guaire Aidne fugit Conall mac Maelduiḃ fugit, 7 cecidit rex nepotum Maein:—

Ni torċair di Connaċtaiḃ,
Nic aṫcumai ind ḟeisir,
Maelduin, Maelruain, Maelcalcaiċ,
Conall, Maeldub, Maelbresail.

Uisio quam uidit Fursseus religiosus episcopus.

.b. Kt. Ianair. (6 f., l. 20.) Anno domini dc.° xx.° uii.° (alias 28°). Bellum Boilgg luaṫa, in quo Faelan filius Colmain rex Laegen uictor erat. Bellum Doṫ in quo Suibne menn mac Fiaċna uictor erat, 7 Domnall mac Aeḋo fugit. Occisio Suibne menn mic Fiaċna mic Feradaig mic Muireadaig mic Eoġain, ri Erenn, i Taerr brem (.i. la Conġal caeċ mac Scannlain). Pausa

---

[1] *Lethet-Midind.*—The *Four Mast.* (an. 622) say that the battle of Lethet-Midind was fought at a place called Drung. In the *Book of Leinster* the battle is simply called caṫ druing, "battle of Drung," (fol. 41, col. 3). Neither place has been identified.

[2] *Bolg-luatha.*—"Sack of Ashes." A nickname applied to Crundmael, son of Ronan, King of South Leinster (or Ui-Cennselaigh), as appears from a marginal note in the *Book of Leinster*, p. 316. He is called Crunnmael *erbuilg*, C. of the big "sack," or "belly," in the *Ann. Four Mast.*, at 650, and "Crunnmael Builg-luatho" at the year 646 *infra.*

[3] *Ard-Corann.*—This place is also mentioned as battle-ground at the years 464, 506, and 510, *supra.* See note[3] under the year 464. According to the *Four Mast.* (624) and *Chron. Scot.* (627), this battle of Ard-Corrann was gained, and Fiachna slain, by *Conadh Cerr*, king of the Scotch Dalriads (and son of Eochaid Buidhe, son of Aedhan, son of Gabhran). The death of Conad Cerr is entered under the year 628 *infra.*

[4] *Carn-Feradhaigh in Cliu.*—Cliu (or Cliu Mail mic Ugaini, *i.e.*, Cliu of Mal son of Ugaini) was the d Irish name of a territory in the S.E. of the present co. Limerick. Carn-Feradhaigh, "Feradach's Cairn," is

Lethet-Midind,[1] in which fell Fiachna Lurgan. Fiachna son of Deman was victor. The besiegement of Bolg-luatha[2] by the Ui-Neill.

Kal. Jan. (Thurs., m. 9.) A.D. 626. The battle of Ard-Corann.[3] The Dalriata were victors; in which fell Fiachna son of Deman. The battle of Carn-Feradhaigh in Cliu,[4] in which Failbhe Flann of Feimin was victor. Guaire Aidhne fled. Conall, son of Maeldubh, fled; and the King of Ui-Maini was slain. [626.]

There fell[5] of the Connaughtmen,
At Ath-cuma-ind-seisir,[6]
Maelduin, Maelruain, Maelcalcaigh,
Conall, Maeldubh, Maelbresail.

The vision which Fursa,[7] the devout bishop, saw.

Kal. Jan. (Frid., m. 20.) A.D. 627 (alias 28).[8] The battle of Bolg-luatha,[9] in which Faelan,[10] son of Colman, King of Leinster, was victor. The battle of Both,[11] in which Suibne Menn, son of Fiachna, was victor, and Domnall, son of Aedh, fled. The killing of Suibne Menn, son of Fiachna (son[12] of Feradach, son of Muiredach, son [627.] BIS.

---

upposed by O'Donovan to be the ld name of Seefin, a hill in the bar. f Coshlea, in that county. *Four Mast.*, A.M. 3656, note *g*.

[5] *There fell.*—Nı τορċαıρ ("there ll not"), A., which seems a mistake r Nı τορċαıρ. The *Four Mast.* ave το ροċαıρ, which is better.

[6] *Ath-cuma-ind-seisir.*—The "ford the slaughter of the Six." Not entified. The orig. text of these nes (a fragment of some poem) is lded, in orig. hand, in the lower arg. of fol. 23*a*, in A. It is not in . The account of this battle is ore fully given in the *Ann. Four ast.* (622), where the names of the onnaughtmen slain are mentioned the prose entry. The *Chron. Scot.* count (627) is somewhat confused.

[7] *Fursa.*—The death of St. Fursa is entered at the year 660 *infra*.

[8] *Alias* 28°.—Added in very old hand in A. Not in B.

[9] *Bolg-luatha.*—See above under the year 625, and under 646 *infra*.

[10] *Faelan.*—In the list of the Kings of Leinster in the *Bk. of Leinst.* (p. 39, col. 2), Faelan, who is stated to have reigned 30 years, is called ταλτα Cαemgın, or St. Kevin's "foster-son," he having been educated by that Saint.

[11] *Both.*—Pronounced *Boh.* Not identified.

[12] *Son.*—The original of the parenthetic clause, interlined in B., is added in an old hand in the margin in A.

Columbam filii Bairrdaeni, abbatis Clono. Iugulatio Cummeni filii Colmain. Uastatio Lagen la Domnall. Domnall mac Aeḋa mic Ainmireaċ regnare incipit.

Kl. Ianair. (1 f., l. 1.) Anno domini dc.° xx.° iiii.° Bellum Feda euin, in quo Maelcaiċ mac Scannail rex Cruiṫne uictor fuit. Dal Riati ceciderunt. Conid cerr rex Dal Riati cecidit. Bellum Duin ceiṫirnn in quo Congal caeċ fugit 7 Domnall mac Aeḋo uictor erat, in quo cecidit Guaire mac Forindain. Uel bellum Feḋo euin ubi ceciderunt nepotes Aedain, Rigullon Faelbae. Mors Eċdaċ buiḋe regis Pictorum, filii Aedain. Sic in libro Cuanaċ inueni. Uel sic in libro Duiḃdaleṫe narratur: bellum Leṫirbe etir Cenul mic Erca 7 Cenul Feradaig, in quo Maelfiṫriċ cecidit. Ernaine mac Fiaċna uictor erat.

Kl. Ianair. (2 f., l. 12.) Anno domini dc.° xx.° ix.° Bellum Leiṫirḃe inter genus Eugain inuicem, in quo Maelfiṫriċ cecidit, 7 bellum Mitani. Taerr Breni comburitur, 7 iugulatio Branduiḃ mic Maelecoḃo.

Fol. 23ab. Kl. Ianair. (3 f., l. 23.) Anno domini dc.° xxx.° Bellum filii Ailli, 7 mors Cinedon filii Lugṫreni regis Pictorum.

---

[1] *Taerr-Breni.*—A., B., and Clar. 49. O'Conor renders it "in regione Brefniæ!" But *Taerr-Breni* should be "Traig-Breni" ("strand of Bren"), as in the *Four Mast.*, *Chron. Scot.*, *Book of Leinster* (25*a*), and other authorities. O'Donovan identifies Traig-Breni (or Brena) with a strand on the shore of Lough Swilly, in the bar. of Inishowen, co. Donegal. *Four Mast.*, at 623, note *u*. The place is again referred to at the year 629.

[2] *Cluain, i.e.*, Clonmacnoise.—The *Four Masters* (at 623) write the name of Columban *Colman Mac Ui Barddani* ("C. son of the descendant of Bardani"), and add that he was of the Dal-Barrdaine.

[3] *Fidh-eoin.*—"John's Wood," or the "Bird's Wood." Not identified.

[4] *Maelcaich.*—His death is entered at the year 665 *infra*.

[5] *Conad Cerr.*—See note 3, p. 96, *supra*.

[6] *Dun-Ceithirnn.*—Now known as the "Giant's Sconce," a cyclopean stone fort on the summit of a hill in the par. of Dunboe, co. Londonderry

[7] *Rigullon* [*and*] *Failbe.*—Rigullon was the son of Conang, son of Aedan Mac Gabhrain; and Failbe son of Eochaidh Buidhe, Conang's brother.

f Eoghan), King of Ireland, in Taerr-breni,[1] by Congal
'aech, son of Scanlan. The rest of Columban, son of
Barrdaeni, abbot of Cluain.[2] Murder of Cummen, son of
'olman. The wasting of Leinster by Domnall. Domnall,
on of Aedh, son of Ainmire, begins to reign.

Kal. Jan. (Sund., m. 1.) A.D. 628. The battle of [628.]
'idh-eoin,[3] in which Maelcaich,[4] son of Scannal, King
f the Cruithni, was victor. The Dalriata were slain.
'onad Cerr,[5] King of Dalriata, fell. The battle of Dun-
'eithirnn,[6] in which Congal Caech fled, and Domnall,
on of Aedh, was victor; and in which fell Guaire, son
f Forindan. Or, the battle of Fidh-eoin,[3] in which fell
.edan's grandsons, Rigullon [and] Failbe.[7] The death of
ochaidh Buidhe, King of the Picts, the son of Aedan.
o I find in the Book of Cuanu. Or thus[8] it is related
the Book of Dubhdalethe: the battle of Lethirbhe,[9]
etween the Cenel-mic-Erca and the Cenel-Feradaigh, in
hich Maelfithrich fell. Ernaine, son of Fiachna, was victor.

Kal. Jan. (Mond., m. 12.) A.D. 629. The battle of [629.]
ethirbhe, between the Cinel-Eoghain themselves, in
hich Maelfithrich fell; and the battle of Mitan. Taerr-
'eni[10] is burned; and the killing of Brandubh, son of
aelcobha.

Kal. Jan. (Tues., m. 23.) A.D. 630. The battle of [630.]
e son of Alli,[11] and the death of Cined,[12] son of Lugtren,
ing of the Picts.

---

dan's death is entered at the year
; *supra*, and Conang's at 621.
'onor prints the names of Rigullon
l Failbe *re guillon Faelbe*, and trans-
s "a servo Falbi!"

Or thus.—The orig. of this entry,
ich is in the text in B. (at 628), is
ed in the margin in A. Clar. 49
no notice of it.

Lethirbhe.—This place has not
i identified.

[10] *Taerr-breni.*—See this place referred to at 627, and note there.

[11] *Son of Alli.*—Eadwin, son of Ælla, King of Northumbria, who was slain in A.D. 633, according to the *Anglo-Sax. Chron.*

[12] *Cined* (genit. *Cinedon*).—The "Cinioth filius Lutrin" of the Pictish Chronicle. See Skene's *Chron. Picts and Scots*, p. 7, *et passim.*

.b. Kl. Ianair. (4 f., l. 4a.) Anno domini dc.° xxx.° i.° Bellum Caṫloen regis Britonum 7 Anfriṫ. Comburtio Bennċoir moer in Britannia, 7 iugulatio Ronain mic Baetain. Bellum aṫo aublo in quo cecidit Diċuill mac Fergusa tuile la Mumain. Insola Medgoeṫ fundata est. Mor ṁuṁan ingean Aeḋa Beannain mortua est.

Kl. Ianair. (6 f., l. 15.) Anno domini dc.° xxx.° ii.° Bellum Iudris regis Britonum. Bellum Aṫo goan i n-iartar Lifi, in quo cecidit Cremtann mac Aeḋo filii Senaiċ ri Lagenorum.

Kl. Ianair. (7 f., l. 26.) Anno domini dc.° xxx.° iii.° Iugulatio duorum filiorum Aeḋa slane la Conall mac Suibne ecc Loċ Threitni ar Fremuin .i. Congal ri Breg, 7 Ailill cruitire senaṫair sil Dluṫaig.

Kl. Ianair. (1 f., l. 7a.) Anno domini dc.° xxx.° iiii.° Occisio Conaill mic Suiḃne i tiġ mic Nafraiċ la Diarmait mac Aeḋa slane. Bellum Cuile coelaen re n-Diarmait mac Aeḋa slane, in quo cecidit Maelumai mac Oengussa. Aecclesia Reċrann fundata est. Nix magna occidit multos in campo Breġ. Quies Fintain

[1] *Cathloen.*—Cadwalla. Regarding this king, see Reeves' *Adamnan* (notes at pp. 13, 14, 16, 34).

[2] *Anfrith.*—Eanfrith, son of Æthelfrith, King of Bernicia. Slain by Cadwalla, King of the Britons (in the year 634, according to *Flor. of Worcester*).

[3] *Ath-abla.*—"Ford of the Apple-tree." Not identified.

[4] *Fergus Tuile.*—O'Conor, in his ed. of these Annals, separates the epithet *Tuile* (which signifies a "flood") from the proper name Fergus, and prints *Tuile la mumain*, which he translates "Inundationes in Momonia!"

[5] *Inis-Medgoeth.*—Farne, or Lindisfarne (Holy Island), off the coast of Northumberland. For evidence as to which of these islands is meant, see Reeves' *Adamnan*, p. 374, note *r*. The *Four Mast.* have the entry at the year 627; but the correct date is 635.

[6] *Mor-Mumhan.* — Mor ṁugan, A. Morr mugan, B. Mor-Mumhan ("Mor of Munster") was wife to Finghin, King of Munster, ancestor of the O'Sullivans. She is described as the paragon of the Irishwomen of her time, in several old authorities. A very curious account of her life and adventures is contained in the *Book of Leinster*, p. 274, *sq.*

[7] *Ath-goan in Iarthar Lifi.*—Athgoan has not been identified. *Iarthar-Lifi*, or "West of Liffey," was a name for that part of the co. Kildare lying along the river Liffey on the west.

Kal. Jan. (Wed., m. 4.) A.D. 631. The battle of Cathloen,[1] King of the Britons, and of Anfrith.[2] The burning of Great Bangor, in Britain; and the killing of Ronan, son of Baetan. The battle of Ath-abla,[3] in which Dichuill, son of Fergus Tuile,[4] was slain by Munstermen. Inis-Medgoeth[5] was founded. Mor-Mumhan,[6] daughter of Aedh Bennan, died. [631.] BIS

Kal. Jan. (Frid., m. 15.) A.D. 632. The battle of Iudris, King of the Britons. The battle of Ath-goan in Iarthar-Lifi,[7] in which fell Crimthann,[8] son of Aedh, son[9] of Senach, King of the Leinstermen. [632.]

Kal. Jan. (Sat., m. 26.) A.D. 633. The murder of two sons of Aedh Slanè, by Conall son of Suibhne, at Loch-Treithni on Fremhuin,[10] viz.:—Congal, King of the Brega, and Ailill Cruitire,[11] ancestor of Sil-Dluthaigh. [633.]

Kal. Jan. (Sund., m. 7.) A.D. 634. Murder of Conall son of Suibhne, in the house of the son of Nafraech, by Diarmait son of Aedh Slanè. The battle of Cuil-Caelain by Diarmait, son of Aedh Slanè, in which fell Maelumai son of Oengus.[12] The church of Rechra[13] was founded. A great snow killed many in Magh-Bregh. The repose of Fintan[14] [634.]

---

[8] *Crimthann.*—In the list of the Kings of Leinster contained in the *Book of Leinster* (p. 39, col. 2), he is called "Crimthand Cualand" ("C. of Cualand"), and the duration of his reign set down as 28 years. The death of his predecessor, Ronan son of Colman, is given by the *Four Mast.* at 610, and in *Chron. Scot.* under 615.

[9] *Son.*—ꝼ̄ıl̄ꞅ (ꝼılıuꞅ) for ꝼılıı, A., B.

[10] *Loch-Treithni on Fremhuin.*—Loch-Treithni (now called Lough-Drin, a little to the east of the town of Mullingar, co. Westmeath,) is not *on* the hill of Fremhuin (or Frewin), but about a mile and a half to the east of it.

[11] *Ailill Cruitire*, *i.e.*, "Ailill the Harper."

[12] *Oengus.*—This was Aengus (or Oengus), son of Colman Mór, whose "Jugulatio" is entered at the year 620 *supra*.

[13] *Rechra* (gen. Rechrann).—Lambay Island, a few miles to the north of Howth, co. Dublin. See Reeves' *Adamnan*, p. 164, note *b*.

[14] *Fintan son of Telchan.*—Otherwise called Munnu, or Mundu. He was the founder of the monastery of Tech-Munna, now Taghmon, in the county of Wexford. In the *Felire of Aengus*, at his festival (21 October), his father, Tulchan (or Telchan), is stated to have been a Druid.

mic Telċain, 7 Ernaini mic Cresseni. Mors Gartnain mic Foiṫ. Eċuiḋ Liss moir obiit. Bellum Seguisse in quo ceciderunt Loċene mac Nectain cennḟotai, 7 Cumuscaċ mac Aengusso, 7 Gartnaith mac [F]oith.

.b. Kl. Ianair. (2 f., l. 18.) Anno domini dc.° xxx.° u.° Iugulatio Ernani mic Fiaċae qui uicit Maelfiṫriċ filium Aeḋo alddain, alias uairidnaiġ, in bello Leiṫirbe, 7 effugatio Carṫaiġ di Raiṫiun in diebus pasca.

Fol. 23ba. Kl. Ianair. (4 f., l. 29.) Anno domini dc.° xxx.° ui.° Bellum Roṫ 7 bellum Sailtire in una die facta sunt. Conall coel mac Maelecobo, socius Domnaill, uictor erat de genere Euagain in bello Saeltire, 7 mors Faelbe flainn Feimin regis Muman. Much-autu Raṫin pausat.

Kl. Ianair. (5 f., l. 10.) Anno domini dc.° xxx.° uii.° Bellum Glinne Mureson 7 obsesio Etin. Cronan mac U Loeġdae abbas Cluana mic U Nois obiit.

Kl. Ianair. (6 f., l. 21.) Anno domini dc.° xxx.°

---

[1] *Ernaine.*—Otherwise called Mernocc (=Mo-Ernocc). According to the *Felire of Aengus* (18th Aug.), he was the founder of the churches of Rathnew (co. Wicklow), and Kildreenagh) co. Carlow.

[2] *Gartnan son of Foith.*—The "Garnard filius Wid" of the *Chron. Pictorum.* See note [6] *infra.*

[3] *Lis-mor.*—The Lismore in Scotland is here referred to; not Lismore, co. Waterford.

[4] *Seguis.*—See under the year 501 *supra,* note [5].

[5] '*Cennfota.*'—"Long-head."

[6] *Gartnaith son of Foith.*—This is also in B., and in Clar. 49. But it is probably only a repetition of the record of the death of *Gartnan son of Foith,* just given (see note [2]), as it is not found in *Tigernach,* nor in the *Chron. Scot.*

[7] *Vanquished.*—See under the year 629.

[8] *Flight.* — effugatio, A. effugatio, B. Do ionnarbadh ("was banished"), *Four Mast.* (631.)

[9] *Carthach.* — Otherwise called Mochuta. See note [11] *infra.*

[10] *Raithin.*—Rahan, in the bar. of Ballycowan, King's co.

[11] *Battle of Roth.*—Adamnan writes the name *Roth* (*Vit. Columb.* iii., 5). Better known as the "battle of Magh-rath." The place where this famous battle was fought is now known as Moira, a village in a parish of the same name, bar. of Lower Iveagh, co. Down. A romantic, but valuable, account of the battle has been edited

son of Telchan, and of Ernaine[1] son of Cresen. The death of Gartnan son of Foith.[2] Eochaidh of Lis-mor[3] died. The battle of Seguis,[4] in which fell Lochene son of Nechtan 'Cennfota,'[5] and Cumuscach son of Aengus, and Gartnaith son of Foith.[6]

Kal. Jan. (Mond., m. 18.) A.D. 635. The killing of [635.] BIS.
Ernaine son of Fiacha, who vanquished[7] Maelfithrich son of Aedh Aldan (alias Uairidnach), in the battle of Leth-irbhe; and the flight[8] of Carthach[9] from Raithin,[10] at Easter-tide.

Kal. Jan. (Wed., m. 29.) A.D. 636. The battle of [636.]
Roth,[11] and the battle of Saeltirè, were fought on the same day; Conall Cael, son of Maelcoba, colleague[12] of Domnall, of the Cinel-Eogain, was victor in the battle of Saeltirè; and the death of Failbhe Flann of Femhin,[13] King of Munster. Mochuta[14] of Raithin rests.

Kal. Jan. (Thurs., m. 10.) A.D. 637. The battle of [637.]
Glenn-Mureson[15] and the siege of Etin.[15] Cronan Mac U Loeghde, abbot of Clonmacnoise, died.

Kal. Jan. (Frid., m. 21.) A.D. 638. The killing of [638.]

---

by O'Donovan, from the *Yellow Book of Lecan*, for the Irish Archæol. Soc. (Dublin, 1842.) See Reeves' *Adamnan*, p. 200, note *n*.

[12] *Colleague.*—focius. Conall Cael ("Conall the Slender") was not the colleague of King Domhnall son of Aedh in the sovereignty, but of his own brother Cellach. See under the year 642 *infra*.

[13] *Failbhe Flann of Femhin.*—For the situation of Femhin, see p. 64, note [1]. Failbhe Flann was the ancestor of the powerful Munster sept of the MacCarthys.

[14] *Mochuta.*—Muchautu, A. Corrected to Moċuta in the margin. After his "effugatio" from Rahan (see notes [9], [10]), St. Mochuta, or Carthach, founded a religious establishment at Lismore, co. Waterford, which subsequently became a bishop's see, and was united to that of Waterford, A.D. 1363. Lanigan gives a very interesting account of St. Mochuta. *Eccl. Hist. of Ireland*, vol. 2, pp. 350–6.

[15] *Glenn-Mureson — Etin.* — Dean Reeves thinks Glenn-Mureson was the name of "a tract in the debateable ground of West Lothian," and that by Etin was not meant Edinburgh, as some suppose, but "*Cair-Eden* . . . . now Carriden, a parish on the Forth, in Linlithgowshire." *Adamnan*, p. 202, note.

iiii.° Iugulatio Congaile mic Dunchada. Obitus Duinsicae uxoris Domnaill. Bellum Osubaldi regis Saxonum. Quies Cridaen i Noendruim 7 Aeda duiḃ abbaid Cille daro, episcoporum. Dolaissi mac Cuimde abbas Leiṫglinne pausauit. Mors Ailella mic Aeḋo róen. Eraclas cum matre sua Martina annis .ii. regnauit.

.b. Kl. Ianair. (7 f., l. 2.) Anno domini dc.° xxx.° ix.° Bellum Caṫraċ cinnċon. Oengus liaṫdana uictor erat. Maelduin mac Aeḋa bennain fugit.

Kl. Ianair. (2 f., l. 13.) Anno domini dc.° xl.° Mors Maeluiḋir caiċ regis Orientalium. Mors Bruidi filii Foiṫ. Domnall mac Aeda castrametatus est i n-Druimm náo. Naufragium scaphae familiae Iae. Obsesio Rithae. Combustio Maeleduin in insola Caini. Iugulatio Maeleduin mic Fergusa 7 Maeleduin mic Colmain.

Kl. Ianair. (3 f., l. 24.) Anno domini dc.° xl.° i.° Mors Domnaill mic Aeḋo regis Hibernie in fine Ianuarii. Postea Domnall brecc in bello sraiṫ Cairuin in fine anni in Decembri interfectus est ab Hoan rege Britonum; annis .xu. regnauit. Iugu-

---

[1] *Domnall.*—Domnall son of Aedh, King of Ireland.

[2] *Saxons.*—Oswald was King of the Northumbrians. He was slain by Penda, King of the 'Southumbrians,' in the year 642, according to the Anglo-Saxon Chronicle.

[3] *Nendruim.* — Otherwise "Naendruim." Nendrum, or Mahee Island, in Strangford Lough.

[4] *Aedh Dubh.*—"Black Aedh." Originally King of Leinster, which position he is stated to have resigned in the year 591, afterwards becoming abbot of Kildare. His name occurs under the form "Aed Cerr" in the List of Kings of Leinster contained in the *Book of Leinster*, p. 39, col. 2.

[5] *Dolaissi, son of Cuinid.*—Mac Cuimdae, A. Dolaissi is a variation of Molaissi, and Laisren, by either of which names the Saint is better known. His festival in the Calendar is 18 April. In the *Book of Leinster*, (p. 349, col. 4), and in other old authorities, the father of St. Molaissi is called Cairill.

[6] *Heraclas.* — Eraclas, A., B. Apparently Heracleonas, son of the Emperor Heraclius. (See under 616)

[7] *Cathair-Cinncon.* — O'Donovan says that this was the name of a stone

Congal, son of Dunchad. The death of Duinsech, wife of Domnall.[1] The battle of Oswald, King of the Saxons.[2] The repose of Cridan in Nendruim,[3] and of Aedh Dubh,[4] abbot of Cill-dara, bishops. Dolaissi, son of Cuinid,[5] abbot of Leithglinn, rested. Death of Ailill, son of Aedh Róen. Heraclas,[6] with his mother Martina, reigned two years.

Kal. Jan. (Sat., m. 2.) A.D. 639. The battle of Cathair-Cinncon.[7] Aengus Liathdana was victor. Maelduin, son of Aedh Bennan, fled. [639.] BIS.

Kal. Jan. (Mond., m. 13.) A.D. 640. Death of Maelodhar Caech, King of the Airthera. Death of Bruide son of Foith.[8] Domnall, son of Aedh, pitched his camp in Druim-Náo. Wreck of a boat of the family of Ia. Siege of Ritha.[9] Burning of Maelduin in Inis-Cain.[10] Murder of Maelduin son of Fergus, and of Maelduin son of Colman. [640.]

Kal. Jan. (Tues., m. 24.) A.D. 641. The death of Domnall, son of Aedh, King of Ireland, in the end of January. Domnall Brecc[11] was slain afterwards, at the end of the year, in December, in the battle of Srath-Caruin[12] (by Hoan,[13] King of the Britons). He reigned 15 years. The killing of Ailill, son of Colman, King of [641.]

---

fort near Rockbarton, bar. of Small County, co. Limerick. (*Four Mast.*, A.D. 636, note *t.*) See under the year 642 *infra*.

[8] *Bruide son of Foith.*—The "Breidei filius Wid" of the *Chron. Pictorum*.

[9] *Ritha.*—Not identified.

[10] *Inis Cain.*—Inishkeen, co. Louth, according to O'Donovan (*Four Mast.*, A.D. 636, note *x*).

[11] *Domnall Brecc.*—The 11th King of the Scotch Dalriada, and son of Eochaidh Buidhe (8th King), whose obit is given above at the year 628. See under 685 *infra*, where the death of Domnall Brecc is again entered.

[12] *Srath-Caruin.* — The "*Srath*" (=stratum), or holm, of "Carun." Dean Reeves thinks that this battle was fought in the valley of the Carron in Stirlingshire. *Adamnan*, p. 203, note.

[13] *Hoan.*—Probably the *Auin*, the obit of whose son Domnall, "King of Ailcluaite," is recorded under 693 *infra*. The orig. of this clause, added in the margin in A., is in the text in B.

latio Ailello mic Colmain, regis generis Loiġaire. Fol. 23bb. Constantinus filius Eracli mensibus .ui. regnauit. Bellum Ossu contra Britones.

Kl. Ianair. (4 f., l. 5.) Anno domini dc.° xl.° ii.° Mors hUaisle filiae Suibni. Quies Cronain epscoip Noindromma. Bellum Cinnċon. Loscoṫ Iarnnboidḃ mic Gartnaiṫ. Cellaċ 7 Conall c[a]el, da mac Mael-ċoba mic Aeda mic Ainmireċ, regnare incipiunt ut alii dicunt. Constantinus filius Constantini annis .xx. uiii. regnauit. Hic dubitatur quis regnauit post Domnall. Dicunt alii historiagraphi regnasse iiii. reges .i. Cellaċ 7 Conall c[a]el, 7 duo filii Aeḋo Slane (mic Diarmada mic Fergusa cerrḃeoil mic Conaill Cremṫainde mic Neill .ix. ġiallaiġ) .i. Diarmait 7 Blaṫmac, per commixta regna.

Kl. Ianair. (5 f., l. 16.) Anno domini dc.° xl.° iii.° Iugulatio duorum nepotum Bogaine .i. Maelbresail 7 Maelanfaiṫ. Guin Flainn' aenaiġ. Mors Bresail mic Seċnasaiċ.

Kl. Ianair. (7 f., l. 27.) Anno domini dc.° xl.° iiii.° Mors Furudrain mic Becce mic Cuanaċ ri ua micc Uais. Loċeni mac Fingin ri Cruiṫne obiit.

Kl. Ianair. (1 f., l. 8, alias 9.) Anno domini dc.° xl.° u.° Guin Scannail mic Becce mic Fiacraċ regis Cruitne. Mac Lasre abb Bennċair quieuit.

---

1 *Constantine.*—The word imperator is added in the margin in A.

2 *Against.*—MS. A. has the abbreviation for "contra," MS. B. that for "inter."

3 *Britons.*—Probably the Britons of Strathclyde. This battle is not noticed in the Anglo-Sax. Chron.

4 *Uaisle, daughter of Suibhne.*—The *Four Mast.* (642), and the *Chron. Scot.* (641), state that she was queen of Faelan, King of Leinster, whose obit is given by the F. M. at the year 665.

5 *Battle of Cenn-con.*—Apparently an inaccurate repetition of the entry under the year 639, where the name is more correctly written "Cathair-Cinncon."

6 *Gartnat.* — Evidently the "Gartnan son of Foith," referred to under the year 634 *supra.* O'Conor has strangely misunderstood this entry, which he prints wrongly, and renders

Cinel-Loeghaire. Constantine,[1] son of Heraclius, reigned six months. The battle of Ossa [Oswy] against[2] the Britons.[3]

Kal. Jan. (Wed., m. 5.) A.D. 642. Death of Uaisle, daughter of Suibhne.[4] The repose of Cronan, bishop of Nendruim. The battle of Cenn-con.[5] The burning of Iarnbodb, son of Gartnat.[6] Cellach and Conall Cael (*i.e.*, two sons[7] of Maelcoba, son of Aedh, son of Ainmire), begin to reign, as others say. Constantine, son of Constantine, reigned twenty-eight years. Here it is doubted who reigned after Domhnall. Other historiographers say that four kings reigned, viz., Cellach and Conall Cael, and the two sons of Aedh Slane (son of Diarmait,[8] son of Fergus Cerrbheoil, son of Conall Cremthainn, son of Niall Nine-hostager), viz.:—Diarmait and Blathmac, in joint sovereignty. [642.]

Kal. Jan. (Thurs., m. 16.) A.D. 643. Murder of two grandsons of Boghaine, viz.:—Maelbresail and Maelanfaith. The killing of Flann Aenaigh. The death of Bresal, son of Sechnasach. [643.]

Kal. Jan. (Sat., m. 27.) A.D. 644. Death of Furudran, son of Becc,[9] son of Cuanu, King of Ui-Mic-Uais. Locheni, son of Fingin, King of the Cruithni,[10] died. [644.]

Kal. Jan. (Sund., m. 8, alias 9.) A.D. 645. The wounding of Scannal, son of Becc, son of Fiachra, King of the Cruithni.[10] Mac Lasre, abbot of Bangor, rested. [645.]

---

by "Comburitur postea propter boves filii Garthnat!"

[7] *Sons.*—The orig. of this clause, added in *al. man.* in the margin in A., is not in B., nor in Clar. 49.

[8] *Son of Diarmait.*—The orig. of this clause, which also is neither in B. nor in Clar. 49, is interlined in A.

[9] *Becc.*—This person was slain in the battle of Dun-bolg, along with King Aedh, son of Ainmire. See above, at the year 597.

[10] *Cruithni.* — These were the Cruithni (or Picts) of Ireland. Skene thought the Picts of Scotland were meant, as he has included these two entries in the extracts regarding Scotch events, taken by him from these Annals. *Chron. Picts and Scots*, (p. 348). See Reeves *Adamnan*, p. 94, note *h*, and Todd's *Irish Nennius*, Add. Notes, p. xlvii.

Kl. Ianair. (2 f., l. 19, alias 20.) Anno domini dc.° xl.° ui.° Maelcoḃo mac Fiaċna iugulatus est, rex Uloṫ. Dunchaṫ aue Ronain iugulatur. Bellum Colgan mic Crunnmael Builgg luaṫo riġ huae Ceinnselaiġ.

.b. Kl. Ianair. (3 f., l. 30, alias 1.) Anno domini dc.° xl.° uii.° Fursu craiḃdeċ obiit.

Kl. Ianair. (5 f., l. 11, alias 12.) Anno domini dc.° xl.° uiii.° Guin Raġallaig mic hUataċ riġ Con-
Fol. 24aa. nacht. Bellum Cairnn Conaill ubi Guaire fugit, 7 Diarmait uictor erat, mac Aeḋo slaine. Mors Oengusa bronbaċlae regis Ceniuil Coirpri. Cocaṫ huae n-Aeḋain 7 Gartnaiṫ mic Accidain. Quies Fursi in Barruna.

Kl. Ianair. (6 f., l. 22, alias 23.) Anno domini dc.° xl.° ix.° Bellum Ossu fri Pante. Bellum duin Craumtain in quo cecidit Oengus mac Domnaill. Filii Maelcoḃa uictores erant .i. Ceallaċ 7 Conall c[a]el. Mors Caṫusaiġ mic Domnaill bricc. Mors Cronain maiġi bile. Hoc anno Beda natus est.

Kl. Ianair. (7 f., l. 3, alias 4.) Anno domini dc.° l.° Quies Aedain episcopi Saxonum 7 iugulatio duorum filiorum Blaimicc mic Aedo slane .i. Dunchad 7 Conall.

---

[1] *Crunnmael Bolg-luatha.*—Mentioned by his epithet "*Bolg-luatha*" under 625 and 627 *supra*, where see notes. The death of a "Crunnmael *Erbuilg*," King of the Leinstermen, is entered *infra*, at the year 655, who seems to be the same person, *Erbuilg* (of the "big sack" or "belly") being probably a variation of the epithet *Bolg-luatha*.

[2] *Fursa.*—Repeated under the next year.

[3] *Guaire.*—Guaire Aidhne, King of Connaught, whose obit is given by the *Four Mast.*, and also *infra*, at A.D. 662. On the lower margin of MS. A., fol. 23*b*, four stanzas in Irish are written (which are not in B.), without any sign to indicate where they should be introduced into the text, if they were intended to be so introduced. The three first are ascribed to Cumeni, and the fourth to Guaire. But as they are somewhat corrupt, and contain no historical fact, it has not been considered necessary to reproduce them here.

Kal. Jan. (Mond., m. 19, alias 20.) A.D. 646. Maelcobha, son of Fiachna, King of Ulad, was slain. Duncath, descendant of Ronan, slain. The battle of Colgu, son of Crunnmael Bolg-luatha,[1] King of the Ui-Ceinnselaigh. [646.]

Kal. Jan. (Tuesd., m. 30, alias 1.) A.D. 647. Fursa[2] the Pious died. [647.] BIS.

Kal. Jan. (Thurs., m. 11, alias 12.) A.D. 648. The killing of Raghallach, son of Uada, King of Connaught. The battle of Carn-Conaill, where Guaire[3] fled, and Diarmait, son of Aedh Slanè, was victor. The death of Oengus Bron-bachal,[4] King of Cinel-Coirpri. The war of the descendants of Aedan,[5] and of Gartnat son of Accidan. The repose of Fursa[6] in Peronne. [648.]

Kal. Jan. (Frid., m. 22, alias 23.) A.D. 649. The battle of Ossu [Oswiu] against Pante [Penda]. The battle of Dun-Cremtain, in which fell Oengus son of Domnall. The sons of Maelcobha were victors, viz.:— Cellach and Conall Cael. The death of Cathasach, son of Domnall Brecc.[7] Death of Cronan of Magh-bilè. In this year Bede was born[8]. [649.]

Kal. Jan. (Saturd., m. 3, alias 4.) A.D. 650. The repose of Aedan, bishop of the Saxons; and the killing of two sons of Bla[th]macc, son of Aedh Slanè, viz.:— Dunchad and Conall. [650.]

---

[4] *Oengus Bron-bachal.*—The "Oingusius cujus cognomentum Bronbachal" of *Adamnan* (i., 13). See Reeves' ed., p. 41, note *a*.

[5] *Aedan.*—Aedan son of Gabran, King of the Scotch Dalriads, whose death is recorded at the year 605 *supra*.

[6] *Fursa.*—His death is entered under the previous year, and also at 660 *infra*. The 'Vision' of St. Fursa is entered above under the year 626.

[7] *Domnall Brecc.*—"Domnall the speckled," King of Dalriada in Scotland, whose death is recorded above at the year 641, and again, by a great mistake, under 685.

[8] *Born.*—This entry is added in *al. man.* in A. B. has merely natiuitas bede. See under the year 653 *infra*.

Blaṫmac mac Aeḋa, in ri,
Ruc a mac ar digu;
Beraiḋ hiru a da mac
Ina ḋiġail ar Blaṫmac.

Maelodran cecinit.

A muilinn,
Ce ro milt mor di ṫuirinn,
Ni bo ċomailt far serbainn
[A] ro milt for uib Cerḃaill.

An men meiles in muilind,
Ni corca acht dergṫuirind;
Is di ḟoglu in cruinn mair
Foṫa muilind Maelodrain.

Iugulatio Oisseni mic Oirirgg.

.b. Kl. Ianair. (1. f., l. 14, alias 15.) Anno domini dc.° l.° i.° Obitus Segeni abatis Iae .i. filii Fiacnae, 7 quies Aidlogo mic Camain abatis Cluana mic Nois, 7 dormitatio Mancheni abbatis Menodroċit. Imairicc Cule corre in quo cecidit Culene mac Forindain. Maeldeich 7 Oncu uictores erant.

Kl. Ianair. (3 f., l. 25, alias 26.) Anno domini dc.° l.° ii.° (alias 3°). Mors Feriṫ mic Toṫolain, 7 Tolairg mic Fooiṫ regis Pictorum. Iugulatio Conaill

---

[1] *Blathmac.*—The original of this stanza is written on the lower margin of fol. 22*b* in A.; but it seems to belong to this place. It is not in B.

[2] *O, mill.*—A muilinn. These words should be repeated, to complete the line, according to a practice frequently followed by Irish Poets. In the *Ann. Four Mast.* (647), the authorship of these verses is ascribed to Maelodran. But in a curious account of the catastrophe, and the cause thereof, contained in the MS. Rawlinson, B. 502, Bodleian Lib. (fol. 73, *b* 2), the composition is attributed to Ultan (*i.e.*, St. Ultan of Ardbrackan). In this account, three persons are stated to have been killed, viz.:—Dunchad, Conall, and Maelodhar, who are represented as the sons of Diarmait MacCerbhaill (sl. 564 *supra*). But this last statement must be an error. The event is thus referred to in Mageoghegan's Transl. of the Annals of Clonmacnoise, at the year 648. "The two sons of Hugh Slane, Donogh and Conell, were killed by the Lynstermen, near Mollingar,

Blathmac,[1] son of Aedh, the King,
Gave his sons for . . . .
Jesus shall take his two sons
From Blathmac, in revenge therefor.

Maelodran sang :—

O, mill,[2]
Though much of wheat thou didst grind,
It was not the grinding of oats
Thou didst grind on Cerbhall's descendants.

The stuff which the mill grinds
Is not oats but red wheat.
Of the saplings of the great tree
Is the 'feed' of Maelodrain's mill.

he killing of Oissen son of Osirg.[3]

Kal. Jan. (Sund., m. 14, alias 15.) A.D. 651. Death [651.] BIS.
Segene, abbot of Ia, *i.e.*, son of Fiachna ; and the repose
Aedlug, son of Caman, abbot of Cluain-mic-Nois ; and
e falling asleep of Manchen, abbot of Menadrochit.[4] The
nflict of Cul-corra,[5] in which Culene,[6] son of Forindan,
as slain. Maeldeich and Onchu were victors.

Kal. Jan. (Tues., m. 25, alias 26.) A.D. 652 (alias 653). [652.]
e death of Ferith son of Totholan, and of Tolarg son
Foith,[7] King of the Picts. The murder of Conall

the mill of Oran, called Mollen-
an." See O'Donov. *Four Mast.*,
. 647, note *d*.

[3] *Oissen son of Oisirg.*—Oswine,
of Osric, King of Deira from 647
651, when he was slain. See
glo-Sax. Chron., and Bede's *Eccl.*
st, III., 14.

[4] *Menadrochit.*—Now Mondrehid,
ish of Offerlane, in the Queen's co.

[5] *Cul-corra.*—The "recess of the
ir." O'Donovan states that this
ce is now known as Coolarn, near
ltrim, co. Meath.

[6] *Culene.*—It is stated in the *Ann. Four Mast.* (648), and *Chron. Scot.* (649), that Culene was King of Ui-Failghe, or Offaly.

[7] *Tolarg son of Foith.*—Foith is the form in which the Irish writers generally represent the "Wid" of the Pictish Chronicle, in which the name of Talorc (for Tolarg) appears after the names of "Garnard filius Wid," and "Breidei filius Wid," with the addition "frater eorum." See Skene's *Chron. Picts and Scots*, p. 7.

cail. Bellum Connacht in quo cecidit Marcan filius Tomaini.

Kl. Ianair. (4 f., l. 6, alias 7.) Anno domini dc.° l.° iii.° Iugulatio Conaill mic Moelcoḃa .i. la Diarmuid mac Aeḋa slane. Colman epscop macc U Telduiḃ, 7 Ossene fota, duo abbates Cluano iraird, obierunt. Duchuae Loċrae abb Fernann quieuit. Iugulatio Fergusso mic Domnaill, 7 Fergusso mic Rogaillniġ, 7 Aedo bedri, 7 Cummeni. Bellum Sraṫo eṫairt ubi Duncaṫ mac Conaing cecidit. [Mors] Aeḋo roin mic Maelcoḃo. Beda hoc anno natus est.

Fol. 24ab. Kl. Ianair. Anno domini dc.° l.° iiii.° Nem mac hui Birn pausat.

Kl. Ianair. Anno domini dc.° l.° u.° Bellum Cumascaiġ mic Ailello in quo cecidit. Crunnmael Mac Suibne uictor erat. Bellum Pante regis Saxonum. Ossu uictor erat. Bellum Annae. Mors

---

[1] *Conall Cael.*—Joint-King of Ireland. See under the next year.

[2] *Marcan.*—It is stated by the *Four Mast.* (649), and the *Chron. Scot.* (650), that Marcan was chief of Ui-Maine (Hy-Many).

[3] *Conall.*—The Conall Cael who shared the sovereignty of Ireland with his brother Cellach. Their accession is entered at the year 642 *supra.* The *Four Masters* give Conall's death under the year 656, the same year in which they have his brother Cellach's obit. See *Chron. Scot.*, p. 92, note 6, and *infra*, under the year 657.

[4] *By*—The original of this clause is added by way of gloss in A. and B. It is not in Clar. 49.

[5] *Mac-Ui-Telduibh.*—Son of "Ua Telduibh" ("descendant of Teldubh,") Telduiḃ in orig. texts.

[6] *Duchua Lochra.*—Duchua (or Dachua) of "Luachair." Also called Mochua and Cronan. His festival is given as 22nd June in the Calendar, at which date the *Martyr. Donegal* has "Cronan, that is Mochua of Luachair, Abbot of Fearna (Ferns, co. Wexford ").

[7] *Aedh Bedri — Cummen.* — The *Four Masters* (649), and the *Chron. Scot.* (651), state that Aedh *Bedri* (or *Beathra*) was the son of Cummen.

[8] *Srath-Ethairt.* — The *Srath* (or *Strath*=stratum), or "holm," of Ethart. Not identified. Dean Reeves thinks it was the name of a place in Perthshire. *Adamnan*, p. 375, note *u.* The record of this battle is more fully given in the *Chron. Scot.*, at the year 651.

[9] *Conang.*—The Conang, son of

el.[1] The battle of Connaught, in which fell Marcan,[2] the
ı of Tomain.

Kal. Jan. (Wedn., m. 6, alias 7.) A.D. 653. The [653.]
lling of Conall,[3] son of Maelcobha, *i.e.*, by[4] Diarmait,
ı of Aedh Slane. Bishop Colman Mac-Ui-Telduibh,[5] and
sene Fota, two abbots of Cluain-Iraird, died. Duchua
chra,[6] abbot of Ferns, rested. The killing of Fergus,
ı of Domnall, and of Fergus, son of Rogaillnech, and of
dh Bedri,[7] and of Cummen.[7] The battle of Srath-
hairt,[8] in which Duncath, son of Conang,[9] was slain.
he death] of Aedh Roin, son of Maelcobha. Beda[10] was
rn in this year.

Kal. Jan. A.D. 654. Nem Mac-Ui-Birn[11] rests.

Kal. Jan. A.D. 655. The battle of Cumascach[12] son of [654.]
lill, in which he fell. Crunnmael son of Suibhne was [655.]
ctor. Battle of Pante,[13] King of the Saxons. Ossu[14]
ıs victor. Battle of Anna.[15] The death of Crunnmael
buile,[16] son of Ronan, King of the Leinstermen. The

---

lhan, whose death by drowning is
ered under the year 621 *supra*.

[10] *Beda.*—This entry is added in *al.*
m. in A. B. has Uel hic natiui-
r Bede. The birth of Bede is
recorded at the year 649 *supra*.

[1] *Nem Mac-Ui-Birn.*—"Nem, son
the descendant of Birn." O'Conor
y inaccurately prints the name
ıı mc hui Ibirubir! The *Four*
sters state (654) that Nem was a
cessor of Enne of Ara. (St. Enna,
Enda, of Aranmore Island, in Gal-
y Bay). Nem's day in the Calen-
is June 14.

[2] *Battle of Cumascach.*—The *Four*
st. (650) call this the battle of
scach, and add that Cumascach,
of Ailill, was Chief of Ui Cremh-
ion. The site (Flescach) has not
n identified. By "battle of Cumascach," the Annalist meant that it was
a battle in which Cumascach was
slain. There are numerous examples of
this practice throughout these Annals.

[13] *Battle of Pante* (*i.e.*, Penda).—
This is one of the examples referred to
in the last note. Penda was slain in
the battle of Widwinfield (Wingfield),
in the year 655, according to the
Anglo-Sax. Chron.

[14] *Ossu.*—Oswiu, King of the Northumbrians, whose death is entered in
the *Anglo-Sax. Chron.* at the year
670.

[15] *Battle of Anna.*—By this is meant
that Anna (King of the East Angles)
was slain in a battle. The *Anglo-*
Sax. Chron. has Anna's death under
the year 654. See note [13].

[16] *Crunnmael Erbuilc.*—See at the
year 646 *supra*.

Crunnmael erbuilc mic Ronain regis Lagenensium. Mors Maelaiċtein Tire da glas. Guin Raġallaich mic Uadaċ riġ Connacht. Uel hic Fursa secundum alios. Moċoeṁog Leith mois quieuit.

Kl. Ianair. (1 f., l. x.) Anno domini dc.° l.° ii.° Obitus Subni mic Cuirṫri abbatis Iae, 7 Ultain mic U Chonċobair. Bellum Delend in quo interfectus est Maeldeiṫ mac Conaill. Mors Tolargain mic Anfriṫ regis Pictorum. Mors Cellceni Loṫri. Orta est uacca illaṫruiġ Briuin que .iiii. uitulos peperit.

Kl. Ianair. (2 f., l. 21.) Anno domini dc.° l.° iii.° Mors Ceallaig mic Maelecoḃo, 7 Cellaig mic Sarain (no Ronain), 7 Fiaċraċ telnain, 7 Blaiṫmicc mic Ronain mic Coluimb. Mors Guret regis Alocluaṫe, Fergaile que filii Domnaill. Uentus maġnus. Tomain mac Taiṫein moritur.

Kl. Ianair. (3 f., l. 2.) Anno domini dc.° l.° iiii.° Dimma niger epscop Condire, 7 Cummeni epscop Náendroma, 7 Duncaḋ mac Aeḋo slane, mortui sunt, 7 iugulatio Orcdoiṫ mic Seċnusaiġ 7 Concenn mic Laiḋgnein 7 Flodubuir rex Francorum.

---

[1] *Raghallach.*—The killing of Raghallach is entered also above at the year 648. This and the two following entries, added in *al. man.* in A., are in the text in B.

[2] *Fursa.*—The death of St. Fursa is entered above, under the years 646 and 647. O'Conor prints *frosa* for Fursa, and translates "Pluvia mirabilis"! But his own blunder is more wonderful. This entry is not in Clar. 49.

[3] *Mac-Ui-Conchobair.* — "Son of the descendant of Conchobar." See O'Donovan's *F. Mast.*, at 656, note *d*, *Martyrology of Donegal*, at September 4th, and under 662 *infra*.

[4] *Delend.* — This is in the genit. form. The nomin. form should probably be *Deliu*. O'Donovan thinks that Delenn may be *Telenn*, in the west of the co. Donegal. *Four Mast.*, A.D. 654, note *a*.

[5] *Maeldeith son of Conall.* — The *Four Masters* (654) and the *Chron. Scot.* (653) have "Maeldoid son of Conaing"; to which the latter authority adds "or of Conall."

[6] *Tolargan son of Anfrith.*—The "Talorcen filius Enfret" of the *Pictish Chron.*

[7] *Lothra.*—Lorrha, in the bar. of Lower Ormond, co. Tipperary.

[8] *Lathrach-Briuin.*—Now Laraghbryan, bar. of North Salt, co. Kildare. This prodigy is noticed in the *Book of Leinster* (p. 25, col. 1), thus:—"Vacca quatuor vitulos in una die peperit."

ath of Maelaichthen of Tir-da-glas. The killing of
ighallach[1] son of Uada, King of Connaught. Or, in
is year [the death of] Fursa,[2] according to others.
ɔchaemhog of Liath-mor rested.

Kal. Jan. (Sund., m. 10.) A.D. 656. The death of [656.]
ıibne, son of Curthri, abbot of Ia, and of Ultan Mac-Ui-
ınchobair.[3] The battle of Delend,[4] in which Maeldeith
n of Conall[5] was slain. Death of Tolargan, son of
ıfrith,[6] King of the Picts. Death of Cellcen of Lothra.[7]
ıere appeared a cow at Lathrach-Briuin,[8] which calved
ır calves.

Kal. Jan. (Mond., m. 21.) A.D. 657. Death of Cel- [657.]
ːh[9] son of Maelcobha, and of Cellach, son of Saran (or
ınan),[10] and of Fiachra Telnan, and of Blathmac, son of
ıman, son of Columb.[11] Death of Guret, King of Al-
uathe,[12] and of Fergal[13] son of Domnall. A great storm.
ımain, son of Taithen, dies.

Kal. Jan. (Tues., m. 2.) A.D. 658. Dimma Dubh,[14] [658.]
ıhop of Connor, and Cummeni, bishop of Naendruim,
d Dunchadh son of Aedh Slanè, died; and the slaying
Orcdoith son of Sechnasach, and of Concenn son of
ıdgnen, and of Flodubur[15] King of the Franks.

Cellach.—King of Ireland con-
ıtly with his brother Conall, whose
th is entered above at the year
(where see note), and again at 663.

[10] *Or Ronan.*—This is the name in
But the *Four Mast.* say that
llach was son of Saran, and abbot
Othan-mór, now Fahan, bar. of
ıhowen, co. Donegal.

[11] *Columb.*—"Colman," Clar. 49.

[12] *Al-Cluathe*, genit. form *Alo-
athe.* — The *Petra Cloithe* of
ımnan (ii., 15). Now Dumbarton
Scotland. See Reeves' *Adamnan*,
43, 44, and at the years 693, 721,
and 869, *infra.*

[13] *And of Fergal.*—Fergaile que,
a curious combination of *Fergaile*, the
genit. case of the name *Fergal*, and
the Lat. conjunction *que.*

[14] *Dubh.*—The "black." Latinized
niger in the origl. texts. But Dimma
is better known to the student of
Eccl. History as Dimma *Dubh.*

[15] *Flodubur.* —Flodubuir, in the
genit. case, in A. and B. (although
O'Conor prints "*Clodubuir* [Clodo-
væi.]" The date of the entry might
probably indicate that Clovis II. (ob.
655) was meant, rather than his son,
Clothair III. (ob. 670.) But an
Irish writer would be more likely to
represent *Clothair* than *Clovis* by the
form in the text.

b. Kl. Ianair. (4 f., l. 13.) Anno domini dc.° l.° ix.° Obitus Finnani episcopi filii Rimedo, 7 Colman Glinne da Locho quieuit, 7 Daniel episcopus Cinngaradh. Mors Echdach mic Blaithmicc. Conall Crannamna moritur. Eughanan mac Tothalain defunctus est.

Fol. 24*ba* Kl. Ianair. Anno domini dc.° lx.° Tommene (.i. mac Ronain) epscop Ard machae, 7 Conainn nepos Daint abb Imlecho Ibair, 7 Laidhggen sapiens mac Baithbannaigh, defuncti sunt. Fursu in Perruna pausauit.

Kl. Ianair. Anno domini dc.° lx.° i.° Cummeni longus (lxxii.° anno etatis sue quieuit) 7 Saran nepos Critain, sapientes, dormierunt. Bellum Ogomain ubi ceciderunt Conaing mac Congaile, 7 Ultan mac Ernaine rex Cianachte, 7 Cennfaeladh mac Gerthide. Blamac mac Aedho uictus est, socius Diarmada. Maelduin mac Furudrain mic Becce mortuus est. Maenach mac Fingin (mic Aedha duib mic Crimthainn

---

[1] *Finnan.*—The Finan who succeeded St. Aedan (ob. 650, *supra*), in Lindisfarne, and who was himself succeeded by Colman. See Bede's *Eccl. Hist.*, Book III., chap. 25. His day in the Calendar is variously given as Jan. 8th and Jan. 9th. Neither O'Donovan at *Four Mast.*, A.D. 659), nor Ussher (*Index Chron.*, at the years 651, 661), seems to have perceived the identity of this Finan with the successor of St. Aedan.

[2] *Colman.*—His obit is recorded in *Ann Four Mast.*, under 659, where it is stated that he died on December 2. But his festival is given in the *Martyr. of Donegal*, as Dec. 13.

[3] *Cenngaradh.*—Kingarth, in Bute. The *Martyr. of Donegal* gives his festival as Feb. 18.

[4] *Conall Crannamna.*—Son of Eochaidh Buidhe, son of Aedan, and 12th King of the Scotch Dalriads.

[5] *Tothalan.*—The name is otherwise written Tuathalan, and is a diminutive of the name Tuathal. This is the last entry on fol. 24*a* of MS. A., on the upper margin of which a stanza in Irish is written, and two on the lower margin, without any marks to indicate the place in the text where they should be introduced. It is doubtful if they have any particular connection with the text at all, as they do not occur in MS. B., nor in Clar. 49. They do not seem worth printing.

[6] *Ronan.*—This clause, added by way of gloss in *al. man.* in A., is not in B. or Clar. 49.

[7] *Conainn Ua Daint.* — "Conainn descendant of Dant." The Latin equivalent for *Ua* (*nepos*) is written

Kal. Jan. (Wedn., m. 13.) A.D. 659. The death of [659.] BIS.
Bishop Finnan,[1] son of Rimid; and Colman[2] of Glenn-da-locha rested, and Daniel, bishop of Cenngaradh.[3] Death of Eochaidh, son of Blathmac. Conall Crannamna[4] dies. Cuganan, son of Tothalan,[5] died.

Kal. Jan. A.D. 660. Tommene (*i.e.*, son of Ronan[6]), [660.]
bishop of Armagh, and Conainn Ua Daint,[7] abbot of Imlech-Ibair, and Laidhggen the Wise, son of Baeth-bannach, died. Fursa rested in Peronne.[8]

Kal. Jan. A.D. 661. Cummeni the Tall[9] (in the 72nd [661.]
year[10] of his age he rested) and Saran Ua Critain,[11] sages, fell asleep. The battle of Ogoman,[12] in which fell Conaing son of Congal, and Ultan, son of Ernaine, King of Cianachta, and Cennfaeladh son of Gerthide.[13] Bla[th]mac son of Aedh, Diarmaid's colleague,[14] was vanquished. Maelduin, son of Furudran, son of Becc, died. Maenach, son of Finghin (son[15] of Aedh Dubh, son of Crimthann, son

---

nepotis in A. and B., but *nepos* in Clar. 49. For the name "Conainn," the *Four Mast.* and *Chron. Scot.* (657) have "Conaing."

[8] *In Peronne.*—In perruna, A. In prsuna, B. Clar. 49 has "in prisona," although O'Conor states (note 2, ad. an.) that this MS. reads "in propria persona!" The death of St. Fursa is noticed above under the years 646 and 647. The present entry is added in *al. man.* in A. But it is part of the original text in B.

[9] *The Tall.*—The orig. of this clause, added in *al. man.* in A., is part of the text in B. Longus, MSS.

[10] *In the 72nd year.*—The birth of St. Cummeni the Tall, or Cummen *fota* ("long," "tall"), is entered at the year 591 *supra.* Much curious information regarding the alleged incestuous origin, and history, of St. Cummeni Fota has been published by Dr. Todd. See *Book of Hymns*, pt. I., pp. 81–93.

[11] *Saran Ua Critain.*—"Saran descendant (*nepos*) of Critan." St. Saran is patron of Tisaran, in the bar. of Garrycastle, King's co.

[12] *Ogoman.*—The *Four Mast.* (660) add that Ogaman was oc cinn corbadain, "*at* Cenn Corbadan;" but neither place has been identified. See note [14].

[13] *Gerthide.*—See under the year 593, *supra.*

[14] *Diarmaid's colleague.*—socius Diarmada. The battle of Ogoman seems to have been fought between the two brothers, Diarmaid and Blathmac (sons of Aedh Slaine), who were Joint-Kings of Ireland at this time, and whose death is entered under the year 664 *infra.*

[15] *Son*, &c.—The original of this clause is interlined in A. and B.

mic Feiḋlimiḋ mic Aenġusa mic Naḋfraich), rex Muman, mortuus est. Iugulatio Maelefuataiġ filii Ernani. Scannlan abb Luġmaiḋ quieuit.

Kl. Ianair. (1 f., l. 16.) Anno domini dc.° lx.° ii.° Quies Segain mic U Chuind abb Bennchoir, 7 mors Guaire Aiḋne. Iugulatio duorum filiorum Domnaill filii Aeḋo .i. Conall 7 Colgu. Mors Gartnaiḋ filii Domnaill, 7 Domnaill mic Toṫolain. Mors Tuaṫail mic Morgaind. Tuenog filius Finntin abb Fernann. Indercaċ episcopus, Dima episcopus, quiescerunt. Ultan mac U Chonċuḃair quieuit secundum alium librum.

.b. Kl. Ianair. (2 f., l. 27.) Anno domini dc.° lx.° iii.° Te[ne]brae in Kl. Maii in nona hora, 7 in eadem aestate coelum ardere uisum est. Mortalitas in Hiberniam peruenit in Kl. Augusti. Bellum Luṫo feirnn .i. i Fortrinn. Mors Cernaiġ filii Diarmato mic Aeḋo slane mic Diarmada cerrbeoil mic Conaill cremṫainne, et terremotus in Brittania, 7 Comgan mac U Teiṁne, 7 Beraċ ab Benncair. Baetan macc U Cormaicc abb Cluano obiit. In campo Iṫo Fotart exarsit mortalitas primo in Hibernia. A morte Patricii cc.ª .iii. prima mortalitas .cxii. Ceallaċ mac Maeilecoḃa moritur hic secundum alium librum.

---

[1] *Segain Mac-Ui-Chuind*—"Segain, son of Cond's descendant." His name is written "Seighin" in the *Martyr. of Donegal*, where his festival is given at September 10.

[2] *Guaire Aidhne.*—King of Connaught, celebrated for his hospitality. He is mentioned at the years 626 and 648 *supra*; and his obit is again entered under the year 665 *infra*.

[3] *Domnall, son of Aedh.*—King of Ireland. His obit is entered above under the year 641.

[4] *Gartnaidh.*—A Pictish king. The "Gartnait filius Donnel" of the Pictish Chronicle.

[5] *Finntin.*—*Fintain* (gen. of Fintan), *Four Mast.* (662).

[6] *Indercach.* — This name seems comp. of *in* (the defin. article in Irish) and *dercach* ("charitable").

[7] *Ultan.*—See above, at the year 656. This entry, added in *al. man.* in A., is in the original text in B.

[8] *Luth-feirnn, i.e., in Fortrenn.*—Luth-feirnn has not been identified. Fortrenn was "one of the seven provinces of the Picts, and lay to the west of the River Tay," according to

of Fedhlimidh, son of Aengus, son of Nadfraech), King of Munster, died. The slaying of Maelfuataigh, son of Ernain. Scannlann, abbot of Lughmadh, rested.

Kal. Jan. (Sund., m. 16.) A.D. 662. The repose of [662.]
Segain Mac-Ui-Chuind,[1] abbot of Bangor; and death of Guaire Aidhne.[2] The killing of two sons of Domnall son of Aedh,[3] viz., Conall and Colgu. The death of Gartnaidh,[4] son of Domnall, and of Domnall, son of Totholan. Death of Tuathal, son of Morgand. Tuenog, son of Finntin,[5] abbot of Ferns; Indercach,[6] a bishop, Dima, a bishop, rested. Ultan[7] Mac-Ui-Conchobair rested, according to another Book.

Kal. Jan. (Mond., m. 27.) A.D. 663. Darkness on [663.] BIS.
the Kalends of May, at the ninth hour; and in the same summer the sky seemed to be on fire. A pestilence reached Ireland on the Kalends of August. The battle of Luth-feirnn, *i.e.*, in Fortrenn.[8] Death of Cernach, son of Diarmait, son of Aedh Slanè, son of Diarmait Cerrbeoil, son of Conall Cremthainne; and an earthquake in Britain; and Comgan Mac-Ui-Teimhne,[9] and Berach abbot of Bangor, [died]. Baetan, son of Ua Cormaic, abbot of Cluain,[10] died. The mortality raged at first in Ireland in Magh Itho of Fothart. From the death of Patrick,[11] 203 [years]; the first mortality,[12] 112 [years]. Ceallach, son of Maelcobha dies in this year,[13] according to another Book.

Skene. *Chron. Picts and Scots*, Preface, p. cxx. But Dean Reeves thinks the name was applied to all Pictland. *Adamnan*, pp. 202, 332.

[9] *Comgan Mac-Ui-Teimhne.*—"Comgan, son of the descendant of Teimhne." In the *Martyr. of Donegal*, which gives his festival at Feb. 27, the name of Comgan is written "Commán."

[10] *Cluain.*—Clonmacnoise.

[11] *Patrick.*—The Patrick referred to here must be "Old Patrick" (or *Sen-Patrick*), whose death is entered *supra*, at the year 457, and again (as "Patrick" only) under 461; and not "Patrick the Archbishop," whose *quievit* is recorded at the year 492 (=493). See under 457 *supra*, note [6]; and under 570, note *b*.

[12] *Mortality.* — moꞃꞇaliꞇa, A. The plague, or leprosy, called *Samthrosc*, mentioned at the year 553 *supra*, is probably here referred to.

[13] *In this year.*—hi (for hic) A. B. See under the year 657 *supra*.

Kl. Ianair. (4 f., l. 8.) Anno domini dc. lx.° iiii.° Mortalitas magna. Diarmait mac Aedo slane, 7 Blaimac, 7 Maelbresail filius Maeleduin, mortui sunt .i. don buiḋe ċonaill. Ultan mac Caunga, ab Cluana iraird. Dormitatio Feicheni Fabair (.i. de eodem Fol. 24bb. morbo .i. don buiḋe conaill), 7 Ailerain sapientis, 7 Cronani filii Silni. Cu cen matair mac Caṫail (mic Aeḋa mic Cairbri mic Crimṫain) ri Muman moritur. Blaimac Teṫbae, Oengus Ulaṫ, Manċan Leiṫ, episcopi abbatesque atque alii innumerabiles mortui sunt. Colman cass abb Cluana mic Noais, Cummeni abb Cluano mic U Nois, dormierunt.

Kl. Ianair. (5 f., l. 20.) Anno domini dc.° lx.° u.° Mors Ailella flainnesso filii Domnaill filii Aeḋo filii Ainmereaċ. Maelcaiċ mac Scannail di Cruiṫniḃ, Maelduin filius Scannail rex generis Coirpri, obierunt. Eochaid iarlaiṫi rex Cruiṫne moritur. Dubinnrecht mac Dunchada rex .h. mBriuin Ai moritur. Mors Ceallaiġ mic Guaire. Guaire Aiḋne mortuus est secundum alium librum.

Kl. Ianair. (6 f., l. 1.) Anno domini dc.° lx.° ui.° Mortalitas in hibernia. Bellum Aene itir Arada 7 hUi Fiḋgenti, ubi cecidit Eugen filius Crunnmail. Cearnaċ sotal mac Diarmata quieuit.

---

[1] *Diarmait—Blathmac.*—Brothers, and Joint-Kings of Ireland.

[2] *Buidhe-chonaill.*—The original of this clause is added by way of gloss (though a little displaced) in A. and B.

[3] *Ultan the son of Cunga.*—Ultan m caunga, A. B. The *Four Masters* write the name mac hui cunga ("son of the descendant of Cunga.")

[4] *Buidhe-chonaill.*—The orig. of this, not in A. or Clar 49, is added by way of gloss in B. See note [5], p. 54 *supra*.

[5] *Son of Silne.*—Called "Cronán, son of Sinill" in the *Martyr. of Donegal*, at the 11th of Nov., where his festival is given.

[6] *Son.*—The original of this clause, which is added by way of gloss in A., is not in B.

[7] *Dies.*—The obit of Cu-cen-mathair ("Canis sine matre") is wrongly entered above at A.D. 603, instead of his birth.

[8] *Liath.* — *Liath-Manchain*, or Lemanaghan, King's co.

[9] *Other persons.*—Alii, B. Not in A.

Kal. Jan. (Wedn., m. 8.) A.D. 664. A great mortality. [664.]
rmait,[1] son of Aedh Slane, and Bla[th]mac,[1] and elbrcsail, son of Maelduin, died (*i.e.*, of the 'Buidhe naill')[2]. Ultan the son of Cunga,[3] abbot of Cluain-ird, [died]. The 'falling asleep' of Feichen of Fabhar ., from the same distemper, *i.e.*, the 'Buidhe chonaill'),[4] l of Aileran the Wise, and of Cronan, son of Silne.[5] -cen-mathair, son of Cathal (son[6] of Aedh, son of Cairbre, of Crimthan), King of Munster, dies.[7] Bla[th]mac of thba, Oengus Uladh, Manchan of Liath,[8] and bishops l abbots, and other persons[9] innumerable, died. Colman s, abbot of Cluain-mic-Nois, [and] Cummeni, abbot of iain-mic-Nois, slept.

Kal. Jan. (Thurs., m. 20.) A.D. 665. The death of [665.]
ill Flannessa, son of Domnall, son of Aedh, son of mire. Maelcaich,[10] son of Scannal, of the Cruithni,[11] d] Maelduin, son of Scannal, King of Cinel-Coirpri, d. Eochaid Iarlaithi, King of the Cruithni,[11] dies. bhinnrecht, son of Dunchad, King of Ui-Briuin-Ai, s. Death of Cellach son of Guaire.[12] Guaire Aidhne[13] d, according to another Book.

Kal. Jan. (Frid., m. 1.) A.D. 666. A mortality in [666.]
land.[14] The battle of Aine[15] between the Arada and -Fidhgenti, in which fell Eugen son of Crunnmael. rnach Sotal,[16] son of Diarmait, rested.

---

[10] *Maelcaich.*—Mentioned at 628 ra.

[11] *Cruithni.* — The Cruithni (or ts) of Dalaraide, co. Antrim.

[12] *Guaire.* — The Guaire Aidhne ing of Connaught) referred to in next entry.

[13] *Guaire Aidhne.*—See at the year , *supra*, where the death of Guaire already noticed. This entry is led in *al. man.* in A B. has rely Uel mc Guaire aidne.

[14] *In Ireland.* — in hibernia, B. The same words seem to have been added as a gloss over mortalitas in A.; but they are now almost illegible.

[15] *Aine.* — Any, or Knockany, in the barony of Smallcounty, co. Limerick.

[16] *Cernach Sotal.* — The Cernach, son of Diarmait, son of Aedh Slanè, &c., whose death is entered above under 663. This entry is added in the later hand in A.

.b. Kl. Ianair. (f., l. .) Anno domini dc.° lx.° uii.° Mortalitas magna .i. an buiḋe ċonaill. Bellum Fertsi inter Ultu 7 Cruitne, ubi cecidit Caṫusaċ mac Luirggeni. Nauigatio Columbani episcopi [cum] reliquis sanctorum ad insolam uaccae albae, in qua fundauit aecclesiam, 7 nauigatio filiorum Gartnaiḋ ad hiberniam cum plebe sceṫ. Ferġus mac Muccedo mortuus est. Diarmait 7 Blaṫmacc da riġ Erenn, 7 Feichin Foḃair, 7 alii multi mortui sunt .i. don buiḋ ċonaill, secundum alium librum.

Kl. Ianair. Anno domini dc.° lx.° uiii.° Obitus Cummeni albi abbatis Iae, 7 Critani abbatis Benn-ċair, 7 Mucuae micc hUirt, 7 mors Maelefoṫartaiġ mic Suiḃne regis nepotum Tuirtri.

Cennfaelaḋ cecinit:—
Ni dilu
Nach ri limsa alaliu,
O breṫa Maelfoṫartaiġ
Ina geimnen do ḋairiu.

Itarnan 7 Corindu apud Pictores defuncti sunt. Iugulatio Maeleduin mic Maenaiċ.

---

[1] *A great mortality.*—The words magna .i. an buiḋe ċonaill, which are not in B., are added as gloss over mortalitas in A. The writing is now extremely faint. Clar. 49 has "Mortalitas magna called Buichoinnell." See note [6], p. 54 *supra*.

[2] *Fertais.*—Fertsi (genit. of fertais). See O'Donovan's *Four Masters*, A.D. 665, note *u*, where the Editor expresses the opinion that from this "Fertais" the name of Belfast (bel fertsi; "mouth of the ford"), has been derived.

[3] *Colman.*—Columbani (in the genit. case), A., B., and Clar. 49; in which latter MS. an old hand has written *Colmani* in the margin. Colman's death is recorded at the year 675 *infra*.

[4] *With the relics of the Saints.*—reliquis s̄corum, A., B., and Clar 49. O'Conor, however, prints "cum reliquis Scotor." The entry of Colman's retirement to Ireland in the *Book of Leinster* (p. 24, col. 1), has cum reliquis s̄cor. The *Four Masters* say (667) go naoṁaib oile imaille friu, "together with other Saints."

Kal. Jan. A.D. 667. A great mortality,[1] *i.e.*, the [667.] BIS.
uidhe chonaill.' The battle of Fertais[2] between the
uid and the Cruithni, in which fell Cathusach son of
rgein. Voyage of Bishop Colman,[3] with the relics of
Saints,[4] to Inis-bo-finde, in which he founded a
urch; and the voyage to Ireland of the sons of Gartnat,
th the people of Sceth.[5] Fergus son of Muccid died.
armaid[6] and Blathmacc, the two Kings of Ireland, and
ichin of Fobhar,[7] and many others died, *i.e.*, of the
uidhe chonaill,' according to another Book.

Kal. Jan. A.D. 668. Death of Cummene the Fair, [668.]
bot of Ia, and of Critan, abbot of Bangor, and of Mocua
ı of Ust; and the death of Maelfothartaigh, son of
ibhne, King of the Ui-Tuirtri.

Cennfaeladh sang[8]:—

Not dearer
Is either king than another to me,
Since Maelfothartaigh was borne
In his bier to Derry.

arnan[9] and Corindu died[10] among the Picts. Assassina-
on of Maelduin, son of Maenach.

---

[5] *Sceth.*—The Isle of Skye. In the ok *of Leinster* (p. 358, col. 3), the ne is written ꞅcecha. For various er forms of this curious name con- t Reeves' *Adamnan*, p. 62, note *b*. Armstrong's *Gaelic Dictionary*, der the word *sgiathanach*, where a od deal of nonsense regarding the mology of the name "Skye" is nted.

[6] *Diarmaid.*—This entry is repre- ted in B. by Uel hic Diaꞃmaic Blaimac 7 Fecin moꞃcui ꞅunc don buiꝺe conaill. ("Or in s year Diarmait, and Blai[th]mac, d Fechin died, *i.e.*, of the 'Buidhe-chonaill.'") The decease of all three is entered above at the year 664.

[7] *Fobhar.*—Fore, in the bar. of the same name, co. Westmeath. For some curious notices regarding Fore, see O'Donovan's *Four Mast.*, at A.D. 1176, note *s*.

[8] *Cennfaeladh sang.*—The following stanza, which is not in B., is written on the lower margin of fol. 25*a* in A.

[9] *Itarnan.*—O'Conor mistook this name for the name of a place. See his ed. of these Annals at the same date.

[10] *Died.*—deꝼuncꞇi ꞅunc ꞅunc, A.

Kl. Ianair. Anno domini dc.° lx.° ix.° Nix magna facta est. Oscolt mor. Iugulatio Moeleduin nepotis Ronain. Mors Blaṫmicc mic Maelecoḃo, 7 iugu-
Fol. 25aa. latio Cuanai filii Cellaiġ. Uenit genus Gar[t]nait de Hibernia. Iugulatio Brain finn mic Maelefoṫartaiġ. Mors Dunchado hui Ronain.

Kl. Ianair. Anno domini dc.° lxx.° Mors Ossu filii Eitilbriṫ regis Saxonum. Fergus mac Crunnmail moritur. Iugulatio Seċnusaiġ filii Blaimic regis Temoirie, initio hiemis;

Ba sruanaċ, ba echlascaċ
A tech ambiḋ Sechnasach;
Ba himḋa fuiḋel for slaitt
Hi taiġ i m-bith mac [B]laiṫmeicc.

Dubduin rex generis Coirpri iugulauit illum; 7 Bran finn mac Maeleoctraiċ moritur. Bellum Droma cepais. Mailrubai in Britanniam nauigat.

.b. Kl. Ianair. (5 f., l. 26.) Anno domini dc.° lxx.° i.° Bellum Dungaile mic Maeletuile, 7 combustio Aird maċae 7 domus Tailli filii Segeni, deleti sunt ibdig. Mors Cummascaiċ mic Ronain. Mes mor. Cenn-

[1] *Fell.*—facta est, A. Not in B.

[2] *Famine.* — Oscolt. Otherwise written ascalt (see *Chron. Scot.* at A.D. 962). See also Stokes's ed. of *Cormac's Glossary*, p. 1. O'Conor erroneously prints *Scol mor.*, and more erroneously translates "mortalitas magna armentorum." Clar. 49 reads "Great sleaing of chattle."

[3] *Family of Gartnat.* — genus Gartnait. See under 667. Regarding the identity of this Gartnat, see Reeves' *Adamnan*, p. 290.

[4] *Son of Maelfothartaigh.*—The death of another "Bran Finn," stated to have been the son of a "Maelochtraich," is entered under the next year.

[5] *Ossu.*—Oswiu, King of the Northumbrians.

[6] *Eitilbrith.*—Æthelfrith, slain in 617, according to the *Anglo-Sax. Chron.*

[7] *Full of bridles.*—The original of this stanza, which is not in B., is written on the lower margin of fol. 25a in A.

[8] *Cinel-Coirpre, i.e.*, the race of Cairbre, son of Niall Nine-hostager, who were at this period seated in the present bar. of Granard, co. Longford, but whose descendants afterwards gave name to the districts now represented by the baronies of Carbury, in the cos. of Kildare and Sligo.

[9] *Bran Finn.*—Bran the "Fair."

Kal. Jan. A.D. 669. Great snow fell.[1] A great famine.[2] [669.]
e murder of Maelduin Ua Ronain. The death of
ıthmac, son of Maelcobha, and the murder of Cuana,
ı of Cellach. The family of Gartnat[3] comes from
land. The assassination of Bran Finn, son of Mael-
hartaigh.[4] The death of Dunchad Ua Ronain.

Kal. Jan. A.D. 670. The death of Ossu,[5] son of Eitilbrith,[6] [670.]
ng of the Saxons. Fergus, son of Crunnmael, dies.
e assassination of Sechnusach, son of Bla[th]mac, King
Tara, in the beginning of winter:—

Full of bridles,[7] full of horse-whips, was
The house where Sechnasach was wont to be.
Many were the leavings of plunder,
In the house in which Blathmac's son used to be.

ıblıduin, King of Cinel-Coirpre,[8] slew him. And Bran
un,[9] son of Maelochtraich, dies. The battle of Druim-
pais.[10] Maelruba[11] passes over to Britain.

Kal. Jan. (Thurs., m. 26.) A.D. 671. The battle of [671.] BIS.
ıngal,[12] son of Maeltuile; and the burning of Armagh,
d of the house of Taille,[13] son of Segene. [Many] were
stroyed there.[14] The death of Cummascach, son of Ronan.
·eat fruit. Cennfaeladh, son of Blathmac, begins to reign.

---

e assassination of a "Bran Finn." of Maelfothartaigh, is recorded der the preceding year.

[0] *Druim-Cepais.*—Not identified. ır. 49 has "Druim-cexais."

[1] *Maelruba.*—See under the year 2.

[2] *Battle of Dungal.*—bellum ıngaıle.—This idiomatic form of pression is used very frequently in se Annals, to indicate that the son whose battle is thus noticed s himself slain therein. This battle called the battle of Tolach-ard high hill") in *Three Fragments of nals*, at A.D. 672.

[13] *The "House of Taille."*—Tech-Taille. Now Tehelly, in the par. of Durrow, bar. of Ballycowan, King's co. See O'Donovan's *Four Mast.*, A.D. 670, note *u*. The domuſ taıllı of the original text is printed *do mgtalli* by O'Conor, who translates it "duo Mactallii!"

[14] *[Many] were destroyed there.*—The original, deleti ſunt ıbdıg, seems corrupt, and should probably be corrected to et multı delecı ſunt ıbı (or ıbıdem). For ıbdıg, O'Conor reads *ibi*, as does the "translator" (?) of Clar. 49.

faelaḋ mac Blaṫmaic regnare incipit. Expulsio Drosto de regno, 7 combustio Bennċair Brittonum.

Kl. Ianair. Anno domini dc.° lxx.° ii.° Combustio maige Lunge. Iugulatio Domangairt mic Domnaill bricc regis Dal Riatai. Gabail Eliuin mic Cuirp 7 Conamail filii Canonn, 7 Cormacc [mac] Maele-foṫartaiġ moritur. Nauigatio Faelbei abbatis Iae in Hiberniam. Mailrubai fundauit aecclesiam Aporcrosan. Constantinus filius superioris Constantini regnauit annis x. 7 iiii.

Kl. Ianair. Anno domini dc.° lxx.° iii.° Iugulatio Congaile cennḟoti mic Dunchado, regis Uloṫ. Becc Bairche interfecit eum. Iugulatio Doir mic Maelduiḃ regis Cianaċte. Mors Scannlain mic Fingin regis .h. Meiṫ. Nubes tenuis 7 tremula ad speciem celestis arcus .iiii. uigilia noctis ui.a feria ante pasċa ab oriente in occidentem per serenum coelum apparuit. Luna in sanguinem uersa est.

Kl. Ianair. (2 F., l. 29.) Anno domini dc.° lxx.° iiii.°
Fol. 25ab. Bellum Cindḟaelaḋ filii Blaṫmaic filii Aeḋo slane, in quo Cindfaelaḋ interfectus est. Finechta mac Dunchada uictor erat. Iugulatio Airmedaiġ hui Guaire. Mors Noe mic Danel. Mors filii Pante.

---

[1] *Magh-luinge.* — The "Campus Lunge" of *Adamnan* (i., 30; ii., 15). An establishment founded by St. Colum-Cille in the island of Tiree. See Reeves' *Adamnan*, p. 59, note *f*, and *Ulster Jl. of Archæol.*, Vol. II., pp. 233–244.

[2] *Domnall Brecc.*—See under the year 641 *supra*.

[3] *Of Elvin, son of Corp.* Eliuin mc Cuirp, A., B.—The translation of this clause in Clar. 49 is "the captivitie of Eolvin mc Cairbre and Conmaoil mc Canonn. Cormac Maile fothart moritur." But this is plainly wrong. Although the text of B. is at one with A., O'Conor incorrectly prints *Gabhail Eluan mc Coirpre*, &c. ("Capture of Elua, son of Coirpre,"&c.)

[4] [*Son.*]—See *Fragments of Annals*, p. 69.

[5] *To Ireland.*—The return of Failbhe from Ireland is entered under the year 675.

[6] *Aporcrosan.* — Applecross, in Ross-shire, Scotland. The death of St. Maelrubha, in the 80th year of his age, is recorded at the year 721 *infra*.

ulsion of Drost from the kingship; and the burning Bangor of the Britons.

Kal. Jan. A.D. 672. The burning of Magh-luinge.[1] killing of Domangart, son of Domnall Brecc[2] King Dalriata. The capture of Elvin son of Corp,[3] and amail son of Cano; and Cormac, [son[4]] of Maelartaigh, dies. Voyage to Ireland[5] of Failbhe, abbot Ia. Maelruba founded the church of Aporcrosan.[6] stantine,[7] son of the previous Constantine, reigned[8] enteen years. [672.]

Kal. Jan. A.D. 673. The assassination of Congal nfota,[9] son of Dunchad, King of Uladh. Becc Bairche[10] ed him. The assassination of Doir, son of Maeldubh, g of Cianachta. Death of Scannlan, son of Fingin, g of Ui-Meith. A thin and tremulous cloud, in the n of a rainbow, appeared at the fourth watch of the it, on the Friday[11] before Easter Sunday, [extending] 1 east to west, in a clear sky. The moon was turned blood. [673.]

al. Jan. (Mond., m. 29.) A.D. 674. The battle of nfaeladh, son of Blathmac, son of Aedh Slanè, in ch[12] Cennfaeladh was slain. Finachta, son of Dunchad victor. The assassination of Airmedach, descendant uaire. Death of Noe, son of Danel. Death of the [674.]

---

estival appears in the Calendar ril 21.

onstantine.—This was Constantine II., Emperor of the East, who d from 668 to 685. *Art de V. tes*, t. 1, p. 417.

eigned.—ɼeᵹıɼ, for ɼeᵹnaꞇ, ᵹnauıꞇ, A., B., and Clar. 49.

ngal Cennfota.—"Congal Long-"

Becc Bairche.—In the list of the of Ulad, contained in the *Book inster*, (p. 41, col. 3), Becc Bairche is stated to have been king of that province for 24 years, and to have died in pilgrimage.

[11] *Friday.*—uıᵃ ɼeɼıa, or sixth day of the week. The *Chron. Scot.* has uᵃ ɼeɼıa, or Thursday.

[12] *In which.*—The original of this clause, which is part of the text in B., is interlined in *al. man.* in A. Cennfaeladh only commenced to reign in A.D. 671, and was succeeded in the kingship by his slayer, Finachta, who was Cennfaeladh's second cousin.

Mors Scannlain mic Fingin regis nepotum Meiṫ. Finachta regnare incipit, scilicet Finachta fleaḋaċ mac Duncaḋa mic Aeḋa slaine.

.b. Kl. Ianair. (3 f., l. x.) Anno domini dc.° lxx.° u.° Columbana episcopus insolae uaccae albae, 7 Finan filius Airennain pausant. Iugulatio Maeleduin filii Rigullain 7 Boidb filii Ronain hoi Congaile. Multi pictores dimersi sunt illaind abae. Distructio Ailċe fringrenn la Finechtae. Faelbe de Hibernia reuertitur. Congal mac Maeleduin, 7 filii Scannail, 7 Airṫulae iugulati sunt.

Kl. Ianair. (5 f., l. 21.) Anno domini dc.° lxx.° ui.° Stella cometes uisa luminosa in mense septimbris 7 octimbris. Dunchad mac Ultain occisus est i n-dun Forggo. Bellum inter Finsnecta 7 Lagenos in loco proximo Loċo gabar, in quo finsnechta uictor erat. Iugulatio Cuandai mic Euganain. Congressio Cule

---

[1] *Son of Penda.* — Apparently Wulfhere, son of Penda, King of Mercia, whose obit the *Anglo-Sax. Chron.* has at A.D. 675. The name of Penda is written Pante in the MSS.

[2] *Scannlan.*—The death of this Scannlan is already entered under the year 673.

[3] *Finachta the Festive.*—Finachta fleaḋaċ. The original of this clause is added in *al. man.* in A., and in the original hand in B. For some curious information regarding King Finachta, see *Fragments of Irish Annals* under the year 677.

[4] *Columban.*—This is the Colman whose voyage (from Lindisfarne) to Inis-bo-finde (*Inishbofin*, off the W. coast of Mayo) is entered at the year 667 *supra*. Bede devotes a good deal of attention to St. Colman, *Eccl. Hist.*, Book III., caps. 25, 26.

[5] *Finan.*—The festival of this Finan is given in the *Martyr. of Donegal* under Feb. 12, where his father's name is written "Erannan," a mere variation of "Airennan."

[6] *Son.*—fli, A., B.

[7] *Rigullan.*—This was probably the Rigullan whose death is noticed at the year 628 *supra*, and who was son of Conang (see at A.D. 621), son of Aedan Mac Gabrain, King of the Scotch Dalriads (whose obit is given above at the year 605).

[8] *Ronan Ua Congaile.* — Ronain hoi Congaile, A., B. But O'Conor blunderingly prints hoi (*nepotis*) "hoc est." Ronan Ua Congaile means "Ronan descendant of Congal."

›f Penda.[1] Death of Scannlan,[2] son of Fingin, King ̄i-Meith. Finachta begins to reign, viz., Finachta ?estive,[3] son of Dunchad, son of Aedh Slanè.

ıl. Jan. (Tuesd., m. 10.) A.D. 675. Columban,[4] ›p of Inis-bo-finne, and Finan,[5] son[6] of Airennan, d. The assassination of Maelduin, son of Rigullan,[7] of Bodb, son of Ronan Ua Congaile.[8] A great many were drowned in Land-abae.[9] The destruction of ıh-Frigrenn[10] by Finachta. Failbhe[11] returned from nd. Congal son of Maelduin, and the sons of nal, and Aurthula, were slain. [675.] BIS.

ıl. Jan. (Thurs., m. 21.) A.D. 676. A bright comet seen in the months[12] of September and October. ıhad[13] son of Ultan was slain in Dun-Forgo. A e between Finachta[14] and the Leinstermen, in a place Loch-gabar, in which Finachta[14] was victor. The sination of Cuanda son of Eoganan. The encounter [676.]

'our Masters, who often ignore connected with Scotch history, no reference to the death of uin son of Rigullan, or of Bodb : Ronan Ua Congaile, having :ntly regarded them as members Gaelic family of Alba (or nd).

nd-abae.—Not identified. See s' *Adamnan*, p. 60, note *b.* (*Chron. Picts and Scots*, Index *ndabae*), says it is "Lundaff Kinloch, Perthshire," without safing any authority for the ıent.

ilech Frigrenn. — Ailech, or , as the name is now written, Lough Swilly, in the bar. of wen West, co. Donegal.

ıilbhe.—The voyage to Ireland of Failbhe is noticed at the year 672. His obit appears under 678 *infra*.

[12] *In the months.*—ın menſe, A., B., and Clar. 49. The appearance of this comet is noticed in the *Anglo-Sax. Chron.* at the year 678, where it is stated that it shone every morning for three months like a sunbeam. Its appearance is likewise recorded in the *Chron. Scot.* and *Annals of Clonmacnoise*, at the year 673, but under 677 (which is the proper year) in Tigernach.

[13] *Dunchad.* — The *Four Masters* state that Dunchad was chief of the Oirghialla.

[14] *Finachta.*—Finnſnechτα ("white-snow"), in original. This was Finachta, King of Ireland. See under the year 674.

Maein, ubi ceciderunt filii duo Maeleaichdin. Beccan Ruimm quieuit.

Kl. Ianair. (6 f., l. 2.) Anno domini dc.° lxx.° uii.° (alias uiii.) Mors Colggen mic Failbhei flainn regis Muman. Daircill mac Curetai epscop Glinne da locha, Coman epscop Fernann, pausant. Interfectio generis Loairnn i Tiriinn. Toimsnamho rex Osraighi. Bellum Duin locho, 7 bellum liacc Moelain, 7 doirad Eilind. Mors Drosto filii Domnaill. Bellum i Calathros in quo uictus est Domnall brecc.

Kl. Ianair. (7 f., l. 13.) Anno domini dc.° lxx.° uiii.° Quies Failbi abbatis Iae. Cennfaelad mac Ailella mic Baetain, sapiens, pausauit. Bellum Finnsnechta contra Beicc mBairche. Dormitatio Nectain neir. Domnall mac Suibni la hUltu moritur.

Fol. 25ba. .b. Kl. Ianair. Anno domini dc.° lxx.° ix.° Colman abas Benncair pausat. Iugulatio Fiannamla mic Maeletuile regis Lagenorum. Cathal mac Roghaillig moritur. Bellum Saxonum ubi cecidit Ailmine

---

[1] *Cul-Maini.* — According to O'Donovan, Cuil-Maini (or Cuil-Maine), was the ancient name of the parish of Clonmany, in the north-west of the barony of Inishowen, co. Donegal. (*Four Mast.*, A.D. 1499, note *k*.) But as there were other places of the name, it is not certain that the Cul-Maini above referred to was the Clonmany in Donegal.

[2] *Beccan Ruimm.*—Plainly so written in A. and B. But Clar. 49 incorrectly reads *Ruinim*, whilst O'Conor prints *Beccan puim* . . . . . The *Four Masters*, who write the name "Becan Ruimind," state (675) that he died in Britain, on March 17th, which is his festival day in the *Martyr. of Donegal.*

[3] *Slain.*—Clar. 49, and O'Conor following it, have "quievit" which is wrong. The *Four Masters* (at 676), state that "Tuaimsnamha" was slain by Faelan Seanchostol. Faelan Senchustul is in the list of Kings of the Ui-Cendselaig in the *Book of Leinster*, p. 40, col. 1, where he is stated to have fought seven battles against the Ossorians, in the last of which Tuaimsnamha was slain.

[4] *Battle in Calathross.*—This entry is quite out of place here, and should appear under the year 634 *supra*. The death of Domnall Brecc is recorded above at the year 641, and again inaccurately at 685 *infra*. See Reeves' *Adamnan*, p. 202, note.

[5] *Failbhe.*—Abbot of Hi from 669

'ul-Maini,[1] in which two sons of Maelaichdin were
ı. Beccan Ruimm[2] rested.
al. Jan. (Frid., m. 2.) A.D. 677 (alias 678). The [677.]
h of Colggu, son of Failbhe Flann, King of Munster.
'cill, son of Cureta, bishop of Glenn-da-locha, and
ıan, bishop of Ferns, rest. Slaughter of the
ıl-Loarnn, in Tirínn. Toimsnamho, King of Ossory,
n.][3] The battle of Dun-locha, and the battle of
ıc-Moelain, and the enslavement of Elend. The death
)rost son of Domnall. A battle in Calathross,[4] in
ch Domnall Brecc was vanquished.
al. Jan. (Sat., m. 13.) A.D. 678. The repose of [678.]
bhe,[5] abbot of Ia. Cennfaelad,[6] son of Ailill, son of
tan, a wise man, rested. The battle of Finsnechta[7]
nst Becc Bairche. The falling asleep of Nechtan
r. Domnall, son of Suibne, dies by the Ulaid.[8]
al. Jan. A.D. 679. Colman, abbot of Bangor, rests. [679.] BIS.
assassination of Fianamail,[9] son of Maeltuile, King
ıe Leinstermen. Cathal, son of Raghallach, dies. A
le of the Saxons, in which Ailmine son of Ossu[10] was

9, and predecessor of Adamnan. he is mentioned above at the 672, 675.

nnfaelad.—This seems to have the remarkable man who lost his n of forgetfulness" (*inchind der-*, through a wound received in ead, at the battle of Magh-Rath 636, *supra*). See O'Donovan's the account of this battle, pub. by the *Irish Archæol. Society* lin, 1842), p. 278, note *e*.

attle of 'Finsnechta' (or 'Fin-.')—The *Four Masters* (at the 677) call this the battle of ltiu" (now Teltown, co. Meath.)

ies by the Ulaid.—"Killed by orthern men." Clar. 49.

ianamail.—In the *Ann. Four Mast.*, at A.D. 678, Fianamail is stated to have been slain by one of his own people, at the command of Finachta *Fledach*. But in the list of Leinster Kings in the *Book of Leinster* (p. 39, col. 2), Fianamail (the term of whose reign is given as 12 years), is stated to have been slain by the Ui-Cend-selaigh in the battle of Aife, or of Selga, in the *fortuatha* ("borders") of Leinster, or by one of his own people. In the *Fragments of Irish Annals*, the beginning of Fianamail's reign is erroneously entered under the year 679.

[10] *Ailmine son of Ossu.*—Ælfwine son of Oswy. See *Anglo-Sax. Chron.* at the year 679.

filius Orru. Obsessio Duin baitte. Dunchad filius Euganain iugulatur est. Mors Maelefoṫartaiġ episcoip Ard sraṫo. Bellum i m-Bodbgnu ubi cecidit Conall oirggneċ. Lepra grauissima in Hibernia que uocatur bolgcach.

Kl. Ianair. Anno domini dc.° lxxx.° Combustio regum i n-dun Ceiṫirnn .i. Dungal mac Scannail rex Cruiṫne, 7 Cennfaelad rex Cianaċtae, .i. mac Suibni, in initio aestatis, la Maelduin mac Maelefitriċ. Bellum Blaisleib postea in initio hiemis, in quo interfectus est Maelduin filius Maelefiṫriċ. Iugulatio Conaill ċoil filii Dunchado i Ciunn tire. Iugulatio Seċnasaiġ mic Airmedaiġ 7 Conaing mic Congaile. Obsessio duin Foiṫer.

Kl. Ianair. Anno domini dc.° lxxx.° i.° Iugulatio Cinnfaelad mic Colgen regis Conacht. Bellum raṫa more maiġi line contra Britones, ubi ceciderunt Caṫurac mac Maeleduin ri Cruiṫne, 7 Ultan filius Dicolla, 7 iugulatio Muirmin in mano. Obitus Suibne filii Maeleumai principis Corcoiġi. Orcades deletae sunt la Bruide.

Kl. Ianair. Anno domini dc.° lxxx.° ii.° Dunchad

---

[1] *Dun-Baitte.*—Not identified. Apparently the name of some place in Scotland.

[2] *Bodbgna.*—This was the name of a hilly district in the east of the present co. Roscommon. The name is still preserved in that of the well-known mountain *Sliabh-Badbgna* (*anglicè*, *Slieve Bawne*), in the barony of Roscommon.

[3] *Conall Oirgnech.*—"Conall the Plunderer." The *Four Masters* add that he was "Chief of the Cinel-Cairbre" (678).

[4] '*Bolgach.*'—The Irish name for the small-pox is *bolgach beg*, or "little *bolgach*."

[5] *Dun-Ceithirnn.*—Now known as the "Giant's Sconce," in the parish of Dunboe, in the north of the co. Londonderry.

[6] *Cruithni.* — The Cruithni (or Picts) of Ireland.

[7] *Cianachta.*—The "Cianachta of Glenn-Gaimhin," whose territory is now represented by the barony of *Keenaght*, co. Londonderry.

[8] *Bla-sliabh.*—Not identified.

[9] *Cenn-tire.* — "Land's Head." Cantyre, in Scotland.

[10] *Dun-Foither.* —Now known as "Dunnottar in the Mearns" (Scotland), according to Skene. *Chron.*

n. The siege of Dun-Baitte.[1] Dunchad, son of ;anan, was slain. The death of Maelfothartaigh, iop of Ard-Sratha. A battle in Bodbgna,[2] in which iall Oirgnech[3] was slain. A most severe leprosy reland, which is called 'bolgach.'[4]

Kal. Jan. A.D. 680. Burning of the Kings in Dun-thirnn,[5] viz., Dungal son of Scannal, King of the ithni,[6] and Cennfaelad, King of the Cianachta,[7] *i.e.*, son of Suibne, in the beginning of summer, by elduin son of Maelfitrich. The battle of Bla-sliabh[8] rwards, in the beginning of winter, in which Maelduin, of Maelfitrich, was slain. The killing of Conall l, son of Dunchad, in Cenn-tire.[9] The killing of hnasach, son of Airmedach, and of Conang, son of igal. The siege of Dun-Foither.[10] [680.]

Kal. Jan. A.D. 681. The slaying of Cennfaelad,[11] of Colgu, King of Connaught. The battle of Rath-r of Magh-Linè[12] against Britons, in which fell Cathasach of Maelduin, King of the Cruithni,[13] and Ultan son Dicuill; and the killing of Murmin 'in mano.'[14] Death Suibne, son of Maelduin, abbot of Corcach.[15] The cneys were destroyed by Bruide. [681.]

Kal. Jan. A.D. 682. Dunchad Mursce,[16] son of Mael- [682.]

---

and Scots. See the Index thereto, *unfother.*

Cennfaelad.—In the *Ann. Four* (680) it is stated that Cenn-dh was slain after the house in h he was sheltered had been red against him; and that his r was one Ulcha Derg ("Red d") of the "Conmaicne Cuile."

Rath-mor of Magh-Linè.—Now more, par. of Donegore, bar. of r Antrim, co. Antrim. A place famous in Irish history. See r *na hUidre*, p. 133*a*; and es' *Eccl. Antiqq.*, p. 69, note *s.*

Cruithni.—The Cruithni (or Picts) of Dalaraide in Antrim. Not the Picts of Scotland.

14 *Murmin 'in mano.'*—Of the person called Murmin, or the addition 'in mano,' the Editor is unable to give any satisfactory explanation. Dean Reeves prints 'in manu.' *Adamnan*, p. 377.

15 *Corcach.*—Coꞃcoiġi, the genit. form. Ware has no notice of this successor of St. Barra, or Finnbarr, founder of the Monastery of Cork.

16 *Dunchad Mursce.*—In his ed. of these Annals, O'Conor ignorantly renders *Mursce* by "Dux maritimus." But the epithet *Mursce* means that

mursce filius Maeleduibh iugulatus est. Bellum Corainn in quo ceciderunt Colgu filius Blaimaic 7 Fergus mac Maeleduin rex generis Coirpri. Obsesio Duin att, 7 obsessio Duin duirn. Initium mortalitatis puerorum in mense Octimbris. Dormitatio Airmedaigh na Craeibe.

.b. Kl. Ianair. Anno domini dc.° lxxx.° iii.° Mortalitas paruulorum. Mors Maini abbatis Noindromo,
Fol. 25bb. 7 mors Dergorgaill. Mors Concoluim. Bellum Cairpil finnbair. Loch Eachach do soudh hi fuil hoc anno.

Kl. Ianair. Anno domini dc.° lxxx.° iiii.° Uentus magnus. Terremotus in insola. Saxones campum Bregh uastant, 7 aecclesias plurimas, in mense Iuni. Mors Congaile mic Guaire, 7 mors Bresail filii Fergusso morbo.

Kl. Ianair. Anno domini dc.° lxxx.° u.° Bellum duin Nechtain uicisimo die mensis Mai sabbati die factum est, in quo Etfrith mac Ossu rex Saxonum, .xu.° anno regni sui consummata magna cum caterua

---

Dunchad (who was King of Connaught) had lived, or been fostered, in the territory of "Muirisc," in the north of the present barony of Tireragh, co. Sligo. See O'Donovan's *Hy Fiachrach*, p. 314, note *f*.

[1] *Dun-Att.*—"Dunad, in the parish of Glassary in Argyle." Reeves' *Adamnan*, p. 377, note *b*.

[2] *Dun-Duirn.*—Dean Reeves thinks that this may be "Dundurn, at the east end of Loch-Earn in Perthshire" (*Adamnan*, p. 377, note *c*.)

[3] *Of October.*—Octobri, B. See Reeves' *Adamnan*, p. 182, note *a*, in which the learned Editor, with characteristic industry, has collected numerous references to the pestilences which prevailed in this country anciently.

[4] *Craebh.*—Craebh-Laisre, or the "Tree of St. Lasair," a monastery said to have been near Clonmacnoise. See Todd's *Irish Nennius*, p. 208, note *x*. The site of the monastery is not now known.

[5] *Of Noendruim.*—Clar. 49 reads "abb Aondromo," "abbot of Aondruim." A very old hand, like that of Ussher, writes "Antrim" in the margin. But *Nendrum* (Mahee Island, in Strangford Lough) seems to have been meant. See Reeves' *Eccl. Antiqq.*, p. 149.

[6] *Death.*—morss, A.

[7] *Loch Echach.* — Lough Neagh. The words hoc anno are omitted in B.

[8] *In the Island.*—in insola, A., B. in insula, Clar. 49. The *Chron. Scot.* (681=684) has in hibernia

ɔh, was slain. The battle of Corand, in which were n Colgu son of Blathmac, and Fergus, son of Mael-n, King of the Cinel-Coirpri. The siege of Dun-Att,[1] l the siege of Dun-Duirn.[2] The beginning of the rtality of children, in the month of October.[3] The ing asleep of Airmedach of the Craebh.[4]

Kal. Jan. A.D. 683. Mortality of children. The [683.] BIS. ,th of Maine, abbot of Noendruim;[5] and the death[6] of rforgall. The death of Cucoluim. The battle of ssel-Finnbair. Loch Echach[7] was turned into blood ;his year.

Kal. Jan. A.D. 684. A great storm. An earthquake [684.] the Island.[8] The Saxons wasted[9] Magh-Bregh, and eral churches, in the month of June. The death of ıghal son of Guaire, and the death of Bresal,[10] son of :gus, from disease.

Kal. Jan. A.D. 685. The battle of Dun-Nechtain[11] was [685.] ght on the 20th day of May, on Saturday, in which 'rith,[12] son of Oswy, King of the Saxons, the 15th year ıis reign being ended,[13] was slain, together with a great

---

ɔla ("in the Island of Ireland"), :h seems more correct.

Wasted.—Under this year, the *lo-Sax. Chron.* states that "Ecg-ı sent an army against the Scots, Berht, his aldorman, with it; miserably they afflicted and ıed God's churches." Thorpe's *ıslation*, London, 1861. Ecgferth eeded his father Oswy (whose is entered at A.D. 670 *supra*), ing of the Northumbrians. See :'s account of the transaction, . *Hist.*, Book 4, chap. 26. The h of Ecgferth (or *Etfrith*, as the e is there written), is entered ır the next year in these Annals.

Bresal.—The *Four Masters* state . 683) that Bresal was chief of ıa (or Ui-Echach-Cobha), now represented by the baronies of Iveagh, co. Down. Reeves' *Eccl. Antiqq.*, pp. 348–352.

[11] *Dun-Nechtain.* — "Nechtan's Fort." Supposed to be "the modern Dunnichen, which is situated in a narrow pass in the range of the Sidlaw hills, which separate Strathmore from the plains of Forfarshire." Skene (*Chron. Picts and Scots*, Pref. cxix.)

[12] *In which Etfrith.*—The "Ecg-ferth" of the *Anglo-Sax. Chron.* See note under preceding year. O'Conor, in his ed. of these Annals (note 1, *ad an.*), wrongly observes that the words *in quo* are wanting in Clar. 49.

[13] *Ended.*–conſummata, in A., B., and Clar. 49. Probably a mistake for conſummato, as in Tigernach.

militum suorum interfectus est, 7 comburit tula aman duin Ollaiġ. Talorgg mac Aciṫaen, 7 Domnall brecc mac Echaċ, mortui sunt. Iugulatio Rotachtaiġ 7 Dargarto mic Finnguine. Mors Banbain oscaċ sapientis.

Kl. Ianair. Anno domini dc.° lxxx.° ui.° Iugulatio Feradaiġ mic Congaile. Quies Doċumaiconoc abbatis uallis da loċo. Dormitatio Rosseni abbatis Corcaiḋe mare. Mors Osseni episcopi monosteri Finntin filii Finnguine. Adomnanus captiuos reduxit ad Hiberniam .lx.

Kl. Ianair. Anno domini dc.° lxxx.° uii.° Quies Segeni (o aċaḋ ċlaidib) episcopi Ardmaċae. Occisio Canonn filii Gartnaiḋ. Finsnechta clericatum suscepit. Bellum Imleċo piċ ubi ceciderunt Dubdainber rex Arda Cianacta, 7 hUarcride nepos Osseni, 7 Congalaċ mac Conaing fugitiuus euasit. Niall mac Cernaiġ uictor erat.

---

[1] *Tula-aman.*—The meaning of this is unknown to the Editor, who is unable to say whether it is the name of a person, or a term for some fiery element. O'Conor translates "*Tula* regalia"!

[2] *Dun-Ollaigh.*—Dunolly, in Argyllshire. Referred to as *Duin-onlaigh* (in the genit. form), at the year 700 *infra*, and in the accus. form *arcem ollaigh*, at the year 733. The nomin. form, Dun-ollaigh, occurs at the year 713.

[3] *Domnall Brecc.*—If this is the same Domnall Brecc referred to above at the years 641 and 677, as no doubt he is, there is much confusion regarding him, not only in these Annals, but also in the Annals of Tigernach. See Reeves' *Adamnan*, pp. 202-3. The *Chron. Scot.*, at the year 682 (=685), records the death of Domnall Brecc in nearly the same words as are used in the entry at 641 *supra*.

[4] *Banban Oscach.* — The epithet *oscach* is possibly for *os cach*, "beyond all." He is called "Banban egnaidh," or "Banban the learned," at his festival day (9th May), in the *Martyr. of Donegal*, and "Banban sapiens" in the *Martyr. of Tallaght*. In the *Fragments of Annals*, at 686, Banban is called "Scribe of Kildare."

[5] *Corcach-mor*; or the "Great marsh." Now known as Cork, in the south of Ireland. mare, gen. of mar, "great," A.; maire, B.

[6] *Finntan son of Finnguine.*—The *Ann. Four Mast.* (685), and the

ıltitude of his soldiers; and Tula-aman[1] burned Dun-
laigh.[2] Talorg, son of Acithaen, and Domnall Brecc,[3]
ı of Eocha, died. The killing of Rothachtach, and of
ırgairt, sons of Finnguine. The death of Banban
scach'[4] the Wise.

Kal. Jan. A.D. 686. The killing of Feradach, son of [686.]
ngal. The repose of Dochuma-Conoc, abbot of Glenn-
-locha. The 'falling asleep' of Rosseni, abbot of
ırcach-mor.[5] The death of Osseni, bishop of the
onastery of Finntan son of Finnguine.[6] Adamnan
ought back 60 captives[7] to Ireland.

Kal. Jan. A.D. 687. The repose of Segeni, from [687.]
:hadh-claidib,[8] bishop of Ard-Macha. Murder of Cano,
n of Gartnaid. Finsnechta[9] entered into religion. The
ttle of Imlech-Pich,[10] wherein fell Dubhdainbher, King
Ard-Cianachta,[11] and Uarcride[12] Ua Osseni; and
ıngalach, son of Conang, escaped by flight. Niall, son
Cernach,[13] was victor.

---

ron. *Scot.* 683 (=687), state that ıntan (called *Munnu*) was the son of ılcan. This Finntan was the founder the monastery of Tech-Munnu, or ıghmon, co. Wexford. But Osseni usually regarded as abbot of onenagh, Queen's co., with which nntan (Munnu) was also conıcted.

[7] *Captives.*—In the *Frag. of Irish ınals*, it is stated that these were the captives whom the Saxons had rried off from Ireland," on the casion, apparently, of the deedation recorded above at the year 34.

[8] *Achadh-claidib.*—The situation of is place, which would be translated Sword-field," is not known to the litor.

[9] *Finsnechta.*—Finnachta, King of Ireland. The *Four Mast.* say that Finnachta went "on his pilgrimage." His return to the kingship is mentioned under the next year.

[10] *Imlech-Pich.* — Emlagh, in a parish of the same name, bar. of Lower Kells, co. Meath.

[11] *Ard-Cianachta.* — Now represented by the bar. of Ferrard, co. Louth.

[12] *Uarcride.*—The *Four Mast.* state that Uarcride was King of Conaille-Muirthemne, a district in the present co. Louth.

[13] *Cernach.*—This is the Cernach [Sotal, or "the haughty"], son of Diarmait, son of Aedh Slanè, whose death is noticed at the year 663 *supra.*

Bronaig Conailli indiu,
Deiṫbir doaiḃ iar n-Uaircridiu;
Ni ba ellṁu bias gen
I n-Aird iar n-Duḃdainber.

Sirecṫaċ,
Bronan file for tir Taiḋgg;
Cen Dubcuile cen mac m-Brain,
Cen Du bdainber ar aird.

Sirechtaċ,
Sella fria leċt leacca,
Far coin, far milcoin, far mna,
Dobuid la far n-eċtrata.

Mona icad dam amne,
Mac Crunnmael dom [f]irichte,
Roptis fola ocus cro
Mo der do marb Imblecho.

Kl. Ianair. Anno domini dc.° lxxx.° iiii.° Iolan espcop Cinngaraṫ obiit. Finsnechta reuertitur ad regnum. Iugulatio Diarmato midi filii Airmedaig ceci. Mors Caṫusaig nepotis Domnaill bricc. Obitus Docinni Daire murċairi. Mors Feradaiġ mic
Fol. 26aa. Tuaṫalain. Mors Maeleduin mic Conaill crannaṁna. Obscurata est pars solis.

Kl. Ianair. Anno domini dc.° lxxx.° ix.° Conġal mac Maeileduin mic Aeḋo bennain, rex Iarmuman, 7

---

[1] *Sad.* — The following stanzas, which are not in B., are written on the lower margin of fol. 25 *b* in A. The name of the author is not very legible; but it looks like "Gabaircenn." The first stanza occurs in the *Frag. of Irish Annals*, at the year 686, where the authorship is ascribed to "Gabhorchenn."

[2] *Ard.*—Put for "Ard-Cianachta."

[3] *The land of Tadhg.* — Tir Taiḋgg. A Bardic name for the land of the sept which gave name to *Ard-Cianachta*, and which was descended from Tadhg, son of Cian, son of Oilill Oluim (King of Munster in the 2nd century).

[4] *Cenngarath.*—Kingarth, in Bute, Scotland.

[5] *Returns to the kingship.*—See the entry under last year regarding Finnachta.

Sad[1] are the Conailli this day.
They have cause, after Uarcride.
Not readier shall be the sword
In Ard,[2] after Dubhdainbher.

Sorrowful,
The grief that is in the land of Tadhg,[3]
Without Dubcuile, without Bran's son,
Without Dubhdainbher over Ard.[2]

Sorrowful,
To look at their stony graves—
To see your dogs, your grayhounds, your women,
In the possession of your foes.

If Crundmael's son had not healed
My sorrow for me, truly,
Of blood and gore my tears would be,
For the dead of Imlech.

Kal. Jan. A.D. 688. Iolan, bishop of Cenngarath,[4] [688.]
ed. Finnachta returns to the kingship.[5] The killing of
armait of Midhe, son of Airmedach 'caech.'[6] Death
Cathasach,[7] grandson of Domnall Brecc. Death of
ochinni of Daire-murchaisi.[8] Death of Feradach, son
Tuathalan. The death of Maelduin, son of Conall
annamhna.[9] Part of the Sun was darkened.

Kal. Jan. A.D. 689. Congal, son of Maelduin, son of [689.]
edh Bennan, King of Iar-Mumha, and Duinechaid son

Airmedach 'caech,' i.e., Airme-h "the blind." cecī, for caeci, B.

Cathasach.—This was Cathasach, son of Domangart (sl. 672 *supra*), o was son of Domnall Brecc.

Daire-murchaisi.—O'Conor ab-dly translates this "Monasterii oreti maritimi." The *Four Mas-* (688) write the name, and bably more correctly, "Daire-ichaisi," which O'Donovan identifies (note *e*, *ad. an.*) with "Derry-brughis, *alias* Killyman, in the county of Armagh."

[9] *Maelduin, son of Conall Crannamhna.*—Maelduin was the 14th King of the Scotch Dalriads. His father, Conall Crannamhna (whose obit is entered above at the year 659), was the 12th King of the same important tribe, and son of the 8th King, Eochaidh Buidhe (ob. 628 *supra*).

Duineċaid mac Oircdoiṫ, 7 Ailill mac Dungaile Eilne mic Scandail, iugulati sunt. Combustio aird Machae. Mors Finguine longi 7 Feradaiġ meiṫ mic Nechtleicc; 7 Choblaiṫ filia Canonn moritur. Dobécoc Cluana aird pausauit. Iustinianus minor filius Constantini annis .x.

Kl. Ianair. Anno domini dc.° xc.° Cronan mac u Chualne, abbas Bennċuir, obiit. Theodorus episcopus Brittaniae quieuit. Dalriati populati sunt Cruṫniu 7 Ultu. Fiṫceallaċ mac Flainn rex hUa Maine moritur. Uentus magnus .xui. Kl. Octimbris quosdam .ui. ex familia Iae mersit.

Kl. Ianair. (2 f., l. 7.) Anno domini dc.° xc.° i.° Adomnanus .xiiii.° anno post pausam Failbei ad hiberniam pergit. Conċad episcopus moritur. Fergus mac Aedain rex in Ċoicid obiit. Iugulatio Maeleditraiḃ mic Euganain. Luna in sanguineum colorem in natali sancti Martini uersa est. Obsesio Duin deauae dibri.

Kl. Ianair. Anno domini dc. xc.° ii.° Bruide mac Bili rex Fortrend moritur, 7 Alphin mac Nectin.

---

[1] *Orcdoith.*—Probably the Orcdoith, son of Sechnasach, whose death is noticed above, at the year 658.

[2] *Dungal of Eilne.*—He was probably the son of the Scannal referred to above, at the year 665, and was called "Dungal of *Eilne*," from a territory so called, in the present county of Antrim. See O'Donovan's *Four Mast.*, A.D. 557, note *i*. In the corresponding entry in the *Chron. Scot.*, 686=689, Dungal's son, Ailill, is called King of the [Irish] "Cruithne," or "Picts." His name occurs also in the list of Kings of Dalaraide, in the *Book of Leinster*, p. 41, col. 5.

[3] *Tall.*—Or the "Long."

[4] *Dobécoc of Cluain-ard.*—Dobécoc was also called Mobécoc, both being devotional forms of the name *Becan*. The church, anciently called *Cluain-ard-Mobecoc*, is now known, according to O'Donovan, as the old church of Kilpeacan, in the bar. of Clanwilliam, co. Tipperary. (*Ann. Four Mast.*, A.D. 689, note *f*.) This Becan is wrongly said to be of Cluain-Iraird (Clonard, co. Meath), in Tigernach (690), *Four Mast.* (687), and *Frag. of Irish Annals* (690).

[5] *Justinian.*—This entry is somewhat out of place, as Justinian the younger began to reign A.D. 685.

[6] *Of Bangor* [in Down].—Bennċuir, A., B.

[7] *Dalriata.* — "It is doubtful whether these were the people of Scotch or Irish Dalriada. The scene of their depredation was the territo-

Orcdoith,[1] and Ailill, son of Dungal of Eilne,[2] son of annal, were slain. The burning of Armagh. The ath of Finguine the Tall,[3] and of Feradach the Fat n of Nechtlecc; and Coblaith daughter of Cano dies. ɔbécoc of Cluain-ard[4] rested. Justinian[5] the younger, n of Constantine, [reigns] ten years.

Kal. Jan. A.D. 690. Cronan son of Ua Chualne, abbot Bangor,[6] died. Theodore, bishop of Britain, rested. ıe Dalriata[7] spoiled the Cruithni and the Ulaid. Fithellach, son of Flann, King of Ui-Maine, dies. A great ɔrm, on the 16th of the Kalends of October, overhelmed some six persons of the community of Ia. [690.]

Kal. Jan. (Mond., m. 7.) A.D. 691. Adamnan comes Ireland in the fourteenth year[8] after the death of ıilbhe. Conchad the bishop dies. Fergus son of Aedan, ing of the Province,[9] died. The killing of Maeldithibh son of Eoganan. The moon was turned[10] into the ılour of blood on the Nativity of St. Martin. The ege of Dun-Deavæ *dibsi*.[11] [691.]

Kal. Jan. A.D. 692. Bruide son of Bili, King of ɔrtrenn, dies, and Alphin son of Nechtin. The death[12] of [692.]

ʼs of the Cruithne and Ulidians, w the county of Down, and the ıthern half cf Antrim." Reeves' *lamnan*, p. 377, note *d*.

[8] *Fourteenth year.*—The Abbot ıilbhe died on the 22nd March, 679. is death is entered above under the ar 678=679.

[9] *Fergus son of Aedan, King of the rovince.*—By "the Province," is eant Ulidia, generally designated in ish Annals *the* coicid, "fifth," or rovince. The *Four Masters* (689, 'Donovan's ed.) have "Fergus son Lodan." The *Frag. of Ir. Annals* 92) have "Fergus son of Aodhan." ut the name in the list of "Kings Ulad" in the *Book of Leinster* (p. ı, col. 3) is "Oengus son of Aedan," who is stated to have reigned 16 years.

[10] *Was turned.*—Uersa est. Omitted in A.

[11] *Dun-Deavæ 'dibsi.'*—This name must be corrupt, the last member thereof, '*dibsi*,' being quite unintelligible. Dean Reeves thinks that "Dundaff," south of Stirling (Scotland) may have been intended. *Adamnan*, p. 378, note *e*.

[12] *Death.*—Mors, A. MS. B. has the abbrev. for "et" instead of mors, and makes the entry run on as a continuation of the previous sentence, which ends with "Nechtin," in A. Clar. 49 does not exactly agree with A. or B. But the variations are of no importance.

Mors Diraṫ episcopi Fernann, 7 Bran nepos Faelaen rex Lagenentium mortui sunt. Ceallach mac Ronain moir moritur. Bellum inter Osraigi ocus Laigniu in quo cecidit Faelcar nepos Maeleodrae. Iugulatio Ainḟtiġ 7 nieṫ Neill 7 filiorum Boendo. Mors Doergairt mic Finguine. Bellum contra [filium] Pante.

Fol. 26ab.

Kl. Ianair. Anno domini dc.° xc.° iii.° Cron becc abbas Cluana mic U Nois obiit. Beccḟola episcopus quieuit. Iugulatio Cerbaill mic Maeleodrae. Obsesio duin Foṫer. Mors Ferchair mic Conaeṫ cirr. Domnall mac Auin rex Alocluaṫe moritur. Huidreni campi Bile quieuit. Obitus Cronani Balni.

Kl. Ianair. (iii. f., luna x.) Anno domini dc.° xc.° iiii.° Finsneachta rex Teṁro 7 Bresal filius eius iugulati sunt (ag grellaiġ dollaiġ) apud (alias ab) Aeḋ mac Dluṫaiġ (mic Ailella mic Aeḋa slaine) 7 a Congalaċ mac Conaing (mic Congaile mic Aeda slaine).

---

[1] *Of the Leinstermen.*—Lagenentiam, A.

[2] *Died.*—mortui sunt, for mortuus est, in A. Omitted in B.

[3] *Dies.*—mor, for moritur, or mortuus est, A. mortui sunt, B.

[4] *Grandson of Maelodar* (or *Maelodhar*).—Faelchar was son of Forandal, son of Maelodhar, son of Scanlan Mór (King of Ossory; whose obit the *Four Mast.* give under A.D. 640).

[5] *Ainftech — Nieth-Neill—Boenda.* —The bearers of these names have not been identified by the Editor.

[6] *Doergart.*—Apparently the Dargart son of Finnguine, whose killing ("Jugulatio") is noticed above at the year 685. This Finnguine may have been the same as Finghin, fourth in descent from Conall (son of Comghall), 6th King of the Scotch Dalriads. See Reeves' *Adamnan, Geneal. Table of Dalriadic Kings.*

[7] *Against* [*the son of*] *Penda.*—contra Penda, A., B., and Clar. 49. But Penda had been at this time thirty-eight years dead. (See at the year 655, *supra*). The *Chron. Scot.* (689) more correctly reads contra filium penda ("against the son of Penda.") This son of Penda must have been Æthelred, who succeeded to

rath, bishop of Ferns, and Bran grandson of Faelan, ng of the Leinstermen,[1] died.[2] Cellach, son of Ronan ır, dies.[3] A battle between the Osraighi and the instermen, in which fell Faelchar, grandson of ıelodar.[4] The killing of Ainftech,[5] and of Nieth-ill,[5] and of the sons of Boenda.[5] The death of ergart,[6] son of Finguine. A battle against [the son Penda.[7]

Kal. Jan. A.D. 693. Cron Beec, abbot of Cluain-mic- [693.]
is, died. Beccfhola, a bishop, rested. The killing of rbhall, son of Maelodar. The siege of Dun-Fother.[8] ath of Ferchar,[9] son of Connadh Cerr. Domnall, son Auin,[10] King of Al-Cluaith, dies. Huidreni of Magh-è, rested. The death of Cronan of Balna.[11]

Kal. Jan. (Frid., m. 10.) A.D. 694. Finsnechta,[12] [694.]
ng of Tara, and Bresal his son, were slain (at Grellach-laigh[13]), by[14] Aedh, son of Dluthach (son[15] of Ailill, son Aedh Slanè), and by Congalach, son of Conang (son[15] Congal, son of Aedh Slanè).

Kingship of the Mercians in 675, he death of his brother, Wulfhere. the last battle Æthelred is stated ave fought was a battle against ; Ecgferth of Northumbria, in (*Anglo-Sax. Chron.*) In this , the above entry is somewhat out lace. See Lappenberg's *England r the Anglo-Saxon Kings.* ırpe's Transl.), London, 1845, vol. . 291.

Dun-Fother.—See above, at the 680.

Ferchar.—He was the 10th King e Scotch Dalriads.

Auin.—See a note on this name, r the year 641 *supra.*

Balna.—Now Balla, bar. of Clan-is, co. Mayo.

[12] *Finsnechta, i.e., Finnachta.*—An old hand has added fleḋaċ ("the Festive,") in the margin in A.

[13] *At Grellach-Dollaigh.*—O'Donovan thought this the place now called Girley, two miles to the south of Kells, co. Meath. *Ann. Four Mast.*, A.D. 693, note *q*. The name of the place is twice added in A., firstly, a ngreallaig ḋollaiġ ("in Greallach-Dollaigh") over the name of *Finsnechta*, and again, ag greallaiġ ḋollaiġ ("at G—— D——"), over the words filius eius.

[14] *By.*—apud, alias ab, in A. ab, in B.

[15] *Son.*—The original of these clauses is interlined in A. and B.

Moling Loċair cecinit:—

Ba dirsan do ḟinsneċta,
Indiu Laigid crolige;
Rambe la firu nime,
Dilgud ina boraime;

In bern forsmbiṫ Finsneċta
Immasreitis rigriadai,
Aed doith gerisa do ċaill,
Atosrolaic nisriadai.

Occisio Taidgg mic Faelbei in ualle pellis. Quies Minnbairenn abbatis Achaid bo. Gaimide Lugmaiḋ dormiuit. Mors Brain mic Conaill bicc. Tomnat uxor Ferċair moritur. Mors Conaill filii Tuaṫail.

.b. Kl. Ianair. Anno domini dc.° xc.° u.° Iugulatio Domnaill filii Conaill crandamnai. Finnguine mac cainsine matre, rex Muman, moritur. Fergal Aiḋne et Fiannaṁail mac Mennaiċ moriuntur. Loċeni menn sapiens, abbas Cille dara, iugulatus est. Cummene Mugdorne pausat. Congalach mac Conaing filii Congaile filii Aeḋo slane moritur. Loingseċ mac Aengusa regnare incipit.

Kl. Ianair. Anno domini dc.° xc.° ui.° Taraċin de regno expulsus est. Ferchar fota moritur. Adom-

---

[1] *Moling Lochair* (or Moling Luachra), founder, and patron, of Tech-Moling, or St. Mullin's, co. Carlow. The stanzas following, not in B., are written in the lower margin of fol. 26*a* in A., with a mark of reference to their place in the text.

[2] '*Borama.*'—A large tribute exacted by the Kings of Ireland from the Leinstermen, from the time of King Tuathal Techtmar, in the second century, to the time of Finnachta. The circumstances attending the imposition of the *Bórama*, and the way in which St. Moling succeeded in obtaining its remission from King Finnachta, form the subject of a long tract in the *Book of Leinster*, p. 294*b*, *sq.*

[3] *Aed.*—The original text seems corrupt, and therefore difficult of translation.

[4] *Glenn-gaimhin.* — Or "Glenn-geimhin." In ualle pellis, A. B. "Vallis pellis" is an accurate translation of the name Glenn-geimhin, which was the old name of the vale of the River Roe, near Dungiven (Dun-geimhin), in the county of Londonderry.

[5] *Minnbairenn.* — The name is "Meann Boirne" (Meann of Boirend), in the *Ann. Four Mast.* (693).

Moling Lochair[1] sang :—

It were sad for Finsnechta
To lie to-day in his gory bed.
May he be with the men of Heaven,
For the remission of the 'Borama.'[2]

The gap in which Finsnechta was slain—
Round which kingly cavalcades would ride—
Aed[3] . . . .
Since it has hidden him, he'll not ride over it.

e killing of Tadhg, son of Failbhe, in Glenn-gaimhin.[4] e repose of Minnbairenn,[5] abbot of Achadh-bó. imide of Lugmadh[6] slept. Death of Bran, son of nall Becc.[7] Tomnat, wife of Ferchar,[8] dies. Death Conall, son of Tuathal.

Kal. Jan. A.D. 695. The assassination of Domnall,[9] ι of Conall Crandamna. Finnguine, son of Cu-cen-thair,[10] King of Munster, dies. Fergal of Aidhne,[11] and ιnnamhail, son of Mennach, died. Locheni Menn, the ιse, abbot of Kildare, was slain. Cummene, of Mug-ιna, rests. Congalach, son of Conang, son of Congal, ι of Aedh Slanè, dies. Loingsech, son of Aengus, begins reign. [695.] BIS.

Kal. Jan. A.D. 696. Tarachin[12] was expelled from the ιgship. Ferchar the Tall[13] dies. Adamnan proceeded [696.]

Lugmadh.—Now Louth, in the ιty of the same name.

Conall Becc; i.e., "Conall the le."

Wife of Ferchar.—Apparently Ferchar, son of Conad Cerr (King ιe Scotch Dalriads), whose death ιtered under the preceding year.

Domnall.—This was Domnall n (or "Brown Domnall"), 13th ; of Dalriada.

Cu-cen-mathair.—"Canis sine ·e." His death is recorded under rear 664 *supra*.

[11] *Fergal of Aidhne.*—He was King of Connaught, and grandson of Guaire Aidhne, whose obit is given above at the year 662.

[12] *Tarachin.*—King of the Picts of Scotland. Referred to under the form "Tarain" at the year 698. See Reeves' *Adamnan*, p. 134, note *a*.

[13] *Ferchar the Tall.*—Or "Ferchar the Long" (ꝼeꞃcaꞃ ꝼoꞇa). Ferchar was the first Prince of the House of Loarn who became King of the Dalriads, having succeeded to the position on the death (in 688, *supra*)

nanus ad Hiberniam pergit et dedit legem innocentium populis. Echu nepos Domnaill iugulatus est. Maelḟotarṫaiġ mac Maelduiḃ rex na n-Airgialla moritur. Immairecc Crannchae ubi cecidit Feradaċ mac Fol. 26ba. Maeledoiṫ. Bellum Uilcon. Ecomras mac Congaile mic Guaire iugulatus est. Moling Lochair dormiuit. Britones et Ulaiḋ uastauerunt campum Muirteṁne. Cassan scriba o Lusca quieuit. Iugulatio Concoḃo.

Kl. Ianair. Anno domini dc.° xc.° uii.° Bellum i Fernmuiġ ubi ceciderunt Concobor Machae mac Maeleduin ocus Aed aird rex dail Araide. Bellum inter Saxones et Pictos ubi cecidit Bernıṫ qui dicebatur Brectrid. Combustio Duin Onlaiġ. Expulsio Ainfcellaig filii Fercair de regno, et uinctus ad Hiberniam uechitur. Mors Forannain abbatis Cille daro, ocus Maeleduin mic Mongain. Mors Muirgiusa mic Maeleduin, regis generis Coirpri.

Kl. Ianair. Anno domini dc.° xc.° uiii.° Bouina strages in Saxonia. Bellum Fiannamla mic Osseni. Tarain ad Hiberniam pergit.

---

of Maelduin, son of Conall Crannamna, (14th King of Dalriada), and the last King of the line of Fergus Mor Mac-Erca, second King of Dalriada.

[1] *Law of the Innocents.* — See Reeves' *Adamnan*, p. 179. The *Frag. of Annals*, at 696, state the law was against killing children or women.

[2] *Echu.*—Eucha, B. "Eucha," Clar. 49.

[3] *Crannach*, *i.e.* "a place full of trees." Not identified. The word immairecc (translated "conflict") is rendered by "Scirmish" in Clar. 49.

[4] *Battle of Uilcon.*—Bael (for bellum) A. For Uilcon, Clar. 49 has Ulcor. O'Conor prints *Julcon*, and thinks there is something omitted. The Editor cannot explain the entry.

[5] *Congal.* — The death of a "Conghal, son of Guaire," is entered above at the year 684.

[6] *Moling Lochair.* See under the year 694 *supra*.

[7] *Cassan.*—This is the same as the "Caisin" of the *Four Masters* (at the year 695). See Colgan's *Acta Sanctorum*, p. 781.

[8] *Cucobha.*—"The hound of Cobha." Probably some chieftain of the race of Eochaidh *Cobha*, from whom the tribe of Ui-Echach-Cobha derived their descent. See Reeves' *Eccl. Antiqq.*, p. 349.

[9] *Fernmagh.*—Now represented by the barony of Farney, co. Monaghan. The *Four Masters* state (696) that this battle was fought in "Tuloch-Garroisg" in Fernmagh, which place has not been identified.

Ireland, and gave the 'Law of the Innocents'[1] to the
ple. Echu,[2] grandson of Domnall, was slain. Maelartaigh, son of Maeldubh, King of the Airghialla,
s. The conflict of Crannach,[3] in which fell Feradach,
of Maeldoith. The battle of Uilcon.[4] Ecomras, son
Congal,[5] son of Guaire, was slain. Moling Lochair[6]
t. The Britons and Ulidians devastated Magh-
irthemhne. Cassan,[7] scribe of Lusk, rested. The
rder of Cucobha.[8]

Kal. Jan. A.D. 697. A battle in Fernmagh,[9] in which [697.]
ichobar of Macha, son of Maelduin, and Aedh Aird,[10]
ig of Dal-Araide, were slain. A battle between
ons and Picts, in which fell Bernith, who was
ed Brectrid.[11] The burning of Dun-Ollaigh.[12] The
ulsion of Ainfcellach,[13] son of Ferchar, from the king-
, and he was carried[14] in chains to Ireland. The
th of Forannan, abbot of Kildare; and of Maelduin,
of Mongan. The death of Muirges, son of Maelduin,
ig of Cinel-Coirpri.

Kal. Jan. A.D. 698. A mortality of cows in Saxon- [698.]
l.[15] The battle of Fiannamail son of Osseni. Tarain[16]
ceeds to Ireland.

Aedh Aird.—"Aedh of Ard." gh Hugh," Clar. 49. The name itten *Aedh Airedh* in the *Ann. Mast.* (696), and *Aed Airech Aed*] *Ared*, in the list of the s of Dalaraide in the *Book of ter* (p. 41, col. 5), where Aed is l to have been slain in the battle 'ernmag. The entry of this in the *Frag. of Annals* (697) y inaccurate.

Bernith, who was called Brectrid. e "Berctus," or "Behrt," who d the plain of Bregia in 684. above under that year. The -*Sax. Chron.* has the death of rht the aldorman" at the year *Thorpe's Translation*).

[12] *Burning of Dun-Olliagh.*—Com-burti duin Onlaig, A. The name of Dunolly (see note under the year 685 *supra*) is also written duin On-laig, in the genit. case, at the year 700 *infra*.

[13] *Ainfcellach.*—The son of Ferchar Fota (or "Ferchar the Tall.") He was of the House of Loarn Mor, and 17th King of the Scotch Dalriads. The death of Ainfcellach, in the battle of Finn-glenn, is recorded under the year 718 *infra*. See under the years 733 and 735.

[14] *Carried.*—uethitur, B. Vehitur, Clar. 49.

[15] *Saxon-land.*—Saxonia. England.

[16] *Tarain.*—Apparently the Tara-

.b. Kt. Ianair. Anno domini dc.° xc.° ix.° Accensa est bouina mortalitas in Hibernia i Kt. Febrai in campo Trego i Teċbai. Quies Aeḋo anchorite o Sleibtiu. Dormitatio Iarnlaiġ abbatis Lis moir. Fiannamail nepos Dunchado, rex Dal riati, ocus Flann mac Cindfaelaḋ mic Suibne, iugulati sunt. Aurṫuile nepos Crunnmail de regno expulsus in Britanniam pergit. Fames et pestilentia .iii. annis in Hibernia facta est, ut homo hominem comederet. Flann albus mac Maeletuile .i. de genere Eugain, nepos Crunnmail (.i. mic Suibne mind) moritur.

Kt. Ianair. Anno domini dcc.° Bouina mortalitas. Colman auae Oirc, Ceallaċ mac Maeleracho espscop, Diccuill abbas Cluana auis, mortui sunt. Fol. 26bb. Ailill mac Con cen maṫair rex Muman moritur. Feidelmiḋ mac Fergusa mic Aeḋain moritur. Iugulatio Aeḋo Odbae. Aeḋ mac Dluthaiġ, Congal mac Eugânain, mortui sunt. Imbairecc i Scii ubi ceci-

---

chin, whose expulsion from the kingship [of the Picts of Scotland], is mentioned at the year 696 *supra*.

[1] *Aedh.*—O'Donovan says (*Four Mast.*, A.D. 698, note *b*), that "this was the Aidus of Sleibte [Sleaty, bar. of Slievemargy, Queen's county], mentioned in Tirechan's Annotations on the Life of St. Patrick, preserved in the Book of Armagh."

[2] *Iarnlach.*—Skene copies this entry (*Chron. Picts and Scots*, p. 352), under the impression that Iarnlach was abbot of Lismore in Scotland. But Colgan regarded him as connected with Lismore, in the co. Waterford, and the same as the Iarlugh whose festival is given at the 16th January, in the *Martyr. of Donegal.* (*AA. SS.*, p. 155.)

[3] *Fiannamail Ua Dunchada.*—"F. descendant of Dunchad." Probably the same as the "Fiannamail son of Osseni," mentioned under the preceding year.

[4] *Dal-Riata.*—The Irish Dal-Riata, or Dalriads.

[5] *Flann.*—The *Four Mast.* state (A.D. 698), that Flann had been chief of the Cinel-Eoghain.

[6] *Kingship.* — The kingship, or chieftaincy, of the Cinel-Eoghain.

[7] *Suibne Mend.* — The death of Suibne Mend (or Suibhne Menn), who had been king of Ireland, is recorded above at the year 627. This clause, added by way of gloss in A., is not in B.; but it is in the text of Clar. 49.

[8] *Mortality of Cows.* — "Bovina adhuc mortalitas," Clar. 49.

[9] *Colman Ua Oirc, i.e.*, "Colman, grandson (or descendant) of Orc. The *Four Masters* (at A.D. 700) call

Kal. Jan. A.D. 699. A cow mortality broke out in [699.] BIS.
eland, on the Kalends of February, in Magh-Trega in
thba. The repose of Aedh,[1] anchorite, of Sleibhte.
ie falling asleep of Iarnlach,[2] abbot of Lis-mor. Fian-
mail Ua Dunchada,[3] King of Dal-Riata,[4] and Flann,[5]
ı of Cennfaeladh, son of Suibhne, were slain. Aur-
uile, grandson of Crunnmael, having been expelled from
e kingship,[6] goes into Britain. A famine and plague
evailed during three years in Ireland, so that man
ould eat man. Flann Finn, son of Maeltuile, *i.e.*, of
e Cinel-Eoghain, grandson of Crunnmael (*i.e.*, son of
ibne Mend),[7] dies.

Kal. Jan. A.D. 700. A mortality of cows.[8] Colman [700.]
ı Oirc,[9] Cellach son of Maelracha, a bishop, [and]
cuill,[10] abbot of Cluain-eois, died. Ailill, son of Cu-cen-
ıthair,[11] King of Munster, dies. Feidelmidh, son of
rgus, son of Aedhan,[12] dies. The assassination of Aedh
lbha.[13] Aedh, son of Dluthach,[14] [and] Congal, son of
ganan, died. A conflict in Scii[15], in which Conaing, son

ı Colman Ua hEirc ("C. grandson
lescendant) of Erc," and state that
was abbot of Cluain-Iraird
onard in Meath.) The *Martyr of*
negal has his festival at Dec. 5.

[10] *Dicuill.*—O'Conor, in a note on
ecclesiastic (*ad an.*) says that this
the author of the well-known
k *De Mensura Orbis Terræ.* But
work was not written before 825.
Reeves' *Adamnan*, p. 169, note.

[11] *Cu-cen-mathair.* —Lit. "Mother-
Hound." His obit is entered
ve at the year 664.

[12] *Aedhan.*—This was possibly Aed-
, son of Mongan, son of Fiachna
gan (King of Ulad). See note 7,
he year 624 *supra*, and *Book of*
nster, p. 535, col. 7. The death
Aedhan, son of Mongan, is entered
ve at the year 615, where he is
. to have been King of Dalaraide.

[13] *Aedh Odbha.*—"Aedh of Odbha."
Regarding the situation of Odbha, see
O'Donovan's *Four Mast.*, A.M. 3502,
note *i*.

[14] *Aedh son of Dluthach.*—See above
under the year 694, where Aedh is
mentioned as one of the persons engaged in killing King Finachta.

[15] *A conflict in Scii.*—Imbairecc
i Scii. Dean Reeves translates this
"bellum navale" (*Adamnan*, 378),
and Skene "Water battle" (*Chron.*
Picts and Scots, p. 353). Both were
no doubt misled by O'Conor, who
wrongly prints *Imbairecc iscu*, and
translates "prælium navale," con-
founding the words i scii ("in Skye")
with uisce, the Irish for "water."
The name of Skye is written "Scia"
in *Adamnan* (lib. i., cap. 33). See
Reeves' ed., p. 62, note *b*.

derunt Conaing mac Dunchado[1] et filius Cuandai. Distructio duin Onlaiġ[2] apud[3] Sealbaċ.[4] Iugulatio generis Caṫboṫ.[5] Iugulatio Conaill mic Suibne regis na n-Deisi. Conall mac Donennaiġ rex nepotum Finngenti[6] moritur. Occisio Neill mic Cernaig.[7] Irgalaċ nepos Conaing[8] occidit illum.

Kl. Ianair. Anno domini dcc.° i.° Muiredaċ campi Ai (alias mullaċ leaṫan, mac Fergusa) moritur. Irgalaċ nepos Conaing a Britonibus iugulatus est in insi mac Nesan. Faeldobor Cloċair dormiuit. Maccnia rex nepotum Eċtaċ Ulat, Ailill mac Cinnfaelad rex Ciannachta, mortui sunt, ocus Garban Miḋe, ocus Colggu mac Moenaiġ abbas Luscan, ocus Luaṫ foigde ocus Craċeppais, sapientes, mortui sunt. Tiberius cesar annis .uii. regnauit.

Kl. Ianair. Anno domini dcc.° ii.° Bellum campi Culind in airdd nepotum n-Eċdaiġ, inter Ultu et Britones, ubi filius Raḋgainn cecidit, [aduersarius]

---

[1] *Dunchad.* — Probably Dunchad, son of the Conaing, son of Aedhan, whose death by drowning is entered at the year 621, *supra.* The death of Dunchad (or Duncath, as the name is also written), is noticed above at the year 653.

[2] *Dun-Ollaigh.* — Dunolly, near Oban, in Scotland. This place is mentioned at the years 685, 697, *supra*, and at 713, 733, *infra.*

[3] *By.*—apud. Used also in the same sense at the year 713.

[4] *Selbach.*—Son of Ferchar Fada (of the House of Loarn), 15th King of Dalriada, whose death is entered above under the year 696. On the death of his brother, Ainfcellach, in 719, Selbach succeeded to the kingship.

[5] *Of the Cinel-Cathbotha.*—Generis caṫboṫ. Cinel-Cathbotha (or Cinel-Cathbaid) was the tribe-name of the descendants of Cathbad, grandson of Loarn Mor, 1st King of the Scotch Dalriads.

[6] *Ui-Fidgenti.*—For Fidgenti, A. and B. incorrectly read finngenti (which would mean "Fair Gentiles," and was the name applied by the Irish to one class of the Norse invaders of Ireland). For the situation and history of the Ui-Fidgenti, see O'Donovan's *Four Masters*, note *m*, at A.D. 1178.

[7] *Niall, son of Cernach.*—The *Four Masters* (699) have *Nial Ua Cearnaigh* ("Niall, grandson of Cernach"), which is probably wrong. The Niall here referred to was seemingly the Niall, son of Cernach, mentioned above at the year 687; the death of whose father, Cernach [Sotail], is entered under 663, *supra.*

[8] *Irgalach Ua Conaing.*—"Irgalach,

Dunchad,[1] and the son of Cuanna, were slain. The estruction of Dun-Ollaigh[2] by[3] Selbach.[4] The killing of ie Cinel-Cathbotha.[5] The assassination of Conall, son Suibhne, King of the Desi. Conall, son of Donennach, ing of the Ui-Fidgenti,[6] dies. The killing of Niall, n of Cernach.[7] Irgalach Ua Conaing[8] killed him.

Kal. Jan. A.D. 701. Muiredach of Magh-Ai (alias nullach leathan,[9] son of Fergus), dies. Irgalach[10] Ua onaing was slain by Britons, in Inis-mac-Nesan.[11] aeldobhar, of Clochar, slept. Maccnia, King of Ui-chach-Ulad, [and] Ailill son of Cennfaeladh, King of ianachta, died; and Garbhan of Midhe, and Colgu son Maenach, abbot of Lusk, and Luath-foigde, and rach-erpais, sages, died. Tiberius[12] Caesar reigned seven ears. [701.]

Kal. Jan. A.D. 702. The battle of Magh-Culind in rd-Ua-nEchach,[13] between Ulidians and Britons, in hich fell the son of Radhgann [the enemy[14]] of God's [702.]

---

scendant (or grandson) of Conaing." ie *Four Masters* (699) state that galach was "son of Conaing," as in *Frag. of Irish Annals* (A.D. 700, 2). In the latter authority, at the ar indicated, some very curious rticlars are given regarding this narkable character, and his strange itest with Adamnan. See also eves' *Adamnan*, pp. liii., liv., 179. galach's death is entered under the ct year; and his son, Cinaeth, is ntioned at 723.

[9] *Mullach leathan.*—This nick-ne signifies "of the broad crown;" "latus vertex." The clause is not B., or in Clar. 49.

[10] *Irgalach.*—See note [8].

[11] *Inis-mac-Nesan.*—"The Island he sons of Nesan." The old name Ireland's Eye, near Howth, co. blin.

[12] *Tiberius.*—Tiberius Absimarus, Emperor of the East from 698 to 705.

[13] *Magh-Culind, in Ard-Ua-nEchach.*—Magh-Culind has not been identified. Ard-Ua-nEchach ("the height of the Ui-Echach") was probably the name of a district in the present baronies of Upper and Lower Iveagh, co. Down, which represent the Ui-Echach-Ulad (or "descendants of Eocha of Ulster").

[14] *The enemy.*—The word aduersarius, which seems to have been omitted in A., B., and Clar. 49, occurs in the *Chron. Scot.* (at 699), and in the *Frag. of Annals* (703). The name of Rathgann (or Radgund, as it is written in the *Frag. of Ann.*) is omitted in the *Chron. Scot.* O'Conor, with his usual inaccuracy, prints in place of the above clause, "Ecclesiarum Dei [Vindicatores] *Ulait* victores erant."

aecclesiarum Dei. Ulaiṫ uictores erant. Bellum Corainn, in quo ceciderunt Loingseċ mac Oengusa mic Domnaill mic Aeḋo mic Ainmirech, rex Hibernie, cum tribus filiis suis (.i. la Ceallach Loca Cime mac Raḋallaiġ), et duo filii Colgen, et Dubdibergg mac Dungaile et Fergus Forcraiṫ, et Congal Gabra, et ceteri multi duces; iiii. id. Iulii, iii.ª hora diei sabbati hoc bellum confectum est. Colman mac Finnbarr, abbas Lis moir, mortuus est. Ailen daingen aedificatur. Fergussan mac Maelcon mortuus est. Obsessio Riṫe.

.b. Kl. Ianair. Anno domini dcc.° iii.° Strages dal Riati in ualle Limnae. Adomnanus .lxx.° uii.° anno aetatis sue, abbas Iae, pausat. Aldfriṫ mac Ossu, sapiens, rex Saxonum, moritur. Bellum for Cloenaċ ubi uictor fuit Ceallaċ Cualann, in quo cecidit Bodbcaḋ Mide mac Dermato. Foċartach nepos Cernaiġ fugit. Feradaċ mac Maeleduin rex generis Loegaire cecidit.

Fol. 27aa. Kl. Ianair. Anno domini dcc.° iiii.° Cennfaelaḋ nepos Aeḋo bricc, abbas Benncair, dormiebat. Bellum

---

¹ *Corann.*—Another account of this battle is added, in an old hand, on the lower margin of fol. 26 *b*, in A.:—Caṫ Corainn in quo cecidit Loingseċ mac Oengusa, ri Erenn, cum tribus filiis suis, 7 ri Cairpri droma cliab, 7 ri .h. Conaill Gabra, 7 .x. rig do riġaib Erenn imaille riu fein, hi cloinfind hi cind Oenaig Loġa itir Cinel Conaill 7 Connachta. Cellach Cime mac Raġallaiġ mic Uatach, ri Connacht [ ]. "The battle of Corand in which fell Loingsech, son of Oengus, King of Ireland, with his three sons, and the King of Cairpri of Drium-cliabh, and the King of Ui-Conaill-Gabhra, and ten kings of the kings of Ireland along with them. In Cloenfind, at the head of Oenagh-Logha [it was fought], between the Cinel-Conaill and Connaughtmen. Cellach Cime, son of Raghallach, son of Uata, King of Connaught [ ]." A few words have been cut off by the binder.

² *Saturday.*—The criteria above given indicate that the true date of the battle of Corann was A.D. 704, when the 4th of the Ides (or 12th) of July fell on a Saturday. See O'Flaherty's *Ogygia*, p. 432.

³ *Ailen-daingen.*—This name would signify "a strong island," or the "island of two daughters" (*Ailen-da-ingen*). It has not been identified. Its destruction is recorded at the year 713 *infra*.

ırches. The Ulidians were victors. The battle of ɾann,[1] in which were slain Loingsech, son of Oengus, ı of Domnall, son of Aedh, son of Ainmire, King of land, together with his three sons, (*i.e.*, by Cellach of ɔh-Cime, son of Raghallach), and two sons of Colgu, l Dubhdiberg son of Dungal, and Fergus Forcraith, l Conall Gabhra, and many other chieftains. On the ı of the Ides of July, at the 6th hour of Saturday,[2] s battle was fought. Colman, son of Finnbarr, abbot Lis-mor, died. Ailen-daingen[3] is built. Fergussan, ı of Maelcon, died. The siege of Rithe.[4]

Kal. Jan. A.D. 703. Slaughter of the Dal-Riata in ɔnn-Limna.[5] Adamnan, abbot of Ia, rests in the 77th ır of his age. Aldfrith the Wise, son of Oswiu,[6] dies. ɔattle at Cloenath,[7] where Cellach Cualann was victor; which fell Bodbcath of Meath, son of Diarmait. ɔartach,[8] grandson of Cernach, fled. Feradach, son of elduin, King of Cinel-Laeghaire, was slain.[9] [703.] BIS

Kal. Jan. A.D. 704. Cennfaeladh descendant of Aedh ɔcc, abbot of Bangor, slept. The battle of Corc- [704.]

Siege of Rithe.—Obſeſıo, A. ɔeſıo, B. The situation of Rithe s not seem to be known; but it is ɔably in Scotland.

Glenn-Limna.—ın ualle Lımnae. n Reeves thinks that this is the ley of the Levin Water, which s from Loch Lomond to Dumon. *Adamnan*, p. 378, note *g*.

Aldfrith . . . . . . son of Oswiu. ldfrith, who was King of the thumbrians, spent some time in and, where he was known under name of *Flann Fina*. Tigernach, he year 704, in recording his death ı: Alfrıth mac Oſſu .ı. Flanɒ x la Gaeɒelu, "Alfrith son of iu, *i.e.*, *Flann fina* with the Gaedil." A good deal regarding Aldfrith is collected in Reeves' *Adamnan*, p. 185, note *l*. The death of Aldfrith is entered in the *Anglo-Sax. Chron.* under the year 705.

[7] *Cloenath.*—Now Clane, co. Kildare.

[8] *Focartach.*—Wrongly written ḟocaſtaıġ (the genit. form) in A. and B. Focartach, afterwards King of Ireland (see under the years 713, 715, 723 *infra*), was the son of Niall, son of Cernach Sotail. See above at 687.

[9] *Was slain.*—Cecıɒıɒ, A. This entry is wrongly given in Clar. 49, which has "Fergus mac Laoghaire, rex gentis Maoileduin, cecidit."

Corcmodruaḋ ubi cecidit Celeċair mac Comain. Ceallaċ mac Roġallaiġ, rex Conaċt, post clericatum obiit. Iugulatio Conamlo mic Canonn. Congall (ċinnmaġair) mac Fergusa (.i. Fanat) regnare incipit.

Kl. Ianair. Anno domini dcc.° u.° (alias ui.°). Duchanna Daire, et Ossene filius Gallust, abbas Cluana mic u Nois, pausant. Bruide mac Derili moritur. Concobar mac Maeleduin, rex generis Coirpri, iugulatus est. Cellan mac Seċnusaiġ, sapiens, obiit.

Kl. Ianair. Anno domini dcc.° ui.° Conodor Fobair obiit. Occisio Indrechtaiġ mic Dunchada Muirsce. Fergal mac Maeleduin, ocus Fergal mac Loingsiġ, ocus Conall menn rex genntis Coirpri, occiderunt eum. Bec nepos Duncaḋo iugulatus est. Coibenaċ espcop Aird sraṫo quieuit. Duo terremotus septimana in eadem in mense Decimbri in aquilonali parte Hiberniae. Bachall Beicce bairċe. Mors

[1] *Son of Raghallach.* — mac Roġallniġ, for mac Roġallaiġ, A. and B. Clar. 49 has "mac Raghalla." See above under the year 702.

[2] *Conamail, son of Cano.*—The name of Cano (who was also called *Cugarbh*, and Cano-garbh), is usually printed "Canonn" by modern editors. But *Canonn* is the genit. case of Cano. The form in the *Frag. of Annals* (686=687) is Cana. The death of Cano is recorded above under the year 687; and his son Conamail is mentioned at 672.

[3] *Cennmagair-Fanat.*—The original of these two clauses is added by way of gloss in A. and B. Cennmagair is now known as Kinnaweer, in the bar. of Kilmacrenan, co. Donegal; and Fanat is a well-known district in the same barony. Clar. 49, which O'Conor quotes approvingly, has "Congal . . . . . . regnare incipit *in* Cennmagair, *i.e.*, Fanad," which is not correct. See *Ann. Four Mast.* at A.D. 702, where the accession of Congal is noticed.

[4] *Alias* 706.—Added in an old hand in A. Not in B. or Clar. 49.

[5] *Daire*; *i.e.*, *Daire-Dachonna*, or *Daire-Mochonna* (Dachonna's, or Mochonna's, "Oak-wood"). The form of the saint's name, Conna, was changed into Da-chonna and Mochonna, by the use respectively of the devotional prefixes *da* ("thy") and *mo* ("my"). The *Martyr. of Donegal*, at the 12th of April, has "Conda, abbot of Daire-Dachonna, in Ulster."

[6] *Bruide.*—He was King of the Picts of Scotland. See Reeves' *Adamnan*, App. to Pref., p. li; and Skene's *Chron. Picts and Scots*, Introd., p. cxxi. The fettering of his brother Nechtan, by King Drust, is entered at the year 725 *infra*.

druadh, in which Celechair, son of Coman, was
n. Cellach, son of Ragallach,[1] King of Connaught,
d after entering religion. The slaying of Conamail,
of Cano.[2] Congal (of Cennmagair),[3] son of Fergus
Fanat),[3] begins to reign.

Kal. Jan. A.D. 705 (alias[4] 706.) Dachonna of Daire,[5] [705.]
l Ossene, son of Gallust, abbot of Cluain-mic-Ui-Nois,
t. Bruide,[6] son of Derili, dies. Conchobar, son of
elduin, King of Cinel-Coirpri, was slain. Cellan the
se, son of Sechnasach,[7] died.

Kal. Jan. A.D. 706. Conodar of Fobhar[8] died. Mur- [706.]
of Indrechtach, son of Dunchad Muirsce.[9] Fergal
of Maelduin, and Fergal son of Loingsech, and Conall
nn, King of Cinel-Coirpri, slew him. Bec Ua Dun-
da,[10] was slain. Coibdenach,[11] bishop of Ard-sratha,
ted. Two earthquakes[12] in one week, in the month of
cember, in the northern part of Ireland. The 'bachall'[13]
Becc Bairche. Death of Colman, descendant of

Of Sechnasach.—Seċuꞅaıġ, A.

Conodar of Fobhar.—Conodar
s abbot of Fobhar, or Fobhar-
chin, now Fore, co. Westmeath.

Dunchad Muirsce. — Dunchad,
o was King of Connaught, was
led "Muirsce," from having lived,
been fostered, in Muirisc, a district
the north of the bar. of Tireragh,
Sligo. See above under the year
2.

[10] *Bec Ua Dunchada.*—Bec, grand-
, or descendant (*nepos*) of Dunchad.
it it is uncertain who this Dunchad
s.

[11] *Coibdenach.*—Written coıꝺbenac
A. and B.; but "Coivdenach" in
ar. 49, which is nearer the correct
rm "Coibdenach," as the name is
nerally written.

[12] *Earthquakes.* — Teꞃꞃımotuꞅ,

[13] *Bachall.*—This is for "baculum."
Clar. 49 has "the Crostaf [Cross-
staff] of Becc Bairche." The entry
means that Becc Bairche, assumed
the pilgrim's staff; in other words,
became a pilgrim. The *Four Masters*,
under the year 704, state that he
died on his pilgrimage 12 years afterwards. In the list of the Kings of
Ulad in the *Book of Leinster*, p. 41,
col. 3, Becc Bairche, who is stated
there to have reigned 24 years, is
said to have "died in pilgrimage (éc
i n-ailithri). In his Ed. of the
Ann. Ult., at this year (note 1),
O'Conor gives much unnecessary information on the subject of penance.
This Becc Bairche, who was a famous
character in Irish History, is referred
to above under the years 673 and
678.

Colmain aui Suibni. Slogaḋ Congaile filii Fergusa for Laigniu. Dunchad principatum Iae tenuit.

.b. Kl. Ianair. Anno domini dcc.° iii.° Cass Cuarani rex Cruiṫne iugulatus est. Bouina strages iterum incendit. Croen filius Maroit mortuus est.

Kl. Ianair. Anno domini dcc.° iiii.° Bellum dolo in compo Eilni, ubi iugulati sunt Leṫlabar mac Eċḋaċ, Cúallaiḋ, ocus Cudinaisc. Bellum Selggae in fortuaṫaiḃ Laigen, contra nepotes Cennselaiġ, in quo ceciderunt .ii. filii Ceallaiġ Cualann, Fiaċra et

Fol. 27ab. Fiannaṁail, et Luirgg cum Britonibus Ceallaiġ, et post paululum Coirpri mac Concoluinn iugulatus est. Maeldoborcon espcop Cille daro pausauit. Bellum for Orcaib, in quo filius Artablair iacuit. Pestis que dicitur baccach cum uentris profluuio in Hibernia. Macnio mac Duiḃdainber moritur. Iugulatio Conaill mic Feradaiġ.

---

[1] *Congal.*—The King of Ireland at the time.

[2] *Dunchad.*—This entry is a little out of place, as Dunchad did not become abbot of Ia (or I-Colum-Cille) until A.D. 710. See Reeves' *Adamnan*, p. 379.

[3] *Cucuarain.*—Cass cuarain, A., B. The *Four Masters*, at A.D. 706, say that Cucuarain was "King of the Cruithni (*i.e.*, the Picts of Dalaraide, in Antrim), and the Ulaid," and that the name of his slayer was Fionnchu Ua Ronain. The *Chron. Scot.* (704) agrees with the *Four Mast.*, except as to the name of Cucuarain's destroyer, whom it calls "Finchu Ua Rebain." In the list of the Kings of Ulad contained in the *Book of Leinster*, p. 41, col. 3, "Cuchuain" (as the name is represented in the Facsimile), is stated to have been 'son of Dungal," to have reigned two years, and to have been slain by one "Scandal Find Ua Redain of the Dalaraide." Elsewhere in the latter authority, however (p. 25, col. 1), the same person is described as Cucuárain ri Ulad 7 Cruthentuaithe ("Cuchuarain, King of Ulad and Pictland"). The name of Cucuarain is correctly included in the list of the Kings of Ulad in Reeves' *Eccl. Antiqq.*, p. 354, where the length of his reign is given as five years.

[4] *Battle of Dolo.*—"Bellum Dolo," in A., B., and Clar. 49. The *Four Mast.*, at 707, have cath dola ("battle of *Dola*"). But the *Chron. Scot.* (705) has caṫ maiġe ele per dolum ("Battle of Magh-Ele, through treachery").

[5] *Magh-Elni.* — "Magh-Ele," in *Four Mast.*, and *Chron. Scot.* This was the name of a plain on the east side of the River Bann, about Coleraine, in the co. Antrim. See Reeves'

bline. A hosting of Congal,[1] son of Fergus, upon the nstermen. Dunchad[2] held the government of Ia.

Kal. Jan. A.D. 707. Cucuarain, King of the Cruithni,[3] [707.] BIS.
s slain. A great cattle-mortality again raged. Croen, of Masot, dies.

Kal. Jan. A.D. 708. The battle of Dolo[4] in Magh- [708.]
ii,[5] in which were slain Lethlabar son of Echaidh, -allaidh, and Cudinaisc. The battle of Selga[6] in the ders of Leinster,[7] against the Ui-Cennselaigh, in which re slain two sons of Cellach Cualann, Fiachra and nnamhail, and Luirgg[8] with Cellach's Britons; and er a little time Coirpri, son of Cucoluinn, was slain. eldoborcon, bishop of Kildare, rested. A battle against Orkneys, in which the son of Artablár was slain. e plague which is called 'baccach,'[9] with dysentery,[10] in land. Macnio, son of Dubh-da-inber, dies. The ling of Conall, son of Feradach.

. *Antiqq.*, p. 330, and O'Donovan's r *Mast.* (A.D. 557, note *i*, and 707, *m*).

Selga.—Selga, or Selggae (as the e is written in the MS. A.), is the t. form of ꞅelᵹ, "hunting," ace." O'Donovan states (*Four t.*, A.D. 707, note *n*), that Selgge "the name of a place near Glen- ugh, in the county of Wicklow." next note.

In the borders of Leinster.—In tuaċaiḃ laiᵹen, A., B. Trans- l "in the outwarde parte of ister," in Clar. 49. In the list of Kings of Leinster in the *Book of ster* (p. 39, col. 2), the death of namail son of Maeltuili, King of Province (sl. 679, *supra*), is ed to have occurred i caṫ aire ꞅelᵹa . . . . i tuaṫaib breᵹ, "in the battle Life, or Selga, ... he borders of Brega." The *For- tuatha of Leinster* comprised that part of the present county of Wicklow containing Glendalough and the Glen of Imail.

[8] *And Luirgg.*—et luirgg, A., B., and Clar. 49. Evidently used as a proper name. But nothing seems known respecting such a person. The corresponding passage in the *Ann. Four Mast.* (707) is 7 araill do ḃretnuiḃ tangatar hi ꞅochraide Ceallaiġ, "and some of the Britons who had joined Cellach's army." Ceallach Cualann, who was ancestor of the Ui-Cellaigh-Cualand, a tribe seated in the north of the present co. Wicklow, was rather a famous person in his time. See at the year 703 *supra*; and again at 714, where his death is recorded.

[9] *Baccach, i.e.*, "Lameness."

[10] *With dysentery* (or *diarrhœa.*)—cum uentriꞅ ꞅrofluuio, A., B. ꞅrofluxio, Clar. 49.

Kl. Ianair. Anno domini dcc.° ix.° Conamail mac Failḃi abbas Iae pausat. Combustio Cille daro. Congal .i. Congal Ċinn maġair mac Fergusa Fanad, [mic Domnaill mic Aeda mic Ainmireċ mic Setna mic Fergusa cinnfoda] mic Conaill gulban, id est rex Temoriae, subita morte perit (.i. do ḃiḋg). Immbairecc apud genus Comġaill, ubi .ii. filii Nectain mic Doirgarto iugulati sunt. Oengus mac Maeleanfaid insci iugulatus est. Fiacra mac Dungaile apud Cruiṫne iugulatus est. Colman mac Seċnusaiġ abbas Loṫri moritur. Iustinianus secundus cum Tiberio filio annis .vi. regnauit. Fergal mac Maileduin regnare incipit.

Kl. Ianair. Anno domini dcc.° x.° Faelan nepos Silni moritur. Bellum nepotum Meiṫ ubi Tnuṫaċ mac Moċloingse rex nepotum Meiṫ, et Cuoi filius Aeḋo filii Dluṫaig, ceciderunt. Strages Pictorum in campo Manonn apud Saxones, ubi Finnguine filius

---

[1] *Son of Domnall*, &c.—The original of the clause within the brackets is not in A., B., or Clar. 49. Its omission would leave the entry very inaccurate, as Congal, King of Ireland, who died in A.D. 709, would appear described as the grandson (!) of Conall Guiban, whose death is recorded in the *Ann. Four Mast.*, under A.D. 465. The geneal. matter supplied has been taken from the authentic pedigree sources.

[2] *Of a fit.*—do ḃiḋg. Not in B., nor in Clar. 49. In the *Book of Leinster*, p. 25, col. 1, Congal is stated to have died do bidg oen uaire "of a fit of one hour." Keating, in his brief account of the reign of Congal of Cenn-Maghair, states that the King's sudden death was in consequence of his having burned Kildare, idir cill et túaiṫ, "both church and territory." The burning of Kildare is the second entry under this year.

[3] *Cinel-Comghaill.*—Genus Comġaill. The descendants of Comghall (4th King of the Scotch Dalriads), whose death is recorded above at the year 537. The Cinel-Comghaill gave name to the district now known as Cowall, in Argyllshire, in Scotland.

[4] *Dargart.*—Probably the "Dargart son of Finguine," referred to above under the year 685, who was the fifth in descent from Comghall, *a quo* "Cinel-Comghaill;" and who is mentioned again at 711 *infra*.

[5] *Maelanfaid 'insci.'*—Maelanfaid 'of the speech.' Clar. 49 has "Maelanfa *in Sci*," as if to convey that Maelanfaid had been slain in Skye. O'Conor, with his usual inaccuracy, misprints "Maelanfaid insci" *Maelean for insci*, and translates *for insci* "supra insulam"!

al. Jan. A.D. 709. Conamail, son of Failbhe, abbot [709.]
ı, rests. The burning of Kildare. Congal, *i.e.*, Congal
enn-Maghair, son of Fergus of Fanad [son[1] of Domnall,
of Aedh, son of Ainmire, son of Sedna, son of Fergus
ı-foda], son of Conall Gulban, *i.e.*, King of Tara, died
lenly (*i.e.*, of a fit).[2] A battle among the Cinel-
ghaill,[3] in which two sons of Nectan, son of Dargart,[4]
e slain. Oengus, son of Maelanfaid '*insci*,'[5] was slain.
hra, son of Dungal, was slain by the Cruithni. Colman,
of Sechnasach, abbot of Lothra, dies. Justinianus[6] II.,
ı his son Tiberius, reigned six years. Fergal, son of
lduin, begins to reign.[7]

al. Jan. A.D. 710. Faelan Ua Silni[8] dies. The [710.]
le of the Ui-Meith,[9] wherein were slain Tnuthach,[10]
of Mochloingse, King of the Ui-Meith, and Curoi, son
edh,[11] son of Dluthach. A slaughter of the Picts in
h-Manonn,[12] by the Saxons, wherein Finnguine son of

---

e copies this entry (*Chron. Picts Scots*, p. 353), as if he thought "Oengus, son of Maelanfaid," ı Scottish character, apparently ut having taken the trouble of aining whether he was Scottish ish.

ustinianus.—Iurτιanur, A., B. leath of Justinian II., Emperor e East, is generally referred to 711.

egins to reign; *i.e.*, as King of ıd. The death of Fergal is led under the year 721 *infra*. herty refers the accession of l to the year 711. *Ogygia*, 2.

aelan Ua Silni; *i.e.*, Faelan, son (nepos) or descendant of

i-Meith.—There were two tribes is name descended from Muire-*Meth* ("the fat"), son of Imchad, son of Colla Da-crioch; one of which gave name to the district called Ui-Meith-Tire (in the present co. Monaghan), and the other Ui-Meith-Mara (in the co. Louth). The sept of Ui-Meith-Mara is probably here referred to. See O'Donovan's ed. of *Leabhar na g-Ceart*, p. 148, note *a*.

[10] *Tnuthach*.—This name, which signifies "envious," was originally written Tuᴅaċ in A., but has been corrected by an old hand to Tnuṫaċ (as in B). Clar. 49 has *Tudach*.

[11] *Aedh*.—This is the Aedh, son of Dluthach, whose obit is given above at the year 700.

[12] *Magh-Manonn*. — See note 8, under the year 581 *supra*, on Manonn. This battle is recorded in the *Anglo-Sax. Chron.* at 710, thus: "The same year the aldorman Beohrtfrith fought against the Picts between Hæfe and Cære."

Deileroiṫ immatura morte iacuit. Cennfaelad abbas Fobair moritur. Congressio Britonum et Dal Riati for Loirgg ecclet, ubi Britones devicti. Murgal filius Noe moritur. Coscrad nepotum Neill ic Cuinciu Robairgi, in quo ceciderunt filius Condi et filii Dibċeini. Diccolan sapiens 7 Ultan mac Cummeni epscop telcae Olaind mortui sunt.

b. Kl. Ianair. Anno domini dcc.° x.° i.° Coeddi episcopus Iae pausat. Combustio Tairpirt boitter. Congal mac Doirgarto moritur. Obsessio Aberte apud Selbaċum. Bellum inter duos nepotes Aeḋo Slane, in quo Mane mac Neill iugulatus est. Flann mac Aeḋo mic Dluṫaiġ victor fuit. Ulaiṫ prostrati, ubi Dubṫaċ filius Becce Bairċe occubuit. Duo filii Feraḋaiġ mic Maeleduin in cede generis Loegaire perierunt. Bellum apud Laginenses desemiores, ubi Bran nepos Maeleduin et filius eius ceciderunt

---

[1] *On Lorgg-ecclet.*—for Loirgg ecclet, A., B. O'Conor, however, wrongly prints *forloingg ecclet*, and translates "in navibus apud Cleti."

[2] *Destruction.* — Coscrad. This word is represented by "fight" in Clar. 49.

[3] *Cuince-Robairgi.*—Not identified. In the *Táin bó Cúailnge* (*Leb. na hUidre*, p. 65*a*) there is mention of a place called cuince (explained as a sliab, or "mountain"), in the district of Cuailnge, in the north of the present co. Louth. The name of Quin, in the co. Clare, was anciently written "Cuinche."

[4] *Were slain.*—cecidit, A. ceci, B.

[5] *Telach-Olaind.*—Incorrectly written Teclae Olaind (for Telcae Olaind, the genit. form), in A and B. Sometimes written Tulach-Ualann, and Telach-Ualand (as at 730, *infra.*) Not identified. See O'Donovan's *Four Mast.*, A.D. 709, note *s.*

[6] *Tairpert-boitter.*—Dean Reeves thinks that this was probably the Tarbert which gave name to East and West Lochs Tarbert, the inlets of the sea which nearly insulate Cantyre on the north. *Adamnan*, p. 380, note *l.* It is again referred to at 730, *infra.*

[7] *Doergart.*—Apparently the "Dargart" mentioned above at 709.

[8] *Aberte.*—"Traces of the old castle of *Dunaverty*, standing on a precipitous rock nearly surrounded by the sea, are to be seen on Dunaverty Bay, at the S.E. extremity of Cantyre, opposite Sanda." Reeves' *Adamnan*, p. 380, note *m.*

[9] *Niall.* — This Niall was son of Cernach (ob. 663, *supra*), son of Diarmait, son of Aedh Slanè (sl. 603 *supra*). The entry of this event is

eileroth, was untimely slain. Cennfaeladh, abbot of ɔbhar, dies. An encounter of Britons and Dalriata, on ɔrgg-ecclet,[1] where the Britons were defeated. Murgal, n of Noe, dies. The destruction[2] of the Ui-Neill at uince-Robairgi,[3] in which the son of Condi, and the ns of Dibhcein, were slain.[4] Diccolan the Wise, and ltan, son of Cummeni, bishop of Telach-Olaind,[5] died.

Kal. Jan. A.D. 711. Coeddi, bishop of Ia, rests. The urning of Tairpert-boitter.[6] Congal, son of Doergart,[7] ies. The siege of Aberte,[8] by Selbach. A battle be-ween two descendants of Aedh Slanè, in which Mane, son Niall,[9] was slain. Flann, son of Aedh, son of Dluthach as victor. The Ulidians were overthrown, where Dub-ach, son of Becc Bairche,[10] was slain. The two sons of 'eradach, son of Maelduin, perished in the slaughter of e Cinel-Loeghaire.[11] A battle among the Lower Lein-ermen,[12] wherein Bran Ua Mailduin and his son were [711.] BIS.

---

accurately given by the *Four Mast.* 'IO), who represent Niall as having en slain in the conflict. But Niall ad been dead very many years at at date.

[10] *Becc Bairche.*—King of Ulidia. ee above, under the year 706, where ecc Bairche is stated to have as-med the pilgrim's staff; or, in other ords, gone on a pilgrimage. His bit is entered at 717 *infra.*

[11] *Cinel-Loeghaire.*—There were two ibes known by this name, both des-ended from Loeghaire (ob. 462 *pra*), monarch of Ireland in St. atrick's time; the one, called Cinel-oeghaire of Midhe (or Meath), and e other, Cinel-Loeghaire of Brega r Bregia, in the S. part of the pre-nt co. Meath). The former tribe ould seem to be here referred to. n the Pedigree of the Cinel-Loeg-aire contained in the *Book of Leinster* the Feradach mentioned in the fore-going entry is set down as seventh in descent from said King Loeghaire, and Cainelban (from whom the terri-tory of the Cinel-Loeghaire of Midhe was sometimes called O'Coindelbhain's country) as fifth in descent from Feradach. See O'Donovan's ed. of *O'Dubhagain*, note 14 (p. iv.)

[12] *Among the Lower Leinstermen.*— apud Laginenses deciores (for deteriores), A., B. "Apud Low Leinster," Clar. 49. The *Four Mas-ters* (712) have la Laignib desgabair ("by the South Leinstermen"). Deteriores is obviously a mistake for dexteriores, or 'Southern.' In a copy of Tigernach contained in the MS. H. 3, 18, Trin. Coll, Dublin, the reading is Lagenensis dexterioris, over which Roderick O'Flaherty has written Laigin desgabair.

Dubgualai abbas Glinne da loċa perit. Dluṫaċ mac Fiṫcellaiġ igne uritur. Beda fecit librum magnum.

Kl. Ianair. Anno domini dcc.° x.° ii.° Baetan episcopus Insolae uaccae albae obiit. Faelbeus modicus abbas Cluana mic U Nois pausat. Filia Ossu in monasterio Ild moritur. Ciniod mac Derili et filius Maiṫgernain iugulati sunt. Dorbeni Kaṫedram Iae obtinuit, et .u. mensibus peractis in primatu, .u. Kl. Nouimbris die sabbati obiit. Cormac mac Ailello rex Muman in bello iugulatus est. Tolargg filius Drostain ligatur apud fratrem suum Nectan regem. Cuċercae rex Ossraigi moritur. Seċnusaċ rex H. Mane mortuus est.

Kl. Ianair. Anno domini dcc.° x.° iii.° Bellum imeseċ in campo Singittae uc Bilin ṫeneḋ in Assal, ubi Flann filius Aiḋo mic Dluṫaiġ et Dubduin nepos Becce ceciderunt in altera congressione belli, et Colgu et Aeḋ mac Dermato in prima congressione belli interfecti sunt. Dun Ollaiġ construitur apud

---

[1] *Beda.*—The original of this entry, which is not in Clar. 49, is part of the text in B. A marg. note in A., in an old hand, reads Beda librum magnum hoc anno fecit.

[2] *Inis-bo-finne.* — Insola uaccae albae; *i.e.*, "Island of the White Cow." Now Boffin (or Bophin) Island, or Inishbofin, off the S.W. coast of the co. Mayo.

[3] *Daughter of Ossu.* — Ælflæd, daughter of Oswiu (or Oswy), King of Bernicia (ob. 670, *supra*).

[4] *Monastery of Ild.*—The monastery of St. Hilda, at Whitby in Yorkshire, of which Ælflæd was abbess. See Lappenberg's *History of England*, I., 289, and Bede's *Eccl. Hist.*, III., chap. xxiv.

[5] *Ciniod.*—This name would now be written "Kenneth." Ciniod was apparently the brother of Brude, son of Derilè (705, *supra*), King of the Picts of Scotland.

[6] *Obtained.*—obtenuit, A. O'Donovan erroneously observes (*Four Mast.*, at A.D. 713, note *f*), that the obit of Dorbeni "is not in the Annals of Ulster." The correct date is 713, according to the criteria. See Reeves' *Adamnan*, p. 381, note *n*.

[7] *Slain in battle.*—In a list of the Christian Kings of Munster contained in the *Book of Leinster* (p. 320, col. 1), Cormac, son of Ailill, son of Maenach (*supra*, 661), is stated to have been slain, after a reign of nine years, in the battle of Carn-Feradhaigh, gained over the *Deis Tuaiscert* (or "Northern Deis.") See above,

in. Dubhguala, abbot of Glenn-da-lacha, perished. uthach, son of Fithchellach, was burned by fire. Beda[1] nposed a great book.

Kal. Jan. A.D. 712. Baetan, abbot of Inis-bo-finne,[2] ed. Failbhe Bec, abbot of Cluain-mic-U-Nois, rests. ie daughter of Ossu[3] dies in the monastery of Ild.[4] niod,[5] son of Derilè, and the son of Mathgernan, were in. Dorbeni obtained[6] the chair of Ia, and having ent five months in the primacy, died on Saturday, the th of the Kalends of November. Cormac, son of Ailill, ng of Munster, was slain in battle.[7] Tolargg, son of rostan, was fettered by his brother, King Nectan. icherca, King of the Osraighi, dies. Sechnasach, King Ui-Maine, died. [712.]

Kal. Jan. A.D. 713. A battle, '*imesech*,'[8] in Magh-ngittae,[9] at Bile-thenedh in Assal,[10] wherein Flann, son Aedh, son of Dluthach, and Dubhduin descendant of ecc, were slain in the latter encounter of the battle; id Colgu, and Aedh son of Diarmait, were killed in the st encounter. Dun-Ollaigh[11] is constructed by Selbach. [713.]

A.D. 626, where Carn-Feradhaigh said to be in *Cliu*, a district in the . Limerick. For the situation of the *is* or *Deise*, see O'Donovan's *Suppl. O'Reilly's Dictionary*, under *Deise* *ig*. In the *Annals of the Four asters* (710), this battle is stated to ve been gained *by* the Northern is, and Cormac is incorrectly said have been the son of Finghin, who is really Cormac's grandfather.

[8] '*Imesech.*' — A variation of the ish adv. *fa-sech* (*fo-sech*, or *mo-h*), meaning "about," "by turns," lternately." O'Conor translates it atrox"; Clar. 49, has "Bellum out Essech." But both are wrong. battle *imesech* would mean a "free ght."

[9] *Magh-Singittae.*—The "Plain of Singitta." Not identified. O'Conor incorrectly prints "in campo *Ettech-gittea*."

[10] *Bile-thenedh in Assal.*—O'Donovan says that Bile-thenedh is now represented by "Billywood," in the par. of Moynalty, bar. of Lower Kells, co. Meath. *Four Mast.*, A.M. 3503, note *k*. The old church of Dulane, situated a little to the north of the town of Kells, was on the *Slige-Assail* (or "Road of Assal"), an ancient road which led westwards from Tara, through Westmeath to the Shannon.

[11] *Dun-Ollaigh.*—See above, at the year 700, where the destruction of Dun-Ollaigh by the same Selbach, 18th King of Dalriada, is recorded.

Selbaċum. Alen daingen distruitur. Fogartaċ .h. Cernaiġ de regno expulsus est, in Britanniam iuit. Corcrad .i. Garbsalċa immMidiu, in quo cecidit Forbasaċ nepos Congaile, rex .h. Failgi, apud uiros Mide, uno die et bellum predictum. Siccitas magna. Bellum inter duos 'filios Becce Bairċe et filium Bresail regem nepotum Eċdaċ, in quo uictores erant filii Becce. In hoc anno interfecti sunt peregrini apud Mumnenses, id est, in Clarainеċ cum omni familia sua. Nox lucida in autumno.

Fol. 27bb Kl. Ianair. Anno domini dcc.° x.° iiii.° Ceallaċ Cualann rex Lagen, Flann febla (mac Sgannlain, do iḃ Meiṫ) abbas Aird maċae, Cilleni episcopus, abbas Fernann, mortui sunt. Iugulatio Murċaḋo mic Dermato filii [Airmedaiċ] ceci, regis nepotum Neill. Aeḋ duḃ rex nepotum Fidgente, Flaiṫnia mac Colggen, sapiens, et Mochonno ċuerni, dormierunt. Sloġaḋ Murchada mic Brain du Chaissil.

.b. Kl. Ianair. Anno domini dcc.° x.° u.° Iugulatio regis Saxonum, Osrit filii Aldfriṫ nepotis Ossu.

---

[1] *Alen-daingen.*—The building of this place is recorded above at the year 702, where see note. The ignorant "translator" of Clar. 49, taking this entry as a continuation of the entry preceding it, joins both together, and out of them makes "Dun olla construitur apud Selvacum, and destroyed by his daughter Alena"!

[2] *Ua Cernaigh.*—"Grandson of Cernach." Fogartach, afterwards King of Ireland, (see 715 and 723 *infra*), was son of Niall, son of Cernach Sotal (ob. 663 *supra*).

[3] *Garbsalach.* — Not identified The name would signify the "Rough-dirty" (or the "Dirty-rough") place. Though evidently the name of a place, O'Conor understood *Garbsalach* to mean "fœda contentio."

[4] *Descendant.*—nepos. Clar. 49 has "nephew," which is incorrect, as in this Chronicle nepos is used to represent "grandson," or "descendant."

[5] *Becc Bairche.* — See above, at A.D. 706.

[6] *Pilgrims.* — perigrini, A., B. Clar. 49 reads "In hoc anno interfecti peregrini apud Mumnenses, that is called Clarainech, cum omni sua familia." The Annals of Clonmacnoise state (710) that "there were certain pilgrims killed by the Mounstermen, viz., Clarinach with all his family."

Alen-daingen[1] was demolished. Fogartach Ua Cernaigh,[2] was banished from the Kingdom, and went into Britain. The slaughter of Garbsalach[3] in Midhe, in which Forba-ach descendant[4] of Congal, King of the Ui-Failghe, was lain by the men of Midhe, on the same day as the afore-aid battle. Great drought. A battle between two sons of Becc Bairche,[5] and the son of Bresal, King of Ui-Echach, n which the sons of Becc were victors. In this year pilgrims[6] were slain by Munstermen, viz., the Claraineach, with his whole family. A bright night in Autumn.

Kal. Jan. A.D. 714. Cellach Cualann,[7] King of Lein- [714.]
ster; Flann Febla, son[8] of Scannlan, of the Ui-Meith, abbot of Armagh, and Cilleni, bishop, abbot of Ferna, died. The killing of Murchadh, son of Diarmait, son of [Airmedach] Caech,[9] King of the Ui-Neill.[10] Aedh Dubh, King of the Ui-Fidhgente; Flaithnia the Wise, son of Colggu, and Mochonna Cuerni,[11] slept. The hosting of Murchadh, son of Bran,[12] to Cashel.

Kal. Jan. A.D. 715. The killing of the King of the [715.] BIS.
Saxons, Osrid,[13] son of Aldfrid, grandson of Oswiu. Garnat

---

[7] *Ceallach Cualann.* — See above, nder the year 703.

[8] *Son.*—The original of this clause added in the margin in A., where lann is called "bishop" of Ard-acha (or Armagh). It is not in lar. 49. The words mac Sgonn-ain ("son of Sgannlan"), are part the text in B., in which do ib eit ("of the Ui-Meith") is inter-ned in the original hand.

[9] *[Airmedach] Caech.* — "Airme-ach the Blind" (or "One-eyed.") he MSS. A. and B., which omit the ame of Airmedach, have ceci for ceci. The *Four Mast.* (713) state at Murchadh was chief of the Ui-eill of Clann-Colmain. But in the ook of Leinster (p. 42, col. 1), his name occurs in the list of the Kings of Uisnach. See under A.D. 688 *supra.*

[10] *Ui-Neill.*—See last note.

[11] *Mochonna Cuerni.*—The *Four Mast.* (713) write *Mochonna Cluana Airdne* ("Mochonna of Cluain-Air-dne.") The festival of Mochonna is given under Sept. 30 in the *Martyr. of Donegal.* But the situation of Cluain-Airdne is not known to the Editor.

[12] *Murchadh, son of Bran.*--King of Leinster. His death is entered at the year 726 *infra.*

[13] *Osrid.*--King of the Northum-brians, and son of Aldfrid, son of Oswiu (ob. 670. *supra*). See the *Anglo-Sax. Chron.*, A.D. 716.

Garnat filius Deileroiṫ moritur. Foġartaċ nepos Cernaiġ iterum regnat. Pasċa commutatur in Eoa ciuitate. Faelċu mac Dorbeni Kaṫedram Columbae .lxx. iiii. aetatis sue anno, in .iiii. Kl. Septimbris, die sabbati, suscepit. Obitus Celi Tigernaiġ abbatis Cluana auis. Flann Foirbṫe mac Fogartaiċ mortuus est. Mors Artbrain mic Maileduin.

Kl. Ianair. Anno domini dcc.° x.° iii.° Dunchad mac Cinnḟaelaḋ abbas Iae obiit. Etulb mac Eculb obiit. Condalach mac Conaing, rex nepotum Crumtain, iugulatus est. Expulsio familiae Iae trans dorsum Brittanniae a Nectano rege. Congressio Dalriati et Brittonum in lapide qui uocatur Minuirc, et Britones deuicti sunt. Commixtio agonis Talten la Fogartaċ, ubi ceciderunt filius Rubai et filius Duibḟleiḃe.

Kl. Ianair. Anno domini dcc.° x.° iiii.° Filius Cuidine rex Saxonum moritur. Becc Bairċe obiit. Bellum Cenindro, ubi Tuaṫal nepos Faelċon, et Cellaċ diaṫraiḃ, et Gormgal mac Aeḋa mic Dluṫaiġ,

---

[1] *Fogartach.*—There is some confusion regarding the length of Fogartach's reign. According to the *Ann. Four Mast.* (719), he was only one year King of Ireland. O'Flaherty, who gives 722 as the date of Fogartach's accession, gives him a year and some months. *Ogygia*, p. 432. Fogartach's expulsion from the Kingdom (*de regno*) is noticed above under the year 713, and his return from his exile in Britain is mentioned by the *Four Mast.* at 714. If he "reigned again" in 715, as above stated, he must have reigned as the rival of Fergal son of Maelduin, who was King of Ireland, according to these Annals, from 709 to the death of Fergal in 722 (*infra*, 721), when Fogartach became undisputed monarch.

[2] *Easter is changed.*—comotatur, A., B. Regarding this change in the observance of Easter, see Reeves' *Adamnan*, p. 28, note.

[3] *Chair of Columba*, *i.e.*, the abbacy of Ia, or Iona.

[4] *Of his age.*—aetatis sue, B. sue is omitted in A. Clar. 49 agrees with B.

[5] *Flann Foirbthe.*—"Old Flan," Clar. 49. But *foirbthe* means "perfect," not "old."

[6] *Condalach, son of Conang.*—Clar. 49 has "Connalach son of *Crimthain*," but this is incorrect.

[7] *Dorsum Britanniæ.*—In Irish *Druim-Bretain*, the "Back (or Ridge)

son of Deleroth, dies. Fogartach,[1] grandson of Cernach, again reigns. Easter is changed[2] in the Monastery of Ia. Faelchu, son of Dorbeni, assumes the chair of Columba,[3] in the 74th year of his age,[4] on the 4th of the Kalends of September, on Saturday. Death of Celi-Tigernaigh, abbot of Cluain-eois. Flann Foirbthe,[5] son of Fogartach, died. Death of Artbran, son of Maelduin.

Kal Jan. A.D. 716. Dunchad, son of Cennfaeladh, [716.] abbot of Ia, died. Etulb, son of Etulb, died. Condalach son of Conang,[6] King of the Ui-Crimthainn, was slain. Expulsion of the community of Ia across Dorsum Britanniæ,[7] by King Nectan.[8] A meeting of the Dalriata and Britons, at the rock called Minuirc;[9] and the Britons were defeated. The disturbance[10] of the Fair of Tailtiu[11] by Fogartach, wherein the son of Ruba[12] and the son of Dubhsleibhe, were slain.

Kal. Jan. A.D. 717. The son of Cuidin,[13] King of the [717] Saxons, dies. Becc Bairche[14] died. The battle of Cenannus,[15] wherein fell Tuathal grandson of Faelchu, and Cellach Diathraibh, and Gormgal, son of Aedh son

---

of Britain." The great mountain chain dividing Perthshire and Argyll, terminating in the Grampian Hills. Also called *Druim-Alban*. (Reeves' *Adamnan*, p. 64, note *a*.) Dr. O'Brien states that *Druim-Alban* was otherwise called *Braid-alban*. *Irish Engl. Dictionary*, voce *Drom-saileach*.

[8] *King Nectan*.—King of the Picts. The "Naiton" of Bede. *Eccl. Hist.*, V., 22.

[9] *Minuirc*.—This place has not been identified.

[10] *Disturbance*. — Comixtio, A., B. Clar. 49 reads "burning"!

[11] *Tailtiu*.—The genit. form is *Tailenn*, from which comes the present name of the place, *Teltown*, in the par. of the same name, bar. of Upper Kells, co. Meath, where there are some remarkable remains of antiquity.

[12] *Son of Ruba*.—The *Four Masters* (A.D. 715) have "Maelruba." But the *Frag. of Annals* say "the son of Maelruba," which is probably more correct. "Ruba" is not found as a proper name.

[13] *Son of Cuidin*.—This was evidently Cenred, son of Cuthwine, who succeeded Osrid (ob. 715 *supra*), as King of the Northumbrians, and died after a reign of two years.

[14] *Becc Bairche*.—See at the year 706 *supra*.

[15] *Battle of Cenannus*.—Ceninnso (genit. form of Cemnnas, for Cenannas, the ancient name of Kells, in the co. Meath).

et Aṁalngaiḋ .h. Conaing, et Fergal frater eius ceciderunt. Conall grant uictor erat, et Conall grant nepos Cernaiġ in fine duorum mensium post
Fol. 28aa. bellum interfectus est la Fergal mac Maeleduin. Cronan Ua Eoain abbas Lis moir moritur. Fiannamail nepos Boġaine mic Finn, insolae princeps Maige saṁ, et Dubduin nepos Faelain, episcopus, abbas Cluana iraird, Corpri mac Congaile cennfotai, ocus Ailill mac Finsnechti, iugulati sunt. Pluit frois melo for Oiṫin becc. Pluit frois sanguinis super fossam Laginarum. Inde uocatur Niall frosaċ, qui tunc natus est, mac Fergaile. Eclipsis lunae in plenilunio suo.

Kl. Ianair. (f. 7.) Anno domini dcc.° x.° uiii.° Airmedaċ mac Taiḋg, et Criċan rex nepotum mic Uais, iugulati sunt; et Ertuile mac Ferġusa guill iugulatus est. Drostan dairtaiġe quieuit i n-ard Breccain. Cuu dinerggo moritur. Tuibride .h. Dunchada iugulatus est. Congressio apud Lage-

---

[1] *Conall Grant, i.e.*, Conall "the grey."—He was the grandson of Cernach Sotal, whose obit. is given above at the year 663.

[2] *Fergal.*—King of Ireland. See under 721 *infra.*

[3] *Cronan Ua hEoain, i.e.*, "Cronan descendant of Eoan." The festival of this Cronan, abbot of Lismor Mochuda (Lismore, co. Waterford), is entered in the *Martyr. of Donegal* under the 1st of June. See Colgan's *Acta Sanctorum*, p. 303.

[4] *Inis-Maighe-Samh.* — Inishmacsaint, bar. of Magheraboy, co. Fermanagh. For insolae princeps maige saṁ, Clar. 49 has "primus Episcopus campi Saimh." But "princeps" is frequently used in these Annals to signify a superior or abbot of an ecclesiastical establishment. O'Conor, in his ed., incorrectly prints "*Maigi Samhin*" (for *Maigi Samh*), note [2], *sub an.*, and translates "Campi Solis"!

[5] *Congal Cennfota.*—Probably the Congal Cennfota, or "Congal Longhead," mentioned above at A.D. 673.

[6] *Othan becc.* — "Little Othan." Apparently a place near Othan-mor, or "Big Othan" (now Fahan, barony of Inishowen, co. Donegal.) O'Conor translates "supra genistas spinosas parvas"!

[7] *On the 'foss' of the Leinstermen.* — super fossam Laginarum. Translated "upon the borders of Leinster," in Clar. 49. The shower of blood is stated in the *Book of Leinster* (p. 274, *a*), to have fallen

Diuthach, and Amalgaidh, grandson of Conaing, and brother Fergal. Conall Grant[1] was victor. And iall Grant,[1] grandson of Cernach, was slain at the end two months after the battle, by Fergal,[2] son of Maeln. Cronan Ua hEoain,[3] abbot of Lis-mor, dies. nnamail, descendant of Boghaine, son of Finn, abbot Inis-Maighe-Samh,[4] and Dubhduin, descendant of ılan, bishop, abbot of Cluain-Iraird; Conri, son of ıgal Cennfota,[5] and Ailill, son of Finsnechta, were n. It rained a shower of honey upon Othan-becc.[6] rained a shower of blood upon the 'foss'[7] of the nstermen. Hence Niall 'Frosach,'[8] son of Fergal, ɔ was born then, was so called. An eclipse of the ɔn at its full.[9]

Kal. Jan. (Saturd.[10]) A.D. 718. Airmedach, son of lhg, and Crichan, King of Ui-Mic-Uais, were slain; l Ertuile, son of Fergus Goll, was slain. Drostan of oratory[11] rested in Ard-Breccain.[12] Cu-dimerggo dies. bride, descendant of Dunchadh, was slain. A battle ɔng the Leinstermen, in which Aedh, son of Cellach,[13] [718.]

;lenɒ Lagen (the "glen," or lley," of Leinster.)

Niall 'Frosach.'—"Niall of the vers," or "N. the Showery." se showers, with some variation heir number and character, are n noticed at the date of Niall ach's accession to the monarchy reland, A.D. 763 *infra*. In the *k of Leinster* (p. 25, col. 2) the vers—one of white silver, one of y, and one of wheat—are stated ave occurred *in the reign* of Niall sach, not at his birth or accession. y were probably meteoric phenoa.

At its full.—in plenilunio ſuo, B., and Clar. 49.

Saturday.—p. 7 (for "seventh day of the week"), added in *al. man.* in A. Not in B.

[11] *Drostan of the oratory.*—Ꝺꞃoꞅtain, A. Ꝺaiꞃtaiġe is the genit. form of ꝺaiꞃtech (variously written ꝺauꞃtech, ꝺuꞃtech, ꝺeꞃtech) which signifies an oratory, or house of penitence. Absurdly translated "manse" in Clar. 49, under the year 1116.

[12] *Ard-Breccain.*—Aꞃꝺ bꞃeccan, A. "Breccan's Height." Now Ardbraccan, co. Meath. The festival of the founder, St. Breccan, occurs at the 16th of July in the Calendar.

[13] *Cellach.*—This was Cellach Cualann, King of Leinster, whose obit is entered at the year 714 *supra*. See Shearman's *Loca Patriciana*, Geneal. Table at p. 138.

nenses ubi Aeḋ mac Ceallaiġ cecidit .i. bellum Finnubraċ. Bellum Finnglinne inter duos filios Ferchair fotti, in quo Ainfceallaċ iugulatus est die quintae feriae, iii. id. septimbris. Bellum maritimum Ardae nesbi, inter Dunchad m-becc cum genere Gabrain et Selbaċum cum genere Loairn, et uersum est super Selbaċum, prid. non. Septimbris (uel Octobris), die .iii. feriae, in quo quidam comites conruerunt. Iugulatio in da tigerna i Loċ hUaitne, .i. da mac Maele-foṫartaiġ, li a m-braṫair .i. Cremtann corraċ. Iugulatio familiae Suibne i n-Ard maċa. Aestas sicca.

.b Kl. Ianair. Anno domini dcc.° x.° ix.° Aestas pluuialis. Sinaċ insolo Croṫrann dormiuit. Murbruċt mar in mense Octobris. Teodorus anno .i.

Kl. Ianair. Anno domini dcc.° xx.° Dunchad becc rex Cinntire moritur. Terrimotus in Octimbre. Bellum inter Conachta et Corco Baiscinn, ubi cecidit

---

[1] *Finnabhair.*—This name would be pronounced Finner, Fennor, or Finure. The site of the battle was most probably Fennor, par. of Duneany, co. Kildare.

[2] *Finn-Glenn.*—Dean Reeves observes that there is a Finglen in Campsie in Stirlingshire, but that the place here mentioned seems to have been in Argyle, in the territory of Lorn. *Adamnan*, p. 381, note *r*.

[3] *Ferchar Fota*; *i.e.*, "Ferchar the Tall" (or "Long"), 15th King of the Scotch Dalriads (ob. 696 *supra*). The opponents in this battle were Ainfcellach 17th King of the Dalriads (who was slain therein), and his brother Selbach, 18th King, whose obit is given at the year 729 *infra*, and who is also mentioned under the years 700, 711, 713 and 722

[4] *The 6th.*—Interlined in *al. man.* in A. Not in B., or Clar. 49.

[5] *Ard-esbi.*—Not identified. It was apparently the name of some place on the S.W. coast of Scotland.

[6] *Dunchad Becc.*—"Dunchad (or Duncan) the Little." Called rex Cinn tire, or King of Cantyre, under the year 720 *infra*.

[7] *Or October.*—uel Octimbris, in orig. hand. in A. Octobris, B. Om. in Clar. 49.

[8] *Loch Uaithne.*—Lough Ooney, bar. of Dartry, co. Monaghan.

[9] *By their brother.*—Li a mbraṫair, A., B. "By their cossen." Clar. 49.

[10] *Suibhne.*—Apparently Suibhne, son of Crunnmael, bishop of Armagh, whose obit is given at the year 729 *infra*. The *Four Masters* have no reference to the outrage here alleged

slain, *i.e.*, the battle of Finnabhair.[1] The battle of n-glenn[2] between two sons of Ferchar Fota,[3] in which fcellach was slain, on Thursday, the 6th[4] of the Ides of tember. The marine battle of Ard-esbi,[5] between achad Becc[6] with the Cinel-Gabrain, and Selbach with Cinel-Loarn; and it was gained over Selbach, on the of the Nones of September (or October),[7] on Friday; which some nobles fell. The assassination of the two ls in Loch-Uaithne,[8] viz., two sons of Maelfothartaigh, their brother,[9] *i.e.*, Crimthann Corrach. The killing the family of Suibhne,[10] in Armagh. A dry[11] summer.

Kal. Jan. A.D. 719. A rainy summer. Sinach of s-Crothrann[12] slept. A great sea-burst[13] in the month October.[7] Theodore,[14] one year. [719.] BIS.

Kal. Jan. A.D. 720. Dunchad Becc,[15] King of Cenn-,[16] dies. An earthquake in October. A battle between men of Connaught and the Corca-Baiscinn,[17] in which [720.]

---

ve been committed on the family, ommunity, of Bishop Suibhne. her is it referred to in Tigernach's als, or in the *Chron. Scotorum*.

Dry.—ꞅiccaꞅ, A., B. *Sicca*, 49.

is-Crothrann—. Rectè *Inis-Cloth-* . An island in the expansion of Shannon called Loch-Ribh, or -Ree, and within the limits of o. Longford. It is said to have called Inis-Clothrann, from hra, the mother of Lugaid nderg, 109th King of Ireland, *ygia*, p. 289), and daughter of aid Feidlech (104th King, *ib.*, . The *Book of Leinster* (p. 124*b*) curious account of the killing of amous Queen Medb of Connaught, 'urbaide, son of King Conor Mac , the particulars of which remind trongly of the legend of William See O'Curry's *Manners and Customs*, Vol. 2, pp. 290-1. O'Donovan erroneously states (*Four Mast.*, 719, note *c*) that the foregoing entry "is not in the Annals of Ulster."

[13] *Sea-burst.*—Muꞃbꞃucc. Incorrectly printed *inmbracht* by O'Conor.

[14] *Theodore.*—By mistake for Theodosius (III.), Emperor of the East. For anno .i., O'Conor prints "anno primo," as in Clar. 49.

[15] *Dunchad Becc.*—See under the year 718.

[16] *Cenn-tire.* — "Land's Head." Cantyre, in Scotland.

[17] *Corca-Baiscinn.* — A sept descended from Cairbre-Baschain, son of Conaire II., King of Ireland (*Ogygia*, p. 322), which at the above date occupied the territory now represented by the baronies of Clonderlaw, Moyarta, and Ibrickan, in the S.W. of the co. Clare.

mac Talamnaig. Iugulatio Condinairc filii Roth[e]gtaig. Mors Mainaig abbatis Lainne Leri. Uastatio
Fol. 28ab. maighi Breg du Cathal mac Finnguine ocus do Murchad mac Brain. Mors Cuannai Rois eu. Innred Laighen la Fergal, ocus maidm inna boraime, ocus maidm na ggiallne Laghen fri Fergal mac Maileduin. Inmerach religiosus legem cum pace Christi super insolam Hiberniae constituit.

Kl. Ianair. Anno domini dcc.° xx.° i.° Maelrubai in Apur chrosan anno .lxxx. etatis. Colggu ri airde Lathrann iugulatus est. Maelcorgis o Druim ing, Bile mac Eilphin rex Alochluathe, moriuntur. Ferdacrich mac Congalaig obiit. Cuanan Cille deilge, ocus Dersis Dam inse nepos Collae, Cuana Dromma Cuilinn, Cillem loco Gerg, moriuntur. Feidlimid principatum Iae tenuit. Faelan Martarthaigi, Sidal droma Laidggin, mortui sunt. Bellum Almuine .iii. id.

---

[1] *Maenach.*—The gen. form, "Mainaigh," is incorrectly printed *Mamaig* by O'Conor. The festival of Maenach is given in the *Martyr. of Donegal*, at Oct. 17.

[2] *Lann-leri.*—Dunleer, co. Louth. See *Chron. Scot.* (ed. Hennessy), p. 136, note 2, and Todd's *Cogadh Gaedhel re Gallaibh*, Introd., p. xl., note 2. O'Donovan thought that Lann-leri was the place now called Lynn, in the barony of Fartullagh, co. Westmeath. (*Four Mast.*, A.D. 740, note *w*, and 825, note *g*.) But he was mistaken.

[3] *Ros-eo.*—The "wood of the yews." Now Rush, in the par. of Lusk, co. Dublin. See the *Felire of Oengus* at the 10th of April.

[4] *Exaction.*—A. and B. have maidm ("breach," "defeat"), which is evidently by mistake for naidm, "exaction," "binding," as in the *Chron. Scot.* and *Ann. Four Mast.* (717). Clar. 49 has "The praying of Leinster by M'Mailedain, and the slaughter of the Boroive, and the slaughter of Gialne in Leinster," which is very wrong. Regarding the '*borama*' (or 'cow-tribute'), see note 2 at p. 18 *supra*.

[5] *By.*— fri ("against"), A., B Clar. 49 has "by." The *Four Mast.* have la, "with," or "by"; which seems more correct.

[6] *Maelruba.*—See under the years 670 and 672, *supra*.

[7] *Apurcrossan*; otherwise written "Aporcrossau." See under A.D. 672, *supra*.

[8] *Maelcorgais.* — Apparently the Maelcorghais whose festival is noted at March 12th, in the *Martyr. of Donegal*.

[9] *Druim-ing.* — "Probably the place now called Dromin, situated

son of Talamhnach was slain. The assassination of linaisc, son of Rothe[c]tach. Death of Maenach,[1] ot of Lann-leri.[2] The laying waste of Magh-Bregh, Cathal son of Finnguine, and Murchad son of Bran. ıth of Cuanna of Ros-eo.[3] The wasting of Leinster by gal, and the exaction[4] of the 'borama,' and the ex- on[4] of the hostages of Leinster, by[5] Fergal, son of ɘlduin. Inmesach the Devout established a Law, h the peace of Christ, over the island of Ireland.

Kal. Jan. A.D. 721. Maelruba[6] [died] in Apurcrossan,[7] [721.] the 80th year of [his] age. Colgu, King of Ard- hrann, was slain. Maelcorgais,[8] of Druim-ing,[9] and ɘ, son of Elpin, King of Al-Cluathe,[10] died. Ferdacrich, of Congalach, died. Cuanan of Cill-deilge;[11] Derir Dam-inis,[12] a descendant of Colla; Cuana of Druim- linn,[13] and Cilleni of Loch-Gerg,[14] died. Fedhlimidh d the government of Ia. Faelan of Martartech,[15] Sidal Druim-Laidggin,[16] died. The battle of Almuin,[17] on the

---

Dunshanghlin, in the county of th." O'Donovan (*Four Masters*, 834, note *d*). The *Dinnsenchas* unt of Druim-ing (*Book of ster*, p. 194*b*) would lead one to k that its situation was much er to Dublin.

Al-Cluathe.—See note [12], at A.D. *supra.*

Cill-deilge.—Kildalkey, co. Meath.

Dam-inis.—Devenish, co. Fer- agh.

Druim-cuilinn. — Now Drum- n, bar. of Eglish, King's ıty.

Loch-Gerg.—This was the old e of Lough Derg, in which is ıted the Island of St. Patrick's gatory. See *Martyr. of Donegal*, d's ed.; App. to Introd., p. xl.

Martartech.—"House of Relics." The genit. case of the name, maрτaр- τaιᵹι, would be Anglicised "Mar- taray," "Martary," or "Martry;" forms which are represented in the Townland Index. (Census of Ireland, 1861.) But the particular place referred to here has not been identified.

[16] *Druim-Laidggin.*—Not identified.

[17] *Almuin.*—Now known as the Hill of Allen, a few miles to the north of the town of Kildare. Called *Almu Lagen* ("Almu of Leinster"), *Book of Leinster*, p. 202*a*. The Hill of Allen is celebrated in Irish legends as one of the residences of Finn Mac Cumhail, the Fingal of Macpherson's *Ossian*. This battle is entered in the *Ann. Four Mast.*, and *Chron. Scot.* under the year 718; but Tigernach notices it at 722, which is the proper year, as indicated by the criteria.

Decimbris die ui^e. feriae, in quo ceciderunt (.i. la Murchad mac m-Brain) Ferġal mac Maeleduin (mic Maileḟiṫriċ mic Aeḋa uairiḋnaiċ), ocus Conall menn rex generis Coirpri, Cloṫgno mac Colggen, Duḃdaċriċ, Flann mac Rogellnaiċ, Aeḋ Laigen mac Fiṫċellaiġ rex nepotum Maini, [Niall] mac Muirgiso, Nuaḋo mac Dunchada, Eicneċ mac Colggen rex Orientalium Fergal nepos Aitechtai.

Kl. Ianair. Anno domini dcc.° xx.° ii.° Combustio Clona mic U Nois. Mors Ailchon moristrech Buiti. Indrechtach mac Muiredaiġ, rex Conacht, moritur. Clericatus Selbaich. Sinaċ Tailten moritur.

.b. Kl. Ianair. Anno domini dcc.° xx.° iii.° Faelċu mac Dorbeni abbas Iae dormiuit. Cillenius Longus ei in principatum Iae successit. Cucongalt .h. Conmeldde, Murdobur granairc, moriuntur. Bellum Cinn Deilggden in quo cecidit Fogartaċ Ua Cernaiġ, mac Neill mic Cearrnaiġ hṡotail mic Diarmoda mic Aeḋa slaine. Cinaeḋ mac Irgalaiġ uictor erat. Cuimnles abbas Cluana mic Nois obiit. Iugulatio

---

[1] *The sixth.*—ui^a, A.

[2] *Son of Bran.*—mac Briain, A., B., and Clar. 49. But it should be mac Brain. The death of Murchad, son of Bran, King of Leinster, the victor in the battle of Almuin, is entered at the year 726, *infra.*

[3] *Son.*—The original of this clause, added in the margin in A., is in a gloss in B. It is not in Clar. 49.

[4] *Dubhdacrich.*—In the *Ann. Four Mast.* (718), and *Chron. Scot.* (id. an.), Dubhdacrich is stated to have been the son of Dubhdainbher, King of Ard-Cianachta (*supra* A.D. 687). For "Dubhdainbher," the *Frag. of Annals* (722) have "Dubhdabhairenn," which seems incorrect.

[5] [*Niall.*]—Supplied from *Frag. of Annals* (A.D. 722).

[6] *Airthera.*—The name of this district is still preserved in the baronies of Lower and Upper Orior, in the co. of Armagh. The names and number of the principal persons who were slain in the battle of Almuin are more fully given in the *Ann. Four Mast.*, and *Chron. Scot.* (718), and *Ann. Clonmacnoise* (720).

[7] *Death of Aelchu.*—Mors Ailchon. Ailchon is the genit. form of Aelchu. His name is not found in the ordinary lists of the abbots of Monasterboice.

[8] *Manistir-Buti.* — Monasterboice, co. Louth.

[9] *The entrance into religion of Selbach.*—Clericati (for clericatus, as in Tigernach), A., B. This entry has been misunderstood by

l of the Ides of December, the sixth[1] day of the
;, in which were slain (*i.e.*, by Murchad, son of
[2]), Fergal, son of Maelduin (son[3] of Maelfithrich, son
edh Uaridnach), and Conall Menn, King of Cinel-
ori; Clothgno, son of Colgu; Dubhdacrich;[4] Flann,
of Rogellnach; Aedh Laigen, son of Fithcellach,
g of Ui-Maine; [Niall[5]] son of Muirges; Nuadha, son
unchad; Eicnech, son of Colgu, King of the Airthera,[6]
Fergal Ua Aitechta.

d. Jan. A.D. 722. The burning of Cluain-mic-U- [722.]
. The death of Aelchu,[7] of Manistir-Buti.[8] Indrechtach,
of Muiredach, King of Connaught, dies. The entrance
religion of Selbach.[9] Sinach, of Tailtiu,[10] dies.

al. Jan. A.D. 723. Faelchu, son of Dorbeni, abbot of [723.] BIS.
fell asleep.' Cillene the Tall succeeded him in the
rnment of Ia. Cucongalt Ua Conmelde, Murdobur
ranasc,[11] died. The battle of Cenn-Delgden,[12] in which
Fogartach, grandson of Cernach, (son of Niall, son of
ach Sotail,[13] son of Diarmait, son of Aedh Slanè).
eth,[14] son of Irgalach, was victor. Cuinnles, abbot
luain-mic-Nois, died. The killing of Lethaithech,[15]

---

or (*Rerum Hib. Script.*, iv.,), and by O'Donovan (*Four* , A.D. 719, note *d*). The for- us blunderingly jumbles three into two: "*Indrechtach mac adaig* rex *Connacht* moritur icatu. *Selbaic Sianac Tailten* ch genealogus Taltinensis] r"! O'Donovan, who ought e known better (and in whose the *Four Mast*, the obit of ch of Tailtiu is given under ear 720) follows the incorrect g of O'Conor. The Annalist meant to convey that Selbach King of the Scotch Dalriads, 9, *infra*) assumed the religious or went on a pilgrimage, in ar 722 (=723 *Tig.*)

[10] *Tailtiu.* — Teltown, barony of Upper Kells, co. Meath.

[11] *Granasc.*—Not identified.

[12] *Cenn-Delgden.*—Another battle at the same place (which has not been identified) is referred to under the year 621 *supra*.

[13] *Cernach Sotail.*—His obit is entered above at A.D. 663.

[14] *Cinaeth.*—He was at the time Monarch of Ireland. His death in battle is recorded at the year 727, *infra*.

[15] *Lethaithech.*—In the *Chron. Scot.*, and *Ann. Four Mast.* (718), and *Frag. of Annals* (722), Lethaithech is stated to have been slain in the battle of Almuin (*supra*, A.D. 721).

Fol. 28ba. Leṫaiṫiġ mic Concarat. Caeċ scuili scriba Daire Calggaiḋ quieuit.

Kl. Ianair. Anno domini dcc.° xx.° iiii.° Cillenein nepos Collae, abbas Oṫnae, Alḋċu Doimliagg, moriuntur. Ailen mic Craiċ construitur. Simul filius Drust constringitur. Colman h-uamaċ scriba ardd Maċae, Rubin mac Connaḋ scriba Muṁan, filiusque Broccain o ṫaiġ ṫeille, qui magister bonus euangelii Christi erat, et Colman banban scriba Cille daro, omnes dormierunt. Mors Brain Muimniġ ocus Chairr Chobo. Luna tenebrosa et sanguinea.xuiii. Kl. Ianuarii. Conġal mac Maeleanfaiṫ. Brecc Fortrend, Oan princeps Ego, moriuntur.

Kl. Ianair. Anno domini dcc.° xx.° u.° Nectan mac Deirile constringitur apud Drust regem. Duchonna craibdeċ episcopus Condere mortuus est. Tolarggan maphan mortuus est. Iugulatio Craumṫain filii Cellaiġ in bello Bealaiġ licce immatura aetate.

---

[1] *Daire-Calgaidh.*—Derry, or Londonderry. See Reeves' *Adamnan*, page 160, note [r].

[2] *Othan.*—Othan-mor, or "Othan Mura" (Othan of St. Mura); now Fahan, near Lough Swilly, in the barony of Inishowen, co. Donegal. See under the years 717, *supra*, and 763, *infra*.

[3] *Damliag.*—Duleek, co. Meath.

[4] *Ailen M'Craich.*—"Mac Crach's Island." Not identified. It was probably the name of some island-fortress in Scotland. O'Conor rashly suggests the translation "Monasterium Insulæ *caorach*, seu ovis"? For construitur, as in A. and B.; Clar. 49 has "constringitur"!

[5] *Son of Drust.*—filius drus, A., B., and Clar. 49.

[6] *Colman Uamach.*—"Colman of the Cave" (*uaim*, a "cave"). The *Martyr. of Donegal*, at November 24, identifies Colman Uamach with Colman, son of Lenin [founder and abbot] of Cloyne, co. Cork; in Irish *Cluain uama* (the *cluain*, or meadow) of the cave. But they were different persons, as the death of Colman, son of Lenin, is given in the *Ann. Four Mast.* under A.D. 600. See Harris's *Ware*, p. 573, and Colgan's *Acta Sanctorum*, p. 539, note [15].

[7] *Tech-Theille.*—See at A.D. 671, *supra*, where the name is "Tech-Taille," or "House of Taille."

[8] *Colman Banban.*—The death of Colman Banban is entered in the *Ann. Four Mast.* at the year 720, and in the *Frag. of Annals* at 725. In the latter authority he is called *saoi* (or "sage") of Cill-Dara (Kil-

ı of Cucarat. Cacch-scuili, scribe of Daire-Calgaidh,[1] ›ted.

Kal. Jan. A.D. 724. Cilleneni Ua Colla, abbot of .han,[2] and Aldchu of Damliag,[3] died. Ailen M'Craich[4] built. Simul, son of Drust,[5] is fettered. Colman ımach,[6] scribe of Armagh; Rubin, son of Conna, scribe Munster, and the son of Broccan, of Tech-Theille,[7] who ıs a good master of Christ's Gospel, and Colman Banban,[8] ribe of Kildare—all 'fell asleep.' The death of Bran, Munsterman, and of Cass of Cobha.[9] A dark and ood-red[10] moon on the 18th of the Kalends of January. ›ngal, son of Maelanfaith; Brecc[11] of Fortrenn;[12] Oan, ıperior of Eg,[13] died. [724.]

Kal. Jan. A.D. 725. Nectan,[14] son of Derile, was put fetters by King Drust. Dachonna the Pious, bishop ' Condere, died. Tolarggan 'maphan'[15] died. The killg of Crimthan, son of Cellach,[16] in the battle of Belachıce, at an immature age. The repose of Manchein of [725.]

re). He was probably the same the "Banban *egnaidh*" ("Banban e Wise"), whose festival is given the *Martyr. of Donegal* at May 9. ıe *Felire of Oengus*, at 26 Nov., ›ntions a "Banban," bishop of ›ighlin, of the Corco-Duibhne, who not noticed in Ware's list of the ›hops of that diocese.

[9] *Cobha.*—Probably put for Magh-›bha, or Ui-Echach-Cobha (Iveagh, . Down). See Reeves' *Eccl. Antiqq.*, 9-350. The name "Cass" does t appear in the ordinary pedigrees the septs anciently inhabiting that rritory.

[10] *Blood-red.*—tenebrosa et sanguinea, A., B. *Sanguinea*, Clar. 49.

[11] *Brecc.*—O'Conor took this name as ı epithet ("maculatus") connected th the name which precedes it.

[12] *Fortrenn.*—Pictland. See note at A.D. 663, *supra*.

[13] *Eg.*—Now Eigg, an island off the coast of Inverness, Scotland. See note [7], at the year 616 *supra*.

[14] *Nectan.*—The Nectan referred to under the year 716 *supra*, as having expelled the community of Ia, or Iona, across Dorsum Britanniæ. See Skene's *Chron. of the Picts and Scots*, Preface, p. clvii.

[15] *Tolargan 'maphan.'*—Tolargan is a Pictish name; but the meaning of the epithet 'maphan' is not known to the Editor.

[16] *Cellach.*—This was the Cellach Cualann, King of Leinster, whose obit is given at the year 714 *supra*. See Shearman's *Loca Patriciana*, Geneal. Table, No. 7.

Quies Mancheine Leṫglinne. Iugulatio Ailello mic Boḋbċoḋa Miḋe.

Kl. Ianair. Anno domini dcc.° xx.° vi.° Mors Ailċon abbatis Cluana iraird. Bellum Droma fornocht inter genus Conaill et Eugain, ubi Flann mac Airtaile et Snedgus dergg nepos m[B]raċidi iugulati sunt. Congressio Irrois Foiċnae, ubi quidam ceciderunt deniḃ Airgiallaib, inter Selbaċam et familiam Eċdaċ nepotis Domnaill. Conall mac Moudain martirio coronatur. Adomnani reliquiae transferuntur in Hiberniam et lex renouatur. Bellum moī itir dia bullaiġniu, in quo cecidit Laidgnean mac Conmaeldae. Dunchad uictor fuit. Murchad mac Brain, rex Laginensium, moritur.

---

[1] *Leth-glenn.*—Now Leighlin, or Old Leighlin, co. Carlow. See Harris's *Ware*, Vol. I., p. 453.

[2] *Bodbchadh.*—This name is written "Bodbchar" in the *Book of Leinster*, p. 43 *a*. See under the year 703, *supra*, where he is described as "Bodbchadh Mide (B. of Meath) son of Diarmait."

[3] *Druim-fornocht.*—The "Naked (or exposed) Ridge." O'Donovan thought that this was "the Druim-fornocht mentioned in the foundation charter of the abbey of Newry, and which comprises the present town-lands of Crobane and Croreagh, in the Lordship of Newry." (*Ann. Four Mast.*, A.D., 721, note *o*.) But in O'Clery's *Pedig.* (p. 31) *Druim-fornocht* is stated to have been the name of a place in the "Lagan" [in the barony of Raphoe, co. Donegal], which is more likely to be correct, considering that the battle in question is stated to have been fought between the Cinel-Conaill and Cinel-Eogain, who occupied respectively the present counties of Donegal and Tyrone.

[4] *Ua Braichidi.*—"Descendant of Braichid." Clar. 49 has "nepos Inrachta." But the *Four Mast.* have "Ua Brachaidhe."

[5] *Irros-Foichne.*—Irrois Foiċnae. Dean Reeves correctly observes that this place, the name of which he prints "Ros-foichne," has not been identified, and that it is doubtful whether the place was in Scotland or Ireland. (*Adamnan*, p. 383, note *x*.) But Skene identifies it with a "Ross-feochan," the situation of which he does not give. (*Chron. Picts and Scots.*, Preface, p. cxxx.) As there is no notice of the conflict in the *Ann. Four Mast.*, it may be presumed that the compilers of that Chronicle considered it to have taken place in Scotland; although the killing of "some of the Airghialla" (see next note) would imply that the fight had occurred in Ireland.

[6] *Of the Airghialla.*—deniḃ Air-

ɜth-glenn.[1] The killing of Ailill, son of Bodbchadh[2] of .eath.

Kal. Jan. A.D. 726. Death of Aelchu, abbot of Cluain- ·aird. The battle of Druim-fornocht,[3] between the inel-Conaill and [Cinel]-Eogain, wherein Flann son of rthaile, and Snedgus 'Derg' Ua Braichidi,[4] were slain. he encounter of Irros-Foichne,[5] wherein some of the irghialla[6] were slain, between Selbach[7] and the family ' Echaid Ua Domnaill.[8] Conall son of Moudan was owned with martyrdom. The relics of Adamnan were anslated to Ireland, and the Law[9] was renewed. The ıttle of Moin between . . . . . in Leinster,[10] in hich fell Laidgnen[11] son of Cumelde. Dunchad was etor. Murchad son of Bran,[12] King of the Leinstermen, [726.]

---

allaib. dendiḃ seems an error : deniḃ, dinaiḃ, or donaiḃ ("of e"; see Ebel's Zeuss, p. 216.) an Reeves renders dendiḃ Air- giallaib by "utrorumque Airg- illa" (*Adamnan*, p. 383), and ene, like Clar. 49, "of the two rgiallas" (*Chron. Picts and Scots*, 355.) But there were not *two* bes of Airghialla.

[7] *Selbach.* — This could scarcely ve been Selbach, 18th King of ılriada, whose *clericatus* (or en- nce into religion) is noticed under year 722 *supra*, and whose obit given at 729 *infra*.

[8] *Echaid Ua Domnaill.*—Echaid, scendant of Domnall. Skene thinks it Echaid, or Echa, was the son of ha, grandson of Domnall Brecc [11th ng of Dalriada, sl. 641 *supra*.]

[9] *The Law, i.e.*, the "Law of Adam- ı." For the provisions of this aw," see Reeves' *Adamnan*, p. 179, l App. to the Pref. thereto, p. 1.

[10] *Battle of Moin between* . . . *in Leinster.*—This entry is decidedly corrupt, the words dia bullaiġniu especially so. The *Frag. of Annals*, in the corresponding place (A.D. 727), have Caṫ Mairtin idir Laiġniḃ féin ("battle of Maistin," or Mullagh- mast, "between the Leinstermen themselves.")

[11] *Laidgnen.*—The *Frag. of Irish Annals* (at A.D. 727) call him "Laid- cend Mac Conmella, King of Ui-Ceinn- sealaigh." In the list of the Kings of Ui-Cendselaig contained in the *Book of Leinster* (p. 40, col. 1), Laid- cend Mac Conmella is stated to have reigned during ten years.

[12] *Murchad son of Bran.*—He was victor in the battle of Almain ("Hill of Allen," co. Kildare), recorded at the year 721 *supra*. See *Chron. Sco- torum*, and *Ann. Four Mast.*, at A.D. 718; *Ann. Clonmacnoise*, at 720; and the very romantic account of the battle given in *Frag. of Annals*, p. 33 *sq*.

Dubdainber mac Congalaiġ, rex Cruiṫne, iugulatus est. Bellum Bairne, no inse Bregainn, in quo ceci-
Fol. 28bb. derunt Etirscel mac Cellaiġ Cualann, ocus Congal mac Brain. Faelan uictor fuit. Dormitatio Ceili Crist.

.b. Kl. Ianair. Anno domini dcc.° xx.° iii.° Bellum Droma corcain inter Flaiṫbertaċ mac Loingsiġ et Cinaeḋ filium Irgalaig (mic Conaing ċumaich mic Congalaiġ mic Aeḋa slaine), in quo Cinaeḋ et Eudus mac Ailello, Maelduin mac Feraḋaiċ, Dunchad mac Cormaic ceciderunt. Bellum Ailenne inter .ii. germanos filios Murċaḋo mic Brain, 7 Dunchad senior iugulatus est. Iunior Faelanus regnat. Flann Ointriḃ abbas Benncuir obiit. Bellum Mónid ċroiḃ inter Pictores inuicem, ubi Oenġus uictor fuit, et multi ex parte Elpini regis perempti sunt. Bellum lacrimabile inter eosdem gestum est iuxta castellum Credi, ubi Elpinus effugit. Domnall mac Cellaiġ rex Connacht moritur. Quies filii Beṫaċ uiri sapientis Muman.

Kl. Ianair. Anno domini dcc.° xx.° iiii.° Eicberiċt Christi miles inn parca die pausat. Bellum Moniṫ carno iuxta stagnum Loogdae, inter hostem Nectain

---

[1] *Cruithni.*—The Picts of Ireland are evidently here referred to.

[2] *Bairin—Inis-Bregainn.* — Bairin seems to be here put for "Bairend," a name now represented by the river Burren, in Carlow. The other name (Inis-Bregainn, or Bregann's Island, some islet in the river Burren), has not been identified.

[3] *Cellach Cualann.*—See under the year 714 *supra*.

[4] *Congal.*—He was brother of Murchad son of Bran. See note[12], last page.

[5] *Faelan.*—The Faelan mentioned under the next year.

[6] *Cele-Crist.*—The *Martyr. of Donegal*, at March 3, mentions a Cele-Crist, bishop of Cill-Cele-Crist, in Ui-Dunchadha, i fforṫaiḃ i Laiġniḃ (for i forṫuaṫaiḃ i Laiġniḃ, in Fortuatha ["border territories"] in Leinster). The territory of Ui-Dunchadha comprised the district through which the river Dodder flows. See O'Donovan's *Four Mast.*, A.D. 1044, note *l*.

[7] *Druim - Corcain.* — "Corcan's Ridge." The *Four Mast.* have "Druim-Corcrain." Keating (in his account of the reign of Cinaedh) calls it "Druim-Carrthoinn." The place has not been identified.

ies. Dubhdainbher, son of Congalach, King of the 'ruithni,[1] was slain. The battle of Bairin,[2] or of Inis-Breainn,[2] in which Etirscel son of Cellach Cualann,[3] and 'ongal[4] son of Bran, were slain. Faelan[5] was victor. 'he 'falling asleep' of Celi-Crist.[6]

Kal. Jan. A.D. 727. The battle of Druim-Corcain,[7] [727.] BIS. etween Flaithbertach son of Loingsech, and Cinaedh, on of Irgalach (son of Conang Cumach,[8] son of Congaach, son of Aedh Slanè), in which Cinaedh, and Eudus on of Ailill, Maelduin son of Feradach, and Dunchad son f Cormac, were slain. The battle of Ailinn between two rothers, sons of Murchadh son of Bran;[9] and Dunchad, he elder, was slain. Faelan,[10] the younger, reigns. 'lann of Ointrebh,[11] abbot of Bangor, died. The battle f Monidcroibh[12] between the Picts themselves, wherein)engus was victor, and a great many were slain on the ide of King Elpin. A lamentable battle was fought beween the same persons, near Castle-Credi,[13] where Elpin ed. Domnall, son of Cellach, King of Connaught, dies. 'he repose of Mac-Bethach, a wise man of Munster.

Kal. Jan. A.D. 728. Ecbericht,[14] a soldier of Christ, [728.] ests on Easter Day. The battle of Monith-carno,[15] near

---

[8] *Cumach.*—This epithet is more orrectly given "Cuirri" by the *Four Tasters* (A D. 720). The original of is clause, which is not in B., is inrlined in *al. man.* in A.'

[9] *Son of Bran.*—See note [12], p. 179.

[10] *Faelan.*—See note [5], *supra*, and *ook of Leinster*, p. 39, col. 2.

[11] *Ointrebh.* — Antrim, in the co. ntrim.

[12] *Monidcroibh.* — According to ean Reeves, this was the old name Moncrieffe, in the barony of Dunrny, in Perthshire. *Adamnan*, p. 33, note *y*.

[13] *Castle-Credi.*—Now "Boot-hill" ectè "Moot-hill"), near Scone, in Scotland. See Reeves' *Adamnan*, p. 383, note *z*.

[14] *Ecbericht.*—The Egbert, or Ecgberct, through whose exertions the change in the time of keeping Easter is stated to have been effected in Ia, or Iona (*supra*, A.D. 715). See Bede's *Eccl. Hist.*, Book 3, chap. 4, and Book 5, chaps. 22, 23; and Reeves' *Adamnan* (*App. to Preface*, p. 1), and 379. The death of St. Egberht, "in Iona,' is entered in the *Anglo-Sax. Chron.*, at A.D. 729.

[15] *Monith-carno.*—This place has not been satisfactorily identified. Skene thinks that Monith-carno was the name of a mountain pass in the Mearns,

et exercitum Oengusa, et exactatores Nectain ceciderunt, hoc est Biceot mac Moneit et filius eius, Finguine mac Drostain, Feroṫ mac Finguinne, et quidam multi; et familia Oengussa triumphauit. Bellum Dromo dergg blaṫuug in regionibus Pictorum, inter Oengus et Drust regem Pictorum, et cecidit Drust. Iugulatio Caṫail cuirc filii Neill.

Kl. Ianair. Anno domini dcc.° xx.° ix.° Terremotus .ui. id. Februarii, iiii. feria. Reuersio reliquiarum Adomnani de Hibernia in mense Octimbris. Bran filius Eugain, Selbaċ mac Fercair, mortui sunt. Suibne nepos Mruiċesaiċ (alias mac Crunnmail) episcopus Airdd maċae, mac Oncon scriba Chille daro, in gall o Lilcaċ, filius Concumbu scriba Cluana mic U Nois dormierunt. Oiteċde mac Baiṫecde filii Blaṫmicc, Oengus mac Becce bairċe, qui-

Fol. 29aa. euerunt. Interfectio filii Cinadon. Commixtio dunaid for Domnall mac Murċaḋo i culaiḃ, id est

called Cairn o' Mounth (*Chron. Picts and Scots*, Preface, p. lxxxii.) See Reeves' *Adamnan*, p. 64, note *b*, and 383, note *c*.

[1] *Loch-Loegde.*—Loch Loogdae, A.

[2] '*Exactors.*' — exactatores, A., and Clar. 49. exactores, B.

[3] *Family of Oengus.*—This Oengus was the head of the Cinel-Oengusa, one of the four chief tribes of the Scotch Dalriada. See *Chron. Picts and Scots*, pp. 316-317; and Reeves' *Adamnan*, p. 434.

[4] *Triumphed.*—trihumpauit, B.

[5] *Druim-Dergblathug.* — Chalmers identifies this place with "Drumderg, an extensive ridge, on the western side of the river Ila [the Isla, in Forfarshire.]" *Caled.*, i., p. 211.

[6] *Relics.* — Their 'translation' to Ireland is noticed at the year 726 *supra.* The note Beda claruit is added in the margin in A., in *al. man.*

[7] *In.*—Supplied from B.

[8] *Selbach.*—He was the 18th King of Dalriada. The 'clericatus' (or entrance into religion) of Selbach is entered above at the year 722.

[9] *Suibhne.* — This was evidently the Suibhne referred to above under A.D. 718, where his family is stated to have been slain in Armagh. As the Lists of Comarbs of St. Patrick (or Bishops of Armagh) generally give 15 years as the length of his episcopacy, Suibhne must have been bishop of that See at the time of the outrage (which outrage, it may be added, is not noticed by the *Four Masters*). The death of Ferdacrich, son of Suibhne, who succeeded Cele-Petair as abbot or bishop of Armagh, in A.D. 757, is given at 767 *infra.*

ch-Loegdae,[1] between the host of Nectan and the army Oengus; and the 'exactors'[2] of Nectan were killed, z., Biceot son of Monet, and his son; Finguine son of rostan; Feroth son of Finguine, and many others; and e family of Oengus[3] triumphed.[4] The battle of Druim-ergblathug[5] in the country of the Picts, between Oengus, d Drust King of the Picts, and Drust was slain. The lling of Cathal Corc son of Niall.

Kal. Jan. A.D. 729. An earthquake on the 6th of the [729.] les of February, the fourth day of the week. Return of e relics[6] of Adamnan from Ireland, in[7] the month of ctober. Bran son of Eugan, Selbach[8] son of Fercar, ed. Suibhne,[9] descendant of Mruichesach (alias son of runnmael),[10] bishop of Armagh; Mac Onchon, scribe of ildare; the Gall from Lilcach,[11] and Mac Concumba, ribe of Cluain-mic-Nois, 'fell asleep.' Oitechde, son of aithechde, the son of Blathmacc, and Oengus son of ecc Bairche, rested. The killing of the son of Cinadon. camp melee against Domnall son of Murchad,[12] in the ula, *i.e.*, 'adaigh noidhe nephain,'[13] or of Imlech-Senaich.

---

[10] *Crunnmael.*—This clause, which not in B., is added in *al. man.* in . In the list of Bishops of Armagh ntained in the *Book of Leinster* . 42, col. 3), it is stated that ibhne was the son of Crunnmael, n of Ronan; and of the Ui-Niallain, local tribe which furnished many shops to the See of Armagh.

[11] *The Gall* [*or Foreigner*] *from ilcach.*—The copy of *Tigernach* in e MS., H. 1, 18, T. C. D., at 729, s an Ȝall ulcach ("the bearded oreigner"), and it is added that he as the most astute man of his time. fter the word Lilcać in A., there is mark like ⁊, which seems to have special signification, unless it re-resents the abbrev. for ετ.

[12] *Domnall, son of Murchad.*—His accession to the Sovereignty of Ireland is recorded at the year 742, *infra.*

[13] '*Adaigh noidhe nephain.*'—This is unintelligible to the Editor, and seems corrupt. Skene has printed this entry among his extracts from this Chronicle, in his *Chron. Picts and Scots* (p. 356), and has given a translation which is quite inaccurate. Dr. O'Conor, in his edition of part of these Annals (at 729), also attempts a translation, which is even worse than that of Skene, for he renders the entry by, "Prælium Dunad, contra Domhnaldum filium Murcadi, in locis Saltibus obsitis in angustiis viarum Nephain, vel Imlecho Senaic;" a translation entirely misleading.

adaiġ noiḋe nephain, no imleċo Senaiċ. Coċul oḋor scriba familie Benncair dormitauit. Bellum Fernmuiġi in quo cecidit Cetomun.

Kl. Ianair. Anno domini dcc.° xxx.° Combustio Cuile raiṫin. Clericatus Eċdaċ filii Cuidini, rex Saxan, et constringitur. Combustio Tairpirt boittir apud Dunġal. Bellum inter Cruiṫne et Dal Riati in Murbuilgg, ubi Cruiṫni deuicti fuerunt. Bellum inter filium Oengusa et filium Congusa, sed Bruideus uicit Talorcum fugientem. Donnġal mac Conġaile filii Fergusa moritur. Faeldobur becc sapiens Fobair, Adomnanus episcopus Raṫo maiġe oinaiġ, Colman nepos Littain religionis doctor, pausauerunt. Iugulatio Moenaiġ mic Seċnusaiġ. Mors Eċdaċ mic Colggen anċoritae airdd Maċae. Colman Telċa h-Ualand, Brecc Berḃa, dormitabant. Coblaiṫ filia Ceallaiċ Cualand moritur.

Kl. Ianair. Anno domini dcc.° xxx.° i.° Mors Flaind sinnae aui Collae, abbatis Cluana mic Nuis. Iugulatio Daiṫgusa mic Baiṫ, regis na n-Deisse. Duḃdaleṫe mac Dunchon, Flann cuirrig mac Aiṫeċdai, moriuntur. Bellum Connacht in quo cecidit Muredaċ mac Indrechtaiġ. Pontifex maiġe hEu Saxonum Garaalt obiit. Magnus filosoḟus hiberniae, nepos

---

[1] *Fernmagh.*—Farney, in the co. Monaghan.

[2] *Cuidin.* — This was probably Cuthwine (son of Leodwald), King of Bernicia. See Lappenberg's *England under the Anglo-Saxon Kings*, Vol. I., p. 289. O'Conor prints the name *Eudini*, for *Cudini*.

[3] *Tairpert-boitter.*—See above, at the year 711.

[4] *Cruithni and Dal-Riata.* — The Irish tribes so called, situated respectively in the cos. of Antrim and Down; not the Scotch tribes similarly named.

[5] *Murbulgg.*—This place gave name to Murlough Bay, on the N.E. coast of the co. Antrim.

[6] *Rath-maighe-oenaigh.* — O'Donovan supposes this place to be represented by the "Church of Rath . . . . near Manor-Cunningham, in the barony of Raphoe, and county of Donegal," *Ann. Four Mast.*, A.D. 779, note *x*.

[7] *Cluain-mic-Nois.* — Cluana m̄ Nuis, A. Cluana m̄ cunois, B.

[8] *Indrechtach.* — Probably the Indrechtach, King of Connaught, whose

Cochul-Odhor, scribe of the family of Bangor, 'fell asleep.' The battle of Fernmagh,[1] in which Cetomun was slain.

Kal. Jan. A.D. 730. The burning of Cul-rathin. The entry into religion of Echaid, son of Cuidin,[2] King of the Saxons; and he was put in fetters. The burning of Tairpert-boitter[3] by Dunghal. A battle between the Cruithni and Dal-Riata,[4] in Murbulgg,[5] wherein the Cruithni were vanquished. A battle between the son of Oengus and the son of Congus; but Bruide conquered Talorg, who fled. Donngal, son of Congal, son of Fergus, dies. Faeldobur Becc, the Wise, of Fobar; Adamnan, bishop of Rath-maighe-oenaigh,[6] and Colman Ua Littain, doctor of religion, rested. The killing of Moenach, son of Sechnasach. The death of Echaid, son of Colggu, anchorite, of Armagh. Colman of Telach-Ualand, [and] Brecc Berbha, slept. Coblaith, daughter of Cellach Cualand, dies. [730.]

Kal. Jan. A.D. 731. The death of Flann Sinna, descendant of Colla, abbot of Cluain-mic-Nois.[7] The killing of Dathgus, son of Baeth, King of the Deise. Dubhdalethe son of Dunchu, Flann Cuirrigh son of Aithechda, died. The battle of Connaught, in which Muiredach son of Indrechtach[8] was slain. The pontiff of Magh-Eo of the Saxons,[9] Gerald, died. A great philo- [731.]

---

obit, "*in clericatu*," is entered above at the year 722. His son, Muiredach, whose death is here recorded, is stated by the *Four Mast.* (A.D. 726), and other authorities, to have been bishop of Magh-Eo; an error which owes its origin to the fusion into one of the above two distinct entries regarding Muiredach, son of Indrechtach, and Gerald of Magh-Eo. O'Conor, for instance, prints both entries as one, thus:—"Bellum *Connacht* in quo cecidit . . . *Muredach mc Inrechtaig* Pontifex *Maigi heu* Saxonum Geraalt obiit."

[9] *Magh-Eo of the Saxons.*—Mayo, the seat of an ancient bishopric, in the parish of Mayo, and county of the same name. See O'Donovan's *Four Mast.*, A.D. 726, note *b*, where some strange mistakes regarding the date of the death of St. Gerald of Mayo, committed by Colgan, Dr. O'Conor, and others, are corrected. For some further account of St. Gerald, who was an Englishman, see Lanigan's *Eccl. Hist.*, Vol. III., pp. 166–168.

Miṫrebṫa, extinctus est. Ceallaċ ingen Dunchada di auib Liaṫain, regina optima et benigna, dormitauit. Teimnen Cille Garaḃ, religiosus clericus, quieuit. Cellaċ mac Tuaṫail, rex nepotum Craumtain, iugu-
Fol. 29 *ab.* latus est. Bellum inter genus Conaill et Eugain, in quo filius Fergaile Aid (.i. Aeḋ) de Flaiṫbertaċo filio Loingriċ (mic Aengusa mic Domnaill mic Aeḋa mic Ainmireaċ) triumphauit; hiis ducibus cessis a dicione eius, Flann gohan filius Conġaile mic Fergusa, Flaiṫgus mac Duibdibergg. Tomaltaċ mac Duineċdo moritur. Bellum inter Laigniu desgaḃair et Muimneċu, in quo Aeḋ mac Colggen uictor erat. Sebdann filia Chuirc, dominatrix Cille daro, obiit. Fergus mac Conaill oircniċ, ocus Ferdomnach scriba airdd Maċae, obierunt. Congalaċ Cnuċo moritur.

Kl. Ianair. Anno domini dcc.° xxx.° ii.° Dungal mac Selbaiċ dehonorauit Toraiċ cum traxit Brudeum ex ea, et eadem uice insola Cuilen rigi inuasit. Muiredaċ mac Ainfcellaċ regnum generis Loairnd assumit. Congressio iterum inter Aeḋ mac Fergaile et genus Conaill in campo Iṫo, ubi ceciderunt Conaing mac Conġaile mic Fergusso et ceteri multi. Natiuitas Donnchada mic Domnaill. Occisio Aedo mic

---

[1] *Ui-Liathain.*—A tribe descended from Eochaidh Liathanach (son of Daire Cerba, ancestor of the Ui-Fidhgeinte), whose territory embraced the greater part of the present barony of Barrymore, co. Cork. The name of the territory and tribe is partly represented by that of the present town of Castlelyons, in the aforesaid barony.

[2] *Cill-Garadh.*—Probably the Cinn-Garadh (Kingarth, in Bute), referred to above at the years 659, 688, and *infra* at 736, 789.

[3] *Devout.*—relegiosus, A. Religiossus, B.

[4] *Aedh.*—Aeḋ. Added in *al. man.* in A., over the form Aid. Clar. 49 writes "Hugh," the English form. Aedh became King of Ireland in A.D. 733, as stated *infra* at that year.

[5] *Over Flaithbertach.*—Monarch of Ireland. de Flaiṫbertac, A. de Flaiṫbertaco, B.

[6] *Son of Aengus.*—The original of this clause, which is interlined in *al. man.* in A., is not in B. It is rather inaccurately written in Clar. 49.

[7] *Aedh, son of Colgu.*—Aedh was King of the Ui-Ceinnselaigh, or South Leinstermen.

ɔpher of Ireland, Ua Mithrebtha, died. Cellach, aughter of Dunchad, of the Ui-Liathain,[1] a most excellent nd gracious queen, slept. Teimnen of Cill-Garadh,[2] a evout cleric,[3] rested. Cellach, son of Tuathal, King of he Ui-Crimthain, was slain. A battle between Cinel-Conaill and [Cinel]-Eogain, in which the son of Fergal, Aid (*i.e.*, Aedh),[4] triumphed over Flaithbertach,[5] son of Loingsech (son of Aengus,[6] son of Domnall, son of Aedh, on of Ainmire), of whose force these leaders were slain: Flann Gohan, son of Congal, son of Fergus, [and] Flaithgus, on of Dubhdiberg. Tomaltach, son of Duinechdo, dies. A battle between the South Leinstermen and the Munstermen, in which Aedh, son of Colgu,[7] was victor. Sebdann, daughter of Corc, abbess[8] of Kildare, died. Fergus son of Conall Oircnech,[9] and Ferdomnach, scribe of Armagh, died. Congalach of Cnucha dies.

Kal. Jan. A.D. 732. Dungal,[10] son of Selbach pro- [732.]
faned Torach, when he took Brude out of it; and on the same occasion he invaded the island of Cuilen-rigi.[11] Muiredach, son of Ainfcellach, assumed the government of the Cinel-Loarnd. Another encounter[12] between Aedh, son of Fergal, and the Cinel-Conaill, in Magh-Itha, wherein were slain Conaing, son of Congal, son of Fergus, and many others. The birth of Donnchad,[13] son of Domnall.

---

[8] *Abbess.* — dominatrix. Clar. 49 renders this by "Lady."

[9] *Conall Oircnech.*—"Conall the Plunderer." O'Conor translates the epithet oirgnech "Præpositus, vulgo *Erenach*," which is incorrect, as oircnech is an adj. derived from orcain, or orcuin, "plunder," "destruction," &c.

[10] *Dungal.* — Referred to again under the years 733 and 735.

[11] *Cuilen-rigi.*—Originally written cuiren rigi in A., but corrected to culren rigi, or cuilen rigi, the form in which the name is given at 802 *infra.* Dean Reeves considers it to be probably the island called Inch, off Inishowen, co. Donegal. *Adamnan*, p. 384, note *f.* MS. B. has culren rigi.

[12] *Another encounter.*—Congressio iterum. The first encounter, or battle, is noticed under the preceding year (731).

[13] *Donnchad.*—Afterwards King of Ireland. His obit is given at the year 796 *infra.*

Conai[n]cc regis Irloċrae. Occisio Eċdaċ cobo filii Bresail. Coscraḋ Caṫail do Domnall a Tailtae, ocus coscraḋ Fallomuin do Chatal a Tlaċtgu. Iugulatio Dunlainge filii Dunċon. Flann fine abbas Cluana mic U Nois obiit. Doċumai bolggan ancorita airdd Maċae pausauit. Uacca uisa est i n-Delggenis Cualann, se cossa leae .i. da corp iar n-íarṫur, oen ċenn fair; doomlaċt fo tri ol nais caiċ m-blegum.

Kl. Ianair. Anno domini dcc.° xxx.° iii.° Reċtabrae nepos Caṫasaiġ rex nepotum Tuirtri moritur.
Fol. 29ba. Eclipsis lunae in .xi. Kl. Februarii. Commotatio martirum Petir ocus Phoil ocus Phatraicc ad legem perficiendam; et occisio Coibdenaiġ filii Flainn hui Congaile. Caintigernd ingen Ceallaig Cualann moritur. Talorgg mac Congusso a fratre suo uinctus est, traditur in manus Pictorum, et cum illis in aqua demersus est. Talorggan filius Drostani comprehensus alligatur iuxta arcem Ollaiġ. Dun Leiṫfinn distruitur post uulnerationem Dungaile, et in Hiberniam a potestate Oengusso fugatus est. Congressio in campo Itho inter Flaiṫbertach filium Loingsich et Aed Allain mac Fergaile, ubi nepotes Eċdaċ (do cinel Eogain) ceciderunt, et ceteri. Taiċleaċ

[1] *Ir-Luachair.*—"Eastern Luachair." A district anciently comprising the S.E. part of the present co. Kerry, with the adjoining parts of Limerick and Cork. The Paps Mountains in Kerry, and the country around Kingwilliamstown (bar. of Duhallow), co. Cork, was included within it. See O'Donovan's ed. of *O'Dugan and O'Huidhrin*, note 656.

[2] *Domnall.*—Most likely the "Domnall, son of Murchad" referred to above at the year 729, and whose accession to the sovereignty of Ireland is recorded under 742 *infra*.

[3] *Tailtiu.*—Teltown, co. Meath, where national games were anciently celebrated.

[4] *Tlachtga.*—The old name of the "Hill of Ward," near Athboy, co. Meath.

[5] *Delginis-Cualand.*—Dalkey Island, near Dublin.

[6] *Having six legs.*—The orig., se cossa leae, is roughly translated "six feet with her," in Clar. 49, which adds "and would yeald milk thrice a yeare." The construction of the Irish part of the entry is very faulty in A. and B.

[7] *Greater.*—ol nais caiċ m-blegum. The meaning is that the

e killing of Aedh, son of Conai[n]g, King of Ir-achair.[1] The killing of Echaid Cobo, son of Bresal. e spoiling of Cathal by Domnall,[2] in Tailtiu ;[3] and the iling of Fallomun by Cathal, in Tlachtga.[4] The killing Dunlaing, son of Dunchu. Flann Finè, abbot of iain-mic-Nois, died. Dochuma Bolggan, anchorite of magh, rested. A cow was seen in Delginis-Cualand,[5] ving six legs,[6] viz. :—Two bodies hindwards, one head front. If milked thrice [in the day], the produce of ch milking was greater.[7]

Kal. Jan. A.D. 733. Rechtabra Ua Cathasaigh, King the Ui-Tuirtri, dies. An eclipse of the Moon on the th of the kalends of February. Transposition[8] of the ics of Peter, and Paul, and Patrick, to fulfil the Law ; d the killing of Coibdenach, son of Flann Ua Congaile. intigernd,[9] daughter of Cellach Cualand, dies. Talorg a of Congus, was manacled by his brother, delivered to the hands of the Picts, and drowned by[10] them. lorgan, son of Drostan, was taken and manacled, near un-Ollaigh. Dun-Leithfinn[11] was destroyed, after the ounding of Dungal ; and he fled to Ireland from the wer of Oengus. An encounter in Magh-Itho, between aithbertach,[12] son of Loingsech, and Aedh Allan, son of rgal, wherein the descendants of Echaid (of the Cinel-gain[13]), and others, were slain. Taichlech, son of [733.]

duce of each successive milking s greater than the previous one. O'Donovan's *Four Mast.*, A.D. , note *h*.

[8] *Transposition.* — Commocacio, commucacio, A., B. By ommutatio martyrum" is meant disinterring and enshrining of cs, according to Dean Reeves *damnan*, p. 313, note *c*, and 441, *Commutatio*).

[9] *Caintigernd.*—The St. Kenti-na of Inch-caileoch ("Nuns' Is-d") in Loch Lomond, who is commemorated in the Scotch Calendar at Jan. 9. The obit of her father, Cellach Cualann, King of Leinster, is given above at the year 714.

[10] *By.*—cum, A., B. *Ab.*, Clar. 49.

[11] *Dun-Leithfinn.*—Not identified.

[12] *Flaithbertach.*—King of Ireland at the time. See under 731 *supra.* The *Four Masters* (729=733 of this Chronicle) state that he died in Armagh, having resigned his kingdom to lead a religious life.

[13] *Of the Cinel-Eogain.* — The

mac Cinnfaelaḋ rex Luiġne moritur. Aeḋ ollan regnare incipit.

Kl. Ianair. Anno domini dcc.° xxx.° iiii.° Oegedċar episcopus Noindromma pausat. Bellum in regionibus Murṫeimne inter nepotes Neill 7 Ultu, ubi Aeḋ roin rex Ulaṫ 7 Conċad mac Cuanaċ, rex Cobo, ceciderunt. Aeḋ mac Fergaile uictor fuit. Bellum inter Mumain 7 Laigniu, ubi multi di Laigniḃ 7 pene innumerabiles de Mumu perierunt, in quo Ceallaċ mac Faelċair rex Osraiġi cecidit; sed Caṫal filius Finnguine, rex Muman, euasit. Airechtaċ nepos Duncaḋo Mursce, rex nepotum Fiaċraċ, 7 Caṫal filius Muiredaiġ, rex Connacht (a quo clann Caṫail muigi hAi), moriuntur. Iugulatio Flainn mic Conaing, abbatis Cille more diṫriḃ. Draco ingens in fine autumni cum tonitruo magno post se uisus est. Beda sapiens Saxonum quieuit.

.b. Kl. Ianair. Anno domini dcc.° xxx.° u.° Oengus mac Fergusso rex Pictorum uastauit regiones Dalriatai, 7 obtenuit Dun at, 7 combussit Creic, 7 duos filios Selbaiċ catenis alligauit .i. Donngal 7 Feradaċ; 7 paulo post Bruideus mac Oengusa filii Fergusso obiit.

---

origiual of this clause, which is not in B., is added in *al. man.* in A.

[1] *Oegedchar.*—The so-called translator of these Annals, whose version is contained in the MS. Clar. 49, represents this name by "Hugh Edchar."

[2] *Murtheimhne.*—Otherwise called Magh-Muirtheimhne, "Plain of Muirtheimhne." See above at the year 696. A large plain comprising nearly the whole of the district forming the present co. of Louth.

[3] *Aedh Roin.*—In the list of the Kings of Ulad contained in the *Book of Leinster* (p. 41, col. 3), it is stated that Aedh Róin, after a reign of 26 years, fell by Aedh Allan "in the battle of Fochard" (now Faughard, a village about two miles to the north of Dundalk, co. Louth). The *Four Mast.*, at A.D. 732, calls this battle the "battle of Fochart in Magh-Muirtheimhne." See last note.

[4] *King of Cobo.*—In the *Frag. of Annals*, at A.D. 732, Conchad is called "King of the Cruithne" (or Picts, of Ulster).

[5] *Aedh.*—Aedh Allan, King of Ireland, who assumed the sovereignty in the preceding year.

nnfaeladh, King of Luighne, dies. Aedh Allan begins reign.

Kal. Jan. A.D. 734. Oegedchar,[1] bishop of Nendrum, [734.]
ₛts. A battle in the regions of Murtheimhne,[2] between
e Ui-Neill and the Ulidians, in which Aedh Roin,[3] King
Uladh, and Conchad, son of Cuanu, King of Cobo,[4] were
in. Aedh,[5] son of Fergal, was victor. A battle between
e Munstermen and Leinstermen, in which perished
ıny of the Leinstermen, and Munstermen[6] almost
thout number; in which Ceallach, son of Faelchar,
ing of Ossory, was slain; but Cathal, son of Finnguine,
ing of Munster, escaped. Airechtach, grandson of
ınchadh Muirsce,[7] King of the Ui-Fiachrach, and Cathal,
n of Muiredach, King of Connaught (from whom are
e Clann-Cathail of Magh-Ai[8]), die. Murder of Flann,
n of Conang, abbot of Cillmor-dithribh.[9] A huge
agon was seen in the end of autumn, with great
under after it. Beda, the wise man of the Saxons, rested.

Kal. Jan. A.D. 735. Oengus, son of Fergus, King of [735.] BIS.
e Picts, devastated the regions of Dalriata, and seized
un-At,[10] and burned Creic;[11] and bound two sons of
lbach in chains, viz.:—Donngal[12] and Feradach. And
on after, Brude, son of Oengus, son of Fergus, died.

---

[6] *Munstermen.* — de mume, A.; momonia, B.

[7] *Dunchad Muirsce.*—The killing this person is recorded above at year 682.

[8] *Clann Cathail of Magh-Ai.*—ınn-Cathail was the tribe-name of O'Flanagans of the co. Roscomn, whose territory was anciently luded in the great plain of Magh-Ai, the district now forming that county. e original of this clause, which is t in B., is added in *al. man.* in A.

[9] *Cillmor-dithribh.* — The "Great urch of the Wilderness." Now lmore, in the barony of Ballintober North, co. Roscommon. See Reeves' *Adamnan*, p. 99, note *g*.

[10] *Dun-At*, or Dun-Att, as the name is otherwise written. See above at the year 682. O'Conor incorrectly renders *Dun-At* by "arces," not considering it a proper name.

[11] *Creic.* — Skene says that this place is Creich, in the Ross of Mull, opposite the Sound of Iona. *Chron. Picts and Scots*, Preface, p. cxxxi. O'Conor, mistaking the name creic for crich (a "territory" or "border"), renders it by *regiones*.

[12] *Donngal.* — The Dungal mentioned above at 732 and 733.

Bellum Cnuicc Coirpri i Calathros uc Etarlindu, itir
Fol. 29bb. Dalriatai 7 Foirtrinn, 7 Talorggan mac Ferguso filium Ainfceallaich fugientem cum exercitu persequitur; in qua congressione multi nobiles conciderunt. Mors Fianamla mic Gertindi abbatis Cluana Iraird, 7 mors Crunnmail filii Colggen abb Luscan. Danel mac Colmain inddinn abb aird Breccain, 7 Colman mac Murcon abb maigi Bile, quieuerunt. Iugulatio Maelefothartaig filii Maeletuile di Laignib. Uir sapiens 7 anchorita Insole uaccae albae, Dublitter, 7 Samson nepos Corcrain, dormierunt. Bodbchath mac Conaill gabrai, rex Coirpri, moritur.

Kl. Ianair. Anno Domini dcc°. xxx°. iii°. Mors Ronain abbatis Cinngarad. Faelbe filius Guaire .i. heres Maelrubi [Apor]crosan in profundo pelagi dimersus est, cum suis nautis numero xx. ii. Conmal nepos Lochene abbas Clona mic U Nois pausat. Congressio inuicem inter nepotes Aedo slane, ubi Conaing mac Amalgaid Cernachum uicit, 7 Cathal mac Aedo cecidit; iuxta lapidem Ailbe ab orientali parte gesta est. Muirgis mac Fergusso forcraid iugulatur est. Bresal mac Concobair aird occisus est.

---

[1] *Calathros.*—Mentioned above at the year 687. See Reeves' *Adamnan*, p. 202, note. Skene suggests that Calathros was the Celtic name of the district comprising the Carse of Falkirk. *Chron. Picts and Scots*, Pref., p. lxxx.

[2] *Etarlindu.*—This place, the situation of which has not been identified, signifies "between linns (or lakes)."

[3] *Fortrenns.*—The Picts of Fortrenn, in Scotland, are frequently designated by the name of their territory, Fortrenn, in the Chronicles. See note [8], p. 118, *supra*.

[4] *Talorgan.*—The Talorgan mentioned as having been slain in the battle of Cat, at the year 749 *infra*, where he is stated to have been the brother of Oengus [king of the Picts], whose obit is given at the year 760.

[5] *Son of Ainfcellach.*—This must have been Muiredach (called *Uaignech*, or "the Lonely"), son of Ainfcellach, 17th king of Dalriada (sl. 718 *supra*). Muiredach, who was of the House of Loarn, became king of Dalriada and Lord of Lorn, in the year 733 (732, *supra*).

[6] *Fianamail.*—His obit is in the *Ann. of the Four Masters* under A.D. 731, where his father's name is given as "Gertidh." Fianamail was brother

ie battle of Cnoc-Coirpri in Calathros[1] at Etarlindu,[2] tween the Dalriata and Fortrenns;[3] and Talorgan,[4] son of rgus, with an army, pursued the son of Ainfcellach,[5] who d; in which encounter many noble persons were slain. ie death of Fianamail[6] son of Gertind, abbot of Cluain-iird, and of Crunnmael son of Colgu, abbot of Lusk. inel, son of Colman 'Indinin,'[7] abbot of Ard-Brecain, d Colman, son of Murcu, abbot of Magh-Bilè, rested. ie killing of Maelfothartaigh, son of Maeltuile, by instermen. Dublittir, a wise man and anchorite of Inis-finne, and Samson, descendant of Corcran, slept. odbthach, son of Conall Gabra,[8] king of Coirpri, dies.

Kal. Jan. A.D. 736. Death of Ronan, abbot of Cenn-radh.[9] Failbhe, son of Guaire, *i.e.* successor[10] of Mael-ba of [Apor]crosan,[11] was submerged in the depth of e sea[12] with his sailors, twenty-two in number. Conmal, scendant of Locheni, abbot of Clonmacnoise, rests. A nflict between each other, among the descendants of edh Slanè, in which Conaing, son of Amalghaidh, van-ished Cernach, and Cathal, son of Aedh, was slain: ar Lic-Ailbhe,[13] on the east side, it was fought. Muir-s, son of Fergus Forcraidh,[14] was slain. Bresal, son of ncobhar of Ard, was slain.[15] Oengus, son of Ailill, king [736.]

Cellach Cualann, king of Leinster, ose obit is entered at the year 714 ra.

Indinin. — Printed *indmin* by onor. "Indinin" is probably a take for *Ind-eidhnen*, "the little " (or ivy-covered church). See *on. Scot.* ed. Hennessy, p. 162, e 2.

Conall Gabra.—Called "Congal ora" at the year 702 *supra.*

Cenngaradh.—Kingarth, in Bute.

Successor.—The Latin equivalent, es, is misplaced in the entry.

Maelruba of [*Apor*]*crosan.*—See e [9] at the year 672 *supra.*

[12] *Of the sea.*—pilagi, A.

[13] *Lic-Ailbhe.*—This was the name of a large stone which stood in the plain of Magh-Ailbhe, in Meath (the name of which plain seems still preserved in that of the townland of Moynalvy, par. of Kilmore, bar. of Lower Deece, co. Meath). The falling of this stone is noticed at the year 998 *infra*, where it is stated that four mill-stones were made of it by King Maelsechlainn.

[14] *Fergus Forcraidh.*—The death of this person, in the battle of Corann, is recorded above at the year 702.

[15] *Was slain.*—occissus est, A.

Oengus mac Ailello ri airddae Ciannachta moritur. Mors Graiḟniġ abbatis imleċo Fia. Dal itir Aeḋ n-aldan 7 Caṫal oc Tir da glas. Lex Patricii tenuit hiberniam. Fiangalaċ mac Murcaḋo, rex hUi Mail, moritur.

Kl. Ianair. Anno domini dcc.° xxx.° iiii.° Faelan nepos Brain, Laginensium rex, immatura aetate ac inopinata morte interiit. Tole episcopus Cluana iraird, dignus Dei miles, pausat. Cernaċ filius Foġartaiġ a suis sceleratis sociis dolose iugulatur, quem uaccarum uituli 7 infimi orbis mulieres tediose fleuerunt. Bellum aṫo Senaiċ (.i. caṫ Uċbaḋ .xiiii. septimbris die .ui. feria) inter nepotes Neill 7 Lagin-
Fol., 30aa. enses crudeliter gestum est, in quo binales reges celsi uigoris pectoris armis alternatim congressi sunt .i. Aeḋ aldan ri Teṁrach 7 Aeḋ mac Colggen .i. ri Laigen, e quibus unus superstes uulneratus uixit, .i. Aeḋ allan: alius uero, .i. Aed mac Colgan, militari mucrone capite truncatus est. Tunc nepotes Cuinn immensa uictoria ditati sunt cum Lagenos suos emulos insolito more in fugam mittunt, calcant, sternunt, subuertunt, consumunt, ita ut usque ad internicionem uniuersus hostilis pene deletus exercitus, paucis nuntiis renuntiantibus; 7 in tali bello

---

[1] *Graiphnech.*—Gen. form Graiphnigh. This name signifies "writer." The *Four Masters*, at A.D. 732, write the name "Graiphnidh."

[2] *Imlech-Fia.*—Now Emlagh, in a parish of the same name, barony of Lower Kells, co. Meath.

[3] *Aedh Aldan*; or Aedh Allan. King of Ireland at the time.

[4] *Cathal.*—*Cathal Mac Finguine*, king of Munster, whose obit is given within at the year 741. Cathal is the hero (or rather the Gargantua) of a remarkable story, written in the Rabelaistic style, contained in the old Irish MS. known as the *Leabhar Breac*, called "Mac Conglinne's Vision"; a translation of which, by the Editor of the present work, was published in *Fraser's Mag.* for September, 1873.

[5] *Tir-da-glas.*—Terryglass.

[6] *Ui-Mail.*—The tribe-name of the descendants of Maine Mal, ancestor of most of the ancient septs of the district now represented by the co. Wicklow. The well-known Glen of Imaile, in the barony of Upper Talbotstown, co. Wicklow, derives its name from the Ui-Mail.

f Ard-Cianachta, dies. Death of Graiphnech,[1] abbot of mlech-Fia.[2] A meeting between Aedh Aldan[3] and 'athal,[4] at Tir-da-glas.[5] The 'Law' of Patrick held Ireland. 'iangalach, son of Murchadh, king of Ui-Mail,[6] dies.

Kal. Jan. A.D. 737. Faelan, grandson[7] of Bran, king f the Leinstermen, died at an unripe age, and unxpectedly. Tole,[8] bishop of Cluain-Iraird, a worthy oldier of God, rests. Cernach, son of Fogartach,[9] is reacherously slain by his own wicked associates; whom he calves of the cows, and the women of this lower orld, in long continued sadness bewailed. The battle f Ath-Senaigh[10] (*i.e.*, the battle of Uchbadh,[11] on the 4th of September, the 6th day of the week), was bstinately fought between the Ui-Neill and the Leinsteren, wherein the two kings respectively, men of heroic alour,[12] encountered each other in single combat, namely, edh Aldan, king of Tara, and Aedh son of Colgu, ing of Leinster; one of whom, Aedh Aldan, left the eld alive, though wounded, while the other, Aedh son ' Colgu,[13] had his head severed by the sword[14] of battle. hereupon the race of Conn enjoyed a signal victory, hilst with unwonted measure they routed, trampled, ushed, overthrew, and consumed their adversaries of einster, insomuch that almost their entire army perished, ıd was only saved from utter annihilation by the escape ' a few, who bore away the tidings of the disaster; and [737.]

---

[7] *Grandson.*—Faelan was the son Murchad (king of Leinster, ob. 6, *supra*), son of Bran, king of inster (ob. 692, *supra*), and the same son stated to have been successful ainst his brother in the battle of inne, recorded above at the year 727.

[8] *Tole.*—This name should be pronced Tó-lè. The *Four Masters* ite the name *Tola*, at A.D. 733.

[9] *Fogartach.*—See above, at the ır 723.

[10] *Ath-Senaigh.*—Now Ballyshannon, in the parish of the same name, barony of West Offaly, co. Kildare.

[11] *Uchbadh.* — Another name for Ath-Senaigh. This clause, added in original hand in A., is not in B.

[12] *Of heroic valour.*—celci rigoris rectores, A., B. Clar. 49 has *celsi vigores rectores.*

[13] *Aedh son of Colgu.*—The original of this is not in B.

[14] *By the sword.*—mocrone, A.

tantos cecidisse ferunt quantos per transacta retro secula in uno subcubuisse impetu 7 feroci fuisse conflictu non comperimus. Ceciderunt autem in hoc bello optimi duces .i. Aeḋ mac Colggen, Bran becc mac Murċaḋo (.i. da rig Laigen), Fergus mac Moenaiġ, Dubdacriċ mac aui Cellaiġ mic Triein, da tigerna Fotharta, Fiangalaċ .h. Maeleaiṫcen, Conall .h. Aiṫechdai, ceiṫre meic Flainn aui Congaile, Eladaċ aui Maeluiḋir, 7 ceteri multi qui compendii causa omissi sunt. Iugulatio Fergussa mic Craumṫain. Mors Corcraiċ mic Nuindenaiġ regis Galeng. Bellum Inseo in quo cecidit Fernbeand. Mors Soċaċaiġ aui Maeletoili. Slogad Caṫail mic Finnguine co Laigniu co rucc giallu O Faelain, 7 corrucc maine mara.

Kl. Ianair. Anno domini dcc°. xxx°. uiii°. Fergus glutt, rex Coḃo, sputis uenenatis maleficorum hominum obiit. Cuana nepos Bessain scriba Treoit pausat. Dormitatio Samḋainne cluano Bronaiġ, 7 dormitatio nepotis Maeledaṫnein episcopi. Comburtio muinntere Domnaill i m-Bodbraiṫ, ubi cecidit Ailill Breg leiṫ in domo cenae. Mors Ailello mic Tuaṫail, regis nepotum Cremṫain. Flann mac Cel-

---

[1] *Aedh.*—Aedh, son of Colgn, otherwise called Aedh Mend, was only king of Ui-Cendselaig, or Southern Leinster, according to a list of kings of that province contained in the Book of Leinster, p. 40, col. 1.

[2] *Fotharta.*—The principal tribes of the Fotharta at the time of the above-mentioned battle, were the two septs who gave name to the districts now represented by the baronies of Forth in the cos. of Carlow and Wexford.

[3] *Who.*—qui. Represented by 7, the sign for *et* or ocus, in A. and B. Clar. 49 reads *qui*.

[4] *Of Inis.*—Inseo. Inis means an "Island." But there is nothing in either MS. to indicate what island is here referred to.

[5] *Cathal, son of Finguine.*—King of Munster. See under the year 736.

[6] *Ui-Faelain.*—This was the tribe-name of the powerful sept descended from Faelan, king of Leinster, whose obit is given among the entries for this year. The name was also applied to the territory occupied by the clan, which included the northern part of the co. of Kildare until shortly after the English invasion, when they were driven out of this district, and settled

ch was the carnage in this battle, that more are reported have fallen in it than we read of ever having perished in y one onslaught and fierce conflict of all preceding ages. ie best captains, also, were slain in this battle, viz.:— ᵭdh,[1] son of Colgu, and Bran Bec, son of Murchadh (two ngs of Leinster), Fergus, son of Moenach, and Dubhcrich, son of the grandson of Cellach, son of Trien, two rds of Fotharta;[2] Fiangalach Ua Maelaithcen; Conall a Aitechta; the four sons of Flann, descendant of Conl; Eladach, descendant of Maeluidhir, and many others ho,[3] for the sake of brevity, are omitted. The killing Fergus, son of Cremthan. The death of Coscrach, son Noindenach, king of the Galenga. The battle of Inis,[4] which Fernbeand was slain. Death of Sothcathach, scendant of Maeltuili. A hosting by Cathal, son of nnguine,[5] to the Leinstermen, when he carried off the stages of the Ui-Faelain,[6] and great spoils.

Kal. Jan. A.D. 738. Fergus Glutt, king of Cobha, ed from the envenomed spittles[7] of evil men. Cuana, scendant of Bessan, scribe of Treoit,[8] rests. The 'fallg asleep' of Samhthann of Cluain-Bronaigh; and the alling asleep' of Ua Maeledathnen, bishop. The burng of the family of Domnall[9] in Bodbrath,[10] where Ailill Brig-Leith was slain in the banquet-house. Death of lill, son of Tuathal, king of the Ui-Cremthainn. Flann, [738.]

---

the east of the present county of icklow. In later times the most pectable representatives of the sept re the families of O'Byrne and ic Eochaidh (or Keogh). The ur Masters (A.D. 733) state that hostages were taken from Bran ; ("Bran the Little"), whose ith is recorded under this year.

[7] *Envenomed spittles.*—ſpuτιſ uenιτιſ. uenenτατιſ, A. The Four sters explain this curious entry by ting (A.D. 734) that it appeared to Fergus Glut that wicked people used to cast spittles, in which they put charms, in his face, which was the cause of his death.

[8] *Treoit.*—Trevet, in the barony of Skreen, co. Meath.

[9] *Domnall.*—Apparently the Domnall, son of Murchad, whose accession to the monarchy of Ireland is recorded at the year 742 *infra*, and who is also referred to above at 729.

[10] *Bodbrath.*—Not identified.

laiġ filii Crundiṁail, episcopus Rechrainne, moritur. Talorggan mac Drostain rex Aṫ foiṫle dimersus .i. la Oengus. Mors Aeḋ filii Garbain.

Fol. 30ab. .b. Kl. Ianair. Anno domini dcc.° xxx.° ix.° In clericatum Domnall exiit. Iugulatio nepotis Ailello tigernae cenuil Fiaċaċ. Terrimotus in Ili .ii. id. Aprilis. Flann nepos Congaile mortuus est. Cubretan mac Congusso mortuus est, 7 mors Cellaiġ filii Seċñdi, abbatis Cluano mic Noais. Dubdabairenn abbas Fobair. Dormitatio Manċeine tomae greine. Dormitatio sancti Brain lainne Ela. Fland feblae abbas Goirt chonaich moritur.

Kl. Ianair. Anno domini dcc.° xl.° Mors Conli Teṫba 7 Amalgaḋo regis Conaille. Iugulatio Murchada filii Fergaile filii Maeleduin, 7 Conall mac Iarlaiṫi moritur. Mors Flainn Aiġle, episcopi Eċdroma. Mors Fuirectaiġ principis innseo Coil. Befail ingen Seċnusaiġ moritur. Bellum Forboros in quo ceciderunt .ii. filii Fiannamlo .i. Indrectaċ 7 Conall, 7 ceteri. Iugulatio Ernani nepotis Ecuilp. Bellum cairn Feraḋaiġ in quo cecidit Torcan tinireid.

---

[1] *Rechra.*—It is not certain whether the place here intended is Rechra, now known as the Island of Lambay, to the north of Howth, co. Dublin, or Raghery (otherwise called Rathlin Island), off the north coast of the co. Antrim. The name "Rathlin," applied to this island, is a corruption of "Rechrainne," the genit. form of "Rechra."

[2] *Ath-Foithle.*—Athol, in Perthshire. For other forms of the name, see Reeves' *Adamnan*, p. 385, note j.

[3] *By Oengus.*—O'Conor reads the orig. (la Oengus) "in *Laaengi*," and translates "in nave"!

[4] *Domnall.*—Evidently Domnall, son of Murchadh, who became king of Ireland in 742, and who is elsewhere referred to in these Annals by his Christian name (Domnall) merely. The re-entrance of Domnall into religion is recorded at the year 743 *infra.*

[5] *Cinel-Fiachach.*—Usually Anglicised Kenaliagh. The territory of the descendants of Fiacha, son of Niall Nine-hostager, which comprised some of the southern part of the present co. Westmeath, and a large portion of the King's county adjoining. It was in later times known as "Mageoghegan's Country." See O'Donovan's ed. of O'Dubhagain, note 30.

[6] *Ile.*—The Island of Islay, Scotland.

[7] *Flann Ua Congaile.* "Flann, de-

on of Cellach, son of Crundmael, bishop of Rechra,[1] dies. Talorgan, son of Drostan, king of Ath-Foithle,[2] was drowned, viz., by Oengus.[3] Death of Aedh, son of Garbhan.

Kal. Jan. A.D. 739. Domnall[4] entered into religion. The killing of Ua Ailella, lord of Cinel-Fiachach.[5] An earthquake in Ile,[6] on the 2nd of the Ides of April. Flann Ua Congaile[7] died. Cubretan, son of Congus, died; and the death of Cellach, son of Secde, abbot of Cluain-mic-Nois. Dubdabairenn, abbot of Fobhar, [died]. The 'falling asleep' of Mancheine of Tuaim-greine.[8] The 'falling asleep' of Saint Bran of Lann-Ela. Flann Febhla, abbot of Gort-chonaich, dies. [739.] BIS.

Kal. Jan. A.D. 740. Death of Conla of Tethba, and of Amalgaidh, king of Conaille. The killing of Murchadh, son of Fergal,[9] son of Maelduin; and Conall, son of Carlaith, dies. Death of Flann Aighle, bishop of Echdruim.[10] Death of Fuirechtach, superior of Inis-Coil.[11] Befail, daughter of Sechnasach, dies. The battle of Forboros,[12] in which Fiannamail's two sons, viz., Indrechtach and Conall, and others, were slain. The killing of Ernaine, son of Eculp. Battle of Carn-Feradhaigh,[13] in [740.]

---

scendant of Congal;" the same person referred to above under the year 737, where four of his sons are stated to have been slain in the battle of Ath-Senaigh. The obit of Flann is given by the *Four Masters* at A.D. 746.

[8] *Tuaim-greine.*—Tomgraney, in the barony of Upper Tulla, co. Clare. The *Chron. Scot.*, at A.D. 964, refers the erection of its *cloigtech* (or Round Tower) to Cormac Ua Cillin, whose obit is given at that year in the same Chronicle. The entry is remarkable as being the first record occurring in the Irish Annals, indicating the date of the erection of a Round Tower.

[9] *Fergal.*—Fergal, king of Ireland, whose death in the battle of Allen (co. Kildare) is recorded at the year 721 *supra*.

[10] *Echdruim.*—Now Aughrim, in the co Galway, the site of the famous "battle of Aughrim," fought on July 12th, 1691, between the Jacobite and Williamite armies, in which the Jacobites were defeated.

[11] *Inis-Coil.*—Now Inishkeel, an island on the south side of Gweebarra Bay, in the barony of Boylagh, co. Donegal.

[12] *Forboros.*—This place has not been identified.

[13] *Carn-Feradhaigh.*—See note [4] at the year 626 *supra*.

Iugulatio Ailello corraiġ mic Flainn, regis Ua Failġe. Bellum droma Caṫmail inter Cruiṫniu 7 Dalriati fri Indrechtaċ. Percussio Dalriatai la hOengus mac Forggusso. Corp Petronille inġine Peadair d'aṫrugad hoc anno, 7 na foccail ro d'faġḃail scriptha do litir Peadair fein annsan aḋlacaḋ ṁarmuir as ar ṫogaḋ hi .i. area Petronille dilectissime filie.

Kl. Ianair. Anno domini dcc.° xl.° i.° Mors Airechtaiġ filii Cuanaċ principis Fernand. Foirtbe ceniuil Fiaċaċ 7 Delmne la Ossaiġe. Mors Caṫail mic Finnguine regis Caisil. Mors Maileoctriġ abbatis Cille foibriġ. Mors Cuidgile scriba 7 abbatis Luġmaiḋ. Mors Aeḋo Ḃailb regis Conacht .i. mac Indreċtaiġ mic Muiredaig. Strangulatio Conaing mic Amalgaiḋ regis Ciannaċtae. Iugulatio Artraċ filii Aiṫecdai, riġ nepotum Craumṫainn. Lepra in

[1] *Flann.*—Better known to the students of Irish (MS.) history as Flann-Dachongal, king of the Ui-Failge for fourteen years. See *Book of Leinster*, p. 40, col. 3.

[2] *Cruithni—Dalriata.*—It is not certain whether these were the Picts (*Cruithni*) and Dalriads of Scotland, or those of Ireland. But they were probably the Pictish and Dalriadic septs of Ireland. "Dalriata" is written Dal reti in A., Dal riati in B., and Dalriada in Clar. 49.

[3] '*Smiting.*'—percutio, A. percusio, B. "Percussio," Clar. 49.

[4] *Petronilla.*—There can be no doubt that there was a very early martyr or confessor of this name, which is a diminutive—not of Peter, as is supposed, but of Petronius, and formed in the same manner as Drusilla and Priscilla; although in French it is *Perrine*. She was probably of the noble Roman "familia Petronia." And as to her relationship to St. Peter, it may, as Baronius suggests, have been in the same sense as "Marcus filius meus." This writer treats of her under the year of Christ 69, (cap. xxxiii.—*Annales*, tom. i., p. 640 *b*—ed. Lucæ 1738). She is commemorated at the 31st of May, in the Roman and other Martyrologies; and all the particulars that are known or conjectured of her history are to be found in the Actt. SS. of the Bollandists at that day. Of her translation (above represented by aṫrugad) the earliest authority is the chronicle of Sigebert of Gemblours, who died in 1113, and, at 758, has the following entry:—"Corpus Sanctæ Petronillæ, Petri apostoli filiæ, a Paulo papa transponitur, in cujus marmoreo sarcophago, ipsius apostoli Petri manu sculptum legebatur: Aureæ Petronillæ, dilectissimæ filiæ.—Pistorius, *Rer. Germ. Script.*, tom. i., p. 776 (ed. Ratisb. 1726). According to most ancient authorities the 'translation' of the remains of St. Petronilla

ʼhich fell Torcan Tinireid. The killing of Ailill Corrach, on of Flann,[1] king of the Ui-Failghe. The battle of)ruim-Cathmail, between the Cruithni[2] and Dalriata,[2] gainst Indrechtach. The 'smiting'[3] of the Dalriata by ʼengus, son of Forgus. The body of Petronilla,[4] daughter f Peter, was translated in this year; and these words ʼere found written, in Peter's own handwriting, in the ıarble tomb out of which it was taken, viz.:—"the place)f rest] of Petronilla, most dearly beloved daughter."

Kal. Jan. A.D. 741. Death of Airechtach, son of uanu, superior of Ferns. The devastation of Cinel-ʼiachach[5] and Delbna,[6] by the Osraighe. Death of athal, son of Finnguine, King of Cashel. Death of ʼaelochtraigh, abbot of Cill-Fobrigh. Death of Cudgilè, ꞔribe and abbot of Lughmadh. Death of Aedh Balb, son f Indrechtach, son of Muiredach, King of Connaught. he strangling of Conaing,[7] son of Amalgaidh, King of ianachta. The killing of Artru, son of Aithechda, King ʼ the Ui-Cremthainn. A leprosy in Ireland. Besiege- [741.]

ıs effected by Pope Paul I., who ıs under the fear that the cemetery which they were deposited might, th other cemeteries, be desecrated. Ɛrat inter alia (Baronius says) vetus ꞔmeterium, S. Petronillæ dictum, ex o idem Pontifex sacrum corpus ısdem sanctæ sublatum, transtulit ud basilicam Vaticanam hoc anno." *ınales*, J. C. 758 (tom. 12, p. 644). e Stoke's ed. of the *Felire of Aengus*, xci.; *Obits and Martyrology of ꞔrist Church, Dublin*, p. 121; and *ıok of Lismore*, fol. 52, *b*, 1. The ıntificate of Pope Paul (I.), 757–766, ıbraces the date of 'Translation' St. Petronilla's remains, as given Sigebert, but is 18 years later than e date in these Annals. It is to be ꞔther observed, that the motto said have been found on her tomb, as given by Aringhi (*Roma Subterranea*) and older writers, commences with the word *aureæ*, whereas these Annals read *area*, in which case the word was probably supposed to bear the interpretation of cœmeterium, or sepulchrum.

[5] *Cinel-Fiachach.*—See note under A.D. 739.

[6] *Delbna.*—Ꝺelmne, A., B. Delvna, Clar. 49. There were several territories in Ireland known by this name. The territory here referred to was probably Delbna-Ethra, in later times called MacCochlan's country, and now represented by the barony of Garrycastle, in the King's county, which adjoined the territory of Cinel-Fiachach.

[7] *Conaing.*—Apparently the Conaing mentioned above at the year 736.

Hibernia. Obsessio Ailiuin filii Cruip. Iugulatio Ceniuil Choirpri i n-Granairet.

Kl. Ian. Anno domini dcc.º xl.º ii.º Mors Affricae dominatricis Cille daro. Bellum Daim dergg in quo ceciderunt Dungal mac Flaind, ri Cul, 7 Fol. 30ba. Fergus mac Ostiċ. Inrechtaċ nepos Conaing uictor erat. Mors Cumene nepotis Ciarain, abbatis Reċrainne. Bellum Seretmaiġe (.i. i Cenannas, la Domnall mac Murċaḋa), in quo ceciderunt Aeḋ oldain mac Fergaile, 7 Cumuscaċ mac Concobair ri na n-Airther, 7 Moenaċ mac Conlaiċ rex nepotum Cremthain [7], Muireḋaċ mac Fergusa forcraiḋ, rex nepotum Tuirtri.

Tiugrand Aeḋa Aldain so:—

Dia nommanred mo Dia dil,
For bru loċa Sailcedain,
Iarum diambeinnsi fri col,
Roraḋ main ar moḋ m'anacol.

Bellum itir aui Maine, 7 Ua Fiaċraċ Aiḋne. Bellum Luirg hitir ui Ailello 7 Gailengo. Haec .iiii. bella pene in una aestate perfecta sunt. Lex nepotis

---

[1] *Son of Crop.*—filii Cruip, A. Cuirp (of Corp) B. Cruip, Clar. 49.

[2] *Granairet.*—"Granard" [co. Longford], Clar. 49.

[3] *Abbess.*—dominatrix, A., B., and Clar. 49, for dominatricis.

[4] *Dam-Derg.*—This place has not been identified. The *Four Mast.* (738) state that it was in Breagh. See next note. The name would signify "Red Ox" (or Red Deer).

[5] *Cul.*—In the *Ann. Four Mast.*, at the year 738, where the battle of Dam-Derg is entered, this name is represented by Fer Cul (genit. of Fir Cul) the name of a district otherwise called Feara Cul Breġ, comprising the baronies of Upper and Lower Kells, in the co. Meath.

[6] *Rechra.*—Either Lambay Island, to the north of Howth, co. Dublin, or Rathlin Island, off the north coast of Antrim.

[7] *Cenannas.*—This was the old Irish name of Kells, co. Meath. This clause, which is added in *al. man.* in A., is not in B. Clar. 49 has "Bellum Sretmaii at Kelles by Daniell M'Murchaa." A marg. note in A. has Domnall mac Murchada uictor fuit.

[8] *Aedh Aldan*, or *Aedh Allan*—Monarch of Ireland.

[9] *Airthera.*—The Oriors. The name of this district, which is often referred

ent of Ailivin, son of Crop.[1] The killing of the Cinel-oirpri in Granairet.[2]

Kal. Jan. A.D. 742. Death of Affrica, abbess[3] of Kil-are. The battle of Dam-Derg,[4] in which Dungal, son ? Flann, King of Cul,[5] and Fergus, son of Ostech, were ain. Indrechtach, descendant of Conaing, was victor. eath of Cumene, descendant of Ciaran, abbot of Rechra.[6] he battle of Sered-magh (*i.e.*, at Cenannas,[7] by Domnall, on of Murchad), in which fell Aedh Aldan,[8] son of 'ergal, and Cumuscach, son of Conchobar, King of the irthera,[9] and Moenach, son of Conlaech, King of the Ji-Cremthainn, and Muiredach, son of Fergus Forcraidh,[10] ing of the Ui-Tuirtri. [742.]

This is Aedh Aldan's last verse[11]:—

"If my dear God protected me,
On the brink of Loch-Sailcedan;[12]
If I were afterwards given to sin,
My protection would be beyond rule."

battle between the Ui-Maine and Ui-Fiachrach of idhne. The battle of Lorg,[13] between the Ui-Ailello,[14] nd Gailenga.[15] These four battles were fought almost

---

as "Orientales," *i.e.*, the eastern rts of the ancient territory of the irghialla, is still represented by the ronies of Lower and Upper Orior, the co. Armagh.

[10] *Fergus Forcraidh.*—The death of is person is recorded at the year 702, *pra.*

[11] *Last verse.* — The lines which llow here are written in the top argin of A., fol. 30 *d.* They are ot in B.

[12] *Loch-Sailcedan.* — Now Lough-llagh, in the parish of Dunboyne, . Meath, according to O'Donovan. *our Mast.*, A.D. 738, note *i.*

[13] *Lorg.*—This place has not been identified.

[14] *Ui-Ailello.* — "Descendants of Ailill." The tribe name of the sept that inhabited the district forming the present barony of Tirerrill (in Irish Tip Ailella, or the land of Ailill).

[15] *Gailenga.*--This was the tribe name of a clan descended from Oilill Oluim, King of Munster, who occupied a large district embracing part of the present counties of Mayo and Sligo. The name of Gailenga is still preserved in that of the barony of Gallen, co. Mayo.

Suanaiġ. Conċenn ingen Cellaiġ Cualann moritur. Iugulatio Duibdoiṫre regis nepotum Briuin. Affiaċ abbas Maiġi bile [moritur]. Commotatio martirum Treno Cille deilgge, 7 in bolgach. Domnall mac Murchada regnare incipit.

.b. Kl. Ian. Anno domini dcc.° xl.° iii.° Iugulatio Laidggnein filii Doimennaiġ, episcopi, abbatis Saiġrae, Domnall in clericatum iterum. Iugulatio Colmain episcopi Lessain, la U Tuirtri. Bellum Cliaċ in quo cecidit Concobar di auib Fidgenti. Bellum Ailiuin daberraċ in quo cecidit Dubdadoss mac Murgaile. Da auae Ceallaiġ cualand, Caṫal 7 Ailill, interfecti sunt. Iugulatio Muirgiussa filii Anluain i Tuilain. Foirddbe Corcumudruaḋ don Deiss. Lex Ciarain filii artificis, 7 lex Brendain simul, la Fergus mac Ceallaiġ. Mors Fergussa mic Colmain cutlaiġ sapientis.

Kl. Ian. Anno domini dcc.° xl.° iiii.° In nocte siġnum horribile 7 mirabile uisum est in stellis. Forannan abbas Cluana iraird obiit, 7 Conġus ancorita Cluana tibrinne. Cummaene aua Moenaiġ, abbas Lainne leire, moritur. Bellum inter nepotes

[1] *Ua Suanaigh.*—"Descendant of Suanach." The "Fidhmuine . . . nepos Suanaich," whose "quies" is recorded at the year 756, *infra*. The 'Law' of Ua Suanaigh is again mentioned at the year 747.

[2] *Dubhdoithre.*—The "Black [man] of the Dothra" (the river Dodder, co. Dublin). This river runs through part of the old territory of the Ui-Briuin-Cualand.

[3] *Bolgach.*—See above, at the year 679.

[4] *Saighir.*—Seirkieran, a parish in the barony of Ballybritt, King's County.

[5] *Again.*—iterum. This seems to have been the second effort of Domnall [son of Murchad, Monarch of Ireland] to assume the religious state. See above, at the year 739. But *clericatus* is sometimes applied to a "pilgrimage," and does not always mean the state of being in priest's orders.

[6] *Lessan.*—Now Lissan, in the parish of the same name, barony of Dungannon Upper, co. Tyrone.

[7] *Cliu.*—See note [4], at A.D. 626, *supra*.

[8] *Ailen-daberrach.* — The "two-peaked Island." Situation unknown. The *Four Mast.* (O'Don. ed.) at A.D. 739, write the name *Ailen* (gen. *Ailiuin*) *da bernach* ("two-gapped Island").

one summer. The 'Law' of Ua Suanaigh.[1] Conchenn, ughter of Cellach Cualann, dies. The killing of ıbhdoithre,[2] King of the Ui-Briuin. Affiath, abbot Magh-Bilè, [dies]. Translation of the relics of Trian Cill-Deilge; and the 'bolgach.'[3] Domnall, son of ırchadh, begins to reign.

Kal. Jan. A.D. 743. The killing of Laidgnen, son of [743.] BIS.
›inennach, a bishop, abbot of Saighir.[4] Domnall enters ain[5] into religion. The killing of Colman, bishop of ›ssan,[6] by the Ui-Tuirtri. The battle of Cliu,[7] in which ll Conchobar of the Ui-Fidgenti. Battle of Ailen-.berrach,[8] in which fell Dubhdadoss, son of Murgal. wo grandsons of Cellach Cualann,[9] Cathal and Ailill, ere slain. The killing of Muirges, son of Anluan, in ıilan.[10] Devastation of the Corca-Modhruadh by the ›isi. The 'Law' of Ciaran,[11] son of the Carpenter, and the ıaw' of Brendan,[12] at the same time, by Fergus,[13] son of ›llach. Death of Fergus, son of Colman Cutlach, a wise an.

Kal. Jan. A.D. 744. A terrible and wonderful sign [744.]
as seen in the stars at night. Forannan, abbot of .uain-Iraird, died; and Conghus, anchorite of Cluain-brinne.[14] Cummaene, grandson of Moenach, abbot of ınn-leire,[15] dies. A battle between the Ui-Tuirtri and

---

9 *Cellach Cualann.*—King of Lein-r. His obit is given above, under e year 714.

10 *Tuilan.*—ı Tuılcaın, A., B. Clar. has "at the hill Tula aoin." ıe place in question was probably ıilen, now known as Dulane, in the rony of Upper Kells, co. Meath.

11 *Ciaran.*—Founder and patron of onmacnoise. His obit occurs at the ar 548, *supra*.

12 *Brendan.*—St. Brendan of Clon-t (ob. 576, *supra*).

13 *Fergus.*—King of Connaught at › time.

14 *Cluain-Tibrinne.*—Now known as Clontivrin, in the par. of Clones, co. Monaghan.

15 *Moenach, abbot of Lann-leire.*—The obit of a Maenach, abbot of Lann-leire, is given above at the year 720. He was probably the same as the Moenach here referred to. Lann-leire, which O'Donovan (*Four Mast.*, A.D. 740, note *w*) would identify with Lynn, in the parish of the same name, barony of Fartullagh, co. Westmeath, has been proved by Dean Reeves to be the place now known as Dunleer, co. Louth. See Todd's *Cogadh*

Tuirtri 7 na hAirṫeru. Congal mac Eicniġ uictor fuit; 7 Cuċongalt filius nepotis Caṫasaiġ fugitiuus euasit; 7 ceciderunt Boċaill mac Concoḃair, 7 Ailill nepos Caṫasaiġ. I n-inis itir da Dabul gestum est. Mors Conaill foltċain scribae. Mors Cinnḟaelad principis Dromo Cuilinn. Mors filii inḋferṫaigse abbatis tiġe Taille.

Fol. 30 bb Kl. Ianair. Anno domini dcc.° xl.° u.° Dormitatio Cormaicc Aṫo Truim. Dracones in coelo uisi sunt. Mors Beoċaill Arda achaiḋ. Imthoitim Dungaile feillae 7 Muircertaiġ filii Caṫail. Conmaicne ceciderunt, 7 Ferggus uictus euasit. Ar .h. Briuin in deisceird la Fergus. Mors Maeleanfaiṫ Cille aċaiḋ drommo foto. Fingal Liss moer. Mors Duibdaḃairend nepotis Beccan, abb Cluana auis. Mors Oengusa filii Tipraiti, abbatis Cluana fota, 7 Ciallṫroġ abbas Glaisse noide moritur. Mors Seċnusaiġ mic Colggen regis nepotum Cennselaiġ. Sarugaḋ domnaiġ Phatraicc, ui. cimmidi cruciati.

Gaedhel re Gallaibh, Introd., p. xl., note [2], and *Chron. Scot.* (ed. Hennessy), page 136, note [2].

[1] *Airthera.* — Clar. 49 translates Airthera by "the East partes." See note under the year 742.

[2] *Congal.*—His death is recorded under 747, *infra.*

[3] *Inis-itir-da-Dabul.*—The "Island between two Dabals." In Clar. 49 it is stated that the battle was fought "at Inis between the two Davuls." Dabhal was the ancient Irish name of the River Blackwater, which forms the boundary, for a long distance, between the counties of Armagh and Tyrone. A tributary to this river, called the "River Tall," which joins the Blackwater, after a circuitous course, a few miles to the north of Charlemont, in the county of Armagh, may be the second Dabhal.

[4] *Conall Foltchain.* — "Conall of the fair (or beautiful) hair."

[5] *Druim-Cuilinn.*—Drumcullen, in the south of the barony of Eglish, King's County.

[6] *Mac-ind-ferthaigse.*—This name would signify "Son of the Œconomus (or steward)." See Reeves' *Adamnan*, p. 365.

[7] *Tech-Taille.*—See note [13], under the year 671, *supra.*

[8] *Ath-truim.*—Trim, co. Meath.

[9] *Ard-achadh.*—"High-field." Ardagh, co. Longford.

[10] *Escaped.* — The Author of the version of these Annals in Clar. 49

Airthera.[1] Congal,[2] son of Eicnech, was victor; Cuchongalt, son of Ua Cathasaigh, escaped by flight; . Bochaill, son of Conchobhar, and Ailill Ua Cathasaigh, e slain. In Inis-itir-da-Dabul[3] it was fought. Death Conall Foltchain,[4] a scribe. Death of Cennfaeladh, erior of Druim-Cuilinn.[5] Death of Mac-ind-ferthaigse,[6] ot of Tech-Taille.[7]

Kal. Jan. A.D. 745. The 'falling asleep' of Cormac Ath-truim.[8] Dragons were seen in the sky. Death Beochall of Ard-achadh.[9] The falling by one another Dungal Feille, and Muirchertach, son of Cathal. The maicne were slain, and Fergus, who was vanquished, aped.[10] A slaughter of the Ui-Briuin, of the South,[11] by gus.[12] Death of Maelanfaith of Cill-achaidh of Druim-a.[13] Fingal of Lis-mor [died]. Death of Dubhdabhairenn, cendant of Beccan, abbot of Cluain-eois. Death of ngus, son of Tipraiti, abbot of Cluain-fota;[14] and lltrogh, abbot of Glais-noide,[15] dies. Death of hnasach, son of Colgu, King of the Ui-Cennselaigh. ofanation of Domnach-Patraicc,[16] and six prisoners tured.[17] [745.]

---

ns to have quite misunderstood entry, for he renders Ϝeꞃgguꞅ cuꞅ euaꞅꞅıꞇ by "Fergus went ly conqueror."

Ui-Briuin of the South.—Probably Ui-Briuin-Seola, who were seated the present barony of Clare, co. lway; and therefore the most thern of all the septs of the Ui-uin in Connaught.

[12] *Fergus.*—This must have been Fergus, son of Cellach, King of naught, mentioned above at the r 743.

[13] *Cill-achaidh of Druim-fota.*—'he church of the field of the long ge." Now Killeigh, in the parish Geashill, King's County.

[14] *Cluain-fota.*—Now Clonfad, in the barony of Farbill, co. Westmeath.

[15] *Glais-noide* — *Rectè* "Glais-noiden." Glasnevin, near Dublin.

[16] *Domnach-Patraicc.* — Donagh-patrick, in the barony of Upper Kells, co. Meath. See under the year 749, *infra.*

[17] *Six prisoners tortured.*—uı. cımmıꝺı cꞃucı̄ (for cꞃucıaꞇı), A., B. The entry is translated in Clar. 49, "The forcible entry (ꞅaꞃuġaꝺ) of Donagh Patrick, and 6 prisoners crucified or tormented." O'Conor renders it by "Violatio Ecclesiæ Dunpatric. Sex primariorum Midiæ suspensi."!

Kl. Ian. (i f., l. xvi.) Anno domini dcc.° xl.° vi.° alias 747. Mors Abeil abbatis Imleċo Fea. Mors Muireḋaiġ minn, regis nepotum Meiṫ. Cuanan Glinne abbas maiġi Bile mortuus est. Aeḋ muinderg mac Flaiṫbertaiġ rex in tuaiscirt [obiit]. Seċnusaċ mac Colgen rex Laigen obiit. Cucuimne sapiens obiit. Muime Ċoncuimne cecinit:—

Cuċuimne
Roleġ suiṫe co drumne;
Alleith naill hiaruṫa
Roleici an ċailleċa.

Ando Coimcuimne rombói
Imrualaid de conid soi;
Roleic cailleċa ha saill,
Roleig alaill arithmbói

Ruman mac Colmain poeta optimus quievit. Mors Sarain abbatis Benncair. Bellum Cairn ailċe la Mumain, in quo cecidit Cairpri mac Condinaisc. Mors Dunlaingi filii Dunċon, regis ceniuil Ardgail. Mors Tuaṫalain abbatis Cinnriġmonai. Iugulatio Aeḋa duiḃ filii Caṫail. Pausatio Comain religiosi .i. ind Róis, 7 quies Firdacriċ abbatis Dairinse. Mors

[1] *Alias* 747.—Added in *al. man.* in A.

[2] *Imlech-Fea.*—The same as the Imlech-Pich mentioned above at the year 687, where see note.

[3] *Magh-Bilè.*—The plain of the *bilè*, or sacred tree. Now Movilla, in the par. of Newtownards, co. Down.

[4] *Tuaiscert.*—"The North." This term was anciently applied to the North of Ireland in general; but in later times it was used to indicate the northern part of the co. Antrim, with the country about Coleraine in Londonderry. For the limits of *Tuaiscert*, see Reeves' *Eccl. Antiqq.*, pp. 71, 324.

[5] *King of Leinster.*—The name of Sechnasach does not appear in the list of the Kings of Leinster, contained in the *Book of Leinster* (p. 39); but his name is included among the Kings of Ui-Cendselaig (or South Leinster) in p. 40, col. 1, where he is stated to have reigned two years.

[6] *Cucuimne.*—The original of these lines, which are not in B., are added in the lower margin, fol. 30 *b*, in A.

Kal. Jan, (Sund., m. 15.) A.D. 746, alias 747.[1] Death [746.]
Abel, abbot of Imlech-Fea.[2] Death of Muiredach Menn,
ng of the Ui-Meith. Cuanan of Glenn, abbot of Magh-
ə,[3] died. Aedh Muinderg, son of Flaithbertach, King
the Tuaiscert,[4] [died]. Sechnasach, son of Colgu,
ng of Leinster,[5] died. Cucuimne, a wise man, died.
cuimne's nurse sang:—

Cucuimne[6]
Read knowledge half through;
The other half . . . .
He abandoned for hags.

Well for Cucuimne, as he was,
When it chanced that he was a sage,
He abandoned hags,
He read again whilst he lived.

man,[7] son of Colman, the best poet, rested. Death of
an, abbot of Bangor. The battle of Carn-Ailche[8] in
nster, in which Cairpre, son of Cudinaisc, was slain.
ath of Dunlang, son of Dunchu, King of Cinel-Artgail.
ath of Tuathalan, abbot of Cinnrighmona.[9] The killing
Aedh Dubh, son of Cathal. The rest[10] of Coman the
us, *i.e.*, of the Róes,[11] and the rest of Ferdacrich, abbot
Dairinis.[12] The death of Rudgal, of the Leinstermen.

---

[7] *uman.*—Called the "Virgil of the hil."

[8] *arn-Ailche.* — O'Donovan sug- (*Four Mast.*, A.D. 742, note *l*) this was probably the place now l Carnelly, near the town of , in the county of Clare.

[9] *innrighmona.*—Called "Cell-onaig" in the *Felire of Aengus*, tober 11. It was the ancient of St. Andrews, in Scotland. See 's *Adamnan*, p. 385, note *l*.

[10] *Rest.*—Pausatio.

[11] *Róes.*—ind rois, "of the Ros," *Four Mast.* (A.D. 742). Supposed, but on no sufficient authority, to be *Ros-Comain*, now Roscommon, in the co. Roscommon. See O'Donovan's ed. of the *Four Mast.*, A.D. 746, note *i*.

[12] *Dairinis.*—"Oak Island." Otherwise called Dairinis-Maelanfaidh. Now known as Molana, an island in the Blackwater, a few miles to the N.W. of Youghal.

Rudgaile di Luigniḃ. Quies Iacobi[1] Farannain, predicatoris maximi tempore suo.

b. Kt. Ianair. Anno domini dcc.° xl.° uii.° Baḋud Arascaiċ abaid Muiccinnse Reguil.[2] Quies Cuain caimb sapientis. Nix insolitae magnitudinis, ita ut pene pecora deleta sunt totius Hibernie; ut postea insolita siccitate mundus exarsit. Mors Indreactaiġ nepotis Conaing regis Ciannaċte. Dormitatio Dodimóc[3] anċoritae, abbatis Cluana iraird 7 Cille daro. Documai[4] sapiens, Muirenn[5] filia Cellaiġ
Fol. 31aa. Cualann, regina Irgalaiġ, moriuntur. Occisio Congaile mic Eicniġ, regis na n-airṫer, irraiṫ Erclai. Lex aui Suanaiċ[6] for Leiṫ Cuinn. Flann forbṫe mac Fogertaiġ, Cuan anchorita o Lilcaċ, moriuntur.

Kt. Ianair. Anno domini dcc.° xl.° uiii.° Iugulatio Caṫusaiġ filii Ailello irraiṫ Beiṫeċ regis Cruiṫne. Mors Bresail mic Colggen, abbatis Fernand. Comburtio Cluana ferta Brendain. Comburtio Cille moire Aedain filii Oengussa. Bellum airde Ciannachtae, in quo cecidit Ailill mac Duibdacriċ, ri Arda oa Cinnfaelaḋ, in quo cecidit Domnall mac Cinadon i frigduin, id est rex qui uicit prius. Mors

---

[1] *Jacob.*—This entry, which is added in *al. man.* in A., is not in B.; but it is in Clar. 49.

[2] *Mucinis Riagail.*—"Riagal's Pig-island." The festival day of St. Riagal, who gave name to this island, is set down in the Calendars of Donegal and Aengus at October 16; and it is stated that the place was in Loch-Deirgdeirc, now Lough-Derg, an expansion of the Shannon between Portumna and Killaloe. O'Conor entirely misunderstood the name *Riagail*, which he renders by "ab alienigenis," as if he thought it represented the words ria gallaib, "by Foreigners."

[3] *Dodimóc.*—"Thy little Dimma." This name is also written *Modimóc*, "My little Dimma."

[4] *Docmuai.*—"Thy Cumai." Also written *Mocumai*, "My Cumai." O'Conor wrongly prints Dochumai *do chuain*, and translates "mœrore," thinking that the Annalist intended to represent Dodimóc, referred to in the preceding entry, as having died "of grief"! O'Donovan falls into the same error. (*Four Mast.*, Vol. I., p. 347, note *o*).

[5] *Muirenn.*—She was the mother of Cinaedh, King of Ireland, whose death is recorded above, at the year 727.

[6] '*Law' of Ua Suanaigh.*—See above at the year 742.

'est of Jacob,[1] descendant of Forannan, the greatest her in his time.

l. Jan. A.D. 747. Drowning of Arascach, abbot of [747] BIS. ıis-Riagail.[2] The rest of Cuan Cam, a wise man. · of unusual quantity, so that almost all the cattle of ıd were destroyed; and the world afterwards was .ed from unusual drought. Death of Indrechtach 'onaing, King of Cianachta. The 'falling asleep' of móc,[3] anchorite, abbot of Cluain-Iraird and Cill-dara. mai,[4] the Wise, Muirenn,[5] daughter of Cellach ınn, queen of Irgalach, died. The slaying of Congal of Eicnech, King of the Airthera, in Rath-escla. 'Law' of Ua Suanaigh[6] over Leth-Chuinn.[7] Flann the,[8] son of Fogartach, and Cuan, anchorite from ch, died.

ıl. Jan. A.D. 748. The killing of Cathasach, son of [748.] ., King of the Cruithni,[9] in Rath-beithech.[10] Death resal, son of Colgu, abbot of Ferna. Burning of ın-ferta-Brendain. Burning of Cill-mor of Aedan[11] the of Oengus. The battle of Ard-Cianachta, in which ., son of Dubhdacrich, King of Ard-Ua-Cinnfaelaidh, slain, and in which fell Domnall, son of Cinadon,[12] in

---

h-Chuinn.—"Conn's Half." The rn half of Ireland.

ınn Forbthe.—The death of a n Forbthe, son of Fogartagh," red under the year 715 *supra.*

uithni.—The Cruithni, or Picts, ıd. The *Four Masters*, who the death of Cathasach at the 49, call him "King of Ulad." me occurs as one of the kings .t province in the list contained *Book of Leinster* (p. 41, col. 3).

ath-beithech.—O'Donovan con- l this place to be Rathbeagh, a ınd in the barony of Galmoy, lkenny. *Four Mast.*, A.D. 749, v. But he was probably in error. The name is written *Rath-betha* in the *Book of Leinster*, p. 41, col. 3.

11 *Cill-mor of Aedan.*—The *Martyr. of Donegal*, at Aedan's day (Nov. 2), states that this church was in Ui-Meith-Macha, a district in the co. Monaghan. The name seems to be now represented by Kilmore, a parish in the barony and county of Monaghan.

12 *Cinadon.*—Ciaᴅo (for Cinaᴅon), the genit. form, A., B. "Ciandon," Clar. 49. The *Four Mast.* (744) write the name "Cionaodo" (gen. form), *i.e.*, "of Cionadh," or Cinaedh, which is probably more correct.

Coirpri mic Murcaḋo Mide 7 Becc Baili mic Eċaċ, 7 Libir abbatis maiġi Bile; 7 uentus magnus. Dimersio familiae Iae. Mors Conaill abbatis Tome greine. Naues in aere uisae sunt cum suis uiris, os cinn Cluana mic Nois.

Kl. Ianair. Anno domini dcc.° xl.° ix.° Combustio Foḃair 7 combustio Domnaiġ Phatraig. Mors Suairliċ episcoip Foḃair. Quies Congusso episcoip aird Maċae. Bellum Cato hic inter Pictones 7 Brittones, in quo cecidit Talorggan mac Ferggussa, frater Oengussa. Mors Caṫail Mainmaiġe, regis nepotum Maine. Au inis deseritur. Mors aui Cuirc Cille daro. Mors comarpaiġ filii Ceallain, abbatis Cille more Einir. Mors Condinaisc nepotis Ferggusso, di auiḃ Fiaċraċ. Iugulatio Fiacraċ mic Ailein regis Moġdairne, 7 Bresail mic Aeḋo roin. Aiṫbe flaṫo Oengussa. Mors Duiḃdaleiṫi abbatis cille Scire. Mac Neṁnaill abbas Biror mortuus est. Mors Conċoṫaiġ filii Moiniġ.

Kl. Ianair. Anno domini dcc.° l.° Mors Flaind nepotis Congaile regis nepotum Foilġi. Mors Fergusa filii Fogertaiġ regis deiscerd Breg. Com-

---

[1] *Family.*—The *Four Mast.*, at 744, say "a great number of the family."

[2] *Fobhar.*—Fore, in the barony of Fore, co. Westmeath; where there are some fine ruins of a monastery, and other ancient remains.

[3] *Domnach-Patraic.* — Donaghpatrick, in the barony of Upper Kells, co. Meath. See above, at year 745, where a curious entry regarding Donaghpatrick is given.

[4] *Congus.* — In the list of the *Comarbs*, or successors, of St. Patrick contained in the *Book of Leinster* (p. 42, col. 3), Congus is distinguished by the epithet scribnid, or "scribe." See Todd's *St. Patrick*, p. 181. The *Ann. Four Mast.*, at A.D. 732, have some Irish verses attributed to Congus.

[5] *Cato.* — The MSS. A. and B. have Catohic; but Clar. 49 has "Bellum Cato hic." *Catohic* may possibly be a mistake for *Catonic.* See Reeves' *Adamnan*, p. 385, note *m.*

[6] *Au-inis.*—The "Island of Au." Not identified.

[7] *Ua Cuirc.* — "Descendant (or grandson) of Corc." This person, whose real name is not known, is not found in the ordinary lists of the abbots or ecclesiastics of Kildare.

[8] *Cill-mor-Einir.* — Or Cill-mor-

heat of battle, to wit, the king who conquered at
. Death of Coirpre, son of Murchadh Mide, and of
c Baili son of Echa, and of Liber abbot of Magh-Bilè;
great wind. Drowning of the Family[1] of Ia. Death
Conall, abbot of Tuaim-greine. Ships, with their
vs, were seen in the air, over Clonmacnoise.

al. Jan. A.D. 749. Burning of Fobhar,[2] and burn- [749.]
of Domnach-Patraic.[3] Death of Suairlech, bishop of
har.[2] The rest of Congus,[4] bishop of Ard-Macha.
battle of Cato,[5] in this year, between the Picts and
ons, in which fell Talorgan son of Fergus, the brother
)engus. Death of Cathal of Maenmagh, King of the
Maine. Au-inis[6] is deserted. Death of Ua Cuirc,[7] of
-dara. Death of Comarpach son of Ceallan, abbot of
-mor-Enir.[8] Death of Cudinaisc, descendant of
gus, of the Ui-Fiachrach. The killing of Fiachra
of Alen, King of Moghdarna, and of Bresal son of
h Roen. End[9] of the reign of Oengus.[10] Death of
)haleithe,[11] abbot of Cill-Scirè.[12] Mac Nemhnaill,
ot of Birr, dies. Death of Cucothaigh son of
nach.

al. Jan. A.D. 750. Death of Flann descendant of [750]
gal,[13] King of the Ui-Failghi. Death of Fergus[14]
of Fogartach, King of the South of Brega. Burn-

---

he Einir, the "big church of -Einir." Now Kilmore, a few to the east of the city of gh.

nd.—aitbe; lit. ebb, decay, or ction. O'Conor inaccurately rs the entry by "Atlii ducis isii."

engus—Seemingly Oengus, son gus, King of the Picts, referred ve at the years 728, 730, 733, nd 740.

)ubhdaleithe.—The *Four Mast.*, ive his obit at A.D. 745, call him dáleithe "of the writing." He was probably the compiler of the work from which a quotation is given in this Chronicle at the year 628 *supra*.

[12] *Cill-Scire.*—Kilskeery, co. Meath.

[13] *Congal.*—Flann descendant of Congal. The Flann Ua Congaile mentioned above at the year 737.

[14] *Fergus.* — Originally written Fergaile (gen. of Fergal) in A., over which name uel Fergusa appears in the original hand; with which correction MS. B. agrees. Clar. 49, however, has "Mors Fergail."

bustio lethairle Cluana iraird in ballenio. Mors Eċdaċ Cille tomae. Mors Celi Dulassi o Daiṁinis.

Fol. 31ab. Mors Colman na m-Bretan mic Faelain, abbatis Slaine, 7 Bran mac Baethbethri moritur. Mors Nuaḋat filii Duibsleiḃe, abbatis Cluana auis. Mors Fursui abbatis Lecnae Miḋe. Mors Maeleimorċair epscoip Eċḋroma.

.b Kl. Ianair. Anno domini dcc.° l.° i.° Mors Cillene droctiġ anċoritae Iae. Caṫal mac Forindain abbas Cille daro, Cummene nepos Becce religiosus Ego, mortui sunt. Mors Diċolla filii Menidi, abbatis innse Muiredaiġ, 7 mors Conġusso ceci scribae, abbatis Leiṫ moir Moċomec. Mors Fiaċna nepotis Macniaḋ, abbatis clona ferta Brenainn. Mors Flaiṫbertaiġ filii Conaill minn, regis generis Coirpri. Indrechtaċ mac Muiredaiġ minn moritur. Mors Foidminn mic Fallaiġ, regis Conaile Muirteiṁne. Mors Cillein filii Congaile in hi. Mors Conaing nepotis Duiḃduin, regis Coirpri Teṫbae. Mors Maeletuile abbatis Tiri da glas. Mors Orbrain

---

[1] '*leth-airle*.'—"half-airle." This means the "half of the granary," according to O'Donovan. (*Four Mast.*, A.D. 746).

[2] *In ballenio.*—'In vellenio,' *Tigernach.* The meaning is not very clear. Clar. 49 has "Combustio lethairle Cluana Iraird m Ballenio," where 'Ballenio' is taken for a man's name. The record possibly means that half the corn of the establishment was burned in the kiln.

[3] *Cele-Dulassi.*—This name signifies the "cele" (*socius*) of "Dulassi," a variation of the name of Molassi, or Molaisse, the founder and patron of Daimhinis, or Devenish (in Loch-Erne).

[4] *Cluain-eois.*—Clones, co. Monaghan.

[5] *Lecan-Midhe.*—"Lecan of Meath." Now Leckin, "an old church, near Bunbrusna, in the bar. of Corkaree, co. Westmeath." See *Four Mast.*, O'Donovan's ed., A.D. 746, note *g*.

[6] *Echdhruim.* — "Horse-ridge." Now Aughrim, in a parish of the same name, and barony of Kilconnell, co. Galway.

[7] *Cillene* '*droctech*.'—"Cillene the 'bridge-maker.'" Although here called merely "anchorite," Cillene appears to have been abbot of Ia, or Iona. See Reeves' *Adamnan*, p. 382. The number 320 is added in the margin in A., probably to signify

; of the 'leth-airle'[1] of Cluain-Iraird in 'ballenio.[2]
ath of Echaid of Cill-toma. Death of Cele-Dulassi[3]
Daimh-inis. Death of Colman of the Britons, son of
elan, abbot of Slane; and Bran, son of Baeth-bethri,
es. Death of Nuadu son of Dubhsleibhe, abbot of
uain-eois.[4] Death of Fursu, abbot of Lecan-Midhe.[5]
ath of Mael-imorchair, bishop of Echdhruim.[6]

Kal. Jan. A.D. 751. Death of Cillene 'droctech,'[7] [751] BIS.
chorite of Ia. Cathal, son of Forandan, abbot of Cill-
ra, and Cummene descendant of Becc, a devout man of
gg,[8] died. Death of Dichuill, son of Menid, abbot of
is-Muiredhaigh;[9] and death of Conghus 'Caech,' scribe,
bot of Liath-mor of Mochoemoc.[10] Death of Fiachna,
scendant of Macniadh, abbot of Clonfert-Brendan.
ath of Flaithbertach, son of Conall Menn, King of the
nel-Coirpri. Indrechtach, son of Muiredach Menn,
es. Death of Foidmenn, son of Fallach, King of
maille Murteimhne. Death of Cillene,[11] son of Congal,
Hi. Death of Conang Ua Dubhduin, King of the
irpri of Tethbha.[12] Death of Maeltuile, abbot of Tir-

---

t this year is the 320th year from commencement of these Annals 1).

Devout man of Egg.—ꞃelegioꞅuꞅ o, A. ꞃeligioꞅꞅuꞅ, B., which ts Ego. The copy of the entry Clar. 49, though confused, is in eement with A. By Egg is meant island of Eigg, off the coast of erness, Scotland. See above, at year 616.

Inis-Muiredhaigh.—Inishmurray, ell-known island off the coast of barony of Carbury, co. Sligo, aining some remarkable remains s ancient importance.

Liath-mor of Mochoemoc.—Now mokevoge, in the parish of Two-Mile-Borris, barony of Eliogarty, co. Tipperary. The obit of its founder, Mochoemhoc, or 'Pulcherius,' is given above at the year 655.

[11] *Cillene.*—Dean Reeves thinks that this Cillene, son of Congal, was probably brother to "Slebhine, son of Congal," abbot of Iona from A.D. 752 to 767. *Adamnan*, p. 385.

[12] *Coirpri of Tethbha.*—The territory of this branch of the powerful tribe of Cinel-Coirpri, is now partly represented by the barony of Granard, in the county of Longford. Tethbha, sometimes written *Tebhtha*, was in later times known as "Teffia," See O'Donovan's ed. of O'Dubhagain's *Topog. Poem*, note [35].

anċorite 7 episcopi Cluana creaṁa. Mors Rectabrat nepotis Guaire, abbatis Tommae greine. Mors Dedimi nepotis Ligain, sapientis Cluana. Foirdbe Brecriġe do ċenul Coirpri i telaiġ Findin. Foirdbe Caillriġe Luirg la uu Briuin.

Kl. Ianair. Anno domini dcc.° l.° ii.° Sol tenebrosus. Dormitatio Maccoiged abbatis Liss Moir. Quies Lucriḋ abbatis clona mic U Nois. Lex Coluim cille la Domnall Mide. Mors Cellain abbatis cluana ferta Brenainn. Mors Scannlain ḋuin leṫglaisi. Eċaiḋ nepos Moinaiġ rex nepotum maccu Uais moritur. Mors Mobai. Mors Ferblai mic Nargusa, sapientis. Interfectio nepotum Ailello la Greccraiġi. Mors Scannlaiġi cluana Bairenn. Mors Fuirri Erro mac n-Eirc. Mil mor dorala docum tire i m-Bairċiu ind aimsir Fiaċnai mic Aeḋa roin riġ Ulaḋ, 7 tri fiacla oir ina chinn, 7 .l. unga in gach fiacail diḃ, co rugad fiacail diḃ, co raibi for altoir Bennchair an bliadain si, scilicet anno domini 752.

---

[1] *Tir-da-glass.*—This name signifies the "land of the two streams." Terryglass, in the barony of Lower Ormond, co. Tipperary.

[2] *Cluain-creamha.* — Now Clooncraff, in the parish of the same name, barony and county of Roscommon. The name *Cluain-creamha* signifies the "Lawn (or meadow) of the Wild Garlic."

[3] *Cluain, i.e.*, Clonmacnoise, in the King's county.

[4] *Brecrighe.*—This was the name of a tribe situated in Magh-Brecraighe, in the N.W. of the co. of Westmeath, adjoining the county of Longford, in which the Cinel-Coirpri were at this time located. O'Conor blunders most egregiously regarding this entry, in his ed. of these Annals.

[5] *Telach-Findin.* — This place, the name of which would now be written Tullafinneen, or Tullyfinneen, has not been identified.

[6] *Calrighe of Lurg.*—A sept of the Calraighe, seated in the district of Magh-Luirg, or Moylorg, co. Roscommon.

[7] *Domnall of Meath*—This was Domnall, son of Murchad, King of Ireland, whose accession is recorded above, at the year 742. He was probably called *Domnall Mide* ("Domnall of Meath"), from having been the first of the Meath branch of the Ui-Neill who became King of Ireland. See *Book of Leinster*, p. 42, col. 1.

[8] *Dun-lethglaisi.* — Downpatrick, co. Down. See note [1], at the year 583, *supra*.

[9] *Ui-mic-Uais.*—See note [12], at A.D. 597, *supra*.

ι-glas.[1] Death of Osbran, anchorite and bishop of uain-creamha.[2] Death of Rechtabrat, descendant of uaire, abbot of Tuaim-greine. Death of Dedimus, 'andson of Ligan, sage of Cluain.[3] The annihilation of .e Brecrighe[4] by the Cinel-Coirpri, in Telach-Findin.[5] The ınihilation of the Callrighe of Lurg,[6] by the Ui-Briuin.
Kal. Jan. A.D. 752. A dark sun. The 'falling' asleep [752.]
' Macoiged, abbot of Lis-mor. The rest of Lucridh, ɔbot of Cluain-mic-U-Nois. The 'Law' of Colum Cille ɣ Domnall of Meath.[7] Death of Cellan, abbot of Clonfert-rendan. Death of Scannlan of Dunlethglaisi.[8] Echaidh, ɘscendant of Moenach, King of the Ui-mac-Uais,[9] dies. eath of Mobai. Death of Ferbla son of Nargus, a wise an. The killing of the Ui-Ailella[10] by the Grecraighi.[11] eath of Scannlach of Cluain-Bairenn.[12] Death of Fursa ˈEs-mac-nEirc.[13] A whale was cast ashore in Bairche,[14] ι the time of Fiachna son of Aedh Roin, King of Ulad, hich had three teeth of gold in its head, and 50 ounces in ıch tooth of them, and one of the teeth was taken to, and 'as on the altar of Bennchair[15] this year, to wit, A.D. 752.

---

[10] *Ui-Ailella.* — "Descendants of lill." See above at the year 742, te.

[11] *The Grecraighi.* — Otherwise lled the "Grecraighi of Loch-chet." Loch Techet was the ancient me of Lough-Gara, between the unties of Sligo and Roscommon. ıe territory of the Grecraighe is lieved to have comprised the entire the present barony of Coolavin, co. igo, and a portion of the co. Roscom-ɔn. See O'Flaherty's *Ogygia*, part I., cap. xlvi.

[12] *Cluain-Bairenn.*—Now known as oonburren, in the barony of Moy-rnan, co. Roscommon.

[13] *Es-mac-nEirc.*—The "Cascade of e sons of Erc." Also called "Es-ıchonna" and "Es-Ui-Fhloinn." Now known as Assylin, near Boyle, co. Roscommon.

[14] *Bairche.*—Dean Reeves has satisfactorily proved that this was the ancient name of the territory now forming the barony of Mourne, co. Down. *Eccl. Antiqq.*, p. 205 *sq.* The Mourne Mountains were known as *Benna Bairche*, the "Peaks of Bairche." The *Four Masters* record this prodigy at the year 739. But Fiachna son of Aedh Roin was not then King of Ulad. His obit is given at the year 788 *infra*; and as the *Book of Leinster* (p. 41, col. 3) gives the duration of Fiachna's reign as 38 years, he could not have been King of Ulad before A.D. 750. Clar. 49 has no notice of the prodigy.

[15] *Bennchair.*—Bangor, co. Down.

Kl. Ianair. Anno domini dcc.° l.° iii.° Mors ḟlaind filii Concobair regis maiġi Ai. Loingseċ mac Flaiṫbertaiġ rex generis Conaill moritur. Sleibene abbas Iae in Hiberniam uenit. Quies
Fol. 31ba. Cerpain Doimliacc. Iugulatio Cinnḟaelaḋ nepotis Cuileni. Foirtbe Foṫart feae do Osrigiu. Bellum aird Noiscan inter nepotes Briuin 7 genus Coirpri, in quo ceciderunt multi. Mors Abeil aṫo Omnae. Bellum inter nepotes Tuirtri inuicem.

Kl. Ianair. Anno domini dcc.° l.° iiii.° Mors Flaiṫniaḋ mic Tnuṫaiġ, regis nepotum Meiṫ. Combustio cluana mic Nois in xii Kl. Aprilis. Mors Fiaċraċ Martarṫaiġe. Felcmaire mac Comgaill, Caṫal mac Diarmata sapiens, Doelgus abbas cille Scire, mortui sunt. Indrectaċ mac Duṫaiġ rex nepotum Maini, Flaiṫnia mac Flainn nepotis Conġaile rex nepotum Foilġi, Fiangalaċ mac Anmchaḋa filii Maelecuraiċ, abb Insi bo finne for loċ Ri, Macc Ronċon di ċenul Coirpri, Sneiṫceirt abb n-Oindroma, mortui sunt.

.O. Kl. Ianair. Anno domini dcc.° l.° u.° Combustio Bennċair moer in feria Patricii. Fergus mac Ceallaiġ (no Fothaiḋ gaiḋeirg mic Muireḋaiġ) ri Connaċt, Ailgal ancorita Cluana Cormaic, Forindan episcopus meṫuis tuirm, Baeṫallaċ mac Colmain

[1] *Daim-liacc.*—"Stone-house" (or "church"). Duleek, co. Meath.

[2] *Fotharta-Fea.*—The tribe-name of a sept inhabiting the district now represented by the barony of Forth, co. Carlow.

[3] *Ard-Noiscan.*—Ardnyskine, near Ardagh, co. Longford, according to O'Donovan; *Four Mast.*, A.D. 749, note *t*. But the site of the battle may have been *Ardneeskan*, in the barony of Tirerrill, co. Sligo.

[4] *Martar-tech.*—This name signifies "House of relics," or "Relic house." It has not been identified.

[5] *Cill-Scirè.* — Kilskeer, in the parish of the same name, barony of Upper Kells, co. Meath.

[6] *Bangor the Great.*—Bennċair moer. The great monastery of Bangor in the co. of Down.

[7] *Fothad gai-deirg*; *i.e.* "Fothad of the red dart" (or "spear").—The original of this clause is added in the margin in A., in a later hand. B. does not mention Cellach, but describes

Kal. Jan. A.D. 753. Death of Fland son of Conchobar, King of Magh-Ai. Loingsech son of Flaithbertach, King of Cinel-Conaill, dies. Sleibene, abbot of Ia, comes to Ireland. The rest of Cerpan of Daim-liacc.[1] The killing of Cennfaeladh descendant of Culeni. The devastation of the Fotharta-Fea,[2] by the Osraigi. The battle of Ard-Noiscan,[3] between the Ui-Briuin and the Cinel-Coirpri, wherein many were slain. Death of Abel of Athomna. A battle among the Ui-Tuirtri, between each other. [753.]

Kal. Jan. A.D. 754. Death of Flaithnia son of Tnuthach, King of the Ui-Meith. Burning of Cluain-mic-Nois, on the 12th of the Kalends of April. Death of Fiachra of Martar-tech,[4] Felcmaire son of Comgall; Cathal son of Diarmaid, a wise man; Doelgus, abbot of Cill-Sciré,[5] died. Indrechtach son of Dluthach, King of the Ui-Maine; Flaithnia, son of Flann Ua Congaile, King of the Ui-Failghi; Fiangalach, son of Anmchad, son of Maelcuraich, abbot of Inis-bo-finde on Loch-Ri; Mac Ronchon, of the Cinel-Coirpri, and Sneithcheist abbot of Nendrum, died. [754.]

Kal. Jan. A.D. 755. Burning of Bangor the Great,[6] on the festival of Patrick. Fergus son of Cellach (or of Fothadh Gai-deirg,[7] son of Muiredach), King of Connaught; Ailgal, anchorite[8] of Cluain-Cormaic;[9] Forindan, bishop of Methus-tuirm,[10] and Baethallach, son of Colman [755] BIS.

Fergus as the son of Fothadh Red-spear, son of Muiredach. Clar. 49 says "Fergus son of Cella," and does not notice the alteration suggested in A. The *Four Mast.*, at A.D. 751, give the obit of "Fergus, son of Ceallach, King of Connaught." Fergus is also called "son of Cellach" (mac Cellaig) in the *Book of Leinster*, p. 41, col. 1). He was probably the "Fergus son of Cellach" mentioned at the year 743 *supra*, in connection with the 'Law' of St. Ciaran, and the 'Law' of St. Brendan.

[8] *Anchorite.*—ancoirita, A.

[9] *Cluain-Cormaic.* — The "Lawn (or meadow) of Cormac." The *Four Mast.*, at A.D. 751, say that Ailgal was anchorite of Imlech-Fordeorach. But neither place has been identified.

[10] *Methus-tuirm.*—So in A. and B. "Methius-truim," Clar. 49. "Methas-Truim" in *Four Mast.* (A.D. 751). This place has not been identified.

nepotis Suibne, mortui sunt. Slogad Laiġen la Domnall fri Niall, co rabadar i maiġ Muirṫeimne. Naufragium Delbnae in stagno Ri erga ducem .i. Diumasaċ, (.i. xxx. eṫar, 7 ni terna dib acht lucht aen eṫair). Bellum Gronnae magnae in quo genus Coirpri prostratum est.

Kl. Ianair. Anno domini dcc.° l.° iii.° Quies Fidṁuine ancoritae Raṫin, id est nepotis Sunaiċ. Edalbald rex Saxonum moritur. Combustio Cille móre diṫraiḃ o auib Cremṫainn. Mors Finċon abbatis Liss moir. Bellum Cinn febrat inter Muiṁnenses inuicem, in quo cecidit Bodbgal princeps Mungairt. Dormitatio Siaḋail Linde duaċail. Ferġus mac Conġaile, Tomaltaċ ri Ciannachta glinne
Fol. 31bb. gaiṁin, Cuidġal ancorita, Ailduib abbas Muccirt, mortui sunt. Iugulatio Duinn mic Cumuscaiġ ri .h. mBriuin in deisceirt. Lex Columbae cille la Sleibene.

Kl. Ianair. Anno domini dcc.° l.° iiii.° Niallġus mac Boiṫ rex na n-Deisse m-Breġ, Muireḋaċ mac Cormaic slana abbas Luġmaiḋ, Caṫal rí nepotum Cennselaiġ, Domnall mac Flainn deirgge, Elpin Glaisse noide, Aeḋ mac Cormaic leṫri Ciannaċt, Fiḋbaḋaċ Cille deilge, mortui sunt. Celepetar (a

---

1 *Over against.* — erga, A. B. The *Four Mast.* (751) say im a ttiġerna, "with their lord."

2 *Boats.* — The original of this clause is interlined in *al. man.* in A., by way of gloss. B. has "xxx etar preter unum," which substantially agrees with the addition in A.

3 *Gronn-mor.*—gronnae magnae, A. B. Clar. 49 reads *Grane magnæ*. The place has not been identified.

4 *Ua Suanaigh* —"Descendant (or *nepos*) of Suanach." See above at the years 741 and 747, where the 'Law' of Ua Suanaigh" is mentioned; and *Martyr. Donegal* at May 16.

5 *Cill-mor-dithraibh.*—See note on this name under the year 734 *supra*.

6 *Cenn-Febrat.* — "This was the ancient name of a part of the mountain of Sliabh Riach, to the south of Kilmallock, on the confines of the counties of Limerick and Cork." O'Donov. *Four Mast.*, A.D. 186, note *x*.

7 *Between each other.*—inuicem, A. B.

Ua Suibne, died. The hosting of Leinster by Domnall, against Niall, until they were in Magh-Murtheimne. Shipwreck of the Delbhna in Loch-Ri, over against[1] their leader, *i.e.*, Diumasach (viz., 30 boats,[2] and only the company of one boat of them escaped). The battle of Gronn-mor,[3] in which the Cinel-Coirpri was overthrown.

Kal. Jan. A.D. 756. Rest of Fidhmuine, *i.e.*, Ua Suanaigh,[4] anchorite of Rathin. Æthelbald, King of the Saxons, dies. Burning of Cill-mor-dithraibh[5] by the Ui-Cremthainn. Death of Finnchu, abbot of Lismor. Battle of Cenn-Febrat[6] among the Munstermen, between each other,[7] in which Bodbgal, superior of Mungairt,[8] was slain. The 'falling asleep' of Siadhal of Linn-Duachail. Fergus, son of Congal; Tomaltach, King of Cianachta of Glenn-geimhin;[9] Cuidghal, an anchorite, and Aildobur, abbot of Muccert, died. The killing of Donn, son of Cumuscach, King of the Ui-Briuin of the South. The 'Law' of Colum-Cille, by Sleibene.[10] [756.]

Kal. Jan. A.D. 757. Niallghus, son of Boeth, King of the Deisi-Bregh;[11] Muiredach, son of Cormac-Slana,[12] abbot of Lughmadh; Cathal, King of Ui-Cennselaigh; Domnall, son of Flann Deirgge; Elpin of Glais-Noiden;[13] Aedh, son of Cormac, half-king of Cianachta, and Fidhbadhach of Cill-deilge, died. Cele-Petair (from Crich-Bresail),[14] [757.]

---

[8] *Mungairt.*—Now Mungret, a few miles to the S.W. of the city of Limerick.

[9] *Cianachta of Glenn-geimhin.*—See note [7] under the year 680, and note [4] under 694, *supra.*

[10] *Sleibene.*—Abbot of Ia from 752 to 767. The 'Law,' or tribute, of St. Colum-Cille is referred to again at the year 777.

[11] *Deisi-Bregh.*—The territory of this tribe, which was otherwise called *Deisi-Temrach* (or "Deises of Tara"), is now represented by the baronies of Upper and Lower Deece, in the county of Meath.

[12] *Slana.* "Of Slane."—The *Four Mast.*, at A.D. 753, write the word *Slaine* (in the genit. case).

[13] *Glais-Noiden.*—Glasnevin, near Dublin.

[14] *From Crich-Bresail.*—The original of this clause, which is not in B., is added in *al. man.* in A. In the List of the *comarbada*, or successors, of St Patrick contained in the *Book of Leinster* (p. 42, col. 3), Cele-Petair is stated to have been "from Druim-

crich Bresail) abbas ard Maċae [obiit]. Marṫu filia maicc Dubain, dominatrix Cille daro, obiit. Bellum Droma robaiġ inter nepotes Fiacrach 7 nepotes Briuin, in quo ceciderunt Tadgg mac Muirdibuir 7 nepotes tres Cellaiċ, Caṫrannaċ, Caṫmuġ, Artbran. Ailill nepos Dunċoḋa uictor fuit.

Kl. Ianair. Anno domini dcc.° l.° uiii.° Slogadaċ mac Donngaile de genere Ċoirpri, Eċaiḋ mac Conaill minn abbas Foibrain, Forduban liḃeċaire, Domnall mac Aeḋa lagen, Siadail mac Luaiṫ doctor, Eċaiḋ mac Fiaċraċ sapiens, mortui sunt. Bellum Emnae Maċae, ubi Dungal nepos Conaing 7 Donnbo interfecti sunt. Fiaċna mac Aeḋo roin uictor fuit.

Nimatulaiġ Donn bo bare
Co farggaiḃ a rige;
Conid fail in adbai huire,
Iar caṫ Chuile cire.

Techt hi sliaḃ dar eisi,
No ac deirgi in daim liac;
Dollotar hi ciunn hitaat;
Suili caich nodċiat.

---

chetna in Ui-Bresail." Ui-Bresail, or Clann-Bresail, was the name of a tribe (and also of their territory) situated in the present barony of Oneilland East, in the county of Armagh.

[1] *Abbess.*—dominatrix, A., B., and Clar. 49.

[2] *Grandsons of Cellach.*—The *Four Mast.*, at A.D. 753, state that the three persons, whose names follow in the entry, were sons of Fergus, son of Roghallach. But this is incorrect, as their father Fergus [vid. 744, *supra*] was son of Cellach [King of Connaught, ob. 704, *supra*], son of Raghallach [also K. of Connaught], whose death is entered above at the year 648.

[3] *Dunchadh*, *i.e.*, Dunchadh Mursce, or "Dunchadh of Muirisc." See note [16], under the year 682, *supra*.

[4] *Foibhran.*—At the year 815 *infra*, (where the name is written *Foibrein*, (genit. of *Foibren*), the place is referred to as in the territory of Graicraigi (or Gregraidhi), which anciently comprised the present barony of Coolavin, co. Sligo, and a considerable portion of the N.W. of the co. Roscommon.

[5] *Emain-Macha.*—Now the Navan fort, about two miles to the west of Armagh. For much useful information as to the way in which several present Irish topographical names, beginning with the letter N, are formed from old names beginning with vowels (as

›t of Armagh, [died]. Marthu, daughter of MacDubhain, ›ss[1] of Cill-dara, died. The battle of Druim-Robaigh, ‹een the Ui-Fiachrach and the Ui-Briuin, in which Tadhg, son of Muirdibur, and three grandsons Cellach[2]—Cathrannach, Cathmugh, Artbran. Ailill, ›dson of Dunchadh,[3] was victor.

›al. Jan. A.D. 758. Slogadach, son of Donngal, of Cinel-Coirpri; Echaidh, son of Conall Menn, abbot Foibhran;[4] Fordubhan Liphechaire; Domnall, son Aedh Lagen; Siadhail, son of Luath, doctor, and aidh, son of Fiachra, a wise man, died. The battle of ›in-Macha,[5] in which Dungal Ua Conaing, and ›nbo,[6] were slain. Fiachna,[7] son of Aedh Roin, was victor. [758.]

Not well[8] did Donn-bo go [on his] career
Until he left his kingship;
Wherefore he is in a house of clay,[9]
After the battle of Cul-Círè.[10]

Going into a sliabh afterwards,
On abandoning the daim-liac,[11]
They went to the point where they are—
The eyes of all see them.

›n from *Emain*), see Joyce's *Irish* ›es *of Places*, First Series, p. 83.

›Donnbo.—Probably the same as Donnbo, son of Cubreatan, by ›n Congal, son of Eignech, lord ›e Airthera (or Oriors) was slain ›D. 743, according to the chron- ›y of the *Four M.* The killing of ›gal is entered in these Annals at year 747; but the name of his ›r is not given. The *Frag. of* ›*Annals*, at A.D. 722 (p. 33, *sq.*), a harrowing, and apparently ›ryphal, account of the history of ›her Donnbo.

[7] *Fiachna.*—See the note on Fiachna ›of Aedh Roin, at the year 752, *a.*

[8] *Not well.*—nımaculaıġ, probably for nımacouluro ("not well did he go"), a form of expression not yet satisfactorily examined or explained, seems cognate with the forms nıma-ꞃucꞅam, nımaloomaꞃ, nımaꞃ[o] ġabꞅamaꞃ ("not well have we gained," "—passed," "—taken"). See *Chron. Scot.*, A.D. 827. These stanzas, which are not in B., or in Clar. 49, are written in the lower margin of fol. 31 *d* in A., with a sign referring to their place in the text.

[9] *House of clay, i.e.*, a grave.

[10] *Cul-Círè.* — Not known. The name may possibly be only a local name for the exact site of the battle of Emain-Macha.

[11] *Daim-liac.* — The name 'Damliac,' which means "stone-church,'

Sirsan duit a cheirchen chochlaiċ,
As nar idir naṫraiċ,[1]
T'etan friad bodbai ndoiċraiḋ,
Do ċul fris in caṫraiġ.[2]

Du leitne fri loċa Eirne,
hErim duit i Míde,
Is do leiṫne alaile
Fri Gleann roglach riġe.[3]

Iugulatio Rectabrat mic Dunċon, regis Muġḋorne. Dubdrumman abbas Tuiliain moritur. Aestas pluuialis. Benn Muilt[4] effudit amnem cum piscibus. Iugulatio Ferdamail mic Cinnḟaelaḋ.

.b. Kl. Ianair. Anno domini dcc.° l.° ix.° Nix magna hi iiii. nonas Februarii. Imairecc Foling[5] in quo ceciderunt Dunchad mac Caṫail 7 Ceiṫernaċ mac Doṫaiḃ. Mors Tairceltaiġ sapientis. Occisio Congalaiġ mic Conaill regis Diaṫraiḃ. Mors Muiredaiġ nepotis Brain regis Lagen. Fames 7 mess mar. Mors Concoḃair nepotis Taidgg teimin; 7 Conait abbas Liss moer, 7 Gaimdibail abbas airne Endai, mortui sunt. Bellum hitir muintir Clono 7 Biroir, imMoin choisse blae. Condam cluana Cuirḟin moritur.

---

when not used in connexion with any establishment in particular, is usually understood as indicating "Daimliac-Chianain," or Duleek, co Meath.

[1] *Amongst worms.*—idir naṫraiċ. Naṫraiċ is put for naṫraiġ, to rhyme with caṫraiġ, the last word in the stanza. The proper form of the accus. plural of nathir (*natrix*), however, is nathracha.

[2] *The city, i.e.*, the "city" of Armagh; or probably by "the city" was meant *Emain-Macha*, or *Emania*, the ancient seat of royalty in Ulster.

[3] *Glenn-rige.* — This was the old name of the valley of the Newry river. See Reeves' *Eccl. Antiqq.*, p. 253.

[4] *Benn-muilt.* — The "point of molt" (*molt* being the Irish for a "wether"; comp. Fr. *mouton*, old Fr. *moulton*, or *multon*). Clar. 49 describes *Benn-muilt* as "a mountain," but gives no clue as to its situation.

[5] *Conflict of Foling.*—Clar. 49 has "the Skirmish of Foling"; but O'Conor, in his ed. of these Annals, renders "*Imairec Foling*" by "Conflictus cruentus." Foling was, however, the name of a place, which has not been identified. This entry is not given by the *Four Masters*.

Alas! for thee, thou hooded little black man;
'Tis a shame [thou should'st be] amongst worms![1]
Thy face towards thy hateful foes,
Thy back towards the city.[2]

Thy side towards the Lakes of Erne,
(A journey thou hadst to Meath);
And thy other side
Towards the angry Glenn-rige.[3]

e killing of Rechtabrat, son of Dunchu, King of ghdhorna. Dubhdrumman, abbot of Tuilen, dies. rainy summer. Benn-muilt[4] poured forth a stream h fishes. The killing of Ferdamal, son of Cennfaelad.
Kal. Jan. A.D. 759. Great snow on the fourth of the [759.] BIS.
nes of February. The conflict of Foling,[5] in which nchad son of Cathal, and Ceithernach son of Dothadh, re slain. Death of Taircelltach, a wise man. Murder Congalach, son of Conall, King of Diathraibh.[6] Death Muiredach, grandson of Bran,[7] King of Leinster. mine, and abundance of acorns. Death of Conchobhar, of Tadhg Teimin; and Conait,[8] abbot of Lis-mor, l Gaimdibail, abbot of Ara-Enda,[9] died. A battle ween the 'families' of Cluain[10] and Biror,[11] in Moin-sse-Blae.[12] Condam of Cluain-Cuifthin[13] dies.

Diathraibh.—The situation of this (or territory) is unknown to the or. The entry is not in the *Ann.* *Mast.* O'Conor blunders, as d, and for "Diathraibh" prints *hib*, and translates "a latere ejus"!

Muiredach, grandson of Bran.—redach (ancestor of the Ui-Muir-gh, the tribe name of the O'Tooles) the son of Murchad (ob. 726 *a*), son of Bran Bec (otherwise d Bran Mut), whose death is rded above at the year 737. See rman's *Loca Patriciana*, Geneal. e at p. 138.

Conait.—This name is written "Condath" by the *Four Mast.* (A.D. 755).

[9] *Ara-Enda.*—Ara of St. Enna (or Enda). Now Aranmore Island, in Galway Bay.

[10] *Cluain; i.e.* Clonmacnoise. This entry is not given by the *Four Mast.*, who persistently ignore incidents of this nature.

[11] *Biror.*—Birr; or, as it is now generally called, Parsonstown.

[12] *Moin-Coisse-Blae.*—This name, which means the "Bog at the foot of (or along) the [river] Bla," is now forgotten in the district.

[13] *Cluain-Cuifthin.*—Now Clonguffin,

Fol. 32*aa*. Kl. Ianair. Anno domini dcc.° lx.° Mors Finsnechti filii Foġertaiġ, nepotis Cernaiġ. Bellum Aṫo dumai inter Ultu 7 nepotes Echaċ, in quo cecidit Ailill mac Feiḋelmṫo. Bellum beluit Gabrain in quo ceciderunt Donngal mac Laiṫgnaen, rex nepotum Ceinnselaiġ, 7 alii reges. Mors Oengusa mic Ferġussa, regis Pictorum.

Kl. Ianair. Anno domini dcc.° lx.° i.° Nix magna 7 luna tenebrosa. Occisio Eutiġirn episcopi a sacerdote, i n-dertaiġ Cille daro. Quies Cormaic abbatis cluana mic U Nois. Nox lucida in autumno. Bellum Caille tuidbig ubi Luigni prostrati sunt. Cenel Coirpri uictoriam accepit. Ferfio mac Fabri sapiens, abas Comraire Mide obiit. Bellum montis Cruim. Roḃartaċ mac Cuanaċ, princeps Oṫnae, mortuus est.

Kl. Ianair. Anno domini dcc.° lx.° ii.° Mors Domnaill mic Murchada, (mic Diarmada guṫḃinn, mic Oirmeaḋaiġ ċaeiċ, mic Conaill mic Suiḃne mic Colmain ṁoir mic Diarmada mic Ferġusa cerrḃeoil), regis Temoriae; in xii. Kalendas Decimbris mortuus est. Bec laitne ab Cluana iraird, 7 Faelċu Finnglaissi, 7 Fidairle Oa Suanaiċ, abb Raṫin, mortui sunt. Mors Reoṫaidi abb Fernann. Mors

---

in the parish of Rathcore, co. Meath. See at the year 770 *infra*, where the name is Cluain-Cuibhtin.

[1] *Fogartach.* — See above, under the year 723.

[2] *Ath - duma.* — "Ford of the Mound." Not identified.

[3] *Belut-Gabrain.* — The "Pass (or Road) of Gabran." The Ballygaveran of early Anglo-Norman documents. Now Gowran, in the co. Kilkenny.

[4] *Oengus.*—The *aithbe* ("ebb," or "decay") of the sovereignty of an Oengus, son of Fergus, is recorded above at the year 749; and the death of another Oengus, son of Fergus, King of Fortrenn (Pictland), is entered at the year 833 *infra*.

[5] *A dark moon.*—An eclipse of the moon occurred in the year 762.

[6] *Caill-Tuidbig.*—The "Wood of Tuidbeg." O'Donovan suggests that this place is probably Kiltabeg, near Edgeworthstown, in the county of Longford. *Four Mast.*, A.D. 757, note *f*, and *Addenda* to vol. I., p. 1192.

[7] *Luigni.*—Clar. 49 has "Luigni of Connaught" [*i.e.* the ancient inhabit-

Kal. Jan. A.D. 760. Death of Finsnechta, son of gartach,[1] grandson of Cernach. The battle of Athma,[2] between the Ulaid and the Ui-Echach, in which ill, son of Feidhilmidh, was slain. The battle of Belutbrain,[3] in which fell Donngal son of Ladgnen, King the Ui-Cennselaigh, and other Kings. Death of ngus[4] son of Fergus, King of the Picts. [760.]

Kal. Jan. A.D. 761. Great snow, and a dark moon.[5] [761.]
e killing of Eutigern, a bishop, by a priest, in the tory of Kildare. The 'repose' of Cormac, abbot of ain-mic-U-Nois. A bright night in autumn. The tle of Caill-Tuidbig,[6] where the Luigni[7] were overown, and the Cinel-Coirpri obtained the victory. fio, son of Fabre, a wise man, abbot of Comrair-Midè,[8] d. The battle of Sliabh-Truim.[9] Robhartach, son of nu, superior of Othan,[10] died.

Kal. Jan. A.D. 762. Death of Domnall, son of [762.]
rchad (son of Diarmaid Guthbhinn,[11] son of Airmedach ech, son of Conall, son of Suibhne, son of Colman the at, son of Diarmaid, son of Fergus Cerrbheoil), King Tara. On the 12th of the Kalends of December he l. Bec-Laitne,[12] abbot of Cluain-Iraird, and Faelchu Finnglais,[13] and Fidairle Ua Suanaigh, abbot of hin,[14] died. Death of Reothaide, abbot of Ferns.

---

of the present barony of Leyny, Sligo.] But the "Luigni of h," who gave name to the barony une in the latter county, were ntly meant.

omrair-Midè. — "Comrair of h." Now Conry, a parish in the y of Rathconrath, co. West-1.

iabh-Truim.—See note [2] under ear 614 *supra*.

thau.—Otherwise called *Othan*-. Fahan, in the present barony ishowen West, co. Donegal.

[11] *Diarmaid Guthbhinn.*—Diarmaid "of the sweet voice." This clause, which is interlined in *al. man.* in A, and which also occurs in Clar. 49, is not in B.

[12] *Bec-Laitne.*—"Bec of the Latin." No specimens of his Latin appear to have survived.

[13] *Finnglais*, *i.e.* the "Bright Stream." Now Finglas, a village a little to the north of Dublin.

[14] *Rathin.*—Otherwise called Rathin-Ui-Suanaigh. Now Rahan, in the parish of the same name, barony of Ballycowan, King's County.

Anfaḋain abbatis Linne Duaċail. Sol tenebrosus in hora tertia diei. Mors Flainn garaḋ regis generis mic Ercae. Duceta Loṫri. Strages Cuilnige mare, ubi Connacta prostrati sunt. Bellum hitir .h. Fidgenti 7 Corcumruaḋ 7 corco Baiscainn. Bruide rex Fortrenn moritur. Niall frossaċ regnare incipit.

.b. Kl. Ianair. Anno domini dcc.° lx.° iii.° Nix magna tribus fere mensibus. Quies Ronain abbatis Cluana
Fol. 32ab. micc U Nois. Mors Cormaic mic Ailella, abbatis mainistreċ Buitti. Int ascalt mor 7 fames. Mors Duiḃdeilgge sapientis. Bellum Argamain inter familiam Cluana micc U Nois 7 Dermaiġi, ubi ceciderunt Diarmait dub mac Domnaill, 7 Diġlaċ mac Duibliss, 7 .cc. uiri de familia Dermaige. Bresal mac Murchada uictor extetit cum familia Cluana. Siccitas magna ultra modum. Ailill aua Duncaḋa, rex Connacht, mortuus est. Scannlan Feimin, mac Aedgaile, moritur. Riuth fola in tota hibernia. Iugulatio Bresail mic Murchada. Bellum Duinbile re Donnchad for firu Telaċ. Mors Fiaċraċ mic

[1] *Duceta of Lothra.* — Duceta Loṫri, A. B. Duceta Lothra, Clar. 49. O'Conor prints duceta Loṫri as part of the preceding entry recording the death of Flann Garadh, and translates "occisi a Lothriensibus," which is surely wrong. Duceta is not mentioned by Tigernach or the *F. M.* Lothra is now known as Lorrha, in a parish of the same name, barony of Lower Ormond, and county of Tipperary.

[2] *Fortrenn.*—Pictland, in Scotland. See note [8], under the year 663 *supra*.

[3] *Niall Frossach.*—"Niall of the Showers." O'Flaherty Latinizes *Frossach* "Nimbosus." *Ogygia*, p. 433. See under the next year.

[4] *Of Clonmacnoise.*—Cluana m̄cu-nois, A. Cluana m̄ nois, B. Cluana m° Nois, Clar. 49. The Irish form of the name of Clonmacnoise is variously written *Cluain-mic-U-Nois* (the "meadow of the son of Nois's descendant"), and *Cluain-mic-Nois* (the "meadow of the son of Nois"); and it is difficult to say which is the more correct form, as the etymology of the name, which is sometimes found written *Cluain-muc-Nois* (the "meadow of Nois's pigs"), is uncertain.

[5] *Manistir-Buiti.*—Now Monasterboice, in the co. Louth; a few miles to the N. W. of Drogheda.

[6] *Famine.*—Probably a return, or continuation, of the famine mentioned above at the year 759.

th of Anfadan, abbot of Linn-Duachail. A darkened at the third hour of the day. Death of Flann Garadh, g of Cinel-Mic-Erca. Duceta of Lothra[1] [died]. The ghter of Cuilnech-mor, where the Connaughtmen e overthrown. A battle between the Ui-Fidgenti, the Corcumruadh and Corco-Baiscinn. Bruide, King 'ortrenn,[2] dies. Niall Frossach[3] begins to reign.

.al. Jan. A.D. 763. Great snow for nearly three [763.] BIS. ths. Repose of Ronan, abbot of Clonmacnoise.[4] Death of nac, son of Ailill, abbot of Manistir-Buiti.[5] The great city and famine.[6] Death of Dubhdeilge the Wise. battle of Argaman, between the 'family' of Clonnoise[4] and [the 'family' of] Dermagh,[7] wherein[8] fell rmait Dubh, son of Domnall, and Dighlach, son of hliss, and 200 men of the family of Dermagh.[7] Bresal, of Murchad, remained victor, with the family of ain.[9] Great drought beyond measure. Ailill, grand- of Dunchad,[10] King of Connaught, died. Scannlan of nin, son of Aedhgal, dies. The bloody-flux[11] in all Irel. The killing of Bresal,[12] son of Murchadh. The battle un-bilè,[13] by Donnchad, over the Fera-Tulach.[14] Death

---

'ermagh. — Otherwise written nagh, Durrow, in the barony of cowan, King's County. For an nt of the foundation of the stery of Durrow, by St. Columsee Reeves' *Adamnan*, p. 23, . This entry, like others of the kind, has been intentionally ed by the *Four Masters*.

'herein.—uibi, A. The words bene" are added in the margin

luain, *i.e.*, Clonmacnoise.

unchad, *i.e.*, Dunchad Mursce 2 *supra*). Ailill was the son of chtach, son of Dunchad Mursce. O'Donovan's Hy-Fiachrach, l. Table, facing p. 476.

'loody flux.—ꞃıuꞇh ꞅola. Clar. 49 has "A runinge flood of blood in whole Ireland." This seems to be the first mention of the prevalence of the bloody flux, or true dysentery, in Ireland.

[12] *Bresal.*—Apparently the Bresal referred to a few lines before, as engaged in the fight between the 'families' of Clonmacnoise and Durrow.

[13] *Dun-bilè.*—This place, the name of which signifies the "Fort of the ancient tree," and which was evidently in the present co. Westmeath, has not been identified.

[14] *Fera-Tulach.* Or *Fir-Tulach.*—The tribe-name of a people who occupied the district now represented by the barony of Fartullagh, co. Westmeath.

Foṫaiḋ abbatis Baslice. Murċaḋ mac Inrechtaiġ (*sic*). Tri frosa do ferṫain i crich Muiredaig i n-Inis Eugain .i. fross d'argut ġil, 7 fros do cruiṫnicht, 7 fros do ṁil.

Tri frosa aird Uilinne,
Ar grad Neill do nim;
Fros argait, fros tuirinne,
Ocus fros do ṁil.

Mac Fergail ba feraṁail,
Oc laechraiḋ a gairm;
O ḟuair cach dia lenaṁain,
Niall frosach a ainm.

Cet n-giall ar caċ oen coiceḋ
Ro ṫobaiġ Niall ní;
Robo croḋa in saer baeded
A tobach foṫri.

Kl. Ianair. Anno domini dcc.° lx.° iiii.° In nocte signum horribile 7 mirabile in stellis uisum est. Mors Flaitbertaiġ mic Loingsiċ, regis Temorie, in clericatu. Quies Tolai aird Brecain. Iugulatio Suibne mic Murcoḋa, cum duobus filiis suis.

---

1 *Baslec.*—Baslick, barony of Castlereagh, co. Roscommon.

2 *Three showers.*—This is possibly an amplification of the entry above given, at the year 717, of the falling of *two* showers (one of honey, and one of blood), in celebration, as the story goes, of the birth of Niall Frossach in that year. The record of the accession of Niall Frossach to the monarchy of Ireland is the last entry under the year 762; wherefore it would appear that the prodigy above mentioned was regarded by the Annalist as signalizing Niall's elevation to the throne. In the *Book of Leinster* (p. 25, col. 2), the three showers are merely stated to have fallen in the reign of Niall (inna ḟlaiṫ). But at p. 274 a, the same MS. contains the statement that the "shrines and precious things" of the saints of Ireland were covered with the silver which fell. These showers may really have been only some phenomena, like showers of shooting stars.

3 *Ard-Uilinne.* — Not identified. The original of these stanzas, which

'iachra, son of Fothad, abbot of Baslec.[1] Murchad, of Innrechtach, [died]. Three showers[2] were shed in h-Muiredaigh in Inis-Eogain, viz. :—a shower of white r, a shower of wheat, and a shower of honey.

The three showers of Ard-Uilinne[3]
From Heaven for love of Niall [fell]:
A shower of silver, a shower of wheat,
And a shower of honey.

Fergal's son was manly;
With heroes was his calling;
Since he found all to follow him—
Niall Frosach his name.

A hundred pledges from each Province
The hero Niall exacted.
Brave was the noble, who boasted
That he had thrice exacted them.

al. Jan. A.D. 764. In the night a terrible and derful sign[4] was observed in the stars. Death of thbertach son of Loingsech, King of Tara, in the ious state.[5] The repose of Tola of Ard-Brecain. killing of Suibhne son of Murchadh, with his two . The battle of Carn-Fiachach[6] between two sons [764.]

›t in B., is written in the top n of fol. 32 *a* in A., with a mark ting the place in the text where night be introduced.

gn.—A similar prodigy is re- l above at the year 744.

ligious state.—The *Four Mast.*, incorrectly give the obit of bertach at the year 729 of eckoniog (=734), and enter it at A.D. 760 (=765), say that ed in Armagh. At the year he *F. M.*, instead of giving eath of Flaithbhertach, should have recorded his retirement from the kingship, and entrance into the religious state, in which he continued until his death. See O'Flaherty's *Ogygia*, p. 433.

[6] *Carn-Fiachach.*—The "Carn (or monumental heap) of Fiacha." This Fiacha, who was son of Niall Nine-hostager, was ancestor of the tribe called Cinel-Fiachach, whose territory lay in the S. of the present co. of Westmeath. Carn-Fiachach, now called Carn, is situated in the barony of Moycashel in the said county.

Bellum cairn Fiaċaċ inter duos filios Domnaill, id est, Donnchad 7 Murchad. Fallomon la Donnchad, Ailgal la Murchad. In bello cecidit Murchad; Ailgal in fugam uersus est. Folaċtaċ abbas Biror mortuus est. Loarnn abbas Clona iraird quieuit. Cellbil cluana Bronaiġ [obiit]. Defectio panis.

Kl. Ianair. Anno domini dcc.° lx.° u.° Dormitatio Craumtain abbatis Cluana ferta. Iugulatio Follaṁain mic Concongalt, regis Midi, dolose. Bellum Sruṫrae itir .h. Briuin 7 Conmaicniu, ubi plurimi ceciderunt di Conmaicniḃ, 7 Aeḋ duḃ mac Toiċliċ cecidit. Dubinnreċt mac Caṫail uictor fuit. Bellum itir Midi 7 Bregu, ubi ceciderunt Maeluṁai mac Toṫail 7 Donngal mac Doreit. Mors Cernaiġ mic
Fol. 32ba. Caṫail 7 Cernaiġ mic Flainn. Suibne abbas Iae in hiberniam uenit.

Kl. Ianair. Anno domini dcc.° lx.° ui.° Conbrann abbas Cille aciḋ mortuus est. Iugulatio Murċada mic Flaiṫbertaiġ righ cenuil Conaill. Fiodbadaċ abbas Benncair quieuit. Dubdainber mac Cormaic abbas mainistreċ Buiti. Quies Sleibeni Iae. Mac ind ṡaer, abbas Enaiċ duiḃ [obiit]. Glaindibur abbas Laṫraiġ Briuin pausat. Cellaċ mac Coirpri filii

---

[1] *Domnall; i.e.* Domnall son of Murchad, king of Ireland, whose obit is entered above at the year 762.

[2] *Donnchad.*—He became king of Ireland in the year 770.

[3] *Falloman.* — The entry of this battle in *Ann. Four Mast.*, at A.D. 760, differs somewhat from the foregoing entry. The *F. M.* represent Falloman as having been *slain by* Donnchad, in place of having assisted Donnchad. The death of 'Follamhan' is the second entry under the next year in these Annals.

[4] *Cluain-Bronaigh.* — The "Lawn (or Meadow) of Bronach." Now Clonbroney, near Granard, in the county of Longford.

[5] *Failure.*—defectio, A. defectus, B.

[6] *Cluain-ferta*; *i.e.* Cluain-ferta-Brenainn (Clonfert-Brendan); Clonfert, in the barony of Longford, co. Galway.

[7] *Follamhan.*—This name is written Falloman in an entry under the preceding year, where see note.

[8] *Sruthair.* —O'Donovan identifies this place with Shrule, or Abbeyshrule, in the barony of Shrule, co. Longford. *Four Mast.*, A.D. 761, note *w*.

'omnall,[1] to wit, Donnchad[2] and Murchad. Falloman[3] with Donnchad; Ailgal with Murchad. Murchad slain in the battle, Ailgal was put to flight. ichtach, abbot of Birr, died. Loarn, abbot of Cluain-rd, rested. Cellbil of Cluain-Bronaigh,[4] [died]. lure[5] of bread.

Kal. Jan. A.D. 765. The 'falling asleep' of Cremthan, [765.] ot of Cluain-ferta.[6] The killing of Follamhan,[7] son Cucongalt, king of Meath, treacherously. The battle Sruthair,[8] between the Ui-Briuin and the Conmaicni, ere great numbers of the Conmaicni fell, and Aedh bh, son of Toichlech, was slain. Dubhinnrecht,[9] son Cathal, was the victor. A battle between the men Meath and the Brega, where Maelumha son of Tothal, l Donngal son of Doreith, were slain. Death of rnach son of Cathal, and of Cernach son of Flann. ibhne, abbot of Ia, comes to Ireland.

Kal. Jan. A.D. 766. Conbrann,[10] abbot of Cill-achaidh,[11] [766.] d. The killing of Murchad, son of Flaithbertach, ng of Cinel-Conaill. Fidbadach, abbot of Bennchair,[12] sted. Dubhdainbher son of Cormac, abbot of Manistir-iiti,[13] [died]. The repose of Sleibene[14] of Ia. Mac-ind-r,[15] abbot of Enach-dubh,[16] [died]. Glaindibur, abbot Lathrach-Briuin,[17] rests. Cellach, son of Coirpri,

---

[9] *Dubhinnrecht.*—The name is writ- "Dubhindreachtach" by the *ur Mast.* (A.D. 761). The obit of bhinnrecht appears under the year 7.

[10] *Conbrann.*—The name of this lesiastic is written "Cubran" in *Ann. Four Mast.*, at A.D. 762. e genit. form of "Cubran" is Conbran."

[11] *Cill-achaidh.*—The "Church of e Field." Now Killeigh, in the rony of Geashill, King's County.

[12] *Bennchair.*—Bangor, in the county Down.

[13] *Manistir-Buiti.*—The "Monastery of Buite" (ob. 518, *supra*). Now Monasterboice, co. Louth. According to the *Ann. Four Mast.* (A.D. 762), Dubhdainbher was drowned in the river Boyne.

[14] *Sleibene.*—Abbot of Ia (or Iona) from A.D. 752 to 767. He is mentioned at the years 753 and 756 *supra.*

[15] *Mac-ind-sair.* — "Son of the Carpenter."

[16] *Enach-dubh.*—Annaduff, in the parish of the same name, co. Leitrim.

[17] *Lathrach-Briuin.*—Laraghbryan, near Maynooth, co Kildare.

Foġertaiġ a latrone iugulatus est. Flaṫġus mac Fiaċraċ mic Caṫail iugulatus est dolore. Lex Patricii.

.b. Kl. Ianair. Anno domini dcc.° lx.° uii.° Dubinnrecht mac Caṫail, rex Connaċt, mortuus est .i. a fluxu sanguinis. Gormgal mac Ailello mortuus est. Aidain abbas Lis moir, h-Uae Miannaiġ abbas sruiṫi Cluana mic Nois, mortui sunt. Ferdacriċ mac Suibne abbas airdd Maċae quieuit. Eiṫne ingen Bresail Breġ, regina regum Teṁoriae, regnum celeste adipisci meruit post poenitentiam. Coibdenaċ abbas cille Tomae pausat. Bellum i Fortrinn itir Aeḋ 7 Cinaeḋ.

Kl. Ianair. Anno domini dcc.° lx.° uiii.° Coscraḋ itir Osraiġi inuicem, ubi filii Ceallaiġ filii Faelcair in fugam uersi sunt. Toimsnama uictor euasit. Bellum Fernand, in quo cecidit Dubcalggaiḋ mac Laidggnen. Cennselaiġ uictor fuit. Quies Murgaile mic Nindedo abbatis Reċrainne. Encoraċ huae Doadain, abbas Glinne da loċa, mortuus est. Longus Coirpri mic Foġertaiġ re n-Donnchad. Terremotus 7 fames, 7 morbus leprae multos inuasit. h-Abundantia

---

1 *The 'Law' of Patrick.*—Regarding the nature of this 'Law,' or system of collecting tribute, see Dean Reeves' observations, *Colton's Visitation*, Pref., p. III., *sq.*

2 *Dubhinnrecht.*—Mentioned above at the year 765.

3 *Aedan.*—Written Aidain in A. and B., and "Aoan" in Clar. 49. The *Four Mast.*, at A.D. 763, have Aeḋan, which seems more correct. The form Aidain in the text is the genit. of Aidan, or Aedan.

4 *Ua Miannaigh, i.e.*, a "descendant (or grandson) of Miannach." The *Four Mast.* (at A.D. 763) have forgla sruiṫe (the "majority of the sruithe," or "religious seniors," as O'Donovan translates). But this is surely wrong. In note *g*, appended to this entry in the *Four Mast.* by O'Donovan, he states that Clar. 49 (ad. an. 767) has "Lyne *sapiens* Cluana-mic-Nois"; whereas this latter authority has really "*Hue* (for *Ua*) abbas et sapiens," the name *Miannaigh* being omitted after *Ua*.

5 *Suibhne.*—This is the Suibhne, bishop of Armagh, mentioned above at the years 718 and 729.

6 *Of kings.*—regum, A. B. "Of the kings," Clar. 49. The *Four Masters* (A.D. 763) say ben ri Temraċ; which O'Donovan renders "wife

of Fogartach, was slain by a robber. Flathgus, of Fiachra, son of Cathal, was treacherously slain. Law' of Patrick.[1]

l. Jan. A.D. 767. Dubhinnrecht,[2] son of Cathal, of Connaught, died, *i.e.*, from 'bloody flux.' Gormgal, of Ailill, died. Aedan,[3] abbot of Lis-mor, Ua naigh,[4] the most learned abbot of Clonmacnoise, Ferdacrich, son of Suibhne,[5] abbot of Armagh, d. Eithne, daughter of Bresal Bregh, the queen of s[6] of Tara, deserved to obtain the heavenly king- after penance. Coibdenach, abbot of Cill-Toma, A battle in Fortrenn,[7] between Aedh and Cinaedh. [767.] BIS.

l. Jan. A.D. 768. A destructive fight[8] among the ighi themselves, where the sons of Cellach, son of char, were put to flight. Toimsnamha escaped rious. The battle of Ferna,[9] in which fell Dubhcal- n, son of Ladgnen. Cennselach[10] was victor. Repose of gal, son of Nindidh, abbot of Rechra.[11] Encorach Dodain, abbot of Glenn-da-locha, died. The banish- t of Coirpre, son of Fogartach, by Donnchad.[12] An quake, and a famine; and a leprous disease attacked [768.]

King of Teamhair [Tara]." ithne may have been the wife re than one King of Tara.

rtrenn. — For Fortrenn, a for the country of the Scotch see note [8], under the year *supra*. The *Four Mast.* (at 63) imply that this Fortrenn Leinster; which seems doubt- Skene quotes the entry (*Chron. and Scots*, p. 358), as an inci- n Scotch history; but it does not , from Skene's quotation, that ene of the battle was in Scotland.

structive fight.—Cорсрaд. The *Mast.* (at the year 764) use the omaірecc, which means "con-

[9] *Ferna.*—Ferns, co. Wexford.

[10] *Cennselach.* — Cennрelaіg (for "Ui-Cennselaigh," the tribe-name of the people of South Leinster), A., B. Clar. 49 has *Cinnselach.* The death of Cennselach, son of Bran (the person meant, no doubt, in the fore-going entry) is recorded among the events of the next year.

[11] *Rechra.* — Dean Reeves thinks that Rathlin, off the coast of Antrim, was meant (*Eccl. Antiqq.*, p. 249). But Lambay Island, off the east coast of Dublin county, also called Rechra, may have been intended.

[12] *Donnchad.*—King of Ireland at the time.

dairmera. Comman Enaiġ daṫe, Conċobur mac Cumascaiċ rex Aiḋne, mortui sunt.

Fol. 32bb. Kl. Ianair. Anno domini dcc.° lx.° ix.° Nargal mac Natsluaiġ mortuus est a fluxu sanguinis. Toimsnaṁa mac Flainn, rex Ossairgi, iugulatus est. Artgal, abbas Cloċair mac Doiṁeni, mortuus est. Bellum inter Lagenenses inuicem for aṫ Orc, ubi Ceallaċ mac Dunchada uictor fuit, 7 ceciderunt Cinaeḋ filius Flainn 7 frater eius Ceallaċ, 7 Caṫnio mac Becce, 7 ceteri multi. Fiaċrai Granairit, Ferrgil Cille more einir, Fergus episcopus filius Caṫail, mortui sunt. Folaċtach tige Tuae, abbas Clona macc U Nois, mortuus est. Bellum inter nepotes Cennselaiġ, ubi cecidit Cennselach mac Brain, 7 Etirscel mac Aeḋa filii Colggen uictor fuit. Congressio etir Donnchad mac Domnaill 7 Cellaċ mac n-Donnchada, 7 exiit Donnchad cum exercitu nepotum Neill cu Laigniu, 7 effugerunt eum Laginenses, 7 exierunt i Sciaiġ Neċtin; 7 manserunt hui Neill . uii . diebus i raiṫ Alinne, 7 accenderunt igni omnes terminos Laginentium. Cosraḋ Builgg boinne for firu deisceirt Breg, ubi ceciderunt Flaitbertaċ mac Flainn filii Rogellniġ, 7 Uarcriḋe mac Baiṫ, 7

[1] *Acorns.*—dairmera, genit. of dairmes, "oak fruit."

[2] *Enach-Dathe.*—This place has not been identified.

[3] *Toimsnamha.* — Or *Tuaimsnama*, See Shearman's *Ossorian Genealogy*, Part I. (*Loca Patriciana*, p. 264).

[4] *Clochar-mac-Doimheni.*—Clogher, in the county of Tyrone.

[5] *Ath-Orc.*—The "Ford of Orc." Not identified. It was probably the name of some ford on the Liffey, or Barrow.

[6] *Cellach.*—King of Leinster, and son of Dunchad, whose death is recorded above at the year 727.

[7] *Granairet.*—Granard, in the co. Longford.

[8] *Cill-mor-Enir.*—Now Kilmore, in the parish of the same name, barony of Oneilland West, co. Armagh.

[9] *Tech-Tua.*—The "House of St. Tua." Now Taghadoe, in the par. of the same name, barony of North Salt, co. Kildare.

[10] *Cennselach.* — See note [10], under the preceding year.

[11] *Donnchad.*—King of Ireland at this time.

[12] *Cellach.*—King of Leinster. See note [6].

[13] *Sciach - Nechtin.* — "Nechtan's

y. Abundance of acorns.[1] Comman of Enach-Dathe,[2] :hobar son of Cumascach, King of Aidhne, died.
al. Jan. A.D. 769. Nargal, son of Natsluagh, died [769.]
he 'bloody flux.' Toimsnamha,[3] son of Flann, King Issory, was slain. Artgal, abbot of Clochar-mac-nheni,[4] died. A battle between the Leinstermen aselves, at Ath-Orc,[5] where Cellach[6] son of Dunchad victor; and where Cinaedh son of Flann, and his her Cellach, and Cathnio son of Becc, and a great y others, were slain. Fiachra of Granairet,[7] Fergil ill-mor-Enir,[8] Fergus son of Cathal, a bishop, died. ıchtach of Tech-Tua,[9] abbot of Clonmacnoise, died. attle among the Ui-Cennselaigh, in which Cenn-:h[10] son of Bran was slain, and Etirscel, son of Aedh, of Colgu, was victor. An encounter between Donn-l[11] son of Domnall, and Cellach[12] son of Donnchad; Donnchad proceeded to Leinster with the army of Ui-Neill. And the Leinstermen eluded him, and t to Sciach-Nechtin.[13] And the Ui-Neill remained n days in Rath-Alinne,[14] and burned all the borders he Leinstermen with fire. The slaughter[15] of Bolg-ıne against the men of South Brega, in which fell thbertach, son of Flann, son of Rogellnach,[16] and cridhe son of Baeth, and Snedgus son of Ainftech,[17]

." The *Four Mast.* (A.D. 766) the name sciaṫ Neaċtain, h O'Donovan correctly translates ıchtain's Shield (note *b*, *ad an.*). *Sciach Nechtin* seems more correct.

Rath-Alinne. – The "Rath of ı." Now the hill of Knockaulin, e parish of Kilcullen, co. Kildare.

Slaughter.—corcraḋ. Clar. 49 "one sett," for "onset," and novan (*F. M.* 765) translates raḋ "battle." But corcraḋ fies more than a battle. See movan's Suppl. to O'Reilly, *v.* raḋ. The so-called translator of these Annals, however, in the MS. Clar. 49, renders the word by "skirmish."

[16] *Son of Rogellnach.*—The *F. M.* (at 765) have mic Rogallaiġ, "son of Roghallach," which is probably correct, although the name is written Rogellnaiċ, in the genit. case (nom. Rogellnaċ), in these Annals at the year 721 *supra*.

[17] *Son of Ainftech.*—mac Ainḟtiġ (for mac Ainḃtiġ, "son of Ainbh-tech," in A). The form in B. would represent mac Ainḟritiġ, "son of Aufritech," which would be incorrect.

Sneidgus mac Ainfciġ, 7 Cernaċ mac Flainn foirbṫe. Coscraḋ aṫa Cliaṫ ria Ciannacht for hU Teig. Ar mor di Laigniḃ. Robbaḋad sochaidi di ċiannacht illan mora oc tinntud. Gormman ingen Flainn mic Aeḋa mortua est. Crunnmael episcopus, abbas Cille more einir, quievit. Mors Conmaic mic Brendain, abbatis Cluana dochre. Maelduin mac Duibinnrecht iugulatus est. Mors hui Becce abbatis Fobair.

Kt. Ianair. Anno domini dcc.° lxx.° Mors Flainn hui Doċuae, abbatis insi cain Deġa. Aedgen Fobair obiit. Becc mac Conlai, ri Teṫbae, mortuus est. Coirpri mac Fogertaig, rex Breġ, mortuus est. Forbasaċ nepos Cernaiġ, abbas Cluana mic U Nois [obiit]. Oengus mac Fogertaiġ, ri cenuil Loeġaire, subita morte periit. Caṫal mac Conaill minn, ri Coirpri moir, Dungalach mac Taiċliċ, dux Luigne, Fol. 33aa. mortui sunt. Coblaiṫ ingin Caṫail, dominatrix Cluana cuiḃtin obiit. Allcellaċ telċa Olann, 7 Aiċleċ huae Cindriaeċ, obierunt. Sloġaḋ isin Foċla la Donnchad.

Kt. Ianair. Anno domini dcc.° lxx.° i.° Mors Airledo Cluana iraird. Iugulatio Concobair .h. Maeleduin. Sloġaḋ Donnchada co cnocc m-Bane.

---

[1] *Flann Foirbthe.* — His obit is entered above at the year 715, at which date Clar. 49 calls him "Old Flann mc Fogarta."

[2] *Ath-cliath.*—Dublin.

[3] *Cianachta.* — The *Four Mast.* (A.D. 765) say "Cianachta-Bregh"; a sept descended from Cian (*a quo* "Cianachta"), son of Oilill Oluim, King of Munster, whose territory seems to have comprised the present town of Duleek, co. Meath, and a large portion of the surrounding country.

[4] *The full tide.*—"In a sea tide," Clar. 49. The situation of the place where this drowning occurred is left to conjecture. But it was probably in the tidal part of the river Liffey, across which the Cianachte, in their return home, would probably have had to pass.

[5] *Cill-mor-Einir.*—See note [8], p. 236.

[6] *Cluain - Dochre.* — "Cluain-Tochne," in the *Four Mast.* (A.D. 765). The *Chron. Scot.* and *Ann. Four Mast.* (at A.D. 977) mention a "Cluain-Deochra," which is stated in O'Clery's Irish Calendar, at 11th January, to have been in the co. Longford, although Archdall (*Monast. Hib.*, p. 708) identifies it with Clonrane, in the bar. of Moycashel, co. Westmeath. It may be the place now called Cloondara, in the parish of Killashee, bar. and county of Longford.

Cernach son of Flann Foirbthe.[1] The massacre of
liath,[2] by the Cianachta, against the Ui-Teig. A
slaughter of the Leinstermen; and numbers of the
ichta,[3] were drowned in the full tide[4] when returning.
an, daughter of Flann, son of Aedh, died. Crunnmael,
hop, abbot of Cill-mor-Einir,[5] rested. Death of
nach, son of Brendan, abbot of Cluain-dochre.[6]
duin, son of Dubhinnrecht, was slain. Death of
Becce, abbot of Fobhar.[7]
al. Jan. A.D. 770. Death of Flann Ua Dachua, [770.]
t of Inis-cain-Degha.[8] Aedgen of Fobhar[7] died. Becc,
of Conla, King of Tethba, died. Coirpri, son of
rtach, King of Bregh, died. Forbasach Ua Cernaigh,
t of Clonmacnoise, [died]. Oengus, son of Fogartach,[9]
of the Cinel-Loeghaire, died suddenly. Cathal, son
onall Menn, King of Coirpri-mor,[10] [and] Dungalach,
of Taichlech, chief of Luighne, died. Coblaith,
hter of Cathal, abbess of Cluain-Cuibhtin,[11] died.
llach of Telach-Olaind,[12] and Aichlech Ua Cindfiaech,
A hosting into the Fochla[13] by Donnchad.[14]
al. Jan. A.D. 771. Death of Airlid of Cluain-Iraird. [771.
killing of Conchobar Ua Maeleduin. A hosting by
nchad to Cnoc-mBanè.[15] The "Fair of the clapping

---

bhar.—Fore, in the barony of
co. Westmeath.

is-cain-Degha.—Inishkeen, in
rony of Farney, co. Monaghan;
name to the parish of Inish-
situated partly in the county of
ghan, and partly in Louth county.

n of Fogartach.—The Four
(at 766) have mac Ḟeraḋaiġ,
of Feradhach."

King of Coirpri-mor.—ri Coir-
noir, "king of the great Coirpri
irbri)," A. B. has ri Coirpri
(for "king of Coirpri, moritur"
'mortuus est"). Clar. 49 has
"moritur." But the reading in
A. is probably correct. The territory
(or tribe) of "Coirpri-mor" is mentioned in the *Ann. Four Mast.* at the years 949, 974, 1029, and 1032.

[11] *Cluain-Cuibhtin.*—See note at the year 759 *supra*, where the name is "Cluain-Cuifthin."

[12] *Telach-Olaind.*—See this place referred to above at the years 710 (note [5], p. 160) and 730.

[13] *Fochla.*—The north of Ireland.

[14] *Donnchad.*—King of Ireland a the time.

[15] *Cnoc-mBanè.* — The "Hill of Banè." See O'Donovan's *Four Mast.* at A.D. 111, note *g*.

Oenaċ inna lamcomarṫae, in quo ignis 7 tonitru similitudine diei iudicii. Ind laṁcomart hi feil Miċel dianepred in tene di nim. Mors Suibne abbatis Iae. Aensit Goiḋil da tredan immelle, 7 oen p̄raind etarru, ar oṁun in teinid̄. Quies Maelaiċthin abb cluana Eiḋniġ. Lex Comain 7 Aedain secunda for teora Connacht. Aeḋ aiṫgin rex hUe Mane, Art mac Flaiṫniaḋ rex Aiḋne, iugulati sunt. Lergus mac Duibcombair mortuus est.

Kl. Ianair. Anno domini dcc.° lxx.° ii.° Moenaċ mac Colmain, abbas Slane 7 cille Foibriċ, a fluxu sanguinis mortuus est. Daniel nepos Foileni, scriba Letubai, quieuit. Donncoṫaiḋ rex Connaċt mortuus est. Insolita siccitas 7 ardor solis, ut pene panis omnis deperiit. Deirmess mor inna dead. Martan inse Eidneċ, Aedan episcopus maiġe hEu, Ceiṫernaċ huae Erumon oabbas cluana ferta Brenainn, mortui sunt. Lerṫan dominatrix Cille daro obiit. Luna tenebrosa in .ii. nonas decimbris. Aeḋ mac Coirpri, princeps Reċrainne, mortuus est.

Kl. Ianair. Anno domini dcc.° lxx.° iii.° Mors Albrain mic Foidmid, abbatis Treoid moir, in sexta

---

[1] "*Fair of the clapping of hands.*"—This evidently refers to a celebration of national games somewhere, during which the people present thereat were so terrified by excessive thunder and lightning, that they clapped their hands in token of horror and despair. Dr. O'Conor, and the so-called 'translator' of Clar. 49, considered *lamcomairt* ("clapping of hands") as the name of the place in which the *oenach* (or "fair") was held. But they were clearly mistaken. A similar incident is noticed at the year 798, *infra*.

[2] *Fasted.*—aensit (for ainsit), A. B. The so-called "translator" of these Annals in Clar. 49 renders this entry "Irishmen fasted for feare of theire destruction, one meale among them in awe of the fyre." Dr. O'Conor (Ann. Ult. ad an.) translates aensith "consensio spontanea," which is as bad. But the translation given in the *Census of Ireland* for 1851 (Part V. vol. 1, p. 57), where aensit is rendered by "all in one place" (as if the original was aen sith) is even worse.

[3] *Two 'tredans'*; *i.e.* two fasts of three days each. See *tredan, i.e. tredenus, i.e.* tres dies. Gloss in *Fel. of Oengus*, at Nov. 16.

[4] *Cluain - Eidhnech.* — Clonenagh, near Mountrath, in the Queen's County.

of hands,"[1] in which occurred lightning and thunder, like unto the day of judgment. The 'clapping of hands'[1] on the festival of St. Michael, of which was said the "fire from Heaven." Death of Suibhne, abbot of Ia. The Goidhil fasted[2] two 'tredans'[3] together, and only one meal between them, through fear of the fire. Repose of Maelaichthin, abbot of Cluain-Eidhnech.[4] The 'Law' of Coman and of Aedan, a second time,[5] over the three divisions of Connaught. Aedh Aithgin, King of the Ui-Maine, and Art son of Flaithniadh, King of Aidhne, were slain. Lergus, son of Dubhcomair, died.

Kal. Jan. A.D. 772. Moenach, son of Colman, abbot of Slane and Cill-Foibrigh, died of the 'bloody flux.' Daniel Ua Foileni, scribe of Letuba,[6] rested. Donncothaidh, King of Connaught, died. An unusual drought and heat of the sun, so that almost all food failed. A great abundance of acorns after it. Martan of Inis-eidnech, Aedan bishop of Magh-Eo,[7] [and] Ceithernach Ua Erumono, abbot of Cluain-ferta-Brenainn, died. Lerthan, abbess[8] of Cill-dara, died. A dark moon on the second of the Nones of December. Aedh son of Coirpri, abbot[9] of Rechru, died. [772.]

Kal. Jan. A.D. 773. Death of Albran, son of Foidmed, abbot of Treoid-mor,[10] on the sixth day between the two [773.]

[5] *A second time.*—ſa (for ſecunda) A. B. O'Conor prints *fa.* Clar. 49 ignores it. The beginning of the third "Law" (*Lex*, or tribute) of Coman and Aedan is noticed under the year 779 *infra.*

[6] *Letuba.*—This place, which has not been identified, is again referred to at the year 778 *infra.*

[7] *Magh-Eo.*—The "Plain of the Yew." Mayo, barony of Clanmorris, co. Mayo.

[8] *Abbess.*—dominatrix. A B.

[9] *Abbot.*—princeps, A. B. Clar. 49 has "prince"; bnt princeps seems used throughout these Annals to signify the abbot or superior of a monastery.

[10] *Treoid-mor*; or "Great Treoid." But there is no mention in these Annals, or in any other authority known to the Editor, of a *Treoid-beg*, or "little Treoid." The place referred to is now known as Trevet, in the parish of the same name, barony of Skreen, and county of Meath. The old name of the place was *Duma-dergluachra* ("Mound of the red rushy-place"), according to a statement in *Lebor-na-hUidri*, p. 119*a*.

feria inter duo pascha. Ultan .h. Berodeirgg, abbas Oṫnae móre, Eirennaċ mac Eiċin abbas Leiṫ-glinne, Forinnain scriba 7 episcopus Treoit, perierunt. Dunlaiṫ ingen Foġertaiġ obiit. Tomaltaċ mac Murġaile, rex Cruaċna Ai, Dodbċad mac Ectgusa, rex cenuil filii Ercae, mortui sunt. Suairleċ .h. Conciarain, abbas Liss moir, Impaiṫeċ glinne Cloiṫiġe, anchorita, mortui sunt. Flaṫruae mac Fiaċraċ, rex Cruiṫne, moritur. Commixtio agonis la Donnchad. Eugan mac Colmain a fluxu sanguinis mortuus est, 7 ceteri multi ex isto dolore mortui sunt.

Fol. 33ab.

Kl. Ianair. Anno domini dcc.° lxx.° iiii.° Mors Cinaḋon regis Pictorum; 7 Donngal mac Nuaḋat abbas Luġmaiḋ, 7 Fianċu abbas Luġmaiḋ, 7 Conall maiġe Luingi, 7 Suairleċ abbas Linne, perierunt. Comburtio airdd Maċae. Comburtio Cille daro. Comburtio Glinne da loċa. Congressio inter Mumanenses 7 nepotes Neill, 7 fecit Donnchad uastationem magnam in finibus Muminensium, 7 ceciderunt multi ti Muimneċaiḃ. Imairecc i Cluain iraird itir Donnchad 7 muintir Cluana iraird. Guier Ciarain craiḋbtiġ .i. Belaig duin. Bellum aċaiḋ liag inter

[1] *Two Easters; i.e.* Easter Sunday and Low Sunday.

[2] *Othan-mor.* — "Great Othan." Now Fahan, barony of Inishowen, co. Donegal.

[3] *Leithglenn.*—Now known as Old-Leighlin, the site of a Bishop's See, in the barony of Idrone West, co. Carlow.

[4] *Treoit.*—Trevet, bar. of Skreen, co. Meath.

[5] *Of Cruachan-Ai.* — The *Four Mast.* (at A.D. 769) have Maiġe hAi, "of Magh-Ai," the name of a well-known district in the co. Roscommon.

[6] *Glenn-Cloitighe.* — O'Donovan thought that this was probably the vale of the river [Clody], near New-town-Barry, in the county Wexford. (*Ann. Four Mast.*, A.D. 769, note *o.*) But this is doubtful. O'Conor absurdly translates the name "vallis illustrium heroum."

[7] *Cruithni, i.e.*, the Cruithni, or Picts, of Dalaraide, in Ireland; although Skene copies the entry as referring to the Scotch Picts (*Chron. Picts and Scots*, p. 358).

[8] *Fair.*—O'Conor thought that the Fair (or assembly) meant was the Fair of Tailltiu (or Teltown), co. Meath; and he was possibly right in this instance.

rs.[1] Ultan Ua Berodeirgg, abbot of Othan-mor[2]; nach, son of Eichen, abbot of Leithglenn,[3] [and] nan, scribe and bishop of Treoit,[4] died. Dunlaith, ıter of Fogartach, died. Tomaltach, son of Murgal, of Cruachan-Ai,[5] [and] Bodbchad, son of Echtgus, of Cinel-mic-Erca, died. Suairlech Ua Conciarain, of Lis-mor, [and] Imraithech of Glenn-Cloitighe,[6] an rite, died. Flathroe, son of Fiachra, king of the ıni,[7] dies. Disturbance of a fair[8] by Donnchad. ı, son of Colman, died from the 'bloody flux,' and others died from that disorder.

. Jan. A.D. 774. Death of Cinadhon, king of the Picts; onngal, son of Nuada, abbot of Lughmadh,[9] and Fian-bbot of Lughmadh, and Conall of Magh-luinge,[10] and ech, abbot of Linn,[11] died. Burning of Ard-Macha. ng of Cill-dara. Burning of Glenn-da-locha. A battle en the Munstermen and the Ui-Neill, and Donnchad[12] itted great devastation in the borders of the Munster- and many of the Munstermen were slain. A conflict ain-Iraird, between Donnchad[12] and the 'family' of ı-Iraird. The repose of Ciaran the pious, *i.e.*, of ı-duin.[13] The battle of Achadh-liag,[14] between the iuin and the [Ui]-Maine, where the [Ui]-Maine [774.]

madh.—Louth, in the co.

h-luinge.—See note [1], at the , *supra.*

. — This should evidently -Duachaill, a place which an identifies with Magheralin, . Down; but on no sufficient , so far as the Editor can *Martyr. of Donegal*, at the April, has "Suairlech, abbot Duachaill, A.D. 774."

chad.—Monarch of Ireland ıe.

[13] *Belach-duin.*—The "Pass" of the "*dun*" (or "fort"). This was the old name of Disert-Chairain, or Castle-keeran, in the barony of Upper Kells, and county of Meath.

[14] *Achadh-liag.*—The "Field of the Stones." Dr. O'Conor (in Ann. Ult. ad. an.) states that this place was Athleague [in the bar. of Athlone, co. Roscommon]. But O'Donovan (*Four Mast.*, A.D. 770, note *x*) thought that the place referred to was "the place now called Achadh-leaga, situated on the east side of the river Suck," in the same barony.

nepotes Briuin 7 Maine, ubi Mane prostratus est. Strages nepotum filiorum Brocc in tempore Colggen mic Cellaiġ. Combustio insole Baiṫeni.

.b. Kl. Ianair. Anno domini dcc.° lxx.° u.° Quies Colmain ḟinn ancoritae. Mors Goidil Cluana Iraird. Mors Forbusaiċ abbatis Raṫo Aiḋo. Mors Collbrainn abbatis Cluana mic U Nois. Comotatio martirum sancti Erce Slane, 7 comotatio martirum Uiniani Cluana Iraird. Mors Maelemanaċ abbatis Cinngaraḋ. Bellum inter dal n-Araide inuicem, i sleib Miss, in quo cecidit Nia mac Conalta. Bellum Druing iterum in eodem anno, itir dal n-Araide, in quo ceciderunt Cinaeḋ cairgge mac Caṫasaiġ, 7 Dungal .h. Fergusa forcraiḋ. Tomaltaċ mac Indrechtaiġ 7 Eċaiḋ mac Fiaċnae uictores erant. Cellaċ mac Dunchada, rex Laiġen, mortuus est.

Fol. 33ba. Bellum Aṫa dumai itir na hAirṫeru 7 .h. Eċoċ Coḃo, in quo cecidit Gormgal mac Conaill crui, rex Coḃo. Eugan mac Roncinn abbas Liss ṁoir, 7 Maelruḃai .h. Moinaiġ, perierunt. Caṫcos[c]rad itir U Neill 7 Muime, in quo familia Dermaigi fuit, 7 filii Tobaiṫ, id est Duineċaiḋ 7 Catrannaċ, 7 alii de filiis

---

[1] *Were overthrown.*—prostratus est, A. and B., with which Clar. 49 agrees. But the name of Mane (or Maine), ancestor of the sept, is put for the sept itself in these authorities. The *Four Mast.* (at A.D. 770) have more correctly in ro meaḃaiḋ for Uiḃ Maine ("in which the Ui-Maine were defeated").

[2] *Colgu.*—King of the Ui-Cremthainn. His obit is given at the year 780, *infra*.

[3] *Inis-Baithin.*—Now Ennisboyne, in the barony of Arklow, co. Wicklow.

[4] *Cluain-Iraird.*—Clonard in the barony of Upper Moyfenrath, co. Meath.

[5] *Rath-Aedha.*—Now Rahugh, in the parish of the same name, barony of Moycashel, and county of Westmeath.

[6] *Of Finian.*—Uiniaui, A. Finniaui, B. "Finiani," Clar. 49, which seems more correct.

[7] *Cenngaradh.*—Kingarth in Scotland.

[8] *Themselves.*—inuicem, A. B. For *invicem* the *Four Masters* generally use fesin ("themselves"), as in this case.

[9] *Sliabh-Mis.*—Slemish, a moun-

vere overthrown.[1] A slaughter of the Ui-Mac-Brocc, in he time of Colgu,[2] son of Cellach. Burning of Inis-Baithin.[3]

Kal. Jan. A.D. 775. The repose of Colman Finn, anchorite. Death of Goidel of Cluain-Iraird.[4] Death of Forbasach, abbot of Rath-Aedha.[5] Death of Colbrand, abbot of Clonmacnoise. 'Translation' of the relics of St. Erc of Slane, and 'translation' of the relics of Finian[6] of Cluain-Iraird. Death of Maelmanach, abbot of Cenngaradh.[7] A battle among the Dalaraide themselves,[8] at Sliabh-Mis,[9] in which Nia, son of Cualta, was slain. A battle of Drung[10] again in the same year, among the Dalaraide, in which fell Cinaedh Cairgge, son of Cathasach, and Dungal, grandson of Fergus Forcraidh.[11] Tomaltach,[12] son of Indrechtach, and Echaidh,[13] son of Fiachna, were victors. Cellach, son of Dunchad, King of Leinster, died. The battle of Ath-duma[14] between the Airthera and the Ui-Echach-Cobha, in which fell Gormgal, son of Conall Crui, King of Cobha. Eugan, son of Ronchenn, abbot of Lis-mor, and Maelrubha Ua Moenaigh, died. A destructive battle between the Ui-Neill and Munstermen,[15] in which were the 'family' of Dermagh,[16] and the sons of Tobath, *i.e.* Duinechaidh and Cathrannach, and others of the sons of [775.] BIS.

ain in the barony of Lower Antrim, n the co. of Antrim.

10 *Drung.*—See note[1], p. 96, *supra.*

11 *Fergus Forcraidh.*—The death of his person is recorded above under he year 702.

12 *Tomaltach.*—This Tomaltach, son f Indrechtach, is mentioned among he kings of Ulad in the list in the *Book of Leinster* (p. 41, col. 3), and lso in the list of kings of Dalaraide p. 41, col. 5). See under the year 789 *infra.*

13 *Echaidh.*—Called "Eocho" in he *Book of Leinster* list of the kings of Ulad (p. 41, col. 3), where he is stated to have reigned 10 years.

14 *Ath-duma.*—A battle of Ath-duma between the Ulidians and the Ui-Echach is mentioned above at the year 760. The place has not been identified.

15 *Munstermen.* -- Muime, A. B. has the abbrev. for Muimnechu (accus. pl. of Muimnech, a "Munsterman").

16 *'Family' of Dermagh.* -- The community of Durrow, in the King's county. The *Four Masters* do not give this entry.

Domnaill; 7 ceciderunt multi de Mume, 7 uictores fuerunt nepotes Neill. Conbadh inna con.

Kl. Ianair. Anno domini dcc.° lxx.° ui.° Iugulatio mac Cumascaich oc Odraib, alius uixit alius mortuus est. Comroid cathimairecc itir da ua Cernaigh, id est Niall 7 Cumuscach, in quo ceciderunt Ectghus mac Baith, 7 ceteri multi, hi faithci Caladromo. Slogad Lagen la Donnchad for Bregа. Ind ule gaim issind samradh .i. flechodh mor 7 gaeth mor. Flathrui filii Domhnaill regis Connacht. Cumuscc ind oenaigh la Donnchad for Ciannacht. In coccadh itir Donnchad 7 Congalach. Strages Calraighi la hUi Fiachrach. Banbodhbhgni sapiens obiit. Ind riuth fola. Galrai imdai olchena, pene mortalitas. In bo ar már.

Kl. Ianair. Anno domini dcc.° lxx.° uii.° In coccadh cetna itir Donnchad 7 Congalach .i. mac Conaing, 7 bellum forcalaid inna forciunn, ubi ceciderunt Congalach mac Conaing, 7 Cuanu mac Ecnid, 7 Dermait mac Clothgni, 7 Dunchad mac Aléni, 7 Flathnia mac Maeleduin, 7 ceteri multi. Donnchad uictor fuit.

---

[1] *Combat of the Cu's.*—Obadh (for conbadh, or combadh) inna con. This would also mean "battle of the dogs," *cu* (gen. pl. and sg. *con.*) a "dog," being frequently used in the formation of the names of remarkable Irishmen in ancient times. This entry may have some reference to the 1st and 2nd entries under the next year.

[2] '*Jugulatio.*'—This word as used in the Irish Annals always means a death inflicted by violence. The *Four Masters*, who have the entry of this event at the year 772, say that the one killed the other; in other words, that they fell by each other.

[3] *Odhra.*—Now Odder, in the parish of Tara, barony of Skreen, and county of Meath.

[4] *Cernach.*—The Cernach, son of Diarmait, son of Aedh Slané, whose death is entered above at the years 663 and 666.

[5] *Caladruim.*—Now Galtrim, in the par. of the same name, barony of Lower Deece, co. Meath.

[6] *King.*—regis, A. B. Clar. 49 has 'rex.' But the older MSS. are probably correct, and as the forms filii and regis are used in connection with "Flathrui" (the genit. form of Flathrue, or Flathru), it follows

)omnall; and many of the Munstermen were slain; and he Ui-Neill were victors. Combat of the Cu's.[1]

Kal. Jan. A.D. 776. The 'jugulatio'[2] of Cumuscach's [776.]
ions, at Odhra,[3]—one lived, another died. A mutual battle between two descendants of Cernach,[4] viz., Niall and Cumuscach, in which fell Echtgus, son of Baeth, and nany others, in the fair-green of Caladruim.[5] The iosting of Leinster by Donnchad upon Breg. Winter .ltogether in the Summer, viz., great rain and great wind. 'lathrui, son of Domnall, King[6] of Connaught. Dis-urbance of the fair,[7] by Donnchad, against the Cianachta. 'he war between Donnchad and Congalach.[8] Slaughter of the Calraighi by the Ui-Fiachrach. Ban-Bodbhgna,[9] , wise man, died. The 'bloody flux.' Many diseases esides; a mortality almost. The great mortality of ows.

Kal. Jan. A.D. 777. The same war between Donn- [777.]
had and Congalach (*i.e.*, son of Conaing[10]); and the attle of Forcalad at the end of it, in which were slain Congalach, son of Conaing, and Cuanu, son of Ecned, nd Diarmait, son of Clothgna, and Dunchad, son of Léne, and Flaithnia, son of Maelduin, and many others.)onnchad was victor.

---

iat some word like mors, or obitus, as been omitted before Flathrui. ut the death of Flaithruae, King of 'onnaught (the same name a little ltered), is entered under the year 78.

[7] *The fair.* — The "Fair" (or national games") celebrated an-ually in Tailltiu, or Teltown, in the arony of Upper Kells, co. Meath. 3e above, at the year 716. O'Conor itirely misunderstood this entry, hich he translates in his ed. of these nnals (ad. an.), "Levis pugua, seu velitatio, facta apud Doenag, a Dunn-chado rege contra Ciannachtenses."

[8] *Congalach.*—The same personage mentioned under the next year.

[9] *Ban-Bodbhgna.*—"Bau of 'Bod-bhgna.'" Bodbhgna is now known as Sliabh-Baune, in the county of Roscommon.

[10] *Son of Conaing.*—The original of this clause is added by way of gloss in B. It is in the text in Clar. 49. Congalach, son of Conaing, was King of the Brega, in Meath.

Do ċath forcalait foroiret
Domnach dubaċ derach;
Ba imda maṫair boed bronaċ
In luan iar na ḃarach.

Combustio cluana micc U Nois hi .vi. idus Iuil. Ind ruaṫ fola. In bo ar már. Lex Coluim Cille la Donnchad 7 Bresal. Mors Etirsceili mic Aeḋo mic Colggene, regis .h. Cennselaiġ. Dormitatio Ainfċel-laiġ, abbatis Conndire 7 Lainne ela. Niall frosaċ mac Fergaile (ann I ċolaim ċille), 7 Niall mac Conaill graint rex deisceirt Breġ, 7 Tuaṫal mac Crem̃tain rex Cualand, 7 Flannabra rex .h. Mail, 7 Aeḋ finn mac Eċdaċ rex Dal Riati, omnes mortui sunt. Siṫmaiṫ abatissa cluana Bairenn mortua est. Finan abbas Cluana auis, 7 Constans sapiens Loċa n-Eirne, quieuerunt. Cedis nepotum Mani in campo Dairben, ubi Artgal uictor erat. Eiṫni ingen Cinaḋon mortua est.

Fol. 33*bb*. Kl. Ianair. Anno domini dcc.° lxx.° viii.° Mors Fulartaiġ episcopi Cluana iraird. Oengus mac Aleni

---

[1] *Forcalad*.—O'Donovan was uncertain whether this should be "Forcalad," or *for Calad* ("upon Calad"); which ("Calad") he regarded as "probably the . . . . Caladh of Calraighe . . . . . in the present parish of Ballyloughloe [co. Westmeath]. *Ann. Four Mast.*, A.D. 773, note *o*. This stanza, which is not in B., is added, in the original hand, in the lower margin of fol. 33*b* in A., with a mark of reference to its place in the text.

[2] *Donnchad*.—Monarch of Ireland. The enforcement, or promulgation, of the 'Law' (or tribute) of St. Colum-Cille by his father Domnall, also monarch of Ireland, is recorded above at the year 752.

[3] *Lann-Ela*.—Now Lynally, in the barony of Ballycowan, King's county.

[4] *Niall Frosach*. — Niall "of the Showers." His accession to the kingship of Ireland is recorded above at the year 762 (=763). In the *Book of Leinster* (p. 25, col. 2), Niall is stated to have died in Hi (Iona), na ailithri, "in his pilgrimage;" and it is added that three remarkable showers fell in his reign, namely, a shower of "white silver," a shower of honey, and a shower of wheat. See under the years 717 and 763, *supra*.

By the battle of Forcalad[1] was caused
A sorrowful, tearful Sunday.
Many a fond mother was sad
On the Monday following.

Burning of Clonmacnoise on the 6th of the Ides of July. The 'bloody flux.' The great mortality of cows. The 'Law' of Colum-Cille by Donnchad[2] and Bresal. Death of Etirscel, son of Aedh, son of Colgu, King of Ui-Cennselaigh. The 'falling asleep' of Ainfcellach, abbot of Connor, and of Lann-Ela[3]. Niall Frosach,[4] son of Fergal, (in I-Colum-Cille[5]), and Niall son of Conall Grant,[6] King of the South of Bregh, and Tuathal son of Cremthan,[7] King of Cualand, and Flannabra, King of Ui-Mail, and Aedh Finn son of Echaidh, King of Dal-riata[8]—all died. Sithmaith, abbess of Cluain-Bairenn,[9] died. Finan, abbot of Cluain-auis,[10] and Constans, a wise man, of Loch-Eirne,[11] rested. A slaughter of the Ui-Mani, in Magh-Dairben,[12] where Artgal[13] was the victor. Eithni, daughter of Cinadhon,[14] died.

Kal. Jan. A.D. 778. Death of Fulartach, bishop of [778.]
Cluain-Iraird. Oengus son of Alene, King of Mughdorne;

[5] *I-Coluim-Cille.* — Iona. This clause is interlined in A and B.

[6] *Conall Grant*; *i.e.* Conall "the Gray." See under the year 717, *supra.*

[7] *Cremthan.*—The Crimthan, son of Cellach Cualand, whose death is entered above at the year 725.

[8] *Dalriata*; *i.e.* the Irish Dalriata, in the co. of Antrim. See Reeves' *Eccl. Antiqq.*, p. 318, *sq.*

[9] *Cluain-Bairenn.* — Cloonburren, in the parish of Moore, barony of Moycarn, and county of Roscommon.

[10] *Cluain-auis.* — Otherwise written Cluain-eois; now Clones, county Monaghan.

[11] *Loch-Eirne.*—Lough Erne, in the co. Fermanagh. But this is probably a mistake. The *Martyr. of Donegal*, at Nov. 14, give the festival of "Constans, Priest and Anchorite, of Eo-inis, in Loch-Eirne in Uladh, A.D. 777;" evidently the same person. But according to the *Ann. Four Mast.*, at A.D. 1231, Eo-inis [Eanish, O'Donov. note *e ad an.*] was in Logh-Oughter [co. Cavan; an expansion of the River Erne further south].

[12] *Magh-Dairben.* — Somewhere in Connaught. Not identified.

[13] *Artgal.*—King of Connaught. See under the year 781 *infra.*

[14] *Cinadhon.*—King of the Scotch Picts, whose obit is given above at the year 774.

rex Muġdorne, Conall hua Osseni abbas Letubai, Ainmeri abbas Raṫo nuae, Conna mac Conain, Moinan mac Cormaic abbas caṫraċ Fursi i Francia, Flaiṫruae rex Connacht, defuncti sunt. Bouum mortalitas non desinit, 7 mortalitas hominum de pennuria. Combustio Cille daro hi .iii. idus Iuin. Combustio cluana moer Maeḋocc. Combustio Cille deilgge. In bolggach for Erinn huile. Uentus maximus in fine autumni. Muiredaċ mac Oengusa, rex arda Cianachta, iugulatus est. Sloġaḋ la Donnchad isin Foċla, co tucc giallu o Domnall mac Aeḋo muindeirg, rege aquilonis. Bellum Mumen inuicem, ubi cecidit Fergal mac Eladaiġ rex Dessmuman. Breislen Berri uictor fuit. Forboraċ mac Maeletolai, abbas Rois chaimm, moritur.

Kl. Ianair. Anno domini dcc.° lxx.° ix.° Combustio Alocluaḋe in Kalendis Ianuarii. Combustio cluana Bairenn 7 combustio Balni. Mors Murċoḋa mic Duiḃdatuaṫ. Bellum do maḋmaim re Colggen mac Cellaiġ forr na hAirṫeru, ubi ceciderunt multi ignobiles. Eilpin rex Saxonum moritur. Mac Leinne abbas innse Bairenn obiit. Fuga Ruadraċ a Oċtur ochae, 7 Coirpri mic Laiḋġnein, cum duobus generibus

[1] *Letuba.*—This monastery is mentioned above at the year 772.

[2] *Fursa's City.* — Peronne, in France. St. Fursa is referred to at the years 626, 647, 648, 655, and 660, *supra.*

[3] *Flathrua.*—See under the year 776.

[4] *Ceased not.*—non desiuit, A. non desinit, Clar. 49. Omitted in B.

[5] *Fochla.*—A name for the North of Ireland.

[6] *Des-Mumha.*—Desmond.

[7] *Breislen of Berre.*—Berre is now represented by the barony of Bear, in the N.W. of the co. Cork. The obit of Breislen of Berre is entered under the year 798 *infra*, and that of his son Maelbracha, lord of Corca-Loighde (a territory to the south of Berre, in the same county), is given by the *Four Masters* at A.D. 800 (=805).

[8] *Ros-caimm.* — Plainly written rois chaimm (in the genit. case) in A. and B., and "Roischaim" in Clar. 49. The *Four Mast.*, at A.D. 774, have rosa Comáin ("of Roscommon"). But the place intended may be Roscam, in the parish of Oranmore, co. Galway. It certainly could not have

onall Ua Osseni, abbot of Letuba;[1] Ainmeri, abbot of ath-nua; Conna, son of Conan; Moenan, son of Cormac, ıbot of Fursa's City[2] in France, [and] Flaithrua,[3] King : Connaught, died. The mortality of cattle ceased ot;[4] and a mortality of men from want. Burning of ill-dara on the 3rd of the Ides of June. Burning of luain-mor-Maedhog. Burning of Cill-deilgge. The nall-pox throughout all Ireland. A very great wind in ıe end of Autumn. Muiredach, son of Oengus, King of .rd-Cianachta, was slain. A hosting by Donnchad into he Fochla,[5] so that he brought hostages from Domnall, ɔn of Aedh Muinderg, King of the North. A battle mong the Munstermen themselves, in which fell Fergal, ɔn of Eladach, King of Des-Mumha.[6] Breislen of ;erre[7] was the victor. Forbasach, son of Maeltola, abbot f Ros-caimm,[8] dies.

Kal. Jan. A.D. 779. Burning of Al-Cluadhe,[9] on the Calends of January. Burning of Cluain-Bairenn,[10] and urning of Balne.[11] Death of Murchadh, son of Dubh-latuath. A battle was broken[12] by Colgu, son of Cellach .pon the Airthera, where many ignoble persons were lain. Eilpin, King of the Saxons,[13] dies. Mac-Leinne, .bbot of Inis-Bairenn, died. The flight of Ruaidhri from)chtar-Ocha,[14] and of Coirpre, son of Ladhgnen, with the [779.]

---

een intended for Ros-Comain (Roscommon).

[9] *Al-Cluadhe.*—Also written Al-Cluaithe, or Al-Cluathe. Dumbarton, ı Scotland. See note 12 at the year 57 *supra.*

[10] *Cluain-Bairenn.*—Cloonburren, o. Roscommon.

[11] *Balne.*—Or *Balna* (Latinized in he genit. form *Balni*). Now Balla, a the barony of Clanmorris, co. Iayo. See above under the year 93.

[12] *Was broken.*—Do maidmaim.)r. O'Conor, in his ed. of these Annals (*ad an.*), mistaking this expression for the name of a place, translates "Prælium Domadhmanense"!

[13] *King of the Saxons.*—This seems a mistake, as Elpin was a Pictish King. See Skene's *Chron. Picts and Scots*, Pref., p. cxxvi. note.

[14] *Ochtar-Ocha.*—Or Uachtar-Ocha ("upper Ocha"). Some place in Leinster; but not identified. O'Donovan says (*Ann. F. M.* A.D. 765, note s) that Ocha was the ancient name of a place near the hill of Tara, in Meath. See note [4] under the year 482 *supra.* Some lines of poetry referring to

Laginentium. Donnchad persecutus est eos cum suis sociis, uastauitque 7 comburrit fines eorum 7 aeclesias. Nix magna in Aprilio. Fergus Maigi dumai mortuus est. Forbflaiṫ ingin Connlai, dominatrix cluana Bronaiġ, mortua est. Augustin Bennċair, 7 Sedraċ mac Sobarṫain, 7 Nadarċu sapiens, mortui sunt. Congressio senodorum nepotum Neill Laginentiumque in opido Temro, ubi fuerunt ancoritae 7 scribe multi, quibus dux erat Dublitter. Macnio mac Ceallaiġ, abbas Duin leṫglaissi, quieuit. Lex tertia Commain 7 Aeḋain incipit.

Kl. Ianair. Anno domini dcc.° lxxx.° Dungalaċ mac Conġaile mortuus est. Magna comixtio in ardd
Fol. 34aa. Machae, in quinquagissima die, in qua cecidit Condalaċ mac Aillello. Senċan abbas Imleċo Ibair, 7 Oraċ abbas Lis moer, abbas insse Daimle, 7 Saerġal hue Edairngnae abbas cluana ferta Moluae, 7 Duḃinnrecht mac Fergusa abbas Fernann, 7 Ailngnaḋ episcopus ard Breccain, 7 Moenaċ .h. Monaiġ abbas Lainne leire, 7 Fectaċ abbas Foḃair, 7 Colggu mac Cellaiġ ri .h. Creṁtain, 7 Ailbran .h. Lugadon abbas cluana Dolcain, Nuada .h. Bolcain abbas Tommae da olann, Dungal mac Flaiṫniaḋ rex .h. Mail, Soergal

---

Ochtar-Ocha are written in the top margin of fol. 34a in A. But they are not worth printing.

[1] *The two tribes of the Leinstermen*, *i.e.*, the North Leinstermen proper, and the South Leinstermen, or Ui-Cennselaigh. Ruaidhri was King of Leinster (see his ob. at 784 *infra*), and Coirpri King of Ui-Cennslaigh. (*Book of Leinster*, p. 39, col. 2, and p. 40, col. 1.)

[2] *Donnchad.*—King of Ireland at the time.

[3] *Of the synods.*—senodorum, A. and B., (though O'Conor prints from the latter MS. "Sinodorum"). "Synodarum," Clar. 49.

[4] *Dubhlitter.* — Probably Dubhlitter, abbot of Finglas (near Dublin), whose obit is given *infra* at the year 795.

[5] *President.* — dux. Clar. 49 translates "Captain."

[6] *Third.*—The "Lex secunda," or second promulgation of the 'Law,' or tribute, of Coman and Aedan, is recorded above at the year 771.

[7] *Quinquagesima.* — "Shrovetide," *Ann. Clonmacnoise*, A.D. 778.

[8] *Imlech-Ibhair.* — Emly, in the barony of Clanwilliam, co. Tipperary.

vo tribes of the Leinstermen.[1] Donnchad[2] pursued iem, with his confederates, and wasted and burned their rritories and churches. Great snow in April. Fergus : Magh-duma dies. Forbflaith, daughter of Connla, bbess of Cluain-Bronaigh, died. Augustin of Bennchair, id Sedrach, son of Sobarthan, and Nadarchu, a wise an, died. A congress of the synods[3] of the Ui-Neill id the Leinstermen, in the town of Tara, where were veral anchorites and scribes, over whom Dubhlitter[4] was resident.[5] Macnio, son of Cellach, abbot of Dun-thglaisi, rested. The third[6] 'Law' of Coman and edan begins.

Kal. Jan. A.D. 780. Dungalach, son of Congal, died. reat confusion in Ard-Macha on Quinquagesima[7] day, i which Condalach, son of Ailill, was slain. Senchan, bbot of Imlech-Ibhair;[8] Orach, abbot of Lis-mor; the bbot of Inis-Daimle;[9] Saerghal Ua Edairngnae, abbot of luain-ferta-Molua[10]; Dubhinnrecht, son of Fergus, abbot ' Ferns; Ailgnadh, bishop of Ard-Brecain; Moenach a Monaigh, abbot of Lann-leire;[11] Fechtach, abbot of obhar;[12] Colgu, son of Cellach, king of the Ui-Cremthain; ilbran Ua Lugadon, abbot of Cluain-Dolcain;[13] Nuada 'a Bolcain, abbot of Tuaim-da-olann;[14] Dungal, son of laithniadh, king of Ui-Mail;[15] Saergal Ua Cathail, a [780.]

---

[9] *Inis-Daimle.*—In the *Martyr. of 'onegal*, at July 4, Inis-Daimle (or iis-Doimhle, as the name is there ritten) is described as between Ui-ennselaigh [county of Wexford] id the Deisi [co. Waterford]. Dr. 'odd thought Inis-Daimle was pro-ably the same as "Little Island," in ie expansion of the Suir, near Vaterford. *War of the Gaedhil*, &c., itrod., xxxvii., note [2].

[10] *Cluain-ferta-Molua.*—See note [10], . 85, *supra*.

[11] *Lann-leire,*—Or *Lann-leri*, as written above at the year 720, where see note [2].

[12] *Fobhar.*—Fore, co. Westmeath.

[13] *Cluain-Dolcain.* — Clondalkin near Dublin. Other members of the Ua Lugadon family seem to have been abbots of Clondalkin. See under the years 789 and 800, *infra*.

[14] *Tuaim-da-olann.*—A variation of the name Tuaim-da-ghualann; Tuam, co. Galway.

[15] *Ui-Mail.* —This territory comprised the well-known Glen of Imaile, in the present county of

.h. Caṫail sapiens, 7 Fergus mac Eċaċ ri Dal Riati, omnes defuncti sunt. Bellum riġe re feraiḃ Breġ for Laiġniu, die samnae, in quo cedidit Cucongalt ri Ratho inbir. Diarmait mac Conaing 7 Conaing mac Dunġaile, da ua Conaing, 7 Maelduin mac Fergusa 7 Foġertaċ mac Cumascaiġ, duo nepotes Cernaiġ, uictores erant belli Rigi.

Lotar Laiġin ar saṁain
Do ṫaiġ daġrir nad carsat;
Nissroġab luga diġi,
For bru Riġi ro arsat.

Eicneċ mac Eirtenaiġ equonimus Doimliacc, 7 Cudinaisc .h. Ciarraige, moriuntur.

Kl. Ianair. Anno domini dcc.° lxxx.° i.° Huarcriḋe .h. Mailetoile, 7 Cormac mac Bresail abbas airdd Breccain 7 aliarum ciuitatum, 7 Dubṫolargg rex Pictorum citra Monoṫ, 7 Muireḋaċ mac Huargaile equonimus Iae, 7 Beccan Liffeċairi, 7 Scannal nepos Taiḋgg abbas Achaid bo in feria Comġaill, dominatus xl.° iii anno, 7 Ban[ban] abb Cloento, 7 Aeḋan abbas Roiss Commain, 7 Ultan equonimus Bennċair, 7 Ferdomnaċ Tomae da ġualann, omnes perierunt.

Wicklow. The *Four Masters* (at A.D. 776) have "Umhall," now represented by the baronies of Murresk and Burrishoole, co. Mayo; which seems wrong.

[1] *Righe.*—O'Donovan (*Four Mast.*, A.D. 776, note *g*) says that this is the River Rye, which unites with the Liffey at Leixlip, after forming the boundary for several miles between the counties of Kildare and Meath. But Shearman would identify it with the King's river, in the centre of Wicklow. *Loca Patriciana*, p. 121.

[2] *Rath-inbhir.* — The "Rath (or 'fort') of the Estuary." According to the Irish life of St. Patrick in the *Leabar Breac* (p. 28, col. *a*) Rath-inbbir was in the country of the Ui-Garchon, which comprised Rathnew, Glenealy, and other places in the present barony of Newcastle, co. Wicklow. It was probably the old name of the present town of Wicklow, which is situated at the mouth (or estuary) of Inbher-Dea, the ancient name of the Vartry river.

[3] *Samhain.*—Allhallowtide.

[4] *Desire of drink* [*i.e.*, *thirst*] *seized them not.*—O'Donovan translates this line "They left not the

e man, and Fergus, son of Echa, king of Dalriata—died. The battle of Righe[1] [gained] by the men of gh over the Leinstermen, on the day of Allhallows, in ich were slain Cucongalt, king of Rath-inbhir.[2] rmait son of Conaing, and Conaing son of Dungal wo descendants of Conaing—and Maelduin, son Fergus, and Fogartach, son of Cumascach—two cendants of Cernach—were victors in the battle of he.[1]

The Leinstermen went on Samhain[3]
To the house of a good man they loved not;
Desire of drink seized them not;[4]
They remained on the brink of Righe.[1]

nech, son of Eistenach, steward[5] of Daimliacc, and linaisc Ua Ciarraighe, died.

Kal. Jan. A.D. 781. Uarcridhe Ua Mailetoile; Cormac [781.]
of Bresal, abbot of Ard-Brecain and other monases; Dubhtolarg, King of the Picts on this side of noth;[6] Muiredach, son of Uargal, steward[7] of Ia; can Liffechaire; Scannal Ua Taidg, abbot of Achadh-(on the festival of Comghall, in the 43rd year of his ernment); Ban[ban],[8] abbot of Cloenad;[9] Aedhan, ot of Ros-Comain; Ultan, steward of Bennchair, and domnach of Tuaim-da-ghualann[10]—all died. The

---

of drink" (*Ann. Four Mast.*, 776). But this is clearly wrong. poet meant to convey that the which remained on the brink ie river *Righe* could not have red from thirst.

Steward. — Or House-steward. onimus, for oeconomus, A., nd Clar. 49.

Monoth.—One of the two mounranges in Scotland called the und," or "Mounth." See es' *Adamnan*, p. 387, note *r*.

[7] *Steward.* — equonimus, MSS. The *Four Mast.* (at A.D. 777), have prioir, or "Prior." See Reeves' *Adamnan*, p. 365.

[8] *Ban[ban].*—ban, A., B. "Banab," Clar. 49; which adds the title "Airchinn," for *Airchinnech*, "Herenach," or "Erenach." The name is written *Banbhan* in the *Ann. F. M.*, which is probably the correct form.

[9] *Cloenad.*—Clane, co. Kildare.

[10] *Tuaim-da-ghualann.*—Tuam, co. Galway.

Baċall Artgaile mic Caṫail regis Connacht, peregrinatio eius in sequenti anno ad insolam Iae. Bellum Cuirriċ in confinio Cille daro in ui. Kalendas septimbris, tertia feria, itir Ruadraiċ mac Faelain 7 Bran mac Muiredaiġ, ubi ceciderunt Mugron mac Flainn rex .h. Failġi, 7 Dubdacriċ mac Laiḋgnein, hi frecur. Ruaiḋri uictor fuit. Bran captiuus ductus est.

Kl. Ianair. Anno domini dcc.° lxxx.° ii.° Occisio Domnaill filii Flaiṫniaḋ, riġ .h. Failġi, i cluain Conaire Maelduiḃ i n-geislinniu. Oengus mac Crunnṁail Fol 34ab. abbas Doimliacc, 7 Ailill .h. Tipraiti, 7 Suairleċ ancorita celibris Liss moer, 7 Baṫallaċ sapiens Senċuae, 7 Domnall mac Ceiternaiġ rex nepotum Carrcon in clericatu, 7 Rectlaiten Foḃair sapiens, 7 Aoron sapiens, 7 Faelgus mac Tnuṫgaile sapiens Cluana iraird, 7 Fergus episcopus Doimliacc, 7 Becc mac Cumuscaiġ, omnes mortui sunt. Combustio aird Maċae 7 maiġi hEu saxonum. Ignis horribilis tota nocte sabbati, 7 tonitruum, hi .iiii. nonas augusti, 7 uentus magnus 7 ualidissimus distruxit monasterium cluana Bronaiġ. Bellum Dumai aċaḋ inter Dal nAraiḋe inuicem, in quo cecidit Focarta nepos

---

[1] *'Bachall' of Artgal.*—This is an idiomatic way of saying that Artgal assumed the pilgrim's staff (*bachal*= baculum). See a similar expression used in reference to Becc Bairchc, King of Ulad, at the year 706 *supra.* The obit of Artgal (whose victory in the battle of Magh-Dairben, over the Ui-Maine, is recorded above at the year 777) is given under 790 *infra.*

[2] *Ia.*—Iona, in Scotland.

[3] *Cuirrech.*—The Curragh of Kildare.

[4] *In mutual combact.*—hi frecur, A., B. Literally meaning "in response" (or "in opposition"). The blundering author of the version in Clar. 49 makes a proper name out of hi frecur, and writes "Duvdacrich Mc Laignen O'Frecar."

[5] *Cluain-Conaire-Maelduibh.*—The "*Cluain-Conaire*" ("Conary's meadow") of Maeldubh, a saint whose festival is mentioned in the *Martyr. of Donegal,* under Dec. 18. Now Cloncurry, in the parish of the same name, barony of East Offaly, co. Kildare; and not Cloncurry, in the barony of Ikeathy and Oughterany, in the same county, which was anciently known as *Cluain-Conaire-Tomain.* See the *Felire of Oengus* at Sept. 16, and *Book of Leinster,* p. 43a.

[6] *In geislinne.* — i ngeislinniu,

:hall' of Artgal,[1] son of Cathal, King of Connaught,
his pilgrimage to the Island of Ia[2] in the following
:. The battle of Cuirrech[3] in the vicinity of Kildare,
he 6th of the Kalends of September, the third day
he week, between Ruaidhri son of Faelan, and Bran
of Muiredach, in which Mugron son of Flann, King
Ji-Failghi, and Dubhdacrich son of Ladgnen, were
ı in mutual combat.[4] Ruaidhri was the victor. Bran
led away captive.

:al. Jan. A.D. 782. The slaying of Domnall son of [782.]
thniadh, King of Ui-Failghi, in Cluain-Conaire-
lduibh,[5] in 'geislinne.'[6] Oengus, son of Crunnmael,
ot of Daimliacc; Ailill Ua Tipraiti; Suairlech, a cele-
ed anchorite, of Lis-mor; Bathallach, a wise man, of
chua; Domnall, son of Ceithernach, King of the Ui-
:con, in religion; Rechtlaiten of Fobhar, a wise man;
on, a wise man; Faelgus, son of Tnuthgal, a wise
, of Cluain-Iraird; Fergus, bishop of Daimliacc,[7] and
:, son of Cumascach—all died. Burning of Armagh,
of Magh-eo[8] of the Saxons. Terrible lightning
ng the entire night of Saturday,[9] and thunder, on
4th of the Nones of August; and a great and mighty
l destroyed the monastery of Cluain-Bronaigh. The
le of Duma-achadh[10] among the Dalaraidhe them-

. "in Geislinne," Clar. 49, "Geislinne" seems to be re- l as the name of a place. Dr. or, in his ed. of these Annals ı.), altogether misrepresents he text and its meaning.

ıimliacc.—Duleek, co. Meath.

ıgh-eo.—Mayo, in the county yo. See notes 8 and 9, under ar 731, pp. 184–5 *supra*.

ıturday. — nocte sabbati. lated "night of Sunday," in the t from these Annals published *Table of Cosmical Phenomena,* ensus of Ireland for the year 1851 (Part V., Vol. I., p. 57). The year 782 of this chronicle corresponds to the year 783 of the common reckoning, the Dominical Letter of which being E., the 3rd of August was Sunday, and the fourth of the Nones (or 2nd) of August was therefore a Saturday.

[10] *Duma-achadh.*—The "mound of the field." O'Donovan, observing that this name is written "Dunaiachaidh" [the gen. case], in the Annals of Ulster, identifies the place with a fort in the parish of Dunaghy, co. Antrim. *Four Mast.*, A.D. 778,

Conalta. Bellum hi Fernae moer inter abbatem 7 equonimum, id est, Caṫal 7 Fiannachtaċ. Moinach nepos Moinaiġ rex nepotum filiorum Cuais, mac Flaiṫniaḋ abbas Cluana ferta, mortui sunt. Scamaċ. Forus ċano Patricii hi Cruaċniḃ, la Dubdaleiṫi 7 la Tipraiti filium Taiḋgg.

.b. Kt. Ianair. Anno domini dcc.° lxxx.° iii.° Reċtnia abbas cluana macc U Nois obiit. Maelduin mac Oengusa, ri cenel Loiġaire, 7 Innrechtaċ mac Dunchada, 7 Ciaran abb Raṫo maiġe oenaiġ 7 tiġe Moḟinnu, 7 Aeḋgal ri hUmaill, 7 Cernaċ mac Suibne equonimus airdd Maċae, 7 Coisenmeċ nepos Predeni rex nepotum Eċdaċ Ulaiṫ, 7 Maelcaeċ mac Cursaiṫ minn, 7 Conall mac Crunnmail abbas Lusca, 7 Cugaṁnae mac Noennenaiġ rex generis ċoirpri, omnes defuncti sunt. Combustio Aṫo truim. Bellum re n-Domnall mac Aeḋo muindeirg for cenel mBoġaine. Baċall Duncaḋo mic Duibdatuaḋ, regis nepotum Maine. Flann episcopus sapiens, abbas innse cain Deġo, ueneno mortificatur est. Bellum cairn Conaill in Aidniu, ubi Tipraiti uictor, 7 nepotes Fiaċraċ uicti. Rigdal itir Donnchad mac nDomnaill

note *t*. But "Duma-achadh" is the form in A. and B. Clar. 49 has "Duma-acha."

[1] *Ferna-mor*.—Ferns, co. Wexford. This battle is not noticed in the *Ann. Four Mast.*, the compilers of which generally omitted entries of this kind, apparently from a disinclination to notice events calculated to bring discredit on the church of which they were such devout members.

[2] *Son of Flaithniadh*.—The corresponding entry in the *Ann. Four Masters*, at A.D. 776, has Flaithniadh, son of Congal, and not *mac Flaithniadh*, or "son of Flaithniadh."

[3] *Scamach*.—Under the year 785, in the MS. Clar. 49, *scamach* is explained by "*scabes*." But *scamach* seems connected with *scaman*, which in the "Lorica of Gildas" (Stokes's *Old Irish Glossaries*, p. 141,) appears to signify "lungs," *cum pulmone* being glossed *cusin scaman* ("with the lungs."). See the same work, p. 150, No. 221.

[4] *Dubhdaleithi* — *Tipraiti*. — The former was Archbishop of Armagh at the time, and the latter King of Connaught. This entry seems to have been quite misunderstood by O'Conor and by the so-called 'translator' of

ːlves, in which fell Focarta Ua Conalta. A battle in erna-mor,[1] between the abbot and the steward, viz:— athal and Fiannachtach. Moinach Ua Moinaigh, King f Ui-Mac-Uais, [and] the son of Flaithniadh,[2] abbot of luain-ferta, died. The 'Scamach.'[3] The promulgation f Patrick's 'Law' in Cruachna, by Dubhdaleithi,[4] and y Tipraiti[4] son of Tadhg.

Kal. Jan. A.D. 783. Rechtnia, abbot of Clonmacoise, died. Maelduin, son of Oengus, King of Cinel-oeghaire; Innrechtach, son of Dunchad; Ciaran, abbot f Rath-maighe-oenaigh and Tech-Mofinnu; Aedhgal, ing of Umhall; Cernach, son of Suibhne, steward of rmagh; Coisenmech Ua Predeni, King of Ui-Echach of lladh; Maelcaich, son of Cuscrad Menn; Conall, son of runnmael, abbot of Lusca, and Cugamhna, son of Noenenach, King of Cinel-Coirpri—all died. Burning of th-truim. A battle [gained] by Domnall,[5] son of Aedh Iuinderg, over the Cinel-Boghaine. The 'bachall' of)unchad,[6] son of Dubhdatuath, King of Ui-Maine. 'lann, a wise bishop, abbot of Inis-cain-Dego, was put o death by poison.[7] The battle of Carn-Conaill[8] in idhne,[9] where Tipraiti[10] was victorious, and the Ui-'iachrach were defeated. A royal meeting between [783.] BIS.

ıese Annals whose version is con-ined in Clar. 49.

[5] *Domnall.* — Originally written)onnchaꝺ in A., but properly cor-ected to Ꝺomnall.

[6] *The 'bachall' of Dunchad.*— his is an idiomatic way of saying ıat Dunchad assumed the 'baculum' pilgrim's staff; in other words went ı a pilgrimage. See above, under ıe year 706, where a similar entry garding Becc Bairche, King of lidia, is recorded; and under the ear 781, in connection with the name of Artgal, King of Connaught.

[7] *By poison.*—ueníno, A.

[8] *Carn-Conaill.*—See under the year 648 *supra*, and O'Donovan's ed. of the *Ann. Four Mast.*, A.D. 645, note *x*.

[9] *Aidhne.*—This was the ancient name of a district co-extensive with the diocese of Kilmacduagh, in the county of Galway.

[10] *Tipraiti.*—King of Connaught at the time. His obit is entered under the year 785 *infra*.

7 Fiaċnae mac nAeḋo roen, occ Innsi narriġ i n-airṫeru Breġ.

Ossi briġ
In dál occ Innsi na riġ;
Donnchaḋ ni dichet for muir,
Fiachna ni tuidecht hi tir.

Aduentus reliquiarum filii Eirc ad ciuitatem Tailten.

Kl. Ianair. Anno domini dcc.° lxxx.° iiii.° Dunchad nepos Daimeni rex nepotum Mani, Maeloċtaraiġ
Fol. 34 ba mac Conaill abbas cille Cuilinn 7 cille Manaċ scriba, 7 Maelduin mac Fergusa rex Loċa gabor, 7 Foelgus nepos Roiċliċ sapiens, 7 Muġṫigernd mac Cellaiġ sapiens abbas Innse celtrae, 7 Iosep .h. Foileni sapiens abbas Biror, 7 Ruaidri mac Faelain rex cunctorum Laginencium, 7 Concobar mac Colgen, omnes perierunt. Commotatio reliquiarum Ultani. Bellum Muaide, ubi Tipraiti uictor fuit. Eċaiḋ mac Focartaiġ, abbas Foċlado 7 insi Croṫrann, mortuus est. Ellbriġ abatissa cluana Bronaiġ mortua est.

Kl. Ianair. Anno domini dcc.° lxxx.° u.° Maelduin mac Aeḋa bennain rex Irloċre, Scannlan mac Flainn

---

[1] *Donnchad.* — Monarch of Ireland.

[2] *Fiachna.*—King of Ulidia. His obit is recorded under the year 788 *infra.*

[3] *Inis-na-righ.* — The "Island of the Kings." Some island off the N.E. coast of the county of Dublin; probably one of the group near Skerries.

[4] *Of what.*—Ossi, A. The *Four Mast.* write Cissi, which is undoubtedly more correct. This stanza, which is not in B., is added in the lower margin of fol. 34*a* in A., with a sign of reference to the proper place in the text.

[5] *Would not come.*—ni tuidecht is seemingly a mistake for ni tuidchet, the proper form.

[6] *Of the son.*—fli, for filii, A. and B. Dean Reeves, however, prints "filiorum Eirc" ("of the *sons* of Erc"). *Adamnan*, p. 387, note t.

[7] *Tailtiu* (gen. *Tailten*).—Teltown, in the parish of the same name, barony of Upper Kells, co. Meath. See Reeves' *Adamnan*, p. 194, note d.

[8] *Cill-manach.*—The *Four Mast.*

Donnchad,[1] son of Domnall, and Fiachna[2] son of Aedh Roen, at Inis-na-righ,[3] in the eastern parts of Bregh.

> Of what[4] effect
> Was the meeting at Inis-na-righ?
> Donnchad would not go upon the sea?
> Fiachna would not come[5] ashore.

Arrival of the relics of the son[6] of Erc at the city of Tailltiu.[7]

Kal. Jan. A.D. 784. Dunchad Ua Daimeni, King of Ui-Maine; Maelochtraigh son of Conall, abbot of Cill-Cuilinn and Cill-manach,[8] a scribe; Maelduin son of Fergus, King of Loch-gabhor; Faelgus Ua Roichlich, a wise man; Mughthigernd son of Cellach, a wise man, abbot of Inis-Celtra; Joseph Ua Foileni, a wise man, abbot of Biror; Ruaidri[9] son of Faelan, King of all the Leinstermen, and Conchobar son of Colgu—all died. 'Translation' of the relics of Ultan.[10] The battle of Muaidh,[11] where Tipraiti was victor. Echaidh son of Focartach, abbot of Fochladh and Inis-Clothrann,[12] died. Ellbrigh, abbess of Cluain-Bronaigh, died. [784.]

Kal. Jan. A.D. 785. Maelduin, son of Aedh Bennan, king of Ir-Luachair;[13] Scannlan, son of Flann, king of [785.]

(at A.D. 780=785) write "Cill-na-manach," the "Church of the monks;" now Kilnamanagh, in the barony of Crannagh, co. Kilkenny. For a weird story, regarding the transformation of human beings into wolves, through the curse of St. Natalis, patron of Kilnamanagh, see Todd's *Irish Nennius*, p. 204, note p, and Girald. Cambr. *Topogr. Hibern.*, Dist. II., cap. 19.

[9] *Ruadri.* — In the list of the Kings of Leinster contained in the *Book of Leinster*, p. 39, col. 2, Ruadri is set down as next in succession to Cellach son of Dunchad, whose obit is given above at the year 775.

[10] *Ultan.* — St. Ultan, patron of Ardbraccan, co. Meath. See above at the years 656 and 662.

[11] *Muaidh.*—The River Moy, in Connaught.

[12] *Inis-Clothrann.* — Inishcloghbran, an island in Lough Ree, in the Shannon. The name is wrongly written ınıꞅ Cꞃoꞇhꞃann in A., B., and Clar. 49.

[13] *Ir-Luachair.*—See note [1], p. 188 *supra.*

ri .h. Fidgenti, 7 Tipraiti mac Ferchair abbas cluana ferta Brenainn, 7 Cellach mac Moinaigh, 7 Tipraiti mac Taidgg ri Connacht, Sneidriaghail abbas cluana mac Nois, Cellach mac Cormaic ri ardae Ciannachta, moriuntur. Uentus maximus in Ianuario. Inundatio in Dairinis. Uisio terribilis hi cluain mac Nois, 7 poenitentia magna per totam Hiberniam. Bellum inter Osraige inuicem, in quo cecidit Faelan mac Forbasaigh. Febordaith abbas Tuilian iugulatus est, 7 ultionem eius (.i. Tuileain, Donnchadh uictor fuit). Bellum Liacfind inter Donnchad 7 genus Aedha slane, in quo ceciderunt Fiachrai mac Cathail, 7 Fogartach mac Cumascaigh rex Locha gabor, 7 duo nepotes Conaing, id est, Conaing 7 Diarmait. Bellum Cenond itir .h. Echach [7] Conaille, in quo ceciderunt Cathrue rex Mughdornae, 7 Rimidh mac Cernaigh. Mors Forbasaigh mic Sechnusaigh, regis gentis Bógaine. Pestis que dicitur scamach.

Kl. Ianair. Anno domini dcc.° lxxx.° iii.° Colggu mac Crunnmhail abbas Luscan, Clemens mac Corbbeni, Lergus nepos Fidcain sapiens cille Maighnenn, Robartach mac Móinaigh equonimus Slane 7 abbas cille Foibrigh, Muiredach mac Cathail abbas Cille daro,

---

[1] *Died.*—moritur, A., B., (though O'Conor prints moritui sunt). "moriuntur," Clar. 49.

[2] *Dairinis.*—"Oak-island." This seems to be the Dairinis, otherwise called Dairinis-Maelanfaidh, from St. Maelanfaidh, its patron; now known as Molana, an island in the southern River Blackwater, a couple of miles to the north of Youghal.

[3] *Tuilan.*—Dulane, in a parish of the same name, barony of Upper Kells, and county of Meath. The original of the parenthetic clause is added in the margin in A.

[4] *Killed.*—The *Four Mast.* (A.D. 781=786) represent Faebordaith as having died naturally. See next note.

[5] *And the avenging of him.*—7 ultionem eius. This entry is very loosely given in the MSS.

[6] *Donnchad.*—Called "Donnchad, son of Murchad," by the *Four Mast.* (A.D. 781=786). But according to the *Book of Leinster* (p. 42 col. 1), the Donnchad here referred to was Donnchad (son of Domhnall, son of Murchadh), King of Ireland at the time,

i-Fidhgenti; Tipraiti, son of Ferchar, abbot of Cluain-ta-Brenainn; Cellach, son of Moenach; Tipraiti, son Tadhg, King of Connaught; Sneidriaghail, abbot of onmacnoise, [and] Cellach, son of Cormac, King of Ard-anachta, died.[1] A very great storm in January. An undation in Diarinis.[2] A terrible vision in Clonmac-ise, and great repentance throughout all Ireland. A ttle between the Osraighe themselves, in which Faelan, n of Forbasach, was slain. Faebordaith, abbot of iilan,[3] was killed;[4] and the avenging of him[5] (*i.e.*, at iilan;[3] Donnchad[6] was victor). The battle of Liac-find, tween Donnchad[6] and the race of Aedh-Slanè, in hich fell Fiachra son of Cathal, and Fogartach, son of imuscach, king of Loch-Gabhor,[7] and two descendants Conaing, viz.:—Conaing and Diarmait. The battle of enond,[8] between the Ui-Echach [and] the Conaille, in hich Cathrae, King of Mughdorna, and Rimidh son Cernach, were slain. Death of Forbasach, son of echnasach, King of Cinel-Boghaine. The plague which called 'scamach.'[9]

Kal. Jan. A.D. 786. Colgu, son of Crunnmael, abbot [786.]
Lusca; Clemens, son of Corbben; Lerghus Ua dhcain, a wise man of Cill-Maighnenn;[10] Robhartach n of Moenach, steward[11] of Slane, and abbot of Cill-ibrigh;[12] Muiredach, son of Cathal, abbot of Cill-dara;

Loch-Gabhor.—An ancient lake, g dried up; now represented by the nlands of Lagore Big and Lagore tle, in the parish and barony of toath, co. Meath.

Cenond.—The site of the battle is t mentioned by the *Four Mast.* D. 784).

'*Scamach.*'—Written *skawaghe* in geoghegan's Translation of the n. Clonmacnoise (at A.D. 783). See e [3], p. 258 *supra.*

[0] *Cill-Maighnenn*; *i.e.*, the Church of St. Maighnenn; now Kilmainham near the City of Dublin. St. Maighnenn's day in the Calendar is December 18.

[11] *Steward.* -- equonimur (for oeconomur), MSS.

[12] *Cill-Foibrigh.*—Written "Kill-favar," in Clar. 49; but incorrectly. O'Donovan thought to identify it with the place now known as Kilbrew, in the barony of Ratoath, co. Meath. *Four Mast.* A.D. 768, note k.

Lomṫuili episcopus Cille daro, Sneidbran episcopus
Fol. 34 ba. Cille daro, Aldċu ancorita Raṫo oinbo, Conall mac Fiḋgaile rex nepotum Mani, mortui sunt. Bellum inter genus Conaill 7 Eogain, in quo uictor fuit Maelduin mac Aeḋa aldain, 7 Domnall mac Aeḋa muindeirg in fugam uersus est. Bellum Goli in quo nepotes Briuin uicti sunt. Caṫmuġ mac Duinncoṫaiġ, 7 Dubdibeirgg mac Caṫail, inuicem ceciderunt. Duḃdaḃairenn abbas Cluana iraird aduisitauit paruchiam crichae Muman. Ar nepotum Briuin hUmil apud nepotes Fiacraċ Muirsce, ubi omnes optimi circa regem Flaṫgalum filium Flannabrat ceciderunt. Rechtabra mac Duiḃcombair abbas Eċdroma obiit.

b. Kl. Ianair. Anno domini dcc.° lxxx.° iii.° Mors Maeleduin mic Aeḋa aldain regis ind Foċlai. Mors Cernaiġ mic Caṫail. Mors Ectgaile filii Baiṫ, abbatis Muccirt. Luna rubra similitudine sanguinis in .xii. Kalendas Martii. Macoac abbas Saigre mortuus est. Colum mac Faelgusa episcopus Loṫri mortuus est. Mors Guaire mic Dungalaiġ regis nepotum Briuin Cualand. Dubdatuaṫ episcopus

---

1 *Aldchu.*—Alḋcu, A. "Allchu," Clar. 49. The name is Aladhċu (Aladhchu) in the *Four Mast.* (782).

2 *Rath-oenbo.* — The "Fort (or Rath) of one cow." Not identified.

3 *Died.*—mor̄ 2, for mortuus est, A. and B. "mortui sunt," Clar. 49.

4 *Ui-Briuin.*—There were several septs the tribe-name of which was Ui-Briuin ("descendants of Brian"). But the site of the battle (Goli) not having been identified, it is impossible to specify the sept here referred to.

5 '*Parochia.*' — 'Parochia' (now understood as simply meaning 'parish'), was used in old Irish records to signify 'diocese;' the corresponding (loan) form in Irish being fairċe. But as regards its use in the above context, Dean Reeves observes "in monastic language a *parochia* was the jurisdiction of a Superior over the detached monasteries of the order." *Adamnan*, p. 336, note g.

6 *Ui-Briuin of Umal.*—The descendants of Brian, son of Eochaidh Muidhmedhoin (King of Ireland in the 4th cent.), who were seated in the 'Owles,' in the co. Mayo. The prevailing surname in later times was (and is) O'Malley.

7 *Where all.*—ube omnes, A. ubi homines, B. Clar. 49, trans-

mthuili, bishop of Cill-dara; Sneidbran, bishop of ll-dara; Aldchu,[1] anchorite of Rath-oenbo,[2] and Conall ı of Fidhgal, King of Ui-Maine, died.[3] A battle tween the Cinel-Conaill and [Cinel]-Eoghain, in which ıelduin, son of Aedh Aldan, was victor, and Domnall, ı of Aedh Muinderg, was put to flight. The battle Goli, in which the Ui-Briuin[4] were defeated. ıthmugh son of Donncothaigh, and Dubhdiberg son of thal, fell by each other. Dubhdabhairenn, abbot Cluain-Iraird, visited the 'parochia'[5] of the territory Munster. A slaughter of the Ui-Briuin of Umal[6] by e Ui-Fiachrach-Muirsce, where all[7] the noblest were ıin around the king, Flathgal son of Flannabhra. ›chtabra, son of Dubhchomair, abbot of Echdruim,[8] ed.

Kal. Jan. A.D. 787. Death of Maelduin, son ef Aedh ldan, King of the Fochla.[9] Death of Cernach, son of ıthal. Death of Echtgal, son of Baeth, abbot of uccert. The moon was red, like blood, on the 12th of e Kalends of March. Macoac, abbot of Saigir,[10] died. ›lum, son of Faelgus, abbot of Lothra,[11] died. Death of ıaire, son of Dungalach, King of the Ui-Briuin-ıaland.[12] Dubhdatuath, a bishop, abbot of Rath- [787.] BIS.

---

es "where all the chiefest;" thus ·eeing with A.

Echdruim.—Aughrim, in the ınty of Galway.

Fochla.—This was a term for ; northern part of Ireland, or pro- ıce of Ulster.

[10] *Saigir*; or Saigir-Chiarain.— rkieran, in the barony of Ballybrit, ng's County.

[11] *Lothra.*—Now Lorrha, in the par- of the same name, barony of wer Ormond, co. Tipperary.

[12] *Ui-Briuin-Cualand.*—In his ed. part of these Annals, O'Conor ›te (2) ad. an.) states that "the O'Byrne's of the co. of Wicklow were meant. But he was wrong. Ui-Briuin-Cualand was the tribe-name of a powerful sept descended from Brian Lethderg (descended in the fourth generation from Cathair Mor, King of Leinster), whose territory comprised the greater part of the present barony of Rathdown, co. Dublin, and a portion of the northern part of the co. Wicklow. The churches of Killiney, co. Dublin, and Delgany in the co. Wicklow, were included in this territory. See Shearman's *Loca Patriciana*, p. 156.

abbas raṫo Aiḋo, pausat. Lex Ciarain for Connachta. Combustio Daire Ċalgaiḋ.

Kl. Ianair. Anno domini dcc.° lxxx.° iiii.° Mors Murgaile abbatis cluana macc U Nois. Fiaċnae mac Aeḋo roen, rex Ulad, mortuus est. Feḋaċ mac Cormaic, abbas Luġmaiḋ 7 Slane 7 Doimliacc, 7 Sloiġeḋaċ rex Conailli, mortui sunt. Gormgal mac Elaḋaiġ, rex Cnoḋbai, in clericatu obiit. Ferfuġaill episcopus cluano Dolcain [obiit]. Combustio Cluana iraird in nocte pasca. Nix magna .iii. Kalendas Maii. Contentio i n-Ard Maċae, in qua iugulatus est uir in hostio oratorii lapidei. Bellum inter Ultu inuicem, in quo cecidit Tomaltaċ mac Caṫail. Eċuiḋ uictor fuit. Occisio cluano ferte Moṅgain la Oengus mac Mugroin, in qua cecidit Aeḋ mac Tomaltaiġ, 7 oratorium combustum. Bellum inter Pictos
Fol. 35aa. ubi Conall mac Taiḋg uictus est 7 euasit, 7 Constantin uictor fuit. Bellum Cloitigi inter genus Eugain 7 Conaill, in quo genus Conaill prostratum

---

[1] *Rath-Aedha.*—Now Rahugh (or Rath-Hugh), barony of Moycashel, co. Westmeath.

[2] *The 'Law' of Ciaran.*—See above under the year 743; and Reeves' *Colton's Visitation*, Introd., p. iv. Mageoghegan, in his translation of the *Annals of Clonmacnoise* (at A.D. 785), says "The rules of St. Keyran were preached in Connaught."

[3] *Daire-Calgaidh.*—Derry, or Londonderry.

[4] *Cnodhba.*—This name is now represented by Knowth, near Slane, co. Meath.

[5] *Cluain-Dolcain.*—Clondalkin, near Dublin.

[6] *Easter night.*—In nocte pasca A. "At Easter eve," Clar. 49.

[7] *Oratory.*—In Clar. 49 this entry is translated "A contention in Ardmacha, wherein a man was killed *with a stone in the oratorie doore.*"

[8] *Son of Cathal.*—In the *Ann. Four Mast.* (at 787=792), Tomaltach is stated to have been the "son of Innreachtach," which is supported by the entry in the List of the Kings of Ulad in the *Book of Leinster*, (p. 41, col. 3), where the length of Tomaltach's reign is given as 10 years. This notice seems out of place, if the entry in the *Book of Leinster* is correct, which represents Tomaltach as reigning 10 years after Fiachna son of Aedh Roen, whose obit is the second entry above given under this year.

a,[1] rests. The 'Law' of Ciaran[2] over the Con-
ıtmen. Burning of Daire-Calgaidh.[3]

l. Jan. A.D. 788. Death of Murgal, abbot of Clon- [788.]
oise. Fiachna, son of Aedh Roen, King of Ulad,
Fedhach, son of Cormac, abbot of Lughmadh,
, and Daimliacc, and Sloighedhach, King of Conailli,
Gormgal, son of Eladhach, King of Cnodhba,[4]
in religion. Ferfughaill, bishop of Cluain-Dolcain,[5]
]. Burning of Cluain-Iraird, on Easter night.[6] Great
on the 3rd of the Kalends of May. A quarrel in
Macha, in which a man was killed in the doorway
e stone oratory.[7] A battle among the Ulidians
selves, in which Tomaltach son of Cathal[8] was
Echaidh[9] was victor. The destruction[10] of Cluain-
-Mongain,[11] by Oengus,[12] son of Mugron, in which
, son of Tomaltach, was slain; and the oratory was
ed. A battle among the Picts, where Conall son of
g was vanquished, and escaped,[13] and Constantine
victor. The battle of Cloitech[14] between the
l-Eoghain and [Cinel]-Conaill, in which the Cinel-

---

haidh.—The son of the Fiachna
l to in the last note. Accor-
› the *Book of Leinster* list, he
led Tomaltach, and reigned 10
His obit is given at the year
ra.

estruction. — Occıꞅꞅıo, A.
ıted "burning," Clar. 49.

ain-ferta-Mongain.—Probably
or for Cluain-ferta-Mughaine,
Kilclonfert, in the barony of
Philipstown, King's County,
the territory of Ui-Failghe.

ngus.— The name of Oengus
Mugron appears in the list of
ings of Ui-Failghe at this
in the *Book of Leinster*, p.
3.

[13] *Escaped.* — euaꞅꞅıꞇ, A. This battle is again referred to under the next year.

[14] *Cloitech.*— The *Four Mast.* (at A.D, 784=789) have ıomaıꞃecc claıꝺıꞡe ("battle of Claidech," which place O'Donovan, note d, *ad an.*, identifies with "Clady, a small village on the Tyrone side of the River Finn, about four miles to the south of Lifford." A marginal note in MS. B. has K. Cleꞇıꞡ la hAeꝺ oıꞃnıꞡe (the "battle of Cletech by Aedh Oirdnidhe"). But Cletech was the name of a place on the Boyne, in Meath, whereas the battle in question must have been fought in the north of Ireland.

est, 7 Domnall euasit. Combustio innse cáin Dego. Feirgil abbas Achaiḋ boo mortuus est. Bellum inter Lagenenses dersgabair, in quo cecidit Oengus mac Murchada. Bellum inter Connachta, id est Droma goise, quo Fogartaċ mac Caṫail uictus euasit. Strages Luigne la .h. Ailello in Achaḋ ablae. Sarugad baċlu Isu 7 minn Patraic, la Donnchad mac n-Domnaill, oc raiṫ airṫir ar oenaċ.

Kl. Ianair. Anno domini dcc.° lxxx.° ix.° Mors Noe abbatis Cinngaraḋ. Cormac mac Fergaile, Dungal mac Loegaire abbas Duin leṫglaisi, Maelcombair abbas Glinne da loċa, Maeltuile mac Oengusa, Siadail abbas Duiblinne, Cinaeṫ mac Anmchada ri .h. Liaṫan, Tomaltaċ mac Innrechtaiġ ri dal n-Araide, mortui sunt omnes. Bellum Aṫo rois re n-Oaib Ailello for Luiġniu, in quo cecidit Duḃdaṫuaṫ mac Flaiṫgusa, dux na tri sloinnte. Combustio Eċtroma mac n-Aeḋo. Comotatio reliquiarum Coimgin 7 Mochuae mic U Lugedon. Caedes

[1] *Domnall.*—The Domnall, son of Aedh Muinderg, King of the North of Ireland, referred to above at the year 786.

[2] *Inis-cáin-Dega.* — Inishkeen, in the county of Louth.

[3] *Fergil.*—The *Four Mast.* (A.D. 784) style him an geometer ("the geometer"). Regarding this remarkable man, see Ware's *Writers of Ireland* (Harris's ed.), p. 49, and O'Conor's *Rerum Hibern. Script.*, tom. iv., p. 173. The so-called 'translator' of these Annals in Clar. 49 writes the name "Ferall," thus indicating his ignorance of the identity of "Fergil the geometer" with the "Virgilius Solivagus" of history.

[4] *Cathal.* — Son of Muiredach of Magh-Ai (King of Connaught), whose obit is entered above at the year 701.

[5] *Luighni.* — Otherwise called "Luighni-Connacht;" a sept that gave name to the district now represented by the barony of Leyny, co. Sligo; known in later times as the country of O'Hara.

[6] *Ui-Ailella.* — A tribe descended from Cian, son of Oilill Olum, King of Munster in the second century. The territory occupied by this tribe is now represented by the barony of Tirerril, co. Sligo.

[7] *Achadh-abla.*—The "Field of the apple-tree." According to the Life of St. Finnian of Clonard, contained in the *Book of Lismore* (fol. 26, page 1,

ill was overthrown, and Domnall[1] escaped. Burn-
of Inis-cáin-Dega.[2] Fergil,[3] abbot of Achadh-bo,
A battle between the South Leinstermen, in which
;us, son of Murchad, was slain. A battle between
Connaughtmen, *i.e.*, [the battle] of Druim-Goise, from
h Fogartach son of Cathal[4] escaped, vanquished.
aughter of the Luighni,[5] by the Ui-Ailella,[6] in
dh-abla.[7] Dishonouring of the Bachall-Isu[8] and the
s of Patrick, by Donnchad,[9] son of Domnall, at Rath-
ir,[10] at a fair.

l. Jan. A.D. 789. Death of Noe, abbot of Cenn- [789.]
lh.[11] Cormac, son of Fergal; Dungal, son of Loegaire,
t of Dun-lethglaise; Maelcombair, abbot of Glenn-
cha; Maeltuile, son of Oengus; Siadail, abbot of
hlinn;[12] Cinaeth, son of Anmchad, King of Ui-
nain, and Tomaltach, son of Innrechtach, King of
raide—all died. The battle of Ath-rois [gained]
he Ui-Ailella[7] over the Luighni,[5] in which fell
ndatuath, son of Flaithgus, chief of the Three
es.[13] Burning of Echdruim-mac-nAedha.[14] 'Translation
e relics of Coemgin and of MochuaMac-U-Lugedon.[15]

.), there was a place called
dh-aballl" in Corann [now
rony of Corran], co. Sligo.

chall-Isu.—"Baculus Iesu,"
me of St. Patrick's crozier.
ne account of this remarkable
ee *Annals of Loch Ce*, at A.D.
nd Todd's *Obits, &c., of Christ*
, Introd., p. viii., *sq.*

nnchad.—King of Ireland at
e.

h-airthir.—The "Eastern Rath
rt)." Now Oristown [in the
of Morgallion, co. Meath],
ng to O'Donovan, *Four Mas-*
D. 784, note f.

ngaradh.—Kingarth, in Bute.

ubhlinn.—Dublin. The name
s "black-pool."

[13] *Three Tribes.*—na tri sloinnte; lit. the "three denominations." Probably a variation of the term "*Teora Connacht*" ("Tripartite Connaught," or "Three Connaughts"), applied to the three aboriginal septs of Connaught, called the "Gamanraide of Irras [Erris]," the "Fir-craibhi," and the "Tuatha-Taidhen." See O'Flaherty's *Ogygia*, p. 175. Clar. 49 renders na tri sloinnte by "The Three Surnames."

[14] *Echdruim-mac-nAedha.*—Aughrim, in the par. of the same name, bar. and co. of Roscommon.

[15] *Mac-U-Lugedon.*—"Son of the descendant of Lugedo." The names of other members of this family are mentioned at the years 780 and 800.

magna Ulad la dal n-Araide. Bellum Conaill 7 Custantin hic scriptum est in aliis libris.

Kl. Ian. Anno domini dcc.° xc.° Cernach mac Muiredaiġ, Freccmarc episcop Luscan, Cudinaisc mac Conasaiċ abbas ard Maċae, Donnġal mac Boċallo rex na n-Airter, Artgal mac Caṫail rex Connaċt in hI, Soerbergg abbas cluana macc U Nois, Caincomracc episcop Finnġlaissi, Sirne abbas Bennċair, Muireḋaċ mac Oengusa ab Luscan, omnes defuncti sunt. Baċaill mac Tuaṫail mortuus est. Amalgaiḋ rex .H. Maini mortuus est. Bellum aird ablae, ubi cecidit Diarmait mac Beicce rex Teṫbae, 7 Fergus mac Ailġaile uictor fuit. Caṫċoscraḋ
Fol. 35 ab. re n-Donnchad a Tailti du cairn mic Cairṫin, for Aeḋ ningor, in quo ceciderunt Caṫal mac Eċdaċ rex nepotum Creṁṫain, Maelḟoṫartaiċ mac Artraċ, 7 Domnall mac Colggen. Dinertac mac Mogadaiġ, ancorita, pausauit.

.b. Kl. Ianair. Anno domini dcc.° xc.° i.° Maelruain Tamlaċtai, Aiḋain Raṫain, Aeḋan .H. Concumbu, episcopi 7 milites Christi, in pace dormierunt; 7 Soerṁuġ Enaiġ duib moritur. Bellum sruiṫe Cluana argai ubi cecidit Cinaeḋ mac Artgaile, 7 Muirġis mac Tomaltaiġ uictor fuit, 7 initium regni eius.

---

[1] *Slaughter.*—Caedis, A. Cedes, B.

[2] *Conall and Constantine.*—Conall son of Tadhg, and Constantine son of Fergus, Kings of the Picts of Fortrenn. The "Jugulatio" of Conall is recorded under the year 807, and the death of Constantine (or "Custantin," as the name is generally written in Irish texts) under 820 *infra.*

[3] *In other books.*—in alis libris, A. secundum alios libros, B.

[4] *Conasach.*—Called "Concas, descendant of Cathbath son of Echaid," in the list of the "Comarbs" (or successors) of Patrick, in the *Book of Leinster*, p. 42, col. 3.

[5] *Artgal.*—The assumption of the pilgrim's staff by Artgal is recorded above at the year 781, as well as his pilgrimage to the island of Ia, or Hi-Coluim-Cille.

[6] *Ard-abla.*—The "height (or hill) of the apple tree." O'Donovan identifies this place with "Lis-ard-abhla," now Lissardowlin, in the parish of Templemichael, co. Longford. *Four Mast.*, A.D. 786, note q.

[7] *By Donnchad.*—re n-Donnchad. The so-called 'translator' of these

great slaughter[1] of the Ulidians by the Dalaraide. e battle of Conall[2] and Constantine[2] is written in this ce in other[3] books.

Kal. Jan. A.D. 790. Cernach, son of Muiredach; [790.] eccmarc, bishop of Lusca; Cudinaisc, son of Conasach,[4] bot of Ard-Macha; Donnghal, son of Bochall, King of Airthera; Artgal,[5] son of Cathal, King of Conight, in Ia; Saerberg, abbot of Clonmacnoise; Caenaracc, bishop of Finnglais; Sirne, abbot of Bennir, and Muiredhach son of Oengus, abbot of Lusca—died. Bachaill, son of Tuathal, died. Amalgaidh, ng of Ui-Maine, died. The battle of Ard-abla,[6] where rmait son of Becc, King of Tethba, was slain, and rgus son of Ailgal was victor. A destructive battle ined] by Donnchad,[7] from Tailtiu to Carn-mic-rthin,[8] over Aedh Ningor, in which were slain Cathal of Echaid, King of Ui-Cremthain, and Maelfothart-h son of Artri, and Domnall son of Colgu. Dinertach of Mogadach, an anchorite, rested.

Kal. Jan. A.D. 791. Maelruain of Tamlacht,[9] Aedhan [791.] BIS. Rathin, Aedhan Ua Concumba, bishops, and solders Christ, slept in peace; and Saermhugh of Enachbh[10] died. The battle of Sruth-Cluana-argai,[11] where aedh, son of Artgal,[12] was slain, and Muirghis son of naltach was victor; and the beginning of his [Muir-

---

als in Clar. 49, mistaking the osition re-n for a proper name, this battle "the battle of *Ren*."

Carn-mic-Cairthin; *i.e.*, the irn (or monumental heap) of hin's son." This entry was ly misunderstood by O'Conor, took *Carn* for a man's name!

Tamlacht.—Tallaght, co. Dublin.

Enagh-dubh; *i.e.*, the "Black h." Now Annaduff, in the h of the same name, co. Leitrim.

[11] *Sruth-Cluana-argai*.—The "river of Cluain-argai" (or "Cluain-arggaid," the nomin. form of the name as given by the *Four Masters*, A.D. 787). The name Cluain-arggaid is now probably represented by that of Cloonargid, in the parish of Tibohine, county of Roscommon.

[12] *Artgal*.—The Artgal whose obit is given at the year 790. See note [5], p. 270.

Bellum Aird maiccrime, ubi nepotes Ailello prostrati sunt, 7 Concobar 7 Airechtaċ nepotes Caṫail ceciderunt, 7 Caṫmuġ mac Flaiṫbertaiġ, rex Coirpri, 7 Cormac mac Duiḃdacriċ, ri Breifni, ceciderunt. Bresal mac Flaiṫri rex dal Araide, Maelbresail mac Aeḋo filii Criċain ri .h. Fiacrach, Donncorci rex dal Riatai, Caṫmuġ rex Calraiġi, Teroc princeps Corcaġi more, obierunt.

Kl. Ianair. Anno domini dcc.° xc.° ii.° Dubdaleiṫi mac Sinaiċ abbas aird Maċae, Cruinnmail Droma in asclann abbas Cluana iraird, Coirpri mac Laiḋgnein ri Laigen desgabair, Doimteċ princeps Treoit moer, Cinaeḋ mac Cumuscaiġ abbas Derṁaigi, Flaiṫgel mac Taiċliċ abbas Droma raṫae, perierunt. Lex Comain la Aildobur 7 Muirġius, for teora Connaċt. Lex Ailḃi for Mumain, 7 ordinatio Artroiġ mic Caṫail in regnum Mumen. Sarugad Fainnelaiġ la Gormġal mac n-Dindanaiġ, 7 eccur 7 innred aird Maċae, 7 guin duine ann la hU Creṁtain. Receptio Foindelaiġ iterum i n-Ard Maċae. Comotatio reliquiarum Toli.

---

[1] *Reign.*—*i.e.* as King of Connaught. The death of Muirghis is recorded at the year 814 *infra.*

[2] *Cathal.*—Probably Cathal, father of the Artgal mentioned at the years 781 and 790.

[3] *Ui-Fiachrach.*—O'Donovan states (*Ann. Four Mast.*, A.D. 787, note u) that the sept of Ui-Fiachrach of Ardsratha (Ardstraw, co. Tyrone), is here meant. See Reeves' *Colton's Visitation*, p. 9, note q.

[4] *Corcach-mor.*—Cork, in Munster.

[5] *Dubhdaleithi.*—In the list of the successors of Patrick in the *Book of Leinster*, p. 42, col. 3, Dubhdaleithi is stated to have ruled during 18 years. Ware gives him only 15 years.

[6] *Druim-Inasclainn.* — Dromiskin, bar. and co. of Louth.

[7] *Ladhgnen.*—The words ri Laiḋgnein, "King of Ladhguen," are added in A. and B., through an oversight.

[8] *South-Leinster.* — Coirpri son of "Ladcnen" is included in the list of Kings of Ui-Cennselaigh, in the *Book of Leinster* (p. 40, col. 1), where the length of his reign is given as 14 years.

[9] *Treoit-mor.* — "Great Trevet." Now Trevet, in the barony of Skreen, co. Meath.

[10] *The 'Law' of Coman.*—See above, under the year 779, for a record of the third imposition of this 'Law, 'lex,' or tribute.

s] reign.[1] The battle of Ard-mic-Rimè, where the
ıilella were overthrown, and Conchobar and Airech-
, grandsons of Cathal,[2] were slain; and Cathmugh
of Flaithbertach, King of Coirpri, and Cormac son
'ubhdacrich, King of Breifni, were slain. Bresal, son
'lathri, King of Dalaraide; Maelbresail, son of Aedh,
ɔf Crichan, King of Ui-Fiachrach;[3] Donncorci, King
'alriada; Cathmugh, King of Calraighe, and Ternoc,
rior of Corcach-Mor,[4] died.

al. Jan. A.D. 792. Dubhdaleithi,[5] son of Sinach, [792.]
ıt of Ard-Macha; Crunnmael of Druim-Inasclainn,
ıt of Cluain-Iraird; Coirpri son of Ladhgnen,[7] King
outh Leinster;[8] Doimtech, superior of Treoit-mor;[9]
.edh son of Cumuscach, abbot of Dermagh, [and]
thgel, son of Taichlech, abbot of Druim-ratha, died.
'Law' of Coman,[10] by Aildobur[11] and Muirghis, over
three divisions[12] of Connaught. The 'Law' of
he over Munster; and the ordaining of Artri, son of
ıal, to the kingship of Munster. The profanation of
ıdelach, by Gormghal[13] son of Dinnanach; and the
ing and spoiling of Ard-Macha, and the killing of a
there, by the Ui-Cremthainn. Reception of Faen-
ch again in Ard-Macha. 'Translation' of the relics
'ole.[14]

ildobur. — He was abbot of omain (Roscommon). His obit ıred at the year 799.

'hree Divisions. — See note [13] the year 789 *supra*.

'ormghal. — *In the Book of er*, p. 42, col. 4, Gormhgal is ɔned as one of the three *Air-chs* (or "Herenachs") who he office of abbot by force, and ıre not commemorated in the See Todd's St. Patrick, p. 181. ıme of Gormghal is not included in Ware's list of the Bishops of Armagh. But under the year 798, *infra*, he is stated to have imposed the 'Law' of Patrick over Connaught; and in the entry of his obit at the year 805, he is described as abbot of Armagh and Clones.

[14] *Tole.*—See note [9] under A.D. 737 *supra*. In the MS. Clar. 49, the words "Ep. Clunard" are added in the handwriting of Archbishop Ussher.

Fol 35 *ba.* Kl. Ianair. Anno domini dcc.° xc.° iii.° Airectaċ .h. Faelain abbas aird Maċae, 7 Affiaṫ episcopus aird Maċae, in pace dormierunt in una nocte. Tomas abbas Bennċair, Ioseṗ nepos Cernae abbas cluana macc U Nois, obierunt. Caṫnia nepos Guaire, abbas Tomae greine, 7 Lerben banairċinneċ cluana Bairenn, pausauerunt. Iugulatio Artraċ filii Faelain. Commotatio reliquiarum Treno. Slogaḋ la Donnchad ad auxilium Laginentium contra Mumenenses. Uastatio omnium insolarum Britanniae a gentilibus. Indred Mugdornne maġen la Aeḋ mac Neill.

Kl. Ianair. Anno domini dcc.° xc.° iiii.° Brann ardcenn rex Lagenentium occisus est, 7 regina eius, Eiṫne ingin Domnaill Miḋe. Finsnechta cetarderc, mac Ceallaiġ, occidit eos hi Cill ċule dumai in sexta nocte post Kalendas Maii, id est .iiii. feria. Occisio Cuinn mic Donnchada hi criċ Oa n-Olcan la Flann mac Congalaiġ. Loscaḋ Reċrainne o geinntiḃ, 7 Sci dosclaḋ 7 do lomraḋ.

[1] *Ua Faelain*; *i.e.* descendant (or grandson) of Faelan. A later hand writes alias O Fleaḋaiġ ("alias Ua Fleadhaigh"), as in B. Clar. 49 has O Fleai. But the orig. text in A. agrees with the *Book of Leinster* (p. 42, col. 3), in which Airectach Ua Faeláin is stated to have been of the Ui-Bresail (a sept which furnished many bishops to the See of Armagh), and his rule is limited to one year. The name of Airectach is not in Ware's list of the prelates of Armagh.

[2] *Abbess.*—banairċinneċ. The *Four Masters* seem to have misunderstood this entry, if they copied it from the original of these Annals, as out of Lerben banairċinneċ they make Learḃanḃan airċinneach ("Learbanbhan, airchinneach," as O'Donovan renders it, *F. M.* 789). But the office of *airchinnech*, as O'Don. himself has explained (*Suppl. to O'Reilly* in voce) was an office filled by one of the male sex, whereas *banairchinnech* is Latinized "antestita" (for "antistita") in the St. Gall MS. (p. 66 *a*). Clar. 49 has "Lerben, the abbates of Cluan Bairenn." Besides, Cluain-Baireann (now Cloonburren, in the barony of Moycarn, co. Roscommon) was undoubtedly a nunnery at this time. O'Conor, of course, also misunderstood the entry.

[3] *By Gentiles.*—a gentibus, B. The Annals of Clonmacnoise, at A.D. 791, say "by the Danes."

[4] *Mughdorna Maghen.*—Now represented by the barony of Cremorne, in the county of Monaghan.

Kal. Jan. A.D. 793. Airectach Ua Faelain,[1] abbot Ard-Macha, and Affiath, bishop of Ard-Macha, slept peace on the same night. Thomas, abbot of Bennir, [and] Joseph Ua Cerna, abbot of Clonmacnoise, l. Cathnia Ua Guaire, abbot of Tuaim-greine, and ben, abbess[2] of Cluain-Bairenn, rested. The killing Artri, son of Faelan. 'Translation' of the relics of an. A hosting by Donnchad, in aid of the nstermen against the Munstermen. Devastation all the islands of Britain by Gentiles.[3] Devastation Mughdorna-Maghen[4] by Aedh,[5] son of Niall. [793.]

Kal. Jan. A.D. 794. Brann Ardcenn,[6] King of the nstermen was slain, and his queen, Eithne, daughter Domnall of Meath. Finsnechta 'Cethar-derc,'[7] son Cellach, slew them in Cill-chuile-duma,[8] on the sixth it after the Kalends of May, i.e., the fourth day of the k. The killing of Conn, son of Donnchad, in Crich-n Olcan,[9] by Flann son of Congalach. The burning Rechra by Gentiles, and Sci[10] was pillaged and wasted. [794.]

---

edh.– Aedh Oirdnidhe, whose sion to the sovereignty of Ire- is noticed under the year 796 . He was the son of Niall ch, King of Ireland, whose obit orded under the year 777 *supra.*

rann Ardcenn.—"Bran of the head (or forehead"). The son of Muiredach, mentioned under the year 781. See note [8].

thar-derc.—"Of the four eyes." ext note.

ll-chuile-duma.—The "Church il-duma." O'Donovan rashly ts (*Four Mast.*, A.D. 790, note l), his was probably the place now Kilcool, in the bar. of New- co. Wicklow. But in the *of Leinster* list of the Kings of er (p. 39, col. 2), Bran Ardcend, Muredach, and his wife, are to have been "burned" in Cill-cule-dumai, in *Laighis-chuile*, which was a district in the present Queen's County.

[9] *Crich-Ua-n Olcan.*—The "territory of the Ui-Olcan." O'Donovan states (*Ann. F. M.*, A.D. 790, note m), that this was the name of "a small district in Meath." But he does not give any authority for the statement.

[10] *Sci.*—The Isle of Skye, in Scotland. The text of this clause in A. and B. has scri (with a "punctum delens" under the letter r) doscrad [evidently for do ċoscraḋ] 7 do lomraḋ, "Sci (Skye) was pillaged and wasted." For sci (Skye) the *Four Masters* (at A.D. 790), have a Sccrine ("its [Rechra's] shrines"), which seems an error. The compiler of these Annals evidently meant to say that Skye was pillaged and wasted.

Foindelach (mac Meanaiġ) abbas airdd Maċae subita morte perit. Murcaḋ mac Feraḋaiġ, Tippraiti mac Ferċair o cloin ferta Brenainn, Guaire h. Tippraiti ab Cluana fota, obierunt.

Kl. Ianair. Anno domini dcc.° xc.° u.° Dublittir Finnglaissi, 7 Colggu nepos Duineċdo, Olcoḃur mac Flainn filii Eirc, rex Muṁan, scribae 7 episcopi 7 ancoritae, dormierunt. Offa rex bonus Anglorum mortuus est. Equonimus airdd Maċae, Eċu mac Cernaiġ, mortuus est inmatura morte. Senċan abbas Cille aċaiḋ droma fota 7 Biror, 7 Suiḃne abbas Aṫa truim, 7 Moenaċ mac Oengusa secnap Luscan, omnes obierunt. Mac Fergg[u]sa ri .h. mBriuin, Duineċaiḋ
Fol. 35 bb. hoa Daire dux Ciarraide, mortui sunt. Caṫ Aṫa fen, ubi Muirgis euasit. Cloṫcu episcopus 7 ancorita Cluana iraird in pace quieuit.

Kl. Ianair. Anno domini dcc.° xc.° ui.° Mors Donnchada (mic Domnaill) regis Teṁro 7 Innrechtaiġ mic Domnaill fratris eius.

O thus domain cialla cain,
U. mile bliadan bossfadaig,
I fos is set seirig sin,
Co clos ec deig mic Domnaill.

Cumuscaċ mac Fogartaiġ, rex deisceirt Breg, in clericatu; Rotechtaċ Croibe, 7 Muireḋaċ mac Flainn garad, rex gentis mic Ercae, 7 Crunmael mac Firdacriċ, 7 Curoi mac Oenġusa rex generis Loigaire,

[1] *Maenach.*—The form of the name (in the genit.) in A. and B. is Meanaiġ, (nomin. Meanach). But in the *Book of Leinster* list (p. 42, col. 3), it is Moenaiġ, in the genit. form; nomin. Moenach.

[2] *Dubhlittir.*—See above at the year 779.

[3] *Of Munster.* — Muṁen, A.; Muṁan, B.

[4] *Offa.*—King of the Mercians. His death is recorded in the Anglo-Saxon Chronicle at the year 794, and again at 796, which latter is the correct date.

[5] *Cill-achaidh of Druim-fota*—Killeigh, in the barony of Geashill, King's county.

[6] *Ath-truim.*—Trim, co. Meath.

[7] *Ciarraidhe.*—The *Four Masters*

ndelach (son of Macnach[1]), abbot of Ard-Macha, died denly. Murchadh, son of Feradhach; Tipraiti, son Ferchar, from Cluain-ferta-Brenainn, and Guaire Ua raiti, abbot of Cluain-fota, died.

Kal. Jan. A.D. 795. Dubhlittir[2] of Finn-glais, and gu Ua Duinechda, Olcobhur, son of Flann, son of , King of Munster,[3] [and] scribes, and bishops, and horites, 'fell asleep.' Offa,[4] a good king of the English, d. Echu, son of Cernach, steward of Ard-Macha, died untimely death. Senchan, abbot of Cill-achaidh of im-fota,[5] and of Biror, and Suibhne, abbot of Ath-im,[6] and Moenach, son of Oengus, vice-abbot of Lusca ll died. Mac Fergg[u]sa, King of Ui-Briuin, [and] inechaidh Ua Daire, chief of Ciarraidhe,[7] died. The tle of Ath-fen,[8] where Muirgis got off. Clothcu, bishop l anchorite of Cluain-Iraird, rested in peace. [795.]

Kal. Jan. A.D. 796. Death of Donnchad (son of mnall), King of Tara, and of Innrechtach, son of mnall, his brother. [796.]

From the world's beginning, meanings fair,
Five thousand momentous years,
Here in happy way it was,
'Till the death of Domnall's good son was heard.

nuscach, son of Fogartach, King of the South of gh, in religion; Rothechtach of Croebh, and Muire-h, son of Flann Garadh, King of Cinel-Mic-Erca, l Crunmael son of Ferdacrich, and Curoi son of

---

.D. 791) write this name "Ciar-ie-Aí," the ancient name of a ict near Castlereagh, in the county Roscommon, subsequently known lann-Keherny.

[8] *Ath-fen*,—Probably the "Ath-" in Ciarraigi-Ai (see last note), mentioned in *Lebor na hUidre*, p. 21 *b*.

[9] *From.*—The original of these lines (which is not in B.) is in the top margin of fol. 35 *b* in A., with a mark of reference to the place where it should be included in the text.

7 Ailmeḋair equonimus cluana mic Nois, omnes mortui sunt. Bellum Droma rig, in quo ceciderunt duo filii Domnaill, id est, Finsnechta 7 Diarmait hodur frater eius, 7 Finsnechta mac Follamain, 7 alii multi qui non numerati sunt. Aeḋ mac Neill filii Fergaile uictor fuit.

Cia dorochair Aeḋ la Domnall, coscar cicar;
Fri Aeḋ finn fir i caṫ Droma riġ ro hicaḋ.

Condal filia Murcoḋa, abatissa tiġe sruiṫe Cille daro, dormiuit. Uastatio Midi la Aeḋ mac Neill frasaiġ, 7 initium regni eius.

Kt. Ianair. Anno domini dcc.° xc.° uii.° Eudus nepos Diċolla, abas Cille daro, mortuus est. Combustio inse Patraicc o genntiḃ, 7 borime na criċ do breiṫ, 7 scrin Doċonna do brisead doaiḃ, 7 innreda mara doaib cene, eitir Erinn 7 Albain. Forinnan Imleċo fia, 7 Condmaċ mac Muirṁeḋo nepos Guaire Oidni, scriba Cluana mic Nois, perierunt.

---

[1] *Ailmedhair.*—O'Conor misprints this name "*Ailine-Daire* [Derrensis]," taking *Ailine* (rectè *Ailme*) as the full name, and *daire* (rectè *dhair*) as representing Derrensis ("Derry"). Clar. 49 gives the name, as it would be pronounced, "Ailmear."

[2] *Druim-righ.*—"Dorsum regis,' or the "King's ridge. O'Donovan (*Ann. Four M.*, A.D. 793, note w) identifies this place with Drumree, in the barony of Ratoath, co. Meath.

[3] *Odur.*—Translated "yellowe," in Clar. 49.

[4] *That are not numbered.*—So in Clar. 49. The original of this clause is not in B., which goes to prove that the so-called translator of Clar. 49 did not follow the text of MS. B.

[5] *Aedh*; *i.e.*, Aedh Oirdnidhe, son of Niall Frasach, King of Ireland.

[6] *Aedh*: *i.e.*, Aedh Allan (or Aedh Aldan), as a gloss over the name indicates. He was King of Ireland, and was slain (see above under the year 742) by Domnall, son of Murchad, who succeeded him in the sovereignty.

[7] *Domnall.*—A gloss over the name in A. has mac Murchada ("son of Murchad"). See last note. These lines (which are not in B.) are written in the lower margin of fol. 35 *b* in A., with a mark of reference to the place where they should be inserted in the text.

[8] *Tech-sruithe.*—The 'translator' in Clar. 49 renders this term by "house of the wise." But over the word

ıgus, King of Cinel-Loeghaire, and Ailmedhair,[1] ward of Clonmacnoise—all died. The battle of Druimh,[2] in which were slain two sons of Domnall, viz.: ısnechta, and Diarmait Odur,[3] his brother, and Finsıhta, son of Follaman, and many more that are not nbered.[4] Aedh,[5] son of Niall, son of Fergal, was tor.

Though Aedh[6] was slain by Domnall,[7] a fierce triumph;
By the true, fair Aedh,[5] in the battle of Druim-righ,[2] it was
avenged.

ndal, daughter of Murchadh, abbess of the Tech-ithe[8] in Cill-dara, slept. The wasting of Midhe by dh,[5] son of Niall Frasach,[9] and the commencement of ; reign.

Kal. Jan. A.D. 797. Eudus Ua Dicholla, abbot of ll-dara, died. Burning of Inis-Patraicc[10] by Gentiles; d they carried off the preys of the districts; and the rine of Dochonna was broken by them; and other eat devastations[11] [were committed] by them both in eland and Alba. Forinnan of Imlech-Fia,[12] and ındmach, son of Muirmidh,[13] descendant of Guaire dhne,[14] scribe of Clonmacnoise, died. [797.]

---

wise," an old hand, probably sher's, has written "q. fire."?

ch-sruithe means "house of se-ırs."

[9] *Frasach.* — ꝼꞃaꞅaıᵹ (the gen. m of ꝼꞃaꞅach, "of the showers"), ted in B. See note [8], p. 169, te [2], p. 230, and note [4], p. 248, *supra*.

[10] *Inis-Patraicc.* — "Patrick's Isıd." O'Donovan thought this was . Patrick's Island, near Skerries, . Dublin. *Four Mast.*, A.D. 793, te y. But Dr. Todd understood el, in the Isle of Man (which was ıciently called Insula Patricii), to ve been intended. *Cogadh Gaedhel re Gallaibh*, Introd., xxxv. note [1].

[11] *Great devastations.* — ınnꝺꞃeꝺa maꞃa. Wrongly translated "the spoyles of the sea," in Clar. 49, and also by Todd, *Cog. Gaedhel*, &c. Introd. p. xxxv.

[12] *Imlech-Fia.*—See note [2], p. 194 *supra*.

[13] *Of Muirmidh.*—Muıꞃṁeꝺo, A. B. The *Ann. Four Mast.* (at A.D. 793) have the name in the genit. form Ꝺuıꞃbotha; the nomin. of which would be Ꝺuꞃbotha.

[14] *Guaire Aidhne.* — Oıꝺnı, in A. and B. See note [2], p. 118 *supra*.

Kl. Ianair. Anno domini dcc.° xc.° iiii.° Bellum Duin ganiba inter Connaċta inuicem, ubi Corcraċ mac Duinn, 7 Gaisceḋaċ, 7 alii multi ceciderunt, 7 Muirgis mac Tomaltaiġ uictor fuit. Bellum Finnubraċ hi Teṫbai, ubi reges multi occisi sunt,
Fol 36aa. id est, Fergus mac Algaile, Corcaraċ mac Ceiṫernaiċ, reges generis Coirpri .i. Dubinnrecht mac Artgaile 7 Murchad mac Condmaiġ. Murchad mac Domnaill uictor fuit. Iugulatio Blaṫmic mic Guaire, abbatis Cluana fota Boetain, o Maelruanaiġ 7 o Follamain filiis Donnchada. Nix magna in qua multi homines 7 pecora perierunt. Domnall mac Donnchada dolose a fratribus suis iugulatus est. Feraḋaċ mac Segeni, abbas Reċrainne, obiit. Anaili abbas cluana mic Nois, Ceiṫernaċ abbas Glinne da loċa, 7 Siaḋal .h. Comain abbas Cille aċaiḋ, 7 Fiannaċtaċ Fernann, 7 Suibne Cille deilgge, 7 Breislen Beirre uitam finierunt. Ind laṁcomart hi feil Miċeil, dia n-erred in tene di nim. Lex Patricii for Connacta, la Gormgal mac Dindataiġ. Ailill mac Indrechtaiġ, rex .h. Maine Connacht, mortuus est. Dunflaiṫ filia Flaiṫbertaiġ mic Loi[n]griċ dormiuit.

Kl. Ianair. Anno domini dcc.° xc.° ix.° Airmeaḋach abbas Benncair, Connlae mac Artgaile, Aildobur abbas Rois Comain, Mimtenaċa abbas Glinne da loċa,

---

[1] *Dun-Ganiba.*—"Dun-Gaibhe," in the *Ann. Four Mast.*, A.D. 794.

[2] *Themselves.* — inuicem, A., B. The corresponding word in the *Ann. Four Mast.* is fesin, "themselves."

[3] *Muirghis.*—King of Connaught at the time.

[4] *Finnabhair.*—Supposed to be the place now called Feunor, in the parish of Rathconnell, bar. of Moyashel and Magheradernon, co. Westmeath.

[5] *Murchad.*—The *Four Mast.* (A.D. 794) write the name "Muireadhach." The death of a "Muiredach son of Domnall, King of Meath," is entered at the year 801 *infra*.

[6] *Cluain-fota-Baetain*; *i.e.*, "Baetan's long meadow." Now Clonfad, in the barony of Farbill, co. Westmeath.

[7] *Rechra.*—Genit. form "Rechrann," or "Rechrainne." This was the old Irish name of Rathlin Island, off the coast of Antrim, and also of

Kal. Jan. A.D. 798. The battle of Dun-Ganiba[1] [798.]
:tween the Connaughtmen themselves,[2] in which
əscrach, son of Donn, and Gaiscedhach, and many
hers, were slain; and Muirghis,[3] son of Tomaltach,
ıs victor. The battle of Finnabhair[4] in Tethba, where
any kings were slain, *i.e.*, Fergus son of Algal,
əscarach son of Ceithernach, [and] the Kings of Cinel-
ıirpri, viz., Dubhinnrecht son of Artgal, and Murchad
n of Condmach. Murchad,[5] son of Domnall, was
ctor. The killing of Blathmac, son of Guaire, abbot
' Cluain-fota-Baetain,[6] by Maelruanaigh and Follaman,
ɪns of Donnchad. Great snow, in which great numbers
' men and cattle perished. Domnall, son of Donnchad,
as treacherously slain by his brothers. Feradhach,
ɪn of Segeni, abbot of Rechra,[7] died. Anaili, abbot of
lonmacnoise; Ceithernach, abbot of Glenn-da-locha;
adhal Ua Comain, abbot of Cill-achaidh;[8] Fiannachtach
f Ferna; Suibhne of Cill-delge, and Breislen of Berre,[9]
ıded their lives. The 'lamchomairt'[10] on the festival
'St. Michael, of which was said the "fire from Heaven."
he 'Law' of Patrick[11] over Connaught, by Gormgal,[12] son
' Dindatach. Ailill, son of Indrechtach, King of Ui-
aine of Connaught, died. Dunflaith, daughter of
laithbertach,[13] son of Loingsech, 'fell asleep.'

Kal. Jan. A.D. 799. Airmedhach, abbot of Bennchair;[14] [799.]
ɔnnla, son of Artgal; Aildobur,[15] abbot of Ros-Comain,

---

mbay Island, off the coast of the Dublin; and it is uncertain which these islands, in each of which ɜre was an ecclesiastical establish-nt of Columbian foundation, is ːe meant.

[8] *Cill-achaidh.*—Killeigh, in the ·ony of Geashill, King's county.

[9] *Breislen of Berre.*—See under ː year 778 *supra.*

[10] '*Lamchomairt.*' — See above ler the year 771; p. 240, note [1].

[11] *The Law of Patrick.*—See under the years 733, 736, 766, and 782 *supra*; and Reeves' *Colton's Visitation*, Introd., p. iv., *sq.*

[12] *Gormgal.*—See above, under the year 792.

[13] *Flaithbertach.*—King of Ireland. His death, "in clericatu," is recorded under the year 764 *supra.*

[14] *Bennchair.*—Bangor, co. Down.

[15] *Aildobur.*—See under the year 792.

perierunt. Loingseċ mac Fiaċnae, abbas Duin Leṫglaissi, Condmaċ mac Donit abbas Corcaiġe móre, perierunt. Feirgil nepos Taiḋgg, scriba Luscan, dormiuit. Ailill mac Fergusa, rex deisceirt Breġ, praiectus est de equo suo in circio feriae filii Cuilinn Luscan, 7 continuo mortuus est. Belliolum inter genus Loiġaire 7 genus Ardgail, in quo cecidit Fiangalaċ mac Dunlainge. Conall mac Neill 7 Conġalaċ mac Aenġusa uictores erant, causa interfectionis fratris sui, id est Failbi. Positio reliquiarum Conlaid hi scrin oir argait. Caṫcoscraḋ itir na hAirṫeru inuicem immaiġ Lingsen, ubi ceciderunt Maeloċtaraiċ abbas Daire eiṫniġ, 7 Conmal mac Cernaiġ.

Kl. Ianair. Anno domini dccc.° Positio reliquiarum Ronaen filii Beriċ in arca auri 7 argenti. Fol. 36 ab. Feidlemid .h. Lugadon, abbas ċluana Dolcan, mortuus est. Bellum inter Ultu 7 nepotes Eċdaċ Coḃo, in quo cecidit Eċu mac Ailella rex Coḃo, 7

---

[1] *Dun-lethglaise.*—Downpatrick, co. Down.

[2] *Corcach-mor; i.e.,* the "Great marsh." Cork, in Munster.

[3] *On the festival of Mac Cuilinn.*—The obit of Mac Cuilinn (whose real name was Cuinnidh), patron of Lusk, co. Dublin, is recorded under the year 497, *supra.* His day in the Calendar is September 6.

[4] *A battle.*—belliolum, A., B. The corresponding word in the *Ann. Four Mast.*, A.D. 795, is iomairecc, a "conflict," or "encounter."

[5] *His brother, i.e., Failbhe.*—Failbhe was apparently the brother of Fiangalach, who was slain in this battle, and therefore son of Dunlaing, chief of Cinel-Ardgail, whose obit is recorded at the year 746, *supra.*

[6] *Conlaed.*—First bishop of Kildare. His obit is given above under the year 591. Regarding the shrine in which his relics were placed, see Messingham's *Florilegium*, p. 199, and Petrie's *Round Towers*, pp. 194–201.

[7] *Airthera.*—A tribe inhabiting a district the name of which has been Latinized "Orientales," and "Regio Orientalium." The territory of this tribe is now represented by the baronies of Lower and Upper Orior, in the "east" of the county Armagh.

[8] *Magh-Lingsen.*—The "Plain of Lingsen." Obviously some plain in the district now forming the baronies of Orior, in the co. of Armagh. Not identified.

[9] *Daire Eithnigh.* — O'Donovan,

[and] Mimtenacha, abbot of Glenn-da-locha, died. Loingsech, son of Fiachna, abbot of Dun-lethglaise;[1] Condmach, son of Donit, abbot of Corcach-mor,[2] died. Fergil Ua Taidhg, scribe of Lusca, slept. Ailill son of Fergus, King of the South of Bregh, was thrown from his horse on the festival of Mac Cuilinn[3] of Lusca, and died immediately. A battle[4] between the Cinel-Loeghaire and Cinel-Ardgail, in which Fiangalach, son of Dunlaing, was slain. Conall son of Niall, and Conghalach son of Aengus, were victors on account of the killing of his brother, *i.e.*, Failbhe[5] [it was fought]. The placing of the relics of Conlaed[6] in a shrine of gold and silver. A destructive battle among the Airthera[7] themselves, in Magh-Lingsen,[8] where Maelochtaraigh, abbot of Daire-Eithnigh,[9] and Conmal, son of Cernach, were slain.

Kal. Jan. A.D. 800. The placing of the relics of Ronan,[10] son of Berach, in a shrine of gold and silver. Feidlimid Ua Lugadon,[11] abbot of Cluain-Dolcain,[12] died. A battle between the Ulaid and the Ui-Echach-Cobho,[13] in which fell Echu, son of Ailill, King of Cobho. And [800.]

---

llowing the *Martyr. Donegal* at November 3, and a note in the *Felirè Oengus* at the same date, which state that there was a "Doire (or Daire)-Ednech," otherwise called "Daire-na-fflann," in Eoghanacht-Caisil, identifies this place with the townland of Derrynavlan, in the parish of Graystown, barony of Slievardagh, co. Tipperary. (*Four Mast.*, A.D. 795, note h.) But the accuracy of this identification seems questionable.

[10] *Ronan.*—He was the patron of the church of Druim-Inasclainn, now Dromiskin, in the barony and county of Louth. His death, from the plague called the '*buidhe-conaill*,' otherwise called '*cron-conaill*' (see note [5], p. 54, *supra*) is entered at the year 664 in the *Ann. Four Mast.*; and in the *Chron. Scotorum* at A.D. 661–664.

[11] *Feidlimid Ua Lugadon.*—"Feidlimid, descendant of Lugadu." See under the years 780 and 789, for mention of other members of the family of Ua Lugadon, abbots of Cluain-Dolcain (Clondalkin, near Dublin).

[12] *Cluain-Dolcain.*—See last note.

[13] *Ui-Echach-Cobho*—.The descendants of Eochaid Cobha, from whom the baronies of Iveagh, (Ui-Echach), in the co. Down have been so called. See Reeves' *Eccl. Antiqq.*, p. 350.

cecidit Caireall mac Caṫail ex parte aduersa belli, 7 exercitus eius uictor fuit. Bresal mac Segeni, abbas Iae, anno principatus sui .xxxi.° dormiuit. Ruamnus abbas domnaiġ Seċnaill mortuus est. Befáil filia Caṫail, regina Donnchada, mortua est. Bresal mac Gormgaile, de genere Loeġaire, a fratribus suis dolose occisus est. Caṫrannaċ mac Caṫail Moenṁaigi, 7 Nindiḋ ancorita, pausant. Aestas pluuialis.

Kl. Ianair. Anno domini dccc.° i.° Muiredaċ mac Domnaill ri Miḋe mortuus est. Sloġaḋ la h Aeḋ for Miḋe, co ro rann Miḋe itir da mac Donnchada, id est, Concoḃar 7 Ailell. Ailill mac Cormaic abbas Slane, sapiens 7 iudex optimus, obiit. Fergal mac Anmcaḋa rex Ossaiġi mortuus est. Macoigi Apuirċrosan abbas Bennċair, Muiredaċ mac Olcobair abbas cluana ferta Brendain, Corcraċ nepos Froiċ abbas Luġmaiḋ, Clemens Tire da glas, omnes feliciter uitam in pace finierunt. Artri mac Ailella, rex Muġḋorne magan, mortuus est. Euginis filia Donnchada, regina regis Temoriae, mortua est. Toġal

---

[1] *Bresal.*—See Reeves' *Adamnan*, p. 386.

[2] *Domnach-Sechnaill*; *i.e.* the "church of Sechnall." Now Dunshaughlin, in the barony of Ratoath, co. Meath.

[3] *Befáil.*—This name means "Woman of Fál," (Fál being a bardic name for Ireland). In the Tract on celebrated women in the *Book of Lecan* (p. 391*a*), where the name is written "Bebail," this lady is stated to have been the daughter of a "Cathal King of Ulad," and the mother of Aengus (the Oengus whose obit is given at the year 829 *infra*), and of Maelruanaidh (ob. 842 *infra*). But the ancient lists of the Kings of Ulad have no king named Cathal.

[4] *Cathal*—See last note.

[5] *Donnchad.* — King of Ireland. His obit is given above at the year 796.

[6] *Summer.*—Estas, B.

[7] *Aedh.*—King of Ireland.

[8] *Aporcrosan.* — Applecross, in Ross-shire, Scotland. The foundation of the church of Aporcrosan by St. Maelrubha, abbot of Bangor in the co. Down, is recorded above at the year 672. Regarding the identification of Aporcrosan, and the etymology

airell, son of Cathal, fell on the other side of the battle; ıd his army was victorious. Bresal,[1] son of Segeni, bbot of Ia, 'fell asleep' in the 31st year of his governıent. Ruamnus, abbot of Domnach-Sechnaill,[2] died. efáil,[3] daughter of Cathal,[4] queen of Donnchad,[5] died. resal, son of Gormgal, of the Cinel-Loeghaire, was eceitfully slain by his brothers. Cathrannach, son of athal of Maenmagh, and Nindidh, an anchorite, rest. rainy summer.[6]

Kal. Jan. A.D. 801. Muiredach, son of Domnall, ing of Midhe, died. A hosting by Aedh[7] upon Midhe, hen he divided Midhe between two sons of Donnchad, iz., Concobhar and Ailill. Ailill, son of Cormac, abbot f Slane, a wise man, and most excellent judge, died. 'ergal, son of Anmchadh, King of the Osraighi, died. lacoigi of Aporcrosan,[8] abbot of Bennchair; Muiredach, ın of Olcobhar, abbot of Cluain-ferta-Brendain;[9] Cosrach Ua Froich, abbot of Lughmadh,[10] and Clemens of 'ir-da-glas[11]—all ended[12] their lives happily in peace. ırtri, son of Ailill, King of Mugdhorna-Magan,[13] died. uginis,[14] daughter of Donnchad,[15] Queen of the King of [801.]

---

the name, see the *Irish Ecclesias-al Journal*, July, 1849, pp. 299, 300.

[9] *Cluain-ferta-Brendain.*—Clonfert, the barony of Longford, co. alway.

[10] *Lughmadh.*—Louth, in the county Louth.

[11] *Tir-da-glas*—Terryglass, in the rony of Lower Ormond, co. Tipperary.

[12] *All ended*, &c.—B. has merely nner ᴅeꝼuncꞇı. But Clar. 49 lows the MS. A.

[13] *Mugdhorna-Magan.*—Otherwise itten Mughdorna-Maighen, and Mughdorne. Now represented by the barony of Cremorne, co. Monaghan.

[14] *Euginis.*—In the *Ann. Four Mast.*, at A.D. 797, the name is more correctly written Eugınıa for "Engenia." But A., B., and Clar. 49 have "Euginis," although O'Donovan, in his ed. of the *Four Masters* (A.D. 797, note s), quoting from the version of this Chronicle in the MS., Clar. 49, prints *Euginia.*

[15] *Donnchad*; *i.e.* Donnchad, son of Domnall, King of Ireland, whose obit is recorded at the year 796, *supra.*

loċa Riaċ la Muirġis. I Columbae cille a gentibus combusta est.

Kl. Ianair. Anno domini dccc.° ii.° Quies Flainn mic Narġaile, qui in temtatione doloris .xiii.° anno incubuit. Airfinnan abbas Taṁlaċtai Maelruain pausauit in pace. Dunchad mac Conġaile, rex Loċa Cal, a fratribus suis iugulatus est. Artgal mac Caṫusaiġ, rex insolae Culenrigi, de genere Eugain, iugulatus est. Bellum Ruḃai Conaill inter duos filios Donnchada, ubi Ailill cecidit et Concobar uictor fuit. Oengus mac Muġroin, rex nepotum
Fol. 36ba. Failġi, iugulatus est dolose a sociis Finsneċte filii Ceallaiċ, consilio regis sui. Belliolum inter Sogen et aicme Moenmaiġi, in quo multi interfecti sunt.

.b. Kl. Ianair. Anno domini dccc.° iii.° Doṁnall mac Aeḋa muindeirg, rex aquilonis, mortuus est. Fiaċra mac Tuaṫail, rex nepotum Teig, mortuus est. Quies Carathbrain abbatis Biror. Cormac mac Conaill, equonimus Lusean, mortuus est. Uastatio Laginentium apud filium Neill duabus uicibus in uno mense. Faelan mac Ceallaiġ princeps Cille daro, et Cernaċ mac Dunchada rex Mugdorne, perierunt. Congressio senatorum nepotum Neill, cui dux erat Condmaċ

---

[1] *King of "Temoria"*; (or K. of 'Tara'). See *Ann. Four Mast.*, at A.D. 797, and O'Donovan's note regarding this entry.

[2] *Loch-Riach.*—The structure here referred to as having been demolished must have been some fortress in Loch-Riach, the lake from which the town of Loughrea, co. Galway, has derived its name.

[3] *Muirghis.* — Muirghis, son of Tomaltach, King of Connaught, the beginning of whose reign is noticed at the year 791, *supra*. O'Conor, with his usual inaccuracy, *translates* the proper name 'Muirghis' by 'prædonibus maritimis.'

[4] *Of Narghal.* — Narġaile, A. Clar. 49 has "Argaile" ("of Argal"). But the *Four Mast.* (798) have Naergaile. MS. B. has Narġaile ("of Narghal.")

[5] *Tamlacht-Maelruain.*—Now Tallaght, in the co. of Dublin.

[6] *Loch-Cal.*—Loughgall, co. Armagh.

[7] *Culen-rigi.*—See note [11], p 187, *supra*.

[8] *Rubha-Conaill.* — Now Rathconnell, in the parish of the same

'emoria,'[1] died. The demolition of Loch-Riach[2] by uirghis.[3] I-Coluim-Cille was burned by Gentiles.

Kal. Jan. A.D. 802. The repose of Flann, son of arghal,[4] who suffered for sixteen years from severe ckness. Airfhinnan, abbot of Tamlacht-Maelruain,[5] sted in peace. Dunchad, son of Conghal, King of ch-Cal,[6] was slain by his brothers. Artgal, son of athasach, King of the Island of Culen-rigi,[7] of the inel-Eogain, was slain. The battle of Rubha-Conaill,[8] etween two sons of Donnchad, where Ailill was slain, nd Concobhar was victorious. Oengus, son of Mughn,[9] King of the Ui-Failghi, was deceitfully slain by e companions of Finsnechta,[10] son of Cellach, by their ing's advice. A little battle between the Sogen[11] and the pt of Maenmagh, in which many persons were slain. [802.]

Kal. Jan. A.D. 803. Domnall, son of Aedh Muinderg, ing of the North,[12] died. Fiachra, son of Tuathal, King the Ui-Teig,[13] died. The repose of Caratbran, abbot of iror. Cormac, son of Conall, steward of Lusca, died. illaging of the Leinstermen, by the son of Niall,[14] twice one month. Faelan, son of Cellach, abbot of Cill-dara, nd Cernach, son of Dunchad, King of Mughdorna, died. n assembly of the senators[15] of the Ui-Neill, in Dun- [803.] BIS.

---

me, a mile and a half to the east Mullingar, in the county of Westath.

[9] *Of Mughron.* — ⁊ Domnaill or of Domnall "), as in the List of ngs of Ui-Falge, *Book of Leinster*, 40, col. 3. *The Four Mast.*, at). 798, write Ua Mughroin, "grand- of Mughron."

[10] *Finsnechta.*—King of Leinster, . A.D. 807, *infra*).

[11] *Sogen.*—*Maenmagh.* Septs of powerful tribe of Ui-Maine (or -Many). See O'Donovan's *Tribes Customs of Hy-Many*, and map fixed.

[12] *King of the North.*—rex aquilonis, A., B. The words ri in tuaiscirt, the Irish equivalent, are added by way of gloss in B.

[13] *Ui-Teig.*—This was the tribename of the Ui-Cellaigh-Cualann (or "descendants of Cellach Cualann," King of Leinster; ob. A.D. 714 *supra*), who were seated in the north of the present county of Wicklow.

[14] *The son of Niall, i.e.*, Aedh Oirdnidhe, King of Ireland, and son of Niall Frosach, also King of Ireland. See above at the years 762, 777.

[15] *Senators.*—senatorum, A. The entry regarding this assembly is more

abbas Airdd maċae, i n-dun ċuaer. Bellum inter nepotes Cremtain inuicem, ubi ceciderunt Eċu mac Caṫail et Domnall mac Eċdaċ, et Dubrois et alii multi, et Donncloċair mac Artraċ uictor fuit. Sloġaḋ n-Aedo oirdniḋi docum Laigen co ru giall Finsnechta ri Laigen do Aeḋ. Tonitruum ualidum cumuento 7 igni in nocte precedenti festam Patricii dissipante plurimos hominum, id est mille et decem uiros i tir Corco baiscinn, et mare diuisit insolam Fitae in tres partes, et illuḋ mare cum harena terram Fitae absconduit, id est ined da boo deac di ṫir. Isin bliadainsi dana ro saeraḋ cleirich hErenn ar fecht 7 ar sluaiged la hAed oirnigi, do ḃreith ḟathaiḋ na Canoine. Taḃairt ċeanannsa cen ċaṫ do ċoluim ċille ċeolach, hoc anno.

Kl. Ianair. Anno domini dccc.° iiii.° Muireḋach mac Aimirgin abbas Leiṫglinne, Dubduin mac hIrgusa, mortui sunt. Cuana, abbas mainistreċ Buitti, [obiit]. Moenaċ mac Colgen, abbas Luscan,

---

fully given by the *Four Masters* (at A.D. 799) than in these Annals.

[1] *Dun-Cuair.*—O'Donovan identifies this place with Rath-Cuair, now Rathcore, in the barony of Lower Moyfenrath, co. Meath. *Ann. Four Mast.*, A.D. 799, note d.

[2] *Son of Artri.*—mac Artraċ. Not in B.

[3] *Oirdnidhe.* — corrigi, A.; the words uel Oirdniġ being written over it. Oirniḋi, B.

[4] *Aedh.*—Here follows, in the text in B., the entry which is the last but one for this year in A.

[5] *Dispersing.*—dissipante, MSS. The corresponding expression in *Ann. Four Mast.* (A.D. 799) is go ro marḃaḋ ("so that there were slain"), and in the *Chron. Scotorum* (804) co ro marb ("which killed"). The *Annals of Clonmacnoise* (Mageoghegan's Transl.) have "put assunder." This great disturbance of the elements forms one of the "Wonders of Ireland," a curious list of which is given in Todd's *Irish Nennius*, pp. 192–219.

[6] *Corco-Bascinn.*—The S.W. part of the co. Clare.

[7] *Island of Fita.*—O'Donovan says that, "according to the tradition in the country, this is the island now called Inis-caerach, or Mutton-Island, lying opposite Kilmurry-Ibrickan, in the west of the county of Clare." *Ann. Four Mast.*, A.D. 799, note g.

r,[1] of which Condmach, abbot of Ard-Macha, was
r. A battle among the Ui-Cremthain themselves,
ein were slain Echu son of Cathal, and Domnall
of Echaidh, and Dubhrois, and many others; and
clochair, son of Artri,[2] was the victor. A hosting by
Oirdnidhe[3] to Leinster, when Finsnechta, King of
ster, submitted to Aedh.[4] Great thunder, with wind
ightning, on the night before the festival of Patrick,
rsing[5] a great number of people, that is, a thousand
en men, in the country of Corco-Bascinn[6]; and the
livided the Island of Fita[7] into three parts. And
ame sea covered the land of Fita with sand, to the
t of the land of 12 cows. In this year, moreover,
lergy of Ireland were exempted from expeditions
hostings, by Aedh Oir[d]nidhe, according to
udgment of Fathad-na-Canoine[8]. The giving of
nnas[9] in this year, without battle, to Colum-Cille
ausical.

l. Jan. A.D. 804. Muiredhach, son of Aimirgin, [804.]
t of Leithglenn, [and] Dubhduin, son of Irgus, died.
a, abbot of Manistir-Buiti,[10] [died]. Moenach, son
lgu, abbot of Lusca, a good lector, unhappily,[11] and

hadh-na-Canoine.—"Fathadh Canon" (or "the Canonist"). try, which is written in the f A., in a later hand, forms the text in B. The exemp- Irish ecclesiastics from mili- rvice, through the alleged of Fathadh (or Fothadh) the t, has been the subject of on by several writers on Irish . See O'Donovan's *Four* D. 799, note e, and the ies there quoted; O'Curry's *aterials*, p. 364, *sq.*; and 's *Eccl.* Hist., III., 244. It hy of observation that the compilers of these Annals seem to have attached but slight importance to an event regarded with such interest by many other Irish Historical writers, ancient and modern.

[9] *Cenannas.* — Kells, co. Meath. This entry, which is part of the text in B., and is added in the margin in A., in *al. man.*, seems to be a quotation from some poem; only that the final words (hoc anno) in A. (not in B.) would spoil the metre.

[10] *Manistir-Buiti.*—Monasterboice, co. Louth.

[11] *Unhappily.*—infoliciter. Not in B.

lector bonus, infeliciter et lacrimabiliter uitam finiuit. Fine abatissa Cille daro obiit. Dubdabairenn .h. Dubain, princeps Cluana irairdd, patribus suis additus est. Cernaċ mac Fergusso, rex Loċa gabor, mortuus est. Sloġaḋ n-Oeḋa co Dun Cuaer, co ro rann Laiġniu itir da Muireḋaċ, id est, Muireḋaċ mac Ruaḋraċ, 7 Muireḋaċ mac Brain. Iugulatio Cormaic mic Muirgiusa abbatis Baslice, et uastatio postea Ciarraiḋe la Muirgis. Muircer-
Fol. 36bb. taċ mac Donngaile, rex Breibne, mortuus est. Cell achaid cum oratorio nouo ardescit.

Kl. Ianair. Anno domini dccc.° u.° In quibus pestilentia magna in hibernia insola orta est. Gormgal mac Dindagaid, abbas aird Maċae 7 Cluana auis, obiit. Conġal mac Moenaiġ, abbas Slane, sapiens, in uirginitate dormiuit. Finsnechta mac Ceallaig regnum suum accepit. Lex Patricii la hAeḋ mac Neill. Mess moer. Loiṫeċ doctur Bennċair quieuit. Familia Iae occisa est a gentilibus, id est .lxuiii. Connmaċ, iudex nepotum Briuin, mortuus est.

---

[1] *Was added.*—additus est, A.

[2] *Loch-Gabor.*—Now Lagore, near Dunshaughlin, co. Meath.

[3] *Dun-Cuair.*—Rathcore, co. Meath. See under the year 803.

[4] *Muiredach.*—His obit is given at the year 828 *infra.*

[5] *Muiredach.*—Ob. 817 *infra.*

[6] *Baslec.*—Baslick, in the barony of Castlereagh, co. Roscommon.

[7] *Ciarraidhe.*—Or Ciarraidhe-Ai, afterwards called, and still known by the name of, Clann-Keherny; a district in the barony of Castlereagh, co. Roscommon. See O'Flaherty's *Ogygia*, pt. III., c. 46.

[8] *Muirgis*; i.e. Muirgis son of Tomaltach, King of Connaught.

[9] *Died.* — mortui sunt (for mortuus est), A. B.

[10] *Cill-achaidh.*—Killeigh, in the parish and barony of Geashill, King's County.

[11] *In which.*—in quibus, A. Not in B. There is evidently some error.

[12] *Broke out.*—The words insola orta est are not in B.

[13] *Gormgal.* — See above at the years 792, and 798.

[14] *Dindagad.*—Written *Dindanaigh* in the genit. form (nomin. Dindanach), at 792 *supra*, and [D]indnataig (nom. [D]indnatach) in the *Book of Leinster*, p. 42. col. 4.

[15] *Cluain-auis.*—A variation of the name usually written "Cluain-eois"; now Clones, co. Monaghan.

lamentably, ended his life. Finè, abbess of Cill-dara, died. Dubhdabairenn Ua Dubhain, abbot of Cluain-Iraird, was added[1] to his fathers. Cernach, son of Fergus, King of Loch-Gabor,[2] died. A hosting of Aedh to Dun-Cuair,[3] when he divided Leinster between two Muiredachs, viz:—Muiredach[4] son of Ruaidhri, and Muiredach[5] son of Bran. The killing of Cormac, son of Muirgis, abbot of Baslec;[6] and the devastation of Ciarraidhe[7] afterwards by Muirgis.[8] Muirchertach, son of Donngal, King of Breifni, died.[9] Cill-achaidh,[10] with the new oratory, was burned.

Kal. Jan. A.D. 805. In which[11] a great plague broke out[12] in the island of Ireland. Gormgal[13] son of Dindagad,[14] abbot of Ard-Macha and Cluain-auis,[15] died. Conghal, son of Moenach, abbot of Slane, a wise man, died in chastity. Finsnechta, son of Cellach, obtained his kingdom.[16] The 'Law' of Patrick by Aedh, son of Niall. Great abundance of acorns. Loithech, doctor, of Bennchair, died. The 'family' of Ia slain by Gentiles, that is, [to the number of] sixty-eight. Connmach, judge of Ui-Briuin, died. Flaithnia, son of Cinaedh, King of [805.]

---

[16] *Obtained his kingdom.*—regnum suum accepit. Finsnechta became King of Leinster, in succession to Bran, son of Muridach, whom he put to death by burning in the year 794, as above recorded under that year. He seems to have afterwards incurred the hostility of the King of Ireland, for under the year 803, *supra*, the latter is stated to have made an expedition into Leinster, and received the submission of Finsnechta. But he seems to have resigned his kingship, or been deposed in the next year (804 of these Annals), when King Aedh is stated to have divided Leinster between "two Muireaachs." The *Four Masters*, at A.D. 800 (=804 of these Annals, and 805 of the common reckoning), represent Finsnechta as having entered into religion. In the List of Kings of Leinster, in the *Book of Leinster*, p. 39, col. 2, Finsnechta is said to have again assumed his kingdom, after twice defeating the two sons of Ruaidhri (one of whom was probably the Muiredach son of Ruaidhri, who was made King of the half of Leinster by King Aedh, as stated at the year 804); which accounts for the use of the word "accepit" in the text. The death of this turbulent prince, in Kildare, is noticed under the year 807 *infra*.

Flaiṫnia mac Cinaeḋa, rex nepotum Foilgi, iugulatur est i rraiṫ Imgain. Tir da glas ardet.

Kl. Ianair. Anno domini dccc.° uii.° Condmaċ mac Duibdaleiṫi, ab aird Maċae, subita morte perit. Occisio Artġaile mic Caṫasaiġ, regis nepotum Cruinn na n-Airṫer. Iugulatio Conaill mic Taiḋg o Chonall mac Aeḋaein i Ciunn tire. Constructio nouae ciuitatis Columbae cille hi Cenunnus. Elarius, ancorita et scriba Loċa creae, dormiuit. Luna in sanguinem uersa est. Murchad mac Flainn, ri .h. Fiḋgente, [obiit]. Gentiles comburerunt insolam Muireḋaiġ, et inuaderunt ross Comain. Bellum inter familiam Corcaiḋe et familiam cluana ferta Brendain, inter quas cedes innumerabilis hominum aeclesiasticorum et sublimium de familia Corcaiġi.

.b. Kl. Ianair. Anno domini dccc.° uiii.° Obitus Torbaiġ (alias Kalbaiċ, o Cluain cracha) scribae, abbatis Airdd Maċae. Tomas episcopus, scriba, abbas Linne Duaċal, quieuit. Faelgus princeps Cille achaid dormiuit. Slogad Muirgiussa mic Tomaltaiġ co Connachtaiḃ, la Conċobar mac n-Donnchada, corici

---

[1] *Rath-Imgain.* — Rathangan, co. Kildare.

[2] *Was burned.*—ardet. do losccaḋ, "was burned," *Four Mast.* (A.D. 800=805).

[3] *Airthera.*—A territory now partly represented by the baronies of Orior, in the co. Armagh.

[4] *Cenn-tire.*—"Head of the land." Latinized "Caput Regionis" by Adamnan, *Vit. Columba*, i. 28. See Reeves' ed. p. 57, note *u*. Cantyre, or Kintyre, in Scotland.

[5] *Cenannus.*—hi Cenunnus, A. B. Kells, co. Meath. See Reeves' *Adamnan*, p. 278. The corresponding entry in *Ann. Four Mast.* (A.D. 802) represents the church as having been razed, or demolished.

[6] *Loch-Crea.* — Otherwise called Inis-Locha-Crea; now known as Monahincha, a couple of miles to the s. e. of Roscrea, co. Tipperary.

[7] *Inis-Muiredaigh.* — Inishmurray, off the coast of the barony of Carbury, co. Sligo.

[8] *Ros-Comain.* — Roscommon, co. Roscommon. It is not easy to understand how the "Gentiles" (or Foreigners), who generally committed their depredations from the sea, or from navigable rivers, could have made their way inland as far as the town of Roscommon. Instead of 'Ross-Comain,' the *Chron. Scot.*, (A.D. 807), has Roiss-caim (in the genit. form: nomin. Ross-cam.

[9] *Corcach.*—Cork, in Munster.

the Ui-Failghi, was slain in Rath-Imgain.[1] Tir-da-glas was burned.[2]

Kal. Jan. A.D. 806. Condmach, son of Dubhdaleithe, [806.] abbot of Ard-Macha, died suddenly. The killing of Artgal, son of Cathasach, King of Ui-Cruinn of the Airthera.[3] The killing of Conall, son of Tadhg, by Conall son of Aedhan, in Cenn-tire.[4] Building of the new church of Colum-Cille in Cenannus.[5] Elarius, anchorite and scribe of Loch-Crea,[6] slept. The moon was turned into blood. Murchad, son of Flann, King of Ui-Fidhgente, [died]. Gentiles burned Inis-Muiredaigh,[7] and invaded Ros-Comain.[8] A battle between the 'family' of Corcach,[9] and the 'family' of Cluain-ferta-Brendain, among whom there was a countless slaughter[10] of ecclesiastical men, and of the noblest of the 'family' of Corcach.[9]

Kal. Jan. A.D. 807. Death of Torbach (otherwise [807] BIS Calbhach[11] from Cluain-cracha), scribe, abbot of Ard-Macha. Thomas, a bishop [and] scribe, abbot of Linn-Duachail, rested. Faelgus, abbot of Cill-achaidh,[12] 'fell asleep.' An expedition by Muirgis[13] son of Tomaltach, with the Connaughtmen, accompanied by Concobhar[14] son of Donnchad, as far as Tir-in-oenaigh.[15] And after three

---

[10] *Slaughter.*—ꞅceꝺeꞅ, for ceꝺeꞅ (cæꝺeꞅ), A., B.

[11] *Calbhach.*—The *alias* is added by way of gloss in A. But B. has obıꞇuꞅ Caluaıċ. The name of Torbach (or Calbhach) does not appear in the list of abbots or bishops of Armagh in the *Book of Leinster*, although it occurs in the other lists published by Dr. Todd from other old Irish MSS. (*St. Patrick*, 174–179). The *Ann. Four Mast.* have his obit at A.D. 807, where he is called "Torbach son of Gorman." The death of "Torbach, abbot of Ard-Macha," is also recorded in the *Chron. Scot.*, at A.D. 808.

[12] *Cill-achaidh.*—Killeigh, in the barony of Geashill, King's County.

[13] *Muirgis.*—King of Connaught.

[14] *Concobhar.*—Afterwards King of Ireland. His death is recorded at the year 832 *infra*.

[15] *Tir-in-oenaigh*, i.e. the "land of the Fair." The place here referred to was probably Tailltiu (Teltown, barony of Upper Kells, co. Meath), where a great national Fair, or assembly, was annually held on the first of August; and where, as O'Donovan alleges, "there is a hollow pointed out still called *Lug-an-aenaigh*, i.e. the "hollow of the fair." *Four Mast.* A.D. 803, note y.

t̆ir in oenaiğ, et fugerunt repente post tres noctes; et migrauit Aed̆ mac Neill in ob[u]iam eorum, et
Fol. 37aa. comburrit terminos Midi, eorumque fuga carris et hinulis simulata est. Iugulatio Cinaeda filii Concobair in campo Cobo, o Cruit̆nib̆. Finṡnec̆ta mac Ceallaiğ, rex Lagen, hi Cill dara de ficu mortuus est.

Kt. Ianair. Anno domini dccc.° uiii.° Dormitatio Toictic̆ (alias Taic̆liğ, a Tir imc̆lair), abbatis ard Mac̆ae. Bellum itir U Ceinnselaig inuicem, ubi cecidit Ceallac̆ tosac̆ mac Donngaile, ri rat̆a Etain. Occisio Dunc̆on principis Telc̆a leiss, hi fail scrine Patraicc i tiğ abaid Telc̆a liss. Baetan Cluana tuaiscirt, Cuu quiaraen secnabb Cluana, dormierunt. Ignis celestis percusit uirum in oratorio Nodan. Finbil abatisa cluano Bronaiğ mortua est. Indred̆ n-Ulad la hAed̆ mac Neill, di sarugad scrine Patraic for Dunc̆oin.

Soissit saer saeṫ laechdaiğ,
Ulaid la hAeḋ forsrubtaid,
Is and ansit fo melai
. . congail Breni brut̆mair.

---

¹ *Aedh.*—King of Ireland.

² *Cruithni.* — The Cruithni, or Picts, of Dalaraide, in the now county of Antrim. See Reeves' *Eccl. Antiqq.* 334–348.

³ *Finsnechta.*—See the note regarding Finsnechta, at the year 805 *supra.*

⁴ *Toichtech.*—The name of Toichtech does not appear in any of the old lists of abbots (or bishops) of Armagh published by Dr. Todd (*St. Patrick,* 174–182) But it occurs in the *Book of Leinster,* p 25, col. 2, among the names of the abbots of Armagh who 'rested' during the reign of Aedh Oirdnidhe, King of Ireland from 796 to 818, according to the chronology of these Annals. In recording his obit, the *Four Masters* and *Chron. Scotorum,* at A.D. 808, give him the title of "abbot of Armagh." But in the *Ann. Inisfall.,* at A.D. 795 (=808), he is merely called ferlegin, or "Lector." His name is not in Ware's list of Archbishops of Armagh.

⁵ *Taichlech.*—This is the name in B., which ignores the form "Toichtech." The clause within the parentheses is in A., not in B.

⁶ *Cellach.* — The epithet *Tosach* means "the first." The name of "Cellach, son of Dungal," appears in the list of the Kings of Ui-Cennselaigh (or South Leinster) in the *Book of Leinster,* p. 40, col. 1, as successor to Coirpre, son of Laidcnen, whose obit is given above under the year 792.

nights they fled suddenly. And Aedh,[1] son of Niall, marched against them, and burned the borders of Meath; and their flight was compared to [the flight of] goats and kids. The killing of Cinaedh son of Conebhar, in Magh-Cobho, by Cruithni.[2] Finsnechta, son of Cellach, King of Leinster, died of 'emeroids,' in Cill-dara.

Kal. Jan. A.D. 808. The 'falling asleep' of Toich- [808.]
tech[4] (alias Taichlech,[5] from Tir-Imchlair), abbot of Ard-Macha. A battle among the Ui-Cennselaigh themselves, where Cellach[6] Tosach, son of Donngal, King of Rath-Etain,[7] was slain. The killing of Dunchu, abbot of Telach-liss,[8] beside the shrine of Patrick, in the abbot's house of Telach-liss.[8] Baetan of Cluain-tuaiscert,[9] [and] Cuchiarain, vice-abbot of Cluain,[10] 'fell asleep.' Lightning killed a man in the Oratory of Nodan.[11] Finbil, abbess of Cluain-Bronaigh, died. The plundering of Ulad by Aedh, son of Niall, [in revenge] for the profanation of the shrine of Patrick against Dunchu.

Heroic[12] nobles return sadly,
Ulidians, injured by Aedh.
Where they stayed, under disgrace,
Was [at][13] . . . . of the active Brenè.[14]

---

[7] *Rath-Etain.*—The *rath*, or fort of Etan. "King of Rath-Etain" was but a bardic name for the king of South Leinster.

[8] *Telach-liss.*—Tullylisb, in the parish of the same name, barony of Lower Iveagh, co. Down. O'Donovan was wrong in identifying this place with Tullalease, in the bar. of Orrery [and Kilmore], co. Cork (*Four Mast.*, A.D. 804, note c).

[9] *Cluain-tuaiscert.*—Now Cloontuskert, in the bar. of Ballintobber South, co. Roscommon.

[10] *Cluain*; i.e. Clonmacnoise, King's County.

[11] *Oratory of Nodan.*—O'Donovan thought, and rightly, that this oratory was probably at "Disert-Nuadhan" (the "desert," or "hermitage," of Nuadu), now absurdly anglicised "Eastersnow," near Elphin, in the co. Roscommon. *Ann. Four Mast.*, A.D. 804, note f, and 1330, note p.

[12] *Heroic.*—The original of these stanzas, not in B., is in the top margin of fol. 37a in A., with a mark of reference to the proper place in the text.

[13] *[At]* . . . . .—The original seems like e congail (the first letter being mutilated by the binder), or ec congail ("at Congal," ec for ic, ac, oc, forms of the Irish preposition signifying "at").

[14] *Brenè.*—"Fretum Brene" was the latinized form of the name of the

Tinscansat imteacht chalad,
In saiṫe uallach ulach ;
Atcessa guib co n-grennaib
Oc teċt do ċeallaib Ulad.

Maelfoṫartaiġ mac Flainn, abbas Finnubraċ abae 7 ċille Moinni, obiit. Bellum la hUltu etir da mac Fiaċnae. Cairill uictor fuit. Eċaid euasit.

Kl. Ianair. Anno domini dccc.° ix.° Caṫina abbas Doimliacc, et Tigernaċ fundator daire Meilli, abbas Cille aċid, et Maelfoṫartaiġ mac Aeḋgaile princeps ind airecuil Dociaroc scriba, Caṫal mac Fiaċraċ rex Raṫo airṫir et uirorum Cul, et Eċaiḋ mac Fiaċnae rex Uloth, et Maelduin mac Donngaile equonimus aird Maċae, et Anlon mac Concobair rex Aiḋne, Macoirbb filius Neutir, et Cellaċ .h. Concodaiġ, moriuntur. Guaire abbas Glinne da loċa dormiuit. Tadgg et Flaṫnia, duo filii Muirgiusso, iugulati sunt o Luiġniḃ. Uastatio Luiġne la Muirgius. Laeċ de Luiġniḃ Conacht cecinit:—

Ro marḃ Muirgis mo macsa,
Ba romor rodomtheissi ;
Is meisi imrubart cailg
For bragait Taiḋg tar a eissi.

---

mouth of Strangford Lough, co. Down. See *Chron. Scotorum* (ed. Hennessy), p. 6, note [8], and Todd's *St. Patrick*, p. 406, n. [4].

[1] *Beaks*; i.e. the beaks of birds of prey were seen with fragments of the slain.

[2] *Finnabhar-abha.*—Fennor, barony of Lower Duleek, co. Meath.

[3] *Cill-Moinni.*—Otherwise Cill-Moena, or church of St. Moena. Now Kilmoone, in the barony of Skreen, co Meath.

[4] *Cathina.*—The name is "Caithnia in the *Ann. Four Mast.* (A.D. 805 =810).

[5] *Doimliacc.*—Duleek, co. Meath.

[6] *Daire-Meilli.*—Colgan states, (*Acta Sanctorum*, p. 796), that this establishment was founded by St. Tigernach for his mother, Mella, on the border of Logh-Melge (now Lough Melvin, in the north of the co. Leitrim). The place is not now known by this name.

[7] *Airecul-Dochiaroc.*—"Dochiaroc's Chamber." Now known as Errigal, in the parish of Errigal-Keerogue, co. Tyrone. This entry is very inaccurately given in O'Conor's edition of this Chronicle.

[8] *Rath-airthir.*—See above at A.D. 788.

They tried to go by the shore,
The proud Ulidian host.
Beaks[1] were seen, with fragments,
Coming from the churches of Ulad.

Maelfothartaigh, son of Fland, abbot of Finnabhar-abha[2] and Cill-Moinni,[3] died. A battle among the Ulaid, between two sons of Fiachna. Cairill was victor. Echaid fled.

Kal. Jan. A.D. 809. Cathina,[4] abbot of Doimliacc;[5] and Tigernach, founder of Daire-Meilli,[6] abbot of Cill-achaidh; and Maelfothartaigh, son of Aedhgal, abbot of Airecul-Dochiaroc,[7] a scribe; Cathal, son of Fiachra, King of Rath-airthir,[8] and Fera-Cul;[9] and Echaidh, son of Fiachna, King of the Ulaid; and Maelduin, son of Donngal, house-steward[10] of Ard-Macha; and Anlon, son of Conchobar, King of Aidhne; Macoirb son of Neuter, and Cellach Ua Conchodaigh, died. Guaire, abbot of Glenn-da-locha, 'fell asleep.' Tadhg[11] and Flathnia, two sons of Muirgis,[12] were slain by the Luighni.[13] Devastation of the Luighni[13] by Muirgis.[12] A hero of the Luighni of Connaught sang:— [809.]

Muirgis slew my son,
Which grieved me very much.
It was I that placed a sword
On Tadhg's neck therefor.[14]

---

[9] *Fera-Cul.*—The name of a tribe inhabiting the district comprising the present baronies of Upper and Lower Kells, co. Meath.

[10] *House-steward.* -- equonimuꞅ (for oeconomuꞅ), A. B. The *Four Mast.* have (A.D. 805) ꝼeꞃꞇíġiꞅ, a title equivalent to "custos monasterii." See Reeves' *Adamnan*, p. 365.

[11] *Tadhg.*—ꞇaeḋgg, B.

[12] *Muirgis*; i.e., Muirgis, son of Tomaltach, King of Connaught, whose death is recorded under the year 814 *infra*.

[13] *Luighni*; i.e. the Luighni of Connaught, whose territory is now represented by the barony of Leyny, in the county of Sligo.

[14] *Therefor.*—ꞇaꞃ a eiꞅꞅi. The *Four Mast.* write ꝺaꞃ éiꞅi. The original of these lines, not in B., is written in the lower margin of fol. 37*a*, in A., with a mark of reference to the place where they should be introduced in the text.

Kl. Ianair. Anno domini dccc.° x.° Nuaḋa abbas aird Maċae migrauit cu Connaċta cum lege Patricii et cum armario eius. Derbaid aige dia saṫairnn

Fol. 37ab oiniġ Tailten, cona reċt eċ na carpat, la Aeḋ mac Neill, id est, muinnter Tamlaċta dodrorbai iar sarugad termainn Tamlaċtai Maeleruain dun Neill, et postea familiae Tamlaċtae multa munera reddita sunt. Admoer ingin Aida Lagen in senectute bona mortua est. Dimman Arad, Muminensis anchorita, uitam feliciter finiuit. Tuaṫgal abbas sruiṫe Cluana mortuus est. Strages gentilium apud Ultu. Blaṫmac nepos Muirdibuir, abbas Dermaiġi, [obiit].

.b. Kl. Ianair. Anno domini dccc.° x.° i.° Flann mac Cellaiċ abbas Finnglaise, scriba et ancorita et episcopus, subita morte perit. Item Eċaiḋ episcopus et ancorita princeps Tamlaċta, quieuit. Coscraċ mac Niallġusa rex Garbrois, et Cernaċ mac Flaṫnia, rex Muġdornae mBreg, mortui sunt. Nuaḋa loċa hUamae episcopus et ancorita, abbas airrd Maċae, dormiuit. Flann mac Congalaiġ rex Ciannaċtai moritur. Oengus mac Dunlainge rex generis Artgail, Flaiṫbertaċ mac Coirpri, princeps Cille more

[1] *Nuadha . . . went.*—migrauit, A. mor (for mortuus est), B. The name of Nuadha does not occur in the *Book of Leinster* list (p. 42) of successors of St. Patrick in the abbacy of Armagh. But at p. 25 b of the same MS., "Nuado" is mentioned among the abbots of Armagh who died during the reign of "Aed Ordnide," who began to reign in A.D. 796, and died in 818, according to these Annals. The *Chron. Scot.* has Nuadha's obit at the year 812. It is entered under the next year in this chronicle.

[2] *To Connaught.*—The MSS. A. and B. have cu ċonnaċta, the first c in ċonnaċta being wrongly marked with the sign of 'infection.'

[3] *Tailtiu.*—Teltown, in the barony of Upper Kells, co. Meath.

[4] *Tamlacht*; or Tamlacht-Maelruain. Tallaght, co. Dublin.

[5] '*Termon*'; i.e., the right of sanctuary, asylum, or protection. The term was also applied to a certain portion of the lands of a monastery. In Clar. 49, Termann' is translated by "privilege."

[6] *Aedh Lagen*, i.e., "Aedh of Leinster." The death of Aedh Laigen, son of Fithcellach, King of Ui-Maine, is entered above at the year 721. In the corresponding entries in *Ann. F.M.*

Kal. Jan. A.D. 810. Nuadha, abbot of Ard-Macha, went[1] to Connaught,[2] with the 'Law' of Patrick, and with his shrine. Prevention of the celebration of the fair of Tailtiu,[3] on a Saturday, so that neither horse nor chariot arrived there, with Aedh son of Niall; i.e. the 'family' of Tamlacht[4] that prevented it, because of the violation of the 'Termon'[5] of Tamlacht-Maelruain by the Ui-Neill; and many gifts were afterwards presented to the 'family' of Tamlacht.[4] Admoer, daughter of Aedh Lagen,[6] died at a good old age. Dimman of Aradh,[7] a Munsterman, anchorite, ended his life happily. Tuathgal, a most wise abbot of Cluain,[8] died. A slaughter of Gentiles by the Ulidians. Blathmac Ua Muirdibhuir, abbot of Dermagh[9] [died]. [810.]

Kal. Jan. A.D. 811. Flann, son of Cellach, abbot of Finnglais,[10] a scribe, anchorite, and bishop, died suddenly. Echaidh, also a bishop and anchorite, abbot of Tamlacht, rested. Coscrach, son of Niallghus, King of Garbhros,[11] and Cernach, son of Flathnia, King of Mughdhorna-Bregh, died. Nuadha of Loch-Uamha,[12] bishop, anchorite, and abbot of Ard-Macha 'fell asleep.' Flann, son of Congalach, King of Cianachta, died. Oengus, son of Dunlaing, King of Cinel-Artgail, and Flaithbertach, son of Coirpre, abbot of Cill-mor-Enir,[13] died. Aedh Roen, King of Corco- [811] BIS.

---

and *Chron. Scot.* (718), the same Aedh is stated to have been the descendant of Cernach, and one of the chiefs of the Southern Ui-Neill slain in the battle of Almuin, or Hill of Allen, in the present county of Kildare. The lady Admoer would therefore seem to have survived her father about 90 years.

[7] *Aradh.*—The old name of the district now forming the northern part of the barony of Owney [*Uaithne*] and Arra, co. Tipperary.

[8] *Cluain*, i.e. Clonmacnoise, in the King's County.

[9] *Dermagh.*—Durrow, in the King's County.

[10] *Finnglais.*—Finglas, near Dublin.

[11] *Garbhros.*—The situation of this place, the name of which signifies the rough "*Ross*" (or "*wooded district*") has not been identified.

[12] *Nuadha of Loch-Uamha.*—See note [1], under previous year. According to Colgan (*Acta SS.*, p. 373), *Loch-Uamha* (the "lake of the cave") was in the district now forming the county of Leitrim.

[13] *Cill-mor-Enir.*—See note [9], p. 236 *supra*.

enir, moriuntur. Aedh roen, ri corco Baiscinn, mortuus est. Ar gennte la firu hUmhall. Ar Conmaicne la gennti. Ar Calraighi Luirgg la hU Briuin. Ar Corco-roidhe Midhe la hUa Macuais. Ar gennte la Mumain, id est, la Cobthach mac Maeleduin, ri Locha Léin. Indred in deisceird la Muirgius mac Tomaltaigh .i. ri Connacht. Lex Darii for Connachtu.

Kl. Ianair. Anno domini dccc.° x.° ii.° Conall mac Daimtigh princeps Treoit moritur. Feradhach mac Scannail scriba et sacerdos, abbas Achaidh boo, feliciter uitam finiuit. Ceallach mac Echdach, princeps Cille tóime, mortuus est. Ar nUmill la gennti, ubi ceciderunt Coscrach mac Flainndabrat, et Dunadach rex hUmill. Loigaire mac Congamna, rex generis Coirpri, moritur. Congaltach mac Eitguine, secnab Cluana ferta, moritur. Karolus rex Francorum, immo totius Europae imperator, in pace dormiuit. Lex Darii la hU Neill.

Fol. 37ba. Kl. Ianair. Anno domini dccc.° x.° iii.° Feidilmidh abbas Cille Moinni et 'moer Breg o Patraic, ancorita precipuus scribaque optimus, feliciter uitam finiuit. Tuathal filius Dudubtae, precipuus

---

[1] *Umhall.*—A district known as the "Owles," and "O'Malley's country;" and comprising the baronies of Murresk and Burrishoole, in the co. Mayo.

[2] *Conmaicni.* — Otherwise called "Conmaicni-Mara," a name now represented by "Connemara," in the W. of the co. Galway.

[3] *Corca-Roidhe.* — A tribe which gave name to the barony of Corkaree, co. Westmeath.

[4] *Ui-Mac-Uais.*—"Descendants of the sons of [Colla] Uais." A sept of the old Oirgiallian stock, from which the name of the barony of Moygoish, co. Westmeath, is derived.

[5] *Loch-Léin.*—The Irish name of the Lakes of Killarney. King of Loch-Léin was a bardic term for "King of West Munster."

[6] *South.*—Apparently the South of Connaught, Muirgis being King of Connaught at the time. Under the year 813 *infra*, a hosting by Muirgis against the Ui-Maine "of the South" is recorded.

[7] *Son of Daimtech.* — O'Conor inaccurately prints *mac Dainlig*, "son of Dainlech."

[8] *Treoit.*—Trevet, in the parish of the same name, barony of Skreen, co. Meath.

Baiscinn, died. A slaughter of Gentiles by the men of Umhall.[1] A slaughter of the Conmaicni[2] by Gentiles. A slaughter of the Calraighi of Lurg, by the Ui-Briuin. A slaughter of the Corca-Roidhe[3] of Meath by the Ui-Mac-Uais.[4] A slaughter of Gentiles by Munstermen, *i.e.*, by Cobthach son of Maelduin, King of Loch-Léin.[5] Devastation of the South[6] by Muirgis son of Tomaltach, *i.e.*, King of Connaught. The 'Law' of Dari over Connaught.

Kal. Jan. A.D. 812. Conall, son of Daimtech,[7] abbot of Treoit,[8] died. Feradhach son of Scannal, scribe and priest, abbot of Achadh-bo, ended his life happily. Cellach son of Echaid, abbot of Cill-Toma,[9] died. A slaughter of [the men of] Umhall[10] by Gentiles, in which were slain Coscrach son of Flandabrat, and Dunadach, King of Umhall. Loegaire, son of Cugamna, King of the Cinel-Coirpri, died. Congaltach, son of Etguine, vice-abbot of Cluain-ferta,[11] dies. Charles,[12] King of the Franks, or rather Emperor of all Europe, slept in peace. The 'Law' of Dari[13] by the Ui-Neill. [812.]

Kal. Jan. A.D. 813. Feidilmidh, abbot of Cill-Moinne,[14] and steward[15] of Bregh on the part of Patrick, an eminent anchorite and most excellent scribe, ended his life happily. Tuathal, son of Dudubhta,[16] a famous [813.]

---

[9] *Cill-Toma.* — Kiltoom, in the barony of Fore, co. Westmeath.

[10] *Umhall.* — See under the preceding year; note [1], last page.

[11] *Cluain-ferta;* i.e. Cluain-ferta-Brendain. Clonfert, in the barony of Longford, co. Galway.

[12] *Charles.* — Charlemagne. The correct date of Charlemagne's death is 28th Jan., 814.

[13] *'Law' of Dari.*—The imposition of this 'Law' over Connaught is the last entry under the preceding year.

[14] *Cill-Moinne.* — Kilmoone, in the barony of Skreen, co. Meath.

[15] *Steward.* — moeṙ; translated "Serjeant" in Clar. 49. The office of "steward" or "serjeant" (moeṙ) here referred to, consisted in collecting Patrick's dues, or tribute, in Bregia, by the authority of the archbishop of Armagh.

[16] *Dudubhta.* — The *Four Mast.* (A.D. 809) have the name "Dubhta" which seems the more correct form.

scriba et doctor cluana mac U Nois, dormiunt. Eitirscel mac Ceallaiġ, episcopus Glinne da Loċa et Cinaeḋ mac Ceallaiġ episcopus et abbas Trelic moer, obierunt. Maelduin episcopus, aircinneċ Eċdroma, iugulatus est. Suibne mac Moenaiġ equonimus Slane, et Gormgal mac Neill filii Fergaile, mortui sunt. Slogad la Muirgius et Forceallaċ for Uu mMaine deissoicc, ubi plurimi interfecti sunt innocentes. Forceallaċ Fobair, abbas cluana mic Nois, et Orṫanaċ abbas Cille fobric, Ronan nepos Loċḋeirc episcopus, omnes dormierunt. Bellum inter Lagenenses inuicem, ubi nepotes Cennselaiġ prostrati sunt, et filii Brain uictoriam acceperunt. Ceallach abbas Iae, finita constructione templi Cenindsa, reliquit principatum, et Diarmitius alumnus Daigri pro eo ordinatus est. Broen mac Ruadraċ satrapa Lagenarum moritur. Lex Ciarani for Cruaċna eleuata est la Muirġius. Saeṫ mor 7 tromgallra. Niall mac Aeḋa, rex nepotum Cormaicc, repentina morte moritur. Blaṫmac mac Ailgusa, abbas tire da ġlais, et Blaṫmac dalta Colggen, abbas insolae uaccae albae, obierunt.

---

1 *Trelic-mor*; i.e. "great Trelic." The place referred to is now called Trillick, and is in the barony of Omagh, co. Tyrone. Dr. O'Conor turns it into "Magni Tralee," taking Trelic as a form of the name of Tralee in Kerry. But he was wrong.

2 *Steward.* — equonimus, for oeconomus. Muiredhach, son of Uargal, called equonimus of Ia, at the year 781 *supra*, is described as prioir ("prior") in *Ann. Four M.*, at the corresponding date (A.D. 777). See Reeves' *Adamnan*, p. 365.

3 *Muirgis*; i.e. Muirgis, son of Tomaltach, King of Connaught, whose obit is the first entry under the next year.

4 *Forchellach.* — Abbot of Clonmacnoise. See next entry.

5 *Cill-Fobric.* — Or Cill-Fobrigh Probably Kilbrew, in the barony of Ratoath, co. Meath.

6 *Cenannas.* — Kells, co. Meath. The genit. form Cenindsa (nom. Cenindas) is wrong; the more usual nom. form being Cenannus (genit. Cenannsa).

7 *Diarmait.* — Diarmitius, A. Diarmicius, B.

8 *Foster-son.* — alumnus. A. alumpnus, B.

9 *Ruadhri.*—Apparently the Ruai-

scribe and doctor of Cluain-Mic-U-Nois, 'fell asleep.' Etirscel, the son of Cellach, bishop of Glenn-da-locha, and Cinaedh son of Cellach, bishop and abbot of Trelic-mor,[1] died. Maelduin, a bishop, 'herenagh' of Echdruim, was slain. Suibhne son of Moenach, steward[2] of Slane, and Gormgal, son of Niall, son of Fergal, died. A hosting by Muirgis[3] and Forchellach[4] upon the Ui-Maine of the South, when many innocent people were slain. Forchellach of Fobhar, abbot of Cluain-mic-Nois, and Orthanach abbot of Cill-Fobric,[5] [and] Ronan Ua Lochdeirc, a bishop—all 'fell asleep.' A battle among the Leinstermen themselves, wherein the Ui-Cennselaigh were overthrown, and the sons of Bran obtained the victory. Cellach, abbot of Ia, the building of the church of Cenannas[6] being finished, resigned the abbacy; and Diarmait,[7] foster-son[8] of Daigre, was ordained in his place. Broen, son of Ruadhri,[9] a satrap of the Leinstermen, died. The 'Law' of Ciaran[10] was proclaimed over Cruachan[11] by Muirgis. Great suffering and heavy diseases.[12] Niall, son of Aedh, King of the Ui-Cormaic, died suddenly. Blathmac, son of Ailgus, abbot of Tir-da-glas,[13] and Blathmac, foster-son of Colgu, abbot of Inis-bo-finne,[14] died.

---

dhri, son of Faelan, King of all the Leinstermen, whose obit is entered above at the year 784.

[10] *Of Ciaran*; i.e. St. Ciaran of Clonmacnoise. quiaραιn, A., B.

[11] *Cruachan*.—A famous plain in Roscommon, the principal fort (or *rath*) in which, Rathcroghan, near Belanagare, was anciently the chief seat of the Kings of Connaught. See above under the year 782, where the 'Law' of Patrick is stated to have been proclaimed hi Cρuachnib.

[12] *Heavy diseases*.— τροmgalaρ, "heavy disease," B.

[13] *Tir-da-glas*.—Terryglass, barony of Lower Ormond, co. Tipperary.

[14] *Inis-bo-finne*.—"Island of the white cow." There are two islands thus named, seats of ancient ecclesiastical establishments, viz., Inishbofin, an island off the coast of the barony of Murrisk, co. Mayo (see above at the year 667), and Inishbofin in Logh-Ree (an expansion of the river Shannon), which is regarded as part of the barony of Kilkenny West, co. Westmeath, and is the island here referred to.

Kl. Ianair. Anno domini dccc.° x.° iiii.° Mors Muirgiusa riġ Connact.

Ri derg daiġtheċ cen dimbaiġ,
Muirgius de Cruachain clannaiġ,
Ro ḟaiġ mac Cellaig cuirriġ
Ander din Berba bannaiġ.

Cele Iheru abbas cille Moinne [obiit]. Iugulatio Corcraiċ mic ḟinsnechti. Conall mac Neill, rex deisceirt Breg, moritur. Colman mac Neill iugulatur est a genere Conaill. Slogad la Aeḋ iarum for cenel Conaill, itorcair Rogaillneċ mac Flaiṫgusa. Maelcanaiġ ancorita Lugmaiḋ, Cellaċ mac Congaile abbas Iae, dormierunt. Orgain Cluana cremha, 7 guin duine indi, do feraib Breibne 7 do ṡil Caṫail. Focarta mac Cernaiċ, leṫ ri deisceirt Breg, mortuus est.

Fol. 37bb. .b. Kl. Ianair. Anno domini dccc.° x.° u.° Dungal mac Cuanaċ rex Rois, Tuaṫal mac Domnaill rex airter Liḟi, Irgalaċ mac Maelehumai rex corco Sogain, Conan mac Ruaḋraċ rex Britonum, Caṫal mac Artraċ rex Mugdornae, omnes defuncti sunt.

---

[1] *Cruachan.*—See the entry regarding Cruachan under last year, and the note thereon (p. 303, note [11]).

[2] *Son of Cellach.*—Probably Finsnechta son of Cellach, King of Leinster, whose obit is given at the year 807 *supra*.

[3] *Cuirrech.*—The Curragh of Kildare. The Kings of Leinster are sometimes styled "Kings of Cuirrech," in bardic compositions.

[4] *Cill-Moinne.*—Kilmoone, in the barony of Skreen, co. Meath.

[5] *Aedh*, i.e. Aedh Oirdnidhe, King of Ireland.

[6] *Lughmadh.*—Louth, in the county of Louth.

[7] *Cluain-cremha.*—See note [2], p., 216, *supra*. Dr. O'Conor, in his ed. of these Annals, makes a most extraordinary blunder regarding this entry, which is plainly written in A. And O'Donovan (*Four Mast.*, A.D. 810, note u) is scarcely more happy. It is a pity that the latter did not consult the MS. A. before constructing the note in question.

[8] *Men of Breifni*, i.e. the men of the Western Breifne, or Breifni-Ui-Ruairc (Brefny-O'Rourke).

[9] *Sil-Cathail*, i.e. the "Seed (or descendants) of Cathal." Otherwise designated by the name of Clann-Cathail. This was the tribe-name of

Kal. Jan. A.D. 814. Death of Muirgis, King of Connaught. [814.]

A fierce plundering king, without grief;
Muirgis of fruitful Cruachan;[1]
Who helped the son of Cellach[2] of Cuirrech,[3]
From the south, from the flowing Barrow.

Celi-Isa, abbot of Cill-Moinne[4], [died]. The killing of Coscrach, son of Finsnechta. Conall, son of Niall, King of the South of Bregh, died. Colman, son of Niall, was slain by the Cinel-Conaill. A hosting by Aedh[5] afterwards upon the Cinel-Conaill, in which Rogaillnech son of Flaithgus was slain. Maelcanaigh, anchorite of Lughmadh,[6] and Cellach son of Congal, abbot of Ia, 'fell asleep.' The plundering of Cluain-cremha,[7] and the killing of a man therein, by the men of Breifni[8] and the Sil-Cathail.[9] Focarta son of Cernach, half-king of the South of Bregh, died.

Kal. Jan. A.D. 815. Dungal, son of Cuanu, King of [815.] BIS. Ros;[10] Tuathal, son of Domhnall, King of Airther-Liphè;[11] Irgalach, son of Maelumhai, King of Corco-Soghain;[12] Conan,[13] son of Ruadhri, King of the Britons, and Cathal, son of Artri, King of Mughdorna—all died. Dubh-

---

a respectable branch of the great Sil-Muiredhaigh stock of Connaught, whose chief took the name of O'Flanagan, when the adoption of surnames became general. The Clann-Cathail were seated in the barony and county of Roscommon.

[10] *Ros.* — A district in the co. Monaghan, the name of which seems to be preserved in that of the parish of Magheross ("Machaire-Rois"), in the barony of Farney, in the same county.

[11] *Airther-Liphè.*—"East of *Liphè* (or Liffey)." That part of the plain of Kildare lying to the east of the River Liffey.

[12] *Corco-Soghain*, i.e. the race of Soghan *sal-bhuidhe* ("*yellow heel*"), son of Fiacha Araidhe, King of Ulster. There were several distinct septs of this race in Ireland. See O'Donovan's Hy-Many, pp. 72, 159.

[13] *Conan.*—"Cinan rex moritur." (Ann. Cambriæ, A.D. 816). The obit of "Kynon," King, is entered in the *Brut y Tywysogion*, under 817.

Dubdaleiṫi mac Tomaltaiġ dux namne, omnes perierunt. Mors Ioseṗ scribae Rois Commain. Combustio Cluana mic Nois de media ex maiore parte. Mors Suibne mic Cuanaċ, abbatis Cluana mic Nois. Ceallaċ mac Muirgissa, abbas Dromma caro, iugulatus est o Gertidiu mac Tuaṫail. Uentus magnus in Kalendis Nouembris. Bellum do maḋmaim for hU Fiaċraċ Muirsce re n-Diarmait mac Tomaltaiġ, 7 loscaḋ 7 orggain Foibrein i criċ Graicraigi, ubi plurimi occisi sunt ignobiles. Mors Caṫail mic Ailello regis nepotum Fiacraċ. Oratorium Fobair comburtum est.

Kl. Ianair. Anno domini dccc.° x.° ui.° Mors Daṫail episcopi, scribae et ancoritae, hui Duiblein. Mors Conchruiṫne scribae principis lainne Ela. Tipraiti abbas cluana ferta Brendain, Cumuscaċ mac Cernaiġ equonimus airdd Maċae, obierunt. Belliolum itir firu deisceirt Breg et Ciannachtu, i torcradar ili di ċiannachtaib. Bellum ante Caṫal mac Dunlainge, et re muinntir tiġi Mundu, for muinntir Fernand, ubi .cccc. interfecti sunt. Maeltuile abbas Benncair exulat. Maelduin mac

---

[1] *Namne.*—This place (or tribe) has not been identified. Namne may have been written in mistake for U mane (Ui-Maine, or Hy-Many, in Connaught).

[2] *All died.*— omnes perierunt. Not in B., in which the next entry is joined to this one.

[3] *Death.*—mors. Not in B.

[4] *Ros-Comain.* — Roscommon, in the county of Roscommon. The words mortui sunt are added in B., in which this entry forms part of the previous entry.

[5] *Of the half.*—de media. Not in B. The expression "*de media ex majore parte*" occurs more than once in the MS. A. text of this Chronicle. (See at the year 833 *infra*); but B. does not employ the words *de media*.

[6] *Druim-cara.* — Drumcar, in the parish of the same name, barony of Ferrard, and county of Louth. This place is called "Druim-cara of *Ard-Cianachta*" (the old name of the district now represented by the barony and name of *Ferrard*), under the year 869 *infra*.

[7] *Foibren.—Graicraighe.* See note [4], p. 222, *supra*.

[8] *Ailill.*—This Ailill was son of Innrechtach, son of the Dunchad Mursce whose death is entered at the year 681. See note [16], p. 133, *supra*.

daleithi, son of Tomaltach, chief of Namne,[1]—all died.[2] Death[3] of Joseph, scribe of Ros-Comain.[4] Burning of the greater part of the half[5] of Cluain-mic-Nois. Death of Suibhne, son of Cuanu, abbot of Cluain-mic-Nois. Cellach, son of Muirghis, abbot of Druim-cara,[6] was slain by Gertide son of Tuathal. Great wind on the Kalends of November. A battle was gained over the Ui-Fiachrach of Muirisc by Diarmait son of Tomaltach; and the burning and plundering of Foibren[7] in the district of Graicraighe,[7] where a great number of the common people were slain. Death of Cathal, son of Ailill,[8] King of the Ui-Fiachrach. The oratory of Fobhar[9] was burned.

Kal. Jan. A.D. 816. Death of Dathal Ua Duibhleni, [8. 6.]
a bishop, scribe, and anchorite. Death of Cucruithne, a scribe, abbot of Lann-Ela.[10] Tipraiti, abbot of Cluain-ferta-Brendain, Cumuscach son of Cernach, steward of Ard-Macha, died. A battle between the men of the south of Bregh and the Cianachta, wherein a great number of the Cianachta were slain. A battle by[11] Cathal,[12] son of Dunlaing, and by[11] the 'family' of Tech-Munnu,[13] against the 'family' of Ferna,[13] wherein 400 persons were slain. Maeltuile, abbot of Bennchair, lived in exile.[14] Maelduin, son of Cennfaeladh, abbot of

[9] *Oratory of Fobhar.* — Oratorium Fobair. For oratorium the *Four Mast.* (at A.D. 812), have Derṫeaċ. Fobhar is now known as Fore, in the county of Westmeath.

[10] *Lann-Ela.*—Lynally, in the parish of the same name, barony of Ballycowan, King's co.

[11] *By.*—ante. This is the ordinary Latin equivalent of Irish ria, or ré; but the Irish preposition re, with its variations ria and ra, has also the meaning of "by," and "with."

[12] *Cathal.* — King of Ui Cennselaigh, or South Leinster. His obit is entered in the *Ann. Four Mast.* under the year 817.

[13] *Tech-Munnu.*—*Ferna.* Taghmon and Ferns, in the present county of Wexford. The *Four Masters* have no notice of this battle.

[14] *Lived in exile.* — exultat (for exulat, or exsulat), A. B. The "quievit" of Maeltuile is entered at the year 819 *infra.* The *Four Masters* (at 812=816 of these Annals) record the obit of Maeltuile, and repeat it at the year 818.

Cinnḟaelaḋ princeps Raṫo boṫ, de familia Columbae cille, iugulatus est. Muinntir Coluim cille do dul i Temhair do escuine Aeda. Maelduin rex Rois moritur. Dongall mac Tuaṫail, ri Ardae, moritur. Cilleni abbas Fernann [obiit]. Fergus raṫa Luraiġ, abbas Finnglaissi, obiit. Siadal, abbas et episcopus roiss Commain, dormiuit.

Kl. Ianair. Anno domini dccc.° x.° uii.° Muireḋaċ mac Brain, leiṫri Laigen, moritur. Aig anaiccenta
Fol. 38 aa. 7 sneachta mar robatar o notlaic stellae co h-init. Imtech[t] Boinde cosaib tirmaiḃ 7 alanaile n-aband. Fon oin cumai ind loċae. Ete 7 fianlaiġi iar loċ Eċoċ. Oiss allti do ṫofunn. Solaiċ daurṫige iarmae o ċete iar loċaiḃ Eirne a tirib Connaċt hi tir hUa Crauimtain; aliaque incognita per gelu et grandines in hoc anno facta. Ceallach mac Scannlain abbas cille Foibrig, Cernaċ mac Congalaiġ rex Cnoḋbai, moriuntur. Cuanu abbas Lugmaiḋ, co scrin Moċtai, do dula a tire Muman for longais. Artri airchinnech aird Maċae, co scrin Patraicc, do dul a Connaċta. Aeḋ mac Neill co sluagaiḃ co Dun

---

[1] *Rath-both.*—Now Raphoe, the seat of an ancient bishopric, in the county of Donegal. Regarding the foundation of the monastery of Raphoe, see Reeves' *Adamnan*, p. 280.

[2] *Temhair.*—Tara, co. Meath.

[3] *To curse Aedh*, i.e. Aedh Oirdnidhe, King of Ireland. do escmine (for do escuine, "to curse") A., B. The cause of this 'cursing,' or excommunication, of Aedh may have been for his invasion of Cinel-Conaill as recorded above under the year 814, or for complicity in the murder of the abbot Maelduin. See Reeves' *Adamnan*, p. 389, note x.

[4] *Ros.*—Otherwise written "Fera (or Fir) Rois"; *i e.*, "Men of Ros." See note on the name, under the year 815; p. 305.

[5] *Ard.*—Ard-Cianachta, a district in the co. Louth, now represented by the barony of Ferrard.

[6] *Finnglais*—Finglas, near Dublin.

[7] *Epiphany.*—notlaic stellae, "Christmas of the star," A., B. The *Four Mast.* (A.D. 815) have ó nottlaic, "from Christmas," as in Clar. 49.

[8] *Loch-Echach.*—Lough Neagh.

[9] *Roofing.*—Solaiċ. This word does not occur in any of the ordinary Irish Glossaries. It is rendered by "timber" in Clar. 49, in which the translation of the full entry is loosely

Rath-both,[1] of the 'family' of Colum-Cille, was slain. The 'family' of Colum-Cille went to Temhair,[2] to curse Aedh.[3] Maelduin, King of Ros,[4] died. Donngal, son of Tuathal, King of Ard,[5] died. Cilleni, abbot of Ferna, [died]. Fergus of Rath-Luraigh, abbot of Finnglais,[6] died. Siadal, abbot and bishop of Ros-Comain, 'fell asleep.'

Kal. Jan. A.D. 817. Muiredhach son of Bran, half-king of Leinster, died. Unprecedented frost and great snow from Epiphany[7] to Shrovetide. The Boyne and other rivers were traversed with dry feet, and the lakes in like manner. Herds and multitudes [went] upon Loch-Echach,[8] and wild deer were hunted. The roofing[9] of an oratory was afterwards [brought] by carriage-way[10] across the lakes of Erne, from the lands of Connaught to the land of Ui-Cremthainn; and other unprecedented things were done in this year through frost and hail. Cellach son of Scannlan, abbot of Cill-Foibrigh,[11] [and] Cernach son of Congalach, King of Cnodhba,[12] died. Cuanu, abbot of Lughmadh,[14] went in exile to the land of Munster, with the shrine of Mochta.[15] Artri, superior[16] of Ard-Macha, went to Connaught, with the shrine of Patrick. Aedh,[17] son of Niall, [went] with [817.]

---

made. But the construction of the original is very faulty.

10 *Carriage-way.* — o ċeṫe. ceṫe is explained by conaiṗ, ſeṫ, a "road," "way," in the *Félire of Oengus* (Laud copy), at Dec., 20. See Stokes' ed., p. clxxix.

11 *Cill-Foibrigh.*— See note 12, p. 263 *supra.*

12 *Cnodhba.*—See note 4, p. 266 *supra.*

13 *Cuanu.*—His obit is entered at the year 824 *infra.*

14 *Lughmadh.*—Louth, in the co. Louth.

15 *Mochta.*—The St. Mochta, abbot or bishop of Louth, whose obit is recorded at the year 534 *supra.*

16 *Superior.* —aiṗ̄ (for aiṗchinnech), A. B. In the entry of the obit of Artri, at A.D. 832 *infra* (where see note), Artri is described as abbot (abbaſ) of Ard-Macha. Regarding the meaning of the title aiṗchinnech, see Reeves' *Adamnan*, p. 364, note m, and O'Donovan's *Ann. Four Mast.*, A.D. 1179, note o. In the corresponding entry in the *Chron. Scotorum* (A.D. 818), Artri is called ṗṗinceṗſ ("abbot" or "superior").

17 *Aedh*; i.e., Aedh Oirdnidhe, monarch of Ireland.

Cuaer co ro rand Laigniu itir da huae Brain. Airchinnech Cille moire Enir do sarugad, 7 Dubinnrecht a seccnap do guin ar a incaiḃ, la Laiġniu. Orggain coccae du Cellach mac Foġertaiċ for Concobar mac Muireḋaiċ .i. mac riġ Laigen. Bellum actum est in regione Delḃnae Nodot, .i. caṫ Foraṫ, ubi nepotes Mani cum rege eorum id est Caṫal mac Murcaḋo, et alii plurimi nobiles, prostrati sunt. Reges nepotum Briuin, id est Diarmait mac Tomaltaiġ 7 Maelcoṫaiġ filius Foġertaiġ, uictores erant. Rectaḃra nepos Andola, abbas Daminnsi, moritur. Cluen mac Nois iterum .xii. Kalendas Nouembris arsit tertia ex parte sui.

Kt. Ianair. Anno domini dccc.° x.° uiii.° Uastatio Laigen la hAed mac Neill .i. tir Cualann usque Glenn duorum stagnorum. Mors Aeḋa mic Neill iuxta uadum duarum uirtutum in campo Conaille. Belliolum inter genus Eugain 7 genus Conaill, in quo cecidit Maelbresail mac Murcaḋo rex generis Conaill. Murcaḋ mac Maeleduin fuit uictor. Belliolum itir Ultu inuicem, in quo cecidit Cairell filius Fiaċnae, et Muireḋaċ mac Eċaċ uictor fuit. Catal mac Dunlainge rex nepotum Cennselaig et secnap Fernann moritur. Crunnmael mac Ailello princeps

---

[1] *Dun-Cuair.* — See above, at the year 804.

[2] *Superior.* — airchinnech. See note 16, p. 309.

[3] *Cill-mor-Enir.*—See note [8], p. 212, *supra*.

[4] *Fought.*—actum est, A. gestum est, B.

[5] *Delbhna-Nodot.*—Delḃnae Lodot, A. B. But the proper form is Delḃna Nodot (= D. Nuadat), the ancient name of a district between the rivers Shannon and Suck, in the southern part of the co. Roscommon. See O'Donovan's ed. of *Leabhar na g-ceart*, p. 105, note n.

[6] *Many.*—plurimi, A. multi, B.

[7] *Diarmait.*—The Diarmait son of Tomaltach, King of Connaught, whose obit is entered at the year 832 *infra*.

[8] *Daiminis.*—Devenish, in Lough Erne, in Fermanagh county.

[9] *Of the Kalends.*—Kt. dis, A. Kt., B.

[10] *Aedh* —Monarch of Ireland.

[11] *Ath-da-ferta.* — iuxta uadum duarum uirtutum (Mirabilium,

armies to Dun-Cuair,[1] when he divided Leinster between two grandsons of Bran. The superior[2] of Cill-mor-Enir[3] was profaned, and its vice-abbot, Dubhinnrecht, was wounded whilst under his protection, by the Leinstermen. A battle—slaughter by Cellach, son of Fogartach, over Conchobar son of Muiredhach, *i.e.*, son of the King of Leinster. A battle was fought[4] in the country of Delbhna-Nodot,[5] *i.e.* the battle of Forath, wherein the Ui-Maine, with their king, *i.e.* Cathal son of Murchadh, and many[6] other nobles, were overthrown. The Kings of the Ui-Briuin, viz., Diarmait[7] son of Tomaltach, and Maelcothaigh son of Fogartach, were victors. Rechtabhra Ua Andola, abbot of Daiminis,[8] dies. Cluain-mic-Nois was again burned on the 12th of the Kalends[9] of November—the third part of it.

Kal. Jan. A.D. 818. The wasting of Leinster by [818.]
Aedh[10] son of Niall, *i.e.* the country of Cualann as far as Glenn-da-locha. Death of Aedh[10] son of Niall, near Ath-da-ferta[11] in Magh-Conaille. A battle between the Cinel-Eoghain and Cinel-Conaill, in which Maelbresail son of Murchadh, King of the Cinel-Conaill,[12] was slain. Murchadh,[13] son of Maelduin, was victor. A battle among the Ultonians themselves, in which Cairell[14] son of Fiachna was slain, and Muiredhach son of Echaidh was victor. Cathal son of Dunlaing, King of Ui-Cennselaigh, and vice-abbot of Ferna,[15] died. Crunnmael son of

---

O'Conor); over which an old hand has written aᵹ aċ ꝺa ꝼeꞃτa (a literal translation), in A.

[12] *Cinel-Conaill.*—ᵹenıꞃıꞅ Con-aıll, A.

[13] *Murchadh.*—King of the Cinel-Eoghain, or descendants of Eoghan, son of Niall Nine-hostager, who were otherwise known as the Ui-Neill of the North.

[14] *Cairell.*—According to a statement in the *Book of Leinster* (p. 41, col. 3), Cairell (or Cairill, as the name is there written) reigned nine years, and was slain in a battle between the Ulaid and the Ui-Echach-Cobha, fought at a place called Lapast, in Carn-Cantain. But the situation of Lapast, or of Carn-Cantain, is not now known.

[15] *Ferna.*—Ferns, in the county of Wexford.

Doimliacc, et Muiredaċ filius Crunnmail abbas Disirt Ternoc, defuncti sunt. Congalaċ mac Fergusa
Fol. 38 ab. rex Cul moritur. Cengciges airdd Maċae cen aigi cen tucbail scrine, 7 cumusc ann i torċair mac Eċdaċ mic Fiaċnae. Foṫud foṫnae mortuus est.

b. Kl. Ianair. Anno domini dccc.° x.° ix.° Dalaċ mac Conġusa, princeps Doimliacc, mortuus est. Slogad la Murchad do druim ind eiċ co n-Oib Neill in tuaiscirt. Concobar co n-Oib Neill in deiscirt andes, 7 co Laigniḃ, donec deus eos separauit per suam magnam potentiam. Custantin mac Fergusa, rex Fortrenn, moritur. Maeltuile abbas Bennċair quieuit. Feiḋlimiḋ mac Criṁtain accepit regnum Caissil.

Kl. Ianair. Anno domini dccc.° xx.° Crunnmael mac Oḃrain, abbas Cluana iraird, obiit. Comulf rex Saxonum moritur. Orggan Etir o genntib; praed mor di mnaiḃ do brid ass. Ceannfaelad mac Rumain, scriba et episcopus et ancorita, abb Aṫo truim, dormiuit. Slogad la Conċobur mac n-Donn-

---

[1] *Daimliag.*—Duleek, co. Meath.

[2] *Disert-Ternóc.*—The "desert," or hermitage, of Ternóc. In the *Martyr. of Donegal*, at Feb 8, there is mention of Ternócc, an anchorite, whose place was on the west of the river Barrow. But the exact situation is not indicated.

[3] *Son of Fergus.*—The *Four Mast.* (at A.D. 817) have mac Ferġaile ("son of Fergal.")

[4] *Cul*; i.e. Fir-(or Fera-)Cul; otherwise called Fera-Cul-Bregh, a territory anciently comprising the barony of Kells, co. Meath. See note [5], p. 202 *supra*, and O'Donovan's *Ann. F. M.*, A.D. 693, note p.

[5] *Whitsuntide in Ard-Macha.*—Cengciges airdd Maċae (literally "Whitsuntide of Armagh"). This entry is not found in the other Annals; not certainly in the *Ann. of the Four Masters*, the compilers of which studiously suppress notices of events calculated to reflect, in their opinion, on the character of churchmen.

[6] *Elevation of a shrine.*—tucbail scrine. Some Whitsuntide ceremony, or procession, at Armagh, of which no notice occurs elsewhere, as far as the Editor is aware.

[7] *Fothud of Fothan.*—Fothud (or Fothad) of Fahan, in the barony of Inishowen, co. Donegal. See note [6], p. 289, *supra*.

[8] *Daimliag.*—Duleek, co. Meath.

[9] *Murchadh;* i.e. Murchadh son of Maelduin, King of Cinel-Eoghain.

Ailill, abbot of Daimliag,[1] and Muiredhach son of Crunnmael, abbot of Disert-Ternóc,[2] died. Congalach, son of Fergus,[3] King of Cul,[4] died. Whitsuntide in Ard-Macha[5] without celebratiou, and without the elevation of a shrine;[6] and a disturbance there, in which the son of Echaid, son of Fiachna, was killed. Fothud of Fothan[7] died.

Kal. Jan. A.D. 819. Dalach, son of Congus, abbot of [819.] BIS
Damliag,[8] died. A hosting by Murchadh[9] to Druim-ind-eich,[10] with the Ui-Neill of the North. Conchobar[11] [came] from the South, with the Ui-Neill of the South, and the Leinstermen, until God separated them by His great power. Custantin, son of Fergus, King of Fortrenn,[12] died. Maeltuile, abbot of Bennchair, rested. Fedhlimidh, son of Cremthan, obtained the kingdom of Cashel.

Kal. Jan. A.D. 820. Crunnmael son of Odhran, abbot [820.]
of Cluain-Iraird, died. Comulf,[13] King of the Saxons, died. Plundering of Etar,[14] by Gentiles; a great prey of women being taken therefrom. Cennfaeladh son of Ruman, scribe, bishop, and anchorite of Ath-truim,[15] 'fell asleep.' A hosting by Conchobar[16] son of Donnchad to

---

[10] *Druim-ind-eich.* — The "ridge (or back) of the horse." O'Donovan suggests (*Four Mast.*, A.D. 818, note x), that this is probably the place called Drimnagh, near Dublin.

[11] *Conchobar.*—King of Ireland at the time.

[12] *Fortrenn.*—Pictland. See note [8], p. 118 *supra.*

[13] *Comulf.*—This name may be also read comulf, as Dr. O'Conor prints it from MS., B. The person whose 'moritur' is here recorded was evidently Cenwulf, King of the Mercians, whose obit is entered in the *Anglo-Saxon Chron.* at the year 819, and who was succeeded by his brother Ceolwulf. See Lappenberg's *History of England*, Vol. I., p. 291.

[14] *Etar.* — This was the ancient name of the peninsula of Howth, to the N.E. of Dublin. The Hill of Howth is still called *Benn-Etair*, the "summit of Etar," by those who speak the native language. Dr. O'Conor represents orggan Etir by *Orggan e tir*, which he most inaccurately translates "Devastatio Regni."

[15] *Ath-truim.*—The "Ford of the Elder-tree." Trim, on the Boyne, in the county of Meath.

[16] *Conchobar* —King of Ireland. O'Flaherty refers the commencement

chada co h-ard achadh Sleibe fuait. Uastatio na n-Airther corice Emain Machae.

Kl. Ianair. Anno domini dccc.° xx.° i.° Macriaghoil nepos Magleni, scriba et episcopus, abbas Biror, periit. Aig anaicenta, 7 ruireset inna muire 7 inna locha 7 inna aibni, co ructa graige 7 eti 7 fedman iarmaibh. Sloiged la Murchadh mac Mailedúin co feraib ind fochli corici aird m-Brecan. Eludh iarum do feraib Breg cuice .i. Diarmait mac Neill co sil Aedha slane, co rugiallsat ic druim Ferguso do Murchadh. Indred fer m-Bregh la Concobar mac n-Donnchadha, condersidh ecc Gualait. Indred deisceird Breg leis aitherrach in Kalendis Nouembris, co torchair sluagh dimor leiss de feraib deisceirt Bregh, 7 co ru giallsat hui Cernaigh ar eicin. Mors Forbusaich
Fol. 38 ba. abbatis Achaidh bó Cainnig. Cumuscach mac Tuathail, rex airde Ciannachta, iugulatur est la Murchadh. Bellum Tarbgi inter Conachta inuicem. Nepotes Briuin prostrati sunt, plurimi nobiles interfecti sunt erga duces, id est, Dunchad mac Móinaigh et Gormgal mac Duncado. Nepotes Mani uictores erant, et Diarmait mac Tomaltaigh. Strages uirorum

---

of Conchobar's reign to the year 819. *Ogygia*, p. 433. His death is recorded under the year 832 *infra*.

[1] *Ard-achadh of Sliabh Fuaid.*—The name *Ard-achadh* would be Anglicised 'High-field.' *Sliabh-Fuaid*, the 'Hill of Fuad,' was the ancient name of a hill near the town of Newtown-Hamilton, in the county of Armagh, according to O'Donovan. *Four Mast.*, A.D. 819, note b.

[2] *Airthera.*—See note [7], p. 282, *supra*.

[3] *Macriaghoil.*—Supposed to be the scribe of the beautiful copy of the Gospels known as the Gospels of MacRegol, preserved in the Bodleian Library, Oxford. See O'Conor's *Proleg. ad Annales*, Part II., p. cxlii.

[4] *Murchadh.* — Chief of Cinel-Eoghain.

[5] *Ard Brecain.* — Ardbraccan, co. Meath.

[6] *Druim-Ferguso.* — The "Ridge (or Long Hill) of Fergus." The situation of this place is not known at present.

[7] *At Gualat.*—ecc gualait. The situation of Gualat has not been identified.

[8] *Ui-Cernaigh*; i.e. the "descendants of Cernach." A branch of the

Ard-achadh of Sliabh-Fuaid.[1] Devastation of the Airthera[2] as far as Emhain-Macha.

Kal. Jan. A.D. 821. Macriaghoil[3] Ua Magleni, a scribe and bishop, abbot of Biror, died. Unusual frost; and the seas, and lakes, and rivers were frozen, so that droves, and cattle, and burdens, could be conveyed over them. A hosting by Murchadh[4] son of Maelduin, with the men of the North, as far as Ard-Brecain.[5] The men of Bregh thereupon went secretly to him, viz., Diarmait son of Niall, with the race of Aedh Slanè, and gave hostages to Murchadh at Druim-Ferguso.[6] The plundering of the men of Bregh by Conchobar,[4] son of Donnchadh, when he rested at Gualat.[7] The plundering of the South of Bregh by him again, on the Kalends of November, when a great multitude of the men of South Bregh were slain by him, and the Ui-Cernaigh[8] submitted through compulsion. Death of Forbasach, abbot of Achadh-bó-Cainnigh.[9] Cumuscach son of Tuathal, King of Ard-Cianachta,[10] was slain by Murchadh.[11] The battle of Tarbga among the Connaughtmen themselves. The Ui-Briuin were overthrown; a great many nobles were slain opposite[12] their leaders, viz., Dunchadh son of Moenach, and Gormgal son of Dunchadh. The Ui-Maini were victors, and Diarmait[13] son of Tomaltach. A slaughter of the men of Breifne, opposite[12] their King, [821.]

powerful sept of Sil-Aedha Slanè or "Race of Aedh Slanè" (see under A.D. 603 *supra*), who derived their tribe-name from Cernach (ob. A.D. 663 *supra*), son of Diarmait, son of Aedh Slanè (King of Ireland).

[9] *Achadh-bó-Cainnigh.*—The "Field of (St.) Cainnech's cows." Now Aghaboe, in the parish of the same name, Queen's county.

[10] *Ard-Cianachta.*—See note [11], p. 137 *supra*.

[11] *Murchadh.*—Murchadh son of Maelduin, chief of the Cinel-Eoghain; referred to in the 3rd entry for this year.

[12] *Opposite.*—eṗ̇ga, B. eṗgo, A.

[13] *Diarmait son of Tomaltach.*—His obit is given at the year 832 *infra*, where he is described as King of Connaught. But in the list of Kings of that province, contained in the *Book of Leinster* (p. 41, col. 1) where the name of Diarmait occurs next after that of Muirghis son of Tomaltach

breibne erga regem suum, id est, Maelduin mac Eċtgaile, la cenel Feiḋilmṫo. Roiniuḋ for firu airde Ciannachta re Cumuscaċ mac Congalaiġ, ubi ceciderunt Eudus mac Tigernaiġ et alii multi. Euċu nepos Tuaṫail, ancorita et episcopus, abbas Lugmaid, dormiuit. Roiniuḋ re n-oaib Garbain 7 Cuircniu 7 Fellu for Delbnai.

Kl. Ianair. Anno domini dccc.° xx.° ii.° Dermait mac Donnchada, abbas Roiss eċ, obiit. Dubdacriċ mac Maeletoli, abbas Cille achaid, dormiuit. Feċnusaċ Loċa cendin, episcopus et ancorita, pausauit. Conaing mac Congail, rex Teṫbae, moritur. Lex Patricii for Mumain la Feidlimṫe mac Cremtain, et la hArtriġ mac Concobair (.i. escop ard Maċa)- Ronan abbas cluana mic Nois reliquit principatum suum. Aṫri do ḋenum do Murċaḋ mac Maeleduin, la Niall mac Aeḋo 7 la cenel n-Euġain. Genntiles inuaserunt Bennċur mor. Galinne na m Bretan

(ob. 814 *supra*), his father's name is stated to have been Tadc, who was the father of Tomaltach, father of Muirgis. From which it would appear that Diarmait was the uncle of Muirgis, his predecessor in the kingship of Connaught.

[1] *Ard-Cianachta.* — See note [11], p. 137 *supra*.

[2] *Euchu.* — This name is written Eocha by the *Four Mast.* (A.D. 820).

[3] *Anchorite.*—ancorrita, A.

[4] *Lughmadh.*—Louth, in the county of Louth.

[5] *Cuircni.*—A tribe descended from Corc, son of Lugaid, King of Munster in the 5th century; which gave name to the district of Cuircne, now represented by the barony of Kilkenny West, co. Westmeath, and was for some centuries known as "Dillon's Country."

[6] *Fella.*—A tribe inhabiting a territory bordering on the expansion of the Shannon called Loch-Ree, probably on the western side of the lake. O'Donovan identifies the territory of the Fella with Tuath-n-Ella. *Four Masters*, A.D. 927, note e.

[7] *Delbhna.*—The people here referred to were evidently that branch of the great tribe of the Delbhna (descended from Lugaidh Delbhaedh, son of Cas, ancestor of the Dal-Cais of Thomond), which occupied, and gave name to, the territory of Delbhnamor, now the barony of Delvin, co. Westmeath.

[8] *Loch-Cendin.*—This name is now corruptly represented by "Lough-Kinn," the name of a lake near Abbeylara, in the county of Longford.

[9] *Tethba.*—A territory comprising the most of the eastern part of the

i.e. Maelduin son of Echtgal, by the Cinel-Feidhilmtho. A victory over the men of Ard-Cianachta,[1] by Cumuscach son of Congalach, in which fell Eudus son of Tigernach, and a great many others. Euchu[2] Ua Tuathail, an anchorite[3] and bishop, abbot of Lughmadh,[4] 'fell asleep.' A victory by the Ui-Garbhain, and the Cuircni,[5] and the Fella,[6] over the Delbhna.[7]

Kal. Jan. A.D. 822. Dermait, son of Donnchad, abbot of Ross-ech, died. Dubhdacrich, son of Maeltoli, abbot of Cill-achaidh, 'fell asleep.' Sechnasach of Loch-Cendin,[8] a bishop and anchorite, rested. Conaing son of Congal, King of Tethba,[9] died. The 'Law' of Patrick[10] [established] over Munster by Feidhlimidh[11] son of Crimthan, and by Artri son of Conchobar (*i.e.*, bishop[12] of Ard-Macha). Ronan, abbot of Cluain-mic-Nois, resigned his government. Murchadh, son of Maelduin, was deposed[13] by Niall[14], son of Aedh, and the Cinel-Eoghain. The Gentiles invaded Bennchair the Great[15]. Gailinne[16] [822.]

county of Longford, and the western half of the co. Westmeath. It was divided by the River Inny into North and South Tethba (or Teffia). According to the *Táin bo Cualnge* story in *Lebor na hUidre* (p. 57, a), Granard (in the present county of Longford) was in *Tethba tuascirt*, or Northern Teffia. See O'Donovan's ed. of *O'Dubhagain*, note [35].

[10] *'Law' of Patrick.*—See note [1], p. 234 *supra.*

[11] *Feidlimidh.* —King of Munster. His obit is given at A.D. 846 *infra.*

[12] *Bishop.*—See under the year 817 *supra*, where Artri is described as *airchinnech* of Armagh. The original of this clause, which is not in B., is added in *al. man.* in A. In the entry recording his death at the year 832 *infra*, Artri is described as "abbot" of Armagh.

[13] *Murchadh . . . was deposed.*—The original is αϲρι το ᵭenum do Muρċαᵭ; lit. "an ex-king was made of Murchadh."

[14] *Niall.*—Niall Caille, son of Aedh Oirdnidhe. The beginning of his reign as King of Ireland is recorded at the year 832 *infra.*

[15] *Bennchair the Great.*—Bangor, in the co. Down.

[16] *Gailinne.* — Now Gallen, in the barony of Garrycastle, King's county. The church, or monastery, was called "*Gailinne na mBretan* ("Gailinne of the Britons") from a tradition which attributed its foundation to a Saint Mochonóg, son of a king of Britain (or Wales). See *Mart. Donegal*, at Dec. 19, and Shearman's *Loca Patriciana*, p. 156. Dr. O'Conor blunders greatly (note [1], Rer. Hib. Script., Vol. IV., p. 204) in thinking

exustum est o Feiḋlimtiḋ, cum tota habitatione sua, et cum oratorio. Tene di nim forsa forut n-abbaḋ i n-ard Maċae, conidroloiscc.

Kt. Ianair. Anno domini dccc.° xx.° iii.° Niall mac Fergusa dux nepotum Fornndain moritur. Orggain Benncair ac airtiu o gentib, 7 coscraḋ a derṫaigi, 7 reilgi Comġaill do croṫaḋ as a scrin.

Biḋ fir fir,
Do ḋeoin airdriġ ina riġ;
Berṫair mo ċnama cen ċron
O Benncor baġa d'Oentrob.

Bellum inter uiros Teṫbae inuicem, id est bellum Findubraċ, in quo ceciderunt Aeḋ mac Fogertaiġ et alii multi. Ross Commain exustum est magna ex parte. Bellum inter Connaċta inuicem, in quo ceciderunt plurimi. Belliolum inter Dunchad et Cumuscaċ duos reges Ciannachtae, in quo multi interfecti sunt. Dunchad uictor fuit; Cumuscaċ
Fol. 38 bb. euasit. Eochaid mac Bressail, ri dal Araide in tuaiscert, iugulatus est a sociis suis. Spelan mac Sloġaḋaiġ, rex Conaille Muirṫemni, moritur. Eitgal Sceiligg a gentibus raptus est, et cito mortuus est fame et siti.

Kt. Ianair. Anno domini dccc.° xx.° iiii.° Cuanu Lugmaiḋ, sapiens et episcopus, dormiuit. Diarmait huae Aeḋa roin, anċorita et religionis doctor totius

---

"Gailinne" the same as "Gallovigia" (or Galloway).

[1] *Burned.*—exarsum, apparently corrected to exussum, A.; exhaustum, B. The *Chron. Scot.*, which has a corresponding entry at A.D. 823 (the correct year), has exussum.

[2] *Fedhlimidh.*—King of Munster. His obit is given at A.D. 846 *infra.*

[3] *Bennchair.* — Bangor, in the co. Down.

[4] *True.*—The original of these lines, not in MS. B., is in the lower margin of fol. 38*b* in A., with a mark to signify the place where it should be introduced into the text. It is stated in the *Ann. Four Mast*, at A.D. 822, that the composer was Saint Comghall himself.

[5] *Oentrobh.*—Antrim, in the county of Antrim.

of the Britons was burned[1] by Fedhlimidh,[2] with all its dwelling-place, and with the oratory. Fire from heaven fell on the Abbot's mansion in Ard-Macha, and burned it.

Kal. Jan. A.D. 823. Niall son of Fergus, chief of the Ui-Forindain, died. The plundering of Bennchair[3] in the Ards, by Foreigners, and the spoiling of its oratory; and the relics of Comghall were shaken out of their shrine. [823.]

'Twill be true, true,[4]
By the will of the supreme King of Kings,
My stainless bones shall be taken
From beloved Bennchair to Oentrobh.[5]

A battle among the men of Tethba[6] themselves, *i.e.* the battle of Finnabhair,[7] in which Aedh son of Fogartach, and many others, were slain. Ros-Comain was in great part burned. A battle among the Connaughtmen themselves, wherein a great many were slain. A battle between Dunchad and Cumuscach, two Kings of Cianachta, in which many persons were slain. Dunchad was victor; Cumuscach escaped.[8] Eochaid[9] son of Bressal, King of Dal-Araidhe of the North, was killed by his confederates.[10] Spelan son of Sloghadhach, King of Conaille-Muirthemnè, died. Etgal of Scelig[11] was carried off by Gentiles, and died soon after of hunger and thirst.

Kal. Jan. A.D. 824. Cuanu of Lughmadh, a wise man and bishop, 'fell asleep.' Diarmait, grandson of Aedh Roin, anchorite[12] and doctor of religion of all [824.]

---

[6] *Tethba.* — See note [9] under the year 822.

[7] *Finnabhair.* — Fennor, in the parish of Rathconnell, co. Westmeath.

[8] *Escaped.*— euαγγιτ, A. euαγιτ, B.

[9] *Eochaid.* — See *Book of Leinster*, p. 41, col. 5.

[10] *By his confederates.*—α γοcιγ γuιγ, A.

[11] *Scelig*; or *Scelig-Michil* ("St. Michael's Scelig"). The "Great Skellig" island, off the south-west coast of the county of Kerry. See Todd's *Cogadh Gaedhel re Gallaibh* (Introd.), p. xxxviii, note [1], and p. 223, note [1].

[12] *Anchorite.*—ancoριτα, B.

Hiberniae, obiit; et Cuimneċ abbas Finnglaissi, Aedan abbas Taṁlaċtae, Flannabra princeps Maige bile moriuntur. Colman filius Ailello, abbas Slane et aliarum ciuitatum in Francia et in Hibernia, periit. Fergal mac Caṫrannaiġ, rex Loċa Riaċ, moritur. Maelbresail mac Ailello Cobo, rex Dal Araide, moritur. Magna pestilentia in Hibernia insola senioribus et pueris et infirmis; magna fames et defectio panis. Oenġus mac Maeleduin rex Loċa Gabor moritur. Slat Duin leṫglaisi du genntib. Loscuḋ Maiġi bile cona derṫigib o ġentiḃ. Roiniuḋ imMaiġ inis re.n-Ultaiḃ for gentib, in quo ceciderunt plurimi. Roiniuḋ for Osraigi re n-genntiḃ. Fland mac Forceallaig, abbas Lis moir, in pace dormiuit. Lex Patricii for teora Connaċta la Artriġ mac Concobair (.i. episcopus ard Maċa). Orgain innsi Daimle o genntib. Fallomon mac Fogertaiċ iugulatus est a fratre suo qui nominatur Ceallaċ. Martre Blaiṁicc mic Flainn o genntib in hI Coluim Cille.

Kl. Ianair. Anno domini dccc.° xx.° u.° Diarmait mac Neill, rex deiscert Breġ, moritur. Niall mac Diarmata, rex Miḋe [obiit]. Mac Loingsiġ, abbas

---

[1] *Of all Ireland.* — tocius Hibernie, B.

[2] *Magh-Bilè.* — See note [8], p. 80 *supra.*

[3] *Pestilence.* — pestilencia, B. This entry is more briefly given in B., thus:—Magna pestilencia in hibernia 7 magna fames panis.

[4] *Loch-Gabhor.*—See note [7], p. 263 *supra.*

[5] *Dun-lethglaise.*—Downpatrick, in the present county of Down.

[6] *Over Gentiles.*— for gennti, A. for gentib, B.

[7] *The 'Law' of Patrick.*—See note [11], p. 281 *supra.*

[8] *Three divisions of Connaught.*—See note [13], p. 269 *supra.*

[9] *Artri.*—See above under the year 817, where Artri is described as airchinnech ("herenagh") of Armagh.

[10] *Bishop.* — The original of this clause, which is not in B., is added in *al. man.* in A., over the name Artri.

[11] *Inis-Daimhle.*—The situation of this island has not been satisfactorily identified. The *Martyr. of Donegal,* at July 4, states that it was *between* Ui-Cennselaigh [the co. Wexford] and the Deisi [the baronies of Decies in the south of the co Waterford.]

Ireland,[1] died; and Cuimnech abbot of Finnglais, Aedhan abbot of Tamlacht, Flannabra abbot of Magh-Bilè,[2] died. Colman son of Ailill, abbot of Slane, and of other churches in France and Ireland, died. Fergal son of Cathrannach, King of Loch-riach, died. Maelbresail, son of Ailill of Cobha, King Dal-Araidhe, died. A great pestilence[3] in the island of Ireland among the old people, children, and infirm; a great famine and failure of bread. Oenghus son of Maelduin, King of Loch-Gabhor,[4] died. Plundering of Dun-lethglaise[5] by Gentiles. Burning of Magh-Bilè, with its oratories, by Gentiles. A victory in Magh-inis by the Ulidians over Gentiles,[6] in which a great many were slain. A victory over the Osraighi by Gentiles. Fland son of Forcellach, abbot of Lis-mor, slept in peace. The 'Law' of Patrick[7] [was promulgated] over the three divisions of Connaught,[8] by Artri[9] son of Conchobar (*i.e.* bishop[10] of Ard-Macha). Plundering of Inis-Daimhle[11] by Gentiles. Falloman, son of Fogartach, was slain by his brother, who was named Cellach. Martyrdom of Blamacc,[12] son of Flann, by Gentiles, in I-Coluim-Cille.

Kal. Jan. A.D. 825. Diarmait, son of Niall, King of the South of Bregh, died. Niall,[13] son of Diarmait, King of Midhe, [died]. MacLoingsigh,[14] abbot of Ard-Macha, died [825.]

Dr. Todd (*Cogadh Gaedhel re Gallaibh*, Introd., p. xxxvii., note [2]), would identify it with *Little Island* in the river Suir, near Waterford. See O'Donovan's *Four Masters*, Index Locorum, *sub voce*; and *Chron. Scotorum* (ed. Hennessy), p. 130, note [4].

[12] *Blamacc.*—The proper form of the name is "Blathmac." See Reeves' *Adamnan*, p. 389, note y.

[13] *Niall.*—In the list of the Kings of Uisnech [i.e. of Meath] contained in the *Book of Leinster*, p. 42, col. 1, Niall is stated to have been the son of Diarmait son of Airmedach, and to have been slain by his successor, Muridach son of Domnall, after a reign of seven years.

[14] *MacLoingsigh*; "son of Loingsech".—The *Four Mast.* (at A.D. 825) give his proper name as "Flannghus." The *Chron. Scotorum* (at 823) has "Fergus," which is probably incorrect. It is worth remarking that the name "MacLoingsigh" does not appear in the list of the *Comarbs* (or successors) of Patrick in the *Book of Leinster*, p. 42, though it is in other ancient lists. See Todd's *St. Patrick*, pp. 177–182

ard Maċae, in pace obiit. Art mac Diarmata, rex Teṫbae, per dolum iugulatus est. Clemens episcopus, abbas Cluana iraird, feliciter uitam finiuit. Adomnae mor for hErind n-uile .i. robuḋ plaige o mac Iellaen di Mumae. Maelduin mac Gormgaile, rex nepotum Meiṫ, in clericatu obiit. (Fol. 39aa.) Loscaḋ Beiṫre la Feidlimiḋ, slogaḋ Muman occo. Guin Artraċ mic Muirgesa, riġ Teṫbae. Lex Dari co Connacta iterum. Ruṫnel princeps et episcopus cluana ferta Brenaind moritur.

Kl. Ianair. Anno domini dccc.° xx.° ui.° Eċtgus princeps Tamlaċtae dormiuit. Sarugad Eugain i n-ard Maċae, la Cumuscaċ mac Catail 7 la Artriġ mac Concobair. Orggan Luscan do genntib 7 a loscaḋ, 7 innreaḋ Ciannachta cosici oċtar n-Ugan, 7 orgain Gall ind Airṫir olċena. Bellum Leiṫi ċaim re Niall mac Aeḋa, for hU Cremtain, 7 for Muireḋaċ mac Eaċdaċ rig n-Ulaṫ, in quo ceciderunt Cumuscaċ 7 Congalaċ duo filii Caṫail, et alii reges multi dinaiḃ Airgiallaiḃ. Corcraḋ oinaiġ Taillten

[1] *Fears.* — adomnae. This rare form seems comp. of *ad*, an intensive particle (=*aith*, *ath*), and *omna*, plur. of *oman*, "fear."

[2] *By.*—o, omitted in B.

[3] *Mac Iellaen.* — "Mac Fellaen," Clar. 49. O'Conor prints "*dictae Jellame*," which is very incorrect. Nothing is known at present of this prophet.

[4] *Of Munster.*—di Mumae, A.; di Muimae, B. O'Conor wrongly prints *di muniea.*

[5] *Bethra* : i.e. *Dealbhna-Bethra*, otherwise *Dealbhna-Ethra*, a district comprising the present barony of Garrycastle, in the King's county, with the exception of the parish of Lusmagh, which belonged to the neighbouring territory of the Sil-Anmchada (or O'Maddens), on the Connaught side of the Shannon.

[6] *'Law' of Dari.*—See above under the year 811.

[7] *Ruthnel.* — O'Conor inaccurately prints this name *Bathnell.* The *Four Mast.* (A.D. 824) write it "Ruthmael."

[8] *Cluain-ferta-Brenaind.*—"Clonfert of Brendan;" Clonfert, in the barony of Longford, co. Galway.

[9] *Abbot.*—prinnceps, A.

[10] *Eoghan*—Eoghan 'Mainistrech.' His name appears in the list of *comarbs* (or successors) of St. Patrick, in the *Book of Leinster* (p. 42, col. 4), where he is stated to have been also the successor of St. Finnian, and of St. Buti (of Monasterboice). In this list

in peace. Art, son of Diarmait, King of Tethba, was slain through treachery. Clemens, a bishop, abbot of Cluain-Iraird, ended life happily. Great fears[1] throughout all Ireland, viz., a forewarning of a plague by[2] Mac Iellaen[3] of Munster.[4] Maelduin, son of Gormghal, King of Ui-Meith, died in religion. Burning of Bethra[5] by Feidlimidh; the army of Munster being with him. The killing of Artri, son of Muirghes, King of Tethba. The 'Law' of Dari[6] [proclaimed] to the Connaughtmen again. Ruthnel,[7] abbot and bishop of Cluain-ferta-Brenaind,[8] died.

Kal. Jan. A.D. 826. Echtgus, abbot[9] of Tamlacht, 'fell asleep.' Dishonouring of Eoghan[10] in Ard-Macha, by Cumuscach, son of Cathal, and Artri[11] son of Conchobar. The plundering and burning of Lusca by Gentiles; and the devastation of Cianachta as far as Uactar-Ugan; and the plundering of all the Foreigners of the East.[12] The battle of Lethi-cam[13] by Niall, son of Aedh, over the Ui-Crimthain, and over Muiredach son of Echaid, King of the Ulaid, in which fell Cumuscach and Congalach, two sons of Cathal, and many other kings of the Airghialla. The destruction of the fair of Tailltiu,[14] against the [826.]

---

the name of Eoghan (whose term of government is set down as eight years) is placed after that of Artri son of Conchobar (see at the year 822), who is stated in the above entry to have assisted in "dishonouring" Eoghan. The account of this event in the *Ann. Four Mast.* (at A.D. 825), and in the *Chron. Scotorum* (at 827), is much fuller than that above given. There is much confusion regarding these ecclesiastics. The death of Artri (whose rule as abbot of Armagh lasted only two years, according to the list in the *Book of Leinster*) is entered at the year 832 infra; and that of Eoghan at the year 833. See Harris's *Ware*, Vol. I., pp. 43-45; O'Donovan's *Four Mast.*, A.D. 825, note z, and 832, note s.

11 *Artri.*—See last note.

12 *Foreigners of the East*, i.e., the *Gaill* (or Foreigners) of the eastern part of Meath.

13 *Lethi-Cam.*—In the *Ann. F. M.* (A.D. 825), and in the *Chron. Scotorum* (A.D. 827), Lethi-Cam is stated to have been in Magh-Enir, a plain which included Kilmore (*Cill-mor-Enir*), a place a few miles to the east of the city of Armagh. See note [8], 236 *supra*.

14 *Fair of Tailltiu.*—The fair, or public games, celebrated annually at Teltown (*Tailltiu*), in the co. Meath

for Gailengaiḃ la Concobar mac nDonnchada, in quo ceciderunt multi. Coscraḋ oenaiġ Colmain la Muireḋaċ for Laigniu desgabair, in quo ceciderunt plurimi. Moenaċ mac Crunnmail, secnap fer Rois, mortuus est. Abnier abbas Cille aċid dormiuit. Coscraḋ dunaiḋ Laiġen do gentiḃ, ubi ceciderunt Conall mac Concongalt, rex na Fortuaṫ, et alii innumirabiles. Riġḋal occ Birraib itir Feidlimiḋ 7 Concobair.

b. Kl. Ianair. Anno domini dccc.° xx.° ui.° hUaṫa mac Diarmata, ri Teṫḃae, interfectus est. Robartaċ mac Caṫasaiġ princeps cluana moer Ardae, Muirċiu abbas Drom[a] in asclaind, Clemens abbas linne Du[a]ċail, dormierunt. Mucar mar di muccaiḃ mora in airer n-ardae Ciannaċta o gallaiḃ, 7 martre Teṁnen anċorat. Guin Cinaeḋa mic Cumuscaiġ, ri ardae Ciannaċtae, o gallaiḃ, 7 loscaḋ Lainne leire Cluana moer o gallaiḃ. Caṫroineḋ re Leṫlaḃar mac Loingsiġ, ri dal Araiḋe, for gennti. Caṫroineḋ aile for genntí re Coirpri mac Caṫail, ri .h. Ceinnselaiġ, 7 re muinntir tiġe Mundu. Ar Dealḃna hi fello.

Fol. 39ab. Kl. Ianair. Anno domini dccc.° xx.° uiii.° Muiredaċ mac Ruaḋraċ ri Laigen, Aeḋ mac Ceallaiġ princeps Cille daro, Maeldoborċon abbas cille Ausaile,

---

[1] *Conchobar.*—King of Ireland at the time.

[2] *The Fair of Colman.*—O'Donovan states that this Fair was held on the present Curragh of Kildare. *Four Mast.*, A.D. 825, note l, and 940 note r.

[3] *Muiredhach.*—Muiredhach, son of Ruaidhri, King of Leinster, whose obit. forms the first entry under the year 828 *infra*.

[4] *A great many.* — plurimi, A. multi, B.

[5] *Birra.*—Otherwise written *Biror* Birr (now generally known as Parsonstown), in the King's County.

[6] *Fedhlimidh.*—King of Cashel (or Munster).

[7] *Cluain-mor-Arda.* — Clonmore, a townland giving name to a parish, in the barony of Ferrard, co. Louth, which represents the name (and territory) of the *Fera-Arda-Cianachta*, or "men of Ard-Cianachta."

[8] *Abbot.*—prinnceps, A.

[9] *Ard-Cianachta.*— See note 7.

[10] *Lann-leire.*—Dunleer, co. Louth. See note 15, p. 205 *supra*. This entry is not in B.

[11] *Tech-Munnu.*–Taghmon, co. Wexford.

[12] *In treachery.*—hi fello is a rude

Gailenga, by Conchobar[1] son of Donnchad, in which a great many were slain. Destruction of the Fair of Colman,[2] by Muiredhach,[3] against the South Leinstermen, in which a great many[4] were slain. Moenach son of Crunnmael, vice-abbot of Fera-Ros, died. Abnier, abbot of Cill-achaidh, 'fell asleep.' Destruction of the camp of the Leinstermen by Gentiles, where Conall son of Cuchongalt, King of the Fortuatha, and others innumerable, were slain. A royal meeting at Birra,[5] between Fedhlimidh[6] and Conchobar.[1]

Kal. Jan. A.D. 827. Uatha, son of Diarmait, King of [827] BIS.
Tethba, was slain. Robhartach, son of Cathasach, abbot of Cluain-mor-Arda;[7] Muirchu, abbot[8] of Druim-Inasclaind, [and] Clemens, abbot of Linn-Duachail, 'fell asleep.' A great slaughter of sea-hogs on the coast of Ard-Cianachta,[9] by Foreigners; and the martyrdom of Temhnen, anchorite. The killing of Cinaedh, son of Cumuscach, King of Ard-Cianachta,[9] by Foreigners; and the burning of Lann-leire[10] and Cluain-mor,[7] by Foreigners. A battle was gained by Lethlabhar son of Loingsech, King of Dal-Araidhe, over Gentiles. Another battle was gained over Gentiles by Coirpri, son of Cathal, King of Ui-Cennselaigh, and the 'family' of Tech-Munnu.[11] Slaughter of the Delbhna in treachery.[12]

Kal. Jan. A.D. 828. Muiredach,[13] son of Ruadhri, King [828.]
of Leinster; Aedh son of Cellach, abbot[14] of Cill-dara; Maeldoborchon, abbot of Cill-Ausaille;[15] Cinaedh son of

---

way of representing, in Latin form, the Irish ı ꝼeall ("in treachery"). The ignorant so-called 'translator' of these Annals, whose version is contained in the MS. Clar. 49, in the British Museum, renders this entry thus:—"The slaughter of the Delvinians by murther or in guilefull manner."

[13] *Muiredach.*—See under the year 826 *supra*, p. 324, note 3.

[14] *Abbot.*—prinncepp, A.

[15] *Cill-Ausaille.* -The church of (St.) Auxilius. Now Killashee, near Naas, in the co. Kildare. See note [3], p. 19 *supra*.

Cinaeḋ mac Muġroin rex nepotum Failġi, Cormac mac Muirgiusso princeps Sentruiḃ, Cerball mac Finsnechta ri Delbna, Maelumai mac Ceiṫernaiġ equonimus Findubrach, Drucan mac Taiḋg rex nepotum Meiṫ, omnes mortui sunt. Iugulatio Conaing mic Ceallaiġ o Eċoiġ mac Cernaiġ, per dolum. Diarmait abbas Iae do ḋul a n-Albain co minnaib Coluim cille. Roineḋ for Connaċta re feraiḃ Mide, in quo ceciderunt multi.

Kl. Ianair. Anno domini dccc.° xx.° ix.° Oengus mac Donnchada rex telach Mide moritur. Cormac mac Suiḃne abbas Cluana iraird, scriba et episcopus, in pace quieuit. Ceallaċ mac Concaṫraige, princeps Aċiḋ ċrimtain, moritur. Loscaḋ Foire la Feidlimiḋ. Folloṁan mac Donncaḋa iugulatus est a Muiminensibus. Cumbae hUae mBriuin in deiscirt la Feidlimiḋ. Ioseṗ mac Neċtain abbas roiss Commain quieuit. Finsnechta mac Boḋbcoḋa, rex generis filii Ercae,

---

[1] *Sentrebh.*—Lit. "old habitation." Now Santry, a village a few miles to the N. of the city of Dublin.

[2] *Delbhna.*—The *Four Mast.* (A.D. 827) write *Delbhna Beathra*, the old name of the district now represented by the barony of Garrycastle, in the King's County.

[3] *Steward.*—equonimus (for oeconomus), A. B. The *Four Mast.* (A.D. 827) write prioir, "Prior." See Reeves' *Adamnan*, p. 365.

[4] *Finnabhair.*—O'Donovan identifies this place with "Fennor, near Slane, in the county of Meath." (*Four Mast.*, A.D. 827, note s.); but does not give his authority for the identification. There were many places called "Finnabhair."

[5] *By Echaidh.* — o Eċoiġ, A. o Eoch[aid], B.

[6] *To Alba.*—a nAlbain; i.e. to Scotland.

[7] *With the reliquaries.*—co minnaib, A. B. "With . . . reliques," Clar. 49. For the meaning of *minna* (plur. of *minn*, dat. *minnaib*), see Reeves' *Adamnan*, p. 315, note r.

[8] *Victory.*—Roineḋ (for sroineḋ), lit. "breaking," or "dispersion," A. Reineḋ, B.

[9] *Telach-Midhe.*— O'Donovan explains this name by "Hill of Meath," which he would identify (*Four Mast.* A.D. 828, note w) with Tealach-ard, or Tullyard, near the town of Trim, in Meath. The name is corruptly written, as the proper genit. form of *Telach-Midhe*, should be *Telcha* (or *Telaig*)-*Midhe*.

[10] *Achadh-Crimthain.*—"Crimthan's Field." Not identified.

Mughron, King of Ui-Failghi; Cormac son of Muirghis, abbot of Sentrebh;[1] Cerbhall son of Finsnechta, King of Delbhna;[2] Maelumai son of Ceithernach, steward[3] of Finnabhair,[4] and Drucan son of Tadhg, King of Ui-Meith —all died. The killing of Conang, son of Cellach, by Echaidh[5] son of Cernach, by treachery. Diarmait, abbot of Ia, went to Alba,[6] with the reliquaries[7] of Colum-Cille. A victory[8] over the Connaughtmen by the men of Midhe, in which many were slain.

Kal. Jan. A.D. 829. Oengus, son of Donnchad, King of Telach-Midhe,[9] died. Cormac, son of Suibhne, abbot of Cluain-Iraird, a scribe and bishop, rested in peace. Cellach, son of Cucathraige, abbot of Achadh-Crimthain,[10] died. Burning of Foir,[11] by Fedhlimidh.[12] Follomhan, son of Donnchadh, was slain by the Munstermen. Destruction[13] of the Ui-Briuin of the South,[14] by Fedhlimidh.[15] Joseph, son[16] of Nechtan, abbot of Ros-Comain, rested. Finsnechta,[17] son of Bodhbchadh, King of Cinel-mic-Erca, [829.

---

[11] *Foir.*—Fobhar, or Fore, in the barony of Fore, co. Westmeath.

[12] *Fedhlimidh;* i.e Fedhlimidh, son of Crimthan, King of Cashel (or Munster).

[13] *Destruction.* — Cumbae. This word, which is of rare occurrence by itself, is often met in composition with the particle *aith* (or *ath*), in old and modern Irish texts, in such forms as atcuma ("wounding, laceration;" O'Don. *Suppl. to O'Rielly*), and *aithchumbe* (gl. "cauteria et combustiones," Ebel's ed. of *Zeuss* (p. 881). For Cumbae (as in A.), MS. B. has Cuimbae, which O'Conor wrongly translates "Conventio."

[14] *Ui-Briuin of the South,*—There were several septs in Connaught called "Ui-Briuin," who were descended from Brian, brother of Niall Nine-hostager. The "Ui-Briuin of the South" was, apparently, another name for the "Ui-Briuin-Seola," otherwise called "Muintir-Murchadha," who were seated in the barony of Clare, co. Galway. On the assumption of surnames by the Irish, the principal family of this tribe took the name of O'Flaherty, from an ancestor Flaithbhertach, who flourished *circa* A.D. 970. See O'Flaherty's *Iar Connaught* (Hardiman's ed.), p. 368.

[15] *Fedhlimidh*; i.e. Fedhlimidh, the son of Crimthan, King of Munster, whose obit. is entered at the year 846 *infra*.

[16] *Son.*—mac. Omitted in B.

[17] *Finsnechta.*—Finechta, B.

[obiit]. Suibne mac Forannan, abbas duorum mensium i n-ard Maċae, obiit.

Kl. Ianair. Anno domini dccc.° xxx.° Diarmait do tiachtain i n-hErind co mindaiḃ Coluim cille. Muirenn abatissa Cille dara dormiuit. Airmeḋaċ princeps Maigi bile dimersus est. Cernaċ mac Duncon, scriba et sapiens et sacerdos aird Maċae, pausauit. Oenaċ Tailten do cumusc oc foraḋaib im Scrin mic Cuilind 7 im minda Patraicc, condid apṫa ili de. Indred Conaille do genntiḃ, conarrgabad Maelbriġti airri, 7 Canannan a braṫair, 7 co rucṫa

Fol. 39*b*a. illonga. Caṫ do maḋmaim i n-Aiġneċaib re genntib, for muinntir n-aird Maċae, conairgabṫa roċaide mora diib. Mors Dunchada filii Conaing, regis Cianaċtae. Sarugad Eugain mainistreach abbaid aird Maċae, hi Foigaillnaig, la Conċobar mac n-Donnchada, conairgabṫa a muinnter 7 corucṫa a graigi. Feiḋlimiḋ mac Crem̄tain co sluaġ Muġan 7 Laigen do ṫuiḋecht i Fiambur do innriuḋ fer m-Breġ. Indred Liḟi la Concobar.

---

[1] *Suibhne, son of Forannan.*—Suibne mac Fairnig ("S. son of Fairnech"), in A. Called S. mac Forannan ("S. son of Forannan") in B. The name of this Suibhne does not occur in any of the ancient lists of the "Comarbs," or successors of St. Patrick. The *Four Mast.* however, in noticing his death under A.D. 829, agree with this Chronicle in stating that Suibhne was abbot of Ard-Macha for the space of two months.

[2] *Diarmait.*—Abbot of Hi (or Iona). See Reeves' *Adamnan*, pp. 315, 388. Another voyage of Diarmait, to Alba (or Scotland), is recorded above at the year 828.

[3] *Abbot.*—prinncepp, A.

[4] *Tailtiu.* — Teltown, co. Mea h See note [11], p. 167 *supra.*

[5] *Forads.*—In old Irish glossaries *fora* (or *foradh*) is explained by a "seat' or "bench" (*i.e.* the station) of the person who presided over an assembly, or celebration of national games. See O'Brien's *Ir. Dict.*, voce fora; O'Curry's *Mann. and Cust.*, I. ccxxxiii, and 3, 541, and *Leabh. Gabhala*, p. 44.

[6] *MacCuilind.*—Bishop of Lusk, in the county of Dublin. His obit is entered under the year 495 *supra.*

[7] *Aighnecha.*—The plural form of Aighnech, which was probably the name of a district in the n.e. of the county of Louth, near Carlingford Lough (the ancient Irish name of which was Snamh-aignech." — See Reeves *Eccl. Antiqq.*, p. 252, note z). According to a statement in *Leb. na*

[died]. Suibhne, son of Forannan,[1] abbot for two months in Ard-Macha, died.

[830] Kal. Jan. A.D. 830. Diarmait[2] came to Ireland, with the reliquaries of Colum-Cille. Muirenn, abbess of Cill-dara, 'fell asleep.' Airmedhach, abbot[3] of Magh-bilè, was drowned. Cernach, son of Dunchu, scribe and wise man, and priest of Ard-Macha, rested. Disturbance of the fair of Tailtiu,[4] at the Forads,[5] about the shrine of MacCuilind[6] and the reliquaries of Patrick, and a great many persons died thereof. The plundering of the Conailli by Gentiles; and their King, Maelbrighte, and his brother Canannan, were taken captive, and carried off in ships. A battle was gained in Aighnecha,[7] by Gentiles, over the 'family' of Ard-Macha, great numbers of whom were taken captive. Death of Dunchad, son of Conaing,[8] King of Cianachta. The dishonouring of Eogan Mainistrech,[9] abbot of Ard-Macha, in *foigaillnaig*,[10] by Conchobar[11] son of Donnchad, when his 'family' were made prisioners, and his herds were carried off. Fedhlimidh son of Crimthann, with the army of Munster and Leinster, came to Fiambur,[12] to plunder the men of Bregh. The plundering of Liphè by Conchobar.[11]

---

hUidre (p. 75 b) *Fochaird* (Faughard in the barony of Lower Dundalk, co. Louth), remarkable as the birth-place of St. Bridget, and the scene of the death of Edward Bruce, in the year 1318, was anciently known by the name of Ard-Aignech.

[8] *Son of Conaing*.—filii Conaill, corrected to filii Conaing in A.

[9] *Eogan Mainistrech*.—"Eogan of the Monastery" (*i.e.* Manistir-Buti, or Monasterboice, co. Louth). Eogan had been Lector of that Monastery. The entry of this incident in MS. B. is slightly inaccurate. Regarding the circumstances attending the elevation of Eogan from the Lectorship of Monasterboice to the Abbacy of Armagh, see *Ann. Four Mast.*, at A.D. 825, and *Chron. Scot.* at 827.

[10] *In foigaillnaig*.—hi foigaillnaig. This clause, which is probably corrupt, is unintelligible to the Editor. Dr. O'Conor renders it by "incursione nocturna." *Rer. Hib. Script.*, Vol. IV., p. 208. The entry has been omitted by the *Four Mast.*

[11] *Conchobar*.—King of Ireland.

[12] *Fiambur*.—The *Four Masters*, in the corresponding entry (A.D. 829), write 'Fionnabhair-Bregh' (Fennor, near Slane, co. Meath), which is probably correct. In Clar. 49, the name is written "Finnuir."

.b. Kl. Ianair. Anno domini dccc.° xxx.° i.° Cétna orggain airdd Maċae o genntib fo tri in oen ṁís. Orggain Mucsnama 7 Luġmaiḋ 7 Oa Meiṫ 7 Droma mic Ublae, 7 alanaile ceall. Orggain Duimliacc 7 fini Ciannactai cona ċellaiḃ huiliḃ o genntiḃ. Ergabail Ailella mic Colgen o genntib. Tuaṫal mac Feraḋaiċ do breiṫ do genntib, 7 scrin Adomnain, o Domnuċ maġan. Orggain raṫa Luraiġ 7 Connire o genntib. Cinaeḋ mac Eċdaċ, ri dal Araiḋe in tuaiscirt, iugulatus est per dolum a sociis suis. Cinaeḋ mac Artraċ, rex Cualann, et Diarmait mac Ruadraċ rex airṫir Liḟi, mortui sunt. Concoḃar mac Donnchada, ri Erenn, mortuus est.

Kl. Ianair. Anno domini dccc.° xxx.° ii.° Artri mac Concobair, abbas airdd Maċae, et Concobar mac Donncoḋa rex Teṁro, uno mense mortui sunt. Ruaidri mac Maelefoṫartaiġ, leiṫ ri .h. Cremṫain, moritur. Niall Cailli regnare incipit. Roiniuḋ re Niall 7 re Murcaḋ for gallu i n-daire Calgaiḋ. Orggain cluana Dolcan o ġenntiḃ. Caṫroiniuḋ for muinntir Cille daro inna cill, re Ceallaċ mac Brain, ubi

[1] *Kal. Jan.*—The number '400' is written in the margin in A., to indicate that this was the 400th year from the beginning of Chronicle.

[2] *Mucsnamh.*—Mucknoe, co. Monaghan.

[3] *Ui-Meith.*—Otherwise called "Ui-Meith-Macha." For the situation and extent of this territory, see O'Donovan's *Ann. Four Mast.*, A.D. 1178, note c, and the authorities there cited.

[4] *Domnach-Maghen.*-Donaghmoyne, in the barony of Farney, co. Monaghan.

[5] *Rath-Luraigh.*—Now represented by Maghera, the name of a parish in the barony of Loughinsholin, co. Londonderry. See Reeves' *Down and Connor*, p. 27.

[6] *Conchobar.*—Added in later hand in A. See under the next year.

[7] *Artri.*—See note [16], p. 309 *supra*. In the list of the *comarbs*, or successors, of St. Patrick in the abbacy (or episcopacy) of Armagh, contained in the *Book of Leinster* (p. 42), Artri is stated to have ruled for two years, the term accorded to him in the several lists cited by Dr. Todd (*St. Patrick*, pp. 174-183). Ware fixes the beginning of his government in A.D. 822 (Harris's ed., vol. 1, p. 43). See *Chron. Scotorum*, at A.D. 827; and the references to Artri under the years 822 and 826 *supra*.

[8] *Ui-Crimhtain.*—Otherwise written Ui-Cremhthainn. A tribe of the

Kal. Jan.[1] A.D. 831. The first plundering of Ard-Macha by Gentiles, thrice in one month. Plundering of Mucsnamh,[2] and of Lughmadh, and of Ui-Meith,[3] and of Druim-mic-U-Blae, and of other churches. The plundering of Damliag, and of the territory of Cianachta with its churches, by Gentiles. Capture of Ailill, son of Colgu, by Gentiles. Tuathal, son of Feradhach, was carried off by Gentiles, and the shrine of Adamnan, from Domnach-Maghen.[4] Plundering of Rath-Luraigh[5] and Connere, by Gentiles. Cinaedh son of Echaid, King of the Dal-Araidhe of the North, was killed, through treachery, by his associates. Cinaedh son of Artri, King of Cualann, and Diarmait son of Ruadhri, King of Airther-Lifè, died. Conchobar[6] son of Donnchad, King of Ireland, died. [831.] BIS.

Kal. Jan. A.D. 832. Artri,[7] son of Conchobar, abbot of Ard-Macha, and Conchobar son of Donnchad, King of Temhair, died in the same month. Ruaidhri, son of Maelfothartaigh, half-King of Ui-Crimhtain,[8] died. Niall Çailli[9] begins to reign. A victory by Niall[10] and Murçhadh over the Foreigners, in Daire-Chalgaidh.[11] The plundering of Cluain-Dolcain[12] by Gentiles. A battle was gained over the 'family' of Cill-dara, in their church, by Cellach[13] son of Bran, where many were slain, on St. [832.]

Oirghialla seated in the present baronies of Upper and Lower Slane, in the county of Meath. See O'Donovan's *Ann. Four Mast.*, A.D. 832, note t.

[9] *Niall Cailli.*—The *Four Masters* refer the accession of Niall Caille to A.D. 832. But O'Flaherty states that Niall began to reign in 833 (*Ogygia*, p. 434), which is the true year; thus agreeing with the present Chronicle, the chronology of which is ante-dated by one year at this period. The original of the foregoing entry, which is added in an old hand in the margin in A., forms part of the text in B.

[10] *Niall*; i.e. Niall Cailli, King of Ireland, mentioned in the previous entry.

[11] *Daire-Chalgaidh.* —The ancient name of Derry (or Londonderry). This victory is not noticed in the tract on the "War of the Gaedhel with the Gaill," edited by Dr. Todd.

[12] *Cluain-Dolcain.* — Clondalkin, near Dublin.

[13] *Cellach.*—Kfng of Leinster. See the *Book of Leinster*, p. 39, col. 2, and Shearman's *Loca Patriciana*, geneal.; table 11. His obit is recorded under the next year.

iugulati sunt multi in feria Iohannis in autumno. Iugulatio muinntire cluana mic U Nois, 7 loscuḋ a termuinn corici dorus a cille, la Feiḋlimiḋ riġ Caisil. Fon oen cumai muinnter Dermaiġi co dorus a cille. Mors Diarmota filii Tomaltaiġ, regis Connacht.
Fol. 39bb. Mors Cobṫaiḋ mic Maileduin regis Iarmuman. Loscaḋ Liss moer Moċutu 7 ar Dermuman. Loscaḋ Droma in asclaind o genntiḃ. Orggain Loċa Bricerna for Conġalach mac nEċdaċ, 7 a marbad oc longaiḃ iarum. Reċtabra abbas Cille aċaiḋ obiit. Tipraiti mac Ruamlusa, princeps domnaiġ Seċnaill, moritur.

Kl. Ianair. Anno domini dccc.° xxx.° iii.° Oengus mac Fergusa, rex Fortrenn, moritur. Eugan Manistreċ, abb aird Maċae et Cluana Iraird, et Affraic abatissa Cille daro, dormierunt. Ceallaċ mac Brain, ri Laiġen, 7 Cinaeḋ mac Conaing, rex Teṫbae, mortui sunt. Suiḃne mac Artraċ, rex Moġdorne n-uile, interfectus est a fratribus suis. Concobar mac Ailello occisus est a fratribus suis. Conġalaċ mac Oenġusa, rex generis Loeġaire, moritur. Tuatċar episcopus et scriba Cilla daro obiit. Caṫ for Gennti re n-Dunaḋach mac Scannlain, riġ .h.

[1] *Dermagh.*—Durrow, in the barony of Ballycowan, King's County.

[2] *Lis-mor-Mochuta.*—"Mochuta's great fort" (or "inclosure"). Lismore, co. Waterford.

[3] *Druim-Inasclaind.* — Dromiskin, in the parish of the same name, barony and county of Louth.

[4] *Loch-Bricerna.*—So in A and B. But the name should be "Loch-Bricrenn" (the "lake of Bricriu"), as in the *Four Mast.*; now corrupted to Loughbrickland, near a lake of the same name, in the barony of Upper Iveagh, co. Down. The name of this lake is stated to have been derived from Bricriu, a chieftain who flourished in Ulster in the first century, and who, on account of his talent for sarcasm, is nick-named *Bricriu nemthenga* ("*Bricriu* '*poison-tongue*'") in the old Irish stories.

[5] *Cill-achaidh.*—Killeigh, barony of Geashil, King's County.

[6] *Ruamlus.* Under the year 800 *supra*, the obit of a 'Ruamnus,' abbot of Domnach-Sechnaill (Dunshaughlin, co. Meath) is given; who was probably the father of the Tipraite here referred to.

[7] *Fortrenn.*—Pictland. See note [a], p. 118 *supra*.

John's day in Autumn. The killing of the 'family' of Cluain-mic-U-Nois, by Fedhlimidh, King of Cashel; and the burning of its 'termon' to the door of its church. In the same manner [did he treat] the 'family' of Dermagh,[1] to the door of its church. Death of Diarmait, son of Tomaltach, King of Connaught. Death of Cobhthach, son of Maelduin, King of West Munster. Burning of Lis-mor-Mochuta,[2] and the slaughter of South Munster. Burning of Druim-Inasclaind[3] by Gentiles. The plundering of Loch-Bricerna[4] against Congalach, son of Echaid, who was afterwards killed [by the Foreigners] at their ships. Rechtabra, abbot of Cill-achaidh,[5] died. Tipraite son of Ruamlus,[6] abbot of Domnach-Sechnaill,[6] died.

Kal. Jan. A.D. 833. Oengus, son of Fergus, King of Fortrenn,[7] died. Eogan Mainistrech,[8] abbot of Ard-Macha and Cluain-Iraird, and Affraic, abbess of Cill-dara, 'fell asleep.' Cellach,[9] son of Bran, King of Leinster, and Cinaedh, son of Conang, King of Tethba,[10] died. Suibhne, son of Artri, King of all the Mughdhorna, was slain by his[11] brothers. Conchobar, son of Ailill, was slain by his[11] brothers. Conghalach, son of Oengus, King of Cinel-Loeghaire, died. Tuatchar, bishop and scribe of Cill-dara, died. A battle [was gained] over the Gentiles by Dunadhach,[12] son of Scannlan, King of the Ui-Fidgenti,[13] [833.]

[8] *Eogan Mainistrech.*—See the note on this name under the year 830.

[9] *Cellach.*—Mentioned under the preceding year, as the perpetrator of a great outrage against *muinntir*, 'family,' or community of Kildare.

[10] *Tethba.* — In later times called Teffia, a territory comprising adjoining portions of the present counties of Westmeath and Longford. The *Ann. Four Mast.* and the *Chron. Scotorum* state that Cinaedh, son of Conang, was King of Bregh, the ancient name of a district in the present county of Meath. A stanza in Irish regarding Cinaedh, son of Conang, written in the top margin of fol. 39 *b* in MS. A., has been partially mutilated by the binder.

[11] *His.*—ſuiſ. Omitted in A.

[12] *Dunadhach.*—The name of this chieftain is written *Dunchadach* in B. (which O'Conor prints *Dunchach*), and *Dunchadh* in the *Chron. Scotorum.* But the *Four Mast.* write it *Dunadhach.* See the entry of his obit under the next year, where the name is written *Dunadhaigh,* in the genit. form (nomin. *Dunadhach*).

[13] *Ui-Fidgenti.*—A powerful tribe anciently inhabiting an extensive ter-

Fidgennti, du itorchratar ili. Orgain Glinne da locha o Genntib. Orgain Slane 7 Finnubrach habae o Gentib. Loscaḋ cluana mic U Nois de media ex maiore parte. Guin Broccain mic Cenderchain i n-Aiḋniu.

Kt. Ianair. Anno domini dccc.° xxx.° iiii.° Slogaḋ la Niall co Laiġniu corordigestar ri forraiḃ .i. Bran mac Faelan. Cinaeḋ mac Neill mic Aeḋa iugulatus est la hUltu. Indreḋ Mide la Niall, co rolosccaḋ condici teċ Maelċonoc. Cumuscaċ mac Oengusa, secnap cluana micc U Nois, moritur. Orggain Fernann 7 cluana moer Moeḋoc o Genntiḃ. Coemċluḋ abbaḋ i n-ard Maċa .i. Forindan (o Raṫ mic Malais) i n-inad Dermota (o ṫiġearnan). Eċaiḋ mac Conċongalt rex nepotum Tuirtri, 7 Caincomrac mac Siadail equonimus ċille daro, 7 Bresal mac Cormaic princeps Cille dumai glinn et aliarum ciuitatum, moriuntur, 7 Muircertaċ mac Gormġaile, omnes mortui sunt. Ferġus mac Boḋbcaḋa, rex Cairge braċaiḋe, iugulatus

Fol. 40aa. est a Muminensibus. Mors Dunaḋaiġ mic Scannlain regis .h. Fiḋgenti. Loscaḋ Cluana mac Nois tertia parte sui .ii. non marta. Loscaḋ Mungairit 7 ala-

---

ritory which included the present barony of Coshma, in the co. Limerick. See the interesting note regarding the territory occupied by this tribe in O Donovan's *Annals of the Four Masters* (A.D. 1178, note m).

[1] *Finnabhair-abha.* — The ancient name of Fennor, in the parish of Fennor, barony of Lower Duleek, and county of Meath.

[2] *Of the greater part.*—The MS. A. has "de media ex majore parte." But B. has merely "ex majore parte." See note [5], p. 306 *supra*.

[3] *Aidhne.*—The ancient name of a territory comprising the present barony of Kiltartan in the county of Galway.

[4] *Niall*; i.e. Niall Caille, monarch of Ireland.

[5] *When he ordained.*—The original in A. is corodigestar, and in B. also corodigestar, both MSS. in this case being obviously corrupt. The *Four Masters* (*ad an.*) more correctly write co ro ordaig ("when he ordained").

[6] *Tech-Maelchonoc.*—The "House of Maelchonoc." In the *Ann. Four Masters*, under A.D. 834, the house of Maelchonoc, lord of Dealbhna Beathra (a territory now represented by the barony of Garrycastle, King's County), is stated to have been situated at a place called Bodhammar But it has not been identified.

wherein many were slain. The plundering of Glenn-da-locha by Gentiles. The plundering of Slane and Finnabhair-abha,[1] by Gentiles. Burning of the greater part[2] of Cluain-mic-U-Nois. The mortal wounding of Broccan, son of Cendercan, in Aidhne.[3]

Kal. Jan. A.D. 834. A hosting by Niall[4] to the Leinstermen, when he ordained[5] a King over them, to wit, Bran son of Faelan. Cinaedh, son of Niall, son of Aedh, was killed by the Ulidians. The ravaging of Meath by Niall,[4] when it was burned as far as Tech-Maelchonoc.[6] Cumuscach, son of Oengus, Vice-abbot of Clonmacnoise, died. The plundering of Ferna, and of Cluainmor-Moedhoic, by Gentiles. A change of abbots in Ard-Macha, to wit, Forinnan (from Rath-mic-Malais[7]) in the place[8] of Dermot Ua Tighernain.[9] Echaidh, son of Cuchongalt, King of the Ui-Tuirtri; and Caencomrac son of Siadal, steward of Cill-dara, and Bresal son of Cormac, abbot of Cill-duma-glinn[10] and other churches, died, and Muirchertach son of Gormghal—all died. Fergus son of Bodhbchadh, King of Carraig-Brachaidhe,[11] was slain by Munstermen. Death of Dunadach, son of Scannlan, King of Ui-Fidhgenti. Burning of the third part of Cluain-mac-Nois, on the second of the nones of March. Burning of Mungairit, and other churches of [834.]

---

[7] *Rath-mic-Malais.* — The "fort" (or "rath") of the son of Malas. Added by way of gloss over the name Forindan, in A. and B. Now known as "Rackwallace," a townland in the parish and county of Monaghan, containing an old graveyard. The identification of this place is due to Dean Reeves. O'Conor did his best to prevent the possibility of identification, by printing the name *Raithinnmhalais.*

[8] *In the place.*—ı n-ınαᴅ. ınᴅon, A.; ınnon, B.; both of which are corrupt. The *Four Mast.* write ı n-ıonαᴅh, which is more correct.

[9] *Ua Tighernain.*—Descendant (or grandson) of Tighernan. Regarding these abbots (or bishops) of Armagh, see the lists published by Todd, *St. Patrick*, pp. 175-187; and Harris's *Ware*, vol. 1, p. 45. And see also at the year 851 *infra.*

[10] *Cill-duma-glinn.*—Now Kilglinn, barony of Upper Deece, co. Meath.

[11] *Carraig-Brachaidhe.*— This was the name of a territory forming the north-west portion of the present barony of Inishowen, co. Donegal.

naile ċeall Imumen o gentiḃ. Orggain droma hIung o gallaiḃ.

b. Kl. Ianair. Anno domini dccc.° xxx.° u°. Suiḃne mac Ioseṗ abbas Glinne da Loċa; Soergus nepos Cuinneda abbas Dermaiġe, Forḃurać episcopus et ancorita Luscan, omnes feliciter uitam finierunt. Dunlaing mac Caṫusaiġ, princeps Corcaiġe moire, mortuus est sine communione i Caisiul regum. Gabail in dairṫige i Cill dara for Forindan abbaid n-aerdd Maċae, co samaḋ Patraic olċena, la Feidlimiḋ co caṫ 7 indnu, 7 ro gabta i cact co n-anhumaloit friu. Dermait do dul co Connaċta cum lege et uexillis Patricii. Ceall dara do orgain do gentiḃ o Inbir deaae, 7 rolloscad a leaṫ na cille. Coirpri mac Maeleduin, rex Loċa gaḃor, iugulatus est o Maelcernai, et Maelcerna iugulatus est o Coirpriu in eadem hora; et mortui sunt ambo in una noċte. Prima preda gentilium o deisciurt Breġ .i. o telcaiḃ Droman 7 o Dermaiġ Britonum, et captiuos tam plures portauerunt et mortificauerunt multos et captiuos plurimos asstulerunt. Mes mor etir cnomes 7 daurmes, 7 ro iaḃ glasa cos anrat di ruiṫ. Caṫ Druing etir Connaċta inuicem, dú itorċair Ceallać mac Forbasaiġ princeps Roiss caim, 7 Adoṁnan mac

---

[1] *Druim-hIng.*—O'Donovan thought that this was probably the place now called Dromin, near Dunshaughlin, co. Meath. *Four Mast.*, A.D. 834, note d.

[2] *Dermagh.*—Durrow, in the barony of Ballycowan, King's County.

[3] *Ended life happily.*—B. has defuncti sunt.

[4] *Corcach-mor.*—The "great *corcach* (or *marsh*)." Cork, in Munster. The *Four Masters* (A.D. 835), in noticing the obit of Dunlaing, style him *comarba* (or successor) of Bara, the first bishop of Cork. But Ware has no reference to him in his list of bishops of that See.

[5] *Forindan.*—See under the last year; and also Todd's *Cogadh Gaedhel re Gallaibh*, Introd., p. xlv.

[6] *Feidlimidh.*—Feidhlimidh, son of Crimthann, King of Cashel.

[7] *Dermait.*—The Dermot Ua Tighernain mentioned under last year as having been displaced from the abbacy of Armagh, in favour of Forinnan (or "Forannan," as the name is written in the *Book of Leinster*, p. 42, col. 4).

Ormond, by Gentiles. The plundering of Druim bIng[1] by Foreigners.

Kal. Jan. A.D. 835. Suibhne son of Joseph, abbot of [835.] BIS
Glenn-da-locha; Soergus Ua Cuinneda, abbot of Dermagh;[2] Forbasach, bishop and anchorite of Lusca—all ended life happily.[3] Dunlaing, son of Cathasach, abbot of Corcach-mor,[4] died without communion, in Cashel of the Kings. The taking of the oratory in Cill-dara against Forindan,[5] abbot of Ard-Macha, with Patrick's congregation besides, by Fedhlimidh,[6] by battle and arms; and they were taken prisoners, with great disobedience towards them. Dermait[7] went to Connaught, with the 'Law' and 'ensigns' of Patrick. Cill-dara was plundered by Gentiles from Inbher-Dea;[8] and half the church was burned. Coirpri, son of Maelduin, King of Loch-Gabhor,[9] was killed[10] by Maelcerna, and Maelcerna was killed[10] by Coirpri at the same moment; and they both died in the one night. The first prey taken by Gentiles from the South of Bregh, i.e., from Telcha-Droman, and from Dermagh of the Britons; and they carried off[11] several captives, and killed a great many, and carried away a great many captives. Great produce, between nut-crop and acorn-crop, which closed up streams, so that they ceased to flow. The battle of Drung between the Connaughtmen themselves, in which were slain Cellach, son of Forbasach, abbot of Ros-cam,[12] and Adomnan, son of

---

[8] *Inbher-Dea.*—The mouth of the Vartry River, which flows into the sea at the town of Wicklow, in the co. Wicklow.

[9] *Loch-Gabhor.*—Lagore, near Dunshaughlin, co. Meath.

[10] *Killed.*—By iugulatus est, the compiler probably meant to convey that Coirpri and Maelcerna were mortally wounded in mutual conflict.

[11] *Carried off.*—For portauerunt, B. has duxerunt. The entry is rudely constructed.

[12] *Abbot of Ros-cam.*—In the *Ann. Four Mast.*, at the same year, Cellach is described as *airchinnech* (or "herenagh") of Ros-Commain, now Roscommon, in the county of Roscommon. The authority of the F. M. is followed by Colgan. *Acta SS.*, p. 334.

Aldaileḋ, 7 Connṁaċ mor uictor fuit. Uastatio crudelissima a gentilibus omnium finium Connaċtorum. Ar caṫa forsin Deis tuaisciurt o genntiḃ.

Kl. Ianair. Anno domini dccc.° xxx.° ui.° Flaiṫroa abbas monistreċ Buti, episcopus et ancorita, Martan episcopus Cluana cain, requieuerunt. Maelduin mac Seċnusaiġ, ri fer-Cul, Tuaṫal mac Fianġalaiġ ri ceniuil Ardgail, Riacan mac Finsneċti leiṫri Laigen, mortui sunt. Longas tre ḟichet long di Nordmannaiḃ for Boinn. Longas eile tre ḟiċet long for abaind Liḟi. Ro slatsat iarum in di longais sin maġ Lipi 7 maġ mBreġ etir cealla 7 dune 7 treba. Roiniuḋ re feraiḃ Breġ for Gallaiḃ ec Deoninni i Muġdornaiḃ Breġ, coniddorcradar se fiċit diib. Bellum re genntiḃ oc Inbiur na m-barc for hU Neill o Sinaind co muir, dú irrolaḋ ár nadráirmeḋ, sed primi reges euasserunt. Loscaḋ Innseo cealtrae o gentiḃ. Cella loċa Eirne n-uile, im ċluain Eoais 7 Daiminis, do dilgiunn o genntiḃ. Indreḋ ceniuil Coirpri cruim la Feiḋilmiḋ. Roiniuḋ for Muimneċu re Caṫal mac Muirgesso. Marbaḋ Saxoilḃ toisiġ na n-Gall la Cianaċt.

Fol. 40ab.

[1] *Connmhach Mor.* — His obit is given at the year 845 *infra*, where he is described as rex nepotum Briuin, or King of the Ui-Briuin, a tribe whose territory comprised a large district lying to the east of Lough Corrib, in the co. Galway. See the map prefixed to O'Donovan's ed. of the *Tribes and Customs* of *Hy-Many.*

[2] *Northern Deisi.* — A branch of the great tribe of the Deisi (which has given name to the two baronies of Decies, in the co. Waterford), whose territory embraced a large district lying about Clonmel, in the present co. Tipperary. See O'Flaherty's *Ogygia*, part iii., chap. 69, and Joyce's *Irish Names of Places* (2nd ser., 1875, pp. 425-7).

[3] *Rested.*—quieuerunt, B.

[4] *Abhainn-Liphè.*—The river Liffey; or Anna Liffey, as the name is sometimes incorrectly written.

[5] *Magh-Liphe.* — The "Plain of Liphè" (or Liffey). The flat portion of the present co. Kildare, through which the River Liffey flows.

[6] *Magh-Bregh.* — The "Plain of the Bregha." This comprised the southern portion of the co. Meath washed by the river Boyne. But its exact limits are uncertain.

[7] *Victory.*— roiniuḋ, A. and B. A later hand attempted to alter roiniuḋ to rossaoiniuḋ, by inter-

Aldailedh; and Connmhach Mor[1] was victor. Most cruel devastation, by Gentiles, of all the territories of Connaught. A battle-slaughter upon the Northern Deisi,[2] by Gentiles.

Kal. Jan. A.D. 836. Flaithroa, abbot of Manister-Buti, bishop and anchorite, [and] Martan, bishop of Cluain-cain, rested.[3] Maelduin son of Sechnasach, King of Fir-Cul; Tuathal son of Fianghalach, King of Cinel-Ardgail; [and] Riacan son of Finsnechta, half-King of Leinster, died. A fleet of three score ships of the Norsemen upon the Boyne. Another fleet of three score ships on the Abhainn-Liphè.[4] These two fleets afterwards plundered Magh-Liphè[5] and Magh-Bregh,[6] between churches, and forts, and houses. A victory[7] by the men of Bregh, over the Foreigners, at Deoninne[8] in Mughdorna-Bregh, when six score of them were slain. A battle [was gained] by Foreigners, at Inbher-nambarc, over the Ui-Neill from the Sinainn[9] to the sea, where a slaughter was made that has not been reckoned; but the chief Kings escaped. Burning of Inis-Celtra by Gentiles. All the churches of Loch-Erne, together with Cluain-Eois and Daimhinis, were destroyed by Gentiles. The plundering of the race of Coirpri Crom[10] by Fedhilmidh. A victory over the Munstermen by Cathal,[11] son of Muirghes. The killing of Saxolbh,[12] chief of the Foreigners, by the Cianachta.[13] [836.]

polating the letters srao. But roimiuḋ occurs often in A. and B., and the suggested correction has not therefore been followed.

[8] *Deoninne.*—This place has not been identified. The territory of Mughdorna-Bregh, in which it is stated to have been situated, was in Bregh (or Bregia) in East Meath.

[9] *Sinainn.* — The river Shannon. See O'Donovan's notes regarding the event here recorded. *Four Masters*, A.D. 836, notes, b, c.

[10] *Race of Coirpri Crom.*—A name for the people of Ui-Maine, or the Hy-Many, in the co. Roscommon.

[11] *Cathal.* — King of Connaught. His obit is given by the *Four Mast.* in this year, who add that he "died [soon] after" the victory above referred to. The death of his father Muirges, also King of Connaught, is entered at the year 814 *supra.*

[12] *Saxolbh.* — Saxulf. Regarding this person, see Todd's *Cogadh Gaedhel re Gallaibh*, Introd., pp. lxvi–vii.

[13] *Cianachta.*—The Cianachta-Bregh, or Cianachta of Bregia; a tribe

Kt. Ianair. Anno domini dccc.° xxx.° vii.° Cormac episcopus et scriba Cille Foibriċ, Bran Finnglaisi episcopus et scriba, Tigernaċ mac Aeḋa abbas Finndubraċ abae et aliarum ciuitatum, dormierunt. Domnall mac Aeḋa, princeps Droma urċaille, moritur. Cellaċ mac Coscraiċ princeps ind airicuil Dosenċiarocc, Cellaċ mac Coirpri princeps Aṫo truim, mortui sunt. Congalaċ mac Moenaiġ, rex nepotum filiorum Cuais Breġ, subita morte uitam finiuit. Maelcron rex Loċa lein .i. mac Cobtaiġ, moritur. Rigḋal mor i cluain Conaire Tommain, etir Feiḋlimiḋ 7 Niall. Docutu sanctus episcopus et ancorita Slane uitam senilem feliciter finiuit. Ferrdalaċ equonimus aird Maċae obiit. Bellum re Genntib for Conachta, in quo ceciderunt Maelduin filius Muirgesa et alii multi. Bran mac Faelain rex Laigen moritur.

Kt. Ianair. Anno domini dccc.° xxx.° viii.° Maelgaimrid scriba optimus et ancorita, abbas Bennċair,
Fol. 40ba. pausauit. Colman mac Robartaiġ abbas Slane, Aeḋán abbas Rois crea, Cormac mac Conaill princeps Treoit, Maelruanaiḋ mac Caṫusaiġ secnap Luscan, mortui sunt. Cumascaċ mac Conġalaiġ, rex Ciannactai, moritur. Muireḋaċ mac Eċdaċ, rex coiciḋ Conċobuir, iugulatus est a suis fratribus .i. Aeḋ et Oengus, et

occupying the district about Duleek, co. Meath.

[1] *Finnglais.*—Finglas, a little to the north of Dublin city.

[2] *Finnabhair-aba.*— Fennor, in a parish of the same name, barony of Lower Duleek, and county of Meath.

[3] *Druim-urchaille.* — O'Donovan suggests (*Ann. F. M.*, A.D. 837, note q.), that this may have been the old name of a place called Spancel Hill, in the barony of Bunratty, co. Clare. But Shearman thought, and probably with good reason, that the name Druim-urchaille is now represented by that of Dunmurraghill, in the parish of the same name, in the north of the county of Kildare. See *Loca Patriciana*, p. 112.

[4] *Airicul-Dosenchiarog.* — Another form of the name of a place mentioned above under the year 809. See note [7], p. 296.

[5] *Cluain-Conaire-Tommain.*—Cloncurry, in the barony of Ikeathy and Oughterany, co. Kildare.

[6] *Feidhlimidh.*- King of Cashel (or Munster).

Kal. Jan. A.D. 837. Cormac, bishop and scribe of Cill-Foibrigh; Brann of Finnglais,[1] bishop and scribe, [and] Tigernach son of Aedh, abbot of Finnabhair-aba[2] and other churches, 'fell asleep.' Domnall son of Aedh, abbot of Druim-urchaille,[3] died. Cellach son of Coscragh, abbot of the Airicul-Dosenchiarog,[4] Cellach son of Coirpre, abbot of Ath-truim, died. Congalach son of Moenach, King of Ui-Mac-Uais of Bregh, died suddenly. Maelcron, King of Loch-Lein, viz., the son of Cobhtach, died. A great royal meeting in Cluain-Conaire-Tommain,[5] between Feidhlimidh[6] and Niall.[7] Dochutu, a holy bishop and anchorite of Slane, ended a long life happily. Ferdalach, steward of Ard-Macha, died. A battle by Gentiles over the Connaughtmen, in which Maelduin son of Muirghes, and many others, were slain. Bran,[8] son of Faelan, King of Leinster, died. [837.]

Kal. Jan. A.D. 838. Maelgaimridh, an excellent scribe and anchorite, abbot of Bennchair, rested. Colman son of Robhartach, abbot of Slane; Aedhan, abbot of Roscre;[9] Cormac, son of Conall, abbot of Treoit,[10] [and] Maelruanaidh, son of Cathasach, vice-abbot of Lusca, died. Cumuscach, son of Conghalach, King of Cianachta,[11] died. Muiredach, son of Echaidh, King of Coiced-Conchobair,[12] was slain by his brothers, viz., Aedh and Oengus, [838.]

---

[7] *Niall.*—Monarch of Ireland.

[8] *Bran.* —See above, under the year 834, where Bran is stated to have been ordained King of the Leinstermen, by Niall Caille, Monarch of Ireland. In the list of the Kings of Leinster contained in the *Book of Leinster*, p. 39, the period of Bran's reign is given as four years.

[9] *Ros-cre*—Written ros crae in B. But like ros crea in A. Now Roscrea, in the county of Tipperary.

[10] *Treoit.*—See note [8], p. 300 *supra.* For some curious traditions connected with Treoit (Trevet, co. Meath), and its etymology (tre foit, "three sods"), see the Prophesy of Art son of Conn, *Lebor na hUidre*, p. 119, Lithograph copy, publ. by the R. I. Acad.

[11] *Cianachta.* — The Cianachta of Bregh, a tribe located in the eastern part of the present county of Meath.

[12] *CoicedConchobhair.*—The "Fifth" (or "Province") of Conchobar Mac Nessa; a bardic name for Ulidia. In the list of the kings of Ulidia contained in the *Book of Leinster*, p. 41, the name of "Muridach" appears, the duration of his reign being given as 17 years.

aliis multis. Cenneitiġ mac Congalaiġ, rex nepotum filiorum Cuais Breġ, a suo fratre .i. Ceile, dolose iugulatus est. Crunnṁael mac Fiannamail, equonimus Dermaiġi, iugulatus est o Maelsechnaill mac Maelruanaiḋ. Feċt di Gallaiḃ for Loċ Eċdach, corortadar tuatha 7 cella tuaiscert Erenn ass. Coemċloḋ abbad i n-ard Maċae .i. Dermait (.h. Tiġernaiġ) indon Forinnan (o Raṫ mic Maluis). Bellum re gennib for firu Fortrenn, in quo ceciderunt Euganan mac Oengusa et Bran mac Oengussa, et Aed mac Boanta; et alii pene innumerabiles ceciderunt. Loscaḋ Fernann 7 Corcaiḋe o gennṫiḃ.

.b. Kt. Ianair. Anno domini dccc.° xxx.° ix.° Orggain Luġmaiḋ di Loċ Eċdaċ o gennṫiḃ, qui episcopos et presbiteros et sapientes captiuos duxerunt et alios mortificauerunt. Floriacus imperator Francorum moritur. Loscaḋ aird Maċae cona dertiġiḃ 7 a doimliacc. Feidilmiḋ ri Muman do innriuḋ Mide 7 Breg, coniddeisiġ i Temraiġ, et in illa uice indred Cell 7 Beiṫri la Niall mac Aeḋa.

Is he Feiḋlimiḋ in ri,
Dianid opair oen laiṫi,
Eitrige Connaċt cen caṫ
Ocus Miḋe do manraṫ.

---

[1] *Dermagh.*—Durrow, in the barony of Ballycowan, King's County.

[2] *Maelsechnaill.* — The name is otherwise (and more usually) written Maelsechlainn. He was King of Uisnech (or Meath) for ten years, and his accession to the monarchy of Ireland is recorded at the year 846 *infra.* As Maelsechlainn (or Malachy) I., he occupies a conspicuous place in Irish history because of his sturdy resistance to the Norse and Danish invaders.

[3] *Loch-Echach.*—Lough Neagh.

[4] *Ua Tighernaigh*, i.e., "grandson" (or descendant) of Tigernach. At the year 834 *supra*, where Dermait is stated to have been removed from the abbacy of Armagh in favour of Forannan, he is called O'Thighernan.

[5] *In the place.*—indon (for i ninad), A., B.

[6] *Rath-mic-Malais.*—See note on this name at A.D. 834. This clause is not in B.

[7] *Fortrenn.*—See note [8], p. 118 *supra.*

[8] *Corcach-mor.* — The "Great Marsh," Cork city, in Munster.

[9] *Floriacus.* — For this name we should read "Ludovicus Pius," King of the Franks (who died on the 12th

and by several others. Cenneitigh, son of Conghalach, King of Ui-Mac-Uais of Bregh, was treacherously slain by his brother, *i.e.*, Ceile. Crunnmhael, son of Fiannamhail, steward of Dermagh,[1] was slain by Maelsechnaill,[2] son of Maelruanaidh. An expedition of Foreigners on Loch-Echach,[3] from which they destroyed the territories and churches of the North of Ireland. A change of abbots in Ard-Macha, viz., Dermait (Ua Tighernaigh[4]) in the place[5] of Forindan (from Rath-mic-Malais[6]). A battle by Gentiles over the men of Fortrenn,[7] in which fell Euganan son of Oengus, and Bran son of Oengus, and Aedh son of Boant; and almost countless others were slain. The burning of Ferna, and of Corcach-mor[8], by Gentiles.

Kal. Jan. A.D. 839. The plundering of Lughmadh from Loch-Echach,[3] by Gentiles, who led captive bishops, and presbyters, and wise men, and put others to death. Floriacus,[9] Emperor of the Franks, died. Burning of Ard-Macha, with its oratories and cathedral.[10] Fedilmidh, King of Munster, ravaged Midhe and Bregh, and rested in Temhair;[11] and the plundering of [Fera]-Cell[12] and [Delbhna]-Bethri,[13] on that occasion, by Niall,[14] son of Aedh. [839.] BIS.

Fedhilmidh[15] is the King,
To whom it was but one day's work
[To obtain] the pledges of Connaught without battle,
And to devastate Midhe.

---

of the Calends of July, 840). as O'Conor suggests. *Rer. Hib. Script.*, vol. 4, p. 214, note [1].

[10] *Cathedral.*—doimliacc; literally "stone house" (or "stone church").

[11] *Temhair.*—Tara, in Meath.

[12] *Fera-Cell.*—"This name was long preserved in Fircal, a barony in the King's County, now known as Eglish; but there is ample evidence to prove that Feara-ceall comprised not only the present barony of Eglish, but also the baronies of Ballycowan and Ballyboy, in the same county." O'Donovan's ed. of *O'Dubhagain*, App., p. vi., note [24].

[13] *Delbhna-Bethri.*—The old name of a territory comprising nearly the whole of the present barony of Garrycastle, King's County.

[14] *Niall.*—Monarch of Ireland at the time.

[15] *Fedhilmidh.*—These lines, (not in B.), are written in the lower margin

Morr Murcadha mic Aedha regis Connacht. Guin Cinaedha mic Corcraidh regis Bregmaine, i Tethbai. Iosep Roiss moer, episcopus et scriba optimus et ancorita, abbas Cluana auis et aliarum ciuitatum, dormiuit.

Kl. Ianair. Anno domini dccc.° xl.° Gennti for Loch Eachach beós. Cumsundud for Maelruanaidh mac nDonnchada la Diarmaid mac Concobair, 7 marbad Diarmata iarum la Maelsechnaill in eadem die, et Maelruanaigh in uita remansit. Aedh mac Dunchada
Fol. 40bb. iugulatus est dolose a sociis Conaing mic Flaind in conspectu eius. Longport oc Linn duachaill asa rorta tuatha 7 cealla Tethbai. Longport oc Duiblinn asrorta Laigin 7 Oi Neill etir tuatha 7 cealla, corice sliabh Bladhma. Slogadh la Feidlimid corici Carmain. Slogadh la Niall ar a chenn corice Magh n-Ochtair.

Bachal Feidlimid frighligh,
Foracbadh is na draighnibh,
Dorruc Niall co nert natha,
A cert in catha claidmigh.

---

of fol. 40b in A., with a mark indicating the place where they might be introduced into the text.

[1] *King.*—regis. Om. in B.

[2] *Breghmaine.*—A territory now represented by the barony of Brawny, co. Westmeath.

[3] *Tethba.*—See note [9], p. 316 *supra.*

[4] *Cluain-Eois.*—Written sometimes cluain auis in the text. Clones, in the co. Monaghan. After this entry, the following note is added in a later hand in MS. B.:—Annsa m-bliaghain so tíos tangadur Lochlanaidh a n-Eirinn artus do reir ant sencusa. "In this year below (scil. 840) the *Lochlannachs* came first to Ireland, according to the *senchus* ("history").

[5] *Victory.*—The word in the text is cumsundud, which is decidedly corrupt. In the corresponding entry in the *Ann. Four Masters* (at the same year) the word employed is sraoinead, which means a "breaking," "rout," or "defeat."

[6] *Maelruanaidh.*—King of Uisnech (or Meath); and father of Maelsechnaill (or Malachy I.), who became King of Ireland in A.D. 847. See at the year 846 *infra*, and the note on Maelsechnaill under the year 838 *supra.*

[7] *Linn-Duachaill.*—The "Linn (or 'Pool') of Duachall." The name of some harbour on the coast of the co. Louth; most probably Dundalk harbour. But see Todd's *Cogadh Gaedhel re Gallaibh*, Introd., p. lxii., note [1]. This fortress, or encampment, was of course formed by the Foreigners. It was a long way from it, however, to Tethba, a district comprising parts of the present counties of Westmeath and Longford. See p. 316 *ante*, note [9].

Death of Murchadh, son of Aedh, King[1] of Connaught. The mortal wounding of Cinaedh, son of Coscrach, King of Breghmaine,[2] in Tethba.[3] Joseph of Ros-mor, a bishop and excellent scribe, and anchorite, abbot of Cluain-Eois[4] and other churches, 'fell asleep.'

Kal. Jan. A.D. 840. Gentiles on Loch-Echach still. [840.]
A victory[5] over Maelruanaidh[6] son of Donnchad, by Diarmait son of Conchobar; and Diarmait was afterwards slain by Maelsechnaill the same day; and Maelruanaigh remained alive. Aedh, son of Dunchad, was treacherously slain by the companions of Conaing, son of Fland, in his presence. A fortress at Linn-Duachaill,[7] from which the territories and churches of Tethba[8] were plundered. A fortress at Dubhlinn,[9] from which Leinster and the Ui-Neill were plundered, both territories and churches, as far as Sliabh-Bladhma.[10] A hosting by Feidhlimidh as far as Carman.[11] A hosting by Niall to meet him, as far as Magh-ochtar.[11]

The crozier[12] of vigil-keeping Fedhlimidh,
Which was left on the thorn-trees,
Niall bore off, with usual power,
By right of the battle of swords.

---

[8] *Tethba.*—See last note.

[9] *Dubhlinn.* — Literally, "Blackpool," from which the name "Dublin" is derived. This fortress was also formed by the Foreigners, and is supposed to have been erected on the site of the present Castle of Dublin.

[10] *Sliabh-Bladhma.*—Now known as the Slieve-Bloom Mountains, on the confines of the King's and Queen's Counties.

[11] *Carman—Magh-ochtar.* — The names of two places in the present county of Kildare; the first (Carman) in the south, and the second in the north of the county. O'Donovan was wrong in taking "Carman" to be the same as "Loch-Garman," the old name of Wexford. See his ed. of the *Ann. Four Mast.*, A.D. 840, note h. It is strange that such an acute topographer and scholar, as O'Donovan undoubtedly was, should have considered it likely that King Fedhlimidh, marching from Cashel to meet the King of Ireland somewhere in Kildare, should go round by Wexford, where the Ui-Ceinnselaigh would probably have given him very short shrift. But the correction of the error (which unfortunately has been repeated over and over again in works of seeming authority) would occupy more space than could be devoted to it here.

[12] *Crozier.*—The original of these

Kl. Ianair. Anno domini dccc.° xl.° i.° Muiredaċ mac Cernaiġ, equonimus aird Maċae, moritur. Geinnti for Duiblinn beos. Finsnechta mac Bresail abbas Cille Dumai glinn, Cumsuḋ mac Ruamlusa abbas domnaiġ Seċnaill, omnes mortui sunt. Feidlimiḋ Cille more enir, episcopus, quieuit. Maelduin mac Conaill, ri Calatroma, do ergaḃail do ġenntiḃ. Orggain Cluana mic Nois o genntiḃ di Linn duaċail. Orggain Biror 7 Saiġre o genntiḃ di Duiblinn. Longas Normannorum for Boinn, for Linn roiss. Longas Normannorum oc Linn saileċ la Ultu. Moran mac Indrechtaiġ, abb cloċair mac n-Daimeni, du ergabail du gallaiḃ Linnae, 7 a éc leo iarum. Comman abbas Linne duaċail do guin [do] loscaḋ o genntiḃ 7 goiḋelaiḃ. Orgain tirirt Diarmata o genntiḃ di ċóel uisce. Ceallach mac Caṫgin, abb Droma moer la hU Eċaċ, dormiuit. Dungal mac Ferġaile, ri Ossaiġe, moritur.

Kl. Ianair. Anno domini dccc°. xl°. ii.° Mors Maelruanaiḋ mic Donncaḋa (.i. ri Miḋe 7 athair Maelsechlainn). Mors Caṫail mic Concoḃair. Arttagan mac Domnaill iugulatus est dolose, a Ruargg

lines (not in B.) is written in the top margin of fol. 40*b* in A., with a mark of reference to the proper place in the text. They were meant to be severe against Fedhlimidh, King of Cashel, who was a sort of ecclesiastic.

[1] See note [9], p. 345.

[2] See note [7], p. 344.

[3] *Dublinn.*—The *Four Mast.* (841) say la Gallaiḃ bóinne, "by the Foreigners of the Boyne." But see Todd's *Cogadh Gaedhel re Gallaibh*, p. 17.

[4] *Linn-Rois.*—The "Pool of Ros." That part of the Boyne (according to O'Donovan) opposite Rosnaree, in the barony of Lower Duleek, co. Meath. *Four Mast.*, A.D. 841, note q.

[5] *Clochar-mac-n Daimeni.*—Clogher, in the co. Tyrone. See Reeves' *Adamnan*, p. 111, note c, where some curious information is given regarding the history of this place.

[6] *Linn.*—Apparently the place referred to in the next entry.

[7] *Comman.*—Called Caemhan in the *Ann. Four Mast.*, and *Chron. Scotorum*, in both of which authorities he is stated to have been put to death by Foreigners alone. But the Translator of the Annals of Clonmacnoise (at the year 839) states that "Koewan (abbott of Lyndwachill), was both killed and burnt by the Danes, and some of the Irishmen."

Kal. Jan. A.D. 841. Muiredach son of Cernach, steward of Ard-Macha, died. Gentiles on Dubhlinn[1] still. Finsnechta son of Bresal, abbot of Cill-Duma-glinn; Cumsudh son of Ruamlus, abbot of Domnach-Sechnaill—all died. Feidhlimidh of Cill-mor-Enir, a bishop, rested. Maelduin son of Conall, King of Calatruim, was taken prisoner by Gentiles. The plundering of Cluain-mic-Nois by Gentiles from Linn-Duachail.[2] The plundering of Biror and Saighir by Gentiles from Dubhlinn.[3] A fleet of Norsemen on the Boyne, at Linn-Rois.[4] Another fleet of Norsemen at Linn-sailech in Ulster. Moran, son of Indrechtach, abbot of Clochar-mac-n-Daimeni[5] was taken prisoner by the Foreigners of Linn,[6] and afterwards died with them. Comman,[7] abbot of Linn-Duachail,[8] was wounded and burned by Gentiles and Goidhel. The plundering of Disert-Diarmata,[9] by Gentiles from Cael-uisce.[10] Cellach son of Cathgen, abbot of Druim-mor[11] in Ui-Echach, 'fell asleep.' Dungal, son of Fergal, King of Osraighe, died. [841.]

Kal. Jan. A.D. 842. Death of Maelruanaidh son of Donnchadh, (King of Midhe, and father of Maelsechlainn[12]). Death of Cathal, son of Conchobar. Artagan, son of Domnall, was treacherously slain by Ruarc[13] son of Bran. [842.]

---

[8] *Linn-Duachaill.*—See note [7] under the year 840.

[9] *Disert-Diarmata.* — "Diarmait's Desert" (or "hermitage"). The old Irish name of Castledermot, a place of importance anciently, in the south of the County of Kildare, and about four miles to the eastward of the River Barrow, along which the "Gentiles" from Cael-Uisce probably made their way into that part of Kildare.

[10] *Cael-uisce*; i.e. the "Narrow-water," between the head of Carlingford Lough and Newry, co. Down.

[11] *Druim-mor*; i.e., the "great ridge." Now Dromore, in the barony of Upper Iveagh, co. Down.

[12] *Maelsechlainn.*—Malachy I., King of Ireland. The name is often found written Maelsechnaill. See note on the name under the year 838 *supra*. This clause, which is not in B., is interlined in a later hand in A.

[13] *Ruarc.*—He was king, or chief, of the powerful Leinster tribe called the Ui-Dunlaing. His death is recorded at the year 860 *infra*. See Shearman's *Loca Patriciana*, geneal. Table xi., facing p. 223.

mac Broin. Cinaeḋ mac Conroi, rex generis Loiġaire, iugulatus est o Delḃni. Cumsuḋ mac Derero et Moinaiġ mac Soṫċadaiġ, duo episcopi et duo ancorite, in una nocte mortui sunt i n-disirt Diarmata. Ferġus mac Foṫaiġ, rex Connacht, moritur. Donnacan mac Maeletuile, scriba et ancorita, in Italia quieuit. Suibne mac Forannain, abbas Imleċo Fio, moritur. Colgu mac Fedaiġ ancorita pausauit.

Fol. 41aa. Kl. Ianair. Anno domini dccc.° xl.° iii.° Maelmiṫiġ mac Cinaeḋa iugulatus est a Gentilibus. Ronan abbas Cluana mic Nois dormiuit. Briccein abbas Loṫra obiit. Loscaḋ cluana ferta Brendain o Gentiḃ do Loċ Ri.

Kl. Ianair. Anno domini dccc.° xl.° iiii° Forindan abbas aird Maċae du ergaḃail du Genntiḃ i Cloen comardai, cona minnaiḃ 7 cona muinntir, 7 a breiṫ do longaiḃ Luimniġ. Orggain duin Masc o Genntiḃ, du in ro marbad Aeḋ mac Duiḃdacriċ abb Tire da ġlas 7 Cluana eiḋniġ, 7 du in ro marbaḋ Ceiṫernaċ mac Condinaisc, secnap Cille daro, 7 alaile ile. Dunaḋ di Gallaiḃ (.i. la Tursgeis) for Loċ Ri, corortadar Con-

---

[1] *Two.*—ii (for duo), A. Omd· in B.

[2] *Night.*—noċte, A. nocte, B.

[3] See note [9], p. 347.

[4] *Imlech-fia.*—See note [2], p. 194 *supra.*

[5] *By Gentiles.*—a genntibus, B.

[6] *Lothra.*—Lorrha, in a parish of the same name, barony of Lower Ormond, and county of Tipperary.

[7] *Forindan.*—Or Forannan. See the entries regarding this ecclesiastic at the years 834 and 838, *supra.* His return from Munster is noticed at the year 845.

[8] *Cluain-comarda.*—Written cloen comardai in A. and B. According to Dean Reeves this place, the name of which signifies the "Lawn (or paddock) of the sign, or token," now known as "Colman's Well," a village in the barony of Upper Connello, in the southern border of the co. Limerick. See Todd's Dano-Irish Wars, Introd., p. civ., note [3].

[9] *Luimnech.*—Limerick.

[10] *Dun-Masc.*—Now known as the Rock of Dunamase, a little to the east of Maryborough, in the Queen's Co.

[11] *Tir-da-glas.*—Terryglass, in the barony of Lower Ormond, county of Tipperary, where there are some ruins, the remains of an imposing monastic establishment.

[12] *Cluain-Eidhnigh.*—Clonenagh, in

Cinaedh, son of Curoi, King of Cinel-Loeghaire, was slain by the Delbhna. Cumsudh son of Derero, and Moinach son of Sotchadach, two bishops and two[1] anchorites, died in the one night[2] in Disert-Diarmata.[3] Fergus, son of Fothach, King of Connaught, died. Donnacan son of Maeltuile, scribe and anchorite, 'rested' in Italy. Suibhne son of Forannan, abbot of Imlech-fia,[4] died. Colgu son of Fedach, an anchorite, rested.

Kal. Jan. A.D. 843. Maelmithigh, son of Cinaedh, [843.]
was slain by Gentiles.[5] Ronan, abbot of Cluain-mic-Nois, 'fell asleep.' Bricceni, abbot of Lothra,[6] died. Burning of Cluain-ferta-Brendain, by Gentiles from Loch-Rí.

Kal. Jan. A.D. 844. Forindan,[7] abbot of Ard-Macha, [844.]
was taken prisoner by Gentiles in Cluain-comarda,[8] with his reliquaries and his 'family,' and carried off by the ships of Luimnech.[9] The plundering of Dun-Masc[10] by Gentiles, wherein was slain Aedh son of Dubhdacrich, abbot of Tir-da-glas[11] and Cluain-Eidhnigh,[12] and wherein were slain Ceithernach son of Cudinaisc, vice-abbot of Cill-dara, and several others. A host[13] of the Foreigners (*i.e.* with Turges[14]) on Loch-Rí, so that they destroyed

---

the barony of Maryborough West, Queen's County.

[13] *Host.*—The word in the text is ꝺunaḋ, which signifies 'fortress,' 'encampment,' 'army,' or multitude. In the *Chron. Scotorum*, at A.D. 845, the word used is ḋún, which means a 'fastness,' or 'fortress,' In the *Cogadh Gaedhel re Gallaibh*, the corresponding term is longeꞅ, a fleet (from long, a ship). Todd's ed., p. 12. The *Four Mast.* have ꞅlóiġeḋ, a hosting, or expedition.

[14] *With Turges.*—The original of this parenthetic clause, which is not in B., has been added in *al. man.* in A. The identity of this Turges (or Turgesius, as his name has been Latinized), who seems to have made himself very odious to the Irish by his oppression and cruelty, has for centuries been a subject of idle conjecture. Giraldus Cambrensis, *Top. Hib.* Dist. iii, c. 38, identifies Turgesius with the Gormund of Geoffrey of Monmouth's Chronicle (lib. xi. c. viii.) But Father Shearman tries to prove that this so-called African King Gormundus was a chieftain of the Leinster sept of MacGormans. *Loca Patriciana*, p. 215. See O'Donovan's ed. of *Ann. Four Mast.*, A.D. 843, notes d—g, and Todd's *War of the Gaedhil with the Gaill*, *Introd.*, p. lii.

naċta 7 Miḋe, 7 co ro loscairet Cluain mic Nois cona dertaigiḃ, 7 Cluaen ferta Brenainn, 7 Tir da glass, 7 Loċra 7 alaile caṫraċa. Fiaċna mac Maelebresail, abbas Finnabraċ abae, moritur. Gormgal mac Muiredaiċ, episcopus et ancorita Lainne leire, quieuit. Caṫroiniuḋ for Gennte re Niall mac Aeḋa i maiġ Iṫa. Orggain Donncaḋa mic Follomain 7 Flainn mic Maelruanaig, la Maelseċnaill mac Maelruanaiḋ. Turges du ergaḃail la Maelseċnaill, 7 baduḋ Tuirges illoċ uair iarum. Labraiḋ mac Ailello abbas Slane moritur. Robartaċ mac Bresail, abbas achaid bo Cainniġ, moritur. Robartaċ mac Flainn, abbas Domnaiġ moer, moritur. Dunaḋ di Gallaiḃ Aṫa cliaṫ oc Cluanaib andobuir.

Kl. Ianair. Anno domini dccc.° xl.° u.° Caṫal mac Ailello rex nepotum Maine, Ferrdomnaċ sapiens et scriba optimus aird Maċae, Connmaċ mór mac Corcraiġ rex nepotum Briuin, dormierunt. Orggain
Fol. 41 *ab.* bairlicce do ġenntiḃ. Niall mac Aeda rex Temro (.i. ic linne Neill for Callaind), mersione mortuus est.

---

[1] See note [11], p. 348.

[2] See note [8], p. 348.

[3] *Finnabhair-abha.*—Fennor, near Slane, co. Meath.

[4] *Lann-leire.*—See note [15], p. 205, *supra.*

[5] *Niall.*—King of Ireland.

[6] *Drowning of Turges.*—In none of the Irish Chronicles is it absolutely stated that Turgesius was drowned *by* Maelsechnaill (or Malachy I.); the statement being that Turgesius was drowned after his capture. But Mageoghegan, in his translation of the *Annals of Clonmacnoise*, at A.D. 842, says, "Turgesius was taken by Moyleseaghlyn mac Moyleronie, and he afterwards drownded him in the poole of Loghwarc adjoining to Molyngare." In the *Book of Leinster* also (p. 25, col. b,) it is positively asserted that Turgesius was drowned by Maelsechlainn. The silly story given by Giraldus (Topog. Hib., dist. III., c. 40) alleging that Turgusius was assassinated by 15 young Irishmen, disguised as females, is without any foundation whatever.

[7] *Loch-Uair.*—Now known as Logh-Owel, in the co. Westmeath.

[8] *Achadh-bo-Cainnigh.*—The "field of (St.) Canice's cows." Aghaboe, in the Queen's County.

[9] *Cluana-andobair.*—Cluana antobair, B. This place has not been identified. The *Four Masters*, in the corresponding entry in their Annals (A.D. 843), add that the "fold of Cill-achaidh" (Killeigh, barony of Geashill, King's County,) was burned;

Connaught and Midhe, and burned Cluain-mic-Nois, with its oratories, and Cluain-ferta-Brendainn, and Tir-da-glas,[1] and Lothra,[2] and other establishments. Fiachna son of Maelbresail, abbot of Finnabhair-abha,[3] died. Gormghal son of Muiredach, bishop and anchorite of Lann-leire,[4] rested. A battle was gained over the Gentiles, by Niall[5] son of Aedh, in Magh-Itha. The plundering of Donnchadh son of Fallomhan, and of Flann son of Maelruanidh, by Maelsechnaill, son of Maelruanaidh. Turges was taken prisoner by Maelsechnaill; and the drowning of Turges[6] subsequently in Loch-Uair.[7] Labraidh son of Ailill, abbot of Slane, died. Robhartach son of Bresal, abbot of Achadh-bo-Cainnigh,[8] dies. Robhartach son of Flann, abbot of Domnach-mor, died. An encampment of the Foreigners of Ath-cliath at Cluana-andobair.[9]

Kal. Jan. A.D. 845. Cathal son of Ailill, King of Ui-Maine; Ferdomnach, a wise man, and excellent scribe, of Ard-Macha, [and] Connmhach Mór,[10] son of Coscrach, King of Ui-Briuin, 'fell asleep.' The plundering of Baislic[11] by Gentiles. Niall[12] son of Aedh, King of Temhair, died by drowning (*i.e.*, at Linne-Neill on the Calland[13]). [845.]

---

from which it would appear that Cluana-andobair was in the neighbourhood of Killeigh.

[10] *Connmhach-Mór.*—See above at the year 835.

[11] *Baislic.*—Baslick, in the parish of the same name, barony of Castlereagh, county Roscommon.

[12] *Niall.*—Niall Caille, monarch of Ireland. The name "Niall," with the epithet "Caille," is added in the margin in A., and interlined in B. Niall Caille has been regarded by Irish writers generally as one of the legitimate kings of Ireland. But it is strange that his name does not appear in the list contained in the *Book of Leinster* (pp. 24–26). This may be an accidental omission. The beginning of Niall's reign is noticed at the year 832 (=833), *supra*.

[13] *Calland.*—Represented by ƙct. in A. and B., in each of which the original of the clause is interlined. Supposed to be the River Callan, which flows by Armagh city, and joins the Blackwater a little to the north of Charlemont. O'Donovan thought that the "water" (or river) meant was the Callan (otherwise called King's River), in the co. Kilkenny. (*Four Mast.* A.D. 844, note r.) But this seems unlikely.

Ni caraim in uisci n-duabais
Imteit seoċ toeḃ m'arais,
A Callaind ce nomaide
Mac mna baide ro badis

Maelduin mac Conaill, rex Calatroma, iugulatur a Lagenensibus. Niall mac Cinnfaelaḋ, rex nepotum Fidgennti, moritur. Bellum for Connacta re Gallaiḃ, in quo Rigan mac Fergusa, 7 Moġron mac Diarmota, 7 Aeḋ mac Caṫrannaiġ, et alii multi, ceciderunt. Roiniuḋ re Tigernaċ for Maelseċnaill 7 for Rua[r]cc, in quo trucidati sunt multi. Muiredaċ mac Flaind, abb monistreċ Buti, mortu[u]s est. Forindan abb aird Maċae du tiachtain a tiriḃ Muman, co minnaiḃ Patraicc. Coirpri mac Colmain, abb Aṫa truim, mortuus est. Conaing mac Ferdomnaiġ, abbas domnaiġ Patraicc, mortuus est.

Kl. Ianair. Anno domini dccc.° xl.° vi.° Feiḋlimiḋ (.i. mac Crimtain), rex Muman, optimus Scotorum, pausauit scriba et ancorita. Maelseċnaill mac Maelruanaiġ regnare incipit. Toġal insi loċa Muinremair la Maelseċnaill for fianlaċ mar di maccaiḃ bais Luigne 7 Galeng robatar oc indriuḋ na tuaṫ more Gentilium. Roiniuḋ már re Cerball mac

---

[1] *Ui-Fidgenti.*—See note [6], p. 150 *supra.*

[2] *Maelsechnaill.*—The beginning of his reign as monarch of Ireland is entered under the next year. See a note respecting him at the year 838 *supra.*

[3] *Ruarc.*—Ruarc, son of Bran, chief of the Ui-Dunlaing, and for nine years King of Leinster. See above under the year 842. His death is recorded at 861 *infra.*

[4] *Forindan.*—Mentioned above at years 834 and 838.

[5] *Ath-truim.*—Trim, co. Meath.

[6] *Domnach - Patraic.* — Donaghpatrick, in a parish of the same name, barony of Upper Kells, co. Meath. The first of the entries for this year, namely the obit of Cathal son of Ailill, King of Ui-Maine, is here added in a later hand in A.

[7] *Son of Crimthan.*—The original of this clause is added by way of gloss in A. and B.

[8] *Of the Scoti.*—Scotorum. Om. in B.

I love not the hateful water,
Which flows by the side of my house;
O, Calland, though thou may'st boast of it,
Thou hast drowned the son of a beloved mother.

Maelduin, son of Conall, King of Calatruim, was slain by Leinstermen. Niall son of Cennfaeladh, King of Ui-Fidgenti,[1] died. A battle won over the Connaughtmen, by Foreigners, in which Rigan son of Fergus, and Moghron son of Diarmait, and Aedh son of Cathrannach, and a great many others, were slain. A victory by Tigernach over Maelsechnaill,[2] and over Ruarc,[3] in which many were killed. Muiredach son of Flann, abbot of Manistir-Buti, died. Forindan,[4] abbot of Ard-Macha, came from the lands of Munster, with the reliquaries of Patrick. Coirpre, son of Colman, abbot of Ath-truim,[5] died. Conaing, son of Ferdomnach, abbot of Domnach-Patraic,[6] died.

Kal. Jan. A.D. 846. Fedlimidh (*i.e.* son of Crimthan[7]), King of Munster, the best of the Scoti,[8] a scribe and anchorite, rested. Maelsechnaill, son of Maelruanaidh begins to reign.[9] The demolition of the island of Loch-Muinremar[10] by Maelsechnaill, against a great band of 'sons of death'[11] of the Luighne[12] and Gailenga,[13] who were plundering the districts after the manner of the Gentiles. A great victory by Cerbhall[14] son of Dungal [846.]

---

[9] *Begins to reign.*—As King of Ireland. Added in the margin in A. See under the year 838.

[10] *Loch-Muinremar.*— Now Lough Ramor, near Virginia, in the barony of Castlerahan, co. Cavan.

[11] '*Sons of death*'; i.e. malefactors. O'Conor incorrectly renders the original, *di maccaib bais*, by "Vulgi profani."

[12] *Luighne.*—A district now represented by the barony of Lune, co. Meath.

[13] *Gailenga.*—Otherwise Gailenga-mora. Now known as the barony of Morgallion, in the north of the county of Meath.

[14] *Cerbhall.* — King of Ossory (during 40 years, according to the *Book of Leinster*, p. 40, col. 5). For much interesting information regarding the history of this remarkable man, who is stated to have been King of the Danish settlement in Dublin, and some of whose descendants are

Dungaile for Agonn,[1] in quo ceciderunt da cét déac. Maelgoan mac Eċḋaċ, rex cenuil Bogaine,[2] mortuus est. Ceallaċ mac Maelpatraic, secnab[3] fer Rois des abaind,[4] moritur. Connmaċ mac Cernaiġ, leṫri Ciaraiḋe[5] Connaċt, mortuus est. Artuir mac Muireḋaiġ, rí iarṫair Liphi, mortuus est. Caṫal mac Corcraiċ, rí Foṫart, iugulatus est a nepotibus Neill.

.b. Kl. Ianair. Anno domini dccc.° xl.° vii.° Nix magna in Kalendis Februarii. Finsneċta Luibniġi, anċorita, et rex Connacht antea, mortuus est. Tuaṫcar mac Cobṫaiġ, rex Luiġne, mortuus est. Caṫ re Maelseċnaill for genti i Foraiġ, in quo ceciderunt .uii. cét. Bellum re n-Olcobur ri Muman, 7 re Lorggan mac Cellaig co Laiġniu, for Gennti ecc Sciaiṫ Neċtain, in quo cecidit Tomrair erell tanise riġ

Fol. 41ba. Laiṫlinne, 7 da cet dec imbi. Roiniuḋ re Tigernaċ for Gennti i n-Dairiu disirt Doċonna, in quo ceciderunt da cet decc. Roiniuḋ re n-Euganacht Caisil for Gennti icc Dun Maeletuile, in quo ceciderunt .u. cet.

---

alleged to have become great persons in Iceland (both statements resting, apparently, on insufficient authority). See the references in Todd's *Cogadh Gaedhil re Gallaibh*, indicated in the Index under *Cearbholl, s. of Dungall*, and Shearman's *Loca Patriciana*, pp. 353, 356. The Irish Chronicles make no mention of Cerbhall's kingship of Dublin, or of the alleged connexion of his descendants with Iceland.

[1] *Agonn.* — agon, in A. and B., which O'Conor renders by "de prædonibus." The *Chron. Scotorum* (A.D. 847) has agonḋ. See that Chronicle, ed. Hennessy, p. 148, note [1]. The *Four Mast.*, in the corresponding entry (A.D. 845) write for gallaiḃ Aṫa cliaṫ ("over the Foreigners of Ath-cliath ('Dublin'), which may be correct").

[2] *Cinel-Boghaine.*—See note [9], p. 85, *supra*.

[3] *Vice-abbot.*—secnap. The *Four Mast.* (A.D. 845) write prioir ("prior").

[4] *Fera-Rois, south of the River.*—Probably the River Lagan, which divides the southern part of the co. Monaghan from the counties of Meath and Louth. The territory of the Fera-Rois, a name still represented in Magheross and Carrickmacross, comprised the barony of Farney, in the south of the co. Monaghan, together with adjacent parts of the two latter counties.

[5] *Ciaraidhe* (or Ciarraidhe).— A district afterwards known by the name of Clann Ceithernaigh, or Clankerny, near Castlereagh, in the county of Roscommon.

over Agonn,[1] in which twelve hundred were slain. Maelgoan, son of Echaid, King of Cinel-Boghaine,[2] died. Cellach, son of Maelpatraic, vice-abbot[3] of Fera-Rois, south of the River,[4] died. Connmach, son of Cernach, half-king of Ciaraidhe[5] of Connaught, died. Artuir, son of Muiredach, King of Iarthar-Lifi,[6] died. Cathal, son of Coscrach, King of Fotharta, was slain by the Ui-Neill.

Kal. Jan. A.D. 847. Great snow on the Kalends of February. Finsnechta of Luibnech,[7] an anchorite, and previously King of Connaught, died. Tuathchar, son of Cobthach, King of Luighne, died. A battle [gained] by Maelsechnaill over Foreigners, in Forach,[8] wherein seven hundred were slain. A battle [gained] by Olchobar, King of Munster, and by Lorcan, son of Cellach, with the Leinstermen, over the Foreigners, at Sciath-Nechtain,[9] in which Tomrair Erell,[10] tanist of the King of Lochlann, and twelve hundred along with him, were slain. A victory by Tigernach[11] over the Gentiles in Daire-Disirt-Dochonna,[12] in which twelve hundred[13] were slain. A victory by the Eoghanacht-Caisil over the Gentiles, at Dun-Maeletuile, in which five hundred were slain. A [847] BIS.

[6] *Iarthar-Lifi.*—See note [7], p. 100, *supra.*

[7] *Finsnechta of Luibnech.*- Regarding this Finsnechta (or Finnachta), see the *Chron. Scotorum* (ed. Hennessy), p. 148, note [3]. O'Donovan erred greatly regarding the situation of Luibnech, now Limerick, in the parish of Kilcavan, co. Wexford. See *Ann. Four Mast.*, A.D. 846, note w.

[8] *Forach.* — Now Farragh, near Skreen, in the co. Meath.

[9] *Sciath-Nechtain.* — "Nechtan's Shield (or Bush)." See this place mentioned at the year 769, *supra.*

[10] *Tomrair-Erell.*—Regarding this prominent character, see Todd's "*War of the Gaedhil with the Gaill,*" Introd., p. lxvii., note [4].

[11] *Tigernach.*—In the *Ann. Four Mast.* (846), and the *Chron. Scotorum* (848), Tigernach is called King of Loch-Gabhar, a district the name of which is now preserved in that of Lagore, in the barony of Ratoath, co. Meath.

[12] *Daire - Disirt-Dochonna.* — The "oak-wood of Dochonna's desert." This place has not been identified. Todd states (*War of the Gaedhil*, &c., Introd., p. lxviii., note) that it was in Ulster. But this is unlikely, as the victor was King, or prince, of a district in the south of the co. Meath.

[13] *Twelve hundred.*—The *Four Masters* (846) and *Chron. Scotorum* (848) give the loss of the "Gentiles" at

Coemcloḋ abbad i n-ard Maċae .i. Diermait in uicem Forinnain. Diarmait Cille Can dormiuit.

Kl. Ianair. Anno domini dccc.° xl.° uiii.° Conaing mac Flainn rex Breġ moritur. Coirpri mac Cinaeḋo rex nepotum Mael mortuus est. Finsnechta mac Diarmata abbas Doimliacc, Maelfuataiġ abbas aird Brecain, Oncu episcopus et ancorita Slane, obierunt. Ailill mac Cumuscaiġ, rex Loċa cal, moritur. Flaiṫbertaċ mac Ceileċair occisus est a fratribus suis. Muirḟeċt .uii. xx. long di muinntir riġ Gall du ṫiachtain du tabairt greamma forsna Gaillu robadar ar a ciunn, co commascrat hErenn n-uile iarum. Indrechtaċ abb Iae do ṫiachtain doċum n-Erenn co mindaib Coluim cille. Robartaċ mac Colgen, abbas Slane, exulauit. Flannacan mac Eċdaċ, rex dail Araide in tuaiscirt, iugulatus est a genere Eugain. Maelbresail mac Cernaiġ, rex Muġdorna, iugulatus est a gentilibus post conuersionem suam ad clericos. Airindan abbas Benncair dormiuit. Forbais Maelseċnaill hi Crupait.

Kl. Enair. Anno Domini dccc.° xl.° ix.° Cetaḋaċ abbas Cluana mic U Nois, 7 Tuaṫal mac Feraḋaiċ abbas Rechrand 7 Dermaiġe, 7 Ferċar mac Muireḋaiġ princeps Lainne Lere, defuncti sunt. Oengus mac

---

"twelve score," which seems more reasonable.

[1] *Change of abbots.*—This is the third instance recorded in this chronicle of a change of abbots at Armagh, in connexion with the names of Forindan and Diarmait. See above, at the years 834 and 838.

[2] *Cill-Can.*—So in A. and B. But the *Four Mast.* write the name Cill-Caisi, now known as Kilcash, in the parish of Kilcash, barony of Iffa and Offa East, co. Tipperary.

[3] *Ui-Mail.*—A tribe anciently occupying a district including the Glen of Imail, in the present co. of Wicklow.

[4] *Loch-Cal.* — The name of this territory is still preserved in that of Loughgall, a parish in the county of Armagh.

[5] *Reliquaries.*—In the partial translation of this Chronicle in Clar. 49, Brit. Museum, co mindaib is rendered by with his [Colum Cille's] "oathes or sanctified things."

[6] *Lived in exile.*—exulauit. The

change of abbots[1] in Ard-Macha, to wit, Diarmait in the place of Forindan. Diarmait of Cill-Can[2] 'fell asleep."

Kal. Jan. A.D. 848. Conaing, son of Fland, King of [848.] Bregh, died. Coirpri, son of Cinaedh, King of Ui-Mail,[3] died. Finsnechta son of Diarmait, abbot of Daimliag; Maelfuataigh, abbot of Ard-Brecain, [and] Onchu, bishop and anchorite of Slane, died. Ailill, son of Cumuscach, King of Loch-Cal,[4] died. Flaithbertach, son of Celechar, was killed by his brothers. A naval expedition of seven score ships of the people of the King of the Foreigners came to exercise power over the Foreigners who were before them, so that they disturbed all Ireland afterwards. Indrechtach, abbot of Ia, came to Ireland, with the reliquaries[5] of Colum-Cille. Robartach son of Colgu, abbot of Slane, lived in exile.[6] Flannacan,[7] son of Echaid, King of Dal-Araide of the North, was slain by the Cinel-Eoghain. Maelbresail, son of Cernach, King of Mughdorna, was slain by Gentiles, after his conversion to religion.[8] Airendan, abbot of Bennchair, 'feel asleep.' Encampment of Maelsechnaill in Crupait.[9]

Kal. Jan. A.D. 849. Cetadhach, abbot of Cluain-mic- [849.] U-Nois; and Tuathal son of Feradhach, abbot of Rechra[10] and Dermagh,[11] and Ferchar son of Muiredhach, abbot of Lann-léri,[12] died. Oengus, son of Suibhne, King of Mugh-

---

Four Masters give his obit under the year 847=849.

[7] *Flannacan.*—His name is not in the list of the Kings of Dal-Araide contained in the *Book of Leinster*, p. 41, col. 5.

[8] *Conversion to religion.* — post conuersionem suam ad clericos. This means that Maebresail had embraced a religious life. See the *Ann. Four Mast.* (847), and *Chron. Scotorum* (849).

[9] *Crupait.*—The name is "Crufait" in the Ann. Four Mast. (847), which is also the form in *Lebor na h-Uidre*, p. 127*a*, where the ancient name of the place is stated to have been *Rae ban*, "white plain" (or "field"). It has not been identified. O'Donovan suggests (*F. M.*, A.D. 847, note n) that it may be the place now known as Crohoy, in the barony of Upper Moyfenrath, co. Meath.

[10] *Rechra.*—Lambay Island, to the north of Howth, co. Dublin.

[11] *Dermagh.*—Durrow, in the barony of Ballycowan, King's County.

[12] *Lann-léri.* — Otherwise written *Lann-leire*. See note [15], p. 205 *supra*.

Suibne, rex Mugdorna, iugulatus est o Garfid filio Maelbrigtae. Cinaeḋ mac Conaing, rex Ciannaċtae, du fritċuideċt Maelseċnaill anneurt gall, co r' indriḋ Ui Neill o Sinaind co muir etir cella 7 tuaṫa, 7 co r' ort innsi Loċa gabur dolose, corbo comard fri a lar, 7 corolscad leis dertaċ Treoit 7 tri xx^t dec di doiniḃ ann. Broen mac Ruaḋraċ, rex nepotum Cra-
Fol. 41b. umṫain, et duo germani eius .i. Fogertaċ et Bruatur, iugulati sunt a fratribus suis.

Kl. Ianair. Anno domini dccc.° l.° Colggu mac Ceallaiġ princeps Cille tommae, Scannal mac Tibraiti princeps domnaiġ Seċnaill, Olcobar .i. mac Cinaeda rex Caisil, mortui sunt. Cinaeḋ mac Conaing, rex Ciannachta, demersus est in lacu crudeli morte, o Maelseċnaill 7 o Tigernaċ, di soesmaib deg doine n-Erenn 7 comarbbai Patraic specialiter.

Monuar a doine maiṫi,
Ba ferr a laiṫi cluiċi;
Mór liach Cinaeth mac Conaing
Hi lomand doċum cuiṫi.

Tetact dubgennti du Aṫ cliaṫ, co ralsat ár mór du finngallaiḃ, 7 co ro [s]latsat in longport etir doine 7 moine. Slat do duḃgenntib oc Lind duaċail, 7 ár

---

[1] *Garfidh.*—Garfid, A. The *Four Masters* (848) write the name Gairḃeth.

[2] *Maelsechnaill.*—King of Ireland at the time.

[3] *To the sea*; i.e. from the Shannon eastwards to the sea. The words co muir ("to the sea") are erroneously represented in A. and B. by comm. The liberty has been taken of amending the text, on the authority of the *Ann. Four Mast.* (848), and the *Chron. Scotorum* (850). It appeared plain, besides, that the compiler of this Chronicle intended to use the same form of expression, o Sinaind co muir, employed under the year 836 *supra*, where the extent of the territory of the (southern) Ui-Neill was thus indicated.

[4] *Level with the surface.*—The expression in the text, comard fri a lar, means "equally high with its floor."

[5] *Was burned.*—corolscad, for co ro loscad, A. B.

[6] *Cill-Toma.* — Kiltoom, in the parish of Faughalstown, barony of Fore, and county of Westmeath.

[7] *Cinaedh.*—See under the last year, where his rebellion against King Maelsechnaill (or Malachy I.), and his depredations, are recorded.

dorna, was killed by Garfidh,[1] son of Maelbrigte. Cinaedh, son of Conaing, King of Cianachta, turned against Maelsechnaill,[2] through the assistance of the Foreigners, so that he wasted the Ui-Neill, both churches and districts, from the Sinainn to the sea,[3] and treacherously destroyed the island of Loch Gabhar so that it was level with the surface ;[4] and the oratory of Treoit was burned[5] by him, and 260 men in it. Braen son of Ruadhri, King of Ui-Cremthain, and his two brothers, viz., Fogartach and Bruatar, were slain by their brethren.

Kal. Jan. A.D. 850. Colgu son of Cellach, abbot of Cill-Toma ;[6] Scannal son of Tibraite, abbot of Domnach-Sechnaill, [and] Olchobar, *i.e.*, the son of Cinaedh, King of Caisel, died. Cinaedh[7] son of Conaing, king of Cianachta, was drowned in a pool,[8] a cruel death, by Maelsechnaill and Tigernach,[9] with the approval of the good men of Ireland, and of the successor of Patrick especially. [850.]

Alas,[10] O good people,
His days of play were better !
Great grief that Cinaedh, son of Conaing,
[Should be taken] in ropes to a pool.

The coming of Black Foreigners to Ath-cliath, who made a great slaughter of the White Foreigners; and they plundered[11] the fortress, between people and property. A depredation by the Black Foreigners at Linn-Duachail, and a great slaughter of them [the White Foreigners].[12]

---

[8] *Drowned in a pool.*—in lacu. According to the *Ann. Four Mast.* (849), Cinaedh was drowned in the Ainge (written Angi in the *Chron. Scotorum*) (851), now called the River Nanny, which divides the baronies of Upper and Lower Dulcek, in the county of Meath.

[9] *Tigernach.*—King, or lord, of Loch-Gabhar, in Meath. See under the year 847.

[10] *Alas !*—The original of these lines, not given in B., is added in the lower margin of fol. 41*b*, in A.

[11] *They plundered.*—co rolatsat, for co ro ṡlatsat, A. and B. The *Four M.* (at 849) have co ro indirset; the *Chron. Scotorum* (851) gur indirsiot, conveying nearly the same meaning as the expression in the text.

[12] *White Foreigners.*—Supplied from

mor dub. Congalaċ filius Irgalaiċ, rex Coille Follaṁain, moritur. Riġdal i n-ardd Maċae etir Maelseċnaill co maiṫiḃ Leiṫi Cuinn, 7 Matoḋan co maiṫiḃ coiciḋ Conċobair, 7 Dermait 7 Feṫgna co saṁaḋ Patraicc, 7 Suarleċ co cleirċiḃ Miḋe. Cairell mac Ruaḋraċ, rex Loċa hUaitne, iugulatus est dolose ante portam oratorii Tigernaiġ hi Cluain auis, o Conailliḃ Fernmuiġi. Eċu mac Cernaiġ, rex fer Rois, interfectus est a gentilibus. Tipraiti nepos Baiṫenaig, abbas Liss moer, dormiuit.

.b. Kl. Ianair. Anno domini dccc.° l.° i.° Duo heredes Patricii .i. Forinnan scriba et episcopus et anchorita, et Dermait sapientissimus omnium doctorum Europae, quieuerunt. Uastatio aird Maċae o gallaiḃ Linndae die samċaisc. Luċt ocht xx.it long di ḟindgentiḃ do roaċtadar du caṫ fri Dubgennti do ṡnaṁ Aiġneċ. Tri la 7 tri aiḋċi oc caṫugad doaib, acht is re n-Duibgennti rommeabaiḋ, co farggabsat a ceile allonga leu. Stain fugitiuus euasit, et Iercne decollatus iacuit.
Fol. 42aa. Moenġal abbas Airdde Sraṫa, et Cennfaelad mac Ultain sapiens Boiṫe conais, et Lergal princeps Oṫnae, dormierunt. Fogertac mac Maelebresail, rex

---

Ann. Four Mast. (849), and *Chron. Scotorum* (851).

[1] *Coille-Follamhain.*—According to the *Félire of Oengus*, the church of Rosseach, (Russagh, in the barony of Moygoish, co. Westmeath), was in Caille-Fallamain. See Stokes's ed., p. cxlv.

[2] *Leth-Chuinn.*—"Conn's Half." The northern half of Ireland.

[3] *Matodhan.*—King of Ulidia. His obit is recorded at the year 856 *infra*.

[4] *Province of Conchobar.*—A bardic name for Ulster, over which Conchobar Mac Nessa ruled in the first century of the Christian Era. But Matodhan was only King of Ulidia, or that portion of Ulster comprising the present county of Down, with part of Antrim.

[5] *Diarmait.*—This was the person so often referred to in these Annals, in connexion with the Abbacy of Armagh. See note [4] under the year 847 *supra*.

[6] *Loch-Uaithne.*—This name is now represented by "Loughooney," in the barony of Dartry, co. Monaghan.

[7] *Cluain-auis.* — Clones, county Monaghan.

[8] *Fera-Rois.*—See a note respecting this district, at the year 846 *supra*.

[9] *Heirs.*—In the margin in A. the scribe has added the number 420, that

Congalach, son of Irgalach, King of Coille-Follamhain,[1] died. A royal meeting in Ard-Macha, between Maelsechnaill, with the nobles of Leth-Chuinn,[2] and Matodhan[3] with the nobles of the province of Conchobar,[4] and Diarmait[5] and Fethgna, with the congregation of Patrick, and Suarlech with the clerics of Midhe. Cairell son of Ruadhri, King of Loch-Uaithne,[6] was deceitfully slain before the door of the oratory of Tigernach in Cluain-auis,[7] by the Conailli of Fernmagh. Echu, son of Cernach, King of Fera-Rois,[8] was slain by Gentiles. Tipraite Ua Baithenaigh, abbot of Lis-mor, 'fell asleep.'

Kal. Jan. A.D. 851. Two heirs[9] of Patrick, viz., Forindan, scribe, and bishop, and anchorite, and Diarmait, the wisest of all the doctors of Europe, rested. Devastation of Ard-Macha by the Foreigners of Linn[10] on the day of Sam-chasc.[11] A fleet of eight score ships of White Gentiles came to fight against the Black Gentiles, to Snamh-aignech. They were three days and three nights[12] fighting; but the Black Gentiles were successful, that the others left their ships with them. Stain[13] escaped by flight, and Iercne[14] was beheaded. Moenghal, abbot of Ard-sratha, and Cennfaeladh son of Ultan, wise man of Both-Conais,[15] and Lergal abbot of Othan,[16] 'fell asleep. Fogartach son of Maelbresail, King of the Airghialla, [851.] BIS.

---

being the number of years elapsed since the beginning of the Chronicle (431).

[10] *Linn*; i.e. Linn-Duachaill. See above, at the year 841, and Todd's *War of the Gaedhil*, &c., Introd., p. lxii., note [1].

[11] *Sam-chasc*.—"Summer Easter." The *Four Mast.* (850) write an ꝺomnaċ ıaṗ ccaıꞅc ("the Sunday after Easter," rendered by "the Sunday *before* Easter" in O'Donovan's translation). But according to other authorities, Sam-chasc was a name for the fifth Sunday after Trinity Sunday. See *Chron. Scotorum* (ed. Hennessy), p. 152, note [1].

[12] *Three days and three nights*—.ııı. ła 7 .ııı. aıḋċı, A. B.

[13] *Stain*. — Written like Sꞇam (Stam) in A. and B.

[14] *Iercne*.—Written eıṗcne in B.

[15] *Both-Conais*.—The remains of this ancient ecclesiastical establishment have been discovered by Dean Reeves in the townland of Carrowmore, in the parish of Culdaff, barony of Inishowen East, co. Donegal. *Adamnan*, p. 405, note g.

[16] *Othan*.—Fahan, in the parish of

na n-Airġialla, moritur. Caṫal mac Dubaen, rex Oa n-Duaċ Argatrois, moritur. Forbasaċ mac Maeluiḋir, princeps Cille more Cinneiċ, moritur. Ar di Gallaiḃ oconaiḃ insiḃ airṫir Breg, 7 ar aile uc Raiṫ Aldain la Ciannacht, in uno mense.

Kl. Ianair. Anno domini dccc.° l.° ii.° Ailill mac Robartaiġ princeps Luscan, et Flann mac Rechtabrad abbas Leiṫ Manċain, et Ailgenan mac Donngaile rex Caisil, defuncti sunt. Amlaim mac riġ Laiṫlinde do tuiḋecht a n-Erinn, corogiallsat Gaill Erenn dó, 7 cis o Goiḋelaib. Ectigern mac Guaire, rex Laigen desgabar, iugulatus est dolose a Bruatar filio Aeḋo 7 o Cerball filio Dunġaile; et Bruatar filius Aeḋo iugulatus est dolose a sociis suis viii.° die post iugulationem Eċtigern. Flaṫnia abbas Biror, episcopus, obiit. Cernaċ mac Maelebresail, rex Cobo, moritur. Caṫmal mac Tomaltaiġ, leṫ ri Ulaṫ, a Nordmannis interfectus est.

Kl. Ianair. Anno domini dccc.° l.° iii.° Tuaṫal mac Maelebriġti, rex nepotum Dunlaingi, iugulatus

---

Fahan Upper, barony of Inishowen West, co. Donegal. Formerly called Othan-Mura, from its founder St. Mura, an eminent ecclesiastic and poet. See Todd's *Irish Nennius*, p. 222, note q., and Reeves' *Colton's Visitation*, p. 66.

[1] *Ui-Duach of Argatros.* — The name of the tribe and territory of Ui-Duach is still preserved in that of the parish of Odogh, in the north of the present co. of Kilkenny. But the territory was anciently much more extensive than the present parish of Odogh.

[2] *At the islands* —oconaib insiḃ, A. and B., apparently a mistake for oc naib insiḃ, the more correct form.

[3] *Rath-Aldain.* — According to O'Donovan (*Ann. F. M.*, A.D. 850, note g), this place is now known as Rathallon, in the parish of Moorechurch, barony of Upper Duleek, co. Meath.

[4] *Liath-Manchain* —Lemanaghan, in the barony of Garrycastle, King's County.

[5] *Amhlaim.*—Over the last *m* of the name in A. and B. it is suggested that the name should be "Amhlaip."

[6] *Of Lochlaind.*—Corruptly written Laiṫlinde in A., and Laiṫlinne in B. But it has not been considered necessary to alter the text.

[7] *Echtigern.*—The name of Echtigern appears in the list of the kings

died. Cathal son of Dubhan, King of Ui-Duach of Argatros,[1] died. Forbasach son of Maeluidhir, abbot of Cill-mor-Cinneich, died. A slaughter of the Foreigners at the islands[2] of the east of Bregha; and another slaughter at Rath-Aldain[3] in Cianachta, in the same month.

Kal. Jan. A.D. 852. Ailill son of Robartach, abbot of Lusca; and Flann son of Rechtabhra, abbot of Liath-Manchain;[4] and Ailgenan son of Donngal, King of Caisel, died. Amhlaim[5] son of the King of Lochlaind,[6] came to Ireland, when the Foreigners of Ireland submitted to him, and a tribute [was given] to him by the Gaidhel. Echtigern[7] son of Guaire, King of South-Leinster, was treacherously slain by Bruatar son of Aedh,[8] and by Cerbhall[9] son of Dungal; and Bruatar son of Aedh[8] was treacherously killed by his confederates on the 8th day after the slaying of Echtigern. Flaithnia, abbot of Biror,[10] a bishop, died. Cernach son of Maelbresail, King of Cobha,[11] died. Cathmal son of Tomaltach, half-king of Ulidia, was slain by the Norsemen. [852.]

Kal. Jan. A.D. 853. Tuathal son of Maelbrighte, king of Ui-Dunlaing,[12] was deceitfully killed by his brothers. [853.]

---

of Ui-Cendselaigh, (or South Leinster), in the *Book of Leinster*, p. 40, col. 1, where the duration of his rule is set down as nine years. His slayer is described as Bruatar, son of Dubgilla, King of the Ui-Drona, (a tribe occupying a territory now represented by the barony of Idrone, co. Carlow).

[8] *Bruatar son of Aedh.*—See last note.

[9] *Cerbhall.*—He was King of Ossory during 40 years, according to the *Book of Leinster* (p. 40, col. 5). See a note regarding Cerbhall at the year 846 *supra*. His obit is given at the year 887.

[10] *Biror.*—Birr, in the King's County.

[11] *Cobha.*—The short form of a name otherwise written "Ui-Echach-Cobha, and "Ui-Echach-Ulad." A powerful sept, whose territory is now represented by the baronies of Upper and Lower Iveagh, in the County of Down. See Reeves' *Antiqq. of Down and Connor*, pp. 348–52.

[12] *Ui-Dunlaing.*—This was the tribe name of a powerful family in Leinster, descended from Dunlang, who was King of that Province in the third century. See Shearman's *Loca Patriciana*, Geneal. Table, No. 7. The name of Tuathal occurs in the list of the kings of Leinster in the *Book of Leinster*, p. 39, col. 2.

est dolore a fratribus suis. Maelsechnaill rex Teṁro do dul co firu Muman corici Indeuin na n-Desi, a n-gialla do tabairt. Heres Coluim cille, sapiens optimus, .iiii. id Márta apud Saxones martirizatur. Crech Domnaig moir itir Tigernach 7 Fland mac Conaing, acht is re Fland romemaid.

Kl. Ianair. Anno domini dccc.° l.° iiii.° Caṫan abbatissa Cille daro moritur. Sneachta co fernu fer .ix. Kl. Mai. Crech la hAeḋ mac Neill co hUltu, co
Fol. 42ab. fargab Connecan mac Colmain 7 Flaiṫbertach mac Neill, 7 soċaiḋe cena. Finsneċtai fraude iugulatur est .i. mac Maelbriġti. Ruiḋgus mac Macniaḋ, abbas moinistreċ Buiti, dimersus est. Ailill abbas Achaid boo, Robartach abbas innse cain Deġa scriba, 7 Muireḋaċ ri airde Ciannaċta, mortui sunt.

.b. Kl. Ianair. Anno domini dccc.° l.° u.° Coirsne mor 7 siccet comtar suirri prim loċa 7 prim aibne Erenn du ṫraiġteċaiḃ 7 marclaiġiḃ a .ix. Kl. Decimbris usque ad .uii. idus Ianuarii. Tempestuosus annus et asperissimus. Maelsechnaill mac Maelruanaiġ i cCairiul, co tuc giallu Muman. Cocaḋ mor etir Genti 7 Maelsechnaill co n-Gallġoidelaiḃ leis. Derṫeċ Lusca do loscaḋ a Nordmannis. Roiniuḋ mor re n-Aeḋ mac Neill for Gallgaeiḋelu i n-glinn

[1] *Indeoin-na-nDesi.*—The "Anvil of the Desi." This name is still partially preserved in that of Mullaghnoney (the "summit," *mullach*, of the *inneoin*, or "anvil"), a townland in the parish of Newchapel, barony of Iffa and Offa East, co. Tipperary. See Joyce's *Irish Names of Places*, 2nd Series, pp. 197–8.

[2] *Successor.*—The *Four Masters* (at 852) call him Indreachtach. He is mentioned above at the year 848, as having come to Ireland with the reliquaries of Colum Cille. See Reeves' *Adamnan*, p. 390.

[3] *To the shoulders.*—co fromnu, B. A. has co fernu, "to the shields."

[4] *Manister-Buti.*—Now Monasterboice, co. Louth, founded by Buti (or Buite), son of Bronach, whose obit is given above at the year 518.

[5] *Drowned.*— The *Four Masters* add (A.D. 853), that Ruidhgus was drowned in the Bóinn (Boyne).

[6] *Achadh-bo.* — Or Achadh-bo-Cainnigh. The "field of St. Canice's cows" Now Aghaboe, in the barony of Clarmallagh, Queen's County. The name is written aċiḋ boo in A.; but

Maelsechnaill, king of Temhair, went to the men of Munster as far as Indeoin-na-nDesi,[1] and brought their pledges. The successor[2] of Colum-Cille, the best sage, was martyred by Saxons on the 4th of the Ides of March. The plundering of Domnach-mor, between Tigernach and Fland son of Conaing; but it is by Fland it was won.

Kal. Jan. A.D. 854. Cathan, abbess of Cill-dara, died. [854.
Snow up to the shoulders[3] of men, on the 9th of the Kalends of May. A preying expedition by Aedh son of Niall to the Ulaid, when he lost Connecan son of Colman, and Flaithbertach son of Niall, and many more besides. Finsnechta was slain by treachery, viz., the son of Maelbrighte. Ruidhgus, son of Macniadh, abbot of Manister-Buti,[4] was drowned.[5] Ailill, abbot of Achadh-bo;[6] Robartach, abbot of Inis-cain-Degha,[7] a scribe, and Muiredhach, King of Ard-Cianachta,[8] died.

Kal. Jan. A.D. 855. Great ice and frost,[9] so that the [855.
principal lakes and rivers of Ireland were passable for pedestrians and horsemen, from the 9th of the kalends of December to the 7th of the ides of January. A most tempestuous and harsh year. Maelsechnaill, son of Maelruanaigh, in Caisel, when he brought away the hostages of Munster. A great war between the Gentiles and Maelsechnaill, with whom were the Gall-Gaidel.[10] The oratory of Lusca was burned by the Norsemen. A great victory by Aedh, son of Niall, over the Gall-Gaidel,[10] in

---

achaıᴅ boo in B., which is more correct.

[7] *Inis-cain-Degha.* — Iniskeen, in the barony of Upper Dundalk, co. Louth.

[8] *Ard-Cianachta.* —A district now represented by the barony of Ferrard, in the county of Louth.

[9] *Frost.*—ךıccec, A., B.; probably for ךeccaᴅ, "freezing."

[10] *Gall-Gaidel.* — "Foreign Gael." Dean Reeves regarded them as the descendants of the Irish settlers in the Western Isles [of Scotland]. *Adamnan*, p. 390, note b. For further information regarding these Gall-Gaedhil (or Dano-Irish, as O'Donovan calls them; *Ann. M. F.*, A.D. 854, note t). see *Fragm. of Annals*, pp. 129, 139, 141, 233; and Todd's *War of the Gaedhil*, &c., in the places referred to in the Index under "Gaill-Gaedhil." But Skene, with much reason, suggests that the Gall-Gaidel

Foiċle co ra lad leis ar dimor dib. Horm toiseċ na n-Dubgennti iugulatus est la Ruaḋraiġ mac Meirminn, riġ m-Bretan. Suibne nepos Roiċliċ, scriba et anċorita, abbas Liss moer, Cormac Laṫraiġ Briuin scriba et episcopus, in pace dormierunt. Sodomna episcopus Slane martirizatur.

Kl. Ianair. Anno domini dccc.° l.° ui.° Roiniuḋ re n-Imar 7 re n-Amlaiḃ for Caittil find co na Gall-gaeḋelaiḃ hi tiriḃ Muman. Moengal abb Fobair 7 Siaḋal dirirt ċiarain requieuerunt. Matuḋan mac Muireḋaiġ, rex Ulaṫ, moritur. Triar do loscaḋ i Taillte di ṫeniḋ di nim. Uentus maximus co ra la fiḋar, co comscar innsi loċa. Cellaċ dixit,

O bai senaṫ finn fotail
Necea for soeraiḃ setaib,
Tres bliaḋain ní ar brecaiḃ,
Ar triċuit ar cúic cetaiḃ.

Kl. Ianair. Anno domini dccc.° l.° uii.° Cumsuċ
Fol. 42ba. episcopus et anchorita, princeps Cluana iraird, in pace pausauit. Cinaeḋ mac Ailpin rex Pictorum, 7 Adulf rex Saxan, mortui sunt. Tipraiti ban abbas Tire da glas [mortuus est]. Maelseċnaill mac Maelruanaiġ co feraib Erend do tuiḋecht hi tire

were the people who gave name to the district of Galloway, now forming the counties of Wigtown and Kirkcudbright, in Scotland. *Chron. Picts and Scots*, Preface, pp. lxxix.-lxxx. See also the references in the same work, under the name "Galloway" in the Index.

[1] *Glenn-Foichle.*—Now known as Glenelly, a district coinciding with the parish of Upper Bodoney, barony of Strabane Upper, co. Tyrone. See Dean Reeves' interesting note on this district, *Colton's Visitation*, p. 55, note o.

[2] *Ruadhri.*—Probably Rodhri the Great, whose death is recorded in the *Annales Cambriæ*, and in *Brut y Tywysogion*, at A.D. 877.

[3] *Mermen*, i.e., Mervyn. See *Annales Cambriæ*, and *Brut y Tywisogion*, at the year 844.

[4] *Lis-mor.*—Lismore, in the county of Waterford.

[5] *Lathrach-Briuin.*—Laraghbryan, in the parish of the same name, barony of North Salt, and county of Kildare.

[6] *Caittil Find.*—For other forms of the name of this person, see Todd's *War of the Gaedhil*, &c., Introd., p. lxxi., note [2].

Glenn-Foichle,[1] where a great slaughter was made of them by him. Horm, leader of the Black Gentiles, was slain by Ruadhri,[2] son of Merminn,[3] King of Britain. Suibhne Ua Roichligh, a scribe and anchorite, abbot of Lis-mor,[4] Cormac of Lathrach-Briuin,[5] a scribe and bishop, slept in peace. Sodomna, bishop of Slane, was martyred.

Kal. Jan. A.D. 856. A victory by Imar and Amlaibh, over Caittil Find[6] with his Gall-Gaidhel,[7] in the territories of Munster. Moengal, abbot of Fobhar,[8] and Siadhal of Disert-Chiarain,[9] rested. Matudhan, son of Muiredhach, King of Ulidia, died.[10] Three persons were burned in Tailltiu[11] by fire from heaven. A great storm, which caused great destruction of trees, and broke down lake islands. Cellach said:— [856.]

Since the fair great synod of Nice
Was [held] in noble manner,
The third year, not by false reckoning,
On thirty over five hundreds.[12]

Kal. Jan. A.D. 857. Cumsuth, a bishop and anchorite, abbot of Cluain-Iraird, rested in peace. Cinaedh[13] Mac Alpin, King of the Picts, and Adulf,[14] King of the Saxons, died. Tipraiti Ban[bhan], abbot of Tir-da-glas [died]. Maelsechnaill, son of Maelruanaigh, with the men of Ireland, went into the territories of Munster, and stayed [857.]

---

[7] *Gall-Gaidhel.*—See the note on this name under the last year.

[8] *Fobhar.*—The monastery of Fore, in the barony of Fore, co. Westmeath.

[9] *Disert-Chiarain.* — Now Castlekeeran, in the barony of Upper Kells, co. Meath.

[10] *Died.*—In the list of the Kings of Ulidia in the *Book of Leinster* it is stated (p. 41, col. 3) that Matudan died in pilgrimage.

[11] *Tailltiu.*—Teltown, in the barony of Upper Kells, co. Meath. A place much celebrated in ancient Irish history.

[12] *Hundreds.*—The Council of Nicea was held in A.D. 325; and considering that this Chronicle is antedated by one year at this period, Cellach, who is alleged to have composed the foregoing quatrain, was not very much out in his chronology.

[13] *Cinaedh Mac Alpin.* — Better known by the name of Kenneth Mac Alpin.

[14] *And Adulf.*—The person here meant was probably Æthelwulf, whose death is recorded in the Anglo-Saxon Chronicle at the year 855 (6). The contraction (7) for et is misplaced in

Muman, condeirid .x. naitci oc Neim,[1] 7 a n-innred co muir fadesr iar madmaim for arriga oc carnd Lughdach,[2] co farghadh ann lethri na n-Deise, Maelcron mac Muiredhaigh.[3] Tuc Maelsechlainn iarum giallu Muman o Belut Gabrain[4] co Inis Tarbnai[5] iar n-Ere, 7 o Dun Cermnai[6] co hAraind n-airthir.[7] Pluuialis autumnus et pernicio[si]ssimus[8] frugibus.

Kl. Ianair. Anno domini dccc.° l.° uiii.° Suairlech abbas Achaidh bo,[9] Ailill banbaine abbas Biror, Maelcoba ua Faelan abbas Cluana uamha, Faelgus abbas Rois crea, in pace dormierunt. Slogad mor la hAmlaib 7 Imar 7 Cerbhall i Midhe. Righdhal mathe Erenn oc raith Aedho mic Bricc, im Maelsechnaill rig Temra, 7 im Fethghna comarba Patraicc, 7 im Suairlech comarba Finnio, ic denum sidha 7 caincompaicc fer nErend, conid as in dail sin durat Cerball ri Ossraighi oghreir samtha Patraic 7 a comarba, 7 conidh and do dechaidh Ossraighi i n-dilsi fri leth Cuinn, 7 adrogaidh Maelgualai ri Muman a dilsi. Maelguala rex Muman a Nordmannis occisus est. Sechonnan filius Conaing, rex Cairgi brachaide, moritur.

.b. Kl. Ianair. Anno domini dccc.° l.° ix.° Sloighedh Laigen 7 Muman 7 Connacht, 7 Oa Neill in deiscirt, isin

---

A., where it occurs after the word Saxan.

[1] *Neim.*—This was the ancient name of the southern River Blackwater.

[2] *Carn-Lugdach.*—The cairn (or "monumental heap") of Lughaid. The place has not been identified.

[3] *Half-king.*—The *Four Masters* (at A.D. 856) give Maelcron the title of tanairi, or "tanist."

[4] *Belat-Gabrain.*—Otherwise written "Belach-Gabhrain." The "Road (or Pass) of Gabhran," (Gowran in the co. Kilkenny). This road led from Gowran towards Cashel. See O'Donovan's *Ann. F. M.*, A.D. 756, note. a.

[5] *Inis-Tarbhnai.*—Now known as the "Bull," a small island off Dursey Island, barony of Beare, co. Cork.

[6] *Dun-Cermna.* — This was the ancient name of the Old Head of Kinsale, in the co. Cork.

[7] *Ara-Airthir.*—"East Ara." The most eastern of the Islands of Arran, in Galway Bay, now known by the name of Inisheer.

[8] *Most destructive.*—pernециossimus, A.

[9] *Achadh-bo.*—acidh bo, A. achaidh bo, B.

ten nights at Neim;[1] and he plundered them southwards to the sea, after defeating their Kings at Carn-Lughdach[2] where the half-king[3] of the Deisi, Maelcron son of Muiredhach, was lost. Maelsechlainn afterwards carried off the hostages of [all] Munster from Belat-Gabrain,[4] to Inis-Tarbhnai[5] in the west of Ireland, and from Dun-Cermna[6] to Ara-airthir.[7] A rainy autumn, and most destructive[8] to all kinds of fruit.

Kal. Jan. A.D. 858. Suairlech, abbot of Achadh-bo;[9] [858.]
Ailill Banbaine, abbot of Biror; Maelcobha Ua Faelain, abbot of Cluain-uamha;[10] Faelgus, abbot of Ros-Cre[11]—slept in peace. A great hosting by Amlaiph, and Imar, and Cerbhall;[12] into Meath. A royal assembly of the nobles of Ireland at Rath-Aedha-mic-Bric,[13] including Maelsechnaill, King of Temhair, and including Fethgna successor of Patrick, and Suairlech successor of Finnia,[14] establishing peace and concord between the men of Ireland; and it was in that assembly Cerbhall, King of Osraighi, gave the award of the congregation and successor of Patrick, and it was there the Osraighi entered into allegiance with Leth-Chuinn,[15] and Maelgualai, King of Munster, tendered his allegiance. Maelgualai, King of Munster, was slain by the Norsemen. Sechonnan, son of Conaing, King of Carraig-Brachaidhe,[16] died.

Kal. Jan. A.D. 859. A hosting [of the men] of Lein- [859] BIS
ster, and Munster, and Connaught, and of the Ui-Neill

[10] *Cluain-uamha.*— The "meadow (or paddock) of the cave." Cloyne, in the barony of Imokilly, co. Cork.

[11] *Ros-Cre* —rois ċrea, A. rois crae, B.

[12] *Cerbhall.*—King of Ossory, and at this time in alliance with the Foreigners.

[13] *Rath Aedha-mic-Bric.* — This name, which signifies the "*rath* of Aedh (or Hugh) son of Brec," is now shortened to "Rahugh," the name of a townland and parish in the barony of Moycashel, co. Westmeath.

[14] *Successor of Finnia*; i.e. abbot of Clonard, co. Meath.

[15] *Leth-Chuinn.*—"Conn's Half," or the Northern Half of Ireland, represented at this time by King Maelsechnaill (or Malachy I.)

[16] *Carraig-Brachaidhe.*— The name of this district is still preserved in

foċla, la Maelseċnaill rig Temro, condeisiḋ oc maig duṁai i comḟocus aird Maċae. Do forbairt Aeḋ mac Neill 7 Flann mac Conaing an dunaḋ i n-aiḋċi, co romarbsat doine for lar in dunaiḋ, 7 ro meṁaiḋ for Aeḋ n-iaraiṁ, co farcaib ili stante exercitu Mael-seċnaill in statu suo. Aeḋ mac Duiḃdabairenn, rex Oa Fiḋgennti, moritur. Flannacan mac Colmain moritur. Niall mac Iallain qui passus est pa-
Fol. 42bb. ralisin xxx. iiii. annis, qui uexatur est uisionibus frequentibus tam falsis quam ueris, in Cristo quieuit.

Kl. Ianair. Anno domini dccc.° lx.° Indreḋ Miḋe do Aeḋ mac Neill co n-Gallaiḃ. Gormlaiṫ ingen Donncaḋa, amenissima regina Scotorum, post poenitentiam obiit.

Kl. Ianair. Anno domini dccc.° lx.° i.° Domnall mac Ailpin, rex Pictorum, mortuus est. Aeḋ mac Neill regnare incipit. [Sloicceḋ la] Aeḋ mac Neill co riga Gall im Miḋe, 7 la Flann mac Conaing do indriuḋ Miḋe. Finan cluana cain, episcopus et ancorita, Muirġes ancorita aird Maċa, uitam in pace finierunt. Maelseċnaill mac Maelruanaiġ (mic Donnchaḋa, mic Domnaill, mic Murchaḋa Miḋi, mic Diarmada den, mic Airmeḋaiġ ċaich, mic Conaill

---

that of Carrickabraghy, a townland in the parish of Clonmany, barony of Inishowen East, co. Donegal.

[1] *King of Temair*; i.e. King of Tara, or of Ireland.

[2] *Magh - dumha.* — The "plain (*Magh*) of the mound, or tumulus (*dumha*)." O'Donovan has identified this place with Moy, in the parish of Clonfeacle, barony of Dungannon Middle, co. Tyrone, on the opposite side of the River Blackwater from Charlemont in the co. Armagh. *Ann. F. M.*, A.D. 858, note o.

[3] *Aedh.*—The beginning of Aedh's reign as King of Ireland is recorded under the year 861.

[4] *In its position.*—in statusuo for in statu suo, A. B.

[5] *Ui-Fidhgennti.*—A tribe situated in the co. Limerick. See note [6], p. 150 *supra*.

[6] *Iallan.* — Written Giallain (in the gen. case) in the *Ann. Four Mast.* (A.D. 858). O'Conor prints (from B.) *mac Fallain*, and the translator in Clar. 49 writes *mac Fiallain.*

[7] *Delightful.* — amenissima (for

of the South, into the North, by Maelsechnaill, King of Temair,[1] who rested at Magh-dumha[2] in the vicinity of Ard-Macha. Aedh[3] son of Niall, and Flann son of Conaing, attacked the camp at night, and killed people in the middle of the camp; but Aedh was afterwards defeated, and lost a great number, the army of Maelsechnaill remaining in its position.[4] Aedh, son of Dubhdabhairenn, King of Ui-Fidhgennti,[5] died. Flannacan, son of Colman, died. Niall, son of Iallan,[6] who suffered from paralysis during 34 years, and who was disturbed by frequent visions, as well false as true, rested in Christ.

Kal. Jan. A.D. 860. Plundering of Meath, by Aedh[3] son of Niall, with Foreigners. Gormlaith, daughter of Donnchadh, the most delightful[7] Queen of the Scoti, died after penitence. [860.]

Kal. Jan. A.D. 861. Domnall Mac Alpin,[8] King of the Picts, died. Aedh,[9] son of Niall, begins to reign. [A hosting by] Aedh son of Niall, with the Kings of the Foreigners, into Meath, and by Flann son of Conaing, to plunder Meath. Finan of Cluain-Cain,[10] bishop and anchorite, Muirghes, anchorite of Ard-Macha, made an end of life in peace.[11] Maelsechnaill, son of Maelruanaigh (son of Donnchadh,[12] son of Domnall, son of Murchadh of Meath, son of Diarmaid Dian, son of Airmedach Caech, [861.]

---

amoenissima, A., B. According to the terms used by the *Four Masters* in recording her death (A.D. 859), Queen Gormlaith was not a blameless character.

[8] *Domnall Mac Alpin.*—The brother and successor, as King of the Picts of Scotland, of Kenneth (or Cinaedh) Mac Alpin, whose death is recorded above under the year 857.

[9] *Aedh.*—Aedh Finnliath, son of Niall Caille (whose death by drowning is noticed above at the year 845). The original of this entry, which forms part of the text in B., is added in the margin, in a later hand, in A.

[10] *Cluain-Cain.*—Now Clonkeen, in the barony of Ardee, co. Louth, according to O'Donovan (*Four Masters*, A.D. 836, note *u*).

[11] *In peace.*—For uitam in pace finierunt, as in A., B. has dormierunt.

[12] *Son of Donnchadh.*—This pedigree, which is interlined in A., is not in B.

guṫḃin, mic Suiḃne, mic Colmain moir, mic Diarmada deirg, mic Ferghusa Cerrbeoil), ri hErenn uile, .ii. Kalendas Decembris, .iii. feria, anno regni sui xiii.°, defunctus est. Ruarcc mac Broen, rex nepotum Dunlainge, iugulatus est. Maeloḋor oa Tindriḋ, sui leigis Goiḋeal, mortuus est.

Kt. Ianair. Anno domini dccc.° lx.° ii.° Aeḋ mac Cumuscaiġ, ri .h. Niallan, mortuus est. Muireḋaċ mac Maeleduin, secnap aird Maċae, 7 ri na n-airṫer, iugulatus est o Domnall mac Aeḋo mic Neill. Murecan mac Diarmata, rex Nairr 7 airtir Liphi, a Normannis interfectus est. Uaṁ Aċaiḋ aldai 7 Cnoḋbai, 7 uam feirt Boadan os Dubaḋ, 7 uam mna an gobann ro scruidiset Gaill, quod antea non perfectum est .i. a fecht ro slatsat .iii. riġ Gall feronn Flaind mic Conaing .i. Aṁlaim 7 Iṁar 7 Auisle, 7 Lorcan mac Caṫail leo occa, ri Mide.

.b. Kt. Ianair. Anno domini dccc.° lx.° iii.° Lorcan mac Caṫail, ri Miḋe, do ḋallaḋ la Aeḋ mac Neill riġ Teṁro. Concobar mac Donncaḋa, leiṫri Mide, do marbad i n-uisciu oc Cluain iraird la Amlaiḃ ri

[1] *Ruarc.*—For the pedigree of this chieftain, see Shearman's *Loca Patriciana*, Geneal. Table ii. (facing p. 223).

[2] *Ui-Niallain.*—A powerful tribe, the name of whose territory is still preserved in the baronies of O'Neilland East, and West, in the co. Armagh, and which furnished several bishops to the See of Armagh.

[3] *Airthera.* — Otherwise written Oirthera; and meaning "Easterns," or "Easterlings." The tribe occupying this territory were so called because they were seated in the east of the country of Oirghialla (or, as it was in later times called, Oriel). The Irish name, which has been Latinized "Orientales," and "Regio Orientalium," is now represented by the baronies of Orior, in the east of the county of Armagh.

[4] *Murecan.*—He was King of Leinster for one year, according to the *Book of Leinster* (p. 39), and father of Cerbhall Mac Muirecan, also King of Leinster, whose obit is given at the year 908 (=909) *infra*.

[5] *King of Nas*; i.e., King of Naas, in the county of Kildare. This means that Murecan was King of Leinster.

[6] *Achadh - Aldai.* — O'Donovan thought that this was the ancient name of the great mound of Newgrange. *Four Mast*, A.D. 861, note *b*.

son of Conall Guthbhin, son of Suibhne, son of Colman the Great, son of Diarmaid Derg, son of Fergus Cerrbeoil), King of all Ireland, died on the 2nd of the Kalends of December, on a Tuesday, in the 16th year of his reign. Ruarc,[1] son of Bran, King of the Ui-Dunlaing, was slain. Maelodhar Ua Tindridh, the most learned physician of the Gaedhil, died.

Kal. Jan. A.D. 862. Aedh, son of Cumuscach, King of Ui-Niallain,[2] died. Muiredhach, son of Maelduin, vice-abbot of Ard-Macha, and King of the Airthera,[3] was slain by Domnall, son of Aedh, son of Niall. Murecan,[4] son of Diarmait, King of Nas,[5] and of Airther-Liphè, was slain by Norsemen. The cave of Achadh-Aldai,[6] and [the cave] of Cnodhba,[7] and the cave of Fert-Boadan over Dubadh,[8] and the cave of the smith's wife,[9] were searched by the Foreigners, which had not been done before, viz., on the occasion when three Kings of the Foreigners plundered the land of Flann son of Conaing, to wit, Amhlaim, and Imhar, and Auisle; and Lorcan son of Cathal, King of Meath, was with them thereat. [862.]

Kal. Jan. A.D. 863. Lorcan son of Cathal, King of Meath, was blinded[10] by Aedh son of Niall, King of Temhair. Conchobar son of Donnchadh, half-King of Meath, was killed[11] in a water at Cluain-Iraird,[12] by Amlaiph, [863.] BIS.

---

[7] *Cnodhba.*—Knowth, in the parish of Monknewtown, barony of Upper Slane, co. Meath.

[8] *Fert-Boadan over Dubadh.*—"Fert-Boadan" signifies the "grave of Boadan," and Dubadh is now known as Dowth, on the Boyne, a few miles above Drogheda.

[9] *The cave of the smith's wife.*—uam mna an gobann. The *Four Mast.*, at 861, say that this cave was at droicead ata (Drogheda). See O'Donovan's note on the passage.

[10] *Blinded.*—Apparently in punishment for his participation in the plundering of Meath in the previous year.

[11] *Killed.*—do marbad. In the *Ann. Four Mast.*, at A.D. 862, the expression is do bádhadh, "was drowned."

[12] *Cluain-Iraird.*—Clonard, in the parish of Clonard, barony of Upper Moyfenrath, co. Meath. The "water" in which Lorcan was drowned was evidently the River Boyne, which flows by Clonard.

Fol. 43 aa. Gall. Roiniuḋ mor re n-Aeḋ mac Neill 7 re Flaunn mac Conaing for Anfiḋ mac n-Aeḋo co n-Ultaib, i tir Conailli cerd. Muireḋaċ mac Neill, abb Luġmaiġ 7 alanaile cell, moritur. Aedgen britt episcopus Cille daro, et scriba et anċorita et senex fere .cxvi. annorum, pausauit.

Kl. Ianair. Anno domini dccc.° lx.° iiii.° Eclipsis solis in Kalendis Ianuarii, et eclipsis lunae in eodem mense. Cellach mac Ailella abbas cille daro et abbas Ia, dormiuit in regione Pictorum. Tigernaċ mac Focartai, ri Loċa gaḃor 7 leṫri Breġ, mortuus est. Breatain du indarbu as a tir do ṡaxanaiḃ, corogabaḋ caċt foraib imMaen ċonain. Tadgg mac Diarmata, rex nepotum Cennselaiġ, interfectus est dolose a fratribus suis et a plebe sua. Conmal equonimus Tamlaċta, 7 Tuaṫal mac Artgusso prim-epscop Fortrenn 7 abb duin Caillenn, dormierunt.

Kl. Ianair. Anno domini dccc.° lx.° u.° Amlaiḟ 7 Auisle do dul i Fortrenn co Gallaib Erenn 7 Alban, co r' innriset Cruiṫentuait n-uile, 7 co tucsat a n-giallo. Colgu 7 Aeḋ, da abb mainistreċ Buiti, in uno anno mortui sunt. Cernaċan mac Cumuscaiġ, rex Raṫo airṫir, iugulatus est dolose o Móracain mac Aeḋacain. Aeḋ mac Neill roslat uile longportu

---

[1] *Aedh*; i.e. Aedh Finnliath, King of Ireland.

[2] *Anfidh.*—The name of Anfidh, who was King of Ulidia, is written Anbhith by the *Four Mast.*, and Anbith in the *Book of Leinster*, p. 41, col. 3, where it is stated that he was slain in the country of the "Airthera," (see note thereon, page 372, note [3]), or by the "Conailli-Murtheimne," another name for Conailli-Cerd.

[3] *Lughmagh.*—Louth, in the barony and county of Louth.

[4] *Of the moon.*—Lune, A.

[5] *Cellach.*—See Reeves' Adamnan, p. 390.

[6] *Britons*; i.e. the Welshmen.

[7] *By Saxons.*—do Saxanaċaiḃ, B.

[8] *Maen-Conain.*—Otherwise written "Moin-Conain," and "Mona." The old Irish name of the Island of Anglesey. See Todd's *Irish Nennius*, p. 190, note x. Rowland, (*Mona Antiqua*, p. 20), prints some absurd conjecture regarding the etymology of the name Mona, not being aware of the form in which it is written in

King of the Foreigners. A great victory by Aedh[1] son of Niall, and Flann son of Conaing, over Anfidh[2] son of Aedh, with the Ulidians, in the territory of Conailli-Cerd. Muiredach son of Niall, abbot of Lughmagh[3] and other churches, died. Aedgen Britt, bishop of Cill-dara, and a scribe and anchorite, and an old man of nearly 116 years, rested.

Kal. Jan. A.D. 864. An eclipse of the sun on the Kalends of January, and an eclipse of the moon[4] in the same month. Cellach,[5] son of Ailill, abbot of Cill-dara, and abbot of Ia, 'fell asleep' in the country of the Picts. Tigernach son of Focarta, King of Loch-gabhor, and half-King of Bregh, died. The Britons[6] were expelled from their country by Saxons,[7] so that they were held in subjection in Maen-Conain.[8] Tadhg son of Diarmait, King of Ui-Cennselaigh, was treacherously killed by his brothers and his people. Conmal, steward[9] of Tamlacht, and Tuathal son of Artgus, chief bishop of Fortrenn,[10] and abbot of Dun-Caillenn,[11] 'fell asleep.' [864.]

Kal. Jan. A.D. 865. Amlaiph and Auisle[1] went into Fortrenn,[10] with the Foreigners of Ireland and Alba, when they plundered all Pictland, and brought away their pledges. Colgu and Aedh, two abbots of Manister-Buti, died in the same year. Cernachan son of Cumuscach, King of Rath-airthir,[13] was treacherously slain by Moracan[14] son of Aedhacan. Aedh, son of Niall, plundered all [865.]

Irish texts; "Moin-Conain," or "Maen-Conain," probably representing *Mœnia Conani*, the "stronghold of Conan."

[9] *Steward.*—equonimus, for oeconomus, A. B.

[10] *Fortrenn.*—Pictland. See note [8], p. 118 *supra*.

[11] *Dun-Caillenn.* — Dunkeld, in Perthshire, Scotland.

[12] *Auisle.* — There is great uncertainty regarding the identity of this person. See Todd's *War of the Gaedhil*, &c., Introd., pp. lxxii., lxxix.

[13] *Rath-airthir.*—See at the year 788 *supra*.

[14] *Moracan.*—This name is written "Muiregen" in the *Ann. Four M.*, at A.D. 864.

Gall (.i. airir ind Foċla) etir cenel n-Eugain 7 Dal n-Araide, co tuc a cennlai 7 a n-eti 7 a croḋa allongport er caṫ. Roiniuḋ foraib oc Loċ Febail, ar a tuċta da .xx. deac cenn. Loċ Leibinn do ṡouḋ i fuil co tarla a partiu croo amail sceaṁanu inna imbeċtar.

Kl. Ianair. Anno domini dccc.° lx.° ui.° Maelduin mac Aeḋa, rex Ailiġ, in clericatu dolore extenso Fol. 43ab. quieuit. Robartaċ Finnglaissi episcopus et scriba, et Conall Cille Scire episcopus, et Corcraċ Taiġi Taille scriba et ancorita, et Oegedċar abbas Condire (et Lainne Ela), et Cormac nepos Liaṫain scriba et episcopus et ancorita, in Christo omnes dormierunt. Maeltuile abbas Airne irṫir quieuit. Guaire mac Duibdabairenn moritur. Aban mac Cinaeḋ[a], rigdomna Connaċt, do orcain fri daiġiḋ o Ḟoċlaċan mac Diarmato. Auisle tertius rex gentilium dolo et parricidio a fratribus suis iugulatus est. Bellum for Saxanu tuaiscerta i Cair Eḃroc, re n-Dub Ġallaib, in quo cecidit Alli rex Saxan aquilonalium. Lorcaḋ duine Aṁlaim oc cluain Dolcain la mac n-Gaiṫini 7 la Maelciarain mac Ronain, 7 ar cet cenn di aireċaiḃ

---

[1] *The coast of the Fochla.*—Fochla was a name for the North of Ireland. The original of the clause is added by way of gloss in A. and B.

[2] *Spoils.*—cennlai, A. B.: a word which does not occur elsewhere, and the meaning of which is not clear. The translation is therefore conjectural.

[3] *Over them*; i.e., over the Foreigners.

[4] *Loch-Febhail.* — Lough Foyle, between the counties of Donegal and Londonderry.

[5] *Loch-Leibhinn.*—Lough-Lene, in the barony of Demifore, co. Westmeath; not to be confounded with the more famous lake of the same name in the county of Kerry.

[6] *'Lights'*; i.e. the 'lights,' or lungs, of animals. This is included in the curious list of the "Wonders of Ireland," published by Todd, *Irish Nennius*, p. 193, *sq.*

[7] *Aedh.*—Aedh Oirdnidhe, king of Ireland, whose obit is entered under the year 818 *supra.*

[8] *Finnglais.*—Finglas, near Dublin.

[9] *Cill-Scire.*—Now Kilskeer, in a parish of the same name, barony of Upper Kells, co. Meath.

[10] *Tech-Taille.*—See note [13], p. 12 *supra.*

[11] *Condere.*—Connor, in the county of Antrim.

[12] *Lann-Ela.*—Now Lynally, in the barony of Ballycowan, King's County

the fortresses of the Foreigners (i.e. on the coast of the Fochla[1]), between Cinel-Eogain and Dal-Araide, so that he carried off their spoils,[2] and their flocks and herds, to his camp, after a battle. A victory was gained over them[3] at Loch-Febhail,[4] from which twelve score heads were brought. Loch-Leibhinn[5] was turned into blood, which became lumps of gore like 'lights'[6] round its border.

Kal. Jan. A.D. 866. Maelduin son of Aedh,[7] King of [866.]
Ailech, after lengthened suffering, died in religion. Robhartach of Finnglais,[8] bishop and scribe; and Conall of Cill-Scirě,[9] a bishop; and Coscrach of Tech-Taille,[10] a scribe and anchorite; and Oegedchar, abbot of Condere[11] (and Lann-Ela),[12] and Cormac Ua Liathain, scribe, bishop, and anchorite—all fell asleep in Christ. Maeltuile, abbot of Ara-irthir,[13] rested. Guaire, son of Dubhdabhairenn, died. Aban,[14] son of Cinaedh, 'righdamna' of Connaught, was destroyed with fire by Sochlachan, son of Diarmait. Auisle, third King of the Foreigners, was killed by his brethren in guile and parricide. A battle [was gained] over the Northern Saxons, in Caer-Ebroc,[15] by the Black Foreigners, in which Alli,[16] King of the Northern Saxons, was slain. Burning of Dun-Amhlaim at Cluain-Dolcain,[17] by the son of Gaithin,[18] and by Maelciarain son of Ronan;

The parenthetic clause, which is interlined in the orig. hand in A., is part of the text in B.

[13] *Ara-irthir.* — 'Eastern Ara." The most eastern of the Islands of Aran, in Galway Bay. Mentioned above at the year 857. The adjective irṫir (*rectè* airṫir) is written irtir in A.

[14] *Aban.*—This name is written hUppán (Huppán) in the *Ann. Four M.*, at the year 865.

[15] *Caer-Ebroc.*—York, in England.

[16] *Alli.*—Ælla, King of Northumbria. See *Anglo-Saxon Chron.*, A.D. 867 (868).

[17] *Cluain-Dolcain.*—Clondalkin, near Dublin. Dun-Amhlaim, the fortress of Amlaimh, or Amlaff, must have a Danish fortress in the place.

[18] *Son of Gaithin.*—His name was Cenneidigh. He was lord (or King) of Laighis, or Leix, a district included in the present Queen's County, and a most formidable opponent of the Norse and Danish invaders. See *Fragments of Irish Annals*, pp. 157, 159; and the other references under the name *Cennedigh* in the Index thereto.

Gall in eodem die apud duces predictos in confinio Cluana Dolcain. Muiredaċ mac Caṫail, ri nepotum Creṁṫainn, paralisi longa extinctus est.

.b. Kl. Ianair. Anno domini dccc.° lx.° uii.° Ceallaċ mac Cumuscaiċ, abbas Fobair, iuuenis sapiens et ingeniosissimus, periit. Condmaċ abbas Cluana macc U Nois in nocte Kalendarum Ianuarii in Christo dormiuit. Daniel abb Glinne da laċae 7 Tamlaċtae, Coiṁan mac Dalaiġ ab Doimlacc. Bellum re n-Aeḋ mac Neill oc Cill Ua n-Daiġri for Ou Neill Breg 7 for Laiġniu, 7 for sluaġ mor di ġallaiḃ .i. tri cet uel eo amplius, in quo ceciderunt Flann mac Conaing rig Breġ n-uile, et Diarmait mac Etirsceili ri Loċa gaḃor, et in isto bello plurimi gentilium trucidati sunt, 7 Faċtna mac Maelduin riġdomnai ind Foċlai, doroċair i frituġuin in caṫa, et alii multi.

Flann mac Conaing cosru rig,
Rogab tir ba Taidc maic Cein,
Ro as assiḋ ċerna coir
Gass n-oir ar inchaiḃ sil Neill.

Andam aesiu ind inbir,
hUisse caingen hi cuimniḃ,
Cen laeċ Fernaide foidmin,
Cen ḟlann Bregmaigi buiḋniġ.

---

[1] See note [17], p. 377.

[2] *Glenn-da-lacha.*—Elsewhere written Glenn-da-locha. Glendalough, co. Wicklow.

[3] *Tamlacht.* — Tallaght, in the barony of Uppercross, co. Dublin.

[4] *Diomliacc.*—Duleek, co. Meath.

[5] *Aedh*—The King of Ireland.

[6] *Cill-Ua nDaighri.*—This name would be pronounced *Killoneery*. The place has not been identified, which is somewhat strange, considering the important character of the battle. The late Rev. John F. Shearman was of opinion that Cill-Ua-nDaighri was the same as the place called "Killineer," situated about a mile to the north of Drogheda, which is by no means improbable.

[7] *Three hundred.* — tri cet, A. But B. reads ix. cet, or nine hundred.

[8] *Maelduin.*—The Maelduin, King of Ailech, whose obit is entered at the year 866.

[9] *Tadg son of Cian.*—Cian was son of Oilill Oluim, King of Munster in the 3rd century, and the progenitor of several septs distinguished by the title of *Cianachta* (or descendants of *Cian*). The Cianachta-Bregh (or

and a slaughter of one hundred heads of the chiefs of the Foreigners was made on the same day by the said chieftains, in the vicinity of Cluain-Dolcain.[1] Muiredach, son of Cathal, King of Ui-Cremthainn, died of prolonged paralysis.

Kal. Jan. A.D. 867. Cellach, son of Cumuscach, abbot [867.] BIS.
of Fobhar, a learned and most ingenious young man, died. Condmach, abbot of Clonmacnoise, 'fell asleep' on the night of the Kalends of January. Daniel, abbot of Glenn-da-lacha[2] and Tamlacht,[3] [and] Coemhan son of Dalach, abbot of Doimliacc,[4] [died]. A battle [was gained] by Aedh[5] son of Niall, at Cill-Ua-nDaighri,[6] over the Ui-Neill of Bregh, and over the Leinstermen, and over a great host of Foreigners—viz., three hundred[7] or more; in which fell Flann son of Conaing, King of all Bregh, and Diarmait son of Etirscel, King of Loch-gabhor; and in this battle a great number of Foreigners were slaughtered, and Fachtna son of Maelduin,[8] royal heir of the North, and many others, fell in the mutual wounding of the battle.

Flann son of Conaing, a king up to this,
Possessed the land of Tadg son of Cian.[9]
Out of the *Sidh* of Cerna the just
Grew a golden sprig[10] in presence of Niall's race.

Strange is it to see the Inber![11]
Easier [to keep] a covenant in remembrance!
Without a manly active hero,
Without Flann of the populous Breghmagh.[12]

Cianachta of Bregia, in the co. Meath), of which Flann son of Conaing was king, was perhaps the most powerful of these septs. These stanzas, which are not in B., are added in the lower margin of fol. 43 in A., with a mark of reference to the place where they might be introduced in the text.

[10] *A golden sprig*; i.e. Flann son of Conaing, the subject of this eulogy.

[11] *Inber*.—Inber-Colptha, the old name of the estuary of the Boyne.

[12] *Breghmagh*.—Another form of the name Magh-Bregh, or plain of Bregia, in Meath.

Conġal mac Fedaiġ abbas Cille delga, scriba, quieuit. Erruptio ignota aquae, de monte Cualann, cum pisciculis atris. Uentus magnus in feria Martini. Rechtaḃra mac Murcaḋa, abb Corcaiġe moire, dormiuit.

Kl. Ianair. Anno domini dccc.° lx.° iiii.° Martan abbas Cluana macc U Nois 7 Daiminnsi, scriba, Fol. 43ba. Niallan episcopus Slane, dormierunt. Cormac mac Eladaiġ abbas Saiġre, episcopus et scriba, uitam senilem finiuit. Flann mac Ferċair, equonimus aird Maċa et princeps Lainne leire, heu breuiter uitam finiuit. Maelciarain mac Ronain rignia airṫir Erend, feinid foġla Gall, iugulatus est. Cernaċ mac Eaċaċ, toisech Mugdorna m-Breg, Ruaḋacan mac Neill, toisech Oa Forindan, mortui sunt. Orccain aird Maċa o Amlaim, corolorscaḋ cona derṫaiġiḃ, .x. cet etir briṫ 7 ṁarbad, 7 slat mor ċena. Donnacan mac Cetfada, rex Oa Cennselaig, iugulatus est dolose a socio suo. Ailill Cloċair, scriba et episcopus, abbas Cloċair mac n-Daimen, dormiuit. Dubtaċ mac Maeltuile, doctissimus latinorum totius Europae, in Cristo dormiuit. Maelbrigti mac Spelan, rex Conaille, in clericatu obiit.

Kl. Ianair. Anno domini dccc.° lx.° ix.° Suaisleaċ

---

[1] *Cill-delga.*—Kildalkey, in the barony of Lune, co. Meath.

[2] *Corcach-mor.* — The "great swamp." The ancient name of the site of Cork city.

[3] *Daiminis.*—Devenish Island.

[4] *Saighir.*—Saighir-Ciarain. Now Seirkieran, a parish in the barony of Ballybrit, King's County.

[5] *Lann-leire.*—See note [15], p. 205, *supra.*

[6] *Champion.*—rignia, A., B. The *Four Masters* have (867) treinḟer, lit. "mighty man."

[7] *Mughdorna-Bregh.*—The name of a tribe whose territory was in Bregh (or Bregia), and in the vicinity of Slane, co. Meath. See O'Donovan's *Ann. Four M.*, A.D. 1150, note l.

[8] *Ui-Forindain.*—"Descendants of Forindan (or Forannan)." A sept located in the north of the present county of Tyrone. See Reeves' *Colton's Visitation*, p. 10.

[9] *Was burned.*—co rolcscaḋ, for co rolorscaḋ, A., B.

[10] *Between the captives.*—etir briṫ. The *Four M.* (867) have etir ḃreoaḋ,

Conghal son of Fedach, abbot of Cill-delga,[1] a scribe, rested. A strange eruption of water from Sliabh-Cualann, with little black fishes. A great storm on the festival of St. Martin. Rechtabhra son of Murchadh, abbot of Corcach-mor,[2] 'fell asleep.'

Kal. Jan. A.D. 868. Martan, abbot of Clonmacnoise and Daiminis,[3] a scribe, [and] Niallan, bishop of Slane, 'fell asleep.' Cormac, son of Eladach, abbot of Saighir,[4] a bishop and scribe, ended an old age. Flann, son of Ferchar, steward of Ard-Macha, and superior of Lannleire,[5] alas! ended a short life. Maelciarain son of Ronan, champion[6] of the east of Ireland, a hero-plunderer of the Foreigners, was slain. Cernach, son of Echaidh, chief of Mughdorna-Bregh,[7] [and] Ruadhacan, son of Niall, chief of the Ui-Forindain,[8] died. The plundering of Ard-Macha by Amhlaimh, when it was burned,[9] with its oratories. Ten hundred persons [were lost] between the captives[10] and the slain; and a great depredation besides was committed. Donnacan, son of Cetfaid, King of Ui-Cennselaigh, was treacherously[11] slain by his companion. Ailill of Clochar, scribe and bishop, abbot of Clochar-mac-nDaimen,[12] 'fell asleep.' Dubtach, son of Maeltuile, the most learned of the 'latinists' of all Europe,[13] slept in Christ. Maelbrigti, son of Spelan, King of Conaille, died in the religious state. [868.]

Kal. Jan. A.D. 869. Suairlech Indeidhnen,[14] bishop [869.]

---

which would signify "between burning" (*i.e.*, including the persons burned), which seems incorrect. In the *Fragments of Irish Annals*, and the *Chron. Scotorum*, at A.D. 869, the word used is braid, "captivity."

[11] *Treacherously.*—dolose, A., per dolum, B.

[12] *Clochar-mac-nDaimen.* — The "stony place of the sons of Daimin." Now Clogher, in the county of Tyrone. See Reeves' *Adamnan*, p. iii., note c.

[13] *Of all Europe.* — totius Europae, B.

[14] *Indeidhnen.*—indeiṫnein, A., B. But the form is Indeidhnen in the *Four Masters*, *Fragments of Ir. Annals*, *Chron. Scotorum*, *Martyr. of Donegal*, and other authorities. The name seems to he comp. of ind, the Irish defin. article, and eiḋnen, "ivy," and would be applied to an ivy-covered building. See *Chron. Scot.* (ed. Hennessy), p. 162, note [2]. It

Indeiṫnein, episcopus et ancorita et abbas Cluana Irairdd, optimus doctor relegionis totius Hiberniae, pausauit. Indreḋ Laigen la hAeḋ mac Neill o Aṫ cliaṫ co Gabruan. Cerball mac Dungaile collin adcotada dia n-indruḋ co Dun ṁbolcc. Forroransat Laigin dunaḋ Cerbaill, et mac Gaiṫine et alios occiderunt, et reuersi sunt in fugam cum rege suo .i. Muireḋaċ mac Brain, et trucidati sunt alii de illis. Dalaċ mac Muircertaiġ, dux generis Conaill, a gennte sua iugulatus est. Diarmait mac Dermata interfecit uirum in ard Maċa ante ianuam domus Aeḋo regis Teṁro. Dubdaṫuile abbas Leiṫ moer Moċoeṁoc, et Maeloḋor ancorita abbas Daiminse, et abbas disirt Ciarain Belaig duin .i. Cumscuṫ) scriba et episcopus, Comgan fota ancorita Taṁlactae daltae Maelruain, Condla ancorita Droma casa airde Ciannachta, omnes in Cristo uitam finierunt. Obsesio Aileċ cluaṫe a Nordmannis .i. Amlaiḃ et Iṁar, duo reges Nordmannorum, obsederunt arcem
Fol. 43bb. illum, et destruxerunt in fine .iiii. mensium arcem et praedauerunt. Maelseċnaill mac Neill, leṫri deiscirt Breġ, interfectus est dolose o Ulf dubgall. Cobṫaċ mac Muiredaiġ, princeps Cille daro, dormiuit.

Kt. Ianair. Anno domini dccc.° lxx.° Caṫalan mac Indrechtaiġ, leiṫri Ulaṫ, iugulatus est dolose consilio Aeḋo. Aṁlaiḃ 7 Imar do ṫuidecht afriṫisi du

may be now represented by "Inan," in the parish of Killyon, barony of Upper Moyfeurath, co. Meath, not far from the site of the ancient monastery of Clonard (or Cluain-Iraird), of which Suairlech was abbot.

[1] *Aedh.*—The King of Ireland.

[2] *Gabran.*—Gowran, in the north of the co. Kilkenny.

[3] *Cerbhall son of Dungal.*—King of Ossory.

[4] *Dun-bolc.* — See note [11], p. 77 *supra.* The *Fragments of Annals*, at A.D. 870, contain a pretty full account of the invasion of Leinster here referred to.

[5] *Son of Gaithin.* — Cennedigh, King of Laighis (Leix), mentioned above at the year 866.

[6] *Liath-mor Mochoemhoc.* — Now known as Leamokevoge, in the parish of Two-Mile-Borris, barony of Eliogarty, co. Tipperary.

[7] *Disert-Ciarain.*—The desert, or hermitage, of St. Ciaran. Now Castlekeeran, in the barony of Upper Kells, co. Meath.

[8] *Maelruain*; i.e., St. Maelruain,

and anchorite, and abbot of Cluain-Iraird, the best doctor of religion of all Ireland, rested. The plundering of the Leinstermen by Aedh[1] son of Niall, from Ath-cliath to Gabran.[2] Cerbhall son of Dungal,[3] with the whole of his adherents, plundered them as far as Dun-bolc.[4] The Leinstermen attacked the camp of Cerbhall, and slew the son of Gaithin[5] and others, and returned in flight with their King, *i.e.*, Muiredhach son of Bran; and some of them were butchered. Dalach, son of Muircertach, chief of the Cinel-Conaill, was killed by his own people. Diarmait, son of Diarmait, killed a man in Ard-Macha, before the door of the house of Aedh, King of Temhair. Dubhdathuile, abbot of Liath-mor of Moch-oemhoc;[6] and Maelodhor, anchorite, abbot of Daimhinis; and the abbot of Disert-Ciarain[7] of Belach-duin (*i.e.* Cumscuth), a scribe and bishop; Comgan Fota, anchorite of Tamlacht, foster-son of Maelruain,[8] [and] Condla, anchorite of Druim-Cara[9] of Ard-Cianachta — all ended life in Christ. Siege of Ail-Cluathe[10] by Norsemen; viz., Amhlaiph and Imhar, two Kings of the Norsemen besieged it, and at the end of four months destroyed[11] and plundered the fortress. Maelsechnaill, son of Niall, half-king of the South of Bregh, was deceitfully slain by Ulf,[12] a 'Dubhgall.'[13] Cobthach son of Muiredach, abbot of Cill-dara, 'fell asleep.'

Kal. Jan. A.D. 870. Cathalan son of Indrechtach, half-king of Ulad, was deceitfully slain, through the counsel of Aedh.[14] Amhlaiph and Imhar came again to [870.]

founder and abbot of Tamlacht (Tallaght, in the co. Dublin), whose obit is entered at the year 791 *supra*.

[9] *Druim-cara*.—Drumcar, in the barony of Ardee, co. Louth. See note [6], p. 306 *supra*.

[10] *Ail-Cluathe*.—The old name of Dumbarton in Scotland. See note [12], p. 115 *supra*. Written Aıleċ cluıċe, in the genit. form, in B.

[11] *Destroyed*.—ꝺıſꞇꞃuxeꞃunꞇ, A.

[12] *Ulf*—Called Fulf, in the *Chron. Scotorum*, at A.D. 870.

[13] *Dubhgall*. — This means 'Black Foreigner' (or Dane); from *dubh*, black, and *gall*, the ordinary Irish term for "foreigner."

[14] *Aedh*; i.e. Aedh Finnliath, King of Ireland.

Aċ cliaċ a Albain, diḃ cetaiḃ long, et preda maxima hominum Anglorum et Britonum et Pictorum deducta est secum ad Hiberniam in captiuitate. Expugnatio duin Sobairce, quod antea non perfectum est. Gaill occo la Cenel n-Eugain. Ailill mac Dunlainge regis Lageniensium a Normannis interfectus est. Ailill episcopus, abbas Foḃair, in Christo dormiuit. Curoi mac Alᴅniaḋ inseo Cloṫrann 7 Foċlaḋo Mide, abbas, sapiens, et peritissimus historiarum scotticarum, in Christo dormiuit. Colgu mac Maele-tuile, sacerdos et ancorita, abbas Cluana conaire Tommaen, quieuit. Moengal ailiṫir, abbas Bennċair, uitam senilem feliciter finiuit. Maelmiḋe mac Cumuscaiġ, secnap cluana mic Nois, moritur.

b. Kl. Ianair. Anno domini dccc.° lxx.° i.° Gnia princeps Doimliacc, ancorita et episcopus et scriba optimus, [obiit]. Maelruanaid mac Maelċairarda, dux nepotum filiorum Cuais ind Foċlai, mortuus est. Cennfaelad nepos Moċtigern, rex Caisil, extenso dolore in pace quieuit. Ferdomnaċ princeps Cluana macc U Nois dormiuit. Artġa rex Britanorum sraṫa Cluade, consilio Custantini filii Cinaeḋo, occisus est. Maeltuile episcopus, princeps Tuliain,

---

[1] *Ath-cliath*.—"Ford of hurdles." A name for Dublin.

[2] *Alba*; i.e. Scotland.

[3] *Great multitude of men*.—preda (praeda) maxima hominum, A. B. preda is evidently here used for the Irish braid, which signifies bondage, or captivity, as the concluding words of the entry, in captiuitate, would indicate.

[4] *To Ireland*.—in Hibernium, A. in Hiberniam, B.

[5] *Dun-Sobhairce*.—Dunseverick, in the parish of Billy, barony of Cary, and county of Antrim. A place very famous in ancient Irish history. See Reeves' *Down and Connor*, p. 286, and O'Donovan's *Four Mast.*, at A. M., 3501, note o.

[6] *Of the Leinstermen*.—Lagenencium, A. The text is corrected from B.

[7] *Inis-Clothrann*.—Now Inchcleraun, in Lough Ree; an island regarded as belonging to the barony of Rathcline, co. Longford.

[8] *Scoti*; i.e. the Scoti of Ireland. For scotticarum, as in A., B has scotorum.

[9] *Slept*.—dormiuit, A. quieuit, B.

[10] *Happily*—feliciter. Omitted in B.

Ath-cliath,[1] from Alba,[2] with two hundred ships; and a great multitude of men,[3] English, Britons, and Picts, were brought by them to Ireland,[4] in captivity. The taking by force of Dun-Sobhairce,[5] which had not been done before. Foreigners [were] at it, with the Cinel-Eoghain. Ailill son of Dunlaing, King of the Leinstermen,[6] was slain by the Norsemen. Ailill, bishop of Fobhar, 'fell asleep' in Christ. Curoi son of Aldniadh, abbot of Inis-Clothrann,[7] and of Fochlaidh of Meath, a wise man, and the most learned in the histories of the Scoti,[8] slept[9] in Christ. Colgu son of Maeltuile, a priest and anchorite, abbot of Cluain-Conaire-Tommain, rested. Moengal, a pilgrim, abbot of Bennchair, ended an old age happily.[10] Maelmidhe, son of Cumuscach, vice-abbot[11] of Clonmacnoise, died.

Kal. Jan. A.D. 871. Gnia,[12] abbot of Daimhliacc, an anchorite[13] and bishop, and eminent scribe, [died]. Maelruanaidh, son of Maelchuararda, chief of the Ui-Mac-Uais[14] of the Fochla, died. Cennfaeladh Ua Mochtigern, King of Cashel, after prolonged suffering, rested in peace. Ferdomnach, abbot of Cluain-mac-U-Nois, 'fell asleep.' Artgha, King of the Britons of Srath-Cluade,[15] was killed by the advice of Constantine son of Cinaedh.[16] Maeltuile, [871.] BIS.

---

[11] *Vice-abbot.* — ꞅecnap. In the *Ann. Four Mast.*, A.D. 869, the title is ppioip, i.e. prior.

[12] *Gnia.*—Written like ginα, in B.

[13] *Anchorite.*—ancoριτια, A. B.

[14] *Ui-Mac-Uais.*—The descendants of the sons of Colla Uais, who were seated in the North of Ireland (here called the Fochla). The situation of this tribe has not yet been satisfactorily made out. But in the *Chron. Scotorum* (ed. Hennessy, p. 5), a plain called Lecmagh [Magh-Lí in *Book of Leinster*, p. 5, col. 1] in Ui-Mac-Uais is described as in Ui-Mac-Uais, between Bir (the old name of the Moyola River, co. Londonderry) and Camus (on the Bann, to the south of Coleraine). See Reeves' *Adamnan*, p. 52, note d.

[15] *Srath-Cluade.* —Strathclyde, the ancient name of a district in Scotland. See Skene's *Celtic Scotland*, I. 326, *et passim*.

[16] *Constantine son of Cinaedh* (or Kenneth).—Constantine, son of Kenneth Mac Alpin, or, as he is called, Constantine II., King of the Scots.

in Christo dormiuit. Loingsech mac Foillein, princeps cille Ausili, moritur. Robartach Dermaige scriba optimus pausauit. Mugron mac Maelecotaid lethri Connacht mortuus est.

Fol. 44aa. Kl. Ianair, lunae .xxiii. Anno domini dccc.° lxx.° ii.° Flaithbertach mac Duibroir, rex Corcumdruadh ininis, hUathmaran mac Brocan rex nepotum Fiachrach Aidhne, Dunadach mac Rogaillnich rex generis Coirpri moer, moriuntur. Lethlabar mac Loingsich, rex in coicid, uitam senilem finiuit. Imar rex Normannorum totius Hiberniae et Britanniae uitam finiuit. Dungal mac Moenaigh, princeps Insi cain Dega, in pace quieuit. Donncuan mac Flannacan a Conaing mac Flaind per dolum iugulatus est. Oenach Tailten cen aigi sine causa iusta et digna, quod non audiuimus ab antiquis temporibus cecidisse. Colman episcopus et scriba, abbas n-Oendromo, quieuit. Flaithbertach mac Muircertaigh, princeps duin Chailldeu, obiit.

Kl. Ianair, lunae .ix.a Anno domini dccc.° lxx.° iii.° Aedh mac Fiangusa, princeps Rosa Commain, episcopus et scriba optimus; Maelmordha mac Diarmata

---

[1] *Tulian.*—Otherwise written Tuilen. Now Dulane, in the parish of the same name, barony of Upper Kells, co. Meath.

[2] *Cill-Ausili.*—The church of St. Auxilius (see above, note [3], p. 19); now Killashee, near Naas, in the county of Kildare.

[3] *Corcumdruadh-ininis* [or Ninis]. This territory comprised the present baronies of Corcomroe and Burren, in the county of Clare, with the Arran Islands in Galway Bay, the people inhabiting which were called "Eoghanacht-Ninais" (or descendants of Eoghan [son of Oilill Oluim] of Ninas.)" See *Lebor na h Uidre*, p. 22a, where *Eoganacht Ninussa* is otherwise called *Eóganacht na n-árand*, "the Eugenians of the Aran [Islands]. See also O'Donovan's *Four Mast.*, A.D. 871, note q, and 1482, n. p.

[4] *Ui-Fiachrach of Aidhne.*—For the situation of this tribe, see the Map prefixed to O'Donovan's *Tribes and Customs of Hy-Many.*

[5] *The Province.*—in coicid, lit. "of the fifth;" i.e. of the Province of Ulidia, which in these Annals is always referred to as *the* Fifth. The Provinces of Ireland, even when they were reduced to the present number of four, were each called coiced, or "fifth" by the Irish writers, in consequence of the quinquepartite division made of the country by the five

a bishop, abbot of Tulian,[1] fell asleep in Christ. Loingsech, son of Foillen, abbot of Cill-Ausili,[2] died. Robhartach of Dermhagh, an eminent scribe, rested. Mughron, son of Maelcothaidh, half-king of Connaught, died.

Kal. Jan., m. 27. A.D. 872. Flaithbertach, son of [872.]
Dubhrop, King of Corcumdruadh-Ninis;[3] Uathmaran son of Brocan, King of the Ui-Fiachrach of Aidhne;[4] and Dunadhach son of Rogallnach, King of Cinel-Coirpri-mor, died. Lethlabhar son of Loingsech, King of the Province,[5] ended an aged life. Imhar, King of the Norsemen of all Ireland and Britain, ended life.[6] Dungal son of Moenach, abbot of Inis-cain-Degha,[7] rested in peace. Donncuan, son of Flannacan, was slain through treachery by Conaing, son of Fland. The Fair of Tailtiu[8] not celebrated, without just and sufficient cause, which we have not heard to have occurred[9] from ancient times. Colman, a bishop and scribe, abbot of Nendrum,[10] rested. Flaithbertach son of Muirchertach, abbot of Dun-Cailden,[11] died.

Kal. Jan., m. 9. A.D. 873. Aedh, son of Fiangus, [873.]
abbot of Ros-Comain, a bishop and eminent scribe; Maelmordha son of Diarmait, a bishop and scribe; and Tor-

---

sons of Dela son of Loch (who were of the Firbolg race). See O'Flaherty's *Ogygia*, pars III., c. viii. The tradition of this division seems to have been fresh in the time of Giraldus Cambrensis. *Topogr. Hib.*, Dist. I., cap. viii., and Dist. III., cap. iv. In the list of the Kings of Ulidia contained in the *Book of Leinster* (p. 41, col. 4), Lethlobor (as the name is there written) is stated to have died "of an internal injury," de guin medoin.

[6] *Ended life.*—uitam finiuit, A. B. has in Cristo quieuit

[7] *Inis-cain-Degha.* — *Iniskeen*, in the county of Louth

[8] *Tailtiu.*—Now Teltown, in a parish of the same name, barony of Upper Kells, co. Meath, celebrated for the national fairs, or games, which were wont to be celebrated there every year, from the most ancient times, at the beginning of Autumn. A similar entry occurs at the year 875, but without the additional observation.

[9] *To have occurred.*—cecidit, A. ceci̅ (probably for cecidisse), B.

[10] *Nendrum.* — Mahee Island, in Strangford Lough. See Reeves' *Down and Connor*, p. 148.

[11] *Dun - Cailden.* — Dunkeld, in Perthshire, Scotland.

episcopus et scriba; Torpaiḋ princeps Taṁlaċtae, episcopus et scriba optimus, in Christo dormierunt. Feṫgna episcopus, heres Patricii et caput religionis totius Hiberniae, in pridie nonas Octimbris in pace quieuit. Slogad la hAeḋ mac Neill co Laiġniu, co ro-fasaghat cell Ausili, 7 alaile cealla do loscaḋ cona derṫaigiḃ. Ceall mor muiġi ainir du orgain du Gallaiḃ.

Kl. Ianair, lunae .xx.a Anno domini dccc.° lxx.° iiii.° Moengal tanisi Cluana mac Nois, 7 Robartaċ mac na cerda episcopus Cille daro, et scriba optimus, et princeps Cille achaidh, et Laċtnan mac Moċtigern episcopus Cille daro et princeps Fernann, [obierunt]. Muiredaċ mac Brain cum exercitu Laginensium usque ad montem Monduirnn uastauit, et ad suam iterum regionem ante uesperam reuersus est. Congressio Pictorum fri Dubġallu, et strages magna Pictorum facta est. Oistin mac Amlaiṗ regis Nordmannorum ab Alband per dolum occisus est. Maccoigi princeps Tamlaċtae, et Bennaċta episcopus Luscan, in pace

Fol. 44ab. dormierunt. Feċtnaċ abbas Glinne da loċa obiit.

.b. Kl. Ianair, i.a lunae. Anno domini dccc.° lxx.° u.°

[1] 'Fell asleep.'—dormiuit (for dormierunt) A. qe (with i above) (for quieuerunt?), B.

[2] Of religion.—relegionus, A.

[3] Day before the Nones.—in pridias (for pridie) A. ii. nonas, B.

[4] Cill-Ausili.—See note [3], p. 19 supra.

[5] Cill-mor of Magh-Ainir. — Or Cill-mor of Magh-Enir. See note [8], p. 236 supra.

[6] By Foreigners.—du gullaib, altered to du gallaib, A.

[7] Tanist.—tanisi; i.e. "second," or next in succession to the abbacy.

[8] Mac-na-cerda.—This epithet signifies "son of the artist (or artificer)."

[9] And.—et omitted in B.

[10] Cill-achaidh. — Killeigh, in the parish and barony of Geashill, King's County.

[11] Lachtnan. — Harris blunders greatly in stating (Ware's Works, Vol. I, p. 382), that Colgan (at p. 793 Acta Sanctorum), and the Four Masters, at A.D. 813, mention a "Lactan" as bishop of Kildare at that date, whom Harris would identify with the Lachtnan whose obit is above recorded.

paidh, abbot of Tamhlacht, a bishop and excellent scribe, 'fell asleep'[1] in Christ. Bishop Fethgna, heir of Patrick, and the head of religion[2] of all Ireland, rested in peace on the day before the Nones[3] of October. A hosting by Aedh son of Niall to the Leinstermen, when Cill-Ausili[4] was profaned, and other churches, with their oratories, were burned. Cill-mor of Magh-Ainir[5] was plundered by Foreigners.[6]

Kal. Jan., m. 20. A.D. 874. Moengal, 'tanist'[7] of Clonmacnoise; and Robhartach 'mac-na-cerda,'[8] bishop of Cill-dara, and an excellent scribe, and[9] superior of Cill-achaidh,[10] and Lachtnan[11] son of Mochtigern, bishop of Cill-dara, and superior of Ferna, [died]. Muiredach son of Bran, with an army of Leinstermen, wasted as far as Sliabh-Monduirnn,[12] and returned to his own country before evening. An encounter of the Picts with the Black Foreigners, and a great slaughter of the Picts was committed. Oistin, son of Amlaibh, King of the Norsemen, was deceitfully slain by Alband.[13] Maccoigi, superior of Tamlacht,[14] and Bennachta, bishop of Lusca,[15] slept in peace. Fechtnach, abbot of Glenn-da-locha died. [874.]

Kal. Jan., m. 1. A.D. 875. Custantin[16] son of Cin- [875.] BIS.

---

[12] *Sliabh-Monduirnn.*— Not identified. Sliabh - Modhairn was the ancient name of a range of hills near Ballybay, in the barony of Cremorne, co. Monaghan (according to O'Donovan, *Four Masters*, A. M., 3579, note g). But it could hardly have been the place here intended, being much more than a day's march from Muiredach's home in Kildare.

[13] *Alband.*—Todd took this as meaning the "men of Alba" (or of Scotland), *War of the Gaedhil*, &c., Introd., lxxv., note [4]; and Skene (*Chron. Picts and Scots*, p. 362), quoting from these Annals, represents the ab albanю of the text by "ab Albanensibus." But if the chronicler intended to say that Oistin was slain by the Albans (or Scotch) he would have used the expression ab Albanchaib. The truth seems to be that Oistin was slain by *Alband*, King of the "Black Gentiles;" whose death is recorded under the year 876.

[14] *Tamlacht.* — Tallaght, in the barony of Uppercross, co. Dublin.

[15] *Lusca.*—Lusk, in the barony of Balrothery East, co. Dublin.

[16] *Custantin.*— Constantine, son of

Custantin mac Cinaedha rex Pictorum, Cinaedh abbas achaidh bo Cainnigh, Congalach mac Finsnechta rex na n-Airgialla, Fedhach princeps disirt Diarmata, moriuntur. Coirpri mac Diarmata, rex nepotum Cennselaigh, a fratribus suis occisus est. Oenach Tailten cen aigi sine causa iusta et digna. Domnall episcopus Corcaighe, scriba optimus, subita morte periit.

Kl. Ianair, xii.a lunae. Anno domini dccc.° lxx.° ui.° Eugan et Maeltuile nepos Cuanach, duo abbates Cluana macc U Nois, in pace dormierunt. Donnchadh mac Aedhaccain mic Concobair o Flaunn mac Maelsechnaill per dolum occisus est. Ruaidhri mac Muirminn, rex Brittonum, du tuidhecht docum n-Erenn for teiched re Dubhghallaibh. Maelbrighte episcopus Slane in pace dormiuit. Belliolum occ Loch cuan eitir Finngenti 7 Dubgennti, in quo Albann dux na n-Dubgenti cecidit. Sochartach mac Brocain, dux nepotum Cormaic, mortuus est. Coemchloud abbad i n-ardd Machae .i. Ainmire in uicem Maelcobha. Cathalan mac Cernaigh ri fer Cul moritur.

Kenneth Mac Alpin. Though his simple obit is here recorded, he is stated in other authorities to have been slain in battle by the Norsemen. See Todd's *War of the Gaedhil*, &c., Introd., p. lxxv., note [4], and Skene's *Chron. Picts and Scots*, Introd., cxxxv., and the references given in the Index to that work, regarding Constantine son of Kenneth.

[1] *DisertDiarmata.*— Castledermot, in the south of the county of Kildare.

[2] *Coirpri.*—The name "Cairpri mac Diarmata," or Cairpri son of Diarmait, appears in the list of the Kings of the Ui-Cendselaigh, contained in the *Book of Leinster*, p. 40, col. 2.

[3] *Fair of Tailtiu.*—The National games celebrated annually at Teltown, in the county Meath. See a similar entry at the year 872, where it is stated that the non-celebration of the Fair of Teltown had not been known to have occurred from the most ancient times. The non-celebration is also noticed at 877. But under the year 915 (916) *infra*, the celebration is said to have been renewed by Niall [Glundubh], on his accession to the kingship of Ireland.

[4] *Corcach.*—Cork, in Munster.

[5] *Flann.*—Flann Sinna, afterwards King of Ireland. The date of his accession to the monarchy is not given in these Annals, though his obit is

aedh, King of the Picts; Cinaedh, abbot of Achadh-bo-Cainnigh; Congalach, son of Finsnechta, King of the Airgialla, [and] Fedach, abbot of Disert-Diarmata,[1] died. Coirpri,[2] son of Diarmait, King of Ui-Cennselaigh, was slain by his brothers. The Fair of Tailtiu[3] not celebrated, without just and sufficient cause. Domhnall, bishop of Corcach,[4] an eminent scribe, died suddenly.

Kal. Jan., m. 12. A.D. 876. Eugan and Maeltuile Ua Cuanach, two abbots of Clonmacnoise, slept in peace. Donnchad, son of Aedhacan, son of Conchobar, was slain through treachery, by Flann,[5] son of Maelsechnaill. Ruaidhri,[6] son of Muirmenn, King of the Britons, came to Ireland, fleeing before the Black Foreigners. Maelbrighte, bishop of Slane, slept in peace. A battle at Loch-Cuan,[7] between Fair Gentiles and Black Gentiles, in which Albann,[8] King of the Black Gentiles, was slain. Sochartach, son of Brocan, King of the Ui-Cormaic, died. A change of abbots[9] in Ard-Macha, viz., Ainmirè in the place of Maelcobha. Cathalan, son of Cernach, King of Fera-Cul,[10] died. [876.]

recorded at the year 915 (alias 916) *infra*. The *Four Masters* have his accession at the year 877; but O'Flaherty refers it to 879, (*Ogygia*, p. 434.)

[6] *Ruaidhri.*—Or Rodhri the Great, son of Mervyn Vrycho. The record of his death, by the 'Saxons,' is entered under the next year. The *Annales Cambriæ* and *Brut y Tywysogion* have it also at A.D. 877. See Williams' *Eminent Welshmen*, p. 438, and *Chron. Scotorum* (ed. Hennessy), p. 154, notes 4, 5.

[7] *Loch-Cuan.*—Strangford Lough, in the county Down.

[8] *Albann.*—See the note regarding this person at the year 874.

[9] *Change of Abbots.*—In the margin in A. is written in a small neat hand, the note, "commutatio abbır (abbatır) in Ard Macha." See the note on Maelcobho, at the year 878 *infra*.

[10] *Fera-Cul.*—Otherwise called Fera-Cul-Bregh. A district which seems to have included a large part of the present baronies of Upper and Lower Kell, in the county of Meath. According to the *Martyr. of Donegal*, at 5th April and 26th November, Imlech-Fiarch and Mugh-Bolcc (now represented by the parishes of Emlagh and Moybolgue, in the barony of Lower Kells) were in the territory of Fera-Cul-Bregh

Kl. Ianair, xx.a iii.a lunae. Anno domini dccc.° lxx.° vii.° Ruaiḋri mac Muirminn, rex Britonnum, a Saxonibus interemptus. Aeḋ mac Cinadan, rex Pictorum, a sociis suis occisus est. Garḟiṫ mac Maelbrigte, rex Conaille, decollatus est o auib Eċaċ.

Ruaidri Manann minn n-aine,
Aed a crichaib Cinntire,
Donnchad domna finn flaṫha,
Garbṡiṫ minn Maċa mine;

O doralaim ar m'aire,
Fugerr cricha mo criḋe;
Lecca huara iar n-aire
Baile for barrḟinn bile.

Cumuscaċ mac Muireḋaiġ rex nepotum Cremṫainn o Ulltaib occisus est. Maelpatraicc mac Ceallaiġ princeps mainistreċ Buiti subita morte periit. Ventus magnus et fulgor. Fros fola fluxit co friṫa a parti cro 7 fola fors na maiġiḃ. Oenaċ Tailtin cen aigi sine causa iusta et digna. Eclipsis lunae idibus Octobris, xiiii. lunae; quasi tertia vigilia .iiii. feriae, solisque defectus .iiii. Kl. Novembris, lunae xxviii, quasi .viii. hora diei, .iiii. feriae, solis .xii.

---

[1] *Ruaidhri.*—See the note regarding this King of the Britons (or Welsh), under the preceding year.

[2] *Aedh, son of Cinadh.*—This was apparently Aedh, son of Cinaedh (or Kenneth) Mac Alpin. See Skene's *Chron. of Picts and Scots*, Pref., p. cxxxiv.

[3] *Ruaidhri of Manann.*—Ruaidhri, son of Muirmenn (or Mervyn), seems to have been King of Manann (the Isle of Man). See Williams' *Eminent Welshmen*, p. 438. These stanzas, which are not in B., are written in the top margin of fol. 44 *a* in A., with a mark of reference to the place where they might be introduced in the text.

[4] *Cenn-tirè.*—Kantyre, in Scotland.

[5] *Garbsith.*—The same as the person whose name is written "Garfith" in the preceding prose entry. See *Ann. Four Mast.*, at 875.

[6] The Editor is unable to translate the original, *baile for barrfhinn bile*, which seems devoid of sense or meaning.

[7] *Mainister-Buiti.*—Monasterboice, co. Louth.

Kal. Jan., 23rd of the Moon. A.D. 877. Ruaidhri,[1] son of Muirmenn, King of the Britons, was killed by Saxons. Aedh, son of Cinad,[2] King of the Picts, was killed by his confederates. Garfith, son of Maelbrighte, King of Conaille, was beheaded by the Ui-Echach. [877.]

Ruaidhri of Manann,[3] gem of delight;
Aedh from the lands of Cenn-tirĉ[4];
Donnchad, fair heir of a prince;
Garbsith,[5] ornament of smooth Macha.

It cuts my heart's limits,
When I call to mind
The cold flags over princes!
. . . . .[6]

Cumuscach, son of Muiredach, King of Ui-Cremthainn, was slain by Ulidians. Maelpatraic, son of Cellach, abbot of Mainistir-Buiti,[7] died suddenly. Great wind and lightning. A shower of blood fell, which was found in lumps of gore and blood on the plains.[8] The "Fair" of Tailtiu[9] not celebrated, without just and sufficient cause. An eclipse of the moon on the Ides of October, the 14th of the moon,[10] about the third vigil, on a Wednesday; and an eclipse of the sun on the 4th of the Kalends of November, the 28th of the moon, about the 7th hour of the day, on a Wednesday, 15 solar days intervening.

---

[8] *On the plains.*—In a corresponding entry in the *Chron. Scotorum* (878) these plains are mentioned as in Cianachta, at *Dumha na nDeisi*, some place in the barony of Upper or Lower Deece, co. Meath; though O'Donovan would identify it with Duma-nDresa, a place situated to the north of the well-known hill of Knockgraffon, in the barony of Middlethird, co. Tipperary. See under the year 897 *infra*.

[9] *Fair of Tailtiu.*—See the note regarding this Fair, at the year 875 *supra*.

[10] *Fourteenth of the moon.*—The 4th of the moon, according to the MS. B. The whole of this entry, not fully given in B., is added in the lower margin of fol. 44 *a* in MS. A., with a sign of reference to the place where it should be introduced in the text.

Fol. 44ba. diebus interuenientibus. Scrin Coluim cille 7 a minna[1] olċena du tiaċtain doċum n-Erend for teiċeaḋ ria Gallaiḃ.

Kl. Ianair, iiii. lunae. Anno domini dccc.° lxx.° uiii.° Aeḋ [finnliath] mac Neill [caille],[2] rex Temoriae,[3] in .xii. Kl. Decimbrium i n-Druim in asclaind[4] i criċ Conaille dormiuit.

Duodecem[5] calaind cheolaċ
Decimbir dian a thoiden,
I n-erbailt ainru airiḃ
Aeḋ Ailiġ airdri Gaiḋel.

Fer fial forfaiḋ fernaide,
Diarmbu lan Temair thireċ,
Sciaṫ fri omna ernaide,
Di tein broga mac Miled.

Flann[6] mac Mailseċnaill regnare incipit. Tigernaċ mac Muireḋaiċ episcopus, princeps Droma in asclainn, extenso dolore pausauit. Fergil mac Cumsaid, abb domnaiġ Seċnaill,[7] do marbad i n-duinetaiċiu.[8] Oengus mac Cina[e]ḋa, dux fer n-arda Ciannaċta, moritur. Maelcoḃo mac Crunnṁaeil, princeps aird Maċa, do ergaḃail do Gallaiḃ, 7 in ferleiginn .i. Moċta.

---

[1] *Minna*.—Reliquaries. See Reeves' *Adamnan*, p. 315, note [2], regarding the meaning of the word *minna*.

[2] *Finnliath. Caille*.—These epithets are added in the margin in A, in a very old hand. They are not in B.

[3] *King of Temair* (or of Tara); i.e. King of Ireland.

[4] *Druim-Inasclaind*.—Now Dromiskin, in a parish of the same name, barony and county of Louth.

[5] *Twelfth*.—These stanzas are written in the top margin of fol. of 44 *b* in MS. A., with a mark of reference to the place in which they should be introduced in the text. They are not in B. See the *Ann. Four Mast.*, at the year 876.

[6] *Flann*.—Otherwise called "Flann Sinna." His obit is recorded at the year 915 (=916) *infra*. The original of this entry, which is in the text in B., is added in the margin in A.

[7] *Domnach-Sechnaill*.—Now Dunshaughlin, in the county of Meath.

[8] *In secrecy*.—The so-called translator of these Annals, whose version is preserved in the MS. Clar. 49, British Museum, considered the expression in-duinetaiċiu, (which means killing a person, and hiding the body), as signifying the name of a place. O'Conor renders it by "in depradatione."

The shrine of Colum-Cille, and all his *minna*,[1] arrived in Ireland, to escape the Foreigners.

Kal. Jan., the 4th of the moon. A.D. 878. Aedh [Finnlaith[2]], son of Niall [Caille[2]], King of Temair,[3] 'fell asleep' in Druim-Inasclaind[4] in the territory of Conailli, on the 12th of the Kalends of December. [878.]

On the twelfth[5] of the musical Kalends
Of December, fierce its tempests,
Died the noblest of princes,
Aedh of Ailech, chief King of the Gaedhil.

A steady, manly man [was he],
Of whom territorial Temair[3] was full;
A shield against hidden dangers,
Of the stout stock of Milidh's sons.

Flann[6] son of Maelsechnaill begins to reign. Tigernach son of Muiredhach, a bishop, abbot of Druim-Inasclaind,[4] 'rested' after a protracted illness. Fergil son of Cumsad, abbot of Domnach-Sechnaill,[7] was murdered in secrecy.[8] Oengus, son of Cina[e]dh, chief of the men of Ard-Cianachta,[9] died. Maelcobho[10] son of Crunnmael, abbot of Ard-Macha, was taken prisoner by Foreigners;

---

[9] *Men of Ard-Cianachta.*—Or Fir-Arda-Cianachta; a tribe whose territory is now represented by the barony of Ferrard, in the county of Louth.

[10] *Maelcobho.*—His name is in the list of the *comarbs* (or successors) of St. Patrick contained in the *Book of Leinster* (p. 42, col. 4), where he is represented as having ruled only two years, (Todd wrongly prints v. years, *St. Patrick*, p. 182), and as having been of the 'family' of Cill-mor, or Cill-mor-Ua-Niallain, now Kilmore in the barony of O'Neilland West, in the county of Armagh. See at the year 876 *supra*, where it is stated that there was a change of abbots in Armagh, and that Ainmeri, whose obit is noted under this year in this chronicle, was appointed in the place of Maelcobho, who was displaced. There is a good deal of confusion regarding the succession to the abbacy or bishoprick of Armagh at this time, as appears from the lists published by Todd (*St. Patrick*, pp. 174–182). The oldest list, that in the *Book of Leinster*, which gives the order of succession as *Ainmere*, *Maelcobo*, and *Cathassach*, is probably the most correct. See Harris's *Ware*, Vol. I., p. 46.

Ascolt mor for ceṫraiḃ isind erruċ. Folc mor isind oġomur. Maelcere dux Oa Creiṁtainn occisus est. Ualgarg mac Flaiṫbertaiġ, rigdomna in tuaisceirt, moritur. Finsneċta mac Maelecorcrai, rex Luigne Connaċt, moritur. Ainmeri princeps .ix. mensium i n-ard Maċa dormiuit. Dungal princeps Leiṫglinne moritur.

Kl. Ianair, xv.a lunae. Anno domini dccc.° lxx.° ix.° Feraḋaċ mac Cormaic, abbas Iae, pausauit. Maelciarain mac Conaing, rex Teṫbai, in clericatu uitam senilem finiuit. Duiblitir princeps Cluana auis et tiġe Airindain, mortuus est.

Ni essib bass cen dolmai
Ni roaċt gnas co marbu,
Nir iadad talam trebtaċ
For sencaiḋ baḋid ampu.

Muirecan mac Cormaic, princeps Sentraiḃ, moritur. Maelmiṫiċ mac Duibindreċt occisus est.

Kl. Ianair., vi.a lunae. Anno domini dccc.° lxxx. Ferċair abbas Benncair mortuus est. Crunnmael Cluana cain, episcopus et ancorita, dormiuit. Dertaċ Ciannain do coscraṫ do ġallaiḃ 7 a lan di ḋoiniḃ do briṫ ass, et postea Bariṫ tirannus magnus

---

1 *In the Autumn.*—isind oġomur, for isind foġmur, A. and B.

2 *Luighne of Connaught.*—A very distinguished tribe, whose territory is now represented by the barony of Leyny, in the county of Sligo.

3 *Leith-glenn.*—Now Leighlin, or Leighlin Bridge, in the county of Carlow, the site of a very ancient bishoprick.

4 *Feradhach.* — See Reeves' *Adamnan*, p. 391.

5 *Ia.*—*Iona*, in Scotland.

6 *Tethba.*—See note 9, p. 316 *supra*.

7 *Dubhlitir.* — Literally "Black-letter."

8 *Cluain-Eois.* — Clones, in the present county of Monaghan.

9 *Tech-Airenain.*—The "House of Airenan." Now Tyfarnham, in a parish of the same name, barony of Corkaree, and county of Westmeath.

10 *There tasted not death.*—ni essib bass. This is merely a portion of

and the lector, i.e. Mochta. Great scarcity [of food] for cattle in the spring. Great profusion in the autumn.[1] Maelcere, chief of the Ui-Cremhthain, was slain. Ualgarg son of Flaithbertach, royal-heir of the North, died. Finsnechta son of Maelcorcrai, King of the Luighne of Connaught,[2] died. Ainmeri, abbot of Ard-Macha during nine months, 'fell asleep.' Dungal, abbot of Leith-glenn,[3] died.

Kal. Jan., m. 15. A.D. 879. Feradhach[4] son of Cormac, abbot of Ia,[5] rested. Maelciarain son of Conaing, King of Tethba,[6] ended an old age in a religious state. Dubhlitir,[7] abbot of Cluain-Eois[8] and Tech-Airenain,[9] died. [879.]

There tasted not death[10] quickly,
There went not usually to the dead,
The fruitful land was not closed over
A historian more illustrious.

Muirecan son of Cormac, abbot of Sentrebh,[11] died. Maelmithich,[12] son of Dubhindrecht, was slain.

Kal. Jan., the 6th of the moon. A.D. 880. Ferchair, abbot of Bennchair,[13] died. Crunnmael of Cluain-cain,[14] a bishop and anchorite, 'fell asleep.' The oratory of Cianan[15] was plundered by Foreigners, and its full of people taken out of it; and Barith, a great tyrant of the [880.]

---

some stanzas written on the top margin of fol. 45*a* in MS. A., the beginning of the verses having been mutilated by the binder.

[11] *Sentrebh.*—The "Old House." Santry, a few miles to the north of Dublin.

[12] *Maelmithich.*—The *Four Masters* (at A.D. 877) write the name Maelmithidh, and state that he was slain by the *Airthera*, a powerful tribe whose territory is now represented by the baronies of Orior, in the east of the present co. Armagh.

[13] *Bennhair.*—Bangor, in the county of Down.

[14] *Cluain-cain.*—O'Donovan identifies this place (*Four Mast.*, A.D. 836, note u) with Clonkeen, in the barony of Ardee, and county of Louth.

[15] *The oratory of Cianan.*—This was at Duleek, co Meath, the monastery of which was founded by St. Cianan. See note [6], p. 29 *supra.*

Nordmannorum a Cianano occisus est. Mael-
sincill mac Muġroin rex Ua Failġi moritur. Oenġus
Fol. 44bb. mac Maelċaurardda princeps Aird sraṫa, Oenacan
mac Ruadraċ princeps Luscan, Flaiṫeman mac
Ceallaiġ rex Ua mBriuin Cualann, moriuntur.
Suibne episcopus Cille daro quieuit. Ruiḋgel epis-
copus abbas imleċo Ibair quieuit. Maelfabaill mac
Loingsiġ, rex Cairge braċaide, moritur.

Kl. Ianair, iiii.a lunae. Anno domini dccc.° lxxx.° i.° Sloġeḋ la Flann mac Maelseċlainn co n-Gallaib 7 Goidelaib isa foċla, conderiḋ i Maġ itir da glais co r' innred leis ardd Maċa. Muircertaċ mac Neill, abbas daire Calcaiġ et aliarum ciuitatum, pausauit. Imtoṫaim itir Lorcan mac Coscraiċ, ri O Niallain, 7 Donnacan mac Fogertaiġ riġ Fernmuiġe. Belliolum itir Conaille Muirṫeimne 7 Ultu, itorċair Anḃiṫ mac Aeḋa rex Ulaṫ, 7 Conallan mac Maeleduin rex Coḃo, et alii nobiles ceciderunt. Conaille uictores erant. Scannlan princeps Duin leṫglaissi iugulatus est o Ulltaib. Cormac mac Ciarain, secnap cluana ferta Brenainn et princeps Ṫuama da ġualann, moritur.

---

[1] *Killed by Cianan.*—The *Four Masters* (at A.D. 878) state that Barith was "killed and burned" in Ath-cliath [Dublin] "through the miracles of God and Cianan." The Barith here mentioned was of course a different person from the "Barid son of Ottir" referred to at the year 913 *infra*. See Todd's *War of the Gaedhil*, &c., Introd., pp. lxxiv., lxxxiv., and pp. 273–4.

[2] *Maelsinchill.*—His name occurs in the list of the Kings of Ui-Failge in the *Book of Leinster* (p. 40, col. 3), where he is stated to have reigned during nine years.

[3] *Ard-sratha.*—Ardstraw, in the county of Tyrone.

[4] *Imlech-Ibhair.* — Emly, in the barony of Clanwilliam, co. Tipperary; the seat of an ancient bishoprick.

[5] *Carraig-Brachaidhe.*—See note [11], p. 325 *supra*.

[6] *Magh-itir-da-glas.* — This name signifies the "plain between two rivers." The place has not been identified.

[7] *Daire-Calcaigh.*—The old Irish name of Derry, or Londonderry. See Reeves' *Adamnan*, p. 160, note r.

[8] *Ui-Niallain.*—A branch of the great stock of the Airghialla, whose

Norsemen, was afterwards killed by Cianan.[1] Maelsinchill,[2] son of Mughron, King of the Ui-Failghi, died. Oenghus, son of Maelcaurarda, abbot of Ard-sratha;[3] Oenacan, son of Ruaidhri, abbot of Lusca, [and] Flaitheman, son of Cellach, King of Ui-Briuin-Cualann, died. Suibhne, bishop of Cill-dara, rested. Ruidhgel, a bishop, abbot of Imlech-Ibhair,[4] rested. Maelfabhaill, son of Loingsech, King of Carraig-Brachaide,[5] died.

Kal. Jan., the 7th of the moon. A.D. 881. A hosting by Flann son of Maelsechlainn, with Foreigners and Irish, into the North, when they halted at Magh-itir-daglas,[6] and Ard-Macha was plundered by him. Muirchertach son of Niall, abbot of Daire-Calcaigh[7] and other monasteries, rested. Lorcan son of Coscrach, King of the Ui-Niallain,[8] and Donnacan son of Fogartach, King of Fernmhagh,[9] fell by each other.[10] A battle between the Conaille-Muirthemhne and the Ulidians, in which Anfith[11] son of Aedh, King of Ulidia, and Conallan son of Maelduin, King of Cobho,[12] and other nobles were slain. The Conaille were victors. Scannlan, abbot of Dunlethglaisi, was slain by Ulidians. Cormac son of Ciaran, vice-abbot of Cluain-ferta-Brenainn, and abbot of Tuaim- [881.]

---

tribe name, Ui-Niallain, is still preserved in the names of the baronies of O'Neilland East and West, in the county of Armagh.

[9] *Fernmhagh.*—Now represented by the barony of Farney, in the county of Monaghan.

[10] *Fell by each other.*—The literal translation of the original, imtotaim itir Lorcan . . . . 7 Donnacan, would be "a mutual falling between Lorcan . . . . and Donnacan;" which means that the two fell in mutual conflict.

[11] *Anfith.*—The name is written "Anbith" in a list of the Kings of the Ulaid contained in the *Book of Leinster*, p. 41, col. 3, where he is stated to have reigned ten years, and to have been slain in the country of the "Airthera" (or "Oriors"), at Dabull [a river in the county of Armagh, now known by the name of "the *Tall* river."] See Reeves' *Colton's Visitation*, p. 126.

[12] *Cobho.*—Here used for Ui-Echach Cobho (or descendants of Echaidh Cobho), whose territory is now represented by the baronies of Lower and Upper Iveagh, in the county of Down.

Concobar mac Taiḋg, rex teora Connaċt, uitam senilem finiuit. Aeḋan princeps Cluana iraird in pace quieuit. Dubinnse, princeps innsi cain Dega, moritur.

Ct. Ianair, lunae xiiii. Anno domini dccc.° lxxx.° ii.° Maelruain episcopus Luscan in pace dormiuit. Cumuscaċ mac Domnaill rex Ceniuil Loegaire moritur. Braen mac Tigernaig occisus est o Anfiṫ mac Gairbiṫ.

Broen mac Tigernaig cen goi,
Cadla erclos fon mbiṫ che,
Oengus do guin amal loen,
Cain oen do ḋecraib De.

Mors mic Ausli o mac Iergni 7 o ingain Maelseċnaill. Anfiṫ mac Mugrain, dux Mugḋorna mBreġ, iugulatus est. Eoċoccan mac Aeḋo, leṫ ri Ulad, iugulatus est filiis Anfiṫ mic Aeḋo. Caṫasaċ mac Robartaiċ, princeps aird Maċa, in pace quieuit. Oengus mac Maeleduin, rigdomna in tuaiscirt, decollatur est o dal Araiḋe.

b. Fol. 45aa. Ct. Ianair, lunae xx.a ix.a Anno domini dccc.° lxxx.° iii.° Ailbrenn mac Maiċtiċ, princeps Cluana iraird, extenso dolore dormiuit. Suairleċ princeps aird Brecain uitam senilem finiuit. Domnall mac Muirecain, rex Laginensium, iugulatus est a sociis

---

[1] *Tuaim-da-ghualann.*—Tuam, in the county of Galway.

[2] *A good old age.*—The words uitam senilem finiuit are represented in the *Ann. Four Mast.*, (A.D. 879) by iar ndeiġḃeṫhaiḋ, "after a good life."

[3] *Inis-cain-Dega.*—Inishkeen, in the barony and county of Louth.

[4] *Braen.*—The original of these lines, (not in B.), is written in the lower margin of fol. 44*b* in A., with a sign of reference to the place where they might be introduced into the text.

[5] *Oengus.*—The person whose decapitation forms the last entry for this year.

[6] *Braen.*—The MS. A. has loen, which is obviously a mistake for broen.

[7] *Iergni.*—Called Iercne in MS.

da-ghualann,[1] died. Conchobar son of Tadhg, King of the three divisions of Connaught, ended a good old age.[2] Aedhan, abbot of Cluain-Iraird, rested in peace. Dubhinnse, abbot of Inis-cain-Dega,[3] died.

Kal. Jan., the 18th of the moon. A.D. 882. Maelruain, bishop of Lusca, slept in peace. Cumuscach son of Domnall, King of Cinel-Loegaire, died. Braen, son of Tigernach, was slain by Anfith son of Gairbhith. [882.]

> Braen,[4] son of Tigernach, without guile ;
> Whose renown was great throughout the world.
> Oengus[5] was killed, like Braen.[6]
> He was not one of God's enemies.

Death of the son of Ausli, by the son of Iergni[7] and the daughter[8] of Maelsechnaill. Anfith, son of Mughran, chief of Mughdhorna-Bregh, was slain. Eochocan, son of Aedh, half-king[9] of Ulidia, was slain by the sons of Anfith,[10] son of Aedh. Cathasach,[11] son of Robartach, abbot of Ard-Macha, rested in peace. Oenghus, son of Maelduin, royal heir of the North, was beheaded by the Dal-Araidhe.

Kal. Jan., the 29th of the moon. A.D. 883. Ailbrenn, son of Maichtech, abbot of Cluain-Iraird, died after a long illness. Suairlech, abbot of Ard-Brecain, ended a long life. Domnall, son of Muirecan, King of the Leinstermen, was slain by his associates. [883.] BIS.

A., at the year 851 (=852) *supra*, and Eirene in the corresponding entry in B See Todd's *War of the Gaedhil*, etc., Introd., p. lxiii. The *Chron. Scotorum*, at A.D. 883, gives the name of the son of Iergni (or Eirgni), as "Otir."

[8] *Daughter.*—Her name was Muirgel, according to the *Chron. Scotorum.*

[9] *Half-king.* — In the list of the Kings of Ulidia in the *Book of Leinster*, p. 41, col. 3, Eochocan is set down as full king of that province, the duration of his government being limited to one year.

[10] *Anfith.*—See the record of his death among the entries for the preceding year.

[11] *Cathasach.* — See the note on Maelcobho, at the year 878 *supra.*

suis. Coirpri mac Dunlainge, rex iarṫair Liḟi, mortuus est. Conaing mac Flainn, rigdomna Cianachta, decollatus est a Laginensibus. Donncuan mac Condalaiġ, rex Ciannachta glinne gaimin, moritur. Dunacan mac Tuaṫcair, dux Galeng collumraċ, iugulatus est o Galengaiḃ moraiḃ. Cormac mac Ceiṫernaiġ, secnap Tire da glas 7 cluana ferta Brenainn pausauit. Rogaillneċ abbas Bennċair, Dunacan mac Cormaic abbas mainistreċ Buiti, Conallan mac Maelteimin princeps innsi cain Deġa, dormierunt.

Kl. Ianair, x. lunae. Anno domini dccc.° lxxx.° iiii.° Tuileflaiṫ abatissa Cille daro dormiuit, et Scannal episcopus Cille daro moritur. Domnall mac Cinaeḋa ri ceniuil Loegaire in clericatu obiit. Maeltuile mac Feċtnaiġ, princeps Glaisse noide mortuus est. Maelpatraicc mac Maelecaurarda, rex na n-Airgialla, iugulatus est a sociis suis. Eclipsis solis, et uisae sunt stellae in coelo. Maelduin mac Oengusso, rex coille Follaṁain, moritur. Cormac, princeps Cluana iraird et episcopus Doimliacc, extenso dolore pausat. In mac oc Croeḃ laisse do labraḋ dia da ṁis iar na geinimin, quod ab antiquis temporibus non auditum est. Muireḋaċ mac Brain rex Laginensium et princeps Cille dara, dormiuit. Dunetaṫe do denum i Cill daro. Muġron mac Cinnḟaelad, princeps cluana ferta Brendain, moritur.

---

[1] *Iarthar-Liphe.* Or *Iarthar Lifi.* —See note [7], p. 100 *supra.*

[2] *Cianachta,* i.e. the Cianachta of Bregh (or Bregia), in the present county of Meath; one of several septs descended from Cian, the son of Oilill Oluim, King of Munster in the 2nd century.

[3] *Cianachta-Glinne-gaimhin.* —See note [7], p. 132 *supra.*

[4] *Gailenga-mora.* — The "Great Gailenga." The name is still preserved in that of the barony of Morgallion, in the north of the county of Meath

[5] *Vice-abbot.*—secnap. The *Four M.* (at A.D. 881), say prioir, or prior.

[6] *Glais-noide.* — Usually written "Glais-noidhen;" Glasnevin, to the north of Dublin.

Coirpri son of Dunlaing, King of Iarthar-Liphe,[1] died. Conaing son of Flann, royal heir of Cianachta,[2] was beheaded by Leinstermen. Donncuan son of Condalach, King of Cianachta-Glinne-gaimhin,[3] died. Dunacan son of Tuathcar, chief of Gailenga-Collumrach, was slain by the Gailenga-mora.[4] Cormac son of Ceithernach, vice-abbot[5] of Tir-da-glas and Cluain-ferta-Brenainn, rested. Rogaillnech, abbot of Bennchair; Dunacan son of Cormac, abbot of Mainistir-Buiti; Conallan son of Maeltcimin, abbot of Inis-cain-Dega, 'fell asleep.'

Kal. Jan., the 10th of the moon. A.D. 884. Tuile-flaith, abbess of Cill-dara, 'fell asleep'; and Scannal, bishop of Cill-dara, died. Domnall son of Cinaedh, King of Cinel-Loegaire, died in religion. Maeltuile son of Fechtnach, abbot of Glais-noide,[6] died. Maelpatraic son of Maelcaurarda, King of the Airghialla, was slain by his associates. An eclipse of the sun; and the stars were seen in the heavens. Maelduin son of Oengus, King of Coille-Follamhain,[7] died. Cormac, abbot of Cluain-Iraird, and bishop of Daimliac, rested after prolonged suffering. A boy[8] spoke at Croebh-Laisre,[9] two months after his birth, a thing that had not been heard from ancient times. Muiredhach son of Bran, King of the Leinstermen, and abbot of Cill-dara, 'fell asleep.' A secret murder[10] was committed in Cill-dara. Mughron son of Cennfaeladh, abbot of Cluain-ferta-Brendain, died. [884.]

---

[7] *Coille-Follamhain.* — "Follamhan's (or Fallon's) Wood." A district which included the church (and present parish) of Russagh, in the barony of Moygoish, co. Westmeath.

[8] *A boy.*—In mac, "The boy," A. B. This progidy is included in the list of the "Wonders of Ireland," published by Todd, *Irish Nennius*, p. 193, *sq.*

[9] *Croebh-Laisre.*—The "tree of St. Lasair." The name of a monastery near Clonmacnoise, in the King's county. See Todd's *Irish Nennius*, p. 208, note x.

[10] *Secret murder.* — duneraite. A term used to express an aggravated kind of murder, where the body was concealed afterwards. See O'Donovan's *Four Masters*, A.D. 1349, note h.

Kl. Ianair, xxi. l. Anno domini dccc.° lxxx.° u.° Eiremhon mac Aeḋo, leṫ ri Ulaṫ, o Eloir mac Ergni occisus est. Cloṫobar mac Maeletuile, secnap Fol. 45ab. Cluana iraird, 7 Robartaċ mac Colcan princeps Cille tomae, dormierunt. Fiaċnae mac Ainfiṫ, rex Ulad, a sociis suis iugulatus est. Scannal mac Fergil, princeps domnaiġ Seċnaill, a fratribus suis occisus est.

Kl. Ianair. Anno domini dccc.° lxxx.° ui.° Murcaḋ mac Maeleduin, rigdomna i[n]d Ḟoclai, do marbad o Ḟlannacan mac Fogertaiġ, ri Fernmaiġi. Tigernaċ mac Tolairg, rigdomna deiscirt Breg, iugulatus est a sociis suis. Episcil do ṫiachtain lasin ailiṫir docum n-Erenn, co cain domnaiġ 7 co forcetlaiḃ maiṫiḃ ailiḃ. Eċuiḋ Lainne mac Comġain, episcopus, uitam senilem finiuit. Maelmura riġḟiled Erenn mortuus est.

Ni farlaig talam togu, ni thargai Tempu turu,
Ni taircell Eriu irmar fer fo Mael mi[n]gla[n] Muru.
Ni essiḃ barr cen dolmai, ni roaċt gnas co marbu,
Nir iadad talam trebtaċ for sencaiḋ badid amru.

.b. Kl. Ianair. Anno domini dccc.° lxxx.° uii.° Maelcoba mac Crunnṁail, abbas airdd Maċa, uitam senilem finiuit. Maeltuile mac Cilen, princeps cluana ferta Brenaind, pausauit. Maelpatraicc scriba et sapiens

---

[1] *Eiremhon.*—This name is written "Auromun" in the *Book of Leinster* list (p. 41, col. 3) of the Kings of Ulidia, where Auromun is represented as full King of the province during 3 years.

[2] *Ergne.* — Apparently the Ierene (or Eircne) whose death is recorded above at the year 851.

[3] *Clothobar.*—This name is represented by "Clothchu" in the *Ann. Four M.* (A.D. 884), where he is said to have been "Prior of Cluain-Iraird," instead of vice-abbot.

[4] *Cill-Toma.* — Kiltoom, in the barony of Fore, co. Westmeath.

[5] *The Fochla.*—A name frequently applied in these and other Annals to the North of Ireland.

[6] *Fernmhagh.* — A territory now represented, in name at least, by the barony of Farney, in the county of Monaghan.

[7] '*Cain-Domnaigh.*' — Literally "Sunday Law." A code enforcing the strict observance of Sunday.

[8] *Lann.*—The *Four Masters* (A.D. 884) say that Echaidh was bishop of

Kal. Jan., m. 21. A.D. 885. Eiremhon[1] son of Aedh, half-King of Ulidia, was slain by Eloir son of Ergne.[2] Clothobar[3] son of Maeltuile, vice-abbot of Cluain-Iraird, and Robhartach son of Colcu, abbot of Cill-Toma,[4] 'fell asleep.' Fiachna son of Anfith, King of Ulidia, was slain by his associates. Scannal son of Fergal, abbot of Domnach-Sechnaill, was killed by his brethren. [885.]

Kal. Jan. A.D. 886. Murchadh son of Maelduin, royal heir of the Fochla,[5] was killed by Flannacan son of Fogartach, King of Fernmhagh.[6] Tigernach son of Tolarg, royal heir of the South of Bregh, was killed by his associates. An epistle came with the pilgrim to Ireland, with the 'Cain Domnaigh,'[7] and other good instructions. Echaidh of Lann,[8] son of Comgan, a bishop, ended a long life. Maelmura,[9] King-poet of Ireland, died. [886.]

There trod not[10] the choice earth, there flourished not at Temair the high,
The great Erin produced not a man, like the mild-bright Maelmura.
There sipped not death without sorrow, there went not usually to the dead,
The habitable earth was not closed over, a historian more excellent.

Kal. Jan. A.D. 887. Maelcobha[11] son of Crunnmael, abbot of Ard-Macha, ended a long life. Maeltuile, son of Cilen, abbot of Cluain-ferta-Brenaind, rested. Mael- [887.] BIS.

"Lann-Eala" (now Lynally, in the barony of Ballycowan, King's county).

[9] *Maelmura*.—Otherwise known as "Maelmura Othna" (Maelmura of Othan, or Fahan, near Lough Swilly, in the present barony of Inishowen West, co. Donegal). See an account of Maelmura's compositions in O'Reilly's *Irish Writers*, p. lvi. See Todd's *Irish Nennius*, p. 222, note q.

[10] *There trod not*.—The original of these lines (not in B) is written in the top margin of fol. 45*a*, in A. Some letters have been injured by the binder, in the process of trimming the edges of the MS.

[11] *Maelcobha*.—See above at the year 878, where Maelcobha is stated to have been captured by Foreigners.

optimus, princeps Treoit 7 maer muintiri Patraicc fri sliaḃ andes, quievit. Dunchad mac Duibdabaireann, rex Caisil, moritur. Caṫroiniuḋ for Flann mac Maelseċnaill re n-Gallaib, du itorċair Aeḋ mac Concobair rex Connaċt, 7 Lergus mac Cruinnein episcopus Cille dara, 7 Donncaḋ mac Maeleduin princeps Cille delca et aliarum ciuitatum. Cerball mac Dungaile, rex Ossaiġi, subita morte perit. Cucenmaṫair princeps imleċo Iḃair pausauit. Tolarg mac Cellaiġ leiṫ ri deiscirt Breg uitam senilem finiuit. Siċfriṫ mac Imair rex Nordmannorum a fratre suo per dolum occisus est. Oenaċ Tailten cen aigi cecidit.

Kl. Ianair. Anno domini dccc.° lxxx.° uiii.° Slogad la Domnall mac Aeḋo co feraiḃ tuaiscirt Erenn 7 co nGallaib cu hU Neill in deiscirt. Maelmartain
Fol. 45ba. comarba Cainniġ mortuus est. Moenach princeps Cille aċaiḋ drummota mortuus est. Oenaċ taillten cen aigi.

Kl. Ianair. Anno domini dccc.° lxxx.° ix.° Coelum ardere uisum est in nocte Kalendarum Ianuarii. Maelpatraicc mac Neill, princeps Slane, feliciter dormiuit. Eugan mac Cinnfaelad, princeps imleċo Ibair, iugulatus est. Gibleċan mac Maelbriġte, rex Conaille Muirteimne, moritur. Flann ingen Dungaile, rigan riġ Teṁra, in penitencia dormiuit. Airmedaċ princeps Maiġi bile dormiuit.

---

[1] *Treoit.* — Now Trevet, in the barony of Skreen, co. Meath.

[2] *To the south of the mountain.*— fri sliaḃ a n-des; literally "towards the mountain from the south." The translator in the Clar. 49 version renders the expression "by the mountain southerly," and renders the word maer (or steward) by "Serjeant."

[3] *Flann.*—Flann Sinna, King of Ireland.

[4] *Cu-cen-mathair.*—This name signifies "canis sine matre."

[5] *Imlech-Ibhair.*—Now Emly, the site of an ancient bishopric, in the barony of Clanwilliam, co. Tipperary.

[6] *Tailtiu.*—Now Teltown, in the barony of Upper Kells, co. Meath. The celebration, or non-celebration, of the fairs (or games) of Teltown seemed to be regarded as matters of great importance, judging from the

patraic, a most excellent scribe and sage, abbot of Treoit,[1] and steward of Patrick's 'people' to the south of the mountain,[2] rested. Dunchad son of Dubhdabhairenn, King of Cashel, died. A victory gained over Flann,[3] son of Maelsechnaill, by Foreigners, in which fell Aedh, son of Concobhar, King of Connaught, and Lergus son of Cruinnen, bishop of Cill-dara, and Donnchadh son of Maelduin, abbot of Cill-delga and other religious establishments. Cerbhall son of Dungal, King of Osraighi, died suddenly. Cu-cen-mathair,[4] abbot of Imlech-Ibhair,[5] rested. Tolarg son of Cellach, half-king of the South of Bregh, finished an old age. Sicfrith son of Imar, King of the Norsemen, was deceitfully slain by his brother. It happened that the Fair of Tailtiu[6] was not celebrated.

Kal. Jan. A.D. 888. A hosting by Domnall, son of Aedh, with the men of the North of Ireland, and with Foreigners, to the Ui-Neill of the South. Maelmartain, successor of Cainnech, died. Moenach, abbot of Cill-Achaidh-dromafota, died. The Fair of Tailtiu[6] not celebrated. [888.]

Kal. Jan. A.D. 889. The sky seemed to be on fire on the night[7] of the Kalends of January. Maelpatraic son of Niall, abbot of Slane, 'fell asleep' happily. Eugan son Cennfaeladh, abbot of Imlech-Ibhair,[8] was slain. Giblechan son of Maelbrighte, King of Conailli-Muirtheimhne, died. Flann daughter of Dungal, Queen of the King of Temhair,[9] 'fell asleep' in penitence. Airmedach, abbot of Magh-Bile, 'fell asleep.' [889.]

---

frequent allusions made to them in this and other chronicles. See under the next year, and note 8, p. 387 *supra*.

[7] *On the night.*—ı nocce. A.

[8] *Imlech-Ibhair.*—See a note regarding this place, under the year 887.

[9] *King of Temhair.*—(or Tara); *i.e.* King of Ireland. The *Four Masters* (at A.D. 886) explain that this King was Maelsechnaill son of Maelruanaidh (or Malachy I.), and that Flann Sinna, King of Ireland for nearly 30 years, and whose obit is given at the year 915 (*alias* 916) *infra*, was the son of Queen Flann.

Kt. Ianair. Anno domini dccc.° xc.° (alias xc.° i.°). Flann mac Maeleduin, abbas Ia, in pace quieuit. Concobar mac Flannacan, rex Ua Failgi, do orcain fri daigiḋ i cluain fota. Muintir Fini do sarugaḋ isind eclais, 7 minna Finnia do sarugad oco 7 do loscaḋ. Maelmorḋa mac Gairbiṫ o Ceallaċ mac Flannacain decollatus est .i. rex Conaille Muirteiṁne. Cormac princeps Fobair 7 tanisi abbaid Cluana mic Nois moritur. Cormac mac Fianamla, princeps Droma in asclainn, dormiuit. Seċnusaċ episcopus Luscan dormiuit. Foṫuṫ princeps mainistreċ Buite moritur. Suibne mac Mailehumai, ancorita et scriba optimus Cluana macc U Nois, dormiuit. Banscal rolai an muir a n-Albain, cxc. .u. traigiḋ ina fot, xuii. fot a trillsi, uii. traiġi fot meoir a laime, uii. traiġi fot a srona. Giliṫir geis uile hi. Maelfaḃuill mac Cleiriġ, riġ Aiḋne, mortuus est.

.b. Kt. Ianair. Anno domini dccc.° xc.° i.° (alias xc.° ii.°). Maelbriġte, abbas Cluana mic Nois, in pace dormiuit. Uentus magnus in feria Martini, condarrgar fiḋár mar is naib cailliḃ, 7 coruc na daurṫaiġi as a laṫraigib, 7 na taiġi olcena. Maelcorgis, princeps Lotri,

---

1 *Cluain-fota.*—The "long lawn" (or "meadow"). This entry is rather loosely constructed in the original, and the corresponding record in the *Ann. Four Masters*, A.D. 887, is not more grammatical. The old translator of these Annals in Clar. 49 renders the entry "Conor, &c., dyed of a mortall *flux* [*recte* "was destroyed with fire"] at Clonfad-Mackfini, dishonoured in the church, and the reliques of Finian dishonoured and burnt with him." The meaning of the passage is made clear by a note in the *Book of Leinster* (p. 40, col. 3), which represents Conchobar son of Flannacan as having been slain in Cluain-fota, in the church, when all the writings (screptra) of Finnian were burnt with him, and Finnian's reliquaries profaned about him.

2 *Tanist-abbot.* — Tanist is the Anglicised form of the Irish tanisi (or tanaisi), which means "second," or next in the order of succession

3 *Druim-Inasclainn.* — This form has been corrupted to Dromiskin, the name of a townland and parish in the barony and county of Louth.

4 *Mainistir-Buite.*—Monasterboice, co. Louth.

5 *Suibhne.*—This was an eminent

Kal. Jan. A.D. 890 (alias 891). Flann son of Maelduin, abbot of Ia, rested in peace. Conchobar son of Flannacan, King of Ui-Failghi, was put to death by fire in Cluain-fota.[1] The 'family' of Fini were profaned in the church, and the reliquaries of Finnia were profaned and burned there. Maelmordha son of Gairbhith, *i.e.*, King of Conailli-Muirtheimhne, was beheaded by Cellach son of Flannacan. Cormac, abbot of Fobhar, and tanist-abbot[2] of Cluain-mic-Nois, died. Cormac son of Fianamail, abbot of Druim-Inasclainn,[3] 'fell asleep.' Sechnasach, bishop of Lusca, 'fell asleep.' Fothuth, abbot of Mainistir-Buite,[4] died. Suibhne[5] son of Maelumai, anchorite, and excellent scribe, of Cluain-mac-U-Nois, 'fell asleep.' A woman[6] was cast ashore by the sea, in Alba, whose length was 195 feet. The length of her hair was 17 feet; the length of a finger of her hand was 7 feet; the length of her nose 7 feet. She was altogether whiter than a swan. Maelfabhuill, son of Cleirech, King of Aidhne,[7] died. [890.]

Kal. Jan. A.D. 891 (alias 892). Maelbrighte, abbot of Cluain-mac-Nois, slept in peace. A great storm on the feast of St. Martin, which created great destruction of trees in the forests, and carried away the oratories and other houses from their sites. Maelcorgis, abbot of [891.] BIS.

---

man, and is believed to be the person mentioned by Ussher as "doctor Scotorum [i.e. of the Irish Scoti] peritissimus," *Index Chronol.*, ad an. 891. His name appears printed as "Swifneh," in the *Anglo-Sax. Chron.* and in *Flor. Wigorn*, at 892, and in the *Annales* Cambriae at 889. See Lanigan's *Eccl. Hist.*, vol. 3, p. 330. There is at Clonmacnoise a tombstone inscribed to Suibhne. See Petrie's *Round Towers*, p. 323; and *Chron. Scotorum*, ed. Hennessy, p. 172, note [3].

[6] *A woman.*—Meaning, of course, a mermaid. Banḟcal signifies a "female form." This entry, which is part of the text in B., was added in A. by the hand which made the entry in the latter MS. at the year 752, regarding the mil mor (or whale; lit. "great animal").

[7] *Aidhne.*—Or Ui-Fiachrach. A territory in the south of the county of Galway, which comprised the present barony of Kiltartan.

moritur. Tigernan mac Sellaċain, rex Breifne, moritur.

Kl. Ianair. Anno domini dccc.° xc.° ii.° (alias xc.°
Fol. 45*bb*. iii.°). Moċta dalta Ḟeṫgnai, episcopus ancorita et scriba optimus aird Maċa, in pace quieuit. Cumusc a cengcigis i n-ard Maċa, etir cenel n-Eogain 7 Ultu, du itorcradar ili. Caṫ for Dubġallu re Saxanaiḃ, du itorcradar sluaiġ diairmiḋe. Mescbaid mor for Gallaiḃ Aṫo cliaṫ, condeċadar i n-essiuṫ, in dala rand diḃ la mac n-Imair, ind rann n-aile la Siċfrit n-Ierll. Conġalaċ mac Flannacain, rigdomna m-Breġ, in pace quieuit.

Kl. Ianair. Anno domini dccc.° xc.° iii.° (alias xc.° iiii.°) Maelodar mac Forbusaiġ, maer muinntiri Patraicc o sleib faḋeas, pausauit. Laċtna[n] mac Maelċiarain, rex Teṫbai, moritur. Fergus mac Maelmiṫil, equonimus Cluana mic Nois, dormiuit. Mac Imair iterum docum n-Erend.

Kl. Ianair. Anno domini dccc.° xc.° iiii.° (alias xc.° u.°) Dublaċtnai mac Maelġualai, rex Caisil, moritur. Maelpetair episcopus, princeps Tire da ġlas, moritur. Cellaċ mac Flannacain, ridomna Breġ n-uile, o Ḟoġartaċ mac Tolairg dolore iugulatus est.

Ni fail mac rig rigi tor,
Fo Ceallaċ n-gormaineċ n-glan;
Teglaċ fo teglaċ ind ḟir
Ni fil fo nim niabṫa gal.

---

[1] *Lothra.*—Lorrha, in a parish of the same name, in the barony of Lower Ormond, co. Tipperary.

[2] *Mochta.* — Evidently Mochta, "lector" of Armagh, who is stated, at the year 878 *supra*, to have been taken prisoner, with the Abbot Maelcobha, by Foreigners. Mochta was apparently not Bishop of Armagh, as his name does not appear in any of the ancient lists of the successors (or *comarbs*) of St. Patrick. See Harris's *Ware*, vol. [1], p. 47.

[3] *Ath-cliath.*--The old name of Dublin.

[4] *Maelodhar.*—The *Four Masters*, at the year 889, give the obit of Maelodhar son of Forbassach, chief judge of Leth-Chuinn (i.e. the northern half of Ireland), who must have been the person referred to in the foregoing entry; but without mentioning his office of steward

Lothra,[1] died. Tigernan son of Sellachan, King of Breifne, died.

Kal. Jan. A.D. 892 (alias 893). Mochta,[2] foster son of Fethgna, bishop, anchorite, and eminent scribe of Ard-Macha, rested in peace. A disturbance at Whitsuntide in Ard-Macha, between the Cinel-Eogain and Ulidians, where many were slain. A battle gained over Black Foreigners by Saxons, in which countless numbers were slain. Great confusion among the Foreigners of Ath-cliath,[3] so that they became divided—one division of them [joining] with the son of Imhar; the other division with Earl Sichfrith. Congalach son of Flannagan, royal-heir of Bregh, rested in peace. [892.]

Kal. Jan. A.D. 893 (alias 894). Maelodhar[4] son of Forbusach, steward of Patrick's 'family' from the mountain[5] southwards, rested. Lachtnan, son of Maelchiarain, King of Tethba, died. Fergus son of Maelmithil, house-steward of Clonmacnoise, 'fell asleep." The son of Imar [comes] again to Ireland. [893.]

Kal. Jan. A.D. 894 (alias 895). Dubhlachtna, son of Maelghuala, King of Cashel, died. Maelpetair, a bishop, abbot of Tir-da-ghlas, died. Cellach, son of Flannacan, royal-heir of all Bregh, was deceitfully slain by Fogartach son of Tolarg. [894.]

"There is no son[6] of a King that rules over lords,
Like the mighty pure Ceallach;
A household like the man's household
Is not under heaven of brilliant rays."

(maeṙ) of the "family" (muinnṫiṙ), or "people," of St. Patrick beyond "the mountain" southwards. The jurisdiction of this maeṙ (steward, or "serjeant," as it is rendered by the old translator of these annals in the Clar. 49 MS., Brit. Museum) was evidently the same as that of the Maelpatraic whose "quievit" is noticed above at the year 887.

[5] *The mountain.*—The name of the mountain (or ṡliab) is unfortunately not given. It was probably Sliabh-Fuaid (the Fews Mountains, on the southern border of the county of Armagh). See last note.

[6] *Son.*—The original of these lines, which is not given in B., is added in the top margin of fol. 45*b* in A.

Muiredaċ mac Eoċocain, leṫ ri Uloṫ, o Aeddeid mac Laigne occisus est. Nix magna 7 ascolt mor. Ard maċa do orcain o Gallaib Aṫa cliaṫ .i. o Gluniaraind, corucsat deiċenbur 7 seċt cet i m-brait.

> Truag a noeb Patraic nar anaċt t'ernaicthi
> In Gaill cona tuagaib ic bualad do ḋerṫaigi.

.b. Kl. Ianair. Anno domini dccc.° xc.° .u.° (alias xc.° ui.°) Blamac princeps Cluana mic Nois, Moran Ua Buide princeps Biror, uitam senilem finierunt. Cinaeḋ mac Flannacain ridomna Breg moritur. Sitriucc mac Imair ab aliis Nordmannis occisus est. Mael-moċergi, mac Indrechtaiġ, leṫ ri Ulad, a sociis suis occisus est. Cumuscaċ mac Muiredaiġ, rex fer n-arda Ciannaċta, o Ultaiḃ occisus est. Ar n-Eoganachta la Osraiġi. Ar n-Gall ra Conaillu 7 la mac Laiġne, in qua cecidit Amlaim .h. Imair. Maelaċiḋ, tanasi Cluana mic Nois 7 princeps Daiminsi, do dul martrai la Delmnai. Flannacan mac Ceallaiġ, ri Breaġ, a Nordmannis iugulatur est. Flann mac Lonain .h. guaire do guin las na Deise Muman.

Fol. 46aa. Kl. Ianair. Anno domini dccc.° xc.° ui.° (alias xc.°

[1] *Pity.*—The original of these lines, also not in B., is written in the lower margin of fol. 45*b* in A., with a sign of reference to the proper place in the text.

[2] *Blamac.*—The correct orthography of this name is *Blathmac.* See *Ann. Four Mast.*, at A.D. 891, and *Chron. Scotorum* (at 896). O'Conor, in his edition of these Annales, wrongly prints the name *Blainn.*

[3] *Ua Buide.*—Printed *oa Binde* by O'Conor.

[4] *Cinaedh.*—MS. B. has Cinaeḋo, which is the genit. form of the name.

[5] *Sitriucc.*—Much confusion has been created regarding the genealogy of these Norse and Danish families who settled in Ireland, by the inaccuracy with which the names of the chief men are written, not only in the Irish Annals, but in other contemporary Chronicles. See Todd's *War of the Gaedhel*, &c., p. 271.

[6] *By other.*—ab alis, A.

[7] *Half-king of Ulidia.*—The *Four Mast.* (A.D. 891) say that Maelmocherghi was lord of Leath-Cathail (Lecale, in the county of Down). His name does not appear in the *Book of Leinster* list (p. 41) of the kings of Ulidia.

Muiredach son of Eochacan, half-king of the Ulaid, was slain by Aided, son of Laigne. Great snow and great scarcity. Ard-Macha was plundered by Foreigners from Ath-cliath, *i.e.*, by Glun-iarainn, when they carried away seven hundred and ten persons into captivity.

"Pity,[1] O Saint Patrick, that thy prayers did not stay
The Foreigners with their axes, when striking thy oratory."

Kal. Jan. A.D. 895 (alias 896). Blamac,[2] abbot of [895.] BIS.
Cluain-mic-Nois, Moran Ua Buide,[3] abbot of Birra, ended a long life. Cinaedh,[4] son of Flannacan, Royal-heir of Bregh, died. Sitriucc,[5] son of Imhar, was slain by other[6] Norsemen. Maelmocherghi, son of Indrechtach, half-king of Ulidia,[7] was slain by his associates. Cumuscach, son of Muiredach, King of Fera-Arda-Cianachta,[8] was slain by the Ulidians. A slaughter of the Eoghanachta by the Osraighi. A slaughter of the Foreigners by the Conailli, and by the son of Laighne,[9] in which fell Amlaim, grandson of Imhar. Maelachidh, 'tanist'[10] of Cluain-mic-Nois, and abbot of Daimhinis, underwent martyrdom by the Delbhna. Flannacan, son of Cellach, King of Bregh, was slain by Norsemen. Flann,[11] son of Lonan Ua Guaire,[12] was slain by Deisi of Munster.

Kal. Jan. A.D. 896 (alias 897). Cathusach, son of [896.]

---

[8] *Fera-Arda-Cianachta.*—See note[7], p. 324 *supra*.

[9] *Son of Laighne.* — This was Aidith (or Aideid), King of Ulidia, whose death is recorded at the year 897 *infra*, but by the *Four Masters* at the year 897 (=901), and in the *Chron. Scotorum* at 898. See the entry in the latter Chronicle regarding the battle above referred to (at the year 896), where "Aiteid," son of Laighne, is named as one of the victors.

[10] *'Tanist.'*—This title is represented in the *Ann. Four Mast.* by secnabb .i. prioir ("Vice-abbot," i.e. Prior), at the year 891, where an explanation is given as to the cause of the martyrdom of Maelachidh. See the record of the event in the *Chron. Scotorum*, at A.D. 896.

[11] *Flann.*—A famous poet. In the *Chron. Scotorum* (at A.D. 896) Flann is called Firgil ("Virgil") of the Gaedhil. See O'Reilly's *Irish Writers*, pp. 58–60, and O'Curry's *Manners and Customs*, vol. 2, pp. 98–104.

[12] *Ua Guaire*, i.e. descendant of Guaire (Aidhne), King of Connaught. See note[2], p. 118 *supra*.

uii.°) Caṫusaċ mac Ferġusa, tanase abb aird Maċa, relegiosus iuuenis, pausauit. Caṫroiniuḋ ria Maelfinnia mac Flannacain for Ultu 7 for dal n-Araiḋe, du itorcradar ili im riġ dal Araiḋe .i. im Muireḋaċ mac Mic Etiġ, 7 im mac Maelmoċeirġi mic Indrechtaiġ, ri Leṫi Caṫail, Aiddeit mac Laigni uulneratus euasit. Uaṫmaran mac Concobair, rex .h. Failgi, a sociis suis per dolum occisus est.

Kl. Ianair. Anno domini dccc.° xc.° uii.° (alias xc.° uiii.°). Aideid mac Laigni, rex Uloṫ, a sociis suis per dolum occisus est. Fros fola fluxit i n-aird Ciannachta. Coirpri mac Suibne, aircinneċ Lainne Leire, dormiuit.

Kl. Ianair. Anno domini dccc.° xc.° uiii.° (alias xc.° ix.°). Mescell abbas Imleċo Ibair, Artagan abbas Corcaiġi, Bresal ferleiginn aird Maċa, moriuntur.

Kl. Ianair. Anno domini dccc.° xc.° ix.° (alias dcccc.°) Pluuialis annus. Mac Etiġ mac Leċlabair, rex dail Araiḋe, moritur. Ascolt mar for ceṫraiḃ. Moenaċ mac Coemain, abbas Doimliacc, moritur. Taḋgg mac Concobair, rex teora Connaċt, extenso dolore pausauit. Domnall mac Caustantin, ri Alban, moritur.

Kl. Ianair. Anno domini dcccc.° (alias dcccc.° i.°). Maelruanaiḋ mac Flaind filii Maelseċnaill, rig-

[1] *Mac-Etigh.*—The obit of this person, whose name appears in the list of the Kings of Dal-Araide contained in the *Book of Leinster* (p. 41, col. 5), is given in these Annals at the year 899, where his son Muiredhach (or Muridach, as the name is written) is mentioned as his successor. Mac-Etigh, Muiredhach's father, may have resigned the government before his death. But in the *Book of Leinster*, (loc. cit.), Mac-Etigh is stated to have been slain by Maelfinnia, in the battle of Rath-cro, which was the name of the place where the battle above mentioned was fought, according to the *Ann. Four Mast.* (A.D. 892).

[2] *Son.*—His name is given as "Aindiarraidh" in the *Ann. Four Mast.* and the *Chron. Scotorum*, at the years 892 and 897 respectively.

[3] *Aiddeit* or *Aideid.*—See note [9], on the "son of Laighne," under the year 895.

[4] *Associates.*—soccis, for sociis, A.

[5] *Ard-Cianachta.* — See note [7], p. 324 *supra.*

[6] *Lann-leire.*—See note[15], p. 205 *supra.*

Fergus, tanist-abbot of Ard-Macha, a religious young man, rested. A battle-rout by Maelfinnia, son of Flannacan, over the Ulidians and the Dal-Araidhe, where a great many were slain, including the King of Dal-Araidhe, viz., Muiredhach son of Mac-Etigh,[1] and including the son[2] of Maelmocheirghe, son of Indrechtach, King of Leth-Cathail. Aiddeit[3] son of Laighne, escaped wounded. Uathmaran son of Conchobar, King of Ui-Failgi, was treacherously slain by his associates.

Kal. Jan. A.D. 897 (alias 898). Aideid[3] son of [897.]
Laighne, King of Ulidia, was treacherously slain by his associates.[4] A shower of blood was shed in Ard-Cianachta.[5] Coirpre, son of Suibhne, 'airchinnech' of Lannleire,[6] 'fell asleep.'

Kal. Jan. A.D. 898 (alias 899). Mescell, abbot of [898.]
Imlech-Ibhair;[7] Artagan, abbot of Corcach, and Bresal, lector of Ard-Macha, died.

Kal. Jan. A.D. 899 (alias 900). A rainy year. Mac- [899.]
Etigh,[8] son of Lethlabhar, King of Dal-Araidhe, died. Great scarcity[9] [of food] for cattle. Maenach, son of Caeman, abbot of Daimliacc, died. Tadhg,[10] son of Conchobar, King of the three divisions of Connaught, rested after long suffering. Domnall,[11] son of Custantine, King of Alba, died.

Kal. Jan. A.D. 900 (alias 901). Maelruanaidh, son of [900.]
Flann, son of Maelsechnaill, royal-heir of Ireland, was

---

[7] *Imlech-Ibhair.*—See above at the year 887; p. 406, n. [5].

[8] *Mac-Etigh.*—See note [1].

[9] *Great scarcity.*— The so-called translator of these Annals whose version is contained in the MS. Clarend. 49, Brit. Museum, renders this entry by great fleaing of Chattle.

[10] *Tadhg.*—His name appears also in the *Ann. Four Mast.* (895), and the *Chron. Scotorum* (900), as King of the three Connaughts (or three divisions of Connaught); but it is not found in the list of the Kings of Connaught in the *Book of Leinster* (p. 41). Hence it may be assumed that the "three divisions of Connaught" (ᴛeoꞃa Connaċᴛ, or "three Connaughts," as it is called in old authorities), did not comprise the entire province. See O'Flaherty's *Ogygia*, pp. 175, 269.

[11] *Domnall.*—Regarding this Domnall (or Donald, as the Scotch histo-

domna n-Erend, o Luigniḃ occisus est .i. o maccaiḃ Cernaċain filii Taiḋcc 7 o mac Lorcain mic Caṫail, ubi multi nobiles ceciderunt .i. Maelcron mac Domnaill, rex generis Loeġaire, et princeps Ross eċ .i. Dubcuilind, et alii multi. Fri daiġiḋ ro h-orta uile.
Fol. 45 (recte 46) Tippaiti mac Nuadat, airċinneċ Condaire et aliarum ciuitatum .i. Lainne Ela 7 Laṫraiġ Briuin. Coemcloḋ riġ i Caisiul .i. Cormac mac Cuilennain tareisi Cinngegain .i. Finnguine.

Kl. Ianair. Anno domini dcccc.° i.° (alias dcccc.° ii.°). Finnguine rex Caisil a sociis suis occisus est per dolum. Indarba n-Genti a hEre .i. longport Atha cliaṫ, o Maelfindia mac Flandacain co feraiḃ Breġ, 7 o Cerball mac Muricain co Laiġniḃ, co farcabsat drecht mar di a longaiḃ, conerlasat leṫmarba iar na n-guin 7 a m-brisiuḋ. Fogartaċ mac Flaind, princeps Laṫraiġ Briuin, mortuus est.

Kl. Ianair Anno domini dcccc.° ii.° (alias dcccc.° iii.°). Caincomruc episcopus et princeps Lugmaid, Maelciarain abbas Tire da glas et Cluana eidniġ, Ceallaċ mac Soergusa, anċorita et episcopus aird Maċae, in pace dormierunt. Maelfinnia mac Flannacain, rex Breg, religiosus laicus, mortuus est.

---

rians prefer to write his name), see Skene's *Chron. Picts and Scots*, Pref., p. cxxxviii., and his *Celtic Scotland*, vol. 1, p. 335, and 338–9.

[1] *Luighni.* — A tribe which gave name to a territory which is now represented by the barony of Lune, in the county of Meath.

[2] *Son of Lorcan.* — The name of Lorcan's son is not given in any of the authorities consulted by the Editor. The blinding of Lorcan, by Aedh [Finnliath], King of Tara (i.e. King of Ireland), is mentioned above at the year 863.

[3] *Nobles.*—nobiles. Omitted in B.

[4] *Ros-ech.* — Now Russagh, in a parish of the same name, barony of Moygoish, and county of Westmeath. See Todd's *Irish Nennius*, p. 201, note u.

[5] *Condaire.*—Connor, in the county of Antrim, the ancient site of a bishopric now united with that of Down, both of which form the united Diocese of Down and Connor.

slain by the Luighni,[1] viz., by the sons of Cernachan son of Tadhg, and by the son of Lorcan,[2] son of Cathal, when a great many nobles[3] fell, viz., Maelcron son of Domnall, King of Cinel-Laeghaire, and the abbot of Ros-ech,[4] i.e., Dubhcuilind, and several others. By fire they were all destroyed. Tipraiti son of Nuadu, 'herenagh' of Condaire,[5] and of other establishments, viz., of Lann-Ela[6] and Lathrach-Briuin[7], [died]. A change of kings at Caisel, viz., Cormac MacCuilennain in the place of Cenngegain,[8] i.e. Finnguine.

Kal. Jan. A.D. 901 (alias 902). Finnguine, King of Caisel, was treacherously slain by his associates. Expulsion of Gentiles from Ireland, i.e. [from] the fortress of Ath-cliath, by Maelfindia, son of Flannacan, with the men of Bregh, and by Cerbhall, son of Murican, with the Leinstermen; when they left a great number of their ships, and escaped half-dead, after having been wounded and broken. Fogartach son of Flann, abbot of Lathrach-Briuin,[7] died. [901.]

Kal. Jan. A.D. 902 (alias 903). Caincomrac, bishop and abbot of Lughmadh;[9] Maelciarain, abbot of Tir-daglas and Cluain-eidnech;[10] Ceallach son of Soergus, an anchorite, and bishop[11] of Ard-Macha, 'fell asleep' in peace. Maelfinnia, son of Flannacan, King of Bregh, a religious layman, died. [902.]

---

[6] *Lann-Ela.*—Lynally, in the barony of Ballycowan, King's County.

[7] *Lathrach-Briuin.*—Now Laraghbryan, in the barony of North Salt, co. Kildare.

[8] *Cennyegain.*—This was a nickname for Finnguine. See Stokes's observations on the subject, in his edition of *Cormac's Glossary*, p. 145.

[9] *Lughmadh.*—Louth, in the parish, barony, and county of the same name.

[10] *Cluain-eidnech.*—The "Ivy lawn (or meadow)." Now Clonenagh, in the barony of Maryborough West, Queen's County.

[11] *Bishop.*—The name of Ceallach, son of Soergus, does not appear in any of the old lists of the abbots or bishops of Armagh. See Harris's *Ware*, vol. 1, p. 47.

Mac Derbail oc baiġ ar Bregmaċ,
Briseḋ ceċ drong n-dolbaċ;
Mael fial Finnia foroll febraċ
h-Eo ruaḋ rogorm roglaċ.

Baithiunn ri reim cen gabaḋ,
Archli os Emna oenuch,
Fer adfeidim cen boegul,
Ba riu Eirinn a oenur.

Maelfinnia fer cen h-ulla,
Coimdiu Breg breo dar dinna,
Delbdai ri roġaċ raṫgorm,
Flaiṫ corаċ caṫlonn Crinna.

Cennetiġ mac Gaiṫini rex Laiċse, Ardiarid mac Maelmuire rex Turbi, mortui sunt. Occisio Treoit o Ṁaelṁiṫig mac Flannacain 7 o Oengus nepote Maelsechnaill, per consilium Flainn filii Maelsechnaill.

.b. Kl. Ianair. Anno domini dcccc.° iii.° (alias dcccc. iiii.°) Ioseph abbas Cluana mic Nois in pace quieuit. Sarugad Cenannsa la Flann mac Maelsechnaill, for Donnchad .i. a ṁac faḋesin, 7 alii multi decollati sunt circa oratorium. Dungal episcopus princeps Glinne da Loċo, uitam senilem in Christo finiuit. Imar ua hIṁair do marbad la firu Fortrenn, 7 ár már n-imbi. Flann mac Conaill, abb Imleċa Iḃair.

Fol. 46ba. Kl. Ianair. Anno domini dcccc.° iiii.° (alias dcccc.° u.°). Maelciarain mac Foirtċirn, epscop Lainne Leire,

[1] *Son.*—The original of these stanzas, which are not in B., is added in the lower margin of fol. 46a in A., with a mark of reference to the place where they should be introduced into the text.

[2] The word in the original, here left untranslated, is n-dolbaċ. The metre of the line is faulty, some word having been apparently omitted before n-dolbaċ.

[3] *Crinna.*—This was the name of a place in Meath, where a great battle was fought in the third century, in which Cormac Mac Airt was victorious. See *Ann. Four Mast.*, at A.D. 226.

[4] *Turbhi.*—The name of this district is now represented by that of Turvey, near Donahate, in the north of the co. Dublin.

[5] *Treoit.* — Now Trevet, in the barony of Skreen, co. Meath.

[6] *Flann.* — Flann Sinna, King of Ireland at the time.

The son of Derbhail, battling over Bregh-magh,
Would scatter every . . . . .[2] band;—
Maelfinnia the generous, great and fierce,
Most illustrious, most valiant hero.

He was a king whose career was without danger;
Chief over the 'fair' of Emain:
A man, I assert, without fear,
Who was alone worthy of Ireland.

Maelfinnia, a man without haughtiness,
Lord of Bregh; a torch over fortresses;
A well-shaped king, select, noble,
The famed prince of the battalions of Crinna.[3]

Cennetigh, son of Gaithin, King of Laighis, [and] Anniaraidh, son of Maelmuire, King of Turbhi,[4] died. Destruction of Treoit[5] by Maelmithidh, son of Flannacan, and by Oengus, the grandson of Maelsechnaill, by the advice of Flann,[6] son of Maelsechnaill.

Kal. Jan. A.D. 903 (alias 904). Joseph, abbot of Cluain-mic-Nois, rested in peace. Profanation of Cenannas[7] by Flann,[6] son of Maelsechnaill, against Donnchad, *i.e.* his own son; and a great many people were beheaded around the oratory. Dungal, a bishop, abbot of Glenn-da-locha, ended an old age in Christ.[8] Imhar,[9] grandson of Imhar, was slain by the men of Fortrenn,[10] and a great slaughter about him. Flann son of Conall, abbot of Imlech-Ibhair,[11] [died]. [903.] BIS.

Kal. Jan. A.D. 904 (alias 905). Maelciarain son of Fortchern, bishop of Lann-leire,[12] rested in peace. A [904.]

---

[7] *Cenannas.*—This was the old Irish name of Kells, co. Meath.

[8] *In Christ.*—The Latin equivalent is not in B.

[9] *Imhar.*—Or Ivar, as the name was otherwise written. Regarding this person, see Todd's *War of the Gaedhil,* &c., pp. 278–9.

[10] *Fortrenn.*—See note [8], p. 118 *supra.*

[11] *Imlech-Ibhair.*—Now Emly, in the barony of Clanwilliam, and county of Tipperary.

[12] *Lann-leire*—See note [15], p. 205 *supra.*

in pace quieuit. Slogad la Flann mac Maelseċnaill cu Osraiġi. Laċtnan abbas Ferna mortuus est. Imairi caṫa etir da mac Aeda .i. Domnall 7 Niall, co ro tairmeirsced tria imride ceniuil n-Eogain.

Kl. Ianair. Anno domini dcccc.° ii.° (alias dcccc.° iii.°). Flann mac Domnaill, riġdomna in tuaiscirt, mortuus est. Eicneċan mac Dalaig, rex generis Conaill, mortuus est. Slogad la Flann mac Maelseċlainn co firu Muman, co r' innreḋ leis o Ġabran co Luimneċ. Ciarmac ri .h. Fiḋgenti. Indrechtach abb Bennċair mortuus est.

Kl. Ianair. Anno domini dcccc.° iii.° (alias dcccc.° iiii.°). Colman scriba, episcopus Daimliacc 7 Lusca, in pace quieuit. Fergill, episcopus Finndubraċ abea, 7 princeps Indeidnein, uitam senilem in Christo finiuit. Annus mortalitatis. Dubrinna mac Eilge, rí muigi hIṫa, mortuus [est].

.b. Kl. Ianair. Anno domini dcccc.° iiii.° (alias dcccc.° u.°). Slogad la cenel n-Eogain .i. la Domnall mac Aeḋo 7 la Niall mac Aeḋo, co rolscaṫ leo Tlaċtga. Maelmartain princeps Luġmaiḋ pausauit (i maiġ Ailbe, hi feil Dagain [Inbir] daile .i. in id Septimbir i Mairt 7 i tres dec). Bellum etir firu Muman 7 Leiṫ Cuinn 7 Laiġniu, in quo occisus est Cormac mac Cuileannain rí Caisil, cum aliis regibus preclaris. Hi sunt, Fogartaċ mac Suibne ri Ciarraiḋe, Ceallaċ mac

[1] *Flann.*—King of Ireland.

[2] *Aedh;* i.e. Aedh Finnlaith, King of Tara (or of Ireland), whose obit is given above at the year 878.

[3] *Gabhran.*—Gowran, in the present county of Kilkenny.

[4] *Luimnech.*—Limerick.

[5] *Ciarmac.*—In the *Ann. Four Mast.* (A.D. 901), corresponding to foregoing entry, the name is written Ciarmbacan, who is stated to have been Lord of Ui-Conaill-Gabhra, a territory now represented by the baronies of Lower and Upper Connello, in the county of Limerick.

[6] *Ui-Fidhgenti.*—See note [6], p. 150, and note [13], p. 333, *supra.*

[7] *Magh-Itha;* i.e., the "plain of Ith." The old name "of a district now represented by the southern half of the barony of Raphoe," in the co. Donegal. Reeves' *Colton's Visitation,* p. 69, note a.

[8] *Domnall-Niall.*—The two brothers

hosting by Flann[1] son of Maelsechnaill, to Osraighe. Lachtnan, abbot of Ferna, died. A challenge of battle between two sons of Aedh,[2] viz., Domnall and Niall; but it was prevented through the intercession of the Cinel-Eoghain.

Kal. Jan. A.D. 905 (alias 906). Flann son of Domnall, royal-heir of the North, died. Eicnechan son of Dalach, King of the Cinel-Conaill, died. A hosting by Flann,[1] son of Maelsechlainn, to the men of Munster, when [the country] from Gabhran[3] to Luimnech[4] was devastated by him. Ciarmac,[5] King of the Ui-Fidhgenti,[6] [died]. Indrechtach, abbot of Bennchair, died. [905.]

Kal. Jan. A.D. 906 (alias 907). Colman, a scribe, bishop of Doimliacc and Lusca, rested in peace. Fergil, bishop of Finnabhair-abha, and abbot of Indeidnen, ended an old age in Christ. A year of mortality. Dubhsinna son of Eilge, King of Magh-Itha,[7] died. [906.]

Kal. Jan. A.D. 907 (alias 908). A hosting by the Cinel-Eoghain, *i.e.*, by Domnall[8] son of Aedh, and by Niall[8] son of Aedh, when Tlachtgha[9] was burned by them. Maelmartain, abbot of Lughmadh, rested—(in Magh-Ailbhe, on the festival of Dagan of [Inbher]-Daile,[10] *i.e.*, the Ides of September, on a Tuesday, the 13th). A battle between the men of Munster and the Leth-Chuinn[11] and Leinstermen, in which Cormac Mac Cuilennain, King of Caisel, was slain, together with other famous Kings, viz., Fogartach son of Suibne, King of Ciarraidhe;[12] [907.] BIS

mentioned above at the year 904, as about to engage in battle with each other.

[9] *Tlachtgha.*—This was the old name of the hill now known as the "Hill of Ward," near the town of Athboy, co. Meath.

[10] *Inbher-Daile.*—This is now represented by Ennereilly, in a parish of the same name, barony of Arklow, and county of Wicklow. This clause, which is not in B., is added in the margin in A.

[11] *Leth-Chuinn.*—"Conn's Half," i.e. the Northern half of Ireland.

[12] *Ciarraidhe.*—In the *Ann. Four Mast.* (903), and the *Chron. Scotorum* (907), Fogartach is described as King of "Ciarraidhe-Cuirche," a territory now represented by the barony of Kerricurrihy, co. Cork.

Cerbaill rí Osraiġi, Ailill mac Euġain princeps triuin Corcaiġi, Colman princeps Cinn etiġ, 7 ceteri. Flann mac Maelseċlainn ri Temraċ, Cerball mac Muirecan ri Laigen, Caṫal mac Concobair ri Connact, uictores fuerunt. Caṫ belaiġ Muġna. Diarmait princeps Daire Calgaiġ in pace quieuit. Cormac ancorita princeps Droma moir, moritur. Maeloġrai mac Conġalaiġ, rí Loċa gabor, per dolum occisus est o Foġartaċ mac Tolairgg.

Fol. 45bb. Ḱt. Ianair. Anno domini dcccc.° uiii.° (alias dcccc.° ix.°). Cerball mac Muirecan, rex optimus Laginensium, dolore mortuus est. Muġron mac Soċlaċain rex nepotum Maine. Bec nepos Leṫlabair rex dail Araiḋe, defunctus est. Bouina mortalitas. Amalgaiḋ mac Congalaiċ ridomna Breġ, 7 Indeirġi mac Maeltemin religiosus laicus, decollati sunt o Conaillib Murteimni. Cumuscaċ mac Ailello, equonimus aird Maċa, quieuit.

Ḱt. Ianair. Anno domini dcccc.° ix.° (alias dcccc.° x.°). Caṫroiniḋ re Flann mac Maelseċnaill cum suis filiis for firu Breifne, ubi cecidit Flann mac Tigernain, 7 alii nobiles multi interfecti sunt, Aeḋ mac Maelṗatraicc, rí .h. Fiacraċ, o Niall mac Aeḋo interfectus est.

Ḱt. Ianair. Anno domini dcccc.° x.° (alias dcccc.° xi.°). Fogartaċ mac Celi rex nepotum filiorum Cuais moritur. Eiṫigen mac Fingin, princeps Treoit, senilem uitam finiuit. Di grein do riṫ immalle in una die

---

1 *Cenn-Etigh.*—Now Kinnitty, in the parish of the same name, barony of Ballybritt, King's County.

2 *Flann.*—This entry, which forms part of the text in B. is added in the margin in A.

3 *Belagh-Mughna.*—The Road (or Pass) of Mughna. It is well known as Ballaghmoone, in the south of the county of Kildare. A curious account of this battle has been published in *Fragm. of Irish Annals*, pp. 201–225. See also O'Donovan's *F.M.*, at A.D. 903, under which year the battle is there entered; the correct date being 908.

4 *Of the Leinstermen.*—Laginentium, corrected to Laginensium, A. Laiġi B.

Ceallach son of Cerbhall, King of the Osraighi; Ailill son of Eogan, abbot of Trian-Corcaighe; Colman, abbot of Cenn-Etigh,[1] and others. Flann[2] son of Maelsechlainn, King of Temhair; Cerbhall son of Muirecan, King of Leinster, [and] Cathal son of Conchobar, King of Connaught, were victors. The battle of Belagh-Mughna.[3] Diarmait, abbot of Daire-Calgaigh, rested in peace. Cormac, an anchorite, abbot of Druim-mor, died. Maeloghra son of Conghalach, King of Loch-gabhor, was treacherously slain by Fogartach son of Tolarg.

Kal. Jan. A.D. 908 (alias 909). Cerbhall son of [908.]
Muirecan, a most excellent King of the Leinstermen,[4] died of anguish. Mughron son of Sochlachan, King of Ui-Maine, [died]. Bec, grandson of Lethlabhar, King of Dal-Araidhe, died. A mortality of cattle. Amalgaidh son of Congalach, royal-heir of Bregh, and Indeirghi son of Maelteimin, a religious[5] layman, were beheaded by the Conailli-Muirteimni. Cumuscach son of Ailill, house-steward[6] of Ard-Macha, rested.[7]

Kal. Jan. A.D. 909 (alias 910). A battle-rout by [909.]
Flann[8] son of Maelsechnaill, with his sons, over the men of Breifni, in which Flann[9] son of Tigernan fell, and a great many other eminent persons were slain. Aedh son of Maelpatraic, King of Ui-Fiachrach, was slain by Niall son of Aedh.

Kal. Jan. A.D. 910 (alias 911). Fogartach son of [910.]
Cele, King of Ui-mac-Cuais,[10] died. Eithigen son of Fingin, abbot of Treoit, ended an aged life. Two suns ran together on the same day, viz., the day before the

---

[5] *Religious.* — relegiosus, A. B.

[6] *House-steward.*—equonimus (for oeconomus), A. B.

[7] *Rested.*—quieuit, A. mor (for moritur, or mortuus est), B.

[8] *Flann.*—Flonn, A. Flann was King of Ireland at the time.

[9] *Flann.*—The *Four Mast.* (at A.D. 905), call him Lord of Breifne.

[10] *Ui-mac-Cuais.*—Otherwise, and correctly, written Ui-mac-Uais. The name of this branch of the Airghialla is preserved, but in an altered form, in that of the barony of Moygoish, co. Westmeath.

.i. i pridh nonas Mai. Domnall mac Aeda do gabail bachla.

b. Kl. Ianair. Anno domini dcccc.° xi.° (alias dcccc.° xii.°). Flann mac Mecluiġe, princeps Corcaiġi, dormiuit. Maelbrigte mac Maeldomnaiġ, princeps Lis moir, in Christo quieuit. Cernaċan mac Duilgein, rigdomna na n-Airter, occisus est in lacu crudeli o Niall mac Aeḋo. Muireḋaċ mac Cormaic princeps Droma inasclainn, 7 ridomna Conailli .i. Gairbiṫ mac Mailmorda, do orcain fri daiġiḋ i prainntiġ Droma inasclainn:

Muireḋaċ,
Ced nach cainid a coemu,
Is domna do dunebaḋ;
Is nell co nime noemu,

Mor thesbaiḋ int oirdnigi
Mac Cormaic milib maissi;
A[n] minn foroll forgliḋe,
Ba cainnel ceċa claissi.

Soċlacan mac Diarmata, rex nepotum Maine, in clericatu finiuit. Cleirċen mac Murchada, rí .h. m-Briuin seola, Muiredaċ mac Mugroin dux clainni Caṫail, moriuntur. Taiġi ili do loscaḋ issrait aird Maċa per incuriam. Pluuialis atque tenebrosus annus. Cometes apparuit.

Kl. Ianair. Anno domini dcccc.° xii.° (alias dcccc° Fol. 46aa. xiii.°). Tipraiti mac Maelḟind princeps imleċo Ibair, Maelmuire ingen Cinaeḋa mic Ailpin, Etulb ri Saxan

---

[1] '*In lacu crudeli.*'—This must surely be corrupt. In the *Ann. Four Mast.* (907), and the *Chron. Scotorum* (911), the lake in which Cernachan is stated to have been drowned is called Loch-Cirr, to the west of Armagh. Possibly "crudeli" may be by mistake for "crudeliter."

[2] *Druim-Inasclainn.*—Dromiskin, in the barony and county of Louth. The second member of the name (*Inasclainn*) is not in A., and is represented in B. by ī.

[3] *By fire.*—fri daiġi, A.

[4] *Muiredhach.*—The original of these stanzas, which is not in B., is added in the lower margin of fol. 46*b* in A., with a sign of reference to the

Nones of May. Domnall, son of Aedh, assumed the pilgrim's staff.

Kal. Jan. A.D. 911 (alias 912). Flann son of Macluighe, abbot of Cork, 'fell asleep.' Maelbrigte son of Maeldomnaigh, abbot of Lis-mor, rested in Christ. Cernachan son of Duilgen, royal-heir of the Airthera, was put to death 'in lacu crudeli,'[1] by Niall, son of Aedh. Muiredhach son of Cormac, abbot of Druim-Inasclainn,[2] and the royal-heir of the Conailli, i.e. Gairbith son of Maelmorda, were killed by fire[3] in the refectory of Druim-Inasclainn. [911.] BIS.

Muiredhach,[4]
Who laments him not, ye learned!
It is a cause for plague.
It is a cloud to holy heaven.

Great loss is the illustrious man,
Son of Cormac, of a thousand graces;
The great, illuminating gem,
Who was the lamp of every choir.

Sochlachan, son of Diarmait, King of Ui-Maine, died in the religious state. Cleirchen, son of Murchad, King of Ui-Briuin-Seola,[5] [and] Muiredach, son of Mughron, chieftain of Clann-Cathail, died. Many houses were burned in the 'Rath' of Ard-Macha, through carelessness. A rainy and dark year. A comet[6] appeared.

Kal. Jan. A.D. 912 (alias 913). Tipraite son of Maelfind, abbot of Imlech-Ibhair, Maelmuire daughter of Cinaedh[7] Mac Alpin, Etulb[8] King of the North Saxons, [912.]

place where they might be introduced into the text.

[5] *Ui-Briuin-Seola.* — A powerful tribe, descended from Brian, the son of Eochaidh Muighmedhoin, King of Ireland in the 4th Cent., whose territory was nearly co-extensive with the present barony of Clare, co. Galway. See Hardiman's edition of O'Flaherty's *Iar Connaught* p. 368.

[6] *Comet.*—Cometir, A. Omitted in B.

[7] *Cinaedh.*—Or Kenneth, as the name is usually written by Scotch historians.

[8] *Etulb.*—Æthelwald, King of Northumbria, whose death (in battle) is recorded in the Anglo-Saxon Chronicle at the year 905. See Lappenberg's *Hist. of England*, pp. 85-6.

tuaiscirt, moriuntur. Congalaċ mac Gairbid, rí Conaille, a suis iugulatur est isin nomaḋ mís iar n-orcain in taiġi abaṫ i n-Druim inasclaind for mac Maelmorḋa 7 for Muiredaċ mac Cormaic princeps Droma. Cuilennan mac Maelbrigte in fine eiusdem anni moritur. Caṫroiniud ria n-Donnchad Ua Maelseċnaill, 7 re Maelmiṫiḋ mac Flannacain, for Fogartaċ mac Tolairg ri deiscirt Breġ, 7 for Lorcan mac Donnchada, 7 for Laiġniu, co fargabsat ili itir bas 7 ergabail. Caṫroined re n-Gentiḃ for fairinn noċoblaiġ de Ultaiḃ i n-airiur Saxan, du itorcradar ili im Cumuscaċ mac Maelmoċorġi mac riġ Leiṫi Caṫail. Sloġeḋ la Niall mac n-Aeḋo co Connaċta, 7 caṫroiniuḋ riam for ócu tuaiscirt Connaċt .i. for Ou Amalngaid 7 for firu hUmaill, co fargabsat sochaide itir bas 7 ergabail, im Maelcluiċe mac Concobair. Pluuialis atque tenebrosus annus. Maelbrigte mac Tornain du teċt imMumain do ḟuaslucaḋ ailiṫir do Bretnaiḃ.

Kl. Ianair. Anno domini dcccc.° xiii.° (alias dcccc.° xiiii.°). Indreḋ deiscirt Breġ 7 deiscirt Ciannaċta o Flaunn mac Maelseċnaill. Cealla ili do ṡarugad leis. Maelbrigte mac Gibleċain, rí Conaille, do guin o hUib Eċoch quarto mense regni sui. Slogad la Niall mac n-Aeḋo i n-dail n-Araide Iunio mense,

[1] *Son.*—His name is given as "Gairbith" in the entry regarding the outrage here referred to, under the year 911.

[2] *Grandson.*—Donnchad was the son of Flann Sinna, King of Ireland at this time, who was the son of Maelsechlainn, also King of Ireland (Malachy I.)

[3] *Saxon-land*; i.e. England.

[4] *Including.*—.i. in A. and B., obviously by mistake for im, as in the *Ann. Four Mast.* (908=913).

[5] *Leth-Cathail.*—Now represented by the barony of Lecale, co. Down.

[6] *Ui-Amalgaidh.*—"Descendants of Amalgadh." A powerful tribe, whose name is now represented in that of the barony of Tirawley [tir Amalgaiḋ], co. Mayo.

[7] *Umhall.* — A district comprising the present baronies of Murrisk and Burrishoole, in the county of Mayo.

[8] *Maelbrigte.*—He was bishop (or abbot) of Armagh. His obit is entered at the year 926 *infra*, where he is

died. Congalach son of Gairbhidh, King of the Conailli, was slain by his own people, in the ninth month after destroying the abbot's house in Druim-Inasclainn, against the son[1] of Maelmordha, and against Muiredhach son of Cormac, abbot of Druim. Cuilennan, son of Maelbrigte, died at the end of the same year. A battle was gained by Donnchad, grandson[2] of Maelsechnaill, and Maelmithidh son of Flannacan, over Fogartach son of Tolarg, King of the South of Bregh, and over Lorcan son of Donnchad, and over the Leinstermen, who lost a great number, between those killed, and prisoners. A battle was gained by Gentiles over the crews of a new fleet of the Ulidians on the coast of Saxon-land,[3] where a great many were slain, including[4] Cumuscach son of Maelmocherghi, son of the King of Leth-Cathail.[5] A hosting by Niall, son of Aedh, to Connaught; and he gained a battle over the warriors of the North of Connaught, viz., over the Ui-Amalgaidh,[6] and the men of Umhall,[7] who lost great numbers between slain and prisoners, including Maelcluiche, son of Conchobar. A rainy and dark year. Maelbrigte,[8] son of Tornan, went into Munster, to ransom a pilgrim of the Britons.

Kal. Jan. A.D. 913 (alias 914). Devastation of the South of Bregh, and of the South of Cianachta,[9] by Flann son of Maelsechnaill. Several churches were violated by him. Maelbrigte son of Giblechan, King of Conailli, was killed by the Ui-Echach, in the fourth month of his reign. A hosting by Niall,[10] son of Aedh, into Dal- [913.]

described as "comarb" (or successor) of Patrick and Colum Cille. But in the list of the *comarbs* of St. Patrick in the *Book of Leinster* (p. 42), Maelbrigte is said to have been also a successor (*comarb*) of St. Bridget. See Harris's *Ware*, vol. 1, pp. 46–7.

[9] *Cianachta;* i.e. the Cianachta-Bregh, a district comprising the east of the present county of Meath.

[10] *Niall.*—This was Niall 'Glundubh' (Niall black-knee), afterwards King of Ireland, who was killed in a battle with the Danish invaders, fought at Kilmashogue, in the co. Dublin, in the year 919 (918 of these

Loingseċ .h. Leṫlaḃair, ri dal Araide di a taireċt oc
Fregabul, 7 maidm fair co fargaḃ a braṫair ar a
lurgg .i. Flaṫruae .h. Leṫlabair. Aeḋ mac Eoċocain ri
in coiciḋ, 7 Loingsech ri dal Araide, di a tairecht oc
carn Erenn, 7 maidm foraiḃ. Cernan mac Colman
toiseċ cenel Maelċe, 7 mac Allacain mic Laiċteċain
7 alaile, du ḟacbail ar a lurgg. Aed, imorro, cum
paucissimis ex fuga reuersus 7 acerrime intra fugam
persistens, quosdam ex militibus Neill prostrauit.
Dubgall filius eius uulneratus euasit. Bellum nauale
oc Manainn etir Barid mac n-Oitir 7 Ragnall .h.
Imair, ubi Bare[d] pene cum omni exercitu suo deletus est. Nocoblaċ mar di Gentiḃ oc Loċ dacaeċ. Siḋ
etir Niall mac n-Oeḋo ri n-Ailiġ 7 Aeḋ riġ in coiciḋ,
Fol. 46ab. oc Tealaig occ, i Kl. Nouembir. Slogad ind ḟoċlai
la Niall mac n-Aeḋo hi Miḋe hi mis Decimbir.
Scorais oc Grellaiġ eillti fri Crosa coil aniar. Luiḋ
sloġ h-uaḋ arin dunaḋ du saġaid arba 7 condaiḋ.
Dusnarraid Oengus .h. Maelseċlainn, cona braiṫriḃ
olċena, 7 co sloġ fer Miḋe, co fargabsat coicer ar
ceṫraċait leo im Coinnecan mac Muircertaiċ, 7 im
ḟergal mac Oenġusa, 7 im Uaṫmaran mac n-Ailib, 7
im Erudan mac Gairriḋ toisech .h. mBresail Maċa, 7
im Maelruanaiḋ mac Cumuscaiċ toiseċ sil Duiḃṫire,
7 im Maelmbriġti mac n-Aeḋacain, 7 im mac n-Eru-
main mic Aeḋo, 7 im Fiaċraiġ mac Cellaċain, 7 im

Annals). See Todd's *War of the Gaedhil*, &c., Introd. pp. xc., xci.

[1] *Fregabal.*—A river in the county Antrim, the name of which is now corrupted to the "Ravel Water." See Reeves' *Down and Connor*, pp. 334–5.

[2] *Province*; i.e. the Province of Ulidia, often called *the* Province in these Annals, though it merely represented the greater portion of the present county of Down.

[3] *Carn-Erenn.*—Now Carnearny (according to Dean Reeves), in the parish of Connor, and county of Antrim. *Down and Connor*, p. 341, note.

[4] *Manann.*—The Isle of Man.

[5] *Loch-dacaech.* — The old Irish name of Waterford Harbour.

[6] *Province.*—In coicid (lit. "the

Araidhe, in the month of June. Loingsech Ua Lethlabhair, King of Dal-Araidhe, met them at Fregabal,[1] when he was defeated, and lost his brother out of his army, *i.e.*, Flathrua Ua Lethlabhair. Aedh son of Eochacan, King of the Province,[2] and Loingsech, King of Dal-Araidhe, met them at Carn-Erenn,[3] but were routed. Cerran son of Colman, chief of Cinel-Maelche, and the son of Allacan son of Laichtechan, and others of their army, were lost. Aedh, however, returning from the flight with a very few, and fiercely resisting during the flight, slew some of Niall's soldiers. Dubhgall, his son, escaped wounded. A naval battle at Manann,[4] between Barid, son of Ottir, and Ragnall grandson of Imar, where Barid was killed, together with nearly all is host. A large new fleet of Gentiles at Lochdacaech.[5] Peace [concluded] between Niall son of Aedh, King of Ailech, and Aedh, King of the Province,[6] at Telach-og,[7] on the Kalends of November. A hosting of the Fochla[8] by Niall, son of Aedh, into Midhe, in the month of December. He encamped at Grellach-Eillte,[9] to the west of Crosa-cail.[10] A large party went from him out of the camp to procure corn and fire-wood. Oengus Ua Maelsechlainn, with all his brethren and the army of the men of Meath, overtook them; and they lost 45 men, including Coinnecan son of Muirchertach, and Ferghal son of Oenghus, and Uathmaran son of Ailib, and Erudan son of Gairfidh, chieftain of Ui-Bresail-Macha, and Maelruanaidh son of Cumuscach, chieftain of Sil-Duibhthire, and Maelbrighte son of Aedhacan, and the son[11] of Eruman son of Aedh, and Fiachra son of Cellachan, and

---

fifth"); by which was meant the Province of Ulidia.

[7] *Telach-og.*—Now Tullyhog, in the barony of Dungannon Upper, co. Tyrone.

[8] *Fochla.*—A name for that part of the North of Ireland occupied by the Northern Ui-Neill.

[9] *Grellach Eillte.*—Girley, in the barony of Upper Kells, co. Meath.

[10] *Crosa-cail.*—Crossakeele, in the last named barony and county.

[11] *Son.*—His name is given as Maelmordha, by the *Four Masters*, at A.D. 910.

Maelmuire mac Flannacain rigdomna na n-Airgialla.

Bron do Grellaiġ eillti huair,
Fuaramar cuain na taib;
Asbert Cormacan fri Niall,
Naċ in lecar siar tiagam sair.

Kl. Ianair. Anno domini dcccc.° xiiii.° (alias dcccc.° xu.°). Oengus .h. Maelseċnaill, riġdomna Temraċ, sextimo idus Februarii feria tertia mortuus est.

Beannacht for laim Cirnd mic Birnd,
Ro marb Oengus finn muaḋ Fail:
Maiṫ ind arrain gaiscid geir,
Digail Aeḋa allain ain.

Domnall mac Aeḋo, ri Ailiġ, uerno equinoctio in penitentia moritur. Friṫuiḃecht Flainn mic Maelseċlainn o maccaiḃ .i. o Donnchad 7 o Conċobur, 7 indreḋ Miḋe uadiḃ co Loċ ri. Slogeḋ ind ḟoċlai la Niall mac n-Aeḋa riġ n-Ailiġ co rogaḃ naiḋm Donnchada 7 Conċoḃuir fria reir a n-aṫar, 7 co fargaḃ sraḋ itir Miḋe 7 Breġa. Maelciarain mac Eoċacain, princeps Cluana h-auis 7 episcopus aird Maċa, anno lxx.° aetatis sue, Scannlan airchinnech Taṁlachta 7 Scannlan airchinnech na Congbala glinne Suileḋi, in Christo moriuntur. Ruarcc mac Maelbrigte, ri Muscraide Ṫire,

---

[1] *Grellach-Eillte.*—Girley, in the barony of Upper Kells, co. Meath.

[2] *Cormacan.* — Better known as Cormacan *Eiges* (or C. the "Poet"). His obit is given by the *Four Masters* at the year 946=948. See O'Donovan's ed. of the *Circuit of Ireland by Muircheartach Mac Neill*, printed for the Irish Archæol. Soc., 1842. The original of these lines, which is not in B., is added in the upper margin of fol. 47*a* in A., with a sign of reference to the proper place in the text.

[3] *Royal-heir.*—ridomna, A.

[4] *Died.*—The *Four Masters* (at A.D. 911) say that Oengus died of wounds received by him in the battle of Grellach-Eillte, mentioned under the preceding year (913) in this Chronicle.

[5] *Fal.*—Fal, and Inis-Fail, were bardic names for Ireland. The orig. of these lines (not in B), is added in the lower margin of fol. 47*a* in A, with the usual mark of reference to the proper place in the text.

[6] *Aedh Allan.*—The death in battle of Aedh Allan, King of Ireland, is recorded above at the year 742. The

Maelmuire son of Flannacan, royal-heir of the Airghialla.

Sorrow to the cold Grellach-Eillte,[1]
We found hosts by its side.
Cormacan[2] said to Niall,
"We will not be allowed to go westwards, let us go eastwards."

Kal. Jan. A.D. 914 (alias 915). Oengus Ua Maelsechnaill, royal-heir[3] of Temhair, died[4] on the seventh of the Ides of February, the third day of the week. [914.]

A blessing on the hand of Cernd son of Bernd,
Who slew Oengus Finn, the pride of Fal;[5]
It was a good deed of his sharp valour,
To avenge the noble Aedh Allan.[6]

Domnall son of Aedh, King of Ailech, died in penitence, at the vernal equinox. A rebellion against Flann son of Maelsechlainn by his sons, viz., by Donnchad and Conchobar; and they devastated Midhe as far as Loch-Ri. The army of the North [was led] by Niall son of Aedh, King of Ailech, who received the guarantee of Donnchad and Conchobar that they would be obedient to their father, and left peace between Midhe and Bregh. Maelciarain son of Eochocan, abbot of Cluain-auis[7] and bishop of Ard-Macha,[8] in the 70th year of his age; Scannlan, 'herenagh' of Tamlacht, and Scannlan, 'herenagh' of Congbail[9] of Glenn-Suilidhe, died in Christ. Ruarcc son of Maelbrigte, King of Muscraidhe-thire,[10] was killed

victor in the battle was Domnall son of Murchad, who succeeded Aedh Allan in the sovereignty, and who was the ancestor of Oengus Ua Maelsechlainn.

[7] *Cluain-auis*.—Or Cluain-eois, as it is otherwise written. Now Clones, in the co. Monaghan.

[8] *Ard-Macha*.—There is probably some error here, as the name of Maelciarain does not appear in any of the ancient lists of bishops, or abbots, of Armagh. See the *Chron. Scotorum* (ed. Hennessy), p. 186, note [4].

[9] *Congbail*.—Now Conwal, in the barony of Kilmacrenan, co. Donegal.

[10] *Muscraidhe-thire*.—The old name of a territory comprising the present barony of Lower Ormond, (and part of Upper Ormond), co. Tipperary.

do ġuin tre meḃail 7 ta[n]gnaċt o hUiḃ Dungalaiġ. Tormaċ mar meinic do ġentiḃ do ṫiachtain oc Loċ daċaeċ beos, 7 indreḋ tuaṫ 7 ceall Muman h-uaḋiḃ.

.b. Kt. Ianair. Anno domini dcccc.° x.° u.° (alias dcccc.° xiii.°). Flann mac Maelseċlainn (mic Maelruanaiḋ mic Donnchada), ri Temraċ, regnans annis xxx. et ui., et mensibus .ui. et diebus .u., anno aetatis sue lx.° uiii.°, octaua die Kalendarum Iunii feria septima, hora
Fol. 46ba. diei quasi septima, moritur. Foġartaċ mac Tolairg ri deiscirt Breġ moritur. Annle mac Caṫan, ri Uaṫne Cliaċ, do bas[ugad] o Gallaiḃ Loċa daċaeċ. Aeḋ mac Ailello abbas cluana ferta Brendain, Conligan mac Draignen tosech .h. Lomain Gaela, Martain abbas roiss Commain, moriuntur. Niall mac Aeḋa isriġe Temraċ, 7 oenaċ Tailten do aiġ las, quod multis temporibus preterimissum est. Gaill Loċa dacaeċ beos do indriuṫ Muman 7 Laigen. Maelbarrḟind sacardd Cluana mic Nois moritur. Ard Maċa do loscaḋ diait i quint Kalendas Mai .i. a leith deisceartaċ, cosin tói 7 cosint saboll 7 cusin ċuicin 7 cosind liss abbaid h-uile. Coblaiṫ ingin Duiḃ-duin, comarba Briġti, quieuit.

Kt. Ianair. Anno domini dcccc.° x.° ui.° (alias dcccc.° xiiii.°). Sneaċta 7 h-uaċt diṁar, 7 aig anaicenta, isin bliadain se, comtar suirre prim loċa 7 priṁ abainn Erend, co ro la ar di ceṫraiḃ 7 enaiḃ 7 eicniḃ. Airdi grainndi olċena. Cometis celum ardere uisum est. Dlum ṫeineḋ do arṫrugud co tosainn iar n-Erinn

---

[1] *Son.*—The original of the parenthetic clause, which is added in *al. man.* in A., is written by way of gloss, in the orig. band in B.

[2] *Who reigned.*—regnans, in A. and B.

[3] *Of June.*—Iunia, A. The criteria above given shew that the correct year was 916, according to the common computation.

[4] *Uaithne-Cliach.*—A territory now represented by the barony of Owney-beg, co. Limerick.

[5] *Ui-Lomain-Gaela.*—A sept of the Ui-Maine (or Hy-Many) of Con-

through treachery and malice, by the Ui-Dungalaigh. A great and frequent increase of Gentiles coming still to Loch-dachaech ; and the territories and churches of Munster were plundered by them.

Kal. Jan. A.D. 915 (alias 916). Flann, son of Mael- [915.] BIS.
sechlainn (son[1] of Maelruanaidh, son of Donnchad), King of Temhair, who reigned[2] 36 years, 6 months, and 5 days, died in the 68th year of his age, on the 8th of the Kalends of June,[3] the 7th day of the week, about the 7th hour of the day. Fogartach son of Tolarg, King of the South of Bregh, died. Annle son of Cathan, King of Uaithne-Cliach,[4] was put to death by the Foreigners of Loch-dacaech. Aedh son of Ailill, abbot of Cluain-ferta-Brendain; Conligan son of Draignen, chieftain of Ui-Lomain-Gaela;[5] [and] Martain abbot of Ros-Comain, died. Niall,[6] son of Aedh, in the kingship of Temhair; and the fair of Tailtiu was celebrated by him, which had been omitted for many years. The Foreigners of Loch-dacaech still plundering Munster and Leinster. Mael-barrfind, a priest of Clonmacnoise, died. Ard-Macha was burned by lightning on the 5th of the Kalends of May, viz., the southern half, with the 'Toi'[7] and the 'Saball,'[7] and the kitchen, and the abbot's house all. Coblaith, daughter of Dubhduin, successor of Brigit, rested.

Kal. Jan. A.D. 916 (alias 917). Great snow and cold, [916.]
and unprecedented frost, in this year, so that the chief lakes and rivers of Ireland were passable, which brought great havoc upon cattle, birds, and fishes. Horrid signs besides. The heavens seemed to glow with comets. A mass of fire was observed, with thunder, passing over Ireland from the west, which went over the sea eastwards.

---

naught. See O'Donovan's *Ann. Four Mast.*, A.D. 949, note k.

[6] *Niall*; Niall Glundubh, or Niall "Black-knee." The epithet glun-duḃ is added as a gloss in B., in a very old hand, and the note Niall glunduḃ regnare incipit in the margin in A., in *al. man.*

[7] *Toi — Saball.*—Regarding these churches, see Reeves' *Ancient Churches of Armagh*, pp. 12, 13; and Todd's *St. Patrick*, p. 480.

aníar co n-dechaiḋ dar muir sair. Sitriuc .h. Imair cona ċobluċ do ġabail oc Cinnḟuait i n-airiur Laigen. Ragnall .h. hImair cona ċobluċ aliu co Gallu Loċa daċaeċ. Ar nGall oc neimlid la Mumain. Ar n-aile la Eoganacht 7 Ciarraiḋe. Slogad .h. Neill in deiscirt 7 in tuaiscirt la Niall mac nAeḋa rig nErend co firu Muman, do ċocuḋ fri Genntí. Scorais ala laiṫiu fiċet mís Augaist oc Tobar glethraċ i Maiġ Feiṁin. Dollotar in Genti issin tír isind lau ċetnai. Firruararttadar in Goidil etir ṫeirt 7 meḋoin laei, 7 caṫaiġset co essartain, co torċair amail ċet fer etursu, acht is lia doċer di ġallaiḃ. Dollotar teorcobraid arin longport na nGennti fri tóir ammuintire. Imorroiset in Goidil for culu doċum a n-dunaiḋ fesin toir dedenaiġ .i. re Raġnall ri Duḃgall, co sloġ di Gallaib uime. Luiḋ Niall mac Aeḋa co n-uatib i n-agaiḋ na Genti co tarmarc dia truit an inguin. Anais
Fol. 46bb. Niall iarsin fiċet n-aiḋce a n-dunaḋ fris n[a] Gennti. Asbreṫ uaḋ fri Laigniu ar a n-gabtis caċt dicein fris in longport. Roinis caṫ Cinnḟuait foraib re Sitriuc hUa Imair, condid ann docer Augaire mac Ailello ri Laigen, 7 Maelmorḋa mac Muirecain ri airṫir Liḟi, Maelmoeḋoc mac Diarmata sui et episcopus Laigen, Augran mac Cennetiġ ri Laiċse, et ceteri duces atque nobiles. Sitriuc .h. Imair do tuidecht i n-Aṫ cliaṫ. Eiṫne ingen Aeḋa, in uera poenitentia et in feria Martini, defuncta est.

---

[1] *Cennfuait.* — O'Donovan (*Four Mast.*, A.D. 915, notes, pp. 589, 590) would identify Cennfuait with Confey, in the barony of Salt, co. Kildare. But the above statement represents Cennfuait as on the "border" (i n-airiur) of Leinster, whereas Confey is several miles inland.

[2] *Neimlid.* — The 'Translation' of these Annals in Clar. 49 has "Imly" (i.e. Emly), bar. of Clanwilliam, co. Tipperary.

[3] *Tobar - Glethrach.* — Not now known by this name.

[4] *Magh-Femhin.*—A plain, famous in Irish history and legend, comprising a large district of country about Clonmel.

[5] *Tierce.*—This was the canonical term for the division of time extending from the 9th to the 12th hour of the day.

Sitriuc, grandson of Imar, came with his fleet to Cennfuait[1] on the border of Leinster. Ragnall, grandson of Imar, went with his other fleet to the Foreigners of Loch-Dachaech. A slaughter of the Foreigners at Neimlid[2] in Munster. Another slaughter by the Eoganacht and the Ciarraidhe. A hosting of the Ui-Neill of the South, and of the North, by Niall son of Aedh, to the men of Munster, to wage war against the Gentiles. He encamped on the 22nd of the month of August at Tobar-Glethrach[3] in Magh-Femhin.[4] The Gentiles went into the territory on the same day. The Irish attacked them between tierce[5] and mid-day, and they fought till vesper-time, so that about[6] 100 men fell between them, but most fell on the part of the Foreigners. Reinforcements came from the camp of the Gentiles, to the aid of their people. The Irish returned back to their encampment before [the arrival of] the last reinforcement, i.e. before Ragnall, King of the Dubh-Gaill [arrived], accompanied by an army of Foreigners. Niall, son of Aedh, went with a small force against the Gentiles, so that God prevented their slaughter through him. Niall after this stayed twenty nights encamped against the Gentiles. He sent word to the Leinstermen to beseige the camp from a distance. The battle of Cennfuait[7] was gained over them by Sitriuc grandson of Imar, in which fell Augaire son of Ailill, King of Leinster; and Maelmordha son of Muirecan, King of Airther-Liphè; Maelmoedhoc, son of Diarmait, a wise man, and bishop of Leinster; Augran son of Cennetigh, King of Laighis, and other captains and nobles. Sitriuc, grandson of Imar, came into Ath-cliath. Eithne,[8] daughter of Aehh, died in true penitence, on the feast of St. Martin.

---

[6] *About.*—am̄ (for amail, "like"), A. B. The *Four Mast.* (915) say that 1100 men were slain.

[7] *Cennfuait.*—See note [1]. A marginal note in A. reads du itorcradar u. c. uel paulo plus, "where 500 or more fell."

[8] *Eithne.*—According to the *Ann. Four Mast.* (A.D. 916), she was Queen of the men of Bregh.

Kl. Ianair. Anno domini dcccc.° xuii.° (alias dcccc.° xuiii.°) Maelioin princeps 7 episcopus Roiss creae, Eicneċ princeps Arann airṫir, Daniel Cluana coirpṫe senċa aṁra, in pace dormierunt. Muirenn ingen Suairt, abatissa Cille daro, quieuit. Gaill Loċa dacaeċ do dergiu Erenn .i. Raġnall ri Dubgall 7 na da iarla .i. Ottir 7 Graggabai, 7 sagaiṫ doib iarsin co firu Alban. Fir Alban dono ar a cenn soṁ co comairneċtar for bru Ṫine la Saxanu tuaiscirt. Dogensat in genti ceṫrai caṫa diḃ .i. caṫ la Goṫbriṫ Ua nImair, caṫ las na da iarla, caṫ las na h-óctigerna. Caṫ dano la Raġnall i n-eroloċ nadacadar fir Alban. Roinis re feraiḃ Alban forsna tri caṫa adconncadar, corolsat ár n-dimar di na genntiḃ, im Ottir 7 im Graggabai. Raġnall dono do ḟuabairt iarsuiḋiu illorg fer n-Alban co ro la ar diḃ, acht nadfarcbaṫ ri na mormoer disuidiḃ. Nox praelium diremit. Eiṫilfleiṫ, famosissima regina Saxonum, moritur. Cocaḋ itir Niall mac Aeḋo ri Teṁraċ 7 Sitriuc .H. nImair. Maelmiṫid mac Flannacain ri Cnoġḃai do dul co genti, fri cornum tuaiscirt Breg a muin gente, quod eo nihil contulit.

Kl. Ianair. Anno domini dcccc.° xu. iii.° (alias

---

[1] *Ara-airther.*—The most eastern of the Islands of Aran, in the Bay of Galway.

[2] *Fell asleep.*—dormiuit, A.

[3] *They went.*—sagaiṫ doib [dodib incorrectly for doib], A. B.

[4] *Banks of the Tine*, i.e. the River Tyne.

[5] *North Saxonland.*—Northumbria or Northumberland. The meaning of the expression la saxanu tuais-cirt, which signifies literally "apud Saxones sinistrales," has been misconceived by some writers on Scotch history. There can be no doubt that the foregoing statement, co comair-neċtar for bru Tine la Saxanu tuaiscirt, means that they (i.e. the Dubhgall [or Black Foreigners] and the men of Alba, or Scotland) met on the banks of the Tyne, in Northumbria. Skene, misunderstanding the expression, states that the men of Alba prepared to meet the invaders "with the assistance of the northern Saxons." (*Chron. Picts and Scots*, p. 363). Dr. Todd fell into the same mistake, (*War of the Gaedhil, &c.*, Introd., p. lxxxvi).

[6] *Graggaba.*—Regarding the iden-

Kal. Jan. A.D. 917 (alias 918). Maeleoin, abbot and bishop of Ros-cre; Eicnech, abbot of Ara-airther,[1] [and] Daniel of Cluain-coirpthe, an eminent historian, 'fell asleep[2] in peace.' Muirenn, daughter of Suart, abbess of Cill-dara, rested. The Foreigners of Loch-Dachaech left Ireland, viz., Ragnall King of the Dubhgall, and the two Earls, to wit Ottir and Graggaba. And they went[3] afterwards against the men of Alba. The men of Alba, however, were prepared for them; so that they met on the banks of the Tine,[4] in North Saxonland.[5] The Gentiles divided themselves into four battalions, viz., a battalion with Gothfrith grandson of Imar; a battalion with the two Earls; a battalion with the young lords. There was another battalion under Ragnall, in ambush, which the men of Alba did not see. The men of Alba gained a victory over the three battalions they saw, and made a great slaughter of the Gentiles, including Ottir and Graggaba.[6] Ragnall, however, afterwards attacked the rear of the army of the men of Alba, and made a slaughter of them, but no King or 'Mor-maer'[7] of them perished. Night interrupted the battle. Eithilfleith,[8] most famous queen of the Saxons,[9] died. War between Niall, son of Aedh, King of Temhair, and Sitriuc, grandson of Imar. Maelmithidh son of Flannacan, King of Cnoghbha,[10] went to the Gentiles, with a view to defending the North of Bregh by the aid of the Gentiles; which availed him nothing. [917.]

Kal. Jan. A.D. 918 (alias 919). Easter on the 7th [918.]

---

tity of this person, mentioned in a previous entry under this year, see Todd's work, just cited, Introd., p. lxxxvi, note [1].

[7] *Mor-maer.*—"Great steward."

[8] *Eithilfleith.*—Æthelfled, Queen of the Mercians, whose obit is entered in the Anglo-Saxon Chron. at the year 918, and a second time at 922.

[9] *Queen of the Saxons.*—Æthelflæd, eldest daughter of Alfred the Great, and wife of Æthelred, 'ealdorman' of the Mercians. See the previous note.

[10] *Cnoghbha.*—This name is now represented by Knowth, the name of a townland containing a large mound, in the parish of Monknewtown, barony of Upper Slane, co. Meath.

dcccc.° xix.°) Cairc for sert Kl. Mai, 7 minċairc ala laiṫiu do ṡamrad. Aed Oa Maelseċnaill do ḋallad
Fol. 47aa. le braṫair, la Donnchad ri Miḋe. Bellum re nGentiḃ occ Duiblinn for Goiḋelu, du i torcair Niall (.i. glundub) mac Aeḋo, ri Erenn, tertio anno regni sui, xuii. Kl. Octimbris, iiii. feria, 7 du itorcair Aed mac Eoċocain ri coiciḋ Conċobair, 7 Maelmiṫid mac Flannacain ri Breg, 7 Concobar .h. Maelseċnaill ridomna Temraċ, 7 Flaiṫbertaċ mac Domnaill ridomna ind Ḟoċlai, 7 mac Duibrinaiġ .i. Maelcraibi, ri na n-Airgiallu, et alii nobiles multi.

Bronaċ indiu hErind h-uag,
Cen ruirig ruag rigi giall;
[As deccis nime gan grein,
Fairgsi muiġe Neill gan Niall]

[Ni]sta medair maitius fir,
Nista siṫ na suba sloiġ;
Ni cumaing oenach do ain,
O rosbaid in broenach broin.

[Truáġ] sin a maġ m-Breġ m-buiḋe,
A tir n-alaind n-adguide;
Ro scarais frit riġ ruirech,
Fotracaiḃ Niall niamguinech.

[Caiti mail iartair betha,
Caiti grain] ceċ airmġreṫa;
Indid Niall croḋa Cnuċa
Ro malart a mor truiċa.

Cett mac Flaiṫbertaiġ ri Corc-Modruaġ, Tigernaċ .h. Cleiriġ, ri .h. Fiaċraċ Aiḋne, mortui sunt.

---

[1] *Little Easter.*—minċairc. Low Sunday, *i.e.* the first Sunday after Easter Sunday. The true year was 919, in which Easter Sunday fell on the 7th of the Kalends of May.

[2] *In which fell.*—du i torcair, B. Mutilated in A.

[3] *Glundubh.*—"Black Knee." The epithet is added by way of gloss in B.

[4] *The 17th.*—The corresponding number is not in A., which has been partly injured in this place.

[5] *Province of Conchobar*, (*i.e.* of Conchobar Mac Nessa, King of Ulster in the 1st century). A name for the Province (coiced or "fifth") of Ulster. See note [5], p. 386 *supra*.

of the Kalends of May, and Little Easter[1] on the 2nd day of Summer. Aedh, grandson of Maelsechnaill, was blinded by his brother, Donnchad King of Midhe. A battle gained by Gentiles at Dubhlinn, over Gaedhil, in which fell[2] Niall (*i.e.* Glundubh)[3] son of Aedh, King of Ireland, in the 3rd year of his reign, on the 17th[4] of the Kalends of December, the 4th day of the week; and in which fell Aedh son of Eochacan, King of the Province of Conchobar;[5] and Maelmithidh son of Flannacan, King of Bregh; and Conchobar Ua Maelsechnaill, royal heir of Temhair; and Flaithbertach son of Domnall, royal heir of the Fochla; and the son of Dubhsinach, i.e. Maelcraibhi, King of the Airghialla, and many other nobles.

Sorrowful[6] to-day is noble Ireland,
Without a valiant chief of hostage reign;
[It is seeing the heavens without a sun,
To see Magh-Neill without Niall].

There is no joy in man's goodness;
There is no peace nor gladness among hosts;
No fair can be celebrated,
Since the cause of sorrow died.

[A pity] this, O beloved Magh-Bregh,
Beautiful, desirable country.
Thou hast parted with thy lordly king;
Niall the wounding hero has left thee!

[Where is the chief of the western world?
Where is the hero] of every clash of arms?
Is it the brave Niall of Cnucha
That has been lost, O great cantred!

Cett son of Flaithbertach, King of Corc-Modruagh, [and] Tigernach Ua Cleirigh, King of Ui-Fiachrach-Aidhne, died.

---

[6] *Sorrowful.*—The original of these stanzas, not in B., is written in the top marg. of fol. 47*aa* in A., with a mark of reference to the place where they might be inserted in the text. Some of the words which had been cut off by the binder, have been restored from the copy in the Ashburnham MS. of the *Ann. Four Mast.* in the Royal Irish Academy.

Kl. Ianair. Anno domini dcccc.° x.° ix.° (alias dcccc.° xx.°). Maelmuire, princeps airdd Brecain, moritur. Caṫroiniuḋ re nDonncaḋ .h. Maelseċnaill for Genti, du itorċair ár n-diṁar. Finċar episcopus et scriba optimus Doimliac feliciter pausauit. Scannal Roiss Creae, et scriba Cluana mic Nois, quieuit. Sitriuc ua hImair do dergiu Ata cliaṫ per potestatem diuinam. Domliac Cenannsa do brisiuḋ o Gentiḃ 7 soċaiḋe martrai ann. Domliac Tuileain do loscaḋ in eodem die. Cormac mac Cuilennain ri na nDesi Muman iugulatus est.

Kl. Ianair. Anno domini dcccc.° xx.° (alias dcccc.° xx.° i.°). Moenaċ mac Siaḋail, comarba Comgaill, cenn ecna innse Erenn, dormiuit. Domnall .h. Maelseċlainn per dolum occisus est a fratre suo Donnchad, quod aptum erat. Ciaran abbas Daiminse pausat. Maelseċlainn .h. Flainn ridomna Teṁraċ, Fiaċra mac Caṫalain ri Coille Follaṁain, Ragnall .h. Imair rí Finngall 7 Dubgall, omnes mortui sunt. Goiṫbriṫ .h. Imair i n-Aṫ cliaṫ. Cinaeḋ mac Domnaill, princeps daire Calcaiċ 7 Droma tuama, 7 cenn adċomairc Conaill in tuaisceirt obiit. Muiriuċt do Gallaiḃ illoċ Feḃail .i. Acolb co n-dib longaib trichat. Cenrig i n-inis Euġain do dergiu co cron 7 co leir doiḃ paucis in ea remanentibus per torporem. Fergal mac Domnaill ri ind [ḟ]oċlai i n-escairdiu friu co romarḃ luċt lunga diḃ, 7 co robris in lungai co ruc a fraid.

---

[1] *Scannal.*—In the *Ann. Four Mast.* (at A.D 918), where the name is written Scannlan, he is stated to have been abbot of Ros-cre (Roscrea.)

[2] *The doimliac*; i.e. the "stone church."

[3] *On.*—in, omitted in B.

[4] *Cuilennan.*—No Cormac "son of Cuilennan" appears in the Geneal. of the Desi-Muman (or Desi of Munster). But there is a Cormac "son of Mothla," who was obviously the person intended. The obit of this Cormac son of Mothla, King of the Desi, is given by the *Four Masters* at A.D. 917, and by the *Chron, Scotorum* at the year 918 (=919.) See Harris's *Ware*, vol. 1, p. 549.

[5] *Maelsechlainn*—Maelsechnaill, B.

[6] *Coille-Follamhain*—See note [7], p. 403 *supra*.

[7] *Gothfrith*—He probably succeeded

Kal. Jan. A.D. 919 alias 920). Maelmuire, abbot of Ard-Brecain, died. A breach of battle by Donnchad, grandson of Maelsechnaill, over the Gentiles, where a great slaughter was made. Finchar, a bishop, and excellent scribe of Doimliacc, rested happily. Scannal,[1] of Ros-cre, and scribe of Cluain-mic-Nois, rested. Sitriuc, grandson of Imhar, left Ath-cliath, through Divine power. The 'doimliac'[2] of Cenannas was broken by Gentiles, and great numbers were martyred there. The 'doimliac'[2] of Tuilen was burned on[3] the same day. Cormac son of Cuilennan,[4] King of the Desi-Muman, was slain. [919.]

Kal. Jan. A.D. 920 (alias 921). Moenach son of Siadhal, successor of Comgall, head of the learning of the Island of Ireland, 'fell asleep.' Domnall, grandson of Maelsechlainn,[5] was deceitfully slain by his brother Donnchad, which was meet. Ciaran, abbot of Daiminis, rested. Maelsechlainn, grandson of Flann, royal-heir of Temhair; Fiachra son of Cathalan, King of Coille-Follamhain,[6] [and] Ragnall grandson of Imar, King of the Finn-Gaill and Dubh-Gaill,—all died. Gothfrith,[7] grandson of Imar, in Ath-cliath. Cinaedh son of Domnall, abbot of Daire-Calgaigh and Druim-thuama, and head of council of the [Cinel]-Conaill of the North, died.[8] A fleet of the Foreigners in Loch-Febhail, viz., Acolb with thirty-two ships. Cen-rig[9] in Inis-Eogain was abandoned by them quickly and entirely; a few remaining there, through laziness. Fergal son of Domnall, King of the Fochla, in enmity towards them, so that he killed the crew of one of the ships, and broke the ship, and took [920.]

---

his brother (or cousin) Sitriuc, whose departure from Ath-cliath (Dublin) is recorded under the year 919.

[8] *Died.*— ꝺıem obııṫ, A. obııṫ, B.

[9] *Cen-rig.* — The name of some island off the coast of Inishowen, in the co. Donegal. See above at the year 732, for mention of an island called Culen-rigi, off the same coast. The versions of this entry given in the MS. Clar. 49, and in O'Conor's ed., are very inaccurate.

Longus aile i Ciunn maġair a n-airer ṫire Conaill .i. mac h-Uaṫmaran mic Bairiṫ cum .xx. nauibus. Indreḋ aird
Fol. 47ab Maċa hi .iiii. id Nouembris o Gallaiḃ Aṫa cliaṫ .i. o Goṫbriṫ Ua Iṁair cum suo exercitu .i. h-isint saṫurn ria feil Martain, 7 na taigi aernaiġi do anacal lais cona lucht de ċeiliḃ de 7 di lobraiḃ, 7 in ceall olċeana, nisi paucis in ea tectis exaustis per incuriam. Indred leṫan uadib for ceċ leaṫ .i. siar co h-Inis .h. Labraḋa, sair co Bandai, foṫuaiṫ co Maġ nIllsen. Acht in sluaġ faṫuaiġ dosfarraiḋ Muircertaċ mac Neill, 7 Aignert mac Murcaḋo, co remid foraib 7 co fargabsat ile, paucis elapsis subsidio sublustris noctis. Eclipsis lunae hi .xu. Kl. Ianuarii, .iii. feria, prima hora noctis. Flaiṫbertaċ mac Muircertaiċ, abbas Cluana moer, moritur.

Cudu andud indbais h uaiġ,
Cudu allud [a] deiglois;
Indid Flatbertaċ finn fial,
Roscar fri míaḋ Cluana móir.

Kl. Ianair. Anno domini dcccc.° xx.° i.° (alias dcccc.° xxii.°). Maelpoil mac Ailella, sui 7 epscop sil Aeḋa Slane, Tadc mac Faelain ri .h. Cennselaiġ, Cernaċmac Flainn princeps Lainne Lére 7 moer muinntiri aird Maċa o Belaċ duin co muir, 7 o Boainn co Cossan, cenn comairle 7 adċomairc fer mBreġ n-uile, omnes

[1] *Cenn-Maghair.*—Or Kinnaweer. See note [3], p. 154 *supra*.

[2] *Gothfrith.*—See note [7], page 440.

[3] *Church*; i.e. the Church-town, or the ecclesiastical buildings generally.

[4] *Inis-Ui-Labrada.* — O'Labrada's Island. Not identified.

[5] *Magh-Nillsen.* — Magh-Uillsenn, *Four Mast.* Not identified.

[6] *Cluain-mor.*—O'Donovan suggests (*F. M.*, A.D. 919, note n), that this place is now represented by the place called Clonmore, in the barony of Rathvilly, co. Carlow.

[7] *Foundation.* — andud. The name of the composer of these lines is not given. O'Conor's version of them is very incorrect. They are not divided metrically in A.

[8] *Or* 922.—The suggestion "uel 22," is in B., not in A. The correct year was, of course, 922.

[9] *Maelpoil.*—Regarding this eminent man, and his identity with the Paulinus to whom Probus dedicated his life of St. Patrick, as alleged by Dr. O'Conor (*Ann. Four Mast.*, ed O'Conor, p. 440, note [1]), see O'Donovan's *Four M.*, A.D. 920,

its spoil. Another fleet in Cenn-Maghair,[1] on the coast of Tir-Conaill, *i.e.*, the son of Uathmaran son of Barith, with twenty ships. The plundering of Ard-Macha on the 4th of the Ides of November, by the Foreigners of Ath-cliath, viz., by Gothfrith[2] grandson of Imar, with his army, on the Saturday before the feast of St. Martin. And the houses of prayer, with their company of Celi-De and of sick, were protected by him, and the church[3] besides, except a few houses in it which were burnt through negligence. An extensive devastation by them on every side, *i.e.*, westwards to Inis-Ui-Labradha;[4] eastwards to the Bann; northwards to Magh-Nillseu.[5] But Muirchertach Mac Neill, and Aignert son of Murchad, met the army [that went] northwards, who were defeated and lost a great many, a few escaping by the aid of the glimmering of night. An eclipse of the moon on the 15th of the Kalends of January, a Tuesday, in the first hour of the night. Flaithbertach son of Muirchertach, abbot of Cluain-mor,[6] died.

Where is the foundation[7] of a great treasure?
Where the report of his good fame?
Behold, Flaithbertach the fair, generous,
Has separated from the honours of Cluain-mor.[6]

Kal. Jan. A.D. 921 (or 922).[8] Maelpoil,[9] son of Ailill, a sage and bishop of the race of Aedh Slane; Tadg son of Faelan, King of Ui-Cennselaigh; Cernach son of Flann, abbot of Lann-leire,[10] and steward of the 'family' of Ard-Macha from Belach-duin[11] to the sea, and from the Boinn to Cossan,[12] chief counsellor and protector of all the men of [921.]

---

note tt; and *Chron. Scotorum*, ed. Hennessy, p. 193, note [6].

[10] *Lann-leire.*—See note [15], p. 205 *supra*.

[11] *Belach-duin.*—This was the old name of Disert-Ciarain (or, as it is now called, Castlekieran), in the present barony of Upper Kells, co. Meath.

[12] *From the Boinn to Cossan*; i.e. from some point (not specified) on the River Boyne to Cassan-linè, supposed to be the old name of the Glyde River, which joins the River Dee, not far from a village called *Annagassan*, to the S.E. of Castlebellingham, in the county of Louth. See Todd's *War of the Gaedhil*, &c., Introd., lxii., note [1].

moriuntur. Ruman epscop Cluana iraird, Ferdalaċ epscop cluana mic Nois, Loingseċ mac Oenacain equonimus Doimliac, Colgu mac Maelsempuil abbas Slane, omnes dormierunt. Longus Luimniġ .i. mic Ailċe for Loċ rí, co ro ortatar Cluain mic Nois 7 h-uile innsi ind Loċa, co rucsat sraid mair etir or 7 argat 7 innbusa ili.

Kl. Ianair. Anno domini dcccc.° xx.° ii.° (alias dcccc.° xx.° iii.°). Maelpadraic mac Morainn, princeps Droma cliaḃ 7 Aird sraṫa, mortuus est. Spelan mac Congalaiġ, rí Conaille, per dolum occisus est. Indreḋ fer nArda 7 Lainne lere 7 fer Roiss in eodem mense. Indred Cille sleiḃe o Gentiḃ de snam Aiġneċ, 7
Fol. 47ba. Dublitir sacardd ard Maċa do ḋul martra leu. Cucongalt sacart Lainne lere, 7 tetra Erenn etir guṫ 7 cruṫ 7 soas, in pace quieuit. Maelcluiċe mac Conċobair, ridomna Connaċt, per dolum occisus est. Ligaċ ingen mic Maelseċlainn, rigan riġ Breġ, mortua est. Finn mac Maelmorḋa, ridomna Laigen, a fratre suo occisus est. Maelcallann princeps disirt Diarmata quieuit.

Kl. Ianair. Anno domini dcccc.° xx.° iii.° (alias dcccc.° xx.° iiii.°). Longas di Gallaiḃ for Loċa Eirne, co r' innrisset innsi ind Loċa 7 na tuaṫa imbi sán can. A n-dersge d' ind Loċ isint saṁraḋ ar ciunn. Gaill for Loċ Cuan, 7 Maelduin mac Aeḋa, ridomna in

[1] *Fleet of Luimnech*; i.e. the Foreign Fleet of Limerick.

[2] *Son of Ailche.*—Mentioned again at A.D. 923, and 927, *infra*. According to Dr. Todd his real name was "Tamar." But he was also known by the name of Gormo Gamle, and various other epithets. See *War of the Gaedhil*, &c., Introd., cv., note [3] and pp. 266-7.

[3] *Conaille*; i.e. the tribe (or territory) of Conaille-Muirtheimhne, in the present county of Louth.

[4] *Fera-Arda.*—Or Fera-Arda-Cianachta. See note [7], p. 324 *supra*.

[5] *Lann-leire.*—See note [15], p. 205.

[6] *Cill-sleibhe.*—Or Cill-sleibhe-Cuilinn. Killevy, in the county of Armagh.

[7] *Snamh-aignech.* — Carlingford Lough. First identified by Dean Reeves. See his *Down and Connor*, p. 252.

Bregh—all died. Ruman, bishop of Cluain-Iraird; Ferdalach, bishop of Cluain-mic-Nois; Loingsech son of Oenacan, house-steward of Doimliac; Colgu son of Maelsempuil, abbot of Slane—all 'fell asleep.' The fleet of Luimnech,[1] *i.e.* of the son of Ailche,[2] on Loch-Ri, so that they destroyed Cluain-mic-Nois, and all the islands of the lake, and carried off a great spoil, between gold and silver, and other treasures.

Kal. Jan, A.D. 922 (alias 923). Maelpatraic son of [922.]
Morand, abbot of Druim-cliabh and Ard-sratha, died. Spelan son of Congalach, king of Conaille,[3] was treacherously slain. Plundering of Fera-Arda,[4] and Lann-leire,[5] and Fera-Roiss, in the same month. Plundering of Cill-sleibhe[6] by Gentiles from Snamh-aignech,[7] and Dubhlitir, priest of Ard-Macha, suffered martyrdom by them. Cucongalt, priest of Lann-leire,[5] the *tetra*[8] of Ireland for voice, and figure, and knowledge, rested in peace. Maelcluiche son of Conchobar, royal-heir of Connaught, was slain through treachery. Ligach, daughter of the son[9] of Maelsechlainn, the King of Bregh's queen, died. Finn son of Maelmordha, royal heir of Leinster, was killed by his brother. Maelcallainn, abbot of Disert-Diarmata,[10] rested.

Kal. Jan. A.D. 923 (alias 924). A fleet of Foreigners [923.]
on Loch-Erne; and they plundered the islands of the lake, and the territories round it, to and fro. They departed from the lake in the Summer following. Foreigners on Loch-Cuan; and Maelduin son of Aedh, royal heir

[8] *Tetra.*—This word, which appears to be used here in the sense of "paragon," or "most eminent," is explained in the *Ann. Four M.*, A.D. 921, as signifying "chantor, or orator," (cantaıꞃe no oꞃatoꞃ), a meaning which does not seem consistent with the context. The Translator in Clar. 49 makes Cucongalt "chiefe of Ireland in all virtues." But Dr. O'Conor understands *tetra* and *cruth* as signifying respectively "Tympanista," and "cithara"!

[9] *Son.*—He was Flann Sinna, King of Ireland, whose obit is entered above at the year 915.

[10] *Disert-Diarmata.*—Now known as Castledermot, co. Kildare.

coiciḃ, do ċotaim leu. No ċoblaċ mar de ġallaiḃ loċa Cuan do baḋaḋ oc Fertais Ruġraiġe, du in robaduḋ nói cet aut eo amplius. Sloġaḋ la Goṫbriṫ .h. n-Imair o Aṫ cliaṫ co Luimneċ, co farsbaḋ slog dimar dia muintir la mac n-Ailċe. Moċta epscop Oa Neill 7 sacart aird Maċa in pace quieuit. Muireḋaċ mac Domnall tanase abbad aird Maċa, 7 ardmaer Oa Neill in deiscirt, 7 comarba Buiti mic Bronaiġ, cenn adcomairc Fer mBreg n-uile ocaib cleirċiḃ quinto die Kalendarum Decimbrium uita decessit. Mael-morḋa mac Conġaile princeps Daiminnsi quieuit.

Kl. Ianair. Anno domini dcccc.° xx.° iiii. (alias dcccc.° 25°). Dubġall mac Aeḋa, ri Ulaṫ, a suis iugulatus est. Lorcan mac Dunchada, ri Breġ, senile morte moritur. Caṫal mac Conċobair, ri Connacht, in penitentia obiit. Domnall mac Caṫail do marbad li a braṫair .i. la Taḋc, per dolum, 7 alii preclari de Connaċtaiḃ.

Kl. Ianair. Anno domini dcccc°. xx°. u.° (alias dcccc.° 26°). Orgain duin Sobairċe do Gallaiḃ loċa Cuan, in quo multi homines occisi sunt 7 capti.
Fol. 47bb. Roiniuḋ re Muirceartaċ mac Neill for Gallu oc snam Aigneċ, ubi .cc. decollati sunt. Colman princeps Cluana iraird 7 Cluana mic Nois, 7 scriba 7 episcopus, in Christo quieuit. Fergus mac Duiligen, ri Luirg, do ṁarbad o feraib Breifne. Longus loċa Cuan do

---

[1] *Province*; i.e. of the Province of Ulidia.

[2] *Loch-Cuan.*—Strangford Lough, co. Down.

[3] *Fertas-Rudhraighe.*—The *Four Masters* (at 922), and the *Chron. Scotorum* (923), give the name of the place of this catastrophe as "Loch-Rudhruidhe," or "Loch-Rudhraighe," and the *Ann. Clonmacnoise* (920=924) as "Logh-Rowrie." Loch-Rudhraighe was the old name of the inner Bay of Dundrum, co. Down; and Fertas-Rudhraighe was probably the name of the passage between the inner and outer Bays; the word *Fertas* signifying a ford, crossing, or passage.

[4] *Luimnech.*—Limerick.

[5] *Son of Ailche.*—See note regarding this active depredator, under A.D. 921.

[6] *Successor of Buite.*; *i.e.* abbot of

of the Province,[1] fell by them. A great new fleet of the Foreigners of Loch-Cuan[2] was drowned at Fertas-Rudhraighe,[3] where 900 persons, or more, were drowned. A hosting by Gothfrith grandson of Imar, from Ath-cliath to Luimnech,[4] when a great multitude of his people were slain by the son of Ailche.[5] Mochta, bishop of the Ui-Neill, and priest of Ard-Macha, rested in peace. Muiredhach son of Domnall, tanist-abbot of Ard-Macha, and high-steward of the Ui-Neill of the South, and successor of Buite[6] son of Bronach—the head of counsel of all the men of Bregh, lay and clerical—died on the 5th of the Kalends of December. Maelmordha son of Conghal, abbot of Daiminis, rested.

Kal. Jan. A.D. 924 (alias 925). Dubhgall son of [924.]
Aedh, King of Ulidia, was slain by his own people. Lorcan son of Dunchad, King of Bregh, died in a senile state. Cathal son of Conchobar, King of Connaught, died in penitence. Domnall, son of Cathal, was treacherously killed by his brother, *i.e.*, Tadhg, and other nobles of the Connaughtmen [were also slain].

Kal. Jan. A.D. 925 (alias 926). Destruction of [925.]
Dun-Sobhairche[7] by the Foreigners of Loch-Cuan,[8] in which a great many men were killed and captured. A victory by Muirchertach Mac Neill over Foreigners at Snamh-Aignech,[9] where 200 were beheaded. Colman, abbot of Cluain-Iraird and Cluain-mic-Nois, and a scribe and bishop, rested in Christ. Fergus son of Duligen, King of Lurg,[10] was slain by the men of Breifne. The fleet of Loch-Cuan[8] took up [a position] at

---

Mainister-Buite, or Monasterboice, co. Louth.

[7] *Dun-Sobhairche.*—Now known as Dunseverick, in the parish of Billy, barony of Cary, co. of Antrim; near the Giant's Causeway.

[8] *Loch-Cuan.*—Strangford Lough, co. Down.

[9] *Snamh-Aigneck.* — See p. 444, note [7]. A marg. note, partly mutilated, states that the victor was Muirchertach of the Leather Cloaks, son of Niall Glundubh.

[10] *Lurg.*—Now represented by the barony of Lurg, co. Fermanagh.

ġabail oc Linn h-Uaċaill .i. Alpṫann mac Goṫbriṫ, hi prid nonas Septembris. Roineḋ re Muirceartaċ mac Neill oc droċut Cluana na Cruimṫer in .ii. feria i quinnt Kl. Enair, du itorċair Alpṫann mac Goṫbriṫ cum magna strage exercitus sui. Ro cabaḋ caċt sechtmuine for alleṫ oc aṫ Cruiṫne, co tainic Goṫfriṫ ri Gall o aṫ cliaṫ dia coḃair.

Kl. Ianair. Anno domini dcccc.° xx.° vi.° (alias dcccc.° xx.° vii.°). Maelbrigte mac Tornain, comarba Patraic 7 Coluim cille, felici senectute quievit. Sitriuc .h. Imair, rí Dubgall 7 Finngall, immatura aetate mortuus est. Longas Linne du dergiu, 7 Goffriṫ do deirgiu Aṫa cliaṫ, et iterum Goṫfriṫ reversus est ante finem sex mensium. Coscraḋ n-oenaiġ o mac Neill mic Aeḋo im Donnchad .h. Maelsechlainn, sed dominus reparavit eos sine ulla occisione. Goaċ mac Duibroa, ri Ciannachta Glinne gaimin, occisus est o Muirceartaċ mac Neill. Fuacarta mac Laċtnain, rex Teṫba, dolose a sua familia occisus est. Cormac episcopus Glinne da loċa, 7 airchinnech, quievit.

.b. Kl. Ianair. Anno domini dcccc.° xx.° vii.° (alias dcccc.° xx° viii.°). Baiṫene comarba Brenaind Biror quievit. Murgel ingin Maelseċlaind in senectute obiit. Maelruanaiġ mac Concobair occisus est o Ḋonnchad. Donnchad mac Domnaill mic Aeda a

[1] *Linn-Uachaill.*—Otherwise written Linn-Duachaill. Not identified. Todd thought it was the name of a pool at the mouth of the confluence of the rivers Dee and Glyde, near Castlebellingham, co. Louth. See *War of the Gaedhil*, &c., Introd., lxii.

[2] *Colum-Cille.* — In the list of 'comarbs' (or successors) of Patrick contained in the *Book of Leinster* (p. 42, col. 4), Maelbrigte, the length of whose rule is limited to 33 years, is stated to have been also 'comarb' of St. Brigit. Ware alleges that Maelbrigte was archbishop of Armagh from A.D. 885 to 927. *Works*, Harris's ed., vol. 1, p. 46.

[3] *Linn.*; i.e. Linn-Duachaill. See among the entries for last year, where the arrival of the fleet of Loch-Cuan at Linn-Uachaill is noted.

[4] *Tailtiu.*—See note [6], p. 406 *supra*

[5] *The son of Niall;* i.e. Muirchertach, son of Niall Glundubh. See the *Circuit of Ireland by Muirchertach*

Linn-Uachaill,[1] viz., Alpthann son of Gothfrith, the day before the Nones of September. A victory gained by Muirchertach Mac Neill, at the bridge of Cluain-na-Cruimther, on Thursday, the 5th of the Kalends of January, where Alpthann son of Gothfrith was killed, with a great slaughter of his army. Half of them were besieged for a week at Ath-Cruithne, until Gothfrith, King of the Foreigners, came from Ath-cliath to their aid.

Kal. Jan. A.D. 926 (alias 927). Maelbrigte son of Tornan, 'comarb' of Patrick and Colum-Cille,[2] rested at a happy old age. Sitriuc, grandson of Imar, King of Dubh-Gaill and Finn-Gaill, died at an unripe age. The fleet of Linn[3] retired, and Gothfrith retired from Ath-cliath; and Gothfrith returned again before the end of six months. Interruption of the 'Fair' [of Tailtiu[4]] by the son of Niall[5] son of Aedh, against Donnchad[6] grandson of Maelsechlainn, but God separated them without any loss of life.[7] Goach son of Dubhroa, King of Cianachta-Glinne-gaimin,[8] was slain by Muirchertach son of Niall. Focarta son of Lachtnan, King of Tethba, was treacherously slain by his people. Cormac, bishop of Glenn-da-locha, and 'herenagh,' rested. [926.]

Kal. Jan. A.D. 927 (alias 928). Baithene, comarb of Brenand of Biror, rested. Murgel,[9] daughter of Maelsechlainn, died in old age. Maelruanaigh, son of Conchobar, was slain by Donnchad.[6] Donnchad, son of Domnall, son of Aedh, was slain by Norsemen. The [927.]

---

mac Neill, edited by O'Donovan for the Ir. Archæol. Soc.; Dublin, 1841.

[6] *Donnchad.*—He was King of Ireland at the time, and the son of Flann Sinna, son of Maelsechlainn.

[7] *Without any loss of life.*—ꞅine ulliuꞅ occiꞅione, A., B.

[8] *Cianachta-Glinne-gaimin.* — See note [7], p. 132 *supra*.

[9] *Murgel.*—See above at the year 882, where the daughter of Maelsechnaill (or Maelsechlainn), called Muirgel in the *Chron. Scotorum* (883), is represented as participating in the killing of the son of Ausli, a chieftain of the Foreigners. But the Murgel whose obit is here given is stated in the *Ann. Four Mast.* (926) and *Chron. Scot.* (927) to have been the daughter of Flann, son of Maelsechlainn.

Nortmannis interfectus est. Mac Ailche for Loċ n-Eċaċ co muiriuċt di Gallaiḃ, co ro inder innsi in loċa et conrimia eius. Diarmait mac Cerbaill rí Osraiġi mortuus est. Ceile comarba Comgaill, et apostolicus doctor totius hibernie do dul i n-ailiṫri.

Tri noi, noi ced do bliadnaib,
Rimṫir fo riaġlaiḃ reiliḃ,
O gein Crist gnim cen den,
Co bas caiḋ Ceili clerig.

Ciaran comarba Cainneċ quieuit.

Kt. Ianair. Anno domini dcccc.° xx.° uiii.° (alias dcccc.° xx.° ix.°). Tuaṫal mac Oenacain, scriba et
Fol. 49aa. episcopus Doimliac 7 Lusca, 7 moer muinntiri Patraicc o sleiḃ faḋes, heu immatura etate quieuit. Longas for Loċ Erpren i Connactaiḃ. Ceile comarba Comgaill, scriba et anchorita et apostolicus doctor totius hibernie, lix.° anno etatis sue, xuiii.° die Kt. Octimbris, in peregrinatione feliciter Romae quieuit. Sloġaḋ la Donnchad co Liat druim fri mac Neill.

Abbreḋ nech fri Donnchad donn,
Risin sonnchad slaidi clann,
Cia beiṫ Liaṫ druim ar a chinn,
Ata gilla diardaind and.

Kt. Ianair. Anno domini dcccc.° xx.° ix.° (alias dcccc.° 30.°). Goṫfriṫ .h. Imair co n-Gallaiḃ Aṫa cliaṫ do toġail dercca Ferna, quod non auditum est antiquis temporibus. Fland Foḃair, episcopus et anco-

[1] *Son of Ailche.*—See the note regarding this person, under A.D. 921 *supra*.

[2] *Ceile.*—Successor of Comgall, or abbot of Bangor (co. Down). The *Four Masters* write his name "Celedabhail" (926), and add that he went to Rome.

[3] *Ceile-Clerigh.*—See last note. The original of these lines, which is not in B., is added in the top margin of fol. 49a in A., with a mark of reference to the proper place in the text (which is on fol. 48b).

[4] *Scribe.*—scripa, A.

[5] *To the south of the mountain.*—This is one of many entries in this Chronicle regarding the office of steward of Patrick's 'family;' but the limits of his district are nowhere

son of Ailche[1] upon Loch-Echach, with a fleet of Foreigners, when he plundered the islands of the lake and its borders. Diarmait son of Cerbhall, King of the Osraighi, died. Ceile,[2] comarb of Comgall, and Apostolic doctor of all Ireland, went into pilgrimage.

Thrice nine, nine hundred years,
Are reckoned by plain rules,
Since the birth of Christ, a deed of fame,
To the death of chaste Ceile-Clerigh.[3]

Ciaran, comarb of Cainnech, rested.

Kal. Jan. A.D. 928 (alias 929). Tuathal son of Oenacan, a scribe,[4] and bishop of Doimliacc and Lusca, and steward of Patrick's 'family' to the south of the mountain,[5] rested, alas! at an immature age. A fleet upon Loch-Orbsen[6] in Connaught. Ceile,[7] comarb of Comgall, a scribe and anchorite, and Apostolic doctor of all Ireland, rested happily at Rome, on his pilgrimage, on the 18th of the Kalends of October, the 59th year of his age. A hosting by Donnchad to Liath-druim,[8] against the son of Niall. [928.]

Let some one say to Donnchad the brown,
To the bulwark of plundering clans,
That though Liath-druim[8] is before him,
There is an angry fellow there.

Kal. Jan. A.D. 929 (alias 930). Gothfrith, grandson of Imar, with the Foreigners of Ath-cliath, demolished Derc-Ferna,[9] a thing that had not been heard of from ancient times. Flann of Fobhar, a bishop and anchorite, [929.]

---

defined except at the year 921 *supra*. See also under the years 813, 887, and 893.

[6] *Loch-Orbsen.*—Loċ Eρρpen, in A. and B. Lough-Corrib.

[7] *Ceile.*—See note [2] under the last year, regarding him.

[8] *Liath-druim.*—It is impossible to say which of the numerous places in Ulster called Liath-druim ("Gray-ridge," Anglicised Leitrim) is here referred to. The original of the stanza here printed, which is not in B., is added in the lower margin of fol. 49*a*, in A.

[9] *Derc-Ferna.*—Supposed to be the Cave of Dunmore, not far from the city of Kilkenny, but apparently on insufficient evidence.

rita, in senectute feliciter pausat. Gaill for Loċ Eċaċ, 7 allongport oc Rubu mena. Gaill for Loċ Beaṫraċ i n-Osraiġi.

Kl. Ianair. Anno domini dcccc.° xxx.° (alias dcccc.° xxx.° i.°). Tipraiti mac Ainsene, comarba Ciarain, extempore dolore obiit. Cennfaelad mac Lorcain, princeps Cluana auis 7 Cloċair mac n-Daimein, 7 tanisi n-abaḋ aird Maċa, pausauit. Maeleoin, episcopus et ancorita Aṫo truim, feliciter quieuit. Derbfail ingen Maelḟinnia mic Flannacain, regina Temraċ, mortua est. Cernaċan mac Tigernain, rí Breifne, mortuus est.

.b. Kl. Ianair. Anno domini dcccc.° 31.° (alias dcccc.° 32.°). Ferdomnaċ mac Flannacain princeps Cluana iraird, scriba optimus, quieuit. Torulb iarla do ṁarbad la mac Neill. Maelgiricc comarba Feiċene Fobair dormiuit. Loingseċ .h. Leṫlobair, ri Dal Araiḋe, mortuus est. Airmedaċ princeps Cuile raṫin a Gentilibus interfectus est. Cinaeḋ mac Caindelbain, dux generis Loeġaire, iugulatus est. Longas for Loċ ri.

Kl. Ianair. Anno Domini dcccc.° 32.° (alias dcccc.° 33.°). Roiniuḋ ria Fergal mac Domnaill mic Aeḋo, 7 ria Siċ-
Fol. 49ab. fraiḋ mac h-Uaṫmurain .i. mac ingine Domnaill, for Muircertaċ mac Neill, 7 for Conaing, immaiġ h-Uaṫa, itorċair Maelgarḃ ri Derlais, 7 Conmal rí Tuaiṫi aċaiḋ, 7 .cc. Cuilen mac Cellaiġ, rex Osraiġi, optimus laicus, mortuus est. Maidm ria Conaing mac Neil

---

[1] *Loch-Echach.*—Lough-Neagh.

[2] *Rubha-Mena.*—This, according to Dean Reeves, was the ancient name of a point on Lough Neagh, in the county of Antrim, "where the Main Water flows into that lake, now included in Shane's Castle park." *Adamnan*, p. 430, note n.

[3] *Loch-Bethrach.*—No lake answering to this name has been identified in Ossory.

[4] *Son of Niall.*—The famous Muirchertach "of the Leather Cloaks." This entry, which is added in the margin in A., forms part of the text in B.

[5] *Cul-rathin.*—Now known as Coleraine, co. of Londonderry.

rested happily in old age. Foreigners on Loch-Echach,[1] and their encampment at Rubha-Mena.[2] Foreigners on Loch-Bethrach[3] in Osraighe.

Kal. Jan. A.D. 930 (alias 931). Tipraiti son of [930.]
Annsene, comarb of Ciaran, died after a long illness. Cennfaeladh son of Lorcan, abbot of Cluain-auis and Clochar-mac-nDaimeni, and tanist-abbot of Ard-Macha, rested. Maeleoin, bishop and anchorite of Ath-truim, rested happily. Derbfail, daughter of Maelfinnia son of Flannacan, queen of Temhair, died. Cernachan son of Tigernan, King of Breifne, died.

Kal. Jan. A.D. 931 (alias 932). Ferdomnach son of [931.]
Flannacan, abbot of Cluain-Iraird, a most excellent scribe, rested. Earl Torulb was killed by the son of Niall.[4] Maelgiricc, 'comarb' of Feichen of Fobhar, 'fell asleep.' Loingsech Ua Lethlobair, King of Dal-Araidhe, died. Airmedach, abbot of Cul-rathin,[5] was killed by Gentiles.[6] Cinaedh son of Caindelbhan, chief of Cinel-Loeghaire, was slain. A fleet upon Loch-Ri.

Kal. Jan. A.D. 932 (alias 933). A victory by Fergal,[7] [932.]
son of Domnall, son of Aedh, and by Sichfridh son of Uathmaran, i.e. the son of Domnall's daughter, over Muirchertach son of Niall, and over Conaing,[8] in Magh-Uatha,[9] where were slain Maelgarbh, King of Derlas,[10] and Conmal, King of Tuaith-achaidh, and 200 [others]. Cuilen son of Cellach, King of the Osraighi, an eminent layman, died. A victory by Conaing[8] son of Niall, over the Ulidians at

[6] *By Gentiles.*—a gentilibus, A., a gentibus, B.

[7] *Fergal.*—He was heir to the sovereignty of Ailech, (or, in other words, of Tirconnell), and son of Domnall (son of Aedh Finnliath, King of Ireland), who previously was Prince, or King, of Ailech, and whose obit is given above at the year 914.

[8] *Conaing.*—He was son of Niall Glundubh, monarch of Ireland, and therefore brother of Muirchertach "of the Leather Cloaks."

[9] *Magh-Uatha.*—O'Donovan suggests that this was "a plain in the east of Meath" (*Four Mast.*, A.D. 931, note s). But this is doubtful.

[10] *Derlas.*—In the Egerton copy of the Tripartite Life of St. Patrick, (Brit. Mus.), Derlas is stated to have

ḟor Ultu oc Rubu Conċongalt, i torcratar .ccc. uel paulo plus. Matuḋan mac Aeḋa co coiceḋ Erenn, 7 co n-Gallaiḃ, co ro ortadar co Sliaḃ Beṫa siar, 7 co Mucnam faḋes, conostarraiḋ Muirċertaċ mac Neill, co remaib foraiḃ, 7 co forgaibset da xx^{it} déc cenn, 7 a n-gabail. Ceilican mac Gairbiṫ, dux na n-Airṫer, mortui sunt.

Kl. Ianair. Anno domini dcccc.° 33.° (alias dcccc.° 34.°). Goṫfriṫ .h. h-Imair, ri crudelissimus Nordmannorum, dolore mortuus est. Dubgilla mac Robucan, dux nepotum Cormaic, dolore occisus est.

Kl. Ianair. Anno domini dcccc.° 34.° (alias dcccc.° 35.°). Cormac dalta Moenaiġ, princeps Achaid bo, obiit. Maelbrigte, princeps Mainistreċ, quieuit. Muiredaċ mac Maelbrigte, princeps Doimliac, immatura aetate obiit. Inis Loċa Gaḃar do ṫogail la h-Amlaiḃ .h. n-Imair. h-Uam Cnoġḃai do ṫogail dó isint seċtmain cetnai. Dairṁes díṁar. Cinaeḋ mac Coirpri, dux nepotum Ceinnselaig, cum multis a Nordmannis interfectus est. Concobar mac Domnaill, ridomna Ailiġ, mortuus est, et sepultus est in cimiterio regum in ard Maċa.

.b. Kl. Ianair. Anno domini dcccc.° 35.° (alias dcccc.° 36.°). Ioseṗ princeps aird Maċa, episcopus et sapiens et ancorita, in senectute bona quieuit. Cluain mic

---

been a district situated to the south of Downpatrick, co. Down; where there was a small *civitas*, or ecclesiastical foundation, called mBrechtain, now certainly represented by the parish church of Bright. See Miss Cusack's ed. of the *Trip. Life of St. Patrick* (Hennessy's Transl.), p. 383. And see also Reeves' *Down and Connor*, pp. 35, 292, 295–6.

[1] *Rubha-Conchongalt.*—Not identified.

[2] *Matudhan.*—King of Ulidia at the time.

[3] *Province of Ireland.*—coiceḋ Erenn; lit. *the* "Fifth of Ireland," or Ulidia.

[4] *Mucnamh.*—Mucram, in A. Now Mucknoe, a parish containing the town of Castleblayney, in the co. Monaghan.

[5] *Died.*—The MSS. have mortui sunt for mortuus est.

[6] *Of anguish.*—dolore, A. B.

Rubha-Conchongalt,[1] in which 300 persons or more were slain. Matudhan[2] son of Aedh, with the Province of Ireland,[3] and with the Foreigners, when they plundered as far as Sliabh-Betha westwards, and southwards to Mucnamh;[4] but Muirchertach son of Niall met them, and defeated them; and they left 240 heads, and their spoils. Celican, son of Gairbhith, King of the Airthera, died.[5]

Kal. Jan. A.D. 933 (alias 934). Gothfrith, grandson [933.]
of Imar, a most cruel king of the Norsemen, died of anguish.[6] Dubhgilla son of Robucan, chief of the Ui-Cormaic, was deceitfully slain.

Kal. Jan. A.D. 934 (alias 935). Cormac, foster-son of [934.]
Moenach, abbot of Achadh-bó, died. Maelbrigte, abbot of Mainistir,[7] rested. Muiredach son of Maelbrigte, abbot of Doimliacc, died immaturely. The Island of Loch-gabhar[8] was destroyed by Amlaibh grandson of Imar. The cave of Cnoghbha[9] was plundered by him in the same week. Great produce of acorns. Cinaedh son of Coirpre, chief of the Ui-Ceinnselaigh, was slain, with a great many others, by Norsemen. Conchobar,[10] son of Domnall, royal-heir of Ailech, died, and was buried in the 'cemetery of the kings' in Ard-Macha.

Kal. Jan. A.D. 935 (alias 936). Joseph,[11] abbot of [935.] BIS.
Ard-Macha, a bishop, wise man and anchorite, died in a good old age. Cluain-mic-Nois was plundered by the

---

[7] *Mainistir.* — Mainistir-Buite, or Monasterboice, co. Louth. This and the rest of the entries for this year are added in a different hand in B.

[8] *Loch-gabhar.*—Now represented by the name of Lagore, in the parish and barony of Ratoath, co. Meath. But the *loch* (or lake) is now dried up.

[9] *Cnoghbha.*—Now known as the mound of Knowth, in the parish of Monknewtown, barony of Upper Slane, and county of Meath.

[10] *Conchobar.*—concuḃar, B. The original of this entry is added in the margin in A., by the orig. hand, but in smaller writing.

[11] *Joseph.*—A marginal note in A., in the original hand, states that he was do ċlainn gairb gaela, "of the family of Garbh-gaela."

Nois do orcain o gallaibh Atha cliath, 7 anad da aidhchi doaibh indi, quod antiquis temporibus inauditum est. Maelpatraic mac Maeletuile, princeps aird Macha, in senectute quieuit.

Fol. 49ba. Kl. Ianair. Anno domini dcccc.° xxx.° vi.° (alias dcccc.° 37.°) Diarmait mac Ailello, princeps Cille cuilinn, in senectute quieuit. Bruatar mac Duibgille, rex nepotum Ceinnsealaigh, iugulatus est. Garbsith mac Maeleitigh, rex fer Roiss, a fratribus iugulatus est. Crongilla mac Cuilennain, ri Conaille muirtheimne, dolore moritur. Conaing mac Neill, ridomna nErenn, moritur. Bellum ingens lacrimabile atque horribile inter Saxones atque Normannos crudeliter gestum est, in quo plurima milia Normannorum que non numerata sunt ceciderunt, sed rex cum paucis euassit .i. Amlaibh; ex altera autem parte multitudo Saxonum cecidit. Adalstan autem rex Saxonum magna uictoria ditatus est. Macetigh mac Annsemain, ri Mogdorna magen, mortuus est. Fedhach princeps Slane mortuus est.

Kl. Ianair. Anno domini dcccc.° 37.° (alias dcccc.° 38.°). Dubthach comarba Coluim cille 7 Adomnain in pace quieuit. Maelcairnigh mac Conaill, princeps Tulain, obiit. Fergal mac Domnaill, ri Ailigh, mortuus est. Imnairi catha etir Donnchad mac Flainn 7 Muirchertach mac Neill, co ro sithaigh Dia. Amhlaibh mac Gothfrith i n-Ath cliath iterum. Cell Cuilind do

[1] *Not been heard.*—7 auditum, for inauditum, A. B.

[2] *Cill-Cuilinn.*—Now Old Kilcullen, in the parish and barony of Kilcullen, and county of Kildare; a place of great importance anciently, where there are still the remains of a round tower, and strong fortifications.

[3] *Battle.* — This was the famous battle of Brunanburh, a graphic account of which is given in the Anglo-Saxon Chronicle, at the year 937, which is the correct year.

[4] *Amlaibh.* — Amlaibh (or Olaf) Cuaran. For some interesting particulars regarding his history, see Todd's *War of the Gaedhil*, &c., pp. 280, sq., and the other places indicated in the Index to that work under the name "Olaf Cuaran."

Foreigners of Ath-cliath; and they stayed two nights in it, a thing that had not been heard[1] of from ancient times. Maelpatraic son of Maeltuile, superior of Ard-Macha, rested in old age.

Kal. Jan. A.D. 936 (alias 937). Diarmait, son of Ailill, abbot of Cill-Cuilinn,[2] rested in old age. Bruatar son of Dubhgilla, King of the Ui-Cennselaigh, was slain. Garbhith son of Maeleitigh, King of Fera-Rois, was killed by his brothers. Crongilla son of Cuilennan, King of Conaille-Muirthemhne, died of grief. Conaing son of Niall, royal-heir of Ireland, died. A great, lamentable, and horrible battle[3] was stubbornly fought between the Saxons and Norsemen, in which many thousands of Norsemen, beyond counting, were slain. But the King, *i.e.* Amlaibh,[4] escaped with a few. On the other side, however, a great multitude of Saxons fell. But Athelstan King of the Saxons was enriched with a great victory. MacEtigh son of Anseman, King of Mughdorna-Magen,[5] died. Fedhach, abbot of Slane, died. [936.]

Kal. Jan. A.D. 937 (alias 938). Dubhtach, comarb[6] of Colum-Cille and Adamnan, rested in peace. Maelcairnigh son of Conall, abbot of Tuilain,[7] died. Fergal[8] son of Domnall, King of Ailech, died. A challenge of battle between Donnchad son of Flann, and Muirchertach son of Niall, until God pacified them. Amlaibh,[9] son of Gothfrith, again in Ath-cliath. Cill-Cuilind[10] was [937.]

---

[5] *Mughdorna-Magen.* — A district now probably represented by the parish of Donagbmoyne (Domnach-Magen) in the barony of Cremorne (Crich-Mughdorna), in the county of Monaghan.

[6] *Comarb*; i.e. successor. As successor of Colum-Cille and Adamnan, Dubhtach was abbot of Raphoe in Ireland, and of Hy in Scotland. See Reeves' *Adamnan*, p. 393.

[7] *Tuilain.* — Now Dulane, in the barony of Upper Kells, co. Meath.

[8] *Fergal.*—See above at A.D. 932.

[9] *Amlaibh.*—The Amlaibh (or Olaf) Cuaran referred to under the last year, in the account of the battle of Brunanburh. See note [4].

[10] *Cill-Cuilind.*—Old Kilcullen, in the parish and barony of Kilcullen, co. Kildare.

orcain la Amlaim .h. nImair, quod non auditum est antiquis temporibus. Slogad la Donnchad .h. Mael-seċlainn riġ Temraċ, 7 la Muircertaċ mac Neill riġ n-Ailiġ, do ċaċt for Gallu Aṫa cliaṫ co r' indrired o Aṫ cliaṫ co Aṫ Truisten. Concobar mac Maelcein, ri hU Failġi, iugulatus est o Laignib.

Kl. Ianair. Anno domini dcccc.° 38.° (alias dcccc.° 39.°). Orcain cille Cuilind o Gallaib Aṫo cliaṫ ol-soḋain na pu menic. Criċan mac Maelmuire, ri .h. Fiaċraċ, moritur. Toġal Ailiġ for Muircertaċ mac Neill, 7 a tabairt condici longairs, conid forsailc diaeisi. Slogad la Donnchad i m-Breaġa, 7 Finnabair aba do arcain, 7 in sacart do marbad for lar na cille,
Fol. 49bb. 7 alaile olċena. Maidm ria Congalaċ mac Maelmiṫiḋ for Galenga moraib (7 beccaib), oc Aṫ daloarc, du itorcratar ili. Adalstan ri Saxan, cleiṫi n-ordain iartair domain, secura morte moritur. Finneċta mac Ceallaiġ, comarba Daire, in Cristo quieuit.

.b. Kl. Ianair, xiiii. lunae. Anno domini dcccc.° 39.° (alias dcccc.° 40.°). Slogad la Donnchad 7 la Muircertaċ co Laiġniu 7 co Muimneċu, co tucsat a n-giallu diblinaib. Suibne mac Conbretan do marbad o Gallaib. Niall mac Fergaile do ġuin ocos [do] badud

---

[1] *Ath-Truisten.*—This seems to have been the name of a ford on the river Greece, near Mullaghmast, in the barony of Kilkea and Moone, co. Kildare. See O'Donovan's *Four Mast.*, A.D. 936, note p.

[2] *Cill-Cuilind.*—See note [10], p. 457.

[3] *A thing not often done.*—ol soḋain na pu menic. This is rendered by the translator of these Annals in Clar. 49, by "which till then was not often done." But O'Conor translates "qui plurimas divitias inde diripuerunt!"

[4] *Ui-Fiachrach.*—There were several septs known by the tribe name of Ui-Fiachrach. But the sept here referred to was the Ui-Fiachrach of Ard-sratha (or Ardstraw), descended from Colla Uais (one of the three Collas, founders of the principal families of the Oirghialla), and which inhabited anciently the district adjacent to Ardstraw in the county of Tyrone. See O'Flaherty's *Ogygia*, part 3, chap. 76.

[5] *Donnchad.*—King of Ireland.

[6] *Finnabhair-abha.*—Fennor, near Slane, in the county of Meath.

[7] *Gailenga-mora*; or Great Gailenga.

plundered by Amlaibh grandson of Imar, a thing that had not been heard of from ancient times. A hosting by Donnchad Ua Maelsechlainn, King of Temhair, and by Muirchertach son of Niall, King of Ailech, to besiege the Foreigners of Ath-cliath, when they devastated from Ath-cliath to Ath-Truisten.[1] Conchobar son of Maelcein, King of the Ui- Failghi, was slain by Leinstermen.

Kal. Jan. A.D. 938. (alias 939). Plundering of Cill-Cuilind[2] by the Foreigners of Ath-cliath, a thing not often done.[3] Crichan son of Maelmuire, King of Ui-Fiachrach,[4] died. Demolition of Ailech against Muirchertach son of Niall, who was carried off to the fleet; but he was afterwards redeemed. A hosting by Donnchad[5] into Bregh, when Finnabhair-abha[6] was plundered, and the priest slain on the floor of the church, and others besides. A victory by Congalach, son of Maelmithidh, over the Gailenga-mora[7] (and [Gailenga]-becca),[8] at Ath-da-loarc, where a great many were slain. Athelstan, King of the Saxons, the pillar of dignity of the western world, died a quiet death. Finnechta, son of Cellach, 'comarb' of Daire,[9] rested in Christ. [938.]

Kal. Jan., m. 18. A.D. 939 (alias 940).[10] A hosting by Donnchad and Muirchertach to the Leinstermen and Munstermen, whose pledges respectively they brought. Suibhne, son of Cubretan, was killed by Foreigners. Niall, son of Fergal, was wounded and drowned, *i.e.* [by][11] [939] BIS.

A tribe whose territory is now represented by the barony of Morgallion, co. Meath.

[8] *Gailenga-becca*; or Little Gailenga. O'Donovan (following O'Dugan) states that this was the name of a territory to the north of the River Liffey, comprising Glasnevin, and that the family name was O'hAonghusa, now anglicised Hennessy. (O'Dugan's *Topogr. Poem*, note [57]). The name of Hennessy seems to have been shortened to the form "Ennis," in the counties of Dublin, Meath, and Kildare.

[9] *Daire.*—Derry, co. Londonderry.

[10] *Alias* 940.—The alias reading, or correction, is not in B.

[11] *By.*—The equivalent in Irish [la] has been supplied from *Chron. Scot.*, and *Four Mast.*

.i. [la] Muircertaċ mac Neill. Flann ingen Donnchada, rigan Ailiġ, moritur. Creċ la Donnchad i m-Breġa, co ro ort Lainn lere. Quies Muireḋaiġ comarba Comgaill.

Kl. Ianair, xx. ix. lunae. Anno domini dcccc.° xl.° (alias dcccc.° xli.°). Secc mor combtar ruirissi loċa 7 sroṫa. Natiuitas Briain mic Cennetig. Slogad la Muircertaċ co ro ort Mide 7 hU Failġi co n-deochaid i n-Ossaiġi, co tuc a reir uadiḃ, 7 co r' innir na Deisi, co tuc Ceallaċan ri Caisil lais fri reir n-Donnchada. Maelruanaiġ mac Flainn (.i. ridomna Ailiġ) do marbad do ċeniul Conaill. Eoċu mac Scannail, airchinnech Imleċo Ibair, moritur. Oenacan, sacart Duin Leṫġlaise, moritur.

Kl. Ianair, x. lunae. Anno domini dcccc.° xli.° (alias dcccc.° 42.°). Dunchad mac Suṫainein episcopus Cluana mic Nois, Foelan mac Muiredaiġ ri Laigen, moritur. Caṫroined re n-Uib Failgi for Gallaiḃ Aṫo cliaṫ; sed in precedente anno hoc factum est. Dun Leṫġlairi do arcain do Ġallaib. Do rigal Dia 7 Patraic forru. Tuc Gaillu dar muir, co ro gabra[t] a n-insi forru, co n-erlai in ri, co ro marbsat Goidil for tir. Da mac Lorcain mic Dunchada do marbad do Conġalach mac Maelmiṫiġ. Maelmoċta, airchinneċ Cluana Iraird, quieuit. Cluain mic Nois do indriuṫ do ġentiḃ Aṫa cliaṫ, 7 Ceall dara.

Fol. 50aa. Kl. Ianair, xxi. lunae. Anno domini dcccc.° xlii.°

---

[1] *Lann-lere.*—See note [15], p. 205 *supra.*

[2] *Passable.*—ruirissi; translated "iced," in the MS. Clar. 49.

[3] *Brian.*—The famous Brian Borumha.

[4] *Hosting.*—A marginal note in A., in the original hand, designates this hosting, or expedition, as sluagad na h-uidhri, *i.e.* "the hosting of the frost," in allusion to the time of the year (mid-winter) in which the expedition was undertaken. See the curious account of this expedition written by Cormacan Eiges in the year 942, and edited by O'Donovan for the Ir. Archæol. Soc. (1841), under the title of *Circuit of Ireland by Muircheartach Mac Neill.* From having provided cloaks made of cow-

Muirchertach son of Niall. Flann, daughter of Donnchad, queen of Ailech, died. A depredation by Donnchad in Bregh, when he destroyed Lann-lere.[1] Repose of Muiredach, comarb of Comgall.

Kal. Jan., m. 29. A.D. 940 (alias 941). Great frost, so [940.]
that lakes and rivers were passable.[2] Birth of Brian[3] son of Cennedigh. A hosting[4] by Muirchertach, when he ravaged Midhe and Ui-Failghi, and went into Osraighi, and obtained his demand from them; and he ravaged the Deisi, and brought with him Cellachan, King of Caisel, in subjection[5] to Donnchad. Maelruanaigh, son of Flann, (*i.e.* royal-heir[6] of Ailech), was killed by the Cinel-Conaill. Eochu, son of Scannal 'herenagh' of Imlech-Ibhair, died. Oenacan, priest of Dun-leth-glaise, died.

Kal. Jan., m. 10. A.D. 941 (alias 942.) Dunchad son [941.]
of Suthainen, bishop of Cluain-mic-Nois, [died]. Foelan son of Muiredach, King of Leinster, died. A victory by the Ui-Failghi over the Foreigners of Ath-cliath; but this was gained in the preceding year. Dun-leth-glaise was plundered by Foreigners. God and Patrick avenged it on them; brought Foreigners across the sea, who seized their islands against them; and the King escaped; but the Irish killed him on shore. Two sons of Lorcan[7] son of Dunchad were slain by Conghalach son of Maelmithidh. Maelmochta, 'herenagh' of Cluain-Iraird, rested. Cluain-mic-Nois and Cill-dara were plundered by the Gentiles of Ath-cliath.

Kal. Jan., m. 21. A.D. 942 (alias 943). A victory over [942.]

---

hides for his army on this expedition, Muirchertach acquired the *sobriquet* of Muirchertach *na g-cochall g-croicenn* ("M. of the leather cloaks"). His death is noticed at the year 942 (=943).

[5] *In subjection.*—fri reir. This clause is not very clearly expressed in the original. But the meaning is that Muirchertach brought Cellachan with a view to making him do homage to Donnchad the monarch of Ireland.

[6] *Royal-heir.*— Added by way of gloss, in A. and B.

[7] *Lorcan.*—He was King of Bregh (or Bregia). His obit is recorded above at the year 924.

(alias dcccc.° 43.). Roiniuḋ for Gallu Loċa cuan re leiṫ Caṫail, in quo pene omnes deleti sunt. Muircertaċ mac Neill (.i. Muircertaċ na coċall croicinn), ri Ailiġ, 7 Ectoir iarṫair beaṫa, do marbad do ġentiḃ prima feria, iiii. Kl. Martii, (.i. la Blacair mac Gofraid ri [Dub]gall, ic Glais liaṫain hi taiḃ Cluana cáin fer Ros).

Deissiḋ digal ocus diṫ
For síl clainne Cuinn co braṫ;
Nad mair Muircertaċ ba liaċ,
Dilecta iaṫ Gaiḋel n-gnaṫ.

Ard Maċa do arcain hi teirt Kl. ar a baraċ o na Gallaib ceṫnaiḃ. Lorcan mac Faelain, ri Laiġen, do marbad do ġallaib. Cellach mac Béce, ri dal Araide, do marbad o muinntir trea ṫa[n]gnaċt.

b. Kl. Ianair. Anno domini dcccc.° xl. iii.° (alias dcccc.° 44.°). Flaiṫbertaċ mac Inmainen cenn in pace quievit. Coirpri mac Maelpatraic, ri .h. Liaṫan, Finn mac Mutain, ri Corco Laiġḋi, do marbad do feraiḃ Maiġi Féine. Congalaċ mac Maelmiṫiḋ, 7 Broen mac

---

[1] *Loch-Cuan.*—Strangford Lough.

[2] *Leth-Cathail.*—A district now represented by the barony of Lecale, co. Down.

[3] *Muircertach.*—See note[4], p. 460.

[4] *Blacair.*—The King of the Danes of Dublin at the time. See Todd's *War of the Gaedhil*, &c., p. 287, note [11].

[5] *Glas-liathain.*—The "stream of Liathan." The *Ann. Four Mast.* and *Chron. Scotorum* state that Muirchertach was slain at Ath-Fhirdiadh (Ardee, co. Louth).

[6] *Cluain-cain.*—Clonkeen, in the barony of Ardee, co. Louth.

[7] *Clann-Cuinn.*—The clan, or descendants, of Conn of the Hundred battles. The original of these lines, not in B., is added in the top margin of fol. 50*a* in A., with a sign of reference to the proper place in the text.

[8] *Lorcan.*—In the list of Kings of Leinster contained in the *Book of Leinster* (p. 39, col. 3), Lorcan is stated to have ruled only one year. It is further stated that he was slain by the Foreigners of Dublin (Athcliath) after having defeated them in the early part of the day (iar rói forro i túr lái).

[9] *Malice.*—The translator in Clar. 49 renders trea ṫang[n]aċt by "murtherously."

[10] *Head.*—This entry is obviously imperfect, something being omitted after cenn ("head"). Flaithbhertach was King of Cashel (or Munster) at the time of his death. Before his acces-

the Foreigners of Loch-Cuan[1] by the people of Leth-Cathail,[2] in which they were nearly all destroyed. Muircertach[3] son of Niall (*i.e.* Muircertach, "of the Leather Cloaks"), King of Ailech, and the Hector of the West of the World, was killed by Gentiles, on a Sunday, the 4th of the kalends of March (*i.e.* by Blacair[4] son of Gofraidh, King of the Dubh-Gaill, at Glas-liathain,[5] by the side of Cluain-cain[6] of Fera-Rois).

Vengeance and ruin have fallen
On the Race of Clann-Cuinn[7] for ever.
As Muircertach does not live, alas!
The country of the Gaedhil will ever be an orphan.

Ard-Macha was plundered on the morrow, the third of the kalends, by the same Foreigners. Lorcan[8] son of Faelan, King of Leinster, was killed by Foreigners. Cellach son of Bec, King of Dal-Araidhe, was killed by his people, through malice.[9]

Kal. Jan. A.D. 943. (alias 944.) Flaithbhertach son of Inmhainen, head,[10] rested in peace. Coirpre son of Maelpatraic, King of Ui-Liathain,[11] Finn son of Mutan, King of Corco-Laighdhi,[12] were slain by the Fera-Maighe-Féine.[13] Congalach son of Maelmithidh, and Braen son of [943.] BIS.

---

sion to the kingship (in 913, according to *Frag. of Annals*), he had been abbot of Inis-Cathaigh, or Scattery Island, in the Shannon.

11 *Ui-Liathain.*—This was the name of a territory nearly co-extensive with the present barony of Barrymore, co. Cork, anciently occupied by the descendants of Eochaidh Liathanach, son of Daire-Cerba, who was the ancestor of the powerful sept of Ui-Fidhgeinte. The Irish name of Castle-lyons, in the barony of Barrymore, is *Caislen Ua Liathain.*

12 *Corco-Laighdhi.*—The name of a territory anciently comprising the south-west part of the county of Cork (namely, the present baronies of Carbery, Beare, and Bantry). But after the Anglo-Norman invasion the territory of the *Corco-Luighdhi* (or descendants of Lughaidh son of Ith) was reduced to narrower limits; and in the 16th century the head of the O'Driscolls (who were the inhabitants of the country) had but a scanty estate round the town of Baltimore. See O'Donovan's *Geneal. of Corca Laidhe;* Miscellany of the Celtic Soc., Dublin, 1849.

13 *Fera-Maighe-Féine*—A tribe anciently inhabiting the district now forming the barony of Fermoy (Fera-Maighe), co. Cork.

Maelmorḋa ri Laiġen, do arcain Aṫa cliaṫ co tucsat seotu 7 maine 7 braitt moir. Donnchad mac Flaind (mic Mailtseaċlaind, mic Maeilruanaiġ, mic Donnchada), ri Temraċ, annis .xxu. transactis in regno, moritur. Maelfeċeni comarba Finnia, Dungal mac Caṫain, in Christo dormierunt. Caṫ Goirt rottaċain ri Cellaċan for tuaṫ Mumain, in quo multi ceciderunt.

Kl. Ianair. Anno domini dcccc.° xl. 4° (alias dcccc. 45.). Secc mor anaicenta, comtar suirri na loċa 7 na h-aiḃne. Gaill loċa Eċoċ do marbad la Domnall mac Muircertaiġ 7 li a braṫair .i. Flaiṫbertaċ, 7 orgain a loingsi. Maeltuile mac Dunain, comarba Tigernaiġ 7 Cairniġ, secura morte moritur. Aurċaṫ mac Murcaḋa ri iarṫair Connaċt, Maelduin mac Gairbiṫ secnap aird Maċa. Blacair do ḋelċud Aṫa cliaṫ, 7 Amlaiḃ tar a eisi. Orem do muinntir hUi Chanannan do marbad do Congalaċ 7 Amlaiḃ cuarain i Conaillib.

Kl. Ianair. Anno domini dcccc.° xl. u.° (alias dcccc° 46.°). Cluain mic Nois do orcain do Gallaiḃ Aṫa cliaṫ, 7 cella fer Miḋe olcena. Maelbeṫach airċinnch Daiminnsi moritur.

Kl. Ianair. Anno domini dcccc.° xl. ui.° (alias
Fol. 50ab. dcccc.° 47.°). Slogad la Ruaidri .h. Canannan co Slaine, coniddairṫiter Gaill 7 Goidel .i. Congalaċ mac Maelmitiḋ 7 Amlaiḃ cuaran, co roimiḋ for Gallu Aṫa cliaṫ, in quo multi occisi et mersi sunt. Lan ind [f]innfaiḋis Patraicc do argut gil o Ceniul Eogain do

[1] *Maelsechlaind.*—"Maelsechnaill," in B. The clause is added in a later hand in A.

[2] *Fell asleep.*—dormiuit, A.

[3] *Gort-Rottachain.*—The name of the place where the battle was fought is given as "Magh-Duine" in the *Ann. Four Mast.* (942), and *Chron. Scotorum* (943).

[4] *Tuath-Mumha.*—Thomond. In the *Chron. Scotorum* and *Ann. Four Mast.*, the battle is stated to have been gained over Cennedigh (who was the father of Brian Borumha).

[5] *Alias.*—The *alias* number is not in B.

[6] *Conailli.*—Conailli-Muirtheimhne, a territory in the county of Louth.

[7] *Alias.*—The *alias* number is not in B.

Maelmordha, King of Leinster, plundered Ath-cliath, when they carried off jewels, and treasures, and a great spoil. Donnchad, son of Flann (son of Maelsechlaind,[1] son of Maelruanaidh, son of Donnchad), King of Temhair, having spent 25 years in the sovereignty, died. Maelfecheni, comarb of Finnia, [and] Dungal, son of Cathan, 'fell asleep'[2] in Christ. The battle of Gort-Rottachain[3] [gained] by Cellachan over Tuath-Mumha,[4] in which a great many were slain.

Kal. Jan. A.D. 944 (alias[5] 945). Great, unusual, frost; so that the lakes and rivers were passable. The Foreigners of Loch-Echach were killed by Domnall, son of Muirchertach, and his brother, *i.e.*, Flaithbhertach; and their fleet was destroyed. Maeltuile, son of Dunan, comarb of Tigernach and Cairnech, died a quiet death. Aurchath son of Murchadh, King of the West of Connaught, [and] Maelduin son of Gairbhith, vice-abbot of Ard-Macha, [died]. Blacair abandoned Ath-cliath, and Amlaibh [remained] in his place. A number of Ua Canannan's people were killed by Conghalach and Amlaibh Cuaran, in Conailli.[6] [944.]

Kal. Jan. A.D. 945 (alias[7] 946). Cluain-mic-Nois was plundered by the Foreigners of Ath-cliath, and the churches of Fer-Midhe also. Maelbethach, 'herenagh' of Daiminis, died. [945.]

Kal. Jan. A.D. 946 (alias 947). A hosting by Ruaidhri Ua Canannain to Slane, where the Foreigners and Gaedhil, viz., Congalach[8] son of Maelmithidh, and Amlaibh Cuaran,[9] encountered him, when the Foreigners of Ath-cliath were routed, and a great many were slain and drowned. The full of Patrick's 'Finnfaidhech'[10] of white silver [was given] by the Cinel-Eoghain to Patrick.[11] [946.]

[8] *Conghalach.*—King of Ireland at the time.

[9] *Amlaibh Cuaran.* — 'Amlaimh (Amlaff) of the sock" (or "of the sandal").

[10] *Finnfaidhech.*—" Sweet sounding." The name of one of St. Patrick's bells. See Reeves's *Bell of St. Patrick*, in *Transac.* R.I.A., vol. xxvii.

[11] *To Patrick*, i.e. to the successor of Patrick.

Patraicc. Scolaigi .h. Aeḋacain, ri Dartraigi,[1] 7 Gairbiṫ mac Muireḋaiġ ridomna .h. Cremṫain, 7 Aeḋ .h. Ruairc, mac Tigernain, hi friṫguin.[2] Broen mac Maelmorḋa, ri Laigen, do marbad for creiċ i n-Osraiġiḃ. Caṫusaċ mac Ailci, episcopus Ceneoil Eogain, moritur.

.b. Kl. Ianair. Anno domini dcccc.° xl. uii.° (alias dcccc.° 48.°).[3] Blocair mac Goffriṫ, ri Gall, do mcrbad la Congalaċ mac Maelmiṫiḋ, 7 se cet dec etir guin 7 brait. Aimsere .h. Atlai comarba Ciarain mic int ṡair,[4] Colman mac Maelpatraicc princeps Slaine, do gabail 7 a éc etarru. Gormlaiḋ[5] ingin Ḟlainn mic Maelsechlainn in penitentia mortua est. Natiuitas Maelsechnaill mic Domnaill.

Kl. Ianair. Anno domini dcccc.° xl.° 8.° (alias dcccc.° xl.° ix.°). Sloġaḋ la Matuḋan mac Aeḋo 7 la Niall Ua n-Eruilb, co ro inder Conaillu 7 Druim n-inasclainn 7 Inis cain Deġa. Creċ la .h. Canannan co ro inder firu Lí, 7 co ro marḃ Flaiṫbertaċ .h. Neill. Aeḋan Tuama da ġualann in Cristo pausauit. Foġartaċ mac Donnacain, ri Oirgiall, in penitentia moritur. Slogad la Conġalaċ mac Maelṁiṫiġ, co ro inder .h. Meiṫ 7 Fernmaċ.

Kl. Ianair. Anno domini dcccc.° 49° (alias dcccc.° 50.°). Donnchad mac Domnaill, rí Miḋe, do marbad dia braiṫriḃ. Oel rí Bretan moritur. Scoṫine airchinnech Dairmaiġi, Maelfindan episcopus Cille dara, Cleirċen mac Conallan airchinneċ daire Calgaiġ, in

[1] *Dartraigi.*—Known as the Dartraigi-Coininse, a tribe whose territory is now represented by the barony of Dartry, co. Monaghan.

[2] *Heat of battle.*—This entry evidently appears to be a continuation of the first entry for this year.

[3] *Alias.*—The *alias* number is not in B.

[4] *Ciaran-mac-int-sair*; i.e. "Ciaran son of the Carpenter." St. Ciaran, founder of Clonmacnoise.

[5] *Gormlaidh.*—She was the queen of Niall Glundubb, King of Ireland, whose death in the battle of Athcliath (or Kilmashoge, near Dublin) is recorded above at the year 918 (=919); having been previously married to Cormac Mac Cuilennain

Scolaighe Ua h-Aedhacain, King of Dartraigi,[1] and Gairbhith son of Muiredhach, royal-heir of the Ui-Cremthainn, and Aedh Ua Ruairc, son of Tighernan, [slain] in the heat battle.[2] Braen son of Maelmordha, King of Leinster, was killed on a predatory expedition in Osraighi. Cathasach, son of Ailce, bishop of Cinel-Eoghain, died.

Kal. Jan. A.D. 947 (alias[3] 948). Blacair son of Goth- [947.] BIS.
frith, King of the Foreigners, was slain by Congalach son of Maelmithidh, besides sixteen hundred killed or captured. Anmere Ua Adlai, 'comarb' of Ciaran-mac-int-sair,[4] [died]. Colman son of Maelpatraic, abbot of Slane, was taken prisoner [by the Foreigners], and died among them. Gormlaidh,[5] daughter of Flann son of Maelsechlainn, died in penitence. Birth of Maelsechlainn[6] son of Domnall.

Kal. Jan. A.D. 948 (alias 949). A hosting by [948.]
Matudhan son of Aedh, and Niall Ua h-Eruilb, when they plundered Conailli, and Druim-Inasclainn, and Inis-cain-Degha. A preying expedition by Ua Canannain, when he plundered the Fera-Lí, and killed Flaithbhertach Ua Neill. Aedhan of Tuaim-da-ghualann[7] rested in Christ. Foghartach son of Donnacan, King of Oirghialla, died in penitence. A hosting by Congalach son of Maelmithidh, when he plundered Ui-Meith and Fern-mhagh.

Kal. Jan. A.D. 949 (alias 950). Donnchad son of [949.]
Domnall, King of Midhe, was killed by his brothers. Oel,[8] King of the Britons, died. Scothine, 'herenagh' of Dairmagh; Maelfindan, bishop of Cill-dara, [and] Cleirchen son of Conallan, 'herenagh' of Daire-Calgaigh,

---

(slain A.D. 907, *supra*), and after his death, to Cerbhall son of Muiregan, King of Leinster, by whom Cormac Mac Cuilennain had been slain.

[6] *Maelsechlainn.* — Maelsechlainn Mor, or Malachy the Great, who became King of Ireland in the year 980. The entry is added in the margin in A.

[7] *Tuaim-da-ghualann.*—Tuaim-da-hualann, A. Tuam, in the county of Galway.

[8] *Oel.*—Howel the Good. See *Annales Cambriæ*.

pace quieuerunt. Matudan mac Aeḋa do marbad o Uiḃ Eċoċ .i. o macaiḃ Broin, sed Deus illum u[i]ndicauit in breui tempore in morte ipsorum. Ruaiḋri Ua Canannan do marbad do ġallaib .i. ridomna Erenn, iar forbais re mis for Miḋiu 7 for Breġu, 7 iar cor

Fol. 50ba. air Gall .i. di mile uel plus. Niall Oa Canannan i fritguin, et alii pauci. Mesr mor anaicenta. Cloicteċ Sláne do loscaḋ do ġallaiḃ Aṫa cliaṫ. Baċall ind erlama 7 cloc ba deċ di clocaiḃ, Caeneċair ferleiginn, [7] soċaide mór imbi, do loscaḋ.

Kt. Ianair. Anno domini dcccc.° l.° (alias dcccc.° 51). Maceitiġ mac Cuilennan, ri Conaille; Guaire .h. Forannain airċinneċ Arda sraṫa, moritur. Goṫfriṫ mac Sitriuc co n-Gallaiḃ Aṫa cliaṫ do orcain Cenannsa 7 domnaiġ Patraic, 7 Aird Breccain 7 Tuileain 7 cille Scire, 7 alailiu cealla olċena. A Cenannus ro orta h-uile, ubi capta sunt tria milia hominum uel plus, cum maxima preda boum et equorum auri et argenti. Aeḋ mac Maelruanaiḋ, Becc mac Duinncuan, ri Teṫbai, Cenneitig mac Lorcain rí Tuaṫmuman, Garbiṫ mac Lorcain rí fer Leamna. Niall moṫlaċ do marbad do ċoirppri tria meabail. Beċ dibaid. Clamtrusca mor for Gallaib Aṫa cliaṫ, 7 ruṫ fola.

.b. Kt. Ianair. Anno domini dcccc.° li.° (alias 952°). Scannal airċinneċ domnaiċ Seċnaill, Flann airċinneċ

---

[1] *Two thousand.*—The *Four Masters* (at A.D. 948) estimate the losses of the Foreigners at six thousand men, exclusive of boys and calones. The note bellum muine brocain ("Battle of Muine Brocain") is added in the margin in A., in the original hand. The site of the battle has not been identified.

[2] *Patron saint;* i.e. St. Erc, or "Bishop" Erc, whose obit is recorded at the year 512 *supra*.

[3] *Alias.*—The *alias* number is not in B.

[4] *Cenannas.*—Kells, co. Meath.

[5] *Aedh.*—According to the *Ann. Four Mast.* (949), and *Chron. Scotorum* (950), Aedh was *rigdamna* ("materies regis," or royal-heir) of Temhair, and was slain by Domhnall son of Donnchad, whose obit is entered under the next year.

[6] *Cennetigh.*—The father of Brian Borumha. The entry is imperfect;

rested in peace. Matudhan, son of Aedh, was killed by the Ui-Echach, viz., by the sons of Broen; but God avenged him in a short time, in their death. Ruaidhri Ua Canannan was killed by Foreigners, *i.e.* the royal-heir of Ireland, after a siege of six months against Midhe and Bregha, and after committing a slaughter of the Foreigners, viz., two thousand,[1] or more. Niall Ua Canannan, and a few others, [fell] in the heat of battle. Unusually great 'mast.' The belfry of Slane was burned by the Foreigners of Ath-cliath. The crozier of the patron saint,[2] and a bell that was the best of bells, [and] Caenechair the lector, [and] a multitude along with him, were burned.

Kal. Jan. A.D. 950 (alias[3] 951). MacEtigh son of Cuilennan, King of Conailli, [slain]; Guaire Ua Forannain, 'herenagh' of Ard-sratha, died. Gothfrith son of Sitriuc, with the Foreigners of Ath-cliath, plundered Cenannas,[4] and Domnach-Patraic, and Ard-Breccain, and Tuilean, and Cill-Scire, and other churches besides; from Cenannas[4] they were all plundered; on which occasion three thousand men, or more, were captured, together with a great booty of cows and horses, of gold and silver. Aedh[5] son of Maelruanaidh, Becc son of Donncuan, King of Tethba, [died]. Cennetigh[6] son of Lorcan, King of Tuadh-Mumha; Garbhith son of Lorcan, King of Fir-Lemhna, [died]. Niall Mothlach[7] was killed by the Coirpri, through treachery. A mortality of bees. A great leprosy upon the Foreigners of Ath-cliath, and a bloody-flux. [950.]

Kal. Jan. A.D. 951 (alias[8] 952). Scannal, 'herenagh' of Domnach-Sechnaill; Flann, 'herenagh' of Druim- [951.] BIS.

but the Chronicler evidently intended to record the obit of Cennetigh. See Todd's *War of the Gaedhil*, &c., Introd., p. xcvii.

[7] *Niall-Mothlach.*—He was of the family of Ua Canannain, a powerful family in the territory now forming the county of Donegal.

[8] *Alias.*—The *alias* reading is not in B. The number 520 appears in the margin in A., in the accurate handwriting of the Canon M'Uidhir (or M'Guire), to indicate that this was the 520th year since the commencement of the Chronicle.

Droma cliaḃ, Custantin mac Aeḋa ri Alban, Ferdomnaċ comarba Ciarain, mortui sunt. Caṫ for firu Alban 7 Bretnu 7 Saxanu ria Gallaiḃ. Flann .h. Cleiriġ, ri deiscirt Connaċt, Doṁnall mac Donnchada ridomna Teṁraċ, Cele clam 7 ancorita, Flann mac Maelfiaċraċ, airċinneċ Maiġi etir di glais.

Kl. Ianair. Anno domini dcccc.° lii.° (alias 953.°). Cluain mic Nois do arcain do feraiḃ Muman co n-Gallaiḃ. Maelcoṫaid comarba Comgaill 7 Mocolmoc. Gailenga do arcain o U Cremṫainn. Domnall dia
Fol 50*bb*. tairrecht Muircertaiġ co fargabsat ar cenn. Maelmartain mac Moenaiġ, Ruaḋacan mac Eitigen rí airṫir Gaileng, Maelpatraic mac Coscan ferleigind Ardd Maċa, Maelmuire airċinneċ Taiġi Feṫgnai, Cennfaelad airċinneċ Saiġre, Dermait mac Torpṫa airċinneċ Liss moir Moċutu, Dubinnsi epscob Bennċair.

Kl. Ianair. Anno domini dcccc.° l.iii.° (alias dcccc. 54°). Flannacan mac Allċon comarba mic Nisse 7 Colmain Ela, Maelcoluim mac Domnaill, ri Alban, occisus est. Conn mac Erudain mic Gairbiṫ, ri Muigi dumai, do marbaḋ. Bodibad mor fo Erinn. Ar mor de Coirpri 7 Teṫbai re n-O Ruairc, co torċair ann .h. Ciardai ri Coirpri. Ceileċair comarba Ciarain 7

[1] *Cele, a leper.*—Cele clam. The *Four Mast.* (A.D. 950) join together Cele (the proper name) and clam (a leper), and construct a name Celeclam, which is wrong.

[2] *Magh-etir-di-glais.*—The "Plain between two streams." See note [6], under the year 881 *supra.*

[3] *Alias.*—The *alias* reading is not in B.

[4] '*Comarb*' *of Comgall;* i.e. successor of St. Comgall, the founder and patron of Bangor, co. Down.

[5] *Mocholmoc.*—Patron of Dromore in the county of Down.

[6] *They;* i.e. the Ui-Cremthainn.

[7] *Tech-Fethgna.* — The "House of Fethgna." This place has not been identified. It was probably some church in Armagh, founded by, or called after, Fethgna bishop of Armagh ("hæres Patricii"), whose obit is entered above at the year 872.

[8] *Saighir,* or Saighir-Ciarain. Seirkeiran, in the barony of Ballybrit, King's County, where there are some interesting ruins.

cliabh, Custantin son of Aedh, King of Alba, [and] Ferdomnach, 'comarb' of Ciaran, [died]. A battle [gained] over the men of Alba, and the Britons and Saxons, by Foreigners. Flann Ua Cleirigh, King of the South of Connaught; Domnall son of Donnchad, royal-heir of Temhair; Cele, a leper[1] and anchorite, [and] Flann son of Maelfiachrach, 'herenagh' of Magh-etir-da-glais,[2] [died].

Kal. Jan. A.D. 952 (alias[3] 953). Cluain-mic-Nois was plundered by the men of Munster, along with Foreigners. Maelcothaid, 'comarb' of Comgall[4] and Mocholmoc,[5] [died]. The Gailenga were plundered by the Ui-Cremthainn. Domnall overtook Muirchertach, when they[6] left a slaughter of heads. Maelmartain, son of Maenach; Ruadhacan son of Etigen, King of Eastern Gailenga; Maelpatraic son of Coscan, lector of Ard-Macha; Maelmuire, 'herenagh' of Tech-Fethgna;[7] Cennfaeladh, 'herenagh' of Saighir;[8] Dermait son of Torpath, 'herenagh' of Lis-mor-Mochuta,[9] and Dubhinnsi, bishop of Bennchair, [died.] [952.]

Kal. Jan. A.D. 953 (alias[10] 954). Flannacan, son of Allchu, 'comarb' of Mac Nisse[11] and Colman-Ela,[12] [died]. Maelcoluim son of Domnall, King of Alba, was slain. Conn, son of Erudan, son of Gairbhith, King of Magh-dumha,[13] was killed. A great cow mortality throughout Ireland. A great slaughter of the Coirpri and Tethba by O'Ruairc, in which Ua Ciardha, King of Coirpri, was killed. Ceile- [953.]

---

[9] *Lis-mor-Mochuta.* — "Mochuta's great fort." Lismore, co. Waterford; founded by St. Mochuda (ob. 636). See note [14], p. 103 *supra*.

[10] *Alias.*—The *alias* reading is not in B.

[11] '*Comarb*' *of Mac Nisse*; i.e. Abbot, or bishop, of Connor in the county of Antrim, of which Aengus Mac Nisse was the founder.

[12] *Colman Ela.*—His obit is recorded above at the year 610. His 'comarb,' or successor, would be abbot of Lann-Ela, (Lynally, in a parish of the same name, barony of Ballycowan, King's County). See Reeves' *Down and Connor*. pp. 97–8.

[13] *Magh-dumha.* — The "plain of the Mound." Now represented by the barony of Moydow, co. Longford.

finnain, Roḃartaċ comarba Coluim Cille 7 Adomnain, in Christo pausauerunt. Niall .h. Tolairgg, Ceallaċan ri Cairil, Rectabra airchinneċ Cille achaid, moriuntur. Bran mac Domnaill, ri Cenuil Loeġaire Breġ, iugulatus est.

Kl. Ianair, ui. feria, uiii. lunae. Anno domini dcccc.° l.iiii.° (alias 955°). Oengus mac Conloingsi airċinneċ Maige bile, Oengus mac Maelbrigte airċinneċ Doimliacc, moriuntur. Alene ri Mugdorna Magen 7 Mugdorna Breġ, 7 Indergi mac Moċain do toitim allurg Congalaiġ i Connaċtu. Slogad la Domnall mac Muircertaiġ co longaiḃ o Ṫuaiġ inḃir for loċ n-Eċaċ, for Daball, dars na h-Airgiallu for loċ n-Eirne, iarsin for loċ n-uaċtair, co ro ort in mBreifne, 7 co tuc giallu hUi Ruairc.

.b. Kl. Ianair, uii. feria, xu. lunae. Anno domini dcccc.° l.u.° (alias 956°). Maelpatraic mac Conbretan airċinneċ Slane, Oengus mac nOcain comarba Feċene, gaiṫene sui espuc Duin leṫ glaisi. Taḋc mac Caṫail, ri Connaċt, mortuus est. Conġalaċ mac Maelmiṫiḋ (mic Flannagain mic Ceallaiġ mic Conġalaiġ mic Conaing ċurraiġ mic Congalaich mic Aeḋa slaine), ri Erenn, do marbad do gallaib (Aṫa cliaṫ) 7 Laignib oc Taig giurann illaignib, 7 Aed mac Aicidi ri Teṫba, et alii multi. Moenaċ comarba Finnia 7 ferleiġinn aird Maċa, Maelbrigte mac Eruḋain, comarba Mic

---

1 '*Comarb*' *of Ciaran and Finnan*; i.e. abbot of Clonmacnoise in the King's County, and of Clonard in Meath; founded respectively by Saints Ciaran and Finnan.

2 '*Comarb*' *of Colum-Cille and Adomnan*; i.e. Abbot of Derry and Raphoe.

3 *Alias*.—The *alias* reading is not in B.

4 *Fell in the army*.—do tuitim allurg. This is another way of saying that Alene was slain on an expedition into Connaught, undertaken by Congalach, King of Ireland.

5 *Tuagh-Inbher*.—The old name of the estuary of the River Bann.

6 *Alias*.—The *alias* number is not in B.

7 *Fechin*.—By successor (or 'comarb') of Fechin the Annalist meant abbot of Fobhar (or Fore), co. Westmeath.

8 *Son*.—The original of the paren-

chair, 'comarb' of Ciaran, and Finnan,[1] and Robhartach, 'comarb' of Colum-Cille[2] and Adomnan,[2] rested in Christ. Niall Ua Tolairg, Cellachan, King of Caisel, Rechtabra, 'herenagh' of Cill-achaidh, died. Bran, son of Domnall, King of Cinel-Loeghaire of Bregh, was slain.

Kal. Jan., Friday; m. 4. A.D. 964 (alias[3] 955). Oen- [954.]
gus son of Culoingsi, 'herenagh' of Magh-Bile, [and] Oengus son of Maelbrigte, 'herenagh' of Doimliacc, died. Alene, King of Mughdorna-Maghen and Mughdorna-Bregh, and Indergi son of Mochan, fell in the army[4] of Congalach, in Connaught. An expedition by Domnall son of Muirchertach, with ships from Tuagh-Inbher[5] upon Loch-nEchach, on the Dabhall, across the Airghialla upon Loch-Erne, afterwards on Loch-uachtair, when he devasted the Breifne, and took O'Ruairc's pledges.

Kal. Jan., Saturday; m. 15. A.D. 955 (alias[6] 956) [955.] bis
Maelpatraic, son of Cubretan, 'herenagh' of Slane; Oengus son of Ocan, 'comarb' of Fechin,[7] [and] Gaithene, learned bishop of Dun-lethglaise, [died]. Tadhc son of Cathal, King of Connaught, died. Congalach son of Maelmithidh (son[8] of Flannagan, son of Cellach, son of Congalach, son of Conaing Curraigh, son of Congalach, son of Aedh Slanè), King of Ireland, was killed by the Foreigners of Ath-cliath[9] and Leinstermen, at Tech-Giurann,[10] in Leinster, and Aedh son of Aicid, King of Tethba, and a great many others. Maenach 'comarb' of Finnia,[11] and Lector of Ard-Macha; Maelbrigte son of Erudhan, 'comarb' of Mac Nisse and of Colman-Ela,[12] [and]

---

thetic clause is added in a different hand in A. It is interlined in the original hand in B.

[9] *Of Ath-Cliath.*—The corresponding Irish, Ača cliat, is added in *al. man.* in A., and interlined in the orig. hand in B.

[10] *Tech-Giurann.*—This place has not been identified. The name should be written *Tech-Giugrand*, according to the *Book of Leinster*, p. 25 *b*.

[11] '*Comarb*' *of Finnia*; i.e. successor of St. Finnia, or abbot of Clonard, co. Meath.

[12] '*Comarb*' *of Mac Nisse and Colman Ela*; i.e. abbot of Connor, co. Antrim, of which MacNisse and Colman Ela were joint patrons.

Nisse 7 Colmain h-Ela, Muireḋaċ mac Eicneċain, moriuntur. Domnall regnare incipit.

Fol. 51aa. Kt. Ianair. Anno domini dcccc.° l.vi.° (alias 957°). Caṫasaċ mac Dulgen (o Ḋruim Ḋorraid), comarba Patraic, sui escop Goiḋel, in Christo Iesu pausauit. Maelḟoṫartaiġ ri Caisil, Colman mac Congaile comarba Molaisse, Eċu mac Anluain ri Loċa cal, Scannal mac Luaċduiḃ comarba Liss cr̄ mortui sunt. Maelcoluim .h. Canannan, ri ceniuil Conaill, Moċta mac Gormacain, Flann .h. h-Aeḋacain airċinneċ Glinne da loca.

Kt. Ianair. Anno domini dcccc.° l.vii.° (alias 958). Flann mac Moċloingsi comarba Tigernaiġ 7 Maeldoid. Tanaide mac h-Uidir, comarba Benncair, do marbad do Gallaib. Niall .h. h-Eruilb. Tuaṫal mac Auġaire, rí Laigen, moritur. Lugaid mac Colgan, airċinneċ Slane, in penitentia moritur. Finaċta mac Laċtna, airċinneċ Ferna, moritur.

Kt. Ianair. Anno domini dcccc.° l.viii.° (alias 959°). Cluain mic Nois do arcain do feraiḃ Muman. Martain comarba Coimgen, Dubduin comarba Coluim cille, Oengus .h. Lapan. Duḃdabairenn mac Domnaill, rí Caisil, a suis occisus est. Moenaċ mac Cormaic, airċinneċ Liss moir.

Kt. Ianair. Anno domini dcccc.° l.ix.° (alias 960.°) Slogad la Domnall mac Muircertaiġ co dal n-Araide,

---

[1] *Domnall.*—He was son of Muirchertach "of the leather cloaks," whose death is noticed above at the year 942.

[2] *Alias.*—The alias number, which is added in a different hand from the original in A., is not in B.

[3] *Son of Dulgen.* — Cathasach is called "son of Maelduin," in the list of the 'comarbs' of Patrick in the *Book of Leinster*, p. 42, col. 4.

[4] '*Comarb*' *of Molaisse*; i.e. successor of St. Molaisse, and abbot of Daimhinish (or Devenish, co. Fermanagh).

[5] *Loch-Cal.*— See note [4], p. 356 *supra*.

[6] *Liss-Cr.*—So in A. and B. The so-called Translator of these Annals whose version is preserved in the MS. Clar. 49, British Museum, renders *Liss-Cr* by "Laisserin," and O'Conor prints *Comhorba Lisserin*, which he translates "Vicarius Lasserani." But these renderings seem quite unreliable.

Muiredhach son of Eicnechan, died. Domnall[1] begins to reign.

Kal. Jan. A.D. 956 (alias[2] 957). Cathasach son of Dulgen[3] (from Druim-dorraidh), 'comarb' of Patrick, the most eminent bishop of the Goidhil, rested in Christ Jesus. Maelfothartaigh, King of Caisel; Colman, son of Congal, 'comarb' of Molaisse;[4] Echu son of Anluan, King of Loch-Cal,[5] [and] Scannal, son of Luachdubh, comarb of Liss-Cr̄,[6] died. Maelcoluim Ua Canannain, King of Cinel-Conaill, Mochta son of Gormacan, Flann Ua hAedhacain, 'herenagh' of Glenn-da-locha, [died]. [956.]

Kal. Jan. A.D. 957 (alias 958). Flann, son of Mochloingse, 'comarb' of Tigernach and of Maeldoid,[7] [died]. Tanaidhe MacUidhir,[8] 'comarb' of Bennchair, was killed by Foreigners. Niall Ua h-Eruilb [died]. Tuathal son of Ughaire, King of Leinster, died. Lugaidh son of Colgu, 'herenagh' of Slane, died in penitence. Finachta son of Lachtna, 'herenagh' of Ferna, died. [957.]

Kal. Jan. A.D. 958 (alias 959). Cluain-mic-Nois was plundered by the men of Munster. Martain, 'comarb' of Coemgen;[9] Dubhduin 'comarb' of Colum-Cille,[10] and Oengus Ua Lapain, [died]. Dubhdabairenn son of Domnall, King of Caisel, was slain by his own people. Moenach son of Cormac, 'herenagh'[11] of Lis-mor, died]. [958.]

Kal. Jan. A.D. 959 (alias 960). A hosting by Domnall,[12] son of Muirchertach, to the Dal-Araidhe, when he [959.]

[7] *'Comarb of Tigernach and Maeldoid;* i.e. abbot of Clones and Mucknoe, in the co. Monaghan, of which Sts. Tigernach and Maeldoid were the respective founders.

[8] *Tanaidhe Mac Uidhir;* i.e. "Tanaidhe son of Odhar." This Odhar was the ancestor from whom the name of Mac Uidhir (M'Guire, or Maguire) has been derived.

[9] *'Comarb' of Coemgen;* i.e. abbot of Glendalough. The *Four Mast.*, at A.D. 957, add that Martain was also successor of Maelruain, or abbot of Tallaght (co. Dublin).

[10] *'Comarb' of Colum-Cille;* i.e. abbot of Ia, or Iona. See Reeves' *Adamnan*, p. 394.

[11] *'Herenagh.'*—The *Four Masters* represent Moenach as 'abbot' of Lis-mor.

[12] *Domnall.*—See under the year 955.

co tuc aitire. Carlus mac Cuinn mic Donnchada occisus est i n-Aṫ cliaṫ. Maidm for Camman mac Amlaiṁ mic Goṫfriṫ oc Dub. Muireḋaċ mac Fergussa co ro la morcuairt Connaċt. Caṫṁoġ airċinneċ Lis moir quieuit.

Kl. Ianair. Anno domini dcccc.° lx.° (alias 961.°) Saiġet teneḋ do ṫuiḋecht iar fut Laiġen aniarḋes, co ro marb mile ċet do doeniḃ 7 altaiḃ cotigi Aṫa cliaṫ. Mac Ercaḋa, ri .h. Bruin [S]eola, obiit. Ualgarc ri Dartraiġi a suis occisus est. Fergraiḋ ri Caisil a suis occisus est. Conaing .h. Domnallan, airċinneċ Cloċair mac n-Daimeni, quieuit.

Kl. Ianair Anno domini dcccc.° lx.° i.° (alias 962.°)
Fol. 51ba. Creċ la Flaiṫbertaċ mac Conċobair, la riġ n- iliġ, i n-dal n-Araide, co r' inder Condire, coniḋtarṫetar Ulaiḋ, co ro marbad ann, 7 a da braṫair .i. Taḋg 7 Cond, et alii multi. Eugan mac Muiredaiġ, erri Erenn, do marbad do Uiḃ Failgi. Oengus .h. Mael-doraid a suis iugulatus est.

Kl. Ianair. Anno domini dcccc.° lxii.° (alias 963.°). Longa la Domnall .h. Neill de ḋabull dar Sliaḃ

---

[1] *Conn.*—This was evidently Conn (son of Donnchad, King of Ireland, son of Flann Sinna, King of Ireland), heir to the sovereignty of Ireland, whose death at the hands of the people of Fernmhagh (a territory represented by the present barony of Farney, in the County Monaghan), is noticed in the *Ann. Four Mast.* at the year 942.

[2] *Camman.* — See Todd's *War of the Gaedhil*, &c., Geneal. Table, p. 278, and note [13], p. 288.

[3] *Dubh.*—The River Duff, which flows into the bay of Donegal, after forming the boundary for some distance between the counties of Leitrim and Sligo. Dr. O'Conor, not knowing that *Dubh* was the name of a river, has blundered greatly in his version of this entry. *Rer. Hib. Script.*, vol. iv., p. 274.

[4] *Muiredhach.*—He was one of the successors of St. Patrick in the abbacy (or bishopric) of Armagh. His removal (or resignation) in favour of his successor Dubhdalethe, is noticed at the year 964, and his obit at 965, *infra.*

[5] *As far as Ath-cliath.* — cotigi Aṫa cliaṫ, A. B. The translator of these Annals in Clar. 49, wrongly renders the clause cotigi Aṫa cliaṫ by "with the houses of Dublin burnt."

[6] *Son.*—His name is given as Donn-

took hostages. Carlus, son of Conn,[1] son of Donnchad, was killed in Ath-cliath. A victory over Camman,[2] son of Amlaimh, son of Gothfrith, at Dubh.[3] Muiredhach,[4] son of Fergus, made a full visitation of Connaught Cathmogh, 'herenagh' of Lis-mor, rested.

Kal. Jan. A.D. 960 (alias 961). An arrow of fire came along Leinster, from the south-west, which killed a hundred thousand of men and flocks, as far as Ath-cliath.[5] The son[6] of Erchadh, King of Ui-Briuin-Seola, died. Ualgarg, King of Dartraighi,[7] was slain by his own people. Fergraidh,[8] King of Caisel, was slain by his own people. Conaing Ua Domnallain, 'herenagh' of Clochar-mac-Daimeni, rested. [960.]

Kal. Jan. A.D. 961 (alias 962). A predatory expedition by Flaithbertach son of Conchobar, King of Ailech, to Dal-Araidhe, when he plundered Condere; but the Ulidians overtook him, and he was there slain, with his two brothers, viz., Tadhg and Conn, and a great many others. Eogan son of Muiredhach, champion of Ireland, was killed by the Ui-Failgi. Oengus Ua Maeldoraidh[9] was slain by his own people. [961.]

Kal. Jan. A.D. 962 (alias 963). Ships[10] [were brought] by Domnall Ua Neill from the Dabhall,[11] across Sliabh- [962.]

---

chad, in the *Ann. Four Mast.*, at A.D. 959.

[7] *Dartraighi.* — Otherwise called Dartraighi-Mac Flannchada; the patrimony of the sept of Mac Flannchada (Mac Clancy or Clancy), now represented by the barony of Rossclogher, co. Leitrim.

[8] *Fergraidh.*—This entry, which is in the marg. in A., is in the text in B.

[9] *Ua Maeldoraidh*, or O'Muldory. The family name of a powerful tribe which held the chief sway in Tir-Conaill from the middle of the 9th to the end of the 12th century, when the O'Donnells asserted their supremacy. The Oengus here referred to was the son of Maelbresail (son of Maeldoraidh), whose obit is given in the *Ann. Four Mast.*, at the year 896.

[10] *Ships.*—Longa. These vessels were probably light cots, or boats, capable of being transported on mens' shoulders.

[11] *Dabhall.*—The northern Blackwater River, which flows between the counties of Armagh and Tyrone, into Lough Neagh.

n-uait co Loċ n-Ainnenne, quod non factum est ab antiquis temporibus. Sic in libro Duibdaleiṫi. Eicneċ mac Dalaiġ ri na n-Airġiall, 7 Dubdara a mac, occisi sunt o Murchad mac Dalaiġ, a fratre. Ro marbad dono in Murchad sin focedoir isin mis ċetnai. Maelmuire mac Eochada, comarba Patraic, natus est. Mac Cellaċain ri Caisil moritur. Gofraiḋ mac Amlaiṁ mortuus est, Comarba Tiġernaiġ moritur .i. Coencomrac. hUalgarc .h. Mailtrea occisus est o Mugdornaib maigen.

.b. Kl. Ianair. Anno domini dcccc.° lxiii.° (alias 964°). Is i so in bliaḋain dedenaċ ind lantad ċoir o tainic Patraic i n-Eirind. Maelruanaiḋ mac Flaind mic Eicneċain, 7 a mac, do marbad do ċloinn ḟiangusa. Dubscuile mac Cinaeda, comarba Coluim Cille, quieuit. Furuḋran mac Becce, rí Deslais, do marbad do cenul Eogain tria ta[n]ġnact 7 mebail. Muirceartaċ mac Conġalaiġ mic Maelmiṫiḋ, ridomna Temraċ, o Domnall

---

[1] *Loch-Aininn.*—Lough-Ennell, near Mullingar, co. Westmeath.

[2] *Had not been done.*—See above at the year 954, where Domnall son of Muirchertach (the Domnall Ua Neill of the present entry) is stated to have transported ships from Tuagh-Inbhir (the mouth of the River Bann) across Lough Neagh, along the Dabhall, and over Airghialla (or Oriel) to Loch-Erne.

[3] *Book of Dubhdalethe.*—This Book, which seems to have been a chronicle of Irish affairs, has been referred to before in these Annals. It is mentioned for the last time at the year 1021 *infra*. The compiler of the work is generally supposed to have been Dubhdalethe, successor of St. Patrick (*i.e.* abbot or bishop of Armagh), whose death is entered within at the year 1064 (=1065), and who is represented in the List of the 'comarbs' of Patrick in the *Book of Leinster*, p. 42, col. 4, as having ruled for 33 years. See Harris's *Ware*, Vol. I., p. 50; and Vol. II. (*Irish Writers*), p. 65; and under A.D. 964 *infra*.

[4] *Maelmuire.*—See at the year 1000 *infra*, where Maelmuire's appointment to the abbacy of Armagh is recorded.

[5] *Son.*—His name is given as Donnchadh (Donogh) in the *Ann. Clonmacnoise* (955—963), and by the *Four Mast.* (961).

[6] *'Comarb' of Tigernach;* i.e. abbot of Clones, co. Monaghan.

[7] *Of the 'just completion.'*—ind lantad ċoir. The so-called Translator of these Annals, whose version is preserved in the MS. Clar. 49, renders this clause by "of the full

Fuait, to Loch-Aininn,[1] which had not been done[2] from most ancient times. Thus in the Book of Dubhdalethe.[3] Eicnech son of Dalach, King of the Airghialla, and his son Dubhdara, were slain by his brother, Murchad son of Dalach. This Murchad was also killed soon after, in the same month. Maelmuire[4] son of Eochaid, 'comarb' of Patrick, was born. The son[5] of Cellachan, King of Caisel, died. Gofraidh son of Amlaimh died. The 'comarb' of Tigernach[6] died, *i.e.* Caencomrac. Ualgarg Ua Mailtrea was killed by the Mughdorna-Maighen.

Kal. Jan. A.D. 963 (alias 964). This is the last year of the 'just completion'[7] [of the full period] since Patrick came into Ireland. Maelruanaidh, son of Flann, son of Eicnechan,[8] and his son, were slain by the Clann-Fianghusa. Dubhscuile son of Cinaedh, 'comarb' of Colum-Cille,[9] rested. Furudhran son of Becc, King of Derlas,[10] was killed by the Cinel-Eoghain, through malice and treachery. Muirchertach, son of Congalach,[11] son of Maelmithidh, royal-heir of Temhair, was killed by [963.] BIS.

---

proftt," which seems wrong. O'Conor translates *Lantadhchoir* (as he prints it), by "plenaria numeratio Poetica," and adds "nempe quia numerando a Patricii adventu, anno 432, quingenti anni perfecte intercessere usque ad annum 963, secundum numerationem Poetarum Hiberniae." *Rer. Hibernicarum*, vol. 4, p. 276. The learned Doctor here made a serious slip in his calculation. But it is obvious that neither O'Conor nor the author of the version of these Annals in Clar. 49 perceived that by the words *lantad choir*, ("just [or full] completion"), was meant the Paschal Cycle, or Cycle of 532 years, framed by Victorius (or Victorinus) of Aquitaine. See note [1], p. 14, and note [1], p. 16, *supra*. This entry is very valuable, not only as strengthening the evidence referring the arrival of St. Patrick in Ireland to the year 431 (=432), but also as evincing the watchfulness of the old Irish Annalists in matters connected with chronological *data*.

[8] *Eicnechan.*—This was apparently the Eicnechan son of Dalach, King of Cinel-Conaill, whose obit is entered above at the year 905.

[9] '*Comarb*' *of Colum Cille*; i.e., successor of Colum-Cille, and therefore abbot of Ia, in Scotland, and probably of Kells and other Columbian foundations in Ireland. See Reeves's *Adamnan*, p. 394.

[10] *Derlas.*—See note [10], p. 453 *supra*.

[11] *Congalach.*—He was King of Ireland, and was slain by the Foreigners in the year 955 (=956), as above mentioned under that date.

mac Congalaig occisus est. Ceall dara do argain do Ġallaib, sed mirerabile pietate misertus est tria Niall .h. nEruilḃ, redemptis omnibus clericis pene pro nomine domini .i. lan in taigi moir sanc[t] Brigti, 7 lan in dertaigi, issed do ruagell Niall dib dia argat fesin.

Kt. Ianair. Anno domini dcccc.° lxiiii.° (alias 965°). Gorta mór díulocta i n-Erind, co renaḋ int aṫair a mac 7 a ingen ar biaḋ. Caṫroineḋ ria n-Oib Canannan co torcair and Domnall. Caṫ etir firu Alban imoneitir, ubi multi occisi sunt im Donnchad .i. abb duine Caillen. Coemcloḋ abbad i n-ard Maċa .i. Dubdaleṫe in uicem Muiredaig (o sliab Cuilinn). Slogad la Domnall .h. Neill, la riġ Temraċ, co ro ort Connaċta, 7 co tuc giallu o hU Ruairc. Iosep 7 Dunċaḋ abbaid ṫire ḋa ġlas, Cinaeḋ abb Lis moir Moċutu, in Cristo quieuerunt.

Fol. 51ba. Kt. Ianair. Anno domini dcccc.° lxu.° (alias 966°). Muireḋaċ mac Fergusa, comarba Patraic, Caṫusaċ mac Murcadan escop aird Maċa, Faelan mac Cormaic ri na n-Deise Muman, Faelan ri Laigen, mortui sunt. Maelmuire ingen Neill mic Aeḋa mortua est. Dubdabairenn comarba Buiti uitam finiuit. Fergal .h. Ruairc do marbad la Domnall mac Congalaiġ, la riġ Breġ.

Kt. Ianair. Anno domini dcccc.° lx.ui.° (alias 967°). Dub mac Maelcoluim, ri Alban, do marbad la h-Albanċu fein. Tigernaċ mac Ruairc, ri Cairce

---

[1] *Wonderful.* — mirerabile (for mirabili), A., B.

[2] *Alias.*—The alias reading is in a later hand in A. It is not in B.

[3] *Intolerable.* — díulocta (for díḟulocta), A., B.; díoḟulaing, *Four M.* (963).

[4] *Themselves.* — imoneitir, A.; imonetir, B. An adverb variously written immanetar, immenetor, and manetar; corresponding in meaning to the Latin *invicem*, or *inter se*; and explained by etarru, "amongst them" in O'Donovan's Irish Glossary. See Ebel's ed. of Zeuss' *Gram. Celtica*, p. 614. The author of the so-called Translation in Clar. 49 renders this entry by "Battle

Domuall son of Congalach. Cill-dara was plundered by Foreigners, but it was compassionated by the wonderful[1] piety of Niall Ua h-Eruilb, nearly all the clerics being redeemed for God's name; viz., the full of the great house of St. Bridget, and the full of the oratory, is what Niall ransomed of them with his own money.

Kal. Jan. A.D. 964 (alias[2] 965). A great, intolerable,[3] famine in Ireland, so that the father would sell his son and daughter for food. A victory by the Ui-Canannan, in which Domnall was slain. A battle amongst the men of Alba themselves,[4] in which many were slain, including Donnchad, *i.e.*, abbot of Dun-Caillen.[5] A change of abbots in Ard-Macha, viz., Dubhdalethe in the place of Muiredach[6] (of Sliabh-Cuilinn)[7]. A hosting by Domnall Ua Neill, King of Temhair, when he devastated Connaught and took hostages from O'Ruairc.[8] Joseph and Dunchadh, abbots of Tir-da-glas, [and] Cinaedh, abbot of Lis-mor-Mochuta, rested in Christ. [964.]

Kal. Jan. A.D. 965 (alias 966). Muiredach son of Fergus, comarb of Patrick; Cathasach son of Murchadan, bishop of Ard-Macha; Faelan son of Cormac, King of the Deisi-Muman; Faelan, King of Leinster, died. Maelmuire, daughter of Niall son of Aedh, died. Dubhdabhairenn, comarb of Buite, ended life. Ferghal O'Ruairc[8] was killed by Domnall, son of Congalach, King of Bregha. [965.]

Kal. Jan. A.D. 966 (alias 967). Dubh, son of Maelcoluim, King of Alba, was killed by the men of Alba themselves. Tigernach son of Ruarc, King of Carraic- [966.]

---

between Scottsmen about Etir" (!), where many were killed about (!) Donogh, abbot of Duncallen.

[5] *Dun-Caillen.*—See note [11], p. 375 *supra*.

[6] *Muiredach.* — See above at the year 959.

[7] *Sliabh-Cuilinn.*—Now Slieve-Gullion, a conspicuous mountain in the south-east of the county of Armagh. See O'Donovan's *Four Mast.*, A.D. 965, note c.

[8] *O'Ruairc.*—Ferghal (or Farrell) O'Rorke, King of Connaught.

bracaiḋe, moritur. Caṫ Formaeile (.i. ic Raiṫ bicria) ceniul Eogain for ceniul Conaill, du itorcair Maelisu .h. Canannan, ri ceniul Conaill, 7 Muircertach .h. Taiḋc ridomna Connacht, et alii multi. Aeḋ .h. h-Aitiḋ, ri .h. n-Echach, a suis iugulatur est. Mathgamain mac Cennetig, ri Caissil, do arcain Luimnig 7 dia loscaḋ. Cerball mac Lorcain, ridomna Laigen, do marbad do Domnall, do rig Breg.

b. Kt. Ianair. Anno domini dcccc.° lx. uii.° (alias 968). Ceallach .h. banan, comarba Comgaill, moritur. Muiredach comarba Cainnig, Flaithbertach mac Muiredaich, ri .h. nEchach, moriuntur. Slogad la Domnall .h. Neill co Laignu, coros indir o Berba siar co fairrge, co tuc borama mor lais, 7 cotarat forbaiss for Gallu 7 for Laignu co cenn da mis. Conmach comarba Ultain quieuit.

Kt. Ianair. Anno domini dcccc.° lx. uiii.° (alias 969). Cinaeth .h. Cathmail airchinnech daire Calcaiḋ, Maelfinnen mac Uchtan epscop Cenannsa 7 comarba Ultan 7 Cairnig, Eogan mac Cleirig epscop Connacht, pausauerunt. Soerlaiḋ ingen Elcomaig .c. annis moritur. Beollan mac Ciarmaic, ri Locha gabor, in Christo quieuit.

Kt. Ianair. Anno domini dcccc.° lx. ix°. (alias 970). Cenannus do arcain do Amlaim cuaran. Maidm for
Fol. 51bb. Ualgarc .h. Ruairc ria Concobar mac Taiḋg, co ro marbad cum plurimis. Sloġad la rig nUlath .i. la

---

[1] *Ua Taidhg*; i.e. "grandson (or descendant) of Tadhg." This patronymic is now represented by O'Teige, and also by the form Tighe; names borne by many persons in the counties of Mayo, Roscommon, and Sligo.

[2] *Mathgamain.* — Now generally anglicised Mahon. He was the eldest brother of Brian Borumha. His murder by Maelmuaidh son of Bran (ancestor of the O'Mahonys of South Munster) is recorded at the year 975 (= 976) *infra.* Regarding the career of this Mathgamain, see Todd's *War of the Gaedhil with the Gaill*, places referred to in the Index to that work, under the name Mathgamhain.

[3] *Luimnech.*—Limerick.

[4] *Comarb of Comgall*; i.e. successor of Comgall, or abbot of Bangor, in the county of Down.

Brachaidhe, died. The battle of Formael (*i.e.*, at Rathbec) by Cinel-Eoghain over Cinel-Conaill, in which fell Maelisu Ua Canannan, King of Cinel-Conaill, and Muircertach Ua Taidhg,[1] royal heir of Connaught, and many others. Aedh Ua h-Atidh, King of Ui-Echach, was killed by his own people. Mathgamain[2] son of Cennetigh, King of Caisel, plundered and burned Luimnech.[3] Cerbhall son of Lorcan, royal heir of Leinster, was killed by Domnall, King of Bregh.

Kal. Jan. A.D. 967 (alias 968). Cellach Ua Banan, comarb of Comgall,[4] died. Muiredach, comarb of Cainnech,[5] Flaithbhertach, son of Muiredach, King of Ui-Echach, died. A hosting by Domnall Ua Neill to Leinster, when he plundered from Berbha westwards[6] to the sea, and brought a great prey of cows, and laid siege to the Foreigners and Leinstermen for two months. Conmach, comarb of Ultan,[7] rested. [967.] BIS.

Kal. Jan. A.D. 968 (alias 969). Cinaeth Ua Cathmail, 'herenagh' of Daire-Calgaigh; Maelfinnen son of Uchtan, bishop of Cenannus and comarb of Ultan and Cairnech, [and] Eoghan son of Clerech, bishop of Connaught, rested. Soerlaith, daughter of Elchomach, died [at the age of] 100 years. Beollan son of Ciarmac, King of Loch-gabhor, rested in Christ. [968.]

Kal. Jan. A.D. 969 (alias 970). Cenannus was plundered by Amlaimh Cuaran.[8] A victory over Ualgarg Ua Ruairc, by Conchobar son of Tadhg,[9] when he [Ualgarg] was killed, with many others. A hosting by the King [969.]

---

[5] *Cainnech.*—St. Canice, founder and abbot of Achadh-bo (Aghaboe), in the Queen's County. His obit is given at the year 599 *supra*, and his birth is entered under 526.

[6] *From Berbha westwards.*—This should be from Berbha (the river Barrow) *eastwards*.

[7] *Comarb of Ultan;* i.e. successor of St. Ultan of Ardbraccan, and abbot of that place. The *Four Masters* (at A.D. 966) state that Conmach was also a priest of Cenannus, or Kells.

[8] *Amlaimh Cuaran.*—See note [4], p. 456, and note [9], p. 465, *supra*.

[9] *Conchobar son of Tadhg.*—King of Connaught at the time. His obit is entered under the year 972 *infra*.

h-Artgair mac Matuḋan, co Gallaiḃ, co ro ort Condere, 7 co fargaiḃ ar cenn. Bellum Cille mona ria nDomnall mac Congalaiġ, 7 ria nAṁlaim, for Domnall .h. Neill, du itorċair Artgar mac Matudain, ri Ulad, 7 Donnacan mac Mailmuire, airċinneċ, 7 Cinaeḋ mac Crongaille ri Conaille, cum plurimis. Orcain Lugmaiḋ 7 Droma inasclainn la Murchad, la riġ nAiliġ. Orcain Mainistreċ 7 Lainne leire la Domnall, la riġ nErend, ubi in una domu .cccl. accensi sunt.

Kl. Ianair. Anno domini dcccc.° lxx.° (alias 971). Culen [mac] Illuilb, ri Alban, do marbad do Bretnaiḃ isroi caṫa. Domnall .h. Neill, ri Teṁraċ, do innarbu a Miḋe do claind Colmain. Niall mac Aeḋa, ri Ulaḋ, moritur. Tuaṫal comarba Ciarain, Maelfamna comarba Cainniġ, moriuntur. Ceallaċ .h. Nuaḋat do marbad do Gallaib i n-dorus in proinntiġi. Slogad la Domnall .h. Neill co firu Miḋe, co ro ort a n-ule cella 7 dune, 7 co ro ort .h. Failġi 7 Foṫarta.

b. Kl. Ianair. Anno domini dcccc.° lxx.° i.° (alias 972). Caṫ etir Ultu 7 Dal-nAraide, itorċair rí in coiciḋ .i. Aeḋ mac Loingsiċ, 7 alii. Murchad mac Finn do marbad la Domnall cloen per dolum. Caṫusaċ mac Fergusa, comarba Duin, moritur. Fogartaċ mac

---

[1] *Artgar*, or *Ardgar*.—More correctly written Artghal in the *Ann. Four Masters*, at the year 968. But the name does not appear, in either form, in the list of the Kings of Ulidia contained in the *Book of Leinster*, p. 41.

[2] *Condere.* — Connor, co. Antrim. To palliate the offence committed by Artgar (or Artghal) in plundering an ecclesiastical establishment so famous as Connor, the *Four Masters* (968) insinuate that it was, at the time, in the possession of the Foreigners.

[3] *Cill-mona.*—Apparently the place now known as Kilmona, in the parish of Rahugh, co. Westmeath.

[4] *Mainistir*; i.e. Manistir-Buite, or Monasterboice, in the county of Louth.

[5] *Lann-leire.*—See note [15], p. 205 *supra*.

[6] *Illulb.*—Indulf, son of Constantine, King of Scotland. His "moritur" is entered in the *Chron. Scotorum* at the year 960 (=961), although Skene observes that the "Irish Annals" do not record his death. See *Chron. Picts and Scots*, Pref., p. cxliii.

[7] *Son of Aedh.*—In the list of

of Ulidia, *i.e.* Artgar,[1] son of Matadhan, when he destroyed Condere,[2] and left a slaughter of heads. The battle of Cill-mona[3] [was gained] by Domnall son of Congalach, and by Amlaimh, over Domnall Ua Neill, wherein fell Ardgar[1] son of Matadhan, King of Ulidia, and Donnacan son of Maelmuire, 'herenagh,' and Cinaedh son of Crongaill, King of Conailli, with many more. Plundering of Lughmadh and Druim-inasclainn by Murchad, King of Ailech. Plundering of Mainistir[4] and Lann-leire,[5] by Domnall, King of Ireland, where 350 persons were burned in one house.

Kal. Jan. A.D. 970 (alias 971). Culen, [son of] Illulb,[6] [970.]
King of Alba, was slain by Britons, in the field of battle. Domnall Ua Neill, King of Temhair, was expelled from Midhe by the Clann-Colmain. Niall son of Aedh,[7] King of Ulidia, died. Tuathal, comarb of Ciaran,[8] Maelsamna comarb of Cainnech,[9] died. Cellach Ua Nuadhat was slain by Foreigners in the door-way of the refectory.[10] A hosting by Domnall Ua Neill to the men of Midhe, when he spoiled all their churches and forts; and he spoiled the Ui-Failghi and the Fotharta.

Kal. Jan. A.D. 971 (alias 972). A battle between the [971.] BIS.
Ulidians and the Dal-Araidhe, in which the King of the Province,[11] *i.e.* Aedh son of Loingsech, and others, were slain. Murchad, son of Finn, was deceitfully killed by Domnall Cloen. Cathasach son of Fergus, comarb of Dun,[12]

Kings of Ulidia contained in *Book of Leinster*, p. 41, col. 4, the name of Niall's father is given as Eochaid, with "vel Aed" written over it.

[8] *Comarb of Ciaran;* i.e. abbot of Clonmacnoise, of which St. Ciaran "son of the carpenter" was the founder.

[9] *Cainnech.*—St. Canice, founder of the Monastery of Aghabo, in the Queen's County.

[10] *Refectory.*—The Irish of the words "in the door-way" (ı n-ꝺoꞃuꞅ) is not in B. The name of the church, or monastery, not having been given, it is not easy to identify Cellach Ua Nuadhat.

[11] *The Province;* i.e. the Province of Ulidia. See note [5], p. 386 *supra*.

[12] *Dun.*—Downpatrick, in the county of Down.

Neill .h. Tolairg do marbad la Domnall mac Congalaig, tria meḃail. Crunnmael airċinneċ Glinne da laċa moritur.

Kl. Ianair. Anno domini dcccc.° lxxii.° (alias 973). Concobar mac Taiḋc, ri Connaċt, moritur. Caṫ etir Murchad .h. Flaiṫbertaiġ 7 Connachta, du i torċair Caṫal mac Taiḋc ri Connaċt, 7 Geibennaċ mac Aeḋa ri .h. Maine, 7 alii multi. Maelmuire airċinneċ Dairmaiġi do baṫaḋ i n-Es ruaiḋ. Becan comarba Finnen, Ailill airċinneċ Glinne da laċa, secura morte moriuntur. Dubḋaleṫe comarba Patraic for cuairt Muman, co tuc a reir.

Fol. 55aa Kl. Ianair. Anno domini dcccc.° lxx. 3.° (alias 974°). Murchad .h. Flaiṫbertaiċ do ḋul for creiċ i cinel Conaill, co tuc gabail mór, conitarrlaiḋ oen ġai conerbailt de oc Dun cloitiġe, do cummain 7 aiṫriġe. Diarmait mac Doċartaiġ, comarba Molaire, mortuus est. Donnchad finn, ri Miḋe, do marbad la Agda mac Duibcinn. Roeniuḋ ria nUgaire mac Tuaṫail for Osraiġi, itorċair Diarmait mac Donnchada. Maidm aile dono ria n-Osraigi for hUib Cennselaig, itorcair Domnall mac Cellaiġ.

Kl. Ianair. Anno domini lxx. 4to. (alias 975°). Etgair mac Etmonn, ri Saxan, in Christo pausauit. Domnall mac Eogain, ri Bretan, in ailiṫri, Foġartaċ

---

1 *Murchad Ua Flaithbertaigh;* i.e. "Murchad descendant of Flaithbertach." He was King of Ailech. See above at the year 969.

2 *Dairmagh.* — Durrow, in the barony of Ballycowan, King's County.

3 *Es-Ruaidh.*—Otherwise written Es-Aedha-Ruaidh, the "Cataract of Aedh *ruadh* ('red')." Anglicised "Assaroe," but also known as the Salmon Leap, on the river Erne, at Ballyshannon, co. Donegal.

4 *Comarb of Finnen;* i.e. successor of St. Finnen, founder of the famous monastery of Clonard, in the county of Meath.

5 *Murchad Ua Flaithbertaigh.*—See note 1.

6 *Dun-Cloitighe.*—The "fort (or fortress) of Cloitech." O'Donovan identifies Dun-Cloitighe with Dunglady, a remarkable fort in a townland of the same name, parish of Maghera, and county of Londonderry. *Ann. F. M.*, A.D. 972, note r.

died. Fogartach, son of Niall Ua Tolairg, was treacherously killed by Domnall son of Congalach. Crunnmael, herenagh of Glenn-da-locha, died.

Kal. Jan. A.D. 972 (alias 973). Conchobar son of Tadhg, King of Connaught, died. A battle between Murchad Ua Flaithbertaigh[1] and the Connaughtmen, in which fell Cathal son of Tadhg, King of Connaught, and Geibhennach son of Aedh, King of Ui-Maine, and many others. Maelmuire, herenagh of Dairmagh,[2] was drowned in Es-Ruaidh.[3] Becan, comarb of Finnen,[4] Ailill, herenagh of Glenn-da-locha, died a quiet death. Dubhdalethe, comarb of Patrick, [went] on a visitation of Munster, and obtained his demand. [972.]

Kal. Jan. A.D. 973 (alias 974). Murchad Ua Flaithbertaigh[5] went on a preying expedition into Cinel-Conaill, and made a great capture; but he was hit by one dart, and died thereof at Dun-Cloitighe,[6] after communion and penitence. Diarmait son of Dochartach, comarb of Molaise,[7] died. Donnchad Finn, King of Midhe, was slain by Aghda, son of Dubhcenn. A victory by Ugaire son of Tuathal[8] over the Osraighi, in which Diarmait son of Donnchad was slain. Another victory also by the Osraighi over the Ui-Cennselaigh, in which Domnall[9] son of Cellach fell. [973.]

Kal. Jan. A.D. 974 (alias 975). Edgar[10] son of Edmond, King of the Saxons, paused. Domnall son of Eogan, King of the Britons,[11] in pilgrimage, [and] Foghartach [974.]

---

[7] *Comarb of Molaise*; i.e. abbot of Daimhinis (Devenish Island in Loch-Erne), the monastery of which was originally founded by St. Molaise.

[8] *Tuathal.* — The obit of this Tuathal, the progenitor from whom the name O'Tuathail, or O'Toole, has been derived, is entered above under the year 957.

[9] *Domnall.*—He was King of Ui-Cennselaigh (or South Leinster) for 9 years, according to the list in the *Book of Leinster*, p. 40, col. 2.

[10] *Edgar.*—The death of Edgar is noticed in the *Anglo-Sax. Chron.* at the year 975, which is the correct year.

[11] *Britons.*—The Britons of Strathclyde. See *Chron. Scotorum* (ed. Hennessy), p. 223, note [6].

abb Daire, mortui sunt. Ferdalach airċinneċ Reċrann a gentilibus occisus est. Cinaed .h. Artugan (.i. do sil Cernaiġ sotail), primeceis Erenn, quieuit. Doinenn mor isin bliaḋain sin.

Kl. Ianair. Anno domini dcccc.° lxx. u.° (alias 976°). Maṫġaṁuin mac Cennetiġ, ri Caisil, do marbad la Maelmuaiḋ mac ṁBrain. Donnchad mac Ceallaiġ, ri Ossaigi, Domnall mac Congalaiġ, ri Breġ, mortui sunt. Conaing .h. Finan, comarba Mic Nisi 7 Colman Ela, pausauit. Taḋg .h. Ruaḋraċ ri Cianaċt occisus est i n-Ultaib. Setna .h. Deman, airċinnech nOendroma, in sua domu exustus est.

Kl. Ianair. Anno domini dcccc.° lxx. ui.° (alias 977.°) Muirċertaċ mac Domnaill .h. Neill, 7 Congalaċ mac Domnaill, da riġdomna Erenn, do marbad la hAṁlaim mac Sitriuca. Gillacolaim .h. Canannan do marbad la Domnall .h. Neill. Aṁlaim mac Ailuilḃ (.i. ri Alban) do marbad la Cinaeḋ mac Domnaill. Conaing mac Cadain, comarba Moedoc, mortuus est. In hoc anno Flaiṫbertaċ mac Muirċertaiċ natus est.

Kl. Ianair. Anno domini dcccc.° lxx.° 7.° (alias 978°). Fiaċra airċinneċ Ia quieuit. Caṫ etir Brian mac Cennetiġ 7 Maelmuaḋ ri Desmuman, co torċair Maelmuaḋ ann. Caṫ Biṫlainde for Laiġniḃ ria
Fol. 52ab. n-Gallaiḃ Aṫa cliaṫ, dú itorċair ri Laigen .i. Ugaire

---

[1] *Rechra.*—See note[13], p. 101 *supra.*

[2] *Cernach Sotal*; i.e. Cernach the Arrogant (or haughty). His obit is given above at the year 663. The parenthetic clause, which is not in B., is written in the marg. in A., in the orig. hand.

[3] *Mathgamhain.* — This name is now Anglicised Mahon. The bearer was the elder brother of Brian Borumha.

[4] *Son of Cellach.*—This is in accordance with the list of Kings of Ossory in the *Book of Leinster*, p. 40, col. 5. But Rev. J. F. Shearman states that Donnchad was the *grandson* of Cellach, being the son of Muirchertach son of Cellach, both of whom were slain in the battle of Belach-Mughna, mentioned above at the year 907 (=908). *Loca Patriciana*, Table II., after p. 264.

[5] *Comarb of Mac Nisse and Colman Ela.*—This would mean Abbot of Connor (of which Mac Nisse was the founder), and of Lann-Ela (now

abbot of Daire, died. Ferdal, herenagh of Rechra,[1] was slain by Gentiles. Cinaedh Ua Artagain (of the race of Cernach Sotail),[2] chief poet of Ireland, rested. Great inclemency of the weather in this year.

Kal. Jan. A.D. 975 (alias 976). Mathgamhain[3] son of Cennetigh, King of Caisel, was killed by Maelmhuaidh son of Bran. Donnchad son of Cellach,[4] King of Osraighi, [and] Domnall son of Congalach, King of Bregh, died. Conaing Ua Finan, comarb of Mac Nisse[5] and Colman Ela,[5] paused. Tadhg Ua Ruadhrach, King of Cianachta, was slain in Ulidia. Setna Ua Deman, herenagh[6] of Oendruim, was burned in his own house. [975.]

Kal. Jan. A.D. 976 (alias 977). Muirchertach, son of Domnall Ua Neill, and Congalach, son of Domnall, two royal heirs of Ireland, were killed by Amlaimh son of Sitriuc. Gilla-Coluim Ua Canannan was killed by Domnall Ua Neill. Amlaimh son of Illulb,[7] King of Alba, was killed by Cinaedh son of Domnall.[8] Conaing son of Cadan, comarb of Moedhoc, died. In this year Flaithbertach[9] son of Muirchertach was born. [976.]

Kal. Jan. A.D. 977 (alias 978). Fiachra, herenagh of Ia, rested. A battle between Brian, son of Cennetigh, and Maelmhuaidh,[10] King of Des-Mumha, in which Maelmhuaidh was slain. The battle of Bithlann [was gained] over the Leinstermen by the Foreigners of Ath-cliath, in [977.]

Lynally, in the barony of Ballycowan, King's County, of which St. Colman Ela was the founder). See Reeves's *Down and Connor*, p. 242.

[6] *Herenagh.* — In the *Ann. Four Mast.*, at A.D. 974, Setna is stated to have been abbot of Aendruim.

[7] *Illulb.*—Indulf, or Indulph. See note [6] under A.D. 970.

[8] *Domnall.*—This should probably be Maelcoluim (Malcolm) as in the *Annals of Tigernach.*

[9] *Flaithbertach.* — This was the famous Flaithbertach O'Neill, nicknamed Flaithbertach-an-trostain, or "F—— of the Pilgrim's Staff;" so called for having gone in pilgrimage to Rome. His death is recorded at the year 1036 *infra.*

[10] *Maelmhuaidh.* — The murder of Brian's brother, Mahon, by Maelmhuaidh, is entered above at the year 975.

mac, Tuaṫail, 7 alii multi. Caṫroiniuḋ ria n-Airġiallaib for cenel Conaill, du i torċair Niall .h. Canannan, 7 alii multi. Corcaċ mor Muman do arcain la daiġiḋ. Les mór Moċutu do arcain 7 do l[oscud].

Kl. Ianair. Anno domini dcccc.° lxx°. 8.° (alias 979°). Muirenn ingin Congalaig, comarba Brigte, quieuit. Leṫlaḃor .h. Fiaċna, rí Ḋalaraiḋe, per dolum occisus est. Conċobar mac Finn, ri úa Failġi, mortuus est. Aireċtaċ .h. Caran, cenn ecnai Erenn, in pace quieuit.

.b. Kl. Ianair. Anno domini dcccc.° lxx. 9.° (alias 980). Caṫ Temraċ ria Maelseċnaill mac nDomnaill for Gallaiḃ Aṫo cliaṫ 7 na n-Insreḋ, irrolaḋ derg ar Gall 7 nert Gall a hErinn, dú itorċair Ragnall mac Aṁlaim, mac rig Gall, 7 Conaṁal mac aerri Gall, 7 alii multi. Doṁnall .h. Neill, ardri Erenn, post penitentiam, in ard Maċa obiit. Muġron, comarba Coluim cille etir Erinn 7 Albain, uitam feliciter finiuit. Rumann .h. Aeḋacan, comarba Tigernaig, Murchad mac Riadai, comarba Comain, pausauerunt. Dubġall mac Donnchada, ridomna Ailiġ, a fratre suo .i. o Muireḋaċ mac Flainn, interfectus est. Muiredaċ mac Flainn ante mensem integrum a gente sua decollatus est. Comaltan .h. Cleiriġ, rí .h. Fiaċraċ Aiḋne, moritur. Tigernan, .h. Maeldoraiḋ .i. ri ceniuil

---

[1] *Comarb of Brigit*; i.e. abbess of Kildare.

[2] *Conchobar*.—He was the ancestor of the Ui-Conchobhair Failghe, or O'Conors of Offaly, and, as O'Donovan alleges, the progenitor from whom they took their hereditary surname, though Mac Firbis states that the surname was taken from his grandson, Conchobar, son of Conghalach [ob. 1017]. *Four Mast.*, A.D. 977, note o.

[3] *Maelsechnaill.* — Called "Mor," or the Great. His accession to the monarchy is recorded under the year 979 (=980) by the *Four Masters.*

[4] *Domhnall.* — A marginal note in A. distinguishes him as "Domhnall of Ard-Macha," and adds that he was the son of Muirchertach of the Leather Cloaks, son of Niall Glundubh. A quatrain in Irish, in praise of Domhnall's prowess, quoted as from Mac Coissi, is written on lower marg., fol. 52*a*, in A.

[5] *Mughron.* — See Reeves's *Adamnan*, p. 394. A few lines of poetry

which fell the King of Leinster, *i.e.*, Ugaire son of Tuathal, and many others. A victory by the Airghialla over the Cinel-Conaill, in which fell Niall Ua Canannain, and many others. Corcach-mor, of Munster, was destroyed by fire. Lis-mor-Mochuta was plundered and burned.

Kal. Jan. A.D. 978 (alias 979). Muirenn, daughter of Congalach, comarb of Brigit,[1] rested. Lethlabhar Ua Fiachna, King of Dal-Araidhe, was treacherously killed. Conchobar,[2] son of Finn, King of Ui-Failghi, died. Airechtach Ua Carain, the most learned of Ireland, rested in peace. [978.]

Kal. Jan. A.D. 979 (alias 980). The battle of Temh- [979.] BIS.
air [was gained] by Maelsechnaill,[3] son of Domnall, over the Foreigners of Ath-cliath and the Islands, where a great slaughter of the Foreigners was committed, and their power [banished] from Ireland; and in which Ragnall, son of Amlaimh, King of the Foreigners, and Conamhal son of a Foreign chief, and many others, were slain. Domhnall[4] Ua Neill, Arch-King of Ireland, died in Ard-Macha, after penitence. Mughron,[5] comarb of Colum-Cille both in Ireland and Alba, ended life happily. Rumann Ua Aedhacain, comarb of Tigernach,[6] [and] Murchad son of Riada, comarb of Coman,[7] 'paused.' Dubhgall son of Donnchad, royal-heir of Ailech, was killed by his kinsman, *i.e.* by[8] Muiredhach son of Flann. Muiredhach son of Flann was beheaded by his own people before an entire[9] month. Comaltan Ua Cleirigh, King of Ui-Fiachrach-Aidhne, died. Tigernan Ua Maeldoraidh, *i.e.* King of Cinel-Conaill, was slain by his own

written on the lower marg., fol. 52 *a* in A., fixing the year of Mughron's death at 980 (the correct year), do not seem of sufficient merit to be printed.

[6] *Comarb of Tigernach*; i.e. abbot of Clones, co. Monaghan.

[7] *Comarb of Coman*; i.e. abbot of Ros-Chomain, or Roscommon, in the county of Roscommon.

[8] *By.*—α, uel o, A. o, B; which seems more correct.

[9] *Entire.*—ıncıgꝛuım, A., B.

Conaill a fuis iugulatus est. Broen mac Murcaḋa, ri Laigen, do ergaḃail do Ġallaib, 7 a marbad iarum.

Kl. Ianair. Anno domini dcccc. lxxx.° (alias 981°). Domnall .h. h-Aitiḋ ri .h. nEċaċ, 7 Loingseċ mac Foġartaiċ ri .h. Niallain, do comṫotim. Cleircen mac Donngaile comarba Feiċin, Eogan .h. Cadain comarba Brenainn, Sinaċ mac Muirċilen comarba Comġaill, in Christo dormierunt. Mess anacnata isin bliadain sin.

Kl. Ianair. Anno domini dcccc.° lxxx.° i. (alias
Fol. 52ba. 982°). Bruatar mac Tigernaiġ, ri .h. Cennsealaiġ, moritur. Archu mac Neill do marbad do maccaiḃ Ardġair tria meḃail. Aeḋ .h. Dubdai, ri tuaisceirt Connaċt, secura morte moritur. Orcain Cilli darao Imur Phuirt Lairce.

Kal. Ianair. Anno domini dcccc.° lxxx.° ii.° (alias 983°). Cormac mac Maelciaran, comarba Moċutu, Muireḋaċ mac Muirecan, secnap aird Maċa, moriuntur. Caṫroiniuḋ ria Maelseċnaill mac Domnaill, 7 ria n-Glun-iarn mac Amlaim, for Domnall cloen, for rí Laigen (7 for Iṁar puirt Lairge), du itorcradar ili itir baḋaḋ 7 marbad, im Gilla Patraic mac Iṁair, 7 alii. Aeḋ .h. Moċran, comarba Dairinchill, iugulatus est.

.b. Kl. Ianair. Anno domini dcccc.° lxxx.° iii.° (alias

---

[1] *Bran.* — The name is written Broen in A. and B. But this is a loose form of writing it.

[2] *Ua h-Aitidh*—This name, which is variously written Ua Aidith, Ua Aiteidh, Ua Aiddeidh, seems to have been derived from Aideid, son of Laighne, King of Ulidia, whose death is noticed at the year 897 *supra*.

[3] *Comarb of Fechin;* i.e. abbot of Fobhar (Fore), in the present county of Westmeath.

[4] *Tigernach.*—Other authorities, as the *Four Masters*, the *Chron. Scotorum*, and the lists of Kings in the *Book of Leinster*, write the name Echtigern, which is apparently the proper form. The *Ann. F. M.*, at A.D. 951, record the death of an Echtigern, Lord of Ui-Cennselaigh, who was probably the father of Bruatar.

[5] *Archu.*—According to the *Chron. Scotorum* (980), Archu was royal heir of Ulidia.

people. Bran,[1] son of Murchad, King of Leinster, was captured by Foreigners; and he was killed afterwards.

Kal. Jan. A.D. 980 (alias 981). Domhnall Ua h-Aitidh,[2] King of Ui-Echach, and Loingsech son of Fogartach, King of Ui-Niallain, fell by one another. Cleirchen son of Donngal, comarb of Fechin;[3] Eoghan Ua Cadhain, comarb of Brenaind, [and] Sinach son of Murthuilen, comarb of Comghall, 'fell asleep' in Christ. Unusual abundance of acorns in this year. [980.]

Kal. Jan. A.D. 981 (alias 982). Bruatar son of Tigernach,[4] King of the Ui-Cennselaigh, died. Archu,[5] son of Niall, was treacherously killed by the sons of Ardgar. Ahdh Ua Dubhda, King of the North of Connaught, died a quiet death. Plundering of Cill-dara by Imhar of Port-Lairge.[6] [981.]

Kal. Jan. A.D. 982 (alias 983). Cormac son of Maelciarain, comarb of Mochuta,[7] Muiredach son of Muirecan, vice-abbot of Ard-Macha, died. A battle-rout by Maelsechnaill son of Domnall, and by Glun-iairn son of Amlaimh, over Domnall Cloen, King of Leinster (and over Imhar[8] of Port-Lairge[6]), where a great many perished[9] by drowning and killing, including Gilla-Patraic, son of Imhar, and others. Aedh Ua Mothran, comarb of Dasinchell,[10] was slain.[11] [982.]

Kal. Jan. A.D. 983 (alias 984). Uissine Ua Lapain [983.] BIS.

---

[6] *Port-Lairge.*—The old name of Waterford.

[7] *Comarb of Mochuta;* i.e. abbot, or bishop, of Lismore, co. Waterford. But, for "Mochuta," the *Four Mast.* have "Mochta," which would make Cormac abbot of Louth

[8] *Imhar.*—The orig. of the parenthetic clause, added in the margin in A., is part of the text in B.

[9] *Perished.*—itorcair, A. itorcradar (plur. form), B., which is more correct. The rest of the entry is interlined in A., but is in the text in B.

[10] *Dasinchell.*—A devotional form of the name of Sinchell, made up of *da* ("thy"), being often used for *mo* ("my"), and the saint's name. See *Martyr. of Donegal,* ed. by Todd and Reeves, Introd. xliii., n. 4. St. Sinchell was founder of the monastery of Killeigh, in the barony of Geshill, King's County.

[11] *Slain.*—iugulatus est. The abbrev. for interiit follows (itit), as if by mistake.

984°). Uissine .h. Lapan, airċinneċ daire Calcaiċ, Muiredaċ .h. Flannacain, ferleiġind aird Maċa, pausant. Dubdaraċ mac Domnallan, ri Derlais, a suis interfectus [est]. Domnall cloen, ri Laigen, o hUib Cennselaig occisus est. Flaiṫbertaċ .h. hAnluain, ri .h. Niallain, per dolum occisus est o hUib Bresail.

Kl. Ianair., u.f.; l.u. Anno domini dcccc.° lxxx.° iiii.° (alias 985°). Foġartaċ .h. Congaile airċinneċ Daiminnsi, Flaiṫlem airċinneċ Saiġri, Maelfinnia airċinneċ Domnaiġ Patraic, in Christo quieuerunt. Slogad la Maelseċlainn mac nDomnaill i Connaċtaiḃ, cotarait maġ nAi illuaiṫred. Creċ folaṁa la Connaċta co Loċ nAinind, coro loiscset 7 coro marbsat rí Fer cell. Maeilseaċloinn mac Domnaill do indriuḋ Connacht, 7 do ṫoġail a n-innseaḋ, 7 do marbaḋ a toiseach.

Kl. Ianair. Anno domini dcccc.° lxxx.° u.° (alias 986°). Cumasc mor (.i. i n-ard Maċa) isin domnuċ ria Luġnasaḋ, etir .h. Eċaċ 7 .h. Niallain, du itorċair mac Trenair mic Celecan 7 alii. Na Danair do ṫuidecht i n-airer Dailriatai, .i. teora longa, co ro riagṫa secht fiċit diiḃ, 7 co ro renta olċena. I Coluim cille do
Fol. 52bb. arcain do Danaraiḃ aiḋċi notlaic, co ro marbsat in apaiḋ 7 .xu. uisor do sruiṫiḃ na cille.

Kl. Ianair. Anno domini dcccc.° lxxx.° ui.° (alias

---

[1] *Daire-Calgaigh.*—Derry (or Londonderry).

[2] *Derlas.*—See note [1o], p. 453 *supra.*

[3] *By the Ui-Bresail.*—o hui Bresail, A. o huib Bresail, B.; which is more correct.

[4] *Saighir.* — Better known as Saighir-Chiarain. Now Seirkieran, in the barony of Ballybritt, King's County.

[5] *To ashes.* — Dr. O'Conor, mistaking the signification of illuaiṫreḋ ("into ashes"), translates "vastat planitiem Aoi in regione Luathre."

[6] *Secret.*— folaṁa. The translator of these Annals in Clar. 49 renders creċ folaṁa by "a stealing army." The *Four Masters*, in the corresponding entry (984), for folaṁa have fo a la ṁoḋ, which O'Donovan renders by "in retaliation."

[7] *Loch-Aininn.*—Lough Ennell (or Belvedere Lake, as it has been named

herenagh of Daire-Calgaigh,[1] Muiredach Ua Flannacain, lector of Ard-Macha, rested. Dubhdarach son of Domnallan, King of Derlas,[2] was killed by his own people. Domnall Cloen, King of Leinster, was killed by the Ui-Cennselaigh. Flaithbertach Ua h-Anluain, King of Ui-Niallain, was treacherously slain by the Ui-Bresail.[3]

Kal. Jan. Thursd.; m. 5. A.D. 984 (alias 985). Foghartach [984.]
Ua Conghaile, herenagh of Daimhinis, Flaithlem herenagh of Saighir,[4] Maelfinnia herenagh of Domnach-Patraic, rested in Christ. A hosting by Maelsechlainn, son of Domnall, to Connaught, when he reduced Magh-Ai to ashes.[5] A secret[6] depredation by the Connaughtmen as far as Loch-Aiuinn,[7] when they burned, and slew the King of, Fir-Cell.[8] Maelsechlainn, son of Domnall, plundered Connaught, and destroyed its islands, and killed its chieftains.

Kal. Jan. A.D. 985 (alias 986). A great conflict[9] (*i.e.* [985.]
in Ard-Macha), on the Sunday before Lammas, between the Ui-Echach and the Ui-Niallain, in which the son of Trianar, son of Celechan, and others,[10] were slain. The Danes came on the coast of Dal-Riata, *i.e.* in three ships, when seven score of them were hanged, and the others dispersed. I-Coluim-Cille was plundered by the Danes on Christmas night, when they killed the abbot, and 15 of the seniors of the church.

Kal. Jan. A.D. 986 (alias 987). The battle of Manann[11] [986.]

---

in later times), near Mullingar, in the county of Westmeath.

[8] *Fir-Cell* (or Fera-Cell).—A district which, according to O'Donovan, included the present barony of Eglish (formerly known as Fircal), with the baronies of Ballyboy and Ballycowan, in the King's County. *Irish Topogr. Poems*, App., note [24].

[9] *Great Conflict.*—cumaſc mor. Dr. O'Conor fell into a serious error in his reproduction of this entry, the original of which he misprints, and renders by "Pascha magnum hoc anno Celebratum est, die Dominica ante mensem Augusti"! For cumaſc ("commotion," "conflict"), he read caſc (Pascha). The parenthetic clause ın-aṗdMaċa ("in Armagh"), which is a gloss in the original hand in A., is not in B.

[10] *Others.*—alaili, for aili A., B.

[11] *Manann.*—The Isle of Man.

987). Caṫ Manand ria mac Aralt 7 riar na Danaraib, ubi mille occisi sunt. Beirgdibuḋ mor co ro la ár doeine 7 indeli i Saxanaiḃ 7 Bretnaiḃ 7 Goiḋelaiḃ. Ar mor forr na Danaraiḃ ro oirg I, coro marbṫa tri xx^it. 7 tri cet diiḃ.

.b. Kl. Ianair. i. f., l. ix. Anno domini dcccc.° lxxx.° uii.° (alias 988). Dunlang mac Duiḃdabairenn, ridomna Caisil, 7 Muirġis mac Conċobair, do comtuitim in hUib Briuin Sinna. Congalaċ .h. Cuilennan ri Conaille, 7 Ciarċaille mac Cairellan ri tuaiscirt Breġ, do comṫuitim. Laidgnen mac Cerbaill, ri Fernmuiġi, do marbad i n-ard Maċa la Fergal mac Conaing, ri Ailiġ. Colum airċinneċ Corcaiḋe, Duḃdabairenn airċinneċ Boiṫi Conais, dormierunt.

.b. Kl. Ianair. Anno domini dcccc.° lxxx.° uiii.° (alias 989°). Dunchad .h. Braen, comarba Ciarain, optimus scriba 7 relegiosissimus, do ecaib i n-ard Maċa (in .xiiii. Kl. Februarii) ina ailiṫri. Dunleṫglaisi do arcain do Ġallaib, 7 a loscaḋ. Glun iairn ri Gall do marbad dia moġaiḋ fein i meisce. Goffraiḋ mac Araild, ri innsi Gall, do marbad i n-Dalriatai. Dunchad .h. Robocan, comarba Coluim cille, mortuus est. Eochaid mac Ardgair, ri Ulad, do dul for sluagad i

---

[1] *Son of Aralt.*—This must have been Godfrey, son of Aralt (or Harold) King of Innsi-Gall (or the Hebrides), who was killed by the Dalriads in the year 988 (alias 989) as recorded *infra*.

[2] *Hi;* or I-Coluim-Cille. See under the year 985, where the plundering of Hi is noticed.

[3] *Ui-Briuin-Sinna.*—The name of a well-known district in the co. Roscommon, lying along the Shannon, from which it partly derives its name Ui-Briuin-[na]-Sinna; i.e. the "Ui-Briuin ('descendants of Brian') of the Shannon." See O'Don. *Four Mast.*, A.D. 1196, note k.

[4] *Corcach.*—More frequently called Corcach-mor-Mumhan, ("the great Corcach—or rushy place—of Munster," Cork).

[5] *Both-Conais.*—See note 15, p. 361 *supra*. A note in the margin in A. has No gumaḋ air in Callaind ro buḋ coir Duncad .h. Brain, "or it may be on these Kalends [i.e. in this year] Dunchad Ua Brain should be." The note refers to the entry regarding

[was gained] by the son of Aralt[1] and the Danes, where one thousand were slain. A sudden great mortality, which caused a slaughter of people and cattle in Saxon-land, and Britain, and Ireland. Great slaughter of the Danes who had plundered Hi,[2] so that three hundred and sixty of them were slain.

Kal. Jan. Sund.; m. 9. A.D. 987 (alias 988). Dunlang son of Dubhdabhairenn, royal heir of Caisel, and Muirghes son of Conchobar, fell by one another in Ui-Briuin-Sinna.[3] Congalach Ua Cuilennan, King of Conailli, and Ciarchaille son of Cairellan, King of the North of Bregh, fell by one another. Laidgnen son of Cerbhall, King of Fernmhagh, was killed in Ard-Macha, by Fergal son of Conaing, King of Ailech. Colum, herenagh of Corcach,[4] Dubhdabhairenn, herenagh of Both-Conais,[5] 'fell asleep." [987.] BIS.

Kal. Jan. A.D. 988 (alias 989). Dunchad Ua Brain, comarb of Ciaran,[6] a most excellent and religious scribe, died in Ard Macha (the 14th of the Kalends of February), in pilgrimage. Dun-lethglaise was plundered by Foreigners, and burned. Glun-iairn,[7] King of the Foreigners, was killed by his own servant,[8] in drunkenness. Gofraidh[9] son of Aralt, King of Innsi-Gall,[10] was killed in Dal-Riata.[11] Dunchad Ua Robocain, comarb of Colum-Cille, died. Eochaid son of Ardgar, King of Ulidia, went on a hosting into Cinel-Eoghain, when he [988.] BIS.

Dunchad Ua Brain under the following year.

[6] *Comarb of Ciaran;* i.e. abbot of Clonmacnoise. For some interesting notices regarding Dunchad O'Brain, see Colgan's Life of him, *Acta Sanctorum*, at Jan. 16.

[7] *Glun-iairn.* — "Iron-knee." He was the son of Amlaibh (or Amlaff) Cuaran, by Dunflaith, daughter of Muirchertach of the Leather Cloaks, of the northern O'Neill stock. See Todd's *War of the Gaedhil*, &c., p. 288.

[8] *Servant.*—His name is given as Colbain in the *Ann. Four Mast.*, A.D. 988.

[9] *Godfrey.*—See note[1], last page.

[10] *Innsi-Gall.—Ib.*

[11] *Dal-Riata.* — The Dalriata of Scotland, a district nearly co-extensive with Argyll.

cenel Eogain, co fargaiḃ ann .h. nAitid. Dubdaleiṫi, comarba Patraic, do gabail comarbuis Coluim cille a comairle fer nErenn 7 Alban. Eċmiliḋ mac Ronain, ri na nAirṫer, do marbad do Conailliḃ cerd. Macleiġinn .h. Murċadain, airċinneċ Cuile raṫain, moritur.

Kl. Ianair. Anno domini dcccc.° lxxx.° ix.° (alias 990). Daire Calcaiġ do argain do ḋanaraiḃ. Airard mac Coissi primecess Erend, Aeḋ .h. Maeldoraid .i. ri ceniul Conaill, mortui sunt. Caṫ Cairn fordroma ria Maelseċlainn for Tuaṫmumain, i torċair Domnall mac Lorcain ri .h. Ḟorca, 7 alii multi.

Fol. 53aa. Kl. Ianair. Anno domini dcccc.° xc.° (alias 991). Donnchad .h. Conġalaiġ, ridomna Temrach, per dolum occisus est la Maelsechlainn. Taḋc mac Donnchada, ridomna Osraiġi, o feraiḃ Muman, Aeḋ .h. Ruairc ridomna Connaċt, Dubdaraċ .h. Ḟiaċnai, o ceniul Eogain, occisi sunt.

.b. Kl. Ianair. Anno domini dcccc.° xc.° i.° (alias 992). Maelpetair .h. Tolaiġ, comarba Brenaind, Maelfinnia .h. Maenaig comarba Ciarain Cluana, dormierunt. Donn .h. Duinncuan, ri Teṫba, moritur. Sluagad la Maelseċlainn i Connaċtaiḃ, co tuc gabala

---

[1] *Aitid.*—This was probably the Aideid son of Laighne, King of Ulidia, whose death is mentioned at the year 897 *supra*. See note [2], p. 492 *supra*.

[2] *Successorship of Colum-Cille.*—That is to say, the presidency of the Columbian order. See Reeves's *Adamnan*, p. 396.

[3] *Conailli-cerd.*—Another name for the tribe better known as Conailli-Muirthemhne, which occupied the northern part of the present county of Louth, and some of the adjoining portion of the county of Down.

[4] *Cul-rathain.*—Coleraine, co. Londonderry.

[5] *Airard MacCoissi.*—The obit of this person is entered in the *Annals of Tigernach* at the year 990, and in the *Chron. Scotorum* under 988=990; but not in the *Ann. Four Mast.* At the year 1023, however, the *F. Masters* notice the death, at Clonmacnoise, of an Erard MacCoisse, "chief chronicler" of the Irish. It is probable that Airard MacCoissi the "chief poet," and Erard Mac Coisse the "chief chronicler" were one and the same person, as the

lost the grandson of Aitid.[1] Dubhdalethi, successor of Patrick, assumed the successorship of Colum-Cille,[2] with the consent of the men of Ireland and Alba. Echmilidh son of Ronan, King of the Airthera, was killed by the Conailli-cerd.[3] Macleighinn Ua Murchadhain, herenagh of Cul-rathain,[4] died.

Kal. Jan. A.D. 989 (alias 990). Daire-Calgaigh was [989.]
plundered by Danes. Airard MacCoissi,[5] chief poet of Ireland, [and] Aedh Ua Maeldoraidh, *i.e.*, the King of Cinel-Conaill, died. The battle of Carn-fordroma[6] [was gained] by Maelsechlainn over [the people of] Thomond, in which fell Domnall son of Lorcan, King of Ui-Forga,[7] and many others.

Kal. Jan. A.D. 990 (alias 991). Donnchadh Ua [990.]
Conghalaigh, royal heir of Temhair,[8] was treacherously killed by Maelsechlainn. Tadhg son of Donnchad, royal heir of Osraighi, [was killed] by the men of Munster; Aedh Ua Ruairc, royal heir of Connaught, Dubhdarach Ua Fiachna, were slain by the Cinel-Eoghain.

Kal. Jan. A.D. 991 (alias 992). Maelpetair Ua Tolaigh, [991.]
comarb of Brenaind,[9] Maelfinnia Ua Maenaigh, comarb of Ciaran of Cluain,[10] 'fell asleep.' Donn, grandson of Donnchuan, King of Tethfa, died. A hosting by Maelsechlainn to Connaught, when he brought great spoils

---

Chron. Scot. (at 988=990), and the *Four Mast.* (1023), respectively state that the Airard of this entry, and the Erard of the *F. M.*, died at Clonmacnoise. See O'Donovan's remarks on the subject (*Four Mast.*, note[t] under A.D. 989), and O'Reilly's *Irish Writers*, pp. lxix., lxxii.

[6] *Carn-fordroma.*—The "Cairn of the protended ridge." Not identified.

[7] *Ui Forga.*—O'Donovan thought that this was the name of a tribe seated at and around Ardcroney, near Nenagh, in the county of Tipperary. *Four Mast.*, A.D. 834, note f.

[8] *Of Temhair* (or Tara).—Cempach. Not in A.

[9] *Comarb of Brenaind;* i.e. successor of Brendan, or abbot of Clonfert, in the county of Galway. The name "Brenaind" is represented by bren̄ in B., and rudely written breinind by a later hand in A

[10] *Cluain.*—Clonmacnoise, in the King's County.

mora laiss. Taḋḃriu ingnaḋ aiḋċi feile Stefan, combo croderg in nem̃.

Kt. Ianair. (i. f., l. iiii.) Anno domini dcccc.° xc.° ii.° (alias 993°). Tuaṫal mac Rubai comarba Finnen 7 Mocolmoc, Concobar mac Cerbaill .h. Maelseċlainn, mortui sunt. Maelruanaiḋ .h. Ciarḋai, ri Cairpri, do marbaḋ do feraiḃ Teṫba. Da Ua Ċanannan do marbaḋ. Eicneċ .h. Leogan, ri Luiġne, do marbaḋ la Maelseċlainn i taiġ abbaiḋ Domnaiġ Patraic. Mael-finnian ua hOenaiġ, comarba Feiċini 7 epscop tuaṫ Luiġne, in Christo Iesu pausauit. Cleirċen mac Maeleduin, ri .h. nEċaċ, a suis iugulatus est. Duniḃa mór for dainiḃ, 7 ceṫraiḃ 7 beċaiḃ, fo Erinn uile isin bliadainsiu. Muirecan (o Boiṫ domnaiġ), comarba Patraic, for cuairt i tir nEogain, co ro erleġ graḋ riġ for Aeḋ mac nDomnaill i fiadnuise sam̃ṫa Patraic, 7 co tuc morċuairt ṫuaiscirt Erenn.

Kt. Ianair. Anno domini dcccc.° xc.° iii.° (alias 994°). Fogartaċ mac Diarmada, ri Corcoṫri, do marbaḋ do ġalengaiḃ Corainn. Mac Dubgaill (.i. Aeḋ) mic

---

[1] *Ruba.*—In the *Ann. Four Masters* (at A.D. 992), the name is Maelrubha, which is probably the correct form.

[2] *Comarb of Finnen and Mocholmoc;* i.e. Abbot of Cluain-Iraird (now Clonard), in Meath, of which Finnen was the founder, and Mocholmoc one of the earlier abbots. The obit of Mocholmoc is given at the year 653 *supra*, where his name is written Colman. The expansion of the name into Mocholmoc (=mo-Cholum-oc) arose from the habit of putting the devotional prefix *mo* ("my") before, and adding the adjective *oc* ("young") after, the simple name of a saint, in token of affectionate regard.

[3] *Cairpri.*—Now represented by the barony of Carbury, in the N.W. of the county of Kildare, anciently called Cairpri Ua Ciardha (Carbury-O'Keary, or Carbury-O'Carey).

[4] *Two descendants.*—Their names are given as Domnall and Flaith-bheartach, in the *Ann. Four Mast.*, at A.D. 992.

[5] *Luighne.*—The barony of Lune, co. Meath.

[6] *Domnach-Patraic.* — Donagh-patrick, in the parish of the same name, barony of Upper Kells, co. Meath.

[7] *Comarb of Fechin;* i.e. abbot of Es-dara (now known as Ballysadare), in the county of Sligo, where a monastery was founded in the 7th century by St. Fechin.

[8] *Tuath-Luighne.* — "Territory of

with him. A wonderful appearance on the night of St. Stephen's festival, when the sky was blood-red.

Kal. Jan. (Sund., m. 4.) A.D. 992 (alias 993). Tuathal son of Ruba,[1] comarb of Finnen and Mocholmoc,[2] [and] Conchobar, son of Cerbhall Ua Maelsechlainn, died. Maelruanaidh Ua Ciardha, King of Cairpri,[3] was killed by the men of Tethba. Two descendants[4] of Canannan were slain. Eicnech Ua Leoghan, King of Luighne,[5] was killed by Maelsechlainn in the abbot's house of Domnach-Patraic.[6] Maelfinnian Ua hOenaigh, comarb of Fechin,[7] and bishop of Tuath-Luighne,[8] rested in Jesus Christ. Cleirchen son of Maelduin, King of Ui-Echach, was slain by his own people. Great mortality upon men, and upon cattle and bees,[9] throughout all Ireland in this year. Muirecan from Both-domnaigh,[10] comarb of Patrick, on a visitation in Tir-Eoghain, when he conferred the degree of King on Aedh, son of Domnall, in the presence of Patrick's congregation,[11] and made a full visitation of the north of Ireland. [992.]

Kal. Jan. A.D. 993 (alias 994). Fogartach son of Diarmaid, King of Corcothri,[12] was killed by the Gailenga of Corann.[13] Aedh, son of Dubhgall, son of Donnchadh, [993.]

Luighne." Now represented by the barony of Leyny, co. Sligo. The bishops of Achonry were sometimes called bishops of Luighne. O'Donovan erred in identifying the Tuath-Luighne here referred to with the barony of Lune, co. Meath. *Four Mast.*, A.D. 992, note c.

[9] *Bees.*—See above at the year 950, where a mortality of Bees is for the first time recorded in these Annals.

[10] *Both-domniagh.* — Bodoney, in the barony of Strabane, co. Tyrone.

[11] *Patrick's congregation*—This is probably another way of designating the clergy and dignitaries of the diocese of Armagh.

[12] *Corcothri.* — This is a corrupt form of the old tribe-name of Corca-Firthri, by which the inhabitants of the baronies of Gallen (co. Mayo), Leyny and Corran (co. Sligo), were anciently designated. See O'Flaherty's *Ogygia*, part iii., chap. 69.

[13] *Gailenga of Corran.*—The Gailenga, who gave name to the district now known as the barony of Gallen, co. Mayo, were descended from Cormac *Gaileng*, great grandson of Oilill Oluim, King of Munster in the 2nd century. The baronies of Corran and Leyny, in the co. Sligo, were also inhabited by the same stock.

Donnchada, ridomna Ailiġ, occisus est. Sord Coluim cille do loscaḋ do Maelseċlainn. Cond mac Conġalaiġ, rí .h. Failgi, do marbad. Maelmuire mac Scanlainn, espcop aird Maċa, quieuit. Sitriuc mac Amlaim do innarba a h-Aṫ cliaṫ. Raġnall mac Imair do marbad do Murchad.

Fol. 53ab. Kl. Ianair. Anno domini dcccc.° xc.° iiii.° (alias 995°). Cinaeḋ mac Maelċolaim, ri Alban, do marbad per dolum. Domnaċ Patraic do argain do Ġallaiḃ Aṫa cliaṫ, 7 do Muirceṙtaċ .h. Congalaiġ; sed Deus uindicauit in morte ipsius in fine eiusdem mensis. Colla airchinneċ Innsi caṫaiġ moritur. Clercen mac Leran, sacart ard Maca, quieuit.

.b. Kl. Ianair. Anno domini dcccc.° xc.° u.° (alias 996°). Tene diait do ġabail aird Maċa, co na farcaiḃ dertaċ na damliac na h-erdaṁ na fidnemeḋ ann cen loscaḋ. Diarmait mac Domnaill, ri .h. Ceinnselaig, Gillapatraic mac Donnchada, rí Ossaigi, Cormac .h. Conġalaiġ, comarba Daiminnsi, mortui sunt. Creċ la Conaille 7 Muġdorna 7 tuaiscirt mBreġ co Glenn riġe, conustaraiḋ Aeḋ mac Domnaill rí Ailiġ, 7 cotarat debaid doiḃ 7 coremaiḋ foraiḃ, coro marbad rí Conaille and .i. .h. Cronġilla (.i. Matudan) 7 alii plurimi (.i. da cet).

.b. Kl. Ianair. Anno domini dcccc.° xc.° ui.° (alias 997°). Maidm for hUiḃ Meiṫ ic Sruṫair, ria mac

---

1 *Sord-Choluim-Cille.* — Swords, a few miles to the north of Dublin.

2 *Murchad.*—Murchad son of Finn, King of Leinster. But in the *Ann. Four Mast.* (at 994) it is stated that Raghnall was slain by *the son* of Murchadh, son of Finn, which is more correct. The death of Murchad, son of Finn, is recorded above at the year 971.

3 *Inis-Cathaigh.* — Now known as Scattery Island, in the Lower Shannon.

4 *Lightning.* — tene diait. The corresponding term in the *Ann. Four Mast.* is tene saiġnén. The translator in MS. Clar. 49 renders tene diait by "the fyre Diat," mistaking diait apparently for *divinus*.

5 *Church-grove.* — fidnemed. Translated *turris* by O'Conor. But the term is comp. of fid (a wood, or grove), and nemed, which is glossed by *sacellum*, in the St. Gall Irish MS., fol. 13 *b*, and would therefore seem to signify a grove, or enclosure

royal heir of Ailech, was slain. Sord-Coluim-Cille[1] was burned by Maelsechlainn. Conn son of Congalach, King of Ui-Failghi, was slain. Maelmuire son of Scannlan, bishop of Ard-Macha, rested. Sitriuc son of Amlaimh, was banished from Ath-cliath. Raghnall, son of Imhar, was killed by Murchad.[2]

Kal. Jan. A.D. 994 (alias 995). Cinaedh son of Maelcoluim, King of Alba, was treacherously killed. Domnach-Patraic was plundered by the Foreigners of Ath-cliath, and by Muirchertach Ua Congalaigh; but God avenged it in his [Muirchertach's] death at the end of the same month. Colla, herenagh of Inis-Cathaigh,[3] died. Clerchen son of Leran, priest of Ard-Macha, rested. [994.]

Kal. Jan. A.D. 995 (alias 996). Lightning[4] seized Ard-Macha, so that it left neither oratory, nor stone church, nor porch, nor church-grove,[5] without burning. Diarmait son of Domnall, King of Ui-Ceinnselaigh; Gillapatraic son of Donnchad, King of Osraighi, [and] Cormac Ua Conghalaigh, comarb of Daiminis, died. A preying expedition by the Conailli, and Mughdorna, and the people of the north of Bregha, as far as Glenn-Righe[6]; but Aedh[7] son of Domnall met them, and gave them battle, when they were defeated, and the King of Conailli, *i.e.*, Ua Cronghilla[8] (*i.e.*, Matudan[9]) and many others (*i.e.*, two hundred[9]) were slain. [995.] BIS.

Kal. Jan. A.D. 996 (alias 997). A victory over the Ui-Meith, at Sruthair,[10] by the son of Donnchad Finn,[11] and [996.] BIS.

---

attached to a church or sanctuary. See Petrie's *Round Towers*, pp. 59–62.

[6] *Glenn-Righe.*—The ancient name of the glen, or valley, of the Newry River. See Reeves's *Down and Connor*, p. 253, note a.

[7] *Aedh.*—He was lord, or king, of Ailech. See under A.D. 992.

[8] *Ua Cronghilla.*—This name is now written Cronnelly, without the O'.

[9] *Matudan.—two hundred*—These parenthetic explanations are added by way of glosses in A. and B

[10] *Sruthair.*—O'Donovan identifies this place with Sruveel, in the parish of Tedavnet, barony and county of Monaghan. *Four Mast.*, A.D. 996, note t.

[11] *Son of Donnchad Finn.*—Apparently the Donnchad Finn, King of Meath, whose death is recorded at the year 973 *supra*. See the third entry, p. 505.

nDonnchada finn 7 ria feraibh Rois, co torchair ann rí .h. Meith, 7 alii. Maelsechlainn mac Maelruanaidh, ridomna Ailigh, do éc do feraigi. Cluain Iraird 7 Cennanus do arcain do Gallaib. Domnall mac Donnchada finn do dallad la Maelsechlainn. Maelcoluim mac Domnall, ri Bretan tuaiscirt, moritur.

Kl. Ianair, (uii. f.; l. xx. ix.) Anno domini dcccc.° xc.° uii.° (alias 998°). Slogad la Maelsechlainn 7 la Brian, co tucsat gialla Gall fri sobus do Gaidelaib. Dubhdaleithi, comarba Patraic 7 Coluim cille, lxxx.° iii. anno aetatis sue (.i. i quint non iuin), uitam finiuit. Loscadh aird Macha de media parte. Domnall mac Duinnchuan, ri Dartraighi, do marbad do Galengaibh. Sluagad la Maelsechlainn i Connachtu, co ro innir. Sluagad n-aill la Brian i Laighniu, co ro innir.

Fol. 53ba. Kl. Ianair. Anno domini dcccc.° xc.° uiii.° (alias 999°). Gillaenan mac Agdai do marbad do fhil Ronain tria mebail. Gillacrist .h. Cuilennan do marbad do Airgiallaib, 7 alii multi. Donnchad mac Domnaill, ri Laigen, do ergabail do Sitriuc mac Amlaim .i. ri Gall, 7 do Maelmordha mac Murchada. Righi Laigen do Maelmordhai iarsuidhiu. Lia Ailbe, primh dinsgnai maighi Bregh, do tuitim. Do ronta cetheora clocha muilinn di iartain la Maelsechlainn. Crech mor la Maelsechlainn o Laigniu. Mac Eicnigh mac Dalaigh,

[1] *From sorcery.*—do feraigi The translator in the MS. Clar. 49 renders this "by physic given him." But O'Conor, more correctly, translates "arte Magica." Feraige seems related to fiosaidhe, "a sorcerer," as in O'Reilly's *Irish Dict.*

[2] *Domnall.*—He seems to have been "the son of Donnchad Finn," referred to in the last entry on p. 503.

[3] *For their submission.*—fri sobus. The *Four Mast.* have fri suabais, which O'Donovan translates "to the joy." But the use of the preposition fri, which means "towards," or "in regard to," is incompatible with this rendering.

[4] *Dubhdalethi.*—See above at the year 988.

[5] *On the 2nd of June.*—Both A. and B. have i quint non iuin, "on the 5th of the Nones of June." But this is an error for i quart non iuin (on the 4th of the Nones of June); the Nones being only four.

[6] *Dartraighi.*—Now represented by

by the Fera-Rois, where the King of Ui-Meith and others were slain. Maelsechlainn son of Maelruanaidh, royal heir of Ailech, died from sorcery.[1] Cluain-Iraird and Cenannus were plundered by Foreigners. Domnall,[2] son of Donnchad Finn, was blinded by Maelsechlainn. Maelcoluim son of Domnall, King of the North Britons, died.

Kal. Jan. (Saturd., m. 29.) A.D. 997 (alias 998). A hosting by Maelsechlainn and Brian, when they took the pledges of the Foreigners for their submission[3] to the Irish. Dubhdalethi,[4] comarb of Patrick and Colum-Cille, made an end of life in the 83rd year of his age (viz., on the 2nd of June).[5] Burning of the half part of Ard-Macha. Domnall son of Donncuan, King of Dartraighi,[6] was killed by the Gailenga. A hosting by Maelsechlainn to Connaught, which he devastated. Another hosting by Brian to Leinster, which he devastated. [997.]

Kal. Jan. A.D. 998 (alias 999). Gilla-Enain, son of Aghda,[7] was killed by the Sil-Ronain, through treachery. Gilla-Christ Ua Cuilennain was killed by the Airghialla, and many more. Donnchad son of Domnall, King of Leinster, was taken prisoner by Sitriuc son of Amhlaimh, King of the Foreigners, and by Maelmordha son of Murchad. The kingship of Leinster [was given] to Maelmordha afterwards. Lia-Ailbhe,[8] the principal monument[9] of Magh-Bregh, fell. Four millstones were afterwards made of it by Maelsechlainn. A great prey by Maelsechlainn out of Leinster. MacEicnigh, son of [998.]

---

the barony of Rosclogher, co. Leitrim, anciently called Dartraighi; and in later times Dartraighi-M'Flannchada, or Dartry-M'Clancy, from the chief family of the district.

[7] *Aghda.*—He was king of Teffia. His death is recorded in the *Ann. Four Mast.*, at A.D. 979.

[8] *Lia-Ailbhe.* — The "Stone of Ailbhe" (or of Magh-Ailbhe, a plain in the county of Meath, the name of which is probably still preserved in that of Moynalvy, a townland in the barony of Lower Deece, co. Meath).

[9] *Monument.* — ꝺinꝺgnai. The *Four Masters* (at A.D. 998), state that *Magh-Ailbhe* was the chief *dingna* of Magh-Bregh. But the entry as above given seems more correct.

ri Airgiall, o hUi Ruairc occisus est. Indreḋ .h. nEċaċ la hAeḋ mac Domnaill, co tuc borroma mor ass. Slogad la Brian, ri Caisil, co Gleann mamma, co tangadar Gaill Aṫa cliaṫ dia ḟuabairt, co Laigniḃ imaille friu, co remaiḋ forro, 7 co rolaḋ a n-ár, im Arailt mac Amlaiṁ 7 im Ċulen mac nEtigen, 7 im maiṫiḃ Gall olċena. Do luiḋ Brian iarsin i nAṫ cliaṫ, co ro ort Aṫ cliaṫ leis.

.b. Kl. Ianair, ii. fa., l.xxi. Anno domini dcccc.° xc.° ix.° (alias millessimo). Hic est octauus sexagissimus quincentissimus ab aduentu sancti Patricii ad babtisandos Scotos. Bissextilis 7 embolismus isin bliadain sin. Domnall .h. Domnallan, ri Dersluis, do marbad la hAeḋ .h. Neill. Imar ri Puirt lairgi do ec. In Gaill dorisi i n-Aṫ cliaṫ, 7 a n-geill do Brian. Flaiṫbertaċ .h. Canannan, ri cenuil Conaill, a suis occisus est. Aed .h. Ciardai do ḋallad. Slogad la Brian co ferta nime i maiġ Breġ. Do lotar Gaill 7 Laigin creċ marcaċ rempu i maġ Breġ, conus taraiḋ Maelseċlainn, 7 pene omnes occisi sunt. Doluiḋ Brian tra for a ċulu cen ċaṫ cen indriuḋ, cogente domino.

.b. Kl. Ianair, iiii. feria; l.ii. Anno domini millesimo (alias millesimo primo). Coemċloḋ abad i n-ard

---

[1] *Ui-Echach.*—A marginal note in A. (and also in B.), in the orig. hand, describes this event as in creaċ mór maiġi caba, "the great depredation of Magh-Cobha."

[2] *Glenn-Mama.*—A glen near Dunlavin, in the barony of Lower Talbotstown, county of Wicklow. For an account of this important battle, see Todd's *War of the Gaedhil*, &c., p. 110; and the Introduction to the same work, p. cxliv., note [3], where a most valuable note on the topography of the district, contributed by Rev. J. F. Shearman, is printed.

[3] *Etigen.*—Written "Echtigern," an Irish form, in Todd's original authority. See last note. A marginal note in A. adds that the battle was fought on the 3rd of the Kalends of January (i.e. the 30th Dec.), being a Thursday.

[4] *Alias* 1000.—The alias reading is added, as usual, in a later hand. A marginal note in orig. hand in A. (and also in B.) has, in Irish characters,

Dalach, King of Airghialla, was slain by Ua Ruairc. The plundering of Ui-Echach[1] by Aedh, son of Domnall, who brought a great spoil of cows therefrom. A hosting by Brian, King of Caisel, to Glenn-Mama,[2] where the Foreigners of Ath-cliath, together with the Leinstermen, came to attack him; but they were routed, and put to slaughter, including Aralt son of Amlaimh, and Culen son of Etigen,[3] and other chiefs of the Foreigners. Brian went afterwards into Ath-cliath; and Ath-cliath was pillaged by him.

Kal. Jan. Mond.; m. 21. A.D. 999 (alias 1000).[4] This [999.] BIS.
is the 568th year since the coming of St. Patrick to baptize the Scoti. A bissextile[5] and embolism[5] in this year. Domnall Ua Domnallain, King of Derlas,[6] was killed by Aedh Ua Neill. Imhar, King of Port-Lairge,[7] died. The Foreigners again in Ath-cliath, and in submission to Brian. Flaithbertach Ua Canannain, King of Cinel-Conaill, was slain by his own people. Aedh Ua Ciardha was blinded. A hosting by Brian to Ferta-Nimhe[8] in Magh-Bregh. The Foreigners and Leinstermen with a predatory party of cavalry went before them; but Maelsechlainn met them, and they were nearly all slain. Brian came back, without battle or plunder, through the power of the Lord.

Kal. Jan. Wednesd., m. 2. A.D. 1000 (alias 1001[9]). A 1000. [BIS.]
change of abbots in Ard-Macha, viz., Maelmuire (son of

"hic est millisimus (*sic*) annus ab incarnatione Domini."

[5] *Bissextile and embolism.*—The Latin of this clause is represented by biſ̄ 7 embl in A. and B., which the so-called "translator" of these Annals in Clar. 49 renders by "Plenty of fruit and milke"!

[6] *Derlas.*—See note [10], p. 453 *supra*.

[7] *Port-Lairge.*—The Irish name for the present City of Waterford.

[8] *Ferta-Nimhe.*—Written Fearta-Nemheadh ("Nemedh's Grave") by the *Four Masters*; which is probably the more correct form. O'Donovan conjectures that the name may be represented by Feartagh, in the parish of Moynalty, barony of Lower Kells, co. Meath; but without any apparent authority.

[9] *Alias* 1001.—The alias number is added in a later hand in A., as also in B.

Maċa .i. Maelmuire (mac Eoċaḋa) in uicem Muirecan (o Ḃoiṫ domnaich). Ferġal mac Conaing, ri Ailiġ, moritur. Niall .h. Ruairc do marbad do cenil Eoġain 7 Conaill. Maelpoil comarba Feiċin moritur. Creċ la firu Muman i n-deiscirt Miḋe, conustaraiḋ Oengus mac Carraiġ, co fargaibset na gabala 7 ar cenn léo. Tochur aṫa Luain la Maelsechlainn 7 la Caṫal mac Conċobair.

Fol. 53bb. Kl. Ianair, u. feria; l. x. iii. Anno domini M.° i.° (alias millesimo 2.°). Slogad la Brian co aṫ Luain, co ruc giallu Connaċt 7 fer Miḋe. Slogad Aeḋa mic Domnaill co Tailtin, 7 luiḋ for a ċulu fo ṡiṫ. Tren-ḟer mac Celecain, secnap aird Maċa, do ṁarbad o Macleiġinn mic Cairill, ri Fernṁaiġi. Crechad Connact la Aeḋ mac Domnaill. Merleċan ri Gaileng, 7 Brotuḋ mac Diarmata, occisi sunt la Maelsechlainn. Colum airchinnech imleċa Iḃair, Caṫalan airchinnech Daiminse, moriuntur. Cernaċan mac Flaind, ri Luiġne, do ḋul i Fernmaiġ for creiċ, co romarḃ Muircertaċ .h. Ciarḋai, rigdomna Cairpre. Slogad la Brian 7 la Maelseċlainn co Dun dealga, do ċuinnciḋ giall for Aeḋ 7 for Eochaid, co ro scarsatar fo osaḋ.

Kl. Ianair, iii. f., l. xx. iiii. Anno domini M.° ii.°

---

[1] *Son of Eochaidh.*—Mac Eoċaḋa. With this the entry in *Ann. Four M.* (at 1001) agrees. But in the *Book of Leinster* (p. 42, col. 4), the name of Maelmuire's father is given as "Eochacan." See Ware's *Works* (Harris's ed.), Vol. I., p. 49; and Todd's *St. Patrick*, p. 182.

[2] *Both-Domnaigh.* — Bodoney, in Glenelly, in the barony of Strabane Upper, county of Tyrone. The original is interlined in A. and B. But the interlineation in B. would convey to the reader the idea that the locality was intended to be identified with the name of Maelmuire son of Eochaidh (*rectè* Eochacan); which would be wrong. See at the year 1004 *infra*, where Muirecan is stated to have been "from (or of) Both-Domnaigh."

[3] *Comarb of Fechin*; i.e. abbot of Fore, co. Westmeath. In M'Geoghegan's Transl. of the *Annals of Clonmacnoise*, at A.D. 994 (=1001), it is stated that Maelpoil was also "bushopp of Clonvicknose."

[4] *Carrach.* — Carrach-calma (or Carthach-calma) i.e. "Carrach (or Carthach) the powerful," seems to

Eochaidh[1]) in the place of Muirecan (of Both-domnaigh[2]). Fergal son of Conang, King of Ailech, died. Niall Ua Ruairc was slain by the Cinel-Eoghain and [Cinel]-Conaill. Maelpoil, comarb of Fechin,[3] died. A preying expedition by the men of Munster to the south of Midhe, when Oengus son of Carrach[4] met them, and they left the spoils, and a slaughter of heads besides. The causeway of Ath-Luain[5] [was made] by Maelsechlainn, and by Cathal son of Conchobar.

Kal. Jan. Thursd., m. 13. A.D. 1001 (alias 1002). [1001.]
A hosting by Brian to Ath-Luain,[5] when he carried off the hostages of Connaught, and of the men of Meath. A hosting of Aedh,[6] son of Domnall, to Tailtiu; and he returned in peace Trenfer son of Celechan, vice-abbot[7] of Ard-Macha, was slain by Macleighinn son of Cairell, King of Fernmhagh. The devastation of Connaught by Aedh,[6] son of Domnall. Merlechan, King of Gailenga, and Brotud son of Diarmait, were slain by Maelsechlainn. Colum, herenagh of Imlech-Ibhair, [and] Cathalan, herenagh of Daiminis, died. Cernachan son of Fland, King of Luighne,[8] went on a preying expedition into Fernmagh,[9] when he killed Muirchertach Ua Ciardha, royal heir of Cairpre. A hosting by Brian and Maelsechlainn to Dun-delga,[10] to demand hostages from Aedh[6] and Eochaid,[11] and they separated in peace.

Kal. Jan. Frid., m. 24. A.D. 1002[12] (alias 1003). [1002.]

---

have been an epithet for Donnchad, grandson of Maelsechlainn (King of Ireland, known as Malachy I., ob. 961 *supra*). See *Chron. Scotorum*, ed. Hennessy, at A.D. 967.

[5] *Ath-Luain.* — Athlone, on the Shannon.

[6] *Aedh.*—Aedh, son of Domnall Ua Neill, King of Ailech. His death is recorded under the year 1003.

[7] *Vice-abbot*—ꞅecnap. The *Four Masters* describe Trenfer as "Prior."

[8] *Luighne.* — Now represented by the barony of Lune, co. Meath.

[9] *Fernmagh.* — Farney, in the county of Monaghan.

[10] *Dun-delga.* — Dundalk, in the county of Louth.

[11] *Eochaid.*—Eochaid, son of Ardghar, King of Ulidia.

[12] *A.D.* 1002. — The 'Translator' of the MS. Clar. 49 gives as the first entry under this year "Brienus regnare incepit." But no such entry appears in the MSS. A. and B.

(alias Millesimo 3.º). Flannchad .h. Ruaḋin comarba Ciarain, Dunchad .h. Manċain comarba Coeiṁgin, Donnġal mac Beoan, airchinnech Tuama grene, Eogan mac Cellaig airchinnech arda Brecan, quieverunt in Christo. Sinaċ .h. Uargusa, ri .h. Meiṫ, 7 Caṫal mac Labraḋa, erri Miḋe, do comtuitim. Ceallach mac Diarmata ri Osraiġi, Aeḋ .h. Conḟiacla ri Teṫba, Concobar mac Maelseċlainn ri Corcumdruaḋ, ocus Aċer Ua Traiġteċ, occisi sunt. Aeḋ mac Eċtigern do marbad i n-dairṫaiġ ḟerna mór Moedoic.

.b. Kl. Ianair, uii. f., l. u. Anno domini M.º iii.º (alias Mº 4.º). Oengus mac Bresail, comarba Cainniġ, i n-ard Maċa in peregrinatione quievit. Eochaid .h. Flannacan, airchinnech Lis oiġeḋ 7 Cluana Fiacna, sui ḟilidechta 7 senċusa, lx.º uiiii. anno aetatis sue obiit. Gilla Cellaiġ mac Comaltan, ri .h. Fiaċraċ Aidne, Brian mac Maelruanaig, occisi sunt. Domnall mac Flannacan ri fer Lí, Muiredaċ mac Diarmata ri Ciaraiḋe Luacra, moriuntur. Caṫ Craibe telċa etir

---

[1] *Comarb of Ciaran*; i.e. successor of St. Ciaran (of Clonmacnoise), or abbot of Clonmacnoise.

[2] *Comarb of Coemhgin*; i.e. abbot of Glendalough, co. Wicklow.

[3] *Tuaim-greine*. — Tomgraney, in the parish of Tomgraney, barony of Upper Tulla, and County of Clare.

[4] *Corcumruadh*.—Corcomroe, in the present county of Clare.

[5] *Ua*—(O', or descendant). Inaccurately written na (gen. pl. of the definite article), in A. and B.; which probably misled the translator in Clar. 49 into rendering "Ua Traightech" by "of the feet." But Ua Traightech was a family name in Clare. O'Conor is, in this case, more than usually amusing in his translation, for he renders the proper name "Acher na (recte Ua) Traigtech" by "Historicorum dux præcipuus."

[6] *Ferna-mor*.—The "Great Alder tree." Ferns, in the county of Wexford, which was founded by St. Maedoc (or St. Mogue, as the name is phonetically written).

[7] *Successor of Cainnech*; i.e. abbot of Achadh-bó (Aghaboe), in the Queen's County. St. Cainnech (or Canice) was also founder of the monastery of Drumachose, in the present barony of Keenaght, co. Londonderry. But Saint Canice's successors in Drumachose are usually styled "successors (*comarbs*) of Cainnech in Cianachta," in the Irish Annals.

[8] *Lis-oigedh* — According to the *Ann. Four Mast.*, and the *Chron. Scotorum*, Eochaidh Ua Flannacain was herenagh of the *Lis-oigedh* (or

Flannchad Ua Ruadhin, comarb of Ciaran[1]; Dunchad Ua Manchain, comarb of Coemhgin[2]: Donnghal son of Beoan, herenagh of Tuaim-greine,[3] [and] Eoghan son of Cellach, herenagh of Ard-Brecain, rested in Christ. Sinach Ua h-Uarghusa, King of Ui-Meith, and Cathal son of Labraidh, a champion of Midhe, fell by one another. Cellach son of Diarmait, King of Osraighe; Aedh Ua Confhiacla King of Tethbha; Conchobar son of Maelsechlainn, King of Corcumruadh,[4] and Acher Ua[5] Traightech, were slain. Aedh, son of Echtigern, was killed in the oratory of Ferna-mor[6] of Moedoc.

Kal. Jan. Sund., m. 5. A.D. 1003 (alias 1004). Oengus, [1003.] BIS. son of Bresal, successor of Cainnech,[7] rested in Ard-Macha, in pilgrimage. Eochaid Ua Flannacain, herenagh of Lis-oigedh,[8] and Cluain-Fiachna,[9] a distinguished professor of poetry and history, died in the 69th year of his age. Gilla-Cellaigh, son of Comaltan, King of Ui-Fiachrach-Aidhne, [and] Brian, son of Maelruaniagh, were slain. Domnall son of Flannacan, King of the Fir-Lí, [and] Muiredach, son of Diarmait, King of Cairaidhe-Luachra, died. The battle of Craebh-telcha,[10] between

---

"guest-house") of Armagh. Eochaidh was a writer of great reputation on Irish history and literature, although his name is not mentioned by Ware or O'Reilly in their accounts of Irish writers. The translator of the *Annals of Clonmacnoise* (Mageoghan), who had some of Eochaid's writings, describes him as "Archdean of Armagh and Clonfeaghna." See O'Curry's *MS. Materials*, p. 138 (where it is erroneously stated that Eochaidh Ua Flannacain is mentioned in connexion with the tract on the ancient pagan cemeteries of Ireland, contained in *Lebor na h-uidre* [pp. 50–52], and O'Donovan's *Four Masters*, A.D, 1003, note r. Some lines of poetry in praise of Eochaidh, attributed to [Cuan] Ua Lochain, written on the lower marg. of fol. 53*b* in A., have been partially mutilated by the binder.

[9] *Cluain-Fiachna.*—Clonfeacle, in a parish of the same name, barony of Dungannon Middle, co. of Tyrone.

[10] *Craebh-telcha*—O'Donovan suggests that this place, the name of which signifies the "Spreading Tree of the Hill," may be identified with Crew, in the parish of Glenavy, barony of Upper Massareene, co. Antrim. *Four Masters*, A.D. 1003, note x. But see Reeves's *Down and Connor*, &c., p. 342, where it is stated that Craebh-telcha was probably in the north of the present county of Down, near

Ultu 7 cenel nEogain, co remaiḋ for Ultu, co torchair ann Eochaid mac Ardgair, ri Ulaḋ, 7 Duḃtuinne a braṫair, 7 a da mac .i. Cuduiligh 7 Domnall, 7 ar int sluaiġ archena etir maiṫ 7 saiṫ .i. Gairbiṫ ri .h. nEċdaċ 7 Gilla Patraic mac Tomaltaiġ 7 Cumuscaċ mac Flaṫroi, 7 Dubslanġa mac Aeḋai, 7 Caṫalan mac Etroċ, 7 Conene mac Muirchertaiġ, 7 forglu Ulad
Fol. 54aa. archeana; 7 ro ṡiacht in imguin co dun Eċdach 7 co Druim bó. Do roċair ann dono Aeḋ mac Domnaill .h. Neill, ri Ailiġ (7 alii, xx. nono etatis anno, regni vero x°). Acht asberat cenel nEogain is uaiḋiḃ fein ro marbad. Donnchad .h. Loingsiġ, ri dal nAraide, do marbad do ċenul Eogain per dolum. Slogad la Brian co traċt nEoṫaile, do ḋul timcell, co ro ṫairmisc cenel nEogain. Da Ua Ċanannan do marbad la hUa Maeldoraid. Dubslane .h. Lorcan, airchinnech imleċa Iḃair, quievit. Maelseċlainn ri Teṁraċ do escor, cor bo croliġi báis dó.

.b. Kl. Ianair, ii. f., l. xvi.° Anno domini M° iiii.° (alias 1005°). Aeḋ .h. Flannacan, airchinnech Máin Coluim cille, Ragnall mac Goḟraiḋ, rí na n-innsi, Concobar mac Domnaill, ri Loċa Beiṫeċ, Maelbrigte .h. Rimeda, abb Ia, Domnall mac Macnía, airchinnech Mainistreċ,

---

Castlereagh. A marg. note in A., in orig. hand, states that the battle was fought on the 18th of the Kalends of October [14th Sept.], being the fifth day of the week [i.e. Thursday], which would agree with the year 1003.

[1] *Dun-Echdach*.—Supposed to be now represented by Duneight, in the parish of Blaris, barony of Castlereagh Upper, co. Down.

[2] *Druim-bó;* i.e. the "Ridge of the Cow." Now Drumbo, in the parish of the same name, barony of Upper Castlereagh, co. Down. The note "sic in libro Duibdaleithi" is added in the marg. in A. and B., in the original hands.

[3] *And others.*—The original of the parenthetic clause, which is added in the marg. in A., in the original hand, forms part of the text in B.

[4] *Traig-Eothaile.*—A large strand near Ballysadare, in the county of Sligo, sometimes written "Trawohelly."

[5] *Cinel-Eoghain.*—The *Four Masters* (*ad. an.*), for "Cinel-Eoghain," write the alias name *Ui Neill in tuaisceirt* ("Ui-Neill of the North").

[6] *Imlech-Ibhair.* -- Emly, in the

the Ulidians and Cinel-Eoghain, where the Ulidians were defeated, and Eochaid, son of Ardgar, King of Ulidia, and Dubhtuinne his brother, and his two sons, viz., Cuduiligh and Domnall, were slain, and a havoc was made of the army besides, between good and bad, viz., Gairbhith, King of Ui-Echach, and Gilla Patraic son of Tomaltach, and Cumuscach son of Flathroe, and Dubhslanga son of Aedh, and Cathalan son of Etroch, and Conene son of Muirchertach, and the elect of the Ulidians besides. And the fighting extended to Dun-Echdach,[1] and to Druim-bó.[2] There also fell there Aedh, son of Domnall Ua Neill, King of Ailech, (and others,[3] in the 29th year of his age, and the 10th year of [his] reign). But the Cinel-Eoghain say that he was killed by themselves. Donnchad Ua Loingsigh, King of Dal-Araidhe, was treacherously killed by the Cinel-Eoghain. A hosting by Brian to Traig-Eothaile,[4] to go round [the North of Ireland]; but the Cinel-Eoghain[5] prevented him. Two Ua Canannains were slain by Ua Maeldoraidh. Dubhslane Ua Lorcain, herenagh of Imlech-Ibhair,[6] rested. Maelsechlainn, King of Temhair, was thrown from his horse, so that he was in danger of death.

Kal. Jan., Mond., m. 16. A.D. 1004 (alias 1005). Aedh [1004.] BIS
Ua Flannacain, herenagh of Maein-Choluim-cille;[7] Ragnall son of Gothfraid, King of the Isles; Conchobar son of Domnall, King of Loch-Beithech;[8] Maelbrighde Ua Rimedha, abbot of Ia, [and] Domnall son of Macnia,

county of Tipperary. See note [4], p. 42 *supra*.

[7] *Maein-Choluim-cille.*—Maein of Colum-cille; one of St. Colum-cille's foundations. Now Moone, in the barony of Kilkea and Moone, co. Kildare, where there are some remarkable ancient remains, including a massive sculptured cross. See Reeves's *Adamnan*, p. 280.

[8] *Loch-Beithech.*—The name of this district, sometimes written Loch-Bethadh, seems to be preserved in that of the lake known as Lough Veagh, in the barony of Kilmacrenan, co. Donegal. This lake contained a fortified island, or *crannog*, which is frequently referred to in Irish chronicles. See *Ann. Four Mast.*, A.D. 1258, 1524; and *Ann. Loch-Cé*, 1524, 1540 (*bis*).

in Christo. Gilla Comġaill, ri Ulad, do marbad o Maelruanaiġ, a germano suo. Aeḋ mac Tomaltaiġ do marbad la Flaiṫbertaċ .H. Neill, la indreḋ Leiṫi Caṫail. Muirecan (.i. o Boiṫ ḋomnaiċ), comarba Patraic, lxx.° secundo anno etatis sue, Aeḋ Treoiti sui ind ecnai 7 i crabud, uitam finierunt i n-ard Maċa. Caṫ etir firu Alban immoneitir, i torċair ri Alban .i. Cinaeḋ mac Duiḃ. Roiniuḋ ic Loċ Bricrenn for Ultu 7 hU Eċaċ, ria Flaiṫbertaċ, itorcair Artan riġdomna .H. Eċaċ. Slogad la Brian co rigraiḋ Erenn ime, co h-ard Maċa, co farcaiḃ .xx. unga do ór for altoir Patraic. Luiḋ for a culu co n-etire fer nErenn lais.

Kl. Ianair. iii. f., l. xx. uiii. Anno domini M.° u.° (alias 1006). Airmedaċ mac Coscraiċ episcopus 7 scriba ard Maċa in Christo quieuit, 7 Finġuine abb Ross cre moritur. Maelruanaiḋ .H. Dubtai 7 a mac Maelseċlainn, 7 a braṫair Geibennaċ, mortui sunt. Eċmiliḋ .H. Aitiḋ, ri .H. nEċaċ o Ultaiḃ, Maelruanaiḋ mac Flannacain o Conailliḃ; Caṫalan ri Gaileng, occisi sunt. Slogad timceall Erenn la Brian

---

[1] *Mainister*; i.e. Mainister-Buite (or Monasterboice).

[2] *Ulidia.*—A marg. note in A., in the original hand, adds that Gilla-Comghaill was King of Leth-Cathail (Lecale, co. Down, see note [2], p. 462 *supra*). But his name appears in the list of the Kings of Ulidia contained in the *Book of Leinster*, p. 41, col. 4. This entry is repeated under the next year.

[3] *Leth-Cathail.*—See last note.

[4] *Of Both-Domnaigh.*—The clause o boiṫ ḋompnaiċ, which is added as a gloss, in a later hand in A., is in the marg. in B., where the more correct form, as above given, is written. See above, under A.D. 1000.

[5] *Treoit.*—Trevet, in the parish of the same name, barony of Skreen, co. Meath.

[6] *Cinaedh son of Dubh.*—Or Kenneth, son of Duff (at. 966 *supra*), as he is called in Scotch historical writings. See Skene's *Chron. Picts and Scots*, Introd., pp. cxliii.–cxlvi.

[7] *Loch-Bricrenn.*—See note [4], p. 332 *supra*.

[8] *Flaithbertach.*—i.e. Flaithbertach Ua Neill (or O'Neill), King of Ailech, referred to in the 2nd entry preceding, in connexion with the plundering of Leth-Cathail [Lecale, co. Down], and the killing of its King, Aedh son of Tomaltach.

[9] *Airmedach.*—His name does not

herenagh of Mainistir,[1] [rested] in Christ. Gilla-Comghaill, King of Ulidia,[2] was killed by Maelruanaigh, his own brother. Aedh, son of Tomaltach, was killed by Flaithbertach Ua Neill, who plundered Leth-Cathail.[3] Muirecan (of Both-Domnaigh[4]), comarb of Patrick, in the 72nd year of his age, [and] Aedh of Treoit,[5] a man eminent in knowledge and piety, ended life in Ard-Macha. A battle amongst the men of Alba themselves, in which the King of Alba, *i.e.* Cinaedh son of Dubh,[6] was slain. An overthrow of the Ulidians and Ui-Echach, at Loch-Bricrenn,[7] by Flaithbertach,[8] wherein fell Artan, royal heir of Ui-Echach. A hosting by Brian, accompanied by the princes of Ireland, to Ard-Macha, when he left 22 ounces of gold on Patrick's altar. He came back bringing with him the hostages of Ireland.

Kal. Jan. Tuesd., m. 27. A.D. 1005 (alias 1006). Airmedach[9] son of Coscrach, bishop, and scribe of Ard-Macha, rested in Christ; and Finghuine,[10] abbot of Ros-cre, died. Maelruanaidh Ua Dubhtai,[11] and his son Maelsechlainn, and his brother Geibhennach, died. Echmilidh Ua Aitidh, King of Ui-Echach, by the Ulidians; Maelruanaidh son[12] of Flannacan, by the Conailli; Cathalan,[13] King of Gailenga,[14] were slain. A [1005.]

---

appear in any of the old lists of the bishops of Armagh (or 'comarbs' of St. Patrick). Airmedach may have been a bishop; but he was not bishop, or abbot, of Armagh.

[10] *Finghuine.* — This entry, which forms part of the text in B., is interlined in the original (or in a contemporary) hand in A.

[11] *Ua Dubhtai.*—This seems to be a mistake for *Ua Dubhdai* (O'Dowda). According to the *Ann. Four Mast.*, and the *Chron. Scotorum*, Maelruanaidh Ua Dubhda was King of the Ui-Fiachrach of Muirisc, whose territory is now represented by the barony of Tireragh (*Tir Fiachrach*), in the co. Sligo. See O'Donovan's *Hy-Fiachrach*, p. 350.

[12] *Son.*—mac, A. B. has .h. for ua, grandson, or descendant.

[13] *Cathalan.*—In the *Ann. Four Mast.*, ad an., the name is Cathal son of Dunchadh.

[14] *Gailenga.* — "Gailenga-mora" (Morgallion, a barony in the county Meath), according to the *Ann. Four M.*

i Connachta, for Ers ruaiḋ i tir Conaill, tria cenel Eogain, for fertais Camsa i n-Ultu, i n-oenaċ Conaille, co roaċtadar im Luġnasaḋ co Belaċ n[d]uin, co tarait oiġreir samṫa Patraic 7 a coṁarbai .i. Maelmuire mac Eoċaḋa. Bellum etir ḟiru Alban 7 Saxanu, co remaiḋ for Albanċu, co farsgabsat ar a n-deg ḋaine. Maelnambo (.i. ri .h. Ceinnsealaiġ) a suis occisus est. Gilla Comgaill mac Ardġair mic Madaḋain, .i. ri Ulad, do marbad dia brathair .i. do Maelruanaid mac Ardgair.

Fol. 54ab. Kl. Ianair. iiii. f., l. ix. Anno domini M.° vii.° (alias 1007). Maelruanaiḋ mac Ardġair do marbad o Matuḋan mac Domnaill. Ceallach .h. Menngoran, airchinnech Corcaiḋe, quieuit. Treinḟer .h. Baiġellan, ri Dartraiġi, do marbad do cenel Conaill for Loċ Eirne. Motaḋan mac Domnaill, ri Ulad, do marbad don Durc i n-ecluis Brigte for lar Duin daleṫglas. Cuconnaċt mac Dunadaiġ, toisech sil nAnmchada, do marbad la Brian per dolum. Slogad la Flaiṫbertach .h. Neill i n-Ultaib, co tuc secht n-etire uaidib,

[1] *Brian.*—In the lower margin of fol. 54*a* in A., the following stanza is written, with reference to Brian:—

Ingnaḋ sliaḃ Cua cen choibden,
Gaill cen imram im eiḋnig,
Oen ben do ṫeċt tar Luaċair,
Bai cen buaċail ic neimleiṫ.

"Strange [to see] Sliabh-Cua without a troop,
Foreigners not rowing about . .
A lone woman going over Luachair,
Cows without a herd, lowing."

It is added that this happy condition was "in tempore Briani." The allusion to a lone woman going over Luachair [Sliabh-Luachra, in Munster] seems connected with the tradition on which Moore founded his charming song "Rich and Rare."

[2] *Fertas-Camsa*; i.e. the ford (or crossing) of Camus; a ford on the River Bann, near the old church of Camus-Macosquin. See Reeves's *Down and Connor*, pp. 342, 388.

[3] *Belach-duin.*—See note [11], p. 443 *supra.*

[4] *Mael-na-mbo.*—This was merely a nickname, signifying "cow-boy." His proper name was Donnchad. He was the son of Diarmait (son of Domnall), King of Ui-Ceinnselaigh, whose obit is given above at the year 995.

[5] *His brother.*—According to the *Ann. Four Mast.*, the death of Gilla-Comghaill, already entered under the preceding year, occurred in a conflict with his brother Maelruanaidh, regarding the Kingship of Ulidia. See note [2], p. 514.

[6] *Corcach.*—Cork, in Munster.

hosting round Ireland by Brian,[1]—to Connaught, over Es-Ruaidh into Tir-Conaill, through Cinel-Eoghain, over Fertas-Camsa[2] into Ulidia, to Oenach-Conaille; and they arrived about Lammas at Belach-duin,[3] when he granted the full demand of Patrick's congregation, and of his successor, *i.e.* Maelmuire son of Eochaidh. A battle between the men of Alba and the Saxons, when the men of Alba were defeated, and left a slaughter of their good men. Mael-na-mbo[4] (*i.e.* King of Ui-Ceinnselaigh), was slain by his own people. Gilla-Comghaill, son of Ardghar, son of Madadhan, King of Ulidia, was killed by his brother,[5] *i.e.*, by Maelruanaidh son of Ardghar.

Kal. Jan. Wednesd., m, 9. A.D. 1006 (alias 1007). [1006.] Maelruanaidh, son of Ardghar, was killed by Matadhan son of Domnall. Cellach Ua Menngoran, herenagh of Corcach,[6] rested. Trenfher[7] Ua Baighellan, King of Dartraighi,[8] was killed by the Cinel-Conaill on Loch-Eirne. Matadhan son of Domnall, King of Ulidia, was killed by the Torc,[9] in St. Bridget's church, in the middle of Dun-da-lethglas.[10] Cuchonnacht son of Dunadach, chieftain of Sil-Anmchada,[11] was treacherously slain by Brian.[12] A hosting by Flaithbertach Ua Neill into Ulidia,

---

[7] *Trenfher*; pronounced "Trener." —Treiner, A. B. has treinḟer, which is nearer to the correct form trenḟer (lit. "strong man"), as in the *Ann. Four Mast.*

[8] *Dartraighi.* — Or Dartraighi-Coininse, the present barony of Dartry, in the county of Monaghan, of which the Ui-Baighellain (or O'Boylans) were chiefs.

[9] *The Torc*; i.e. "the Boar;" a nickname for Dubhtuinne, King of Ulidia, whose name does not appear in the list of Kings of Ulidia in the *Book of Leinster*.

[10] *Dun-da-lethglas.*— Downpatrick.

[11] *Sil-Anmchada*; i.e. the race of Anmchad; the tribe name of that powerful branch of the Ui-Maine of Connaught whose descendants assumed the patronymic of O'Madden (now Madden, without the O'), and whose patrimony embraced the present barony of Longford, in the county of Galway, and the parish of Lusmagh, in the barony of Garrycastle, in the King's County, on the east side of the river Shannon.

[12] *Brian*; i.e. *Brian Borumha.* According to the *Ann. Four Mast.* (1006), and the *Chron. Scotorum* (1005), the slayer of Cuchonnacht was Murchadh, son of Brian, which agrees with a marginal note in a later hand in A.

7 co ro marḃ ri Leṫi Caṫail .i. Coinulad mac Oenġusa. Slogad la Brian co Cenel Eogain, .i. co Dun droma i toeḃ aird Maċa, co tuc .h. Criċiden, comarba Finnen Muiġi bile, ro boi i n-etireċt o Ultaib i Cenel Eogain. In Torc, ri Ulad, do marbad do Muireḋaċ mac Motoḋan, i n-diġail a aṫar, tria nert De 7 Patraic. Muiredaċ mac Criċain do ḋeirgiu comarbuis Coluim cille ar ḋia. Aċnuġuḋ aenaiġ Tailltean la Maelseċnall. Ferdomnaċ i comarbus Coluim cille a comairle fer nErenn isin oenaċ sin. Soiscela mor Coluim cille do dubgait is ind aidci as ind iardom iarṫarach in daimliacc moir Cenannsa; prim mind iartair domain arai in comdaig dendai. In soscela sin do ḟogbail dia fiċet [aidċe] ar dib misaib, iar n-gait de a oir, 7 fot tairis. Domnall mac Duibtuinne, ri Ulad, do marbad do Muiredaċ mac Matadain, 7 do Uargaeṫ sleibe Fuait.

.b. Kl. Ianair. u. f., l. xx. Anno domini M.° uii.° (alias 1008). Ferdomnaċ comarba Cenannsa, Ceileċair mac Duinncuain mic Ceinnedig, comarba Coluim mic

---

[1] *Leth-Cathail.*—Now represented by the barony of Lecale, in the county of Down. See Reeves's *Down and Connor*, pp. 357, 358, and other places referred to in the Index to that work under *Leth-Cathail.*

[2] *Dun-droma;* i.e. the "Fort of the Ridge (or Hill)." This name would be Anglicised "Dundrum." There is a townland of Dundrum in the parish of Keady, in the barony and county of Armagh; but it is some miles to the south of the town of Armagh, and not in the territory of Cinel-Eoghain. It may, however, be the place referred to. This entry is very imperfectly given in O'Conor's version of this Chronicle.

[3] *Ua Crichidhen.*—At the year 1025 *infra,* where his obit is entered, he is called Maelbrigte Ua Crichidhen.

[4] *Magh-bilè.* — Movilla, in the county of Down.

[5] See note [3], p. 517.

[6] *Father.*—The killing of Matadhan is the subject of the fourth entry for this year.

[7] *For God.*—The Chronicler should have said that Muiredach resigned his great office of President of the Columbian Order, to become a recluse. His obit is entered at the year 1010 (=1011) *infra.* See Reeves's *Adamnan*, p. 397.

[8] *Tailltiu.*—See note [11], p. 167 *supra.*

when he brought seven hostages from them, and killed the King of Leth-Cathail,[1] *i.e.*, Cu-Ulad son of Oenghus. A hosting by Brian to the Cinel-Eoghain, *i.e.* to Dun-droma[2] by the side of Ard-Macha, when he brought off Ua Crichidhen,[3] successor of Finnen of Magh-bilè,[4] who had been a hostage from the Ulidians in Cinel-Eoghain. The Torc,[5] King of Ulidia, was killed by Muiredach son of Matadhan, in revenge of his father,[6] through the power of God and Patrick. Muiredach, son of Crichan, resigned the successorship of Colum-Cille for God.[7] Renewal of the Fair of Tailltiu[8] by Maelsechnaill. Ferdomnach[9] [was installed] in the successorship of Colum-Cille, by the counsel of the men of Ireland, in that Fair. The great Gospel[10] of Colum-Cille was wickedly stolen[11] in the night out of the western sacristy of the great stone-church of Cenannas—the chief relic of the western world, on account of its ornamental cover. The same Gospel was found after twenty [nights[12]] and two months, its gold having been taken off it, and a sod over it. Domnall son of Dubhtuinne, King of Ulidia, was killed by Muiredach son of Matadhan, and by Uargaeth of Sliabh-Fuait.

Kal. Jan. Thursd.; m. 20. A.D. 1007 (alias 1008). [1007.] BIS. Ferdomnach, comarb of Cenannas;[13] Ceilechair, son of Donnchuan,[14] son of Cennedigh, successor of Colum son of

[9] *Ferdomnach.*—For some information regarding him, see Reeves's *Adamnan*, p. 397.

[10] *Great Gospel.*—This is the splendidly illuminated MS., known as the Book of Kells, preserved in the library of Trinity College, Dublin.

[11] *Stolen.*—The remainder of this entry, which forms part of the text in B., is continued on the top margin of fol. 54*a* in A., apparently by the orig. hand, one line having been cut off by the binder

[12] *Nights.*—Ɑnꝺ, A. and B. Obviously a mistake for aıꝺċe (or aꝺhaıꝺ, as in *Ann. Four Mast.*)

[13] *Comarb of Cenannas* [Kells, co. Meath].—The appointment of Ferdomnach as successor of St. Colum-Cille, and therefore abbot of Kells, is recorded among the entries for last year.

[14] *Donnchuan.*—The death of Donnchuan, who was brother to Brian Borumha, is noticed in the *Ann. Four Mast.* at A.D. 948 (=950).

Cremthainn (alias abb Tire da glas), Maelmuire comarba Cainnich, in Christo dormierunt. Muiredhach mac Matodhain, ridomna Uladh, do marbadh a suis. Fachtna, comarba Finnia Cluana iraird, quieuit. Secc mor 7 snechta o'n uii. id Enair co caisc.

.b. Kt. Ianair. uiii.f.; l. i. Anno domini M.° uiii.° (alias 1009). Crechdighail mor la Maelsechlainn for Laighniu. Cathal mac Carlusa, comarba Cainnigh, Maelmuire .h. Uchtain, comarba Cenannsa, mortui sunt. Maelan (.i. in gai moir), ri .h. Dorthainn, do marbadh do Cheniul Eogain i n-ard Macha for lar trin moir, tria comergi na da sluagh. Donnchadh .h. Ceile do dalladh la Flaithbertach i n-inis Eogain, 7 a marbadh iarum. Maidm for Connachta ria feraibh Breifne. Maidm dana re Connachtu for feraibh Breifne. Crech la Flaithbertach .h. Neill co firu Bregh, co tuc borroma mor. Maelmordha, ri Laigen, do escur co robrised a choss. Dubchablaigh ingen righ Connacht .i. ben Briain mic Ceinneitigh, mortua est. Oratorium aird Macha in hoc anno plumbo tegitur. Clothna mac Aengusa, primfile Erenn, moritur.

---

[1] *Tir-da-glas.*—Terryglass, in the barony of Lower Ormond, co. Tipperary. The original of this clause is added in the margin in A., and also in B.

[2] *Successor of Cainech;* i.e. abbot of Aghaboe, Queen's County.

[3] *The 6th of the Ides*; i.e. the 8th of January. In the corresponding entry in the *Chron. Scotorum* and *Ann. Four Mast.*, the date given is the 8th of the Ides, or 6th of January.

[4] *Comarb of Cenannas.* — Maelmuire was abbot of Kells. See Reeves's *Adamnan*, p. 397.

[5] *Ui-Dorthainn.*—Otherwise written (and more correctly) Ui-Tortain, or "descendants of Tortan," who was descended in the fourth generation from Colla Dachrioch, one of the three ancestors of the Airghialla. The Ui-Dorthainn were seated near Ardbraccan, in the present county of Meath. See O'Donovan's ed. of *Leabhar na g-ceart*, p. 151. This entry is not given in the *Ann. Four Mast.*

[6] *Trian-mor.*—"Trian-mor" means the "great third." According to Dr. Reeves, that portion of ancient Armagh outside the *Rath* (or rampart) was divided into three divisions, one of which, Trian-mor, included the

Cremthann (alias abbot of Tir-da-glas),[1] [and] Maelmuire, successor of Cainech,[2] 'fell asleep' in Christ. Muiredach son of Matadhan, royal heir of Ulidia, was killed by his own people. Fachtna, successor of Finnia of Cluain-Iraird, rested. Great frost and snow from the 6th of the Ides[3] of January to Easter.

Kal. Jan. Saturd.; m. 1. A.D. 1008 (alias 1009). A great retaliatory depredation by Maelsechlainn on the Leinstermen. Cathal son of Carlus, comarb of Cainech,[2] [and] Maelmuire Ua Uchtain, comarb of Cenannas,[4] died. Maelan (*i.e.* "of the great spear"), King of the Ui-Dorthainn,[5] was killed by the Cinel-Eoghain in Ard-Macha, in the middle of Trian-mor,[6] through an uprising of the two armies. Donnchad Ua Ceile was blinded by Flaithbertach,[7] in Inis-Eoghain; and he was killed afterwards. A victory over the Connaughtmen by the men of Breifni.[8] A victory also by the Connaughtmen over the men of Breifni. A preying expedition by Flaithbertach Ua Neill to the men of Bregha, when he took a great cattle spoil. Maelmordha, King of Leinster, was thrown from his horse, so that his leg was broken. Dubhchablaigh, daughter of the King of Connaught,[9] *i.e.*, the wife of Brian,[10] son of Cennetigh, died. The oratory of Ard-Macha was roofed with lead in this year. Clothna son of Aengus, chief poet of Ireland, died. [1008] BIS.

---

space now occupied by "Irish-street, Callan-street, and the western region of the town." See *Ancient Churches of Armagh*; Lusk, 1860; pp. 19-20.

[7] *Flaithbertach.*—Flaithbertach Ua Neill, lord of Ailech (i.e. chief of the Ui-Neill of the North), nicknamed Flaithbertach "in trosdain" (F. "of the pilgrim's staff"), in allusion to his journey to Rome, noticed at the year 1030 *infra.* His death in penitence, after a turbulent career, is recorded under A.D. 1036.

[8] *Breifni.* — Corruptly written bꝛeıbꝼne, in A.

[9] *King of Connaught.*—He was the Cathal, son of Conchobar, referred to above at the year 1000, as having, in conjunction with King Maelsechlainn, constructed the causeway of Ath-Luain (Athlone), and whose obit is the first entry under the next year.

[10] *Brian.*—Brian Borumha. See Todd's *War of the Gaedhil*, &c., Introd., p. clxi., note [1].

Kl. Ianair. i. f.; l. xii. Anno domini M.° ix.° (alias 1010). Cathal mac Conchobair (ri Connacht, in penitentia moritur). Muiredhach H. Aedha, ri Muscraide, Cathal mac Duibdara, ri Fermanach, mortui sunt. Maelsuthain H. Cerbaill ard sui Erenn 7 ri Eoganachta Locha Lein; Marcan mac Cennetigh, comarba Coluim mic Crimthainn 7 Innsi celtra 7 cille Dalua; Muiredach mac Mochloingsi, airchinnech Mucnama, in Christo dormierunt. Aedh mac Cuinn rigdomna Ailigh, Donncuan ri Mughdorna, occisi sunt. Slogad la Brian co Cloenloch sleibe Fuait, co ro gaibh etire leithe Cuinn. Aestas torrida, autumnus fructuosus. Scanlain H. Dungalain, princeps Duin lethglaisi; sarugud Duin fair, 7 a thabairt amach, 7 a dhallad a Finnabhair, la Niall mac Duibhtuinne. Derbail ingen Taidhg mic Cathail mortua est.

Fol. 54ba.

Kl. Ianair. ii. f., l. xx. iii. Anno domini M.° x.° (alias M.° xi.°). Dunadhach in reiclera Coluim Cille i n-ard Macha. Flaithbertach H. Ceithinan comarba Tigernaigh,

[1] *Penitence.*—The original of this clause, which is added in the margin in A., apparently in the old hand, forms part of the regular text in B.

[2] *Fir-Manach.*—The name of this tribe is still preserved in that of the county of Fermanagh.

[3] *Maelsuthain.*—O'Curry was under the impression that this Maelsuthain was the tutor and "soul-friend" (*anmchara*) of Brian Borumha (*MS. Materials*, p. 76), although the obit of "Maelsuthain, *anmchara* of Brian," is entered in the *Ann. Four Mast.* at the year 1031, where no mention is made of any connexion of this latter Maelsuthain with the Eoghanacht of Loch-Lein, a territory comprising Killarney and an extensive district around it, the patrimony of the older branch of the O'Donoghoe family. It may be added that the name of Maelsuthain does not appear in the ordinary Irish pedigrees of the O'Donoghoes of Loch-Lein. Great interest attaches to the history of the Maelsuthain who was *anmchara* of Brian Borumha, and who, in a note written by him in the *Book of Armagh*, fol. 16 b h, Latinizes his name *calvus perennis*, and states that the note was written by him "*in conspectu Briani imperatoris Scotorum.*"

[4] *Colum son of Crimthann.*—The founder of the monastery of Tir-da-glas (Terryglass), in the barony of Lower Ormond, and county of Tipperary.

[5] *Inis-Celtra.* — Inishcalthra, or Holy Island; an island in the expan-

Kal. Jan., Sund.; m. 12. A.D. 1009 (alias 1010). Cathal son of Conchobar, (King of Connaught, died in penitence[1]). Muiredhach Ua hAedha, King of Muscraidhe, Cathal son of Dubhdara, King of the Fir-Managh,[2] died. Maelsuthain[3] Ua Cerbhaill, chief sage of Ireland, and King of Eoghanacht of Loch-Lein; Marcan, son of Cennetigh, comarb of Colum son of Crimthann,[4] and of Inis-Celtra[5] and Cill-Dalua[6]; Muiredach son of Mochloingsi, herenagh of Mucnamh,[7] 'fell asleep' in Christ. Aedh son of Conn, royal-heir of Ailech, [and] Donncuan, King of Mughdorna, were slain. A hosting by Brian to Cloenloch of Sliabh-Fuaid,[8] when he received the hostages of Leth-Cuinn. A hot summer, a fruitful autumn. Scanlan Ua Dungalain, abbot of Dun-lethglaise, was profaned in Dun;[9] and he was brought out and blinded in Finnabhair, by Niall[10] son of Dubhtuinne. Derbhail, daughter of Tadhg[11] son of Cathal, died. [1009.]

Kal. Jan., Mond.; m. 23. A.D. 1010 (alias 1011). Dunadhach of Colum-Cille's *recles*[12] in Ard-Macha [died]. Flaithbertach Ua Ceithinan, comarb of Tigernach[13] (a [1010.]

---

sion of the Shannon known as Lough-derg, and belonging to the barony of Leitrim, co. Galway.

[6] *Cill-Dalua.*—Killaloe, co. Clare.

[7] *Mucnamh.* — Muckno, in the barony of Cremorne, co. Monaghan.

[8] *Sliabh-Fuaid.*—The old name of the Fews Mountains, near Newtown-hamilton, in the barony of Upper Fews, in the south-west of the co. Armagh.

[9] *Dun;* i.e. Dun-da-lethglas, or Downpatrick.

[10] *Niall.*—He was King of Ulidia for 4 years and 6 months, according to the list of Kings of that province in the *Book of Leinster*, p. 40, col. 4. His death is recorded at the year 1016 *infra*.

[11] *Tadhg.* — King of Connaught, and known as *Tadhg an eich gil*, or "Tadhg of the White Steed." His death is noticed at the year 1030. He was the first who assumed the surname "O'Conchobair (or O'Conor)."

[12] *Recles.* — Dr. Reeves regarded this *recles* as an "abbey church." See his very interesting memoir on the *Ancient Churches of Armagh* (Lusk, 1860), p. 27, where some curious information regarding the *recles* is given.

[13] *Comarb of Tigernach;* i.e. abbot of Cluain-eois (Clones), in the county Monaghan. The original of the parenthetic clause which follows is interlined in a later hand in A., and in the original hand in B.

(seanoir 7 rui espuc, do guin o feraib Breifne, 7 postea in ciuitate sua mortuus est). Muiredaċ mac Criċain, comarba Coluim Cille 7 ferleiginn ard Maċa, in Christo dormierunt. Flaiṫbertaċ .h. Neill (.i. ri Oilig, co n-ocaib in Focla, 7 Murchad mac mBriain co feraib Muman 7 Laigen, 7 .h. Neill in desceirt), do innreḋ ceneoil Conaill, co tuc ccc. do brait, 7 bú imda. Maelruanaiḋ .h. Domnaill, rí ceneoil Luġdaċ, o feraiḃ maiġi Iṫa, Oengus .h. Lapan .i. ri cenel Endai, o cenul Eogain na h-innsi, occisi sunt. Aeḋ mac Maṫgamna, ridomna Caisil, moritur. Slogad la Flaiṫbertach .h. Neill co Dun Eċdaċ, co ro loisc in dun 7 co ro bris a baile, 7 co tuc aitire o Niall mac Duibṫuinne. Slogad la Brian co Maġ corainn, co ruc lais ri cenuil Conaill .i. Maelruanaiḋ .h. Maeldoraiḋ, fri a reir co Cenn coraḋ. Dalaċ disirt Tolai, comarba Feiċin 7 Tolai, in bona senectute mortuus est. Brian 7 Maelsechlainn iterum in clais[s]i sua oc Enach duiḃ.

Kl. Ianair. iii. f., l. iiii. Anno domini M.° x.° i.° (alias M.° 12.°) Teidm tregait isin bliadain sin i n-ard Maċa, co ro marḃ ár. Maelbrigte mac in gobann, ferleiginn aird Maċa, do ec de, 7 Scolaiġi mac

---

[1] *Fell asleep.*—dormierunt, A., B.; seemingly by mistake for dormiebat or dormiuit. A marginal note in A., in the later hand, has lxxx. iiii. anno etatis sue, u. Kl. Enair, in nocte sabati in Christo quieuit; (i.e. "rested in Christ in the 84th [74th, *Four Mast.*] year of his age, on Saturday night, the 5th of the Kalends of January").

[2] *Fochla.*—See note [8], p. 429 *supra.*

[3] *Ua Domhnaill;* or O'Donnell. This is the first notice of the surname O'Donnell to be found in the Irish Annals. The Domnall (or Donnell) from whom the name is derived was son of Eignechan (ob. 905 *supra*), who was King of Cinel-Conaill. See O'Donovan's *Four Mast.*, A.D. 1010, note a.

[4] *Cinel-Lughdach.* — One of the tribe-names of the O'Donnells, who were descended from Lugaid, son of Sedna (who was brother of Ainmire, King of Ireland in the 6th century). The territory of the Cinel-Lughdach comprised a great part of the present barony of Kilmacrenan, co. Donegal.

[5] *Cinel-Enna.*—A tribe descended from Enna, son of Conall Gulban, son of Niall Nine-hostager, whose territory consisted in later times of 30 quarters of land, lying to the south of the barony of Inishowen, co. Done-

senior, and eminent bishop, was wounded by the men of Breifni, and died afterwards in his own monastery). Muiredach son of Crichan, comarb of Colum-Cille, and lector of Ard-Macha, 'fell asleep'[1] in Christ. Flaithbertach Ua Neill, (King of Oilech, with the warriors of the Fochla,[2] and Murchad son of Brian, with the men of Munster and Leinster, and the Ui-Neill of the South), ravaged Cinel-Conaill, and carried off 300 captives, and many cows. Maelruanaidh Ua Domnaill,[3] King of Cinel-Lughdach,[4] was slain by the men of Magh-Itha; Oengus Ua Lapain, King of Cinel-Enna,[5] by the Cinel-Eoghain of the Island.[6] Aedh son of Mathgamain, royal-heir of Caisel, died. A hosting by Flaithbertach Ua Neill to Dun-Echdach,[7] when he burned the *dun*, and broke down the town, and brought pledges from Niall son of Dubhtuinne. A hosting by Brian to Magh-Corainn, when he brought with him the King of Cinel-Conaill, *i.e.* Maelruanaidh Ua Maeldoraidh, in submission, to Cenn-coradh.[8] Dalach of Disert-Tola, comarb of Fechin and of Tola, died at a good old age. Brian and Maelsechlainn again in camp at Enach-duibh.[9]

Kal. Jan., Tuesd.; m. 4. A.D. 1011[10] (alias 1012.) [1011.]
A plague of colic in this year in Ard-Macha, which killed a great number. Maelbrigte Mac-an-gobhan, lector of Ard-Macha, died of it; and Scolaighi son of

gal, and between the arms of the Foyle and Swilly, or between Lifford and Letterkenny. See Colgan's *Acta Sanctorum*, p. 370.

[6] *Cinel-Eoghain of the Island;* i.e. of the island of Inishowen.

[7] *Dun Echdach.*—"Eochaid's *dun* (or *fort*)." See under the year 1003; p. 512, note[1].

[8] *Cenn-coradh.* — "The Head of the Weir." The residence of Brian Borumha at Killaloe. The original of this entry and the one succeeding it is written in a space which appears to have been left blank by the original scribe in A. They form part of the text in B.

[9] *Enach-duibh.*—This name would now be written Annaduff, or Annaghduff. The place referred to was probably Annaduff, in the co. Leitrim or Annaghduff. co. Cavan.

[10] *A.D.* 1011.—The number 580 is added in the margin in A., to signify that so many years had elapsed since the arrival of St. Patrick.

Clercen, sacart ard Maċa, 7 Cennfaelad ant sabaill .i. anmċara toġaiḋe, mortui sunt. Slogad la Flaiṫbertaċ mac Muircertaiċ, la riġ nAiliġ, i cinel Conaill, co roacht maġ Cetne, co tuc boġaḃail moir 7 co tainic imslan. Slogad la Flaiṫbertaċ doridisi i ceinel Conaill, co roact Druim cliab 7 tracht nEothaili, co ro marbsat mac Gillapatraic mic Fergaile .i. Niall, 7 co tucsat maidm for Maelruanaiḋ .h. Maeldoraiḋ, acht ní fargbaḋ neċ ann. Slogad caleic tar a n-eisi la Maelseċlaind i tir nEogain co Maġ daġaḃul, co ro loiscset a creċa telaiġ nOóc, co ruc gaḃail. Slogad
Fol. 54bb. la Flaiṫbertaċ bes corici aird Ulad co ro ort in Aird, 7 co tuc gaḃala is moam tuc ri riam etir brait 7 innile, ce naċ airimter. Slogad la Brian i maġ Muirteiṁne, co tuc ogsoere do ċellaib Patraic do'nt sluagad sin. Maidm for Niall mac Duibṫuinne ria Niall mac Eochada, du itorċair Muircertaċ mac Artan, ridomna .h. nEċoċ, 7 riġaḋ mic Eochada iarum. Coencomrac .h. Scannlan airchinnech Daiminsi, Maclonan airchinnech Rois cre, mortui sunt. Oengus airchinnech Sláne do marbad do airchinnech Dubaḋ. Crinan mac Gormlaḋa, ri Conaille, occisus est o Coinċuailgni.

.b. Kl. Ianair, u. f., l. Anno domini M.° x.° u.° (alias M.° 13°). Creċ la Maelseċlaind i Conailliḃ i n-diġail

---

[1] *Sabhall.*—A church, or oratory, situated within the *rath*, or foss, of Armagh. See Reeves's *Ancient Churches of Armagh* (Lusk, 1860), p. 15.

[2] *Magh-Cetne.*—A plain in the south-west of the county of Donegal, lying between the rivers Erne and Drowse. See O'Donovan's *Four Mast.*, A.D. 1301, note m.

[3] *Druim-cliabh.* — Drumcliff, in a parish of the same name, barony of Carbury, and county of Sligo.

[4] *Traig-Eothaili.*—See note [4] under the year 1003 *supra*.

[5] *Magh-da-gabhul.* — The "Plain of the two forks (or dividing streams)." Not identified.

[6] *Telach-óc.*—Now known as Tullyhog, in the barony of Dungannon Upper, co. Tyrone.

[7] *Ard-Ulad.*—Now known as the baronies of Upper and Lower Ards, in the county of Down.

[8] *Victory.*—Described as caṫ na mullaċ ("battle of the summits"—

Clerchen, priest of Ard-Macha, and Cennfaeladh of the Sabhall,[1] *i.e.* a choice soul-friend, died. A hosting by Flaithbertach son of Muirchertach, King of Ailech, into Cinel-Conaill, until he reached Magh-Cetne,[2] when he took a great cow-spoil, and returned safe. A hosting by Flaithbertach again into Cinel-Conaill until he reached Druim-cliabh[3] and Traig-Eothaili,[4] when they killed the son of Gillapatraic son of Fergal, *i.e.* Niall; and they inflicted a defeat on Maelruanaidh Ua Maeldoraidh; but no one was lost there. A hosting meanwhile by Maelsechlainn, in their absence, into Tir-Eoghain, to Magh-dagabhul,[5] when his plundering parties burned Telach-óc,[6] and took a spoil. Another hosting by Flaithbertach as far as Ard-Ulad,[7] when he plundered the Ard, and brought off the greatest spoils that a King had ever borne, between prisoners and cattle, though they are not reckoned. A hosting by Brian into Magh-Muirtheimne; and he gave full freedom to Patrick's churches on that hosting. A victory[8] over Niall son of Dubhtuinne, by Niall son of Eochaid, in which fell Muirchertach son of Artan, royal heir of Ui-Echach; and the son of Eochaid was afterwards made King. Coencomrac Ua Scannlain, herenagh of Daiminis, MacLonain, herenagh[9] of Ros-cre, died. Oengus, herenagh of Slane, was killed by the herenagh of Dubhadh.[10] Crinan, son of Gormlaidh, King of Conailli,[11] was slain by Cucuailgni.

Kal. Jan. Thursd.; m. A.D. 1012 (alias 1013). A predatory expedition by Maelsechlainn into Conailli,[11] in [1012.] BIS

---

not identified), in the marg. of MSS. A. and B.

[9] *Herenagh.* — In the *Ann. Four Mast.* MacLonain is called "abbot."

[10] *Dubhadh.*—More correctly Dubhath, (the "black ford"). Now known as Dowth, in a parish of the same name, barony of Upper Slane, and county of Meath. The mound of Dowth is a well known and conspicuous object on the northern bank of the River Boyne, a little to the east of the great tumulus of Newgrange. This entry is not given in the *Ann. Four Mast.*, from which records of events calculated to reflect on the church (as the compilers thought) are habitually omitted.

[11] *Conailli.* — i.e. Conailli - Muirtheimhne, or Magh-Muirtheimhne. See Index.

ṡaraiġti finnfaiḋiġ Ṗatraic 7 bristi baċlai Patraic, a forgaire Mailmuire 7 Brian. Creċ mor la hUalgarc .h. Ciardai, la riġ Coirpri, 7 la mac Neill .h. Ruairc, hi Gailenga, conustaraiḋ uathad deg daine do lucht taiġi Mailṡechlainn iar n-ol isin uair sin 7 atte mersa, co tardsat caṫ doiḃ tre dimus, cotorcair ann Donnchad mac Donnchada finn, ridomna Teṁrach, 7 Cernaċan mac Flainn ri Luiġne, 7 Senan .h. Leocain ri Gaileng, 7 alii multi. Maelseċlainn iarum dia torraċtain, co fargabṫa aigi na gabala, 7 co torċair leis hUalgarc .h. Ciardai rí Coirpri, 7 alii multi. Slogad la Flaiṫ-bertaċ la riġ nAiliġ corigi Ed i taeb Cenannsa, co fargaib Maelseċlainn in tailċi ḋo. Gillamoċonna mac Foġartaiġ, ri deisceirt Breġ, do ec ina ċotlud i tiġ Maelseċlainn iar n-ol. Leis dorata na Gaill fon araṫar 7 da Ġall ic foirsed ar a tiaġaiḃ na n-diaiġ. Maidm for firu Miḋe icon Draiġnen, ria n-Galliab 7 Laiġniḃ; c. l. occisi sunt im ḟlann mac Maelsech-lainn. Slogad la Brian co hAṫ in ċairtinn, ubi per tres menses [remansit]. Creċ mór la Murchad

[1] *Finnfaidhech.*—See note [10], p. 465.

[2] *Bachal-Patraic.*—i.e. St. Patrick's *baculum*, crozier, or *crosstafe*, as the word *bachal* is rendered in Clar. 49.

[3] *By the advice.* — a forgaire. Wrongly translated "in the contention," in Clar. 49. Forgaire is put for *hortatio* in the old St. Gall Codex (fol. 161*b*). See Stokes's *Irish Glosses*, p. 146.

[4] *Maelmuire.*—Abbot, or Bishop, of Armagh at the time.

[5] *Cairpre.*—i.e. Cairpre Ua Ciardha, now represented by the barony of Carbury, in the north of the co. Kildare.

[6] *Gailenga.* — Otherwise called Gailenga-mora. Now the barony of Morgallion, in the north of the county of Meath.

[7] *Were.*—atte (for atte, "they were"), A. B.

[8] *Ed.*—There is apparently some error here. The name of the place in the *Ann. Four Mast.*, is "Maighen-attaed." But this has not been identified.

[9] *Tiaga.* — *Tiaga* is the plural of *tiag*, a satchel or bag, and the same as Lat. *theca.* It may possibly be a loan word from the Latin. The entry is not very intelligible. The writer may have intended to say that each plough was drawn by Foreigners, whilst two Foreigners in sacks were drawn after the plough, to do the work of a harrow. The Translator in Clar. 49 states that "the Gentiles" were made to "plough by theire bodies, and two of them by their

revenge of the profanation of the 'Finnfaidhech'[1] of Patrick, and of the breaking of Bachal-Patraic,[2] by the advice[3] of Maelmuire[4] and of Brian. A great depredation by Ualgarg Ua Ciardha, King of Cairpre,[5] and the son of Niall Ua Ruairc, in Gailenga;[6] but a few good men of Maelsechlainn's household, who were after drinking then and were[7] intoxicated, met them and gave them battle through pride, where Donnchad son of Donnchad Finn, royal heir of Temhair, and Cernachan son of Flann, King of Luighne, and Senan Ua Leochain, King of Gailenga, and many others, were slain. Maelsechlainn afterwards overtook them, when the preys were left with him, and Ualgarg Ua Ciardha, King of Cairpre, and several others, were slain by him. A hosting by Flaithbertach, King of Ailech, as far as Ed[8] by the side of Cenannas, when Maelsechlainn abandoned the hill to him. Gilla-Mochonna son of Fogartach, King of the south of Bregha, died in his sleep in Maelsechlainn's house, after drinking. By him the Foreigners were yoked to the plough, and two Foreigners harrowing from their *tiaga*[9] after them. A victory over the men of Midhe, at the Draighnen,[10] by Foreigners and Leinstermen; 150 persons were killed, including Flann son of Maelsechlainn. A hosting by Brian to Ath-in-chairthinn,[11] where he remained three months.[12] A great depredation

tayles harrowing after them." O'Conor's attempt at rendering this entry is even worse.

[10] *Draighnen.* — The "thorny place." Now Drinan in the parish of Kinsaley, barony of Coolock, co. Dublin. This battle is referred to in a stanza (not in B.), written in the lower margin of fol. 54*b* in A., as follows:—

Nimalotar luan for fecht,
Fir Midhe fri forimthecht;
Batar failti Gaill ro clos,
Iccon draighnen don toros.

"Not well went they on Monday, on an expedition—
The men of Meath—towards advancing;
The Foreigners, it was heard, were glad
At the Drinan, because of the trip."

[11] *Ath-in-chairthinn.*—The "ford of the mountain ash" (or "quicken-tree"). Strangely translated "Vadum Officinæ ferrariæ" by O'Conor. Not identified.

[12] *Three months.*—The original of this clause is rather imperfectly given

mac Briain illaignib, co ro oirc in tir co Gleann da loċa 7 co Cill Maighnenn, 7 co ro loisc in tir uile, 7 co ruc gabala móra 7 brait diaṙṁiṫe. Ar Gall la Caṫal mac nDonnchada mic Duiḃdabairenn, du itorċair Amlaiḃ mac Sitriuc .i. mac rig Gall, 7 Maṫgamain mac Duibgilla mic Amlaim, 7 ceteri. Maidm for Connaċta ria nUa Maeldoraiḃ, du itorċair Domnall mac Caṫail (.i. in catt), ridamna Connacht. Muircertaċ mac Aeḋa .h. Neill do marbad do dal Riatai.
Fol. 55aa. Daingin imḋa do denaṁ la Brian .i. Caṫair Cinn coraḋ 7 Inis gaill duiḃ, 7 Inis loċa Sainglenn. Laigin 7 Gaill do ċocaḋ fri Brian, 7 forbais fer Muman 7 Brian ic sleib Mairci co ro innrisett Laiġniu co hAṫ cliaṫ. [Flann mac]Mailseċlainn do marbad do Gallaiḃ Aṫa cliaṫ.

Kt. Ianair. Anno domini M.° x.° iii.°

Kt. Ianair. iii. feria, l.a xx. iii. Anno domini M.° x.° iiii.° Hic est annus octauus cicli decinouinalis, 7 hic est .ccccc. 7 .lxxxii. annus ab aduentu sancti Patricii ad babtisandos Scotos. Feil Grigoir ria n-init 7 minċaisc i samraḋ isin bliadainsi, quod non auditum est ab antiquis temporibus. Slogud la Brian mac Cenneitiġ mic Lorcain, la riġ nErend, 7

in A. and B., which have merely b/u ꝑ mer (rectè mer) m̄ser. The Translator in Clar. 49 writes "where he remayned for three months."

[1] *Cill-Maighnenn.* — Kilmainham, near Dublin.

[2] *Cathal.*—He was King of Des-Mumha, or Desmond. The *Four Masters* state that the slaughter above referred to was inflicted after the burning of Corcach (Cork) by the Foreigners.

[3] *Mathgamain.* — *Dubhgilla.* See Todd's *War of the Gaedhil*, &c., pp. 278, 291, where the name Dubhgilla is printed "Dubhgall," and "Dubhagill."

[4] *Cathair - Cinn - coradh.* — The "stone fort" of Cenn-coradh (or Kincora), at Killaloe.

[5] *Inis-gaill-duibh.*—The "Island of the black Foreigner." Not identified. O'Donovan thought that it was another name for the King's Island, at Limerick.

[6] *Inis-locha-Sainglenn.*—The "Island of Loch-Sainglenn." Loch-Sainglenn is not now known; but the name seems partly preserved in that of Singland, a large townland in the vicinity of Limerick. See Todd's *War of the Gaedhil*, &c., Introd., cxxi., note[3].

by Murchadh, son of Brian, in Leinster, when he plundered the land to Glenn-da-locha and Cill-Maighnenn,[1] and burned the whole country, and carried off great spoils and captives innumerable. A slaughter of Foreigners by Cathal,[2] son of Donnchad, son of Dubhdabairenn, in which fell Amlaibh son of Sitriuc, *i.e.* son of the King of the Foreigners, and Mathgamain,[3] son of Dubhgilla,[3] son of Amlaibh, and others. A victory over the Connaughtmen by Ua Maeldoraidh, in which fell Domnall son of Cathal (*i.e.* the Cat), royal heir of Connaught. Muirchertach, son of Aedh Ua Neill, was slain by the Dal-Riata. Numerous fortresses were constructed by Brian, viz., Cathair-Cinn-coradh,[4] and Inis-gaill-duibh,[5] and Inis-locha-Sainglenn.[6] The Leinstermen and Foreigners made war against Brian; and the Munstermen and Brian encamped at Sliabh-Mairci, and plundered Leinster to Ath-cliath. [Flann,[7] son of] Maelsechlainn was slain by the Foreigners of Ath-cliath.

Kal. Jan. A.D. 1013. [1013.]

Kal. Jan. Frid.; m. 26. A.D. 1014. This is the eighth year of the Cycle of Nineteen; and this is the 582nd year since the coming of St. Patrick to baptise the Scoti. The festival of Gregory[8] was before Shrovetide, and Little Easter[9] in summer, in this year; which had not been heard of from ancient times. A hosting by Brian, son of Cenneidigh, son of Lorcan, King of Ireland, and by Maelsechlainn son [1014.]

---

[7] *Flann.*—This name having been omitted in the orig. MSS., evidently through an oversight, has been supplied on the authority of the *Chron. Scotorum*, and *Ann. Four Mast.* The name of Maelsechlainn, Flann's father, is written in the genit. form, Mailsechlainn in A. and B., which shows that some word or name had been omitted before it. The Translator in Clar. 49 writes "Flann, son of Maelseehlainn, by Genties of Dublin;" which would tend to prove that the original from which he made his version was neither of the MSS. A. and B.

[8] *Festival of Gregory;* i.e. the 12th of March.

[9] *Little Easter;* i.e. Low Sunday, or the first Sunday after Easter. See the *Chron. Scotorum* (ed. Hennessy), p. 250, note [2].

la Maelseċlainn mac Domnaill, la riġ Teṁraċ, co h-Aṫ cliaṫ. Laiġin uile do leir i tinol ar a cinn 7 Gaill Aṫa cliaṫ, 7 a coimlin do Ġallaiḃ Loċlainn leó .i. x.c. luireċ. Gniṫir caṫ croḋa etorra do na frith innsamail. Maiḋir iarum for Gallu 7 for Laiġniu i tosaiġ co rus dileġait uile do leir, in quo bello cecidit ex adversa caterua Gallorum, Maelmorḋa mac Murchada ri Laigen, 7 Domnall mac Fergaile rí na Fortuaṫ. Cecidit uero a Gallis Dubġall mac Amlaim, Siuċraiḋ mac Lodhuir iarla Innsi orcc, 7 Gilla Ciarain mac Gluniairnn, rigdomna Gall, 7 Oittir dub 7 Suartgair, 7 Donnchad .h. Eruilb, 7 Grifine, 7 Luimne, 7 Amlaim mac Laġmainn, 7 Brotor (qui occidit Brian), .i. toiseċ na loingsi Loċlannaiġi, 7 ui. mile itir marbad 7 baṫad. Dorochair imorro a frithguin o Gaiḋelaiḃ .i. Brian mac Cenneitiġ, ardrí Gaiḋel Erenn 7 Gall 7 Bretan, August iartair tuaisceirt Eorpa uile, 7 a mac .i. Murchad, 7 a macsiḋe .i. Toirrdelbach mac Murchada, 7 Conaing
Fol. 55ab. mac Duinnċuan mic Cenneitiġ, rigdomna Muman, 7 Moṫla mac Domnaill mic Ḟaelain, ri na n-Deisi Muman, Eoċo mac Dunaḋaiġ, 7 Niall .h. Cuinn, 7

[1] *Battle.*—The famous battle of Clontarf, which was fought on Good Friday, in the year 1014; a very curious account of which is contained in the Annals of Loch-Cé. But the fullest description of the battle is given in Todd's ed. of the *War of the Gaedhil with the Gaill*, pp. 151–211. See the Introd. to the work, pp. xxvi.–xxvii., and clxvii., *seq.* O'Donovan has illustrated the narrative of the battle, given by the *Four Masters* (at 1013=1014), with many useful notes.

[2] *Fortuatha.*—This name signifies "border territories." See note [7], p. 157 *supra*, and O'Donovan's ed. of *Leabhar na g-ceart*, 207, note d, where for Domnall, son of Fergal, he wrongly prints Domhnall Mac Faelainn.

[3] *Insi-Orc.*—The Orkney Islands.

[4] *Brian.*—The original of this clause is interlined in A. and B. in *man. orig.*

[5] *Donncuan.* — Brother of King Brian.

[6] *Mothla.*—This Mothla was the first person who used the surname "O'Faelain," i.e. "*nepos* Faelani," (now O'Phelan, and Phelan without the O'). The surname was derived from his grandfather, Faelan, the son of Cormac, whose obit is noticed above at the year 965.

of Domnall, King of Temhair, to Ath-cliath. All the Leinstermen were assembled before them, and the Foreigners of Ath-cliath, and an equal number of the Foreigners of Lochlann along with them, viz., 1,000 mail-clad men. A valorous battle[1] was fought between them, for which no likeness has been found. The Foreigners and the Leinstermen were defeated at first, however, so that they were entirely annihilated. In this battle there fell of the hostile band of the Foreigners, Maelmordha son of Murchad, King of Leinster, and Domnall son of Fergal, King of the Fortuatha.[2] But of the Foreigners there fell Dubhgall son of Amlaimh; Siucraidh son of Lodur, Earl of Insi-Orc,[3] and Gillaciarain son of Gluniairnn, royal heir of the Fereigners, and Oittir Dubh, and Suartgair, and Donnchad grandson of Erulb, and Grisine, and Luimne, and Amlaimh son of Lagmann, and Brotor (who slew Brian),[4] *i.e.*, chieftain of the Danish fleet, and 6,000 persons, between killing and drowning. There fell of the Gaedhil, in the mutual wounding, Brian son of Cenneidigh, arch-king of the Gaedhil of Ireland, and of the Foreigners and Britons, the Augustus of all the north-west of Europe, and his son, *i.e.* Murchad, and his [Murchad's] son, *i.e.* Toirdhelbhach, and Conaing, son of Donncuan,[5] son of Cenneidigh, royal heir of Munster, and Mothla,[6] son of Domnall, son of Faelan, King of the Deisi-Mumhan,[7] Eocho son of Dunadhach,[8] and Niall Ua

[7] *Deisi-Mumhan.*—" Deisi of Munster." A powerful tribe descended from Fiacha Suighde, eldest brother of Conn of the Hundred battles, originally seated in the district to the south of Tara known as *Deisi-Temrach*, now forming the baronies of Upper and Lower Deece, co. Meath. But having been expelled from this territory by King Cormac Mac Airt, in the 3rd century, they moved southward, and, after various adventures, succeeded in subduing that part of Munster comprising nearly the whole of the present county of Waterford, with (subsequently) adjacent parts of the co. Tipperary. The name of " Deisi " is still preserved in the barony names Decies Within, and Decies Without, co. Waterford. See O'Flaherty's Ogygia, part III., ch. 69.

[8] *Dunadhach.*—Probably the Dunadhach, son of Diarmaid, lord of

[Cuduiligh] mac Cennetiġ, tri coimṫe Briain; da riġ .h. Maine .h. Ceallaiġ, 7 Maelruanaiġ .h. hEiḋinn ri Aiḋne, 7 Geiḃinnaċ .h. Dubagain ri Fer maiġi, 7 Mac Beaṫaḋ mac Muiredaiġ cloin ri Ciarraiḋe luaċra, 7 Domnall mac Diarmada ri Corco Baiscind, 7 Scannlan mac Caṫail, rí Eoganachta loċa Lein, 7 Domnall mac Eiṁinn mic Cainniġ, mor ṁaer Mair i n-Albain, 7 alii multi nobiles. Luiḋ tra Maelmuire (.i. mac Eochaḋa), comarba Patraic, co sruitiḃ 7 co minnaiḃ, connice Sord Coluim cille, co tuc as corp Briain riġ Erend, 7 corp Murchada a mic, 7 cenn Conaing, 7 cenn Moṫlai, co ro aḋnacht i n-Ard maċa i n-ailaiḋ nuí. Di aiḋċi ḋec imorro do ṡaṁaḋ Patraic ic aire na corp, propter honorem regis positi. Dunlang mac Tuaṫail, ri Laiġen, do éc. Cat etir Cian mac Mailmuaiḋ 7 Domnall mac Duiḃdabairenn, co torċair ann Cian 7 Caṫal 7 Roġallaċ, tri meic Mailmuaiḋ, 7 ár impu. Caṫal mac Domnaill,

Corco-Baiseinn (in the co. Clare), whose death is recorded in the *Ann. Four Mast.*, at the year 992.

[1] *Tadhg Ua Cellaigh.*—This entry is most corruptly given in A. and B., in which the text is da riġ .h. Maine .h. Ceallaiġ, "two Kings of Ui-Maine, Ui-Ceallaigh." But there were not two Kings of Hy-many at the time. It would appear that the first word of the entry, da, (before which a blank has been left in A. and B.), is a mistake for Tadg, and that the name .h. Ceallaiġ has been wrongly transposed. Tadhg Ua Cellaigh (or O'Kelly) is mentioned in all other Irish Chronicles as having fallen in the battle of Clontarf, fighting on the side of Brian; for which reason he is styled in the O'Kelly pedigrees *Tadhg catha Briain*, i.e. "Tadhg of the battle of Brian." See O'Donovan's *Hy-Many*, p. 99.

[2] *Aidhne.*—A territory co-extensive with the diocese of Kilmaeduagh, in the co. Galway. The name Ua hEidhinn is now generally written "Hynes."

[3] *Ua Dubhagain.* — Now written O'Duggan" (or "Duggan," without the O').

[4] *Fer-Maighe.*—"Men of the Plain." Now represented by the barony of Fermoy, co. Cork. Fern maige, A.

[5] *Ciarraidhe-luachra.*—"Ciarraidhe of the Rushes." The northern portion of the present county Kerry, comprising the baronies of Trughenacmy, Clanmorris, and Iraghticonnor, divided from the counties of Cork and Limerick by the range of hills called Sliabh-luachra.

[6] *Corco-Baiscinn.* —This was the tribe-name of the descendants of Cairbre Baschaoin; and also the name of their territory, which anciently com-

Cuinn, and [Cuduiligh] son of Cenneidigh—Brian's three companions; Tadgh Ua Cellaigh,[1] King of Ui-Maine; and Maelruanaidh Ua hEidhinn, King of Aidhne;[2] and Geibhennach Ua Dubhagain,[3] King of Fera-Maighe[4]; and Mac-Beathadh, son of Muiredach Cloen, King of Ciarraidhe-luachra,[5] and Domnall, son of Diarmaid, King of Corca-Baiscinn;[6] and Scannlan son of Cathal, King of the Eoghanacht of Loch-Lein; and Domnall, son of Emhin, son of Cainnech, great steward of Mar in Alba, and a great many other nobles. Maelmuire (son of Eochaidh[7]), comarb of Patrick, went, moreover, with seniors and with relics to Sord-Choluim-Cille, and carried thence the body of Brian, King of Ireland, and the body of his son Murchad, and the head of Conaing,[8] and the head of Mothla, and interred them in Ard-Macha, in a new tomb. Twelve nights, moreover, were the congregation of Patrick waking the bodies, in honour of the dead king. Dunlang, son of Tuathal, King of Leinster, died. A battle between Cian,[9] son of Maelmhuaidh, and Domnall[10] son of Dubhdabairenn, in which Cian, and Cathal, and Raghallach—three sons of Maelmhuaidh, were killed, and a slaughter about them. Cathal, son of

---

prised the present baronies of Clonderalaw, Moyarta, and Ibrickan, in the west of the county of Clare. O'Donovan states that the Domnall referred to in this entry was the ancestor of the family of O'Domhnaill, or O'Donnell, of Clonderalaw. See *Ann. Four Mast.*, A.D. 1013, note q.

[7] *Son of Eochaidh.*—The original of this clause is added by way of gloss in A. and B. In the oldest Irish list of the comarbs of Patrick (i.e. bishops or abbots of Armagh), namely, that contained in the *Book of Leinster*, p. 42, Maelmuire is described as "son of Eochacan."

[8] *Conaing.*—Son of Donncuan, who was brother of Brian Borumha. See note [5], p. 532.

[9] *Cian.*—Ancestor of the O'Mahonys of Ui-Echach (or Iveagh) of Munster, now represented by the O'Mahonys of Cork and Kerry, amongst whom the Christian name Cian (or Kean) is still a favourite name.

[10] *Domnall.*—He was the ancestor of an old and extinct branch of the O'Donoghoe family, the head of which was called O'Donoghoe Mór, and of the branch known as the "O'Donoghoes of the Glen."

ri .h. nEċdaċ, do marbad la Donnchad mac Briain. Maidm ria Taḋg mac Briain for Donnchad mac Briain, co fargbad Ruaidri .h. Donnacan ri Araḋ. Sluagad la .h. Mailoraiḋ 7 la .h. Ruairgg, i maġ Nai, coro marbsat Domnall mac Caṫail, 7 gur innriset in maġ, 7 co rucsat a n-giallu Connaċt, licet non in eadem uice. Maidm for dal n-Araide ria n-Ultaiḃ, ubi multi occisi sunt. Flaiṫbertaċ mac Domnaill, comarba Ciarain 7 Finnen, 7 Ronan comarba Feicin, 7 Conn, .h. Diġraiḋ, in Christo dormierunt. At imda tra airrsi na bliadnasa.

Fol. 55ba. Kl. Ianair. uii. f., l. uiii. Anno domini M.° x.° u.° Domnall mac Duiḃdabairenn do ṁarbad la Donnchad mac Briain a caṫ. Flaiṫbertaċ .h. Neill do ṫecht i Miḋe, do coḃair Mailsechlaind. Maelsechlaind iarum for sluaiġeḋ i lLaiġniu, co ro ort Laiġniu, 7 co tuc boroma mor 7 aitire Laigen lais. Niall mac Fergaile mic Conaing a suo genere occisus est. Muircertaċ mac Muireḋaiġ .h. Neill occisus est o Uib Tuirtre. Donnchad .h. Goaiġ, ri Ciannaċt, do marbad o ċeneol Eogain. Muircertaċ .h. Lorcain airchinneċ

---

[1] *Ui-Echach.* — "Descendants of Echaidh." The tribe-name of the O'Mahonys of Munster, derived from Echaidh, son of Cas, son of Corc Mac Luighdech, King of Ireland in the 5th century. See note [9], p. 535.

[2] *Aradh.*—Also called Aradh-tire and Duharra (Duthaidh-Aradh), now forming part of the barony of Owney and Arra, co. Tipperary.

[3] *Magh-nAi.*—A large and fertile plain in the centre of the present county of Roscommon, lying between the towns of Elphin and Roscommon, Castlereagh and Strokestown. It was otherwise called *Machaire Chonnacht.* The limits of Magh-nAi, are described from local tradition, by O'Donovan, in a note to the *Ann. Four Mast.*, A.D. 1189, note h.

[4] *Although not on that occasion.*—O'Conor erroneously renders the original, licet non in eadem uice, by "prope centum numero, in eadem vice.". The explanation of this apparent enigma is furnished by an entry under the year 1012, recording the defeat of the Connaughtmen by Ua Maeldoraidh, and the killing of Domnall son of Cathal, royal heir of Connaught. See *Chron. Scotorum* (ed. Hennessy), p. 250, note [1].

[5] *Comarb of Ciaran and Finnen*; i.e. abbot of Clonmacnoise and Clonard.

Domnall, King of Ui-Echach,[1] was slain by Donnchad son of Brian. A victory by Tadhg, son of Brian, over Donnchad, son of Brian, in which Ruaidhri Ua Donnacain, King of Aradh,[2] was slain. A hosting by Ua Maeldoraidh and Ua Ruairc into Magh-nAi,[3] when they killed Domnall, son of Cathal, and ravaged the plain; and they carried off the hostages of Connaught, although not on that occasion.[4] A victory over the Dal-Araidhe by the Ulidians, when a great many were slain. Flaithbertach son of Domnall, comarb of Ciaran[5] and Finnen,[5] and Ronan comarb of Fechin,[6] and Conn Ua Digraidh,[7] 'fell asleep' in Christ. Numerous, truly, are the events of this year.

Kal. Jan. Saturd.; m. 7.[8] A.D. 1015. Domnall, son of Dubhdabairenn, was killed by Donnchad, son of Brian, in battle. Flaithbertach Ua Neill came into Midhe, to aid Maelsechlainn. Maelsechlainn went afterwards on a hosting into Leinster, when he plundered the Leinstermen; and he brought away a great prey of cattle, and the hostages of Leinster. Niall, son of Fergal,[9] son of Conaing, was slain by his own people. Muircertach, son of Muiredach Ua Neill, was slain by the Ui-Tuirtre. Donnchad Ua Goaigh,[10] King of Cianachta,[11] was killed by Cinel-Eoghain. Muirchertach Ua Lorcain, herenagh of Lothra; Cernach [1015.]

See the final entry under the next year, where this entry is repeated, but in a very inaccurate form.

[6] *Comarb of Fechin;* i.e. abbot of Fobhar (Fore), co. Westmeath.

[7] *Conn Ua Digraidh.*—In the *Ann. Four Mast.* (A.D. 1013=1014), Conn Ua Digraidhe is stated to have been *comarb*, or successor, of Caeimhghin (St. Kevin); i.e. abbot of Glendalough. His name does not appear in Archdall's inaccurate list of the abbots of Glendalough.

[8] *m. 7.*—The age of the moon is written .1111. (4) in A. and B., which is obviously a mistake for u11., it not being always easy to distinguish between the Roman numerals u. (5) and 11. (2.)

[9] *Fergal*—Apparently the "Fergal son of Conaing," lord of Ailech, whose obit is given in the *Ann. Four Mast.* at A.D. 1000.

[10] *Donnchad Ua Goaigh.*—According to O'Donovan, this name would be Anglicised "Donough O'Goey," or "Denis Gough." *Ann. Four Mast.*, 1014, note g.

[11] *Cianachta.* — The Cianachta of Glenn-gcimhin. Now represented by the barony of Keenaght, co. Londonderry.

Loṫra, Cernaċ mac Caṫusaiġ airchinnech Duin Leṫ-glaisi, Niall mac Dercain airchinnech Mungairde, Donngal .h. Caintein airchinnech Tire da ġlas, in Christo dormierunt. Aeḋ .h. Ruairc, ri Breifne, do marbad la Taḋg, la rig Connacht, dolose .i. ag Loċ Neill i maiġ Ai, do ḟaesaṁ na baċla Isu, conid eḋ sin tall riġi ar a ḟil cenmoṫa Aeḋ a mac amain. Flaiṫbertaċ mac Domnaill comarba Ciarain 7 Finnein 7 Ċronain 7 Ḟeiċin, quieuit.

Kl. Ianair. i. f., l. x.uiii. Anno domini M.° x.° ui.° Flannacan mac Conaing, fosairċinneċ Arda Maċa, 7 Muirġis airċinneċ Lis oeiġeḋ, in Christo dormierunt. Eiṫne ingen .h. Suairt, comarba Brigte, Diarmait .h. Mailtelċa comarba Comġaill, quieuerunt. Macliag ard ollaṁ Erenn mortuus est. Caṫ etir Ultu 7 Dal n-Araide, co remid for Dal n-Araide. Do ḟuit ann Domnall .h. Loingsiġ, ri Dal n-Araide, 7 Niall mac Duibṫuinne, 7 Concobar .h. Domnallan, ri .h. Tuirtri, 7 alii multi. Niall mac Eochada ba coscraċ. Mac Muiredaiġ mic Flaind, ri fer Muiġi Iṫa, a suis occisus est. Donncuan mac Dunlaing, ri Laiġen, 7

[1] *Mungairid.*—Mungret, about three miles to the south of Limerick city.

[2] *Tir-da-glas.* — Now Terryglass, barony of Lower Ormond, county of Tipperary.

[3] *Tadhg.*—Better known to students of Irish history as Tadhg-an-eich-gil, or "Tadhg of the white steed." He was the son of Cathal, son of Conchobar (son of Tadhg), from whom the hereditary surname of O'Conchobhair or O'Conor) has been derived, and whose obit is noticed above at the year 972. The *Four Mast.* state (1014=1015) that Tadhg killed Aedh, in revenge for his brother, Domnall son of Cathal, whose death is recorded under the preceding year.

[4] *Loch-Neill.*—There is no lake now known by this name in Magh-Ai, or the Plain of Connaught.

[5] *Bachal-Isu.*—The "Staff or (Crozier) of Jesus." The so-called 'translator' of a portion of this Chronicle, contained in the MS. Clar. 49, Brit. Museum, renders do ḟaesaṁ na baċla Isu by "rescuing the crostaffe of Jesus," which is wrong; the word faesaṁ (regarded by the translator as meaning "rescuing") signifying "protection." See O'Don. *Supplt. to O'Reilly's* Dict., v. foesaṁ. For some curious information regarding the Bachal-Isu, see O'Curry's *MS. Materials*, App., p. 600, *sq.*

[6] *Cronan and Fechin.* — This is evidently an inaccurate repetition of the last entry under the year 1014;

son of Cathasach, herenagh of Dun-lethglaise; Niall son of Dercan, herenagh of Mungairid,[1] [and] Donngal Ua Caintéin, herenagh of Tir-da-glas,[2] 'fell asleep' in Christ. Aedh Ua Ruairc, King of Breifni, was treacherously killed by Tadhg,[3] King of Connaught, viz., at Loch-Neill,[4] in Magh-Ai, when under the protection of the Bachal-Isu;[5] and it was this [deed] that cut off sovereignty from his race, excepting only his son Aedh. Flaithbertach son of Domnall, comarb of Ciaran and Finnen, and of Cronan and Fechin,[6] rested.

Kal. Jan. Sund.; m. 18. A.D. 1016. Flannacan son of Conaing, vice-herenagh of Ard-Macha, and Muirghes, herenagh of Lis-oiged,[7] 'fell asleep' in Christ. Eithne, daughter of Ua Suairt, comarb of Brigit,[8] [and] Diarmait Ua Mailtelcha, comarb of Comgall,[9] rested. Mac Liag,[10] chief poet of Ireland, died. A battle between the Ulidians and the Dal-Araidhe, when the Dal-Araidhe were defeated. There fell there Domnall Ua Loingsigh,[11] King of Dal-Araidhe, and Niall son of Dubhtuinne, and Conchobar Ua Domnallain, King of Ui-Tuirtre, and many[12] others. Niall son of Eochaidh, was victorious. The son of Muiredach son of Flann, King of Magh-Itha, was slain by his own people. Donncuan, son of Dunlang, [1016.]

---

where, instead of "[comarb] of Cronan and Fechin," the Chronicler correctly says "Ronan, comarb of Fechin." This entry is added in a later hand in A.

[7] *Lis-oiged.*—"Fort of the Guests." The name of a church at Armagh. Mentioned above at the year 1003.

[8] *Comarb of Brigit;* i.e. abbess of Kildare.

[9] *Comarb of Comgall;* i.e. abbot of Bangor, co. Down.

[10] *Mac Liag.*—Called Muirchertach Mac Liag in the *Chron. Scotorum*, A.D. 1014, and *Ann. Four Mast*, A.D. 1015. Said to have been the secretary of King Brian Borumha, a life of whom he is alleged to have written. For some account of Mac Liag's poetical writings, see O'Reilly's *Irish Writers*, pp. 70–72; Hardiman's Irish Minstrelsy, Vol. II., p. 361, and O'Curry's *Manners and Customs*, Vol. II., pp. 99, 116–143, and Vol. III., p. 153.

[11] *Ui Loingsigh.* — "Grandson (or descendant) of Loingsech." The *Four Masters* have "Mac Loingsigh" ("son of Loingsech"). The *Chron. Scotorum* and *Annals of Loch Cé* agree with the present chronicle.

[12] *Many*—mulτι, omitted in B.

Taḋg .h. Riain ri .h. Drona, do marbad la Donnchad mac Gillapatraic, for lar Leiṫglinne. Dun Leṫglaisi do uile-loscaḋ. Cluain mic Nois 7 Cluain ferta 7 Cenannus do loscaḋ. Airbertaċ mac Coisidobrain, airċinneċ Rois ailiṫir, do ec. Siṫ i n-Erinn.

Fol. 55bb. Kl. Ianair. iii. f., l. xx. uiii. Anno domini M.° x.° iiii.° Oengus mac Carraiġ ċalma, riġdomna Teṁraċ, mortuus est. Ferġal mac Domnaill mic Concoḃair, riġdomna Ailiġ, do marbad o cenel Eogain fein. Flann .h. Beicce, ri .h. Meiṫ, a suis occisus est. Cormac mac Lorcan, ri .h. nEċdaċ, do marbad o Uib Trena. Donnchad mac Donnchada .h. Conġalaiġ, riġdomna Erenn, a suis occisus est. Muireḋaċ .h. Duiḃeoin, ri .h. mac Cuais Breġ, do marbad la Flaiṫbertaċ .h. Neill. Ar Gall 7 Laigen i n-ḟodbai la Maelseċlainn. Oengus mac Flaind, airċinneċ Lainne Lere, Cormac .h. Mailmiḋe, airchinneċ Droma raṫe, mortui sunt. Gillacrist .h. Lorcain, ri Caille Follaṁain, do marbad i Cenannus. Conn, mac Concobair mic Eicneċain, mortuus est. Glenn da Loċa do loscaḋ ex maiore parte.

Kl. Ianair. .iiii. f., l. x. Anno domini M.° x.° iiii.° Gormġal in Ard ailean, prim anmċara Erenn, in Christo

---

[1] *Ui-Drona.*—Now the barony of Idrone, co. Carlow.

[2] *Ros-ailithir.*—Now Roscarbery, in the county of Cork.

[3] *Carrach-calma.*—A nickname for Donnchadh Ua Maelsechlainn, whose death is entered in the *Chron. Scotorum* at the year 967.

[4] *Ui-Echach*; i.e. Ui-Echach-Cobha, or Iveagh, in the county of Down; a territory comprising the present baronies of Upper and Lower Iveagh. The name of Cormac does not occur in the list of Kings of Ui-Echach published in Reeves's *Down and Connor*, p. 349, sq.

[5] *Ui-Trena.* — "Descendants of Trian." A sept of the Airghialla, situated in the present county of Armagh; but the exact limits of their territory have not been identified.

[6] *Ua-Duibheoin.*—.h. duibeoin, A.

[7] *Ui-Mic-Uais of Bregha.*—A tribe descended from Colla *Uais*, one of the "Three Collas," progenitors of the Airghialla, anciently seated in Magh-Bregh, in the present county of Meath. See O'Donovan's ed. of *Ann. Four Mast.*, A.D. 837, note u.

[8] *Odba.*—Corruptly written "Fodbai" (dat. form of "Fodba"), in A. B. According to O'Donovan, Odba

King of Leinster, and Tadhg Ua Riain, King of Ui-Drona,[1] were slain by Donnchad, son of Gilla-Patraic, in the middle of Leth-glenn. Dunlethglaise was all burned. Cluain-mic-Nois and Cluain-ferta, and Cenannas, were burned. Airbhertach, son of Cosdobrain, herenagh of Ros-ailithir,[2] died. Peace in Ireland.

Kal. Jan. Tuesd.; m. 28. A.D. 1017. Oenghus, son of Carrach-calma,[3] royal heir of Temhair, died. Ferghal son of Domnall, son of Conchobhar, royal heir of Ailech, was slain by the Cinel-Eoghain themselves. Flann Ua Beicce, King of Ui-Meith, was slain by his own people. Cormac, son of Lorcan, King of Ui-Echach,[4] was killed by the Ui-Trena.[5] Donnchad, son of Donnchad Ua Conghalaigh, royal heir of Ireland, was killed by his own people. Muiredhach Ua Duibheoin,[6] King of Ui-Mic-Uais of Bregha,[7] was killed by Flaithbertach Ua Neill. A slaughter of Foreigners and Leinstermen in Odba,[8] by Maelsechlainn. Oengus son of Flann, herenagh of Lann-leire,[9] Cormac Ua Mailmidhe, herenagh of Druim-rathe,[10] died. Gilla-Christ Ua Lorcain, King of Caille-Follamhain, was killed in Cenannas. Conn son of Conchobar, son of Eicnechan, died. Glenn-da-locha was burned for the most part. [1017.]

Kal. Jan. Wednesd.; m. 10. A.D. 1018. Gormghal of Ard-ailen,[11] chief soul-friend of Ireland, rested in [1018.]

(or Odhbha, as it is written in more modern texts), was the ancient name of a mound near Navan, in the county of Meath. *Ann. Four M.*, A.D. 837, note x.

[9] *Lann-leire.*—See note [15], p. 205 *supra*.

[10] *Druim-rathe.*—This is probably the place now represented by Drum-rat, the name of a parish in the barony of Corran, and county of Sligo. St. Fechin, founder and abbot of the monastery of Ballysodare, in the adjoining barony of Tirerrill, is stated to have founded an abbey here. See Colgan's *AA. Sanctorum*, p. 134.

[11] *Ard-ailen*; i.e. "High Island." An island off the coast of the barony of Ballynahinch, co Galway, where a monastery was erected by St. Fechin, founder of the monasteries of Fore (co. Westmeath), Ballysodare (co. Sligo), and also of Omey Island, which lies between High Island and the mainland. See Ordnance Map

quieuit. Broen mac Maelmordha, ri Laigen, do dallad i n-Ath cliath la Sitriucc mac Amlaim. Maelan, mac Eicnigh .h. Lorcan, ri Galeng 7 tuath Luighne uile, do marbad do Saitnibh. Slogad la Cenel Eogain co Cill Fabricc, co ro marbsat dreimm moir, 7 co fargaibset Gillacrist mac Conaing mic Congalaigh .i. muire clainne Sinaigh. Oentrubh do argain do Feraibh Manach. Domnall .h. Caindelbain, ri Loegaire, 7 Cairmidhe rechtaire Maelsechlainn, do marbad la Firu Cell 7 Eile a tarrucht creiche. Ind retlu mongach do arthrugad in hoc anno fri ré coicthighis i n-aimsir foghamair. Gillacolum mac Muiredaigh .h. Mailtrea, 7 Aedh .h. Erudhain, rí .h. mBresail Macha, mortui sunt.

Kl. Ianair. .ii. f.; l. xxi. Anno domini M.° x.° ix.° Alene mac Osene, ri Mughdorn, 7 Ossene .h. Cadasaigh, ri na Saitne, do marbad la Gailengu. Ceall dara uile

---

of Galway, sheet 21. Colgan (*Acta Sanctorum*, p. 715) mistook Ard-ailen for one of the Arran Islands in Galway Bay; and is followed by Archdall (*Monasticon*, p. 272).

[1] *Broen.*—Properly written Bran in the MS. Clar. 49. From him the powerful family of Ua Brain (now written O'Byrne, and Byrne) of Leinster derive their hereditary surname.

[2] *Ua Lorcain.*—In the Annals of *Tigernach* and the *Four Masters*, the name is written "Ua Leochain," which is undoubtedly the proper form. The name "Ua Leochain" has been corrupted to "Loughan," and is now usually Anglicised "Duck" in the counties of Kildare and Meath; for the reason that *loughan* was regarded as the same as *lachan* the genit. of *lacha*, a *duck*.

[3] *Saithni.*—A tribe occupying a territory in the north of the present county of Dublin, co-extensive with the barony of Balrothery West. The family name was O'Cathasaigh (*i.e.* O'Casey, or Casey). See Dr. Reeves's valuable note regarding the limits of the territory, and its ancient possessors, in the Appendix to O'Donovan's ed. of O'Dugan's Topogr. Poem, note [20]. The Saithni were a branch of the Cianachta-Bregh, a Meath tribe, and may have given name to the townland and parish of Dunsany (Dun-Saithni ?), in the adjoining barony of Skreen, co. Meath.

[4] *Oentrubh.*—Antrim, in the county of Antrim.

[5] *Fera-Manach.*—The tribe-name of the people who inhabited the territory now known as the county of Fermanagh.

[6] *Fera-Cell.*—This was the name of O'Molloy's country in the King's County, which anciently comprised, besides the barony of Fircal (now known by the name of Eglish), the baronies of Ballycowan and Ballyboy.

Christ. Broen[1] son of Maelmordha, King of Leinster, was blinded in Ath-cliath, by Sitriuc son of Amlaimh. Maelan, son of Eicnech Ua Lorcain,[2] King of Gailenga and all Tuath-Luighne, was killed by the Saithni.[3] A hosting by the Cinel-Eoghain to Cill-Fabrig, when they killed a great number, and lost Gilla-Christ, son of Conaing, son of Congalach, *i.e.* steward of Clann-Sinaigh. Oentrubh[4] was plundered by the Fera-Manach.[5] Domnall Ua Caindelbhain, King of Loeghaire, and Caismidhe, Maelsechlainn's steward, were killed by the Fera-Cell[6] and the Eile,[7] in pursuit of a prey. The 'hairy star'[8] appeared this year, during the space of a fortnight, in Autumn time. Gillacoluim, son of Muiredach Ua Mailtrea, and Aedh Ua Erudhain, King of Ui-Bresail-Macha,[9] died.

Kal. Jan. Thursd.; m. 21. A.D. 1019. Alene, son of Ossene, King of Mughdorna, and Ossene Ua Cathasaigh, King of the Saithni,[10] were killed by the Gailenga. Cill- [1019.]

See O'Donovan's ed. of O'Dugan's Topogr. Poem, App., note [24].

[7] *Eile.*—A powerful tribe, whose name was derived from Eile, descended in the ninth generation, according to the *Book of Leinster* (p. 366, col. 8), from Cian, son of Oilill Olum, King of Munster in the third century. The territory of this comprised the present baronies of Eliogarty and Ikerrin in the county of Tipperary, and the baronies of Ballybrit and Clonlisk, in the King's County. The three most prominent families of this tribe were the O'Meaghers of Ikerin (now apparently represented by Joseph Casimir O'Meagher of Dublin), the O'Fogartys and O'Carrolls.

[8] *Hairy star.* — ɼeɼlu mongač. The appearance of this "hairy star," or comet, is not noticed in any of the other Irish Chronicles, with the exception of the *Annals of Loch-Cé*. See Chambers' *Handbook of Descriptive Astronomy*, p. 408 (3rd ed); the author of which does not seem to have known anything of the care with which the compilers of these Annals noted the occurrence of atmospherical and astronomical phenomena.

[9] *Ui-Bresail-Macha.* — A tribe, (otherwise called Clann-Bresail), descended from Bresal, son of Feidhlim, son of Fiachra Casan, son of Colla-da-chrich. See O'Flaherty's *Ogygia*, part III., chap. 76. The territory of the Clann-Bresail seems to have been co-extensive with the present baronies of O'Neilland East and West, in the county of Armagh.

[10] *Saithni.*—See note [3], last page.

do loscaḋ do ṫeiniḋ diaitt. Doṁnall mac Mail-
Fol. 56aa. seċlainn, comarba Finnen 7 Mocolmog, in Christo quieuit. Ardġar 7 Arċu, meic Mailseċlainn mic Maelruanaid, da rigdamna Ailiġ, a suis occisi sunt. Gillacoeimgin mac [Dunlaing], ridomna Laigen, a suis occisus est. Maṫġamain, mac Conaing mic Duinncuan, ridomna Muman, do ecaiḃ. Flaiṫbertaċ .h. Neill do techt i tir Conaill, co ro ort tir nEnna 7 tir Luġdaċ, Ruaiḋri .h. Ailellan, ri .h. nEċdaċ, do marbad la firu Fernmuiġi. Ro marbṫa, immorro, da mac Ceinneitiġ .i. Conġalaċ 7 Gillamuire, ina diġail foceṫoir. Eirce do ṫabairt do hUiḃ Caissein im Donnchad mac mBriain, co ro tescaḋ a bos dear de. Daimliac Dermaiġi do brisiuḋ la Muircertaċ .h. Carraiġ, for Maelmuaiḋ ri fer Cell, 7 a ṫabairt as ar eigin 7 a marbad iarum.

Kl. Ianair. iii. f., l. ii. Anno domini M.° xx.° Ceall dara cona dairtiġ do loscad. Gleann da laċa uile cona dairtiġiḃ do loscaḋ. Cluain iraird, 7 Cluain mic Nois, 7 Sord Coluim cille, tertia parte, cremate sunt. Flaiṫbertaċ .h. Eochada do ḋallad la Niall mac Eochada. Gillaciarain mac Orene, ri Muġdorna, do marbad do feraiḃ Ross. Maelmuaiḋ mac Orene, rí Muġdorna fri re oen lai, do marbad la .h. mac Uair Breġ. Ard Maċa uile do leir do loscaḋ .i. in

[1] *Comarb of Finnen and Mocholmoc;* i.e. abbot of Moville and Dromore, co. Down.

[2] *Maelsechlainn.*—His death, by poison, is noticed at the year 996 *supra.*

[3] *Their own people.*—In the *Ann. Four Mast.*, Ardghar and Archu are stated to have been slain by the Cinel-Eoghain "themselves."

[4] *Conaing.*—This Conaing, who was the son of Donncuan, brother of Brian Borbumha, was slain in the battle of Clontarf. See under A.D. 1014 *supra.*

[5] *Tir-Enna.*—See "Cinel-Enna," under A.D. 1010 (note [5], p. 524).

[6] *Tir-Lughdach.*—See note [4] p. 524 *supra.*

[7] *Ui-Caisin.*—This was the tribe-name of the MacNamaras of Clare.

[8] *Dermagh.*—Durrow, in the barony of Ballycowan, King's County.

[9] *Ua Carraigh;* i.e. grandson of Carrach [-calma]. See note under A.D. 1017; (note [3], p. 540).

dara was all burned by lightning. Domnall son of Maelsechlainn, comarb of Finnen[1] and Mocholmoc,[1] rested in Christ. Ardghar and Archu, sons of Maelsechlainn[2] son of Maelruanaidh, two royal heirs of Ailech, were slain by their own people.[3] Gillacoemghin, son [of Dunlaing], royal heir of Leinster, was slain by his own people. Mathgamain, son of Conaing,[4] son of Donncuan, royal heir of Munster, died. Flaithbertach Ua Neill came into Tir-Conaill, and plundered Tir-Enna[5] and Tir-Lughdach.[6] Ruaidhri Ua Ailellain, King of Ui-Echach, was killed by the men of Fernmhagh. Two sons of Cennedigh, viz., Conghalach and Gillamuire, were immediately slain, moreover, in revenge of him. An assault was given by the Ui-Caisin[7] to Donnchad son of Brian, so that his right hand was cut off him. The stone church of Dermagh[8] was broken by Muirchertach Ua Carraigh,[9] upon Maelmuaidh, King of Fera-Cell,[10] who was forcibly taken thereout, and afterwards killed.

Kal. Jan. Frid.; m. 2. A.D. 1020. Cill-dara, with its oratory, was burned. Glenn-da-locha, with its oratories, was all burned. Cluain-Iraird, and Cluain-mic-Nois, and Sord-Coluim-cille,[11] the third part, were burned. Flaithbertach Ua hEochadha[12] was blinded by Niall son of Eochaidh. Gillaciarain son of Osene, King of Mughdorna, was killed by the Fera-Rois.[13] Maelmuaidh son of Osene, King of Mughdorna during the space of one day, was killed by the Ui-Mac-Uais[14] of Bregha. Ard-Macha was [1020.]

[10] *Fera-Cell.* — "Viri Cellarum." See note [6], p. 542.

[11] *Sord-Coluim-cille.* — Sord of Colum-cille, now Swords in the county of Dublin.

[12] *Ua hEochadha.* — This name, which signifies "descendant of Eochaidh," i.e. of Eochaidh son of Niall, son of Eochaidh, son of Ardghar, King of Ulidia [ob. 976], is now variously written O'Haughey, Haughey, Hoey, and Howe.

[13] *Fera-Rois.*—See note [4], p. 354, *supra.*

[14] *Ui-Mac-Uais.*—A tribe seated in Magh-Bregh (or the Plain of Bregia), in the east of the present county of Meath, to the S.W. of Tara Hill. There were several tribes called Ui-Mac-Uais, all descended from Colla Uais, (*flor.* A.D. 323), one of the "Three Collas," from whom the powerful northern septs of Airghialla were descended. This tribe is to be

damliac mor cona tuiġi do luaiḋe,[1] 7 in cloicṫeċ cona cloccaiḃ, 7 in Saball 7 in Toai,[2] 7 carbat na n-abad, 7 in tsenċaṫair precupta,[3] i teirt Kl. Iuin,[4] 7 illuan re cingcigis. Maelmuire[5] mac Eochaḋa, comarba Patraic, cenn cleireċ iartair tuaisceirt Eorpa uile, in .xx.° anno principatus sui, i teirt non Iuin,[6] dia h-aine ria cingcigis, in Christo quieuit. Amalgaid i comarbus Patraic, doreir tuaiṫi 7 eclaisi.[7] Finnloeċ mac Ruaiḋri, ri Alban, a suis occisus est. Aeḋ .h. Innrechtaiġ, ri .h. Meiṫ, do marbad do Uib Niallain.

Kl. Ianair, .i. f.; l. xiii. Anno domini M.° xx.° i.°

Vol. 56ab. Maidm ria nUgaire[8] mac Dunluing, ri Laigen, for Sitriuc mac Amlaim, ri Aṫa cliaṫ, oc on Deilgne Mogoroc.[9] Fros cruiṫnechta do ferṫain i n-Osraiġiḃ. Creċ la mac Aeḋa .h. Neill dar Uib Dorṫinn batar i maig itechta, 7 romarbrat in Letderg icon tairrecht contair(ṫetar forgla Airgiall ina diaiġ 7 reime. Uel sic in libro Duiḃdaleiṫi narratur, contairetar .h. Meiṫ, rl.) contairṫetar .h. Meiṫ, 7 Mugdorna, 7 na Saitne 7 fir Fernmuiġi, 7 .h. Dorṫain cona riġaiḃ. Robai dono .h. Ceilecan 7 .h. Lorcan, co n-Uib Bresail

---

distinguished from the *Ui-Mac-Uais* of Tethbha (or Teffia), who have given name to the barony of *Moygoish*, co. Westmeath. See note [4], p 300, *supra*.

[1] *Damliac.*—"Stone-church." See Reeves's *Ancient Churches of Armagh*, pp. 12–16.

[2] *Saball—Toi.*—See note [7], p. 433, *supra*.

[3] *Preaching chair.* — Evidently meant for "pulpit."

[4] *The 3rd of the Kalends of June;* i.e. the 30th of May.

[5] *Maelmuire.*—Or Marianus, as the name has been Latinized. See Ware's account of the Archbishops of Armagh (Harris's ed , Vol. i., p. 49), where it is stated that Maelmuire "died of grief, as it was thought, for the universal destruction of Armagh by fire, the month before."

[6] *The 3rd of the Nones;* i.e. the 3rd of June.

[7] *Of the . . . . clergy.*—eclaisi, B. ecailsi, A.

[8] *Ugaire.* — After having been King of Leinster for seven years, according to the *Book of Leinster* (p. 39, col. 3), this brave prince was put to death in a house set on fire, by Donnsleibhe, King of Ui-Faelain, in the year 1024. *Vid. infra.*

[9] *Deilgne - Mogoroc.* — Written "Dergne-Mogoroc" in the *Ann. Four Mast.* Now known as Delgany, in the barony of Rathdown, and county of Wicklow. Regarding the different modes of writing the name, arising from the interchange between the

all burned, viz., the great 'Damliac,'[1] with its roof of lead, and the bell-house with its bells, and the Saball,[2] and the Toi,[3] and the abbots' chariot, and the old preaching chair,[3] on the 3rd of the Kalends of June,[4] the Monday before Whitsunday. Maelmuire[5] son of Eochaidh, comarb of Patrick, head of the clerics of all the north-west of Europe, rested in Christ on the 3rd of the Nones[6] of June, the Friday before Whitsuntide. Amhalgaidh in the successorship of Patrick, by the will of the laity and clergy.[7] Finnlaech, son of Ruaidhri, King of Alba, was slain by his own people. Aedh Ua Innrechtaigh, King of Ui-Meith, was killed by the Ui-Niallain.

Kal. Jan. Sund.; m. 13. A.D. 1021. A victory by Ugaire,[8] son of Dunlaing, King of Leinster, over Sitriuc son of Amlaimh, King of Ath-cliath, at Deilgne-Mogoroc.[9] A shower of wheat[10] was shed in Osraighi. A preying expedition by the son of Aedh Ua Neill, across the Ui-Dorthain[11] who were in Magh-itechta, and they killed the Lethderg in the pursuit; (but the greater part of the Airghialla[12] came together behind him and before him. Or thus it is narrated in the Book of Dubhdaleithe "but the Ui-Meith met him, &c."); but the Ui-Meith, and the Mughdorna, and the Saithni,[13] and the men of Fernmagh,[14] and the Ui-Dorthain,[11] with their Kings, met him. Ua Ceilechan[15] and Ua Lorcain, with the Ui-Bresail and Ui- [1021.]

letters *l* and *r*, so frequently observable in Irish texts, see Joyce's *Irish Names of Places* (Second Series), p. 26.

[10] *Shower of wheat.*—See note [8], p. 169 *supra*.

[11] *Ui-Dorthain* — Otherwise, and more correctly, written Ui-Tortain; a tribe of the Airghialla who were seated near Ardbraccan in the present county of Meath. The events recorded in this entry, which is very inaccurately put together, are not noticed in any of the other Irish Chronicles.

[12] *Airghialla.*—The original of this clause, which is not in B., is added in the margin in *al. man.* in A.

[13] *Saithni.*—See note [3], under A.D. 1018; (p. 542).

[14] *Fernmhagh.*—Now represented by the barony of Farney, co. Monaghan.

[15] *Ua-Ceilechan.* — Written "Ua Celechair" in B., but incorrectly, as the Ua Ceilechains (or O'Callaghans) were at this time the principal family of the Ui-Bresail. See at the year 1037 *infra*, where the death of Archu Ua Celechain, King of Ui-Bresail, is recorded.

7 co n-Uib Niallain ar a cinn a n-Aenaċ Maċa co comrangadar uile ime, co ruc mac Aeḋa a gabail tairrsib uile, 7 ni raibe acht da .xx. deg oglaċ, 7 do cer sochaide etarru for lar Aenaig Maċa. Sic in libro Duibdaleiṫi. Branacan .h. Maeluidir, airri Miḋe, do baṫaḋ dia Belltaine illoċ Ainninde. Amalgaid comarba Patraic do ḋul isin Mumain cetna cur, co tuc mor-ċuairt. Ceallach .h. Caṫasaiġ, ri na Saitne, do marbad do ċenel Eogain. Mac Flainn mic Mailtseċlainn .i. rigdomna Temraċ, Aeḋ .i. rigdomna Ailiġ, 7 Domnall .h. Murchada, occisi sunt.

Kl. Ianair, .ii. f., l. xx.° iiii. Anno domini M.° xx.° ii.° Mac Cerbaill ri Ele, 7 Domnall .h. Cellaig ri Foṫart, Sitriuc mac Imair, ri Puirt Lairgi, occisi sunt. Macleiginn mac Cairill, ri Airġiall, Flann .h. Tacan, airchinnech Dairmaiġi, Lachtnan (.i. i n-Ard Maċa adbaṫ), comarba Innsi cain Dega, in Christo dormierunt. Maelseċlainn mac Domnaill (mic Donnchada, airdri Erenn, tuir Orḋain 7 oirechais iarṫair

---

[1] *Aenach-Macha.* — The "Fair-green of Macha;" the plain immediately surrounding the *rath* called the Navan fort, near Armagh, and including the fort itself.

[2] *Aenach-Macha.*—See last note. A. and B. have over the name Aenaig Macha (the gen. form), ł Aird M. ("or of Ard-Macha").

[3] *Loch-Aininne.*—Now known as Lough-Ennell, near Mullingar, co. Westmeath.

[4] *Saithne* —See note [3], under A.D. 1018; p. 542 *supra.*

[5] *Son.*—The *Four Masters* (ad an.) give his name as Aedh.

[6] *Royal heir of Ailech.*—rigdomna Ailiġ. Not in B. Added as a gloss in A.

[7] *Eli.*—This was the name of a tribe descended from Eli, 8th in descent from Cian, son of Oilill Oluim, King of Munster in the 3rd century. The name of the tribe was applied to the territory, which was anciently called Eli-tuaiscert, or Northern Eli, and in later times Eli-Ua-Cerbhaill (or Eli-O'Carroll), from Cerbhall, who was 15th in descent from the Eli referred to. See the *Book of Leinster*, p. 336, col. 8; and O'Donovan's ed. of *O'Huidhrin*, App., note 759. The territory of Eli-O'Carroll is now represented by the baronies of Clonlisk and Ballybritt, in the King's County. Among the principal representatives of this distinguished Irish sept may be mentioned the Rev. John James O'Carroll, S.J., and his brother, Rev. Fras. Aug., sons of Redmund Peter O'Carroll; Frederick John O'Carroll, B.L., son of Frederick Francis, brother of Redmund; and the Right Hon. John

Niallain, were before him in Aenach-Macha,[1] where they all surrounded him. But the son of Aedh carried his prey through them all; and he had only twelve score good warriors. And a great number fell between them in the middle of Aenach-Macha.[2] Thus in the Book of Dubhdaleithe. Branacan Ua Maeluidhir, a chieftain of Midhe, was drowned on May-day in Loch-Aininne.[3] Amhalgaidh, comarb of Patrick, went to Munster for the first time, and made a great visitation. Cellach Ua Cathasaigh, King of the Saithne,[4] was killed by the Cinel-Eoghain. The son[5] of Flann, son of Maelsechlainn, royal-heir of Temhair; Aedh, *i.e.* royal-heir of Ailech,[6] and Domnall Ua Murchada, were slain.

Kal. Jan. Mond., m. 24. A.D. 1022. The son of Cerbhall, King of Eli,[7] and Domnall Ua Cellaigh, King of Fotharta,[8] and Sitriuc son of Imhar, King of Port-Lairge,[9] were slain. Macleighinn son of Cairell, King of Airghialla; Flann Ua Tacain, herenagh of Dairmagh,[10] and Lachtnan (*i.e.* who died in Ard-Macha[11]), comarb of Inis-cain-Dega,[12] 'fell asleep' in Christ. Maelsechlainn, son of Domnall (son of Donnchad[13]), arch-King of Ireland, pillar of the dignity and nobility of the west of the [1022.]

Naish, eldest son of Anne Margaret (sister of the same Redmund), who married Carroll P. Naish, Esquire, of Ballycullen, co. Limerick.

[8] *Fotharta.* — Fotharta-Fea, or Fotharta O'Nolan; now the barony of Forth, in the county of Carlow, the patrimony of the ancient sept of the Ui-Nuallain, a name now written O'Nolan, and Nolan (without the O'). See O'Flaherty's *Ogygia*, part 3, chap. 64, and *Leabhar na g-ceart* (ed. O'Donovan), p. 211.

[9] *Port-Lairge.*—This is the Irish name of Waterford.

[10] *Dairmagh.*—Durrow, barony of Ballycowan, King's Co. For much information regarding the history of this remarkable establishment in ancient times, see Reeves's *Adamnan* v. *Dairmagh.*

[11] *Died in Ard-Macha.*—The corresponding Irish of this clause is interlined by way of gloss in A. and B., by the original hands.

[12] *Inis-cain-Dega.*—Inishkeen, in the barony of Upper Dundalk, co. Louth, on the borders of the county of Monaghan, a portion of which county is comprised in the parish of Inishkeen.

[13] *Son of Donnchad.*—The original of this, added in the old hand in A., is not in B.

domain do ecaib isin tres bliadain, xl. regni sui, isin tres bliadain lxx. aetatis suae, in .iiii. nonas Septimbris, die uidelicet dominico, secunda lunae. Muirċomrac forrind [ḟ]airce etir Gallu Aṫa cliaṫ 7 Niall mac Eochada, ri Ulad, co ro muiḃ fors na Gallu, 7 co rolaḃ a n-derg ar, 7 co ro dairṫea airṫena. Muircertaċ .h. Carraig .i. ridomna Temraċ, do marbad on Gut .i. la Maelseċlainn. Maidm i Sleiḃ [Ḟ]uait for Airgiallaiḃ ria Niall mac Eochada, co ro cuired derg ar Airgiall and. Maṫgaṁain mac Laidgnen, ri Fernmuiġi, do marbad do ċaṫalan .h. Criċan for lar ċluana Eois. Muiren na tengaḋ occisus est.

Kl. Ianair, .iii. f.; l. u. Anno domini M.° xx.° .iii.°
Fol. 56ba. Ercrai escai i xiiii. escai Enair, i .iiii. id Enair, dia Dardain. Ercrai greine autem i xx. uii. ind escai cetnai, dia Dardain, cinn coectiġes i noi Kl. Domnall mac Aeḋa bic .h. Mailseċlainn do marbad o mac Senan .h. Leoċain. Donnchad .h. Duinn, ri Breġ, do ġabail do ġallaib ina n-airiucht fein, 7 a breiṫ dar muir. Loċlainn mac Maelseċlainn do marbad a suis. Taḋg

---

[1] *The 43rd year.*—The Chronicler here includes, of course, the 12 years during which Brian Borumha usurped the monarchy. The date of this usurpation is not recorded in either of the MSS. A. and B. of these Annals, although the so-called 'translator' of the version in Clar. 49 begins the entries for the year 1002 with "Brienus regnare incipit." The *Chron. Scotorum* refers the beginning of Brian's reign to 999=1001, the date in *Tigernach.* See O'Flaherty's *Ogygia*, p. 435; and Todd's *War of the Gaedhil*, &c., Introd., pp. cliii–clv, where the subject is well discussed. The record of Maelsechlainn's death is given in a fuller manner by the *Four M.*, and in the *Chron. Scot.*

[2] *Sunday.*—The *criteria* here given indicate correctly the year 1022. A few lines of poetry in praise of Maelsechlainn (Malachy II.), not in B., are added in the lower margin of fol. 56*a* in A. But as the text is rather corrupt, it has not been considered necessary to print them.

[3] *Ua Carraigh;* i.e. grandson of Carrach [-calma]. See note [3], p. 540.

[4] *Sliabh-Fuait.*—See note [1], p. 314 *supra.*

[5] *Fernmagh.*—Now the barony of Farney, in the county of Monaghan.

[6] *Of the tongues;* i.e. "of the languages." Nothing further is known to the Editor regarding Muiren's linguistic accomplishments.

[7] *Fourth of the Ides*; i.e. the 10th of January.

world, died in the 43rd year[1] of his reign, the 73rd year of his age, on the 4th of the Nones of September, *i.e.* on Sunday,[2] being the second of the moon. A sea-fight on the sea, between the Foreigners of Ath-cliath and Niall, son of Eochaidh, King of Ulidia, when the Foreigners were defeated, and a great slaughter was made of them; and the rest were made captive. Muirchertach Ua Carraigh,[3] *i.e.* royal heir of Temhair, was killed by the Got, *i.e.* Maelsechlainn. A victory in Sliabh-Fuait,[4] over the Airghialla, by Niall son of Eochaidh, where a great slaughter was made of the Airghialla. Mathgamhain son of Laidgnen, King of Fernmagh,[5] was killed by Cathalan Ua Crichain, in the middle of Cluain-Eois. Muiren, 'of the tongues'[6] was slain.

Kal. Jan. Tuesd.; m. 5. A.D. 1023. An eclipse of [1023.]
the moon on the 14th of the January moon, *i.e.* the 4th of the Ides[7] of January, a Thursday. An eclipse of the sun, also, on the 27th of the same moon, a Thursday, at the end of a fortnight, on the 9th of the Kalends [of February].[8] Domnall, son of Aedh Bec Ua Maelsechlainn, was killed by the son of Senan Ua Leochain.[9] Donnchad Ua Duinn, King of Bregha, was taken prisoner by Foreigners, in their own assembly, and carried across the sea.[10] Lochlainn,[11] son of Maelsechlainn, was killed by his own people. Tadhg, son of Brian,[12] was killed by the

[8] *The 9th of the Kalends [of February]*; i.e. the 24th of January. These criteria correctly indicate the year 1023, when the eclipses above noticed seem to have occurred. See *L'Art de Verif. les dates*, tom. 1, p. 71, ad an. 1023.

[9] *Senan Ua Leochain.* — King of Gailenga-mora and Tuath-Luighne, now represented by the baronies of Morgallion and Lune, in the county of Meath. See above, at the year 1018, where the name Ua Leochain is wrongly written O'Lorcain.

[10] *Carried across the sea.*—The *Four Masters* state (ad an.), that this was in violation of Colum Cille, whose successor was his [Donnchad's] guarantee.

[11] *Lochlainn.* — According to the *Ann. Four M.*, Lochlainn was King of Inis-Eoghain (Inishowen) and Magh-Itha, and was slain by his own brother, Niall, and the Cianachta of Glenn-Geimhin.

[12] *Brian;* i.e. Brian Borumha.

mac Briain do marbad o Eiliḃ. Concobar .h. Carraiġ do marbad la na Gotu. Leobelein ri Bretan do ec. Oenreicc, ri in domain, do ecaiḃ in pace. Tar a eisi rogaḃ Cuana riġe in domain. Da .h. Maċainen do marbad do Ġailengaiḃ. Domnall .h. hEaġra, ri Luiġne Connacht, do marbad do .h. Concobair ri Connacht.

.b. Kl. Ianair, .iiii. f., l. xvi. Anno domini m.° xx.° iiii.° Ugaire mac Dunlaing, ri Laigen, 7 Maelmorḋa mac Lorcan, ri .h. Ceinnselaiġ, teċ do gabail forra ic Dubloċ, la Donnsleiḃe mac Mailmorḋai, la riġ .h. Faelain, 7 a tuitim ann. Donnsleibe iarum do marbad do hUib Muireḋaiġ. Caṫ Aṫa no crois i Corunn, itir .h. Maeldoraiḋ 7 .h. Ruairc, co ro muiḋ for U Ruairc, 7 co ro laḋ a ar. Cuan .h. Loṫcan,

[1] *Eli.*—See note [7], p. 548. Tadhg was killed at the instigation of his brother, Dounchad, according to the *Ann. F. M.* and *Chron. Scot.*

[2] *Conchobar Ua Carraigh.*—Conchobar, son of Aenghus, son of Carrach[-calma]. See note [3] under A.D. 1017; p. 540 *supra.*

[3] *The Gots;* i.e. "the Stammerers"; a nickname borne by several members of a family of the Ui-Mailsechlainns (or O'Melaghlins) of Meath.

[4] *Leobhelin.* — Llewelyn, son of Seisil, King of Wales, whose obit is given in the *Brut y Tywisogion* at the year 1021, and in the *Annales Cambriæ* under A.D. 1023.

[5] *Henry.*—Oenric, for Henricus, A. B. Henry II., Emperor of Germany.

[6] *Cuana.*—This is a curious way of writing the name of Conrad II., the successor of Henry II. in the empire. O'Donovan strangely confounds Cuana (or Conrad II.) with Otho III., who was the predecessor of Henry II. *Ann. Four M.*, A D. 1024, note u.

[7] *Ua Machainens.*—Ua Machainen was the name of the ruling sept at the time in Mughdorna, which was most likely Mughdorna-Bregh (or Mughdorna of Bregia) in the co. Meath; a territory not yet identified, but adjoining the country of the *Gailenga*, the present barony of Morgallion in that county.

[8] *Luighne.*—Now represented by the barony of Leyny, co. Sligo, where the name of Ua hEghra (or O'Hara) is still very general.

[9] *Ua Conchobair;* i.e. Tadhg ("of the white steed") O'Conor, son of Cathal. His death is recorded at the year 1030 *infra.*

[10] *Dubhloch.*—The "Black Lake." In the *Book of Leinster*, p. 39, col. 3, where the death of Ugaire son of Dunlaing is recorded, it is stated that a house was *burned over* him at *Dubloch* in *Laighis-Chule.* Laighis-Chule was the name of one of the seven septs of Laighis (or Leix), and was also, as usual, applied to their

Eli,[1] Conchobar Ua Carraigh,[2] was killed by the Gots.[3] Leobhelin,[4] King of Britain, died. Henry,[5] king of the world, died in peace. Cuana[6] assumed the kingship of the world in his stead. Two Ua Machainens[7] were killed by the Gailenga. Domnall Ua hEghra, King of Luighne[8] of Connaught, was killed by Ua Conchobair,[9] King of Connaught.

Kal. Jan. Wednesd., m. 16. A.D. 1024. Ugaire son 1024. [BIS.]
of Dunlaing, King of Leinster, and Maelmordha son of Lorcan, King of Ui-Ceinnselaigh, had a house taken against them, at Dubhloch,[10] by Donnsleibhe son of Maelmordha, King of Ui-Faelain; and they fell there. Donnsleibhe was slain afterwards by the Ui-Muiredhaigh.[11] The battle of Ath-na-croise[12] in Corann, between Ua Maeldoraidh and Ua Ruairc, when Ua Ruairc was defeated, and put to slaughter. Cuan Ua Lothchain,[13]

---

territory, which appears to have been comprised in the present barony of Stradbally, in the Queen's County. In a short general account of the tribes of Leix, contained in the *Book of Leinster* (p. 318), the *Nuachongbail* (the old name of the village, or church, of Stradbally, in the parish and barony of Stradbally), is otherwise given as *Tulach mic Comgaill*, "the hill of Comgall's son"; and this Comgall appears in the short pedigree of the *Laighis-Cúle* (*loc. cit.*, col. 2), whilst his son, Colman son of Comgall (after whom *Nuachongbail* was called *Tulach mic Comgaill*), is described as *erlam na cilli*; i.e. "founder (or patron) of the church." Colman's day in the Calendar is May 15th. See *Martyr. Doneg.* at that date.

[11] *Ui-Muiredhaigh.*—This was the tribe-name of the O'Tooles, whose country at the date of the event above recorded embraced nearly the southern half of the present county of Kildare. Soon after the Anglo-Norman invasion, the O'Tooles went into the mountains of Wicklow, and settled in the Glen of Imail, and the territory of Fera-Cualann.

[12] *Ath-na-croise.*—The "Ford of the Cross." There is no place now known by this name, or any variation of it, such as Cross-ford, in the barony of Corran, co. Sligo. A stanza in the lower margin of fol. 56*b* in A., which is not in B., referring to this battle, is as follows:—

In caṫ oc aṫ na croisi,
Fechtatar fir cen taisi;
Ro linaḋ collaib Corann;
Is la Conall a maisi.

"[In] the battle at Ath-na-croise
Men fought without weakness.
Corann was filled with corpses;
The Conalls had its glory."

[13] *Cuan Ua Lothchain.*—This name is written Cuan Ua Lochain (or O'Lochain) in other authorities.

primeicer Erenn do marbad i Teḃṫa (ḋ'ḟearaiḃ Teaḃṫa fein). Brenait a n-aen uair in lucht ro marb. Firt filed innsein. Domnall mac Aeḋa, ridomna Ailiġ, do marbad do Gillamura mac Ocan. Maelduin .h. Conċaille, ri .h. Niallain, do marbad do hUib Dorrṫain. Maelruanaiḋ .h. Ciarḋai, ri Cairbri, a ruir occisus est. Creċ la mac .h. Neill co ro ort .h. Meiṫ 7 .h. Dorrṫainn.

Kl. Ianair, iii. f., l. xx. iiii. Anno domini M.° xx.° u.° Flannabra comarba Ia, Muireḋaċ mac Muġroin comarba Ciarain, Maeleoin .h. Doran comarba Daire, Cennfaelad mac Flaiṫbertaiġ, airċinneċ Daiminnsi, Maelbrigte .h. Criċiḋen comarba Finnein 7 Comgaill, Dubinnsi .h. Fairċellaiġ airċinneċ Droma leṫan, Saerbrethach abb Imleċa Iḃair, in Christo dormierunt. Niall .h. Concobair, ridomna Connacht, Gerrgaela ri Breg, occisi sunt. Maelseċlainn gott, ri Miḋe, do ec. Sluagad la Flaiṫbertaċ .h. Neill i
Fol. 56bb. m-Bregaiḃ 7 i n-Gallaiḃ, co tuc giallu Gaiḋel o ġallaib. Creċ la Caṫalan, ri Fernmuiġi, for feraiḃ Manaċ. Creċ la firu Manaċ fo cetoir co Loċ n-Uaiṫne co ro

---

[1] *Became foul.*—The *Ann. Loch-Cé* state that the bodies of the murderers were not buried, but beasts and birds devoured them.

[2] *Ui-Dorthain.*—See note [11], p. 547 *supra*.

[3] *Cairbri;* i.e. Cairbri-Ua-Ciardha, or Carbury-O'Keary. Now represented by the barony of Carbury, county of Kildare. The name O'Keary, now written Keary, and Carey, is still pretty general in the counties of Kildare and Meath.

[4] *Flannabhra.*—See Reeves's *Adamnan*, p. 398.

[5] *Comarb of Ciaran;* i.e. abbot of Clonmacnoise.

[6] *Comarb of Daire;* i.e. abbot of Derry.

[7] *Finnian and Comghall.*—Founders and first abbots, respectively, of Movilla and Bangor, in the co. Down. See at the year 1006 *supra*, where King Brian Borumha is stated to have delivered Ua Crichidben, successor of Finnian, from the hostageship in which he was held in Cinel-Eoghain.

[8] *Druim-lethan.* — The "broad ridge." Drumlane, in the county of Cavan, where St. Maedhog (or Mogue), founder of the monastery of Ferns, is stated to have erected another establishment about the year 600.

chief poet of Ireland, was killed in Tethbha (by the men of Tethbha themselves). The party that killed him became foul[1] in the same hour. This was a 'poet's miracle.' Domnall, son of Aedh, royal-heir of Ailech, was killed by Gillamura son of Ocan. Maelduin Ua Conchaille, King of Ui-Niallain, was killed by the Ui-Dorthain.[2] Maelruanaidh Ua Cairdha, King of Cairbri,[3] was killed by his own people. A preying expedition by the son of Ua Neill, when he plundered Ui-Meith and Ui-Dorthain.[2]

Kal. Jan. Frid., m. 27. A.D. 1025. Flannabhra,[4] comarb of Ia; Muiredhach, son of Mughron, comarb of Ciaran;[5] Maeleoin Ua Dorain, comarb of Daire;[6] Cennfaeladh, son of Flaithbertach, herenagh of Daimhinis; Maelbrigte Ua Crichidhen, comarb of Finnian and Comghall;[7] Dubhinnsi Ua Fairchellaigh, herenagh of Druim-lethan,[8] and Saerbrethach, abbot of Imlech-Ibhair, 'fell asleep' in Christ. Niall Ua Conchobair, royal heir of Connaught, [and] Gerrgaela, King of Bregha, were slain. Maelsechlainn Got,[9] King of Midhe, died. A hosting by Flaithbertach Ua Neill into Bregha, and to the Foreigners,[10] when he brought the hostages of the Gaedhil from the Foreigners. A depredation by Cathalan,[11] King of Fernmagh, upon the Fera-Manach. A preying expedition by the Fera-Manach, immediately afterwards, as far as Loch-Uaithne,[12] which they burned; [1025.]

---

[9] *Maelsechlainn Got.* — See note [3], under A.D. 1023; p. 552. In the *Book of Leinster* (p. 42, col. 2), Maelsechlainn is stated to have died, *dolore extenso.*

[10] *To the Foreigners.*—i n-Gallaib. These were probably the Foreigners occupying Fine Gall (or Fingall), the northern part of the present county of Dublin, bordering on Bregia (or Bregh) in Meath, as suggested in Clar. 49.

[11] *Cathalan.* — In the last entry for this year the patronymic of Cathalan is given as "Ua Crichan," or O Crichain.

[12] *Loch-Uaithne* —Uaithne's Lake. O'Donovan identifies Loch-Uaithne with Lough Ooney, near Smithsborough, in co. Monaghan, where the chiefs of Dartraighe-Coininnse had their principal residence. *Ann. Four Mast.*, A.D. 850, note y.

loiscset, 7 co ro marbsat uii. firu dec for bru ind locha. Termonn Feiċin do arcain do Caṫalan .h. Criċan.

Kl. Ianair, uii. f., l. ix. Anno domini M.° xx.° ui.° Slogad la mac mBriain i Miḋe 7 i mBregu, 7 co Gollu, 7 co Laiġniu, 7 co hOsraigiu, co ruc a n-giallu. Slogad la Flaiṫbertaċ .h. Neill i Miḋe, co tuc giallu, 7 con-dechaid for leic aigriḋ i n-inis Mochta, co ro innis. Slogad la mac Eochada isin uair cetna co Golla, co ro loisc, 7 co tuc brait moir uaiḋiḃ 7 seotu. Gilla-ciarain mac Ualgairg, toisech .h. Duibinnrecht, do ec. Maelruanaid .h. Maeldoraid do ḋul ina ailiṫri. Aṁirgin .h. Morḋa, ri Loigsi, interfectus est. Muircertaċ mac Conġalaiġ ri .h. Failġi interfectus est. Feall la Domnall .h. Ceallaiġ for Muireḋaċ .h. Ceile, co ro marḃ ina airiucht.

Kl. Ianair, i. f., l. xx. Anno domini M.° xx.° uii.° Ruaiḋri mac Fogartaiġ, ri deisceirt Breġ, do ecaib ina ailiṫri. Taḋg mac Gillapatraic do ḋallad la Donnchad mac Gillapatraic, ri Osraigi. Slogad la mac mBriain i n-Osraigib co ro lasat Osraiġi ar a muintire, im Ḋogra mac nDunaḋaiġ, ri sil Anmchada, 7

---

[1] *Termon-Feichin.*—Termonfeckin, in the barony of Ferrard, co. Louth.

[2] *Son of Brian.*—Donnchad, son of Brian Borumha.

[3] *Inis-Mochta.*—"Mochta's Island." Now Inishmot, in a parish of the same name, barony of Lower Slane, co. Meath. The lake in which this island was situated has disappeared, but the ruins of St. Mochta's church are still to be seen in a spot surrounded by low, swampy ground, always flooded in winter. St. Mochta "of the Island," whose day in the Calendar is Jan. 26, is to be distinguished from Mochta of Lughmadh (Louth, ob. A.D. 534 *supra*), whose festival was celebrated on the 19th of August. The *Four Mast.* (A.D. 1026) add that Inishmot was at the time in possession of the Foreigners.

[4] *Son of Eochaidh.*—Niall, son of Eochaidh, King of Ulidia. His obit is given at the year 1063 *infra*, where he is called *Ard-ri* ("arch-king") of Ulidia.

[5] *Went.*—The *Four Masters* say tar muir, "across the sea."

[6] *Son of Brian.*—Donnchad, son of King Brian Borumha.

[7] *Dogra.*—This must certainly be

and they killed seventeen men on the border of the lake. Termon-Feichin[1] was plundered by Cathalan Ua Crichain.

Kal. Jan. Saturd., m. 9. A.D. 1026. A hosting by the son of Brian[2] into Midhe and Bregha, and to the Foreigners, and to the Leinstermen, and to the Osraighi, when he took their pledges. A hosting by Flaithbertach Ua Neill into Midhe, when he took their pledges, and went upon the ice into Inis-Mochta,[3] which he plundered. A hosting by the son of Eochaidh[4] at the same time to the Foreigners, when he burned [their territory], and carried off a great prey from them, and treasures. Gillaciarain son of Ualgarg, chief of the Ui-Duibhinnrecht died. Maelruanaidh Ua Maeldoraidh went[5] on his pilgrimage. Aimhirgin Ua Mordha, King of Laighis, was slain. Muirchertach, son of Congalach, King of Ui-Failghi, was slain. An act of treachery by Domnall Ua Cellaigh against Muiredhach Ua Ceile, whom he killed in his own assembly. [1026.]

Kal. Jan. Sund., m. 20. A.D. 1027. Ruaidhri son of Fogartach, King of the South of Bregha, died in his pilgrimage. Tadhg Mac Gillapatraic was blinded by Donnchad Mac Gillapatraic, King of Osraighi. A hosting by the son of Brian[6] into Osraighi, when the Osraighi committed a slaughter of his people, including Dogra[7] son of Dunadach, King of Sil-Anmchada,[8] and Domnall[9] [1027.]

a mistake for Gadra (or 'Godra' as the name is written in the *Book of Leinster*, p. 338, col. 8), and in the *Chron. Scotorum*, *Ann. Tigern.*, and *Ann. F. M.* See O'Donovan's *Tribes*, &c., of *Hy-Many*, pp. 99, 142, and the *Geneal. Table* prefixed to p. 97. The only other Irish Chronicle in which the name is written "Dogra" is the *Ann. Loch-Cé*, the compiler of which seems to have taken the entry from this Chronicle.

[8] *Sil-Anmchada.* — This was the tribe-name of a branch of the Ui-Maine, who on the formation of surnames took the name of O'Madden, from Madudhan, chief of Sil-Anmchada, whose death is recorded in the *Chron. Scot.* at the year 1007=1009.

[9] *Domnall.*—In the *Ann. Four M.* (ad an.), and *Chron. Scot.* (A.D. 1025=1027), Domnall is described as "son of Senchan, son of Flaithbhertach," and royal heir of Munster.

im Domnall mac Senċan, 7 im sochaide moir arċena. Domnall mac Flaiṫbertaiġ .h. Neill do ecaiḃ. Roin[1] ri Miḋe, 7 Donnchad .h. Duinn ri Breġ, do comtuitim i caṫ. Caṫalan .h. Criċan ri Fernmuiġi, 7 Culoċa .h. Gairbeiḃ, ri .h. Meiṫ, do comtuitim i n-ergail. Creċ la cenel Eogain for Ultaiḃ, co tucsat boroma mor. Dun Caillenn[2] i n-Albain do uile loscad. Donnchad mac Gillamoconna, comarba Seċnaill,[3] sapientissimus Scotorum, in Colonia[4] quieuit.

.b. Kl. Ianair, ii. f., l. i. Anno domini M.° xx.° iiii. Taḋg mac Eachach, airċinneċ cille Dalua,[5] Art airċinneċ Mungairti,[6] in Christo dormierunt. Gillacrist mac Duiḃcuilinn, uasal sacart aird Maċa, do ec i Ros Comain. Brian .h. Concobair 7 Scornn .h.
Fol. 57aa. Ruairc, Flaiṫbertaċ .h. hErudan, Conċobar mac Echada, occisi sunt. Maelmoċta,[7] ri Fer Rois,[8] o Conaillib[9] occisus est. Orccain Doimliacc la firu Manaċ. Mac Concuailgne, ri .h. nEachach, do ec. Sitriuc mac mic Amlaim, ri Gall, 7 Flannacan .h. Ceallaig, ri Breg, a n-dul do Roim. Creċ la Cinel Eogain i tir Conaill, co tucsat gabala mora. Dertaċ Slane do ṫuitim. Donn .h. Conġalaiġ do marbad do ċonaillib.

Kl. Ianair, iiii., f., l. xii. Anno domini M.° xx.° ix.° Donnsleibe mac Brogorbain, ri .h. Foilgi, a suis occisus est. Donnchad .h. Donnacan, ri Fern-

[1] *Roin.*—So in A. and B. The words ni ṫuigim so ("I don't understand this") are written over the name in B., in the orig. hand. In the *Chron. Scot.* the name is written "Raen," but in the *Ann. F. M.* "Roen."

[2] *Dun-Caillen.*—Dunkeld, in Scotland.

[3] *Comarb of Sechnall*; i.e. abbot of Domnach-Sechnaill, now Dunshaughlin, co. Meath.

[4] *Colonia.*—Cologne, in Germany, on the west bank of the Lower Rhine, where an Irish monastery was established.

[5] *Cill-Dalua.*—Killaloe, co. Clare.

[6] *Mungairit.* — Mungret, bar. of Pubblebrien, co. Limerick.

[7] *Maelmochta.*—The *Four Mast* write the name Maelmorda.

[8] *Fera-Rois.*—See note [4], p. 354 *supra.*

[9] *Conailli*; i.e. the Conailli-Muirthemhne, a tribe occupying Magh-Muirthemhne, which included the northern part of the present county of Louth.

son of Senchan, and a great number besides. Domnall, son of Flaithbertach Ua Neill, died. Roin,[1] King of Midhe, and Donnchad Ua Duinn, King of Bregha, fell by each other in battle. Cathalan Ua Crichain, King of Fernmagh, and Culocha Ua Gairbhidh, King of Ui-Meith, fell by each other in a fight. A depredation was committed by the Cinel-Eoghain upon the Ulidians, when they carried off a great prey of cattle. Dun-Caillen[2] in Alba was all burned. Donnchad, son of Gillamochonna, comarb of Sechnall,[3] the wisest of the Scoti, rested in Colonia.[4]

Kal. Jan. Mond., m. 1. A.D. 1028. Tadhg son of [1028.] BIS.
Eochaidh, herenagh of Cill-Dalua,[5] [and] Art, herenagh of Mungairit,[6] 'fell asleep' in Christ. Gillachrist son of Dubhcuilinn, an eminent priest of Ard-Macha, died in Ros-Comain. Brian Ua Conchobair, Scornn Ua Ruaire, Flaithbertach Ua hErudain, and Conchobar son of Echaidh, were slain. Maelmochta,[7] King of Fera-Rois,[8] was killed by the Conailli.[9] The plundering of Doimliacc by the Fera-Manach. The son of Cu-Cuailgne, King of Ui-Echach,[10] died. Sitriuc, grandson of Amlaimh, King of the Foreigners, and Flannacan Ua Cellaigh, King of Bregha, went to Rome. A predatory expedition by the Cinel-Eoghain to Tir-Conaill, when they took great spoils. The oratory of Slane fell down. Donn Ua Conghalaigh was slain by the Conailli.[9]

Kal. Jan. Wednesd., m. 12. A.D. 1029. Donn- [1029.]
sleibhe,[11] son of Brogarbhan, King of Ui-Failghi, was slain by his own people. Donnchad Ua Donnacain,

The Transl. in Clar. 49 wrongly renders Conailli by "the O'Conners."

[10] *Ui-Echach.*—Otherwise called Ui-Echach-Cobha, or "descendants of Eochaidh Cobha;" from which Eochaidh the name of Ui-Echach was adopted as the tribe name, and was also applied to the territory occupied by them, which is now represented by the baronies of Upper and Lower Iveagh, in the county of Down. See Reeves's *Down and Connor*, pp. 348–352.

[11] *Donnsleibhe.*—His name occurs in the list of Kings of Ui-Failghi contained in the *Book of Leinster*, p. 40, col. 3, where the period of his reign is given as three years.

muighi 7 mac Igerrce, ri Conaille, do comtuitim i Cill sleibhe. Brian .h. Concobair, ridomna Connacht, a suis occisus est. Aedh .h. Ruairc, 7 Oengus .h. hOengusa, 7 airchinnech Droma cliabh, 7 tri .xx. duine, do loscad impu i n-inis na lainne. Muirchertach .h. Maeldoraid do marbad do Uib Canannan. Amlaim mac Sitriuc, ri Gall, do ergabail do Mathgamain .h. Riagain, ri Bregh, co fargaibh da .c. dec bo, 7 .ui. xx. each mBretnach, 7 tri .xx. unga do or, 7 cloidim Carlusa, 7 aitire Gaidel etir Laighniu 7 Leth Cuind, 7 tri .xx. unga do argut gil ina ungai geimleach, (conid ceitri fichid bo cuid focall 7 impide, 7 cethri oeitire d'O Riagain fein fri sith, 7 lan logh bragad in tresoeitere). Maelcoluim mac Maelbrigte mic Ruaidhri, Maelbrigde .h. Brolchan, primsaer Erenn, mortui sunt. Fear do tachar a tracht Corcabaiscinn, 7 bathar ocht troighthi etir a chidh 7 a fordrann.

---

1 *Son of Igerrce.*—The *Four Masters* state that his name was Cinaedh, and that he was son of "Angeirrce." In the *Book of Leinster*, p. 335, col. 6, the name is given "Cinaedh son of Ingerrce," and over "Ingerrce" is written the name Muiredach, by way of gloss; from which it would appear that "Ingerrce" was a nickname.

2 See note [9], page 558.

3 *Cill-sleibhe.* — Or Cill-Sleibhe-Cuilinn. Now Killeavy, in the south-east of the county of Armagh, at the foot of the mountain Sliabh-Cuilinn, now corruptly written "Slieve-Gullion."

4 *Druim-cliabh.*—Drumcliff, in the barony of Carbury, county of Sligo.

5 *Inis-na-lainne.* — The 'spear' island. Some island off the northern coast of the co. Sligo. Not identified.

6 *Foreigners.*—The Foreigners of Waterford, according to Todd. *War of the Gaedhil*, &c., p. 295, note [8]. The killing of Amlaimh, on his way to Rome, by Saxons, is recorded at A.D. 1034 *infra*. His departure for Rome is also noticed under last year.

7 *Three score ounces.*—The 'translator' in Clar. 49 has "3 ounces." But the MSS. A. and B. have tri .xx., "three score."

8 *Sword of Carlus.*—This weapon seems to have been regarded as a most sacred object by the Foreigners. The chieftain whose sword it was—Carlus son of Amlaimh, chief of the Foreigners—was slain in the battle of Cill-Ua-nDaighri (note [6], p. 378 *supra*), according to the *Ann. Four Mast.* The same Annals (at A.D. 994), and the *Chron. Scotorum* (933), record the forcible taking by King Maelsechlain, from the Foreigners of Dublin, of the "Sword of Carlus" and the "Ring of Tomar." Dr. Todd suggests that the sword must have been recovered by the Foreigners (or

King of Fernmagh, and the son of Igerrce,[1] King of Conailli,[2] fell by one another in Cill-sleibhe.[3] Brian Ua Conchobair, royal heir of Connaught, was slain by his own people. Aedh Ua Ruairc, and Oengus Ua hOenghusa, and the herenagh of Druim-cliabh,[4] and three score men along with them, were burned in Inis-na-lainne.[5] Muirchertach Ua Maeldoraidh was killed by the Ui-Canannain. Amlaimh, son of Sitriuc, King of the Foreigners,[6] was made prisoner by Mathgamain Ua Riagain, King of Bregha, until he gave 1,200 cows, and six score British [Welsh] horses, and three score ounces[7] of gold, and the sword of Carlus,[8] and the Irish hostages, both of Leinster and Leth-Chuinn,[9] and three score ounces of white silver, as his fetter-ounce;[10] (and four score cows[11] was the proportion for speech and supplication; and four hostages to O'Riagain himself, for peace, and the full compensation for the life of the third hostage). Maelcoluim,[12] son of Maelbrigte, son of Ruaidhri, [and] Maelbrigte Ua Brolchain,[13] chief artificer of Ireland, died. A man was cast ashore on the strand of Corco-Baiscinn; and there were eight feet (in length) between his head[14] and the small of his back.

Danes) of Waterford, because of its having been exacted on this occasion as part of the ransom of Amlaimh, who was chief of the Danish colony of Waterford. See *War of the Gaedhil*, &c., pp. 297–8, and O'Donovan's ed. of *Leabhar na g ceart*; Introd., pp. xxxix, xl.

[9] *Leth-Chuinn.* — "Conn's Half." The northern half of Ireland.

[10] *Fetter-ounce*; i e. the price of his release from his fetters; or his ransom.

[11] *Four score cows.*—The original of this parenthetic clause, which is interlined in a later hand in A., is not in B. But an English version of it is given in Clar. 49. See note [14].

[12] *Maelcoluim.*—King of Alba (or Scotland). See Reeves's *Adamnan*, p. 399, and Geneal. Table facing p. 438 in the same work. See also Stuart's ed. of the *Book of Deer*, Pref., p. li.

[13] *Maelbrigte Ua Brolchain.*—See at the year 1097 *infra*, where the obit is given of a Maelbrigte *mac int sair* ("son of the artificer") O'Brolachain, bishop of Kildare.

[14] *His head.*—a ċiꝺ, for a ċ̄iꝺ (a ċinꝺ), A. The original of this entry, which is written in a later hand in A., is not in B., though it is Englished in Clar. 49, the so-called translator of which is supposed to have made his *quasi* translation from MS. B.

Kt. Ianair, u. f., l. xx. iii. Anno domini M.° xxx.° Bresal Conailleċ, comarba Ciarain, Eochaid .h. Ceiṫnen, comarba Tigernaiġ, ard sui Erend i n-ecnai, i n-ard Maċa quieuerunt. h. Cruimtir, .i. Oengus, comarba Comġaill, do ec. Flaiṫbertaċ .h. Neill do ḋul do Roim. Taḋg .h. Concobair, ri Connacht, 7 in Got, ri Miḋe, occisi sunt. Ruaidri .h. Canannan do marbad la hAeḋ .h. Neill. Taḋg mac Lorcain, ri .h. Ceinnselaig, do éc ina ailiṫri a n-glinn da loċa. Cúmara mac Micliag, ard ollam Erenn, do ec. Eochaid mac ind abaid do marbad don Ure .h. Ruadacan, i meḃail. Cenel Eogain do brisiuḋ luingi .h. Loingsiċ for lar Oentruiṁ. Maelduin mac Ciarmaic, muire ceneoil mBinniġ glinni, do marbad do Conċobur .h. Loingsiġ. Taḋg mac Caṫail mic Concobair interfectus est o Maelseaċlainn .h. Maelruanaiḋ, ri Crimṫainn.

Fol. 57ab Kt. Ianair. ui. f., l. iiii. Anno domini M.° xxx.° i.° Flaiṫbertaċ .h. Neill do ṫiachtain o Roim. Ard

---

[1] *Comarb of Ciaran;* i.e. abbot of Clonmacnoise. Bresal was called "Conaillech," on account of his having been of the Conailli-Muirthemhne.

[2] *Comarb of Tigernach;* i.e. successor of Tigernach, founder and abbot of Clones, in the county Monaghan.

[3] *Flaithbertach Ua Neill.*—Called Flaithbertach *in trostain* (F. "of the pilgrim's staff"), from this journey to Rome. His obit is entered at the year 1036 *infra*.

[4] *Tadhg Ua Conchobair.*—Known in history by the name of *Tadhg an eich ghil*, or Tadhg "of the White Steed." His death is recorded again in the last entry for this year, perhaps through oversight. But in the entry in question, Tadhg is stated to have been slain by Maelsechlainn, grandson of Maelruanaidh, whom the *Four Masters* (1030) describe as the "Got," and "lord of Midhe and Crimthainn."

[5] *The Got;* i.e. the Stammerer. See under the year 1023 *supra*. The person here referred to was Domnall *Got* O'Maelsechlainn, King of Midhe (or King of Uisnech, according to the *Book of Leinster*, p. 42, col. 2).

[6] *Cinel-Binnigh of the Glen.*—The Cinel-Binnigh, who were descended from Eochaidh Binnech, son of Eoghan, son of Niall Nine-hostager, occupied a territory comprised in the present county of Londonderry. The tribe seems in the course of time to have become divided into three or four divisions. But the exact limits of the territory of the original tribe, or of either of the subdivisions, has-

Kal. Jan. Thursd.; m. 23. A.D. 1030. Bresal Conaillech, comarb of Ciaran,[1] Eochaidh Ua Ceithnen, comarb of Tigernach,[2] chief sage of Ireland in learning, rested in Ard-Macha. Ua Cruimtir, *i.e.* Oengus, comarb of Comghall, died. Flaithbertach Ua Neill[3] went to Rome. Tadhg Ua Conchobair,[4] King of Connaught, and the Got,[5] King of Midhe, were slain. Ruaidhri Ua Canannain was killed by Aedh Ua Neill. Tadhg son of Lorcan, King of Ui-Ceinnselaigh, died in his pilgrimage in Glenn-da-locha. Cumhara, son of Macliag, chief poet of Ireland, died. Eochaid, son of the Abbot, was slain by the Orc Ua Ruadacain, in treachery. The Cinel-Eoghain broke the house of Ua Loingsigh, in the middle of Oentruimh. Maelduin son of Ciarmac, steward of Cinel-Binnigh of the Glen,[6] was killed by Conchobar Ua Loingsigh. Tadhg,[7] son of Cathal, son of Conchobar, was slain by Maelsechlainn, grandson of Maelruanaidh, King of Crimthainn. [1030.]

Kal. Jan. Frid.; m. 4. A.D. 1031. Flaithbertach Ua Neill[8] came from Rome. Ard-Brecain was plundered by [1031.]

---

not been ascertained. See Reeves's *Colton's Visitation*, p. 73, note y. The translation of this entry in Clar. 49 is a remarkable instance of the ignorance of Irish of the so-called translator, who thus renders the very simple text above printed:—"Maelduin mac Ciarmaic the *Lady Mary* of Kindred-Binni of Glans, killed by the disease that killeth cattle, in Irish called *Conach.*" !!

[7] *Tadhg.*—Tadhg *an eich ghil*, or Tadhg "of the White Steed," King of Connaught. This entry, which is not in B., nor in Clar. 49, seems to be a repetition of a previous entry under this year, but involving some difference of meaning. See note [4].

[8] *Flaithbertach Ua Neill.*—See note [3]. Some lines of poetry describing the bargains obtainable at Armagh, in the time of Flaithbertach, are added in the lower margin of fol. 57*a* in A. (but are not in B.), viz.:—

Seiſſeḋac do ġran ċorca,
No trian d'airnib dubcorcra,
No do dercnaib darac duinn,
No do ċnoib falaċ finncuill,
Fogabar cen taċa tinn
I n-ard Maċa ar oen pinginn.

"A seisedhach [measure] of oaten grain,
Or a third of [a measure] of purple-red sloes,
Or of acorns of the brown oak,
Or of nuts of the fair hazel hedge,
Was got without stiff bargaining,
In Ard-Macha, for one penny."

mBrecain do argain do Gallaib Atha cliath. Da cet duine do loscadh isin daimliac, 7 da cet do breith i m-brait. Ceall dara do loscadh tria anfaitces drochmna. Slogad la mac Eochada co Telaigh n-oóc, 7 nocho tarraidh ni. Aedh .H. Neill do theacht ina timceall fair, co tuc tri mile do buaibh 7 da cet ar mile di brait. Slogad la mac Eochada i n-Uib Eachach, co ro loisc Cill Combair cona dairtigh, co ro marbh cethrar do cleircibh, 7 co ruc. xxx. do brait. Slogad la mac mBriain i n-Osraighibh, co ro ladh ar a muintire, im Maelcolaim Coimrigech 7 alii multi. Cathasach comarba Coemgin do dhallad la Domnall mac Dunlaing. Creach int sneachta la hAedh .H. Neill i tir Conaill, co ro marbh .H. Canannan, ri ceniuil Conaill. Ua Donnacan, ri Aradh tire, do marbad do .H. Briain .i. Toirrdelbach.

.b. Kl. Ianair. uii. f., l. xu. Anno domini M.° xxx.° ii.° Mathgamain .H. Riacain, ri Breg, do marbad do Domnall .H. Chellaig per dolum. Gilla Comgan mac Maelbrighde, mormaer Murebe, do loscadh co coecait do dainibh ime. Domnall .H. Maeldoraidh, ri cenel Conaill, mac Mathgamna mic Muiredaigh, ri Ciaraidhe, Domnall mac Duinncothaigh, ri Gaileng, occisi sunt. Etru .H. Conaing, ridomna Muman, occisus est o

---

[1] *Son of Eochaid.*—Niall, son of Eochaidh (sl. 1003 *supra*), King of Ulidia; or *ardri*, arch-king, as Niall is called, in the entry recording his obit, at the year 1063 *infra*.

[2] *Telach-og.*—Now Tullyhog, in the parish of Desertcreat, barony of Dungannon Upper, Co. Tyrone.

[3] *Cill-Combair.* — The church of Comar (now Comber, in the barony of Lower Castlereagh, Co. Down). The *b* in the member of the name *Combair*, in the text, is wrong. The proper form of the name is *Cill-Comair*, the Church of the *Comar* (or "Confluence"). See Reeves's *Down and Connor*, p. 338.

[4] *Son of Brian;* i.e. Donnchad

[5] *Cainraighech;* i.e. of Caenraighe a tribe and territory now represented in the name of the barony of Kenry, co Limerick.

[6] *Snow depredation.*—Obviously a depredation committed during a great fall of snow.

[7] *Ua Canannain.*—According to the Four Masters (A.D. 1030), his Christian name was Ruaidhri ("Rory," or "Roderick").

[8] *Toirdhelbhach.* — This name is

the Foreigners of Ath-cliath. Two hundred men were burned in the Daimliac, and two hundred were carried into captivity. Cill-dara was burned through the negligence of a wicked woman. A hosting by the son of Eochaid[1] to Telach-og[2]; but he obtained nothing. Aedh Ua Neill passed round him eastwards, and carried off three thousand cows, and one thousand two hundred captives. A hosting by the son of Eochaid[1] into Ui-Echach, when he burned Cill-Combair,[3] with its oratory, killed four of the clerics, and carried away thirty captives. A hosting by the son of Brian[4] into Osraighi, when a slaughter of his people was made, including Maelcolaim Cainraighech,[5] and many others. Cathasach, comarb of Coemghin, was blinded by Domnall son of Dunlaing. The 'snow-depredation'[6] by Aedh Ua Neill, in Tir-Conaill, when he killed Ua Canannain,[7] King of Cinel-Conaill. Ua Donnacain, King of Aradh-tire, was killed by Ua Briain, *i.e.* Toirdhelbhach.[8]

Kal. Jan. Saturd., m. 15. A.D. 1032. Mathgamain Ua Riacain,[9] King of Bregha, was slain by Domnall Ua Cellaigh, through treachery. Gillacomgan, son of Maelbrighde, great steward of Murebhe,[10] was burned with fifty men about him. Domnall Ua Maeldoraidh, King of Cinel-Conaill; the son of Mathghamain son of Muiredach, King of Ciarraidhe,[11] [and] Domnall[12] son of Donncothaigh, King of Gailenga, were slain. Etru Ua Conaing, royal [1032.]BIS.

pronounced *Threlagh*, and is sometimes written Turlogh, and Anglicised Terence. This Toirdhelbhach, who was the son of Tadhg (sl. 1023, *supra*), son of Brian Borumha, was the first person who adopted the hereditary surname of Ua Briain (or O'Brien).

[9] *Ua Riacain.*—See under the year 1029.

[10] *Murebhe.* — Moray, in Scotland. Gillacomgan was the brother of Maelcoluim (Malcolm), King of Alba (whose obit is entered above at the year 1029), and the father of Lulach, also King of Alba (or Scotland), slain by Malcolm son of Donnchadh (Duncan) in the year 1058, as appears under that year *infra*.

[11] *Ciarraidhe*; i.e. Ciarraidhe-Luachra, the name of which is now represented by that of Kerry (the co. Kerry).

[12] *Domnall.*—This name is written Donnghal in the *Annals of Loch-Cè*, and *Ann. Four Mast.*

muinntir Imleċa. Maidm Droma benncair for Ultaib ria n-Airgiallaiḃ. Maidm inbir Boinne ria Sitriuc mac Aṁlaim, for Conaillib 7 for Uib Dorrṫainn, 7 for Uib Meiṫ, irralaḋ a n-ar. Maeltuile espuc aird Maċa in Christo quieuit. Aeḋ .h. Forreiḋ do ġabail na h-espocoide.

Kl. Ianair. ii. f., l. xx. iii. Anno domini M.° xxx.° iii.° Maidm ria Murchad .h. Maelsechlainn for Concobur .h. Maelseċlainn, co ro marbad Maelruanaiḋ .h. Carraiḋ colma, 7 Lorcan .h. Caindelban, ri Loegaire, 7 alii multi. Conn mac Maelpatraic, airchinnech Mungarti, quieuit. Concobar .h. Muireḋaiġ, ri Ciarraiḋe, occisus est. Aenach Carmain la Donn-
Fol. 57ba. chad mac Gillapatraic, iar n-gabail riġi Laigen. Aṁergin .h. Cerbaill, ri Eile, Cu Mumain mac Ruaidri .h. Cetfaḋa, mortui sunt. Maidm itir Eile i torcair Braen .h. Cleiriḋ 7 Muiredaċ mac mic Gillapatraic, 7 alii multi. Mac mic Boete mic Cinaeḋa do marbad la Maelcolaim mac Cinaeḋa. Oengus .h. Caṫail, ri Eoganachta Loċa Lein. Sgrin Petair 7

---

[1] *The 'family' of Imlech*; i.e. the community of Imlech-Ibhair (Emly, in the barony of Clanwilliam, co. Tipperary.)

[2] *Druim-Bennchair*. — Drumbanagher, in the parish of Killeavy, barony of Lower Orior, co. Armagh.

[3] *Inbher-Boinne*.—The estuary (or mouth) of the River Boyne.

[4] *Maeltuile—Aedh Ua Forreidh*.—These names are not in any of the ancient lists of bishops, or abbots, of Armagh. See Todd's *St. Patrick*, pp. 174–183, and Harris's ed. of Ware, vol. 1, p. 50.

[5] *Carrach-Calma*.—See note [5], p. 508 *supra*.

[6] *Mungairit*.—Mungret, about two miles to the south of the city of Limerick.

[7] *Conchobar*.—Apparently the son of Mathgamain, son of Muiredach (King of Ciarraidhe-Luachra) whose obit is entered above at the year 1003. This Conchobar was the person from whom the hereditary surname of O'Conor-Kerry has been derived.

[8] *Carman*.—See note [11], p. 345 *supra*. Carman has been strangely confounded with Loch-Garman, the Irish name of Wexford, by writers on Irish history generally. But there is no authority for identifying the one place with the other. When Donnchadh MacGillapatrick inaugurated his succession to the kingship of Ossory by the celebration of the Fair (and Games) of Carmau, he was not likely to go to Wexford for the purpose, where he would probably get a

heir of Munster, was killed by the 'family' of Imlech.[1] The victory of Druim-Bennchair[2] was gained over the Ulidians by the Airghialla. The victory of Inbher-Boinne[3] was gained by Sitriuc, son of Amhlaimh, over the Conailli, the Ui-Dorthain, and the Ui-Meith, in which they were put to slaughter. Macltuile,[4] bishop of Ard-Macha, rested in Christ. Aedh Ua Forreidh[4] assumed the bishopric.

Kal. Jan. Mond.; m. 26. A.D. 1033. A victory was [1033.] gained by Murchad Ua Maelsechlainn over Conchobar Ua Maelsechlainn, when Maelruanaidh, grandson of Carrach Calma,[5] and Lorcan Ua Caindelbhain, King of Leoghaire, and many others, were slain. Conn, son of Maelpatraic, herenagh of Mungairit,[6] rested. Conchobar,[7] grandson of Muiredhach, King of Ciarraidhe, was slain. The Fair of Carman[8] [was celebrated] by Donnchad MacGillapatraic, after assuming the Kingship of Leinster. Amhergin Ua Cerbhaill, King of Eli,[9] and Cu-Mumhan,[10] son of Ruaidhri Ua Cetfadha, died. A breach among the Eli,[9] in which fell Braen Ua Cleirigh, and Muiredach MacGillapatraic, and a great many more. The son of Mac Boete,[11] son of Cinaedh,[12] was killed by Maelcolaim,[13] son of Cinaedh. Oengus, grandson of Cathal, King of Eoghanacht of Loch-Lein[14] [was killed]. The shrine of

very warm reception from the Ui-Ceinnselaigh. Carman was really the name of a place in the present county of Carlow.

[9] *Eli*; i.e. *Eli Ua Cerbhaill*, or Eli-O'Carroll. See note [7], p. 548.

[10] *Cu-Mumhan.*—A name signifying "Hound of Munster," The name in B. is *Cu-inmhuin* (i.e. "delightful hound"), which is wrong; the *Ann. Four Mast.*, and *Ann. Loch Cé*, agreeing with the form in the MS. A.

[11] *Son of MacBoete.* — Mac mic boete may mean "son of the son of Boete," or "son of MacBoete," a name formed like MacBethad (Macbeth), but different in derivation as well as in signification.

[12] *Cinaedh.*—Probably Cinaedh (or Kenneth) III., King of Scotland, whose obit is given above at the year 995.

[13] *Maelcolaim.*—Malcolm II., King of Scotland.

[14] *Eoghanacht of Loch-Lein.*—One of the numerous septs called "Eoghanachta" (i.e. descendants of Eoghan Mór, son of Oilill Oluim, King of

Poil ic termann ḟola for altair Patraic i n-ard Maċa, coram omnibus uidentibus. Aeḋ mac [F]laiṫbertaiġ .h. Neill, ri Ailiġ 7 ridomna Erenn, post penitentiam mortuus est aiḋci ḟeili Ainnrias.

Kl. Ianair. iii. f., l. iiii. Anno domini M°. xxx.° iiii.° Maelcoluim mac Cinaeḋa, ri Alban, obiit. Amlaim mac Sitriuc do marbad do Saxanaiḃ, oc dul do Roim. Gillasechnaill, mac Gillamoconna, occisus est. Duḃdaingen, ri Connacht, a suis occisus est. Donnchad mac Briain do innreḋ Ossaiġi do leir. Caṫal mairtir airċinneċ Corcaiḋe, 7 Conn mac Maelpatraic airchinnech Mungarti, in Christo dormierunt. Slogad Ulad i Mide, co teċ mic Mellen. Gilla Fulartaig, ri na nDese Breg, occisus est. Macnia .h. hUchtan, ferleiginn Cenannsa, do bathad ic tiachtain a hAlbain, 7 culebad Coluim Cille, 7 tri minna do minnaib Patraic, 7 triċa fer impu. Suibne mac Cinaeḋa, ri Gallgaiḋel, mortuus est.

Munster in the 3rd century.) This sept was seated in the present barony of Magunihy, county of Kerry, about Lough-Lein. It included the three clans of Ui Donnchadha of Loch-Lein, Ui Donnchadha Mór (i.e. O'Donoghue of Loch-Lein, and O'Donoghue Mór, both now extinct), and *Ui Donnchadha an Glenna* (O'Donoghues of the Glen; i.e. Glenflesg), the present head of which old and distinguished family is Daniel O'Donoghue, known as "O'Donoghue of the Glens."

[1] *Andrew's festival;* i.e. the 30th of November.

[2] *Maelcolaim.*—Malcolm II., King of Scotland.

[3] *Gillasechnaill.*—In the *Ann. Four Mast.*, Gillasechnaill is stated to have been King of South Bregha, and slain by the Fera-Rois.

[4] *His own people.* — The *Chron. Scotorum* (at 1032=1034) states that Dubhdaingen ("son of Donnchadh") was of the Ui-Maine. But the name of Dubhdaingen is not in the list of Kings of Connaught contained in the *Book of Leinster*, p. 41, nor does it appear in the Genealogy of the principal families of the Ui-Maine. See O'Donovan's *Hy-Many*, p. 97.

[5] *Mungairit.*—See note [6], p. 566.

[6] *Tech-mic-Millen*—The "house of Mellen's son." "Mac Millen's house," as rendered in the MS. Clar. 49. Probably now represented by Stamullen, in the parish of the same name, barony of Upper Duleek, co. Meath.

[7] *Deisi.* — This tribe gave their name to the present baronies of Deece (Upper and Lower), co. Meath.

[8] *Ua h Uchtain.*— Several persons of this family were connected, in various

Peter and Paul was dropping blood on Patrick's altar in Ard-Macha, in the presence of all observers. Aedh, son of Flaitbertach Ua Neill, King of Ailech, and royal heir of Ireland, died after penitence, on the night of Andrew's festival.[1]

Kal. Jan. Tuesd.; m. 7. A.D. 1034. Maelcolaim,[2] son of Cinaedh, King of Alba, died. Amlaimh, son of Sitriuc, was killed by Saxons on his way to Rome. Gillasechnaill,[3] son of Gillamochonna, was slain. Dubhdaiugen, King of Connaught, was slain by his own people. Donnchad, son of Brian, plundered all Osraighe. Cathal Martyr, herenagh of Corcach, and Conn, son of Maelpatraic, herenagh of Mungairit[5] 'fell asleep' in Christ. A hosting of the Ulidians into Midhe, to Tech-mic-Mellen.[6] Gilla-Fulartaigh, King of the Deisi[7] of Bregha, was slain. Macnia Ua hUchtain,[8] lector of Cenannas, was drowned coming from Alba, and the *culebad*[9] of Colum-Cille, and three of Patrick's reliquaries, and thirty men about them. Suibhne, son of Cinaedh, King of the Gall-Gaidhel,[10] died. [1034.]

---

capacities, with the monastery of Kells. See Reeves's *Adamnan*, p. 397.

[9] *Culebad.*—The meaning of the word *culebad* has been much discussed. Dr. Reeves thought it was the Irish word for Latin *colobium* (a tunic). *Adamnan*, p. 323. See *Ann. Loch Cé*, A.D. 1034, note [2]. The Rev. Thomas Olden has treated of the nature and use of the *culebad* in an interesting paper published in the *Proceedings of the R. I. Acad.*, ser. II., vol. II., part 7 (Jan. 1886), pp. 355–8. Mr. Olden explains *culebad* (glossed "flabellum," in the authority there cited) as a fan for driving away "flies and other unclean insects which fly past, so that they may not touch the sacred things" (p. 356). See *Ann. Loch Cé* (ed. Hennessy) A.D. 1031, note [2], and 1128, note [6]. See also O'Curry's *MS. Materials*, p. 335, where it is erroneously stated that the "*cuilefadh* of St. Patrick" was alluded to in the Annals of the Four Masters at the year 1128. There is reference to a *cuilebadh*, under that year, in the *Ann. Loch Cé*. (See Hennessy's ed., *ad an.*, note [6]), and also in the present Chronicle under the same date *infra* (where see note).

[10] *Gall-Gaidhel.*—"Foreign Irish." The Gaedhlic (or Celtic) people in the mainland and islands of Scotland who were under the rule of the Norsemen. The name is now represented by Galloway, in Scotland.

Kl. Ianair. iiii. f., l. x.uiii. Anno domini M.° xxx.° u. Cnút mac Sain, ri Saxan, do ec. Caṫal mac Aṁalgaḋa, ri iarṫair Laigen, 7 a ben ingen mic Gillaċoemġin mic Cinaeḋa, 7 a ċu, do marbad i n-aen uair do mac Ceallaiġ mic Dunchada. Flaiṫbertaċ .h. Murchada, rí cenuil Boġaine, cum multis occisus est. Iarnan .h. Flannchada, cu na naeṁ 7 na firen, do ṫeacht for creiċ i n-Delbna, contairtetar uaiti do Delbna im airis co tardsat cliathad dó, 7 co ro marbad Iarnan, 7 ár a muintire, tria neart na naeṁ. Ragnall .h. hIṁair, rí puirt Lairgi, do marbad i n-Aṫ cliaṫ la Sitriuc mac Amlaim. Ard mBrecain do arcain do Sitriuc mac Amlaim. Sord Coluim Cille do arcain 7 do loscad do Concobur .h. Maelsechlainn, ina diġail.

Fol. 57bb. Kl. Ianair. .u. f., l. xx. uiiii. Anno domini M.° xxx.°
.b. ui.° Domnall .h. hUaṫmuran, ri fer Li, o ḋal Araide, Sgolog .h. Flannacan ri Teṫḃa a suis, Domnall .h. Flainn, ridomna Temrach, o feraiḃ Breifne, Murchad .h. Incappail 7 Niall mac Muirgisa, da riġdomna iarṫair Connacht, omnes occisi sunt. Cuchiċe mac Eigneċan, ri cenuil Ennai, obiit. Donnchad mac Dunlaing, ri Laigen, do ḋallad la Donnchad mac Gilla-

---

[1] *Cnút.*—King Canute.

[2] *Sain.* — Sweno, or Svein. The name is written *Stain* in the *Chron. Scotorum* (A.D. 1033=1035).

[3] *West of Leinster.* — iarṫar Laigen. This is probably a mistake for airṫer Laigen (or East of Leinster). The *Four Mast.* state that Cathal was King of Ui-Cellaigh-Cualann, a territory that embraced the north-east portion of the present county of Wicklow.

[4] *Cinel-Boghaine.*—The tribe-name of the descendants of Enna-Boghaine, second son of Conall Gulban, son of Niall Nine-hostager. Their territory is now represented by the barony of Banagh, co. Donegal.

[5] *Hound.*—cu. Translated "persecutor" in Clar. 49, and "canis venaticus" by O'Conor. O'Donovan renders *cu na naemh ocus na firen* by "watchdog of the saints and just men." But as the Chronicler records that Iarnan met his death through the power of the saints, it is obvious that he must have regarded Iarnan as an enemy of all holy and good men.

[6] *Delbhna.* — There were several sub-sections of the great family of Delbhna (descendants of Lughaidh *Delbhaedh*, son of Cas, ancestor of

Kal. Jan. Wednesd.; m. 18. A.D. 1035. Cnút[1] son [1035.]
of Sain,[2] King of the Saxons, died. Cathal son of Amhalgaidh, King of the West of Leinster,[3] and his wife, the daughter of the son of Gillacoemhgin, son of Cinaedh, and his dog, were killed at the same time by the son of Cellach, son of Dunchad. Flaithbertach Ua Murchada, King of Cinel-Boghaine,[4] was slain with many others. Iarnan Ua Flannchadha, 'hound'[5] of the saints and faithful, went on a predatory expedition into Delbhna;[6] but a few of the Delbhna met him about a herd, and gave him battle; and Iarnan was killed, and a slaughter [was made] of his people, through the power of the saints. Ragnall, grandson of Imhar, King of Port-Lairge, was killed in Ath-cliath, by Sitriuc son of Amlaimh. Ard-Brecain was plundered by Sitriuc son of Amlaimh. Sord of Colum-Cille[7] was plundered and burned by Conchobar Ua Maelsechlainn, in revenge therefor.

Kal. Jan. Thursd.; m. 29. A.D. 1036. Domnall Ua [1036.]BIS.
hUathmarain, King of Fir-Li, by the Dalaraidhe; Scolog Ua Flannacain, King of Tethbha, by his own people; Domnall Ua Flainn, royal heir of Temhair, by the men of Breifne; Murchad Ua Incappail, and Niall son of Muirghes, two royal heirs of the west of Connaught—were all slain. Cuchiche, son of Eignechan, King of Cinel-Enna, died. Donnchad son of Dunlaing, King of Leinster, was blinded[8] by Donnchad MacGillapatraic,

---

the Dal-Cais of Thomond) scattered throughout Leinster and Connaught. See O'Donovan's ed. of *O'Dugan's Topogr. Poem*, App., notes [26], [28]. The Delbhna above referred to was probably the branch that gave name to the present barony of Delvin, in the co. Westmeath.

[7] *Sord of Colum-Cille.*—Swords, a few miles to the north of Dublin. From the retaliation here recorded, it would seem that Swords was at the time in the possession of the Foreigners.

[8] *Blinded.*—It is stated in the *Book of Leinster* (p. 39, col. 3) that the operation took place after the victim had been brought out of the church of Disert-Diarmata (i.e. Castledermot, co. Kildare), where he had probably taken refuge.

patraic, conerbailt de. Flaiṫbertaċ .h. Neill, airdri Ailiġ, post penitentiam optimam, in Christo quieuit. Oenġus mac Flainn, comarba Brenaind Cluana, Ceallach .h. Sealbaigh, comarba Barre, in Christo dormierunt. Ruaidri mac Taiḋg mic Lorcain do ḋallaḋ la mac Mailna-mbó.

Kt. Ianair. uii. f., l. x. Anno domini M.° xxx.° uii. Caṫal mac Ruaidri, ri iartair Connacht, do ḋul dia ailitri co hArd Maċa. Flann .h. Maelsechlainn do ḋallaḋ la Concobar .h. Maelsechlainn. Arċu .h. Celecan .i. ri .h. mBresail, 7 Ruaidri .h. Lorcain, ri .h. Niallain, occisi sunt i Croeiḃ ċaille, o Muireḋaċ .h. Ruaḋacain, 7 o hUiḃ Eachach. Cu-inmain .h. Robann, ri Puirt Lairce, a suis occisus est. Cearnaċan goth occisus est la .h. Flannacan do hUiḃ Maine. Tri hUi Maeldoraiḃ do marbaḋ. Fliuċ doinenn mor isin bliadainsi.

Kt. Ianair. i. f., l. xx. i. Anno domini M.° xxx.° uiii.° Cuimniden Coinnsre, comarba mic Nissi 7 Colmain Ela, Colman cam .h. Conġaile, comarba

---

[1] *Flaithbertach.*—A marg. note in the original hand, in A., adds the epithet in trostain, "of the pilgrim's staff," in allusion to Flaithbertach's journey to Rome, recorded above at the year 1030. See note [3], p. 489, *supra.*

[2] *Brenainn of Cluain.*—St. Brendan of Clonfert-Brendan (or Clonfert), in the barony of Longford, co. Galway. The name of Oengus does not appear in Archdall's list of the abbots of Clonfert, nor in Ware's list of the bishops of that ancient See.

[3] *Comarb of Barrè*; i.e. successor of St. Barrè (or Finnbar), abbot or bishop of Cork.

[4] *Tadhg.*—He was King of Ui-Ceinnselaigh. His obit is entered above at the year 1030.

[5] *Son of Mael-na-mbó.*—The name of this son was Diarmait, who, from being King of Ui-Ceinnselaigh (or South Leinster), made himself ruler of all Leinster. His death in battle is recorded at the year 1072 *infra*, where he is called King of Leinster and the "Gentiles" (or Foreigners). *Mael-na-mbo* ("Cow-chief") was a nickname for Donnchad, King of Ui-Ceinnselaigh (slain by his own tribe in 1005, *Four Mast.*), who was the grandfather of Murchadh, King of Leinster (*ob.* 1070, *infra*), from whom the name of Mac Murchadha (or Mac Murrough) has been derived. See note under A.D. 1042.

[6] *Flann— Conchobar*—According to the *Ann. Four Mast.*, they were brothers.

whereof he died. Flaithbertach[1] Ua Neill, chief King of Ailech, after the most perfect penitence, rested in Christ. Oengus son of Flann, comarb of Brenainn of Cluain,[2] [and] Cellach Ua Selbhaigh, comarb of Barrè,[3] 'fell asleep' in Christ. Ruaidhri, son of Tadhg,[4] son of Lorcan, was blinded by the son of Mael-na-mbo.[5]

Kal. Jan. Saturd.; m. 10. A.D. 1037. Cathal, son [1037]
of Ruaidhri, King of the West of Connaught, went on his pilgrimage to Ard-Macha. Flann[6] Ua Maelsechlainn was blinded by Conchobar[6] Ua Maelsechlainn. Archu Ua Celechain,[7] King of Ui-Bresail, and Ruaidhri Ua Lorcain, King of Ui-Niallain, were slain in Craebh-caille,[8] by Muiredach Ua Ruadhacain and the Ui-Echach. Cu-inmain[9] Ua Robann, King of Port-Lairge,[10] was slain by his own people. Cernachan Got[11] was killed by Ua Flannacain of the Ui-Maine. Three Ua Maeldoraidhs were killed. Great rain in this year.

Kal. Jan. Sund.; m. 21. A.D. 1038. Cuinniden[12] [1038.]
Connere, comarb of MacNisse and Colman Ela, Colman Cam[13] Ua Conghaile, comarb of Molaise,[14] rested in

---

[7] *Ua Celechain.*—Anglicised O'Callaghan. This family, which is to be distinguished from the more extensive Cork family of the name, was at one time powerful in that part of the co. Armagh now forming the barony of O'Neilland East. See at the year 1044 *infra.* The late Mr. John C. O'Callaghan, author of the *Green Book* and of the *Irish Brigades in the Service of France*, claimed to be descended from these O'Callaghan's of Ui-Bresail.

[8] *Craebh-caille.* — O'Donovan suggests (*Ann. F. M.*, A.D. 825, note *d*), that this is "probably the place now called Kilcreevy," in the parish of Derrynoose, barony and county of Armagh

[9] *Cu-inmain*; lit. "Delightful Hound." Tigernach writes the name *Cu-Mumhan*, "Hound of Munster."

[10] *Port-Lairge.*— Waterford City. puırт Laırgı, B.

[11] *Cernachan Got*; i.e. Cernachan the "Stammerer." O'Conor renders *got* ("stammerer") by "*statura procerus.*"

[12] *Cuinniden.*—Written "Cuindên" by the *Four Masters*, who describe him as Bishop, Abbot, and Lector, of Condere (Connor). See notes [11], [12], p. 471, and note [12], p. 473, *supra.* The MS. B. has .h. Coımneɲe (for Ua Connere), which seems wrong.

[13] *Cam*; i.e. "bent," or "crooked." The epithet applied to Colman in the *Ann. Four Mast.* is *caech*, "blind."

[14] *Comarb of Molaise*; i.e. successor of St. Molaise, or abbot of Devenish, in Loch Erne.

Molaisi, in Christo quieuerunt. Gillacrist mac Cathbair h. Domnaill do marbad la mac Cuinn h. Domnaill. Cath etir Cuanu ri Allsaxan 7 Otta ri Frangcc, i torchair mile im Otta. Orc allaid h. Ruadhacain, ri h. nEachach, do marbad do claind Sinaig i n-ard Macha, illuan feile Ulltan, i n-digail marbtha Eochada mic ind abaid, 7 i n-digail saraigthi aird Macha. Maidm for hUib Maine ria Dealbna for lar Cluana mic Nois, i n-aine feile Ciarain, in quo multi occisi sunt. Cudulig h. Donnchada, ridomna Caisil, do marbad d' O Faelan.

Fol. 58aa. Kl. Ianair. ii. f., l. ii. Anno domini M.° xxx.° ix.° Iaco ri Bretan a suis, Domnall mac Donnchada ri h. Faelan o Domnall h. Fergaili, Donnchad derg h. Ruairc o hUi Conchobair, Ruaidri ri Fernmuighi a suis, Aed h. Flanacan ri Luirg 7 h. Fiachrach, omnes occisi sunt. Donnchad mac Gillapatraic, airdri Laigen 7 Osraigi, Macnia comarba Buiti,

---

[1] *Cuana.*—Conrad II., Emperor of Germany. See under the year 1023 *supra*; and the *Ann. Loch-Cé* (ed. Hennessy,) Vol. I., p. 40, note [1]. See also Petavius, *Rationar. Temporum*, part I, book viii., chap. xvii.

[2] *Orc-allaidh Ua Ruadhacain.* — The name Ua Ruadhacain is now written O'Rogan (or Rogan without the O'). Orc-allaidh (lit. "wild pig") was probably a nickname for the Muiredach [Ua Ruadhacain] mentioned under the year 1037.

[3] *Clann-Sinaigh;* i.e. the "descendants of Sinach." It would appear from an entry at the year 1059 *infra*, that the Clann-Sinaigh were seated in the *Airthera*, a territory now represented by the baronies of Lower and Upper Orior, co. Armagh.

[4] *Ultan.*—St. Ultan of Ard-Breccain (Ardbraccan, co. Meath), whose festival day is September 4. The Dominical Letter for the year 1038 being A., the 4th of September in that year fell on a Monday.

[5] *Mac-in-abaidh;* i.e. "son of the Abbot." From this form comes the Irish and Scotch surname Mac Nab. The *Four Masters* do not give this entry.

[6] *Delbhna.* — The inhabitants of *Delbhna-Ethra*, or Delvin Mac Coghlan, now the barony of Garrycastle, in the King's County. See *Irish Topographical Poems* (ed. O'Donovan) notes [26], [28].

[7] *Ciaran's festival.*—The festival of St. Ciaran of Clonmacnoise occurs on the 9th of September, which fell

Christ. Gillachrist, son of Cathbar Ua Domnaill, was killed by the son of Conn Ua Domnaill. A battle between Cuana,[1] King of the All-saxan, and Otto, King of the Franks, in which 1,000 men were slain, along with Otta. Orc-allaidh Ua Ruadhacain,[2] King of Ui-Echach, was killed by the Clann-Sinaigh,[3] in Ard-Macha, on the Monday of the festival of Ultan,[4] in revenge of the killing of Eochaidh Mac-in-abaidh,[5] and in revenge of the profanation of Ard-Macha. The Ui-Maine were defeated by the Delbhna[6] in the middle of Cluain-mic-Nois, on the Friday of Ciaran's festival,[7] in which many were slain. Cuduiligh Ua Donnchadha, royal heir of Caisel, was slain by the Ui-Faelain.

Kal. Jan. Mond.; m. 2. A.D. 1039. Iaco[8] King of [1039]
Britain, by his own people; Domnall[9] son of Donnchad, King of Ui-Faelain, by Domnall Ua Fergaile[10]; Donnchad Derg[11] Ua Ruairc, by Ua Conchobair[12]; Ruaidhri,[13] King of Fernmagh, by his own people; Aedh Ua Flannacain, King of Lurg and Ui-Fiachrach[14]—all were slain. Donnchad Mac Gillapatraic, Arch-King of Leinster and Osraighi, [and] Macnia, comarb of Buite,[15] a bishop, and

---

on a Saturday in the year 1038; the vigil of Ciaran's feast day being therefore on a Friday.

[8] *Iaco.*—Printed "Iago, King of Gwynedd," in the *Brut y Tywisogion* (A.D. 1037); and "Iacob rex Venedotiæ" in *Ann. Cambriæ*, A.D. 1039.

[9] *Domnall.*—See the pedigree of this prince in Shearman's *Loca Patriciana*, Table No. 12, between pp. 222 and 223.

[10] *Domnall Ua Fergaile.* — See O'Donovan's *Four Masters*, A.D. 1039, note y.

[11] *Donnchad Derg;* i.e. Donnchad (or Denis), the "Red." He was the son of Art O'Ruairc, King of Connaught (nicknamed *an cailech*, or "the Cock"), whose death is recorded at the year 1046 *infra*.

[12] *Ua Conchobair;* i.e. O'Conor. This was Aedh *an gha bhernaigh* (or Aedh "*of the gapped spear*"), King of Connaught, whose death is recorded at the year 1067 *infra*.

[13] *Ruaidhri.*—The *Ann. of Tigernach*, and the *Four Masters*, have mac Ruaiḋri, "son of Ruaidhri."

[14] *Ui Fiachrach;* i.e. Ui-Fiachrach of Ard-Sratha [Ardstraw], a tribe seated in the north-west of the present county of Tyrone, along the River Derg, and near the barony of Lurg, in the county of Fermanagh.

[15] *Comarb of Buite;* i.e. abbot of Monasterboice, co. Louth.

episcopus et plenus dierum, Ceileċair .h. Cuilennan comarba Tiġernaiġ, suam uitam feliciter finiuit. Muiredaċ mac Flannacain, fosairchinnech aird Maċa, do hUiḃ Eachach. Muireḋaċ mac Flaiṫbertaiċ .h. Neill do marbad do Leiṫrennaiḃ. Cerball mac Faelan o Gallaib occisus est.

.b. Kl. Ianair. iii. f., l. x. iii. Anno domini M.° xl. Hic est annus millissimus 7 xl.mus ab incarnatione domini. Coscraċ mac Aingeda, comarba Flannan 7 Brenainn, Maelmuire .h. Uchtan comarba Coluim cille, Diarmait .h. Seċnusaiġ comarba Seċnaill, in Christo dormierunt. Corcran cleireċ, cenn Eorpa im crabud 7 im ecna, in Christo pausauit. Dunchad .h. Canege, ferleiġinn aird Maċa, mitissimus ac doctissimus, in Christo pausauit. Donnchad mac Crinan, ri Alban, a suis occisus est. Aralt, ri Saxan giuair, moritur. Ceall dara uile do loscaḋ im ḟeil

---

[1] *Comarb of Tigernach;* i.e. successor of St. Tigernach, or abbot of Clones, co. Monaghan.

[2] *Ended.* — finiuit, A. finierunt, B, in which the three obits here recorded are combined in the one entry.

[3] *Flaithbertach Ua Neill.*—Flaithbertach "of the pilgrim's staff," whose obit is entered above at the year 1036.

[4] *Lethrenna.* — This name is a plural noun, the singular of which would be *Lethrinn.* For do Leiṫrennaiḃ, the *Annals of Tigernach* and the *Four Masters* have do Uiḃ Labraḋa, "by the Ui-Labhradha." See *Ann. Loch-Cé* (ed. Hennessy), Vol. I, p. 40, note *l*.

[5] *Comarb of Flannan and Brenainn;* i.e. abbot (or bishop) of Killaloe, in the county of Clare, and of Clonfert, in the county of Galway. But the name of Coscrach does not appear in Ware's lists of the bishops of those Sees.

[6] *Ua hUchtain.* — See Reeves's *Adamnan*, p. 398, and also pp. 279, 321. Maelmuire Ua hUchtain was principal of the Columbian foundations both in Ireland and Scotland.

[7] *Comarb of Sechnall;* i.e. abbot of Dun-Sechnaill (now Dunshaughlin), in the county Meath.

[8] *Corcran Clerech.*—"Corcran the Cleric." After the death of Maelsechlainn the Great (A.D. 1022 *supra*), there seems to have been an interregnum in the government of Ireland, during which the public affairs are alleged to have been carried on by a great poet, Cuan O'Lochain (sl. in 1024), and the Corcran Clerech here referred to. Mr. Moore (*History of Ireland*, vol. II., p. 147, note), states that he could find no authority for

a man full of days, [died]. Ceilechair Ua Cuilennain, comarb of Tigernach,[1] ended[2] his life happily. Muiredach, son of Flannacan, vice-herenagh of Ard-Macha, of the Ui-Echach, [died]. Muiredach, son of Flaithbertach Ua Neill,[3] was killed by the Lethrenna.[4] Cerbhall, son of Faelan, was slain by Foreigners.

Kal. Jan. Tuesd.; m. 13. A.D. 1040. This is the 1040th year from the Lord's Incarnation. Coscrach son of Ainngid, comarb of Flannan and Brenainn[5]; Maelmuire Ua hUchtain,[6] comarb of Colum-Cille, [and] Diarmait, grandson of Sechnasach, comarb of Sechnall,[7] 'fell asleep' in Christ. Corcran Clerech,[8] head of Europe as regards piety and learning, rested in Christ. Dunchad Ua Canege,[9] lector of Ard-Macha, the gentlest and most learned, rested in Christ. Donnchad son of Crinan,[10] King of Alba, was killed by his own people. Aralt, King of the Saxons 'giuais,'[11] died. Cill-dara was all [1040.]BIS.

this allegation in "any of our regular Annals." The portion of the *Book of Leinster* dealing with the succession of the Irish Kings from the earliest period is of an annalistic character; and after the record (p. 26*a*), of the death of Maelsechlainn Mór (or Malachy the Great), the following entry occurs: — comḟlaċiuṙ ṗoṙ hEṙinn ṗṙi ṙe dá bliadain .xl. (no.l.) Cúan .h. Lothcain, Corcṙan cleṙec; i.e. "a joint regnancy over Ireland, for 42 (or 52) years; Cuan Ua Lothchain, and Corcran Clerech." See *Book of Rights* (ed. O'Donovan), Introd., pp. xlii. xliii.

[9] *Ua Canege*; i.e. "grandson (or descendant) of Caneg." The *Four Mast.* have *Ua hAnchainge*, "grandson of Anchaing." This entry is not in B.

[10] *Dunchad son of Crinan.* — The name of Dunchad's father is written "Critan" in the *Chron. Scotorum*, but (correctly) "Crinan" in the *Ann. of Tigernach*. This Dunchad, the Duncan of the play of Macbeth, although stated above to have been slain by his own people (*a suis*), is reported in the Chronicle of Marianus Scotus as having been killed *a duce suo MacBethad mac Finnloech.*" See Skene's *Chron. Picts and Scots*, places referred to in Index under Duncan I.

[11] *Aralt, King of the Saxons 'giuais.* Harold Harefoot, whose obit is also given in the Anglo-Sax. Chronicle and other Old English Chronicles at the year 1040. The meaning of the epithet '*giuais*,' which Dr. O'Conor prints *guiais*, and translates "ferorum," is not plain to the Editor. The Translator in Clar. 49 renders ṙi Saxan giuaiṙ by "King of Saxons of Gills." See *Ann. Loch-Cé* (ed. Hennessy), A.D. 1040, note [11].

Miċeil. Ceanannus do loscaḋ. Dun da leṫglas do loscaḋ 7 ilċealla arċena.

Kt. Ianair .u. f.; l. .xx. iiii. Anno domini M.° xl.° i.° At imḋa ṫra na h-airiri etir marbad doene, 7 éc 7 creċa 7 caṫa. Ni cumaing nech a n-innisin do leir, acht uate do iliḃ diḃ ar daiġ aera na n-doene do ḟis treoṫo. Mac Beathad mac Ainmere ard ollam ard Maċa 7 Erenn arċena. Domnall reṁar ṁac ṁail na mbo do marbad do Laiġniḃ. Muircertaċ mac Gillapatraic do marbad do hUi Ċaillaiḋe a meḃail. Creċ la hAirġiallu i Conailliḃ, co ro brisidar Conaille forro i Maiġ Daċainneċ. Creċ la .h. Neill i
Fol. 58ab. nhUiḃ Eachach Ulad, co tucsat creiċ moir. Gillacomgaill, mac Duinncuan mic Dunlaing, do breiṫ a cill dara ar eicin, 7 a marbad iarum.

Kt. Ianair .ui. f.; l. u. Anno domini M.° xl.° ii.° Fearna mor Moeḋoc do loscaḋ la Donnchad mac mBriain. Glenn Uissen do loscaḋ do mac Mail na mbó, 7 in dairrteċ do brisiuḋ, 7 cet duine do marbad, 7 .iiii. cet do breiṫ eirti, i n-diġail Ferna móre. Loingseċ (.i. h. Flaiṫen), comarba Ciarain 7 Cronain, quieuit. Aeḋ mac ind abaid, (.i. mac Mailmuire 7

[1] *And deaths.*—7 éc, in A. only.

[2] *Domnall Remhar;* i.e., Domnall "the Fat." The proper name of Mael-na-mbo, father of Domnall, was Donnchad. See note [4], p. 516, *supra.*

[3] *Ui-Caellaidhe.* — This name is even yet pretty numerous in the counties of Kilkenny, Queen's county, and Kildare; but under the forms "Kelly" and "Kealy," without the O'

[4] *Magh-Dachainnech.* – Some place in the north of the present county of Louth, which has not been identified.

[5] *Ferna-mor-Moedhoc.* — "Moedhoc's great Alder-tree." Ferns, in the county of Wexford.

[6] *Glenn-Uissen.*—Now represented by Killeshin, in a parish of the same name, barony of Slievemargy, Queen's county. See O'Donovan's *Four Mast.*, A.D. 843, note y.

[7] *Son.*—He was apparently Diarmait, [son of Donnchad, called Mael-na-mbo; see note [4], p. 516 *supra*], at first King of Ui-Ceinnselaigh, but ultimately King of Leinster. The obit of Diarmait is entered under the year 1072 *infra*, where he is described as King of the Leinstermen and Foreigners. See note [5], under A.D. 1036, *supra*.

[8] *Ferna-mór.*—See note [5]. It is stated in the *Ann. Four M.* (A.D. 1041), that the outrages above recorded were committed in revenge not only of the

burned about Michaelmas. Cenannas was burned. Dun-da-lethglas was burned, and many churches besides.

Kal. Jan. Thursd.; m. 24. A.D. 1041. Numerous, truly, are the events [of this year], between the killing of men, and deaths,[1] and depredations, and battles. No one could relate them all; but a few out of many of them [are mentioned], in order that the ages of the people might be known through them. MacBeathad, son of Ainmire, chief poet of Ard-Macha and of Ireland in general, [died]. Domnall Remhar,[2] son of Mael-na-mbo, was killed by the Leinstermen. Muirchertach Mac Gillapatraic was killed by the Ui-Caellaidhe,[3] in treachery. A depredation by the Airghialla in Conaille; when the Conaille routed them in Magh-Dachainnech.[4] A depredation by the Ui Neill in Ui-Echach-Uladh, when they took a great prey. Gillacomghaill, son of Donncuan, son of Dunlaing, was forcibly taken out of Cill-dara, and killed afterwards. [1041.]

Kal. Jan. Frid.; m. 5. A.D. 1042. Ferna-mor-Moedhoc[5] was burned by Donnchad, son of Brian. Glenn-Uissen[6] was burned by the son[7] of Mael-na-mbo, and the oratory was broken, and 100 men were slain, and 400 taken out of it—in revenge of Ferna-mór.[8] Loingsech (i.e. Ua Flaithen), comarb of Ciaran and Cronan,[9] rested. Aedh, son of the Abbot, (*i.e.* son of Maelmuire,[10] and of [1042.]

---

burning of Ferns, but also of the slaying of Domhnall *Remhar*, brother of the [Diarmait] son of Mael-na-mbo, referred to in the last note.

[9] *Comarb of Ciaran and Cronan*; i.e., Abbot of Clonmacnoise and Roscrea.

[10] *Maelmuire.*—The name "Maelmuire" does not appear in any of the ancient lists of Abbots of Cork accessible to the Editor. The only ecclesiastic of the name whose period would correspond to the foregoing entry is Maelmaire (or Maelmuire), abbot, or bishop, of Armagh, whose obit is given at A.D. 1020 *supra*. See under the year 1038, where the then King of Ui-Echach (Iveagh) is stated to have been slain in Armagh, in revenge of the killing of "Eochaidh son of the Abbot" (*Mac-in-abaidh*). It may be added that "Ua Lorcain," or "O'Larkin," was the name of the contemporary ruling family of the Ui-Niallain, a tribe situated in the north of the county of Armagh.

Setaige ingine hui Lorcain), do ec i Corcaig moir Muman. Murchad mac Dunlaing, ri Laigen, 7 Domnall mac Aeḋa, ri .h. Bairrċe, do ṫuitim la Gillapatraic mac n-Donnchada, ri Osraiġi, 7 la Macraiṫ mac Donnchada, ri Eoganachta. Flann mac Mailsechlainn, ridomna Erenn, do marbad tria ṁeabail. Maelpetair .h. hAilecan, ferleiġinn 7 toiseċ macleiġinn aird Maċa, do marbad do feraiḃ Fernṁuiġi. Ailill Mucnoma, cenn ṁanaċ na n-Goeiḋel, in Colonia quieuit.

Kl. Ianair .uii. f.; l. xui. Anno domini M.° xl.° iii.° Caṫal mac Ruaiḋri, ri iarṫair Connacht, do ec ina ailiṫri i n-ard Maċa. Domnall .h. Ferġaile, ri Fortuaṫ Laigen, do marbad dia ḋainib fein. Flann .h. Anbeid, rí .h. Meiṫ, o hUi Cerbuill, o riġ Fernṁuiġi; Aeḋ .h. Conḟiacla, rí Tethba, o Muircertaċ .h. Mailseċlainn; Ceinneitig .h. Cuirc, ri Muscraiḋe, occisi sunt. Ceallach .h. Cleircin, comarba Finnein 7 Moċolmocc, Cairpri .h. Laiḋgnein, airchinnech Ferna 7 tiġi Moling, Gillamoċonna .h. Duibdirma, in pace dormierunt. Maidm Maelecoennaiġ for brú Súire, for Osraiġi 7 for Ermumain, re Carrtaċ mac

[1] *Corcach-mor.* — The "Great Marsh." Cork, in the county of Cork. See last note.

[2] *Domnall.*—The name is Donnchadh in the *Ann. Four Mast.* (1042), and the *Chron. Scotorum* (1040). But the name in the *Ann. Loch-Cé* is Domnall.

[3] *Ui-Bairrche.*—The descendants of Daire *Barrach*, second son of Cathair Mor, King of Leinster in the 2nd century. Their territory comprised the present barony of Slievemargy, Queen's county, and some of the adjacent districts of the co. Carlow.

[4] *Ua Donnchadha.*—("grandson of Donnchad"). mac Donnchada ("son of Donnchad"), A. The obit of Macraith Ua Donnchada (or Macraith O'Donoghoe) is entered at the year 1052 *infra*.

[5] *Eoghanacht.* — Otherwise *Eoghanacht Chaisil;* a sept descended from Eoghan Mor, son of Oilill Oluim, anciently seated around Cashel, in the present county of Tipperary.

[6] *Through treachery.* tria ṁaeabail, A. Tria ṁaeġail, B. Both readings being corrupt.

[7] *Mucnamh.* — Mucknoe, in the barony of Cremorne, co. Monaghan. See Reeves's *Down and Connor*, p. 146, note i.

[8] *Fortuatha-Laighen.*—See note [7], p. 157 *supra.*

Setach, daughter of Ua Lorcain), died in Corcach-mor[1] of Munster. Murchad son of Dunlaing, King of Leinster, and Domnall[2] son of Aedh, King of Ui-Bairrche,[3] fell by Gillapatraic son of Donnchad, King of Osraighi, and by Macraith Ua Donnchadha,[4] King of Eoghanacht.[5] Flann son of Maelsechlainn, royal heir of Ireland, was killed through treachery.[6] Maelpetair Ua h-Ailecain, lector, and chief of the students of Ard-Macha, was killed by the men of Fernmagh. Ailill of Mucnamh,[7] head of the monks of the Gaedhil, rested in Cologne.

Kal. Jan. Saturd.; m. 16. A.D. 1043. Cathal son of Ruaidhri, King of the West of Connaught, died in his pilgrimage in Ard-Macha. Domnall Ua Ferghaile, King of Fortuatha-Laighen,[8] was killed by his own people. Flann Ua Anbheidh, King of Ui-Meith, by Ua Cerbhaill, King of Fernmhagh; Aedh Ua Confiacla, King of Tethba,[9] by Muirchertach Ua Maelsechlainn; Ceinnetigh Ua Cuirc, King of Muscraidhe[10]—were slain. Cellach Ua Cleircein, Comarb of Finnen and Mocholmoc;[11] Cairpri Ua Laidhgnein, herenagh of Ferna and Tech-Moling,[12] [and] Gillamochonna Ua Duibhdirma, 'fell asleep' in peace. The victory of Maelcoennaigh,[13] on the brink of the Suir, over the Osraighi and Irmumha,[14] by Carthach[15] son of Saer- [1043.]

---

[9] *Tethba.*—τebτα, A.

[10] *Muscraidhe.*—Otherwise Muscraidhe-Chuirc("Muskerry-Quirk"); and also called Muscraidhe-Breoghain, and Muscraidhe-Treithirne. This territory comprised the greater part of the present barony of Clanwilliam, in the county of Tipperary.

[11] *Comarb of Finnen and Mocholmoc;* i.e., Abbot of Moville, co. Down, (founded by St. Finnian), and of Dromore, in the same county, (founded by St. Colman, or Mocholmoc).

[12] *Tech-Moling.*—"Moling's House." St. Mullens, in the county of Carlow.

[13] *Maelcoennaigh.*—O'Donovan thought this was the place where "the River Multeen unites with the Suir," about three miles to the west of Cashel, co. Tipperary.

[14] *Irmumha.*—"East Munster." The name is written *Ermumha* in the *Ann. Loch-Ce*, and *Urmumha* by the *Four Masters*. Ormond, in Tipperary, is meant.

[15] *Carthach.*—From this Carthach, whose name signifies "loving," the MacCarthys of Desmond have derived their hereditary surname. His death is noticed at the year 1045 *infra*.

Saerbrethaig,[1] i farcbad .h. Donnacain, ri Arad. Maidm ria cenel Eogain for cenel Conaill i termonn Dabeocc.[2]

b. Kl. Ianair .i. f.; l. xxiii. Anno domini M.° xl.° iiii.°
Fol. 58ba. Cumuscach .h. hAilillen, ri .h. nEchach, do marbad o hUib Caracan.[3] Niall .h. Ceilecan,[4] ri .h. mBresail, 7 a brathair .i. Trenfer,[5] do dallad do macaib Matodain tria mebail. Domnall .h. Cuirc, ri Muscraidhe, do marbad do hUi Laithein 7 do hUi Oissein. Crech la Niall mac Mailsechlainn, la rig nAilig, for hUib Meith 7 for Cuail[n]ge, co ruc da cet déc bó 7 sochaide di braid, i n-digail saraigthi cluicc ind edechta. Crech eile dono la Muirchertach .h. Neill for Mugdorna, co tuc boroma 7 braid i n-digail saraigthi in cluic cetna. In cleirech .h. Conchobair do marbad.

Kl. Ianair .iii. f.; l. ix. Anno domini M.° xl.° u.° Muiredach mac Soersgura airchinnech Daimliac, Catharach .h. Cathail, comarba Coeimgin, Maenach .h. Cirduban, airchinnech Lughmaidh, in pace dormierunt. Congalach .h. Lochlainn, ri Corcumbruadh, Glun iarainn .h. Cleirchen, ri .h. Cairpri, Flaithbertach .h. Canannan ri cenuil Conaill, Domnall .h. Cetfatha,

---

[1] *Saerbrethach*; lit. "noble-judging." A name still in use, as a Christian name, among respectable branches of the MacCarthys of the south of Ireland, in the forms Justin and Justinian.

[2] *Termon-Dabheoc.*—The sanctuary of Dabheoc, for whom see Martyr. of Donegal at 1 January. The church of St. Dabheoc was situated in the island in Lough Derg, co. Donegal, famous in later times as the site of St. Patrick's Purgatory. The church lands included within the limits of Termon-Dabheoc are now known by the name of Termon-Magrath, in the parish of Templecarne, barony of Tirhugh, co. Donegal.

[3] *Ui-Caracain.*—A sept that occupied and gave name to a small tract of land lying on either side of the river Blackwater, and co-extensive with the present parish of Killyman, in the diocese of Armagh. See O'Donovan's *Four Mast.*, A.D. 1044, note f, where further information on the subject is given.

[4] *Ua Ceilechain.*—Or Ua Celechain. See note [7], under the year 1037 *supra*.

[5] *Trenfher* (Pron. *Trenar*); lit. "mighty man," or "champion."

brethach,[1] in which Ua Donnacain, King of Aradh, was slain. A victory by the Cinel-Eoghain over the Cinel-Conaill, in Termon-Dabheoc.[2]

Kal. Jan. Sund.; m. 17. A.D. 1044. Cumuscach Ua [1044.]Bis.
hAilillen, King of Ui-Echach, was killed by the Ui-Caracain.[3] Niall Ua Ceilechain,[4] King of Ui-Bresail, and his brother, *i.e.* Trenfher,[5] were blinded by the sons of Matadhan,[6] through deceit. Domnall Ua Cuirc, King of Muscraidhe,[7] was killed by Ua Laithen[8] and Ua Oissein. A depredation by Niall son of Maelsechlainn, King of Ailech, upon the Ui-Meith and Cualnge, when he carried off 1,200 cows, and a great many prisoners, in revenge of the profanation of *clocc-ind-edechta.*[9] Another depredation, also, by Muirchertach Ua Neill upon the Mughdorna, when he carried off a cattle-spoil, and prisoners, in revenge of the same bell.[10] The Cleirech Ua Conchobair was killed.

Kal. Jan. Tuesd.; m. 9. A.D. 1045. Muiredach, son [1045.]
of Saerghus, herenagh of Daimliacc; Cathasach Ua Cathail, comarb of Coemhgin,[11] [and] Maenach Ua Cirdubhain, herenagh of Lughmadh,[12] 'fell asleep' in peace. Conghalach Ua Lochlainn, King of Corcumruadh, Glun-iarainn Ua Cleirchen, King of Ui-Cairpri; Flaithbertach Ua Canannain, King of Cinel-Conaill, and

---

The name is incorrectly written Treiner (for Treinfer) in A., and Treinfer in B.; the proper form being Trenfer.

[6] *Matadhan.* — Apparently the "Matadhan son of Domnall, King of Ulidia," whose death is recorded above under the year 1006.

[7] *Muscraidhe.*—See note [10], p. 581.

[8] *Ua-Laithen.*—The *Four Masters* write the name "Ua Flaithen," which is probably the correct form.

[9] *Clocc-ind-edechta.* — The "Bell of the Testament." Otherwise called *Clocc-udachta-Patraic*, or the "Bell of Patrick's Will"; because the Saint is alleged to have bequeathed it by will to the church of Armagh. See above at the year 552; Reeves's Essay on the *Bell of St. Patrick*; Trans. Royal Irish Acad., Vol. xxvii., part I. (*Polite Lit. and Antiquities*); and *Antiq. of Down and Connor*, p. 369, *sq.*

[10] *The same Bell.*—See last note.

[11] *Comarb of Coemhgin*; i.e. Abbot of Glenn-da-locha, or Glendalough.

[12] *Lughmadh.*—Louth, in the county of Louth. The name is written Lugh (for Lughad) in B.

ordan Muman, mortui sunt. Airchinnech Leṫglinne do marbad a n-dorus na cille. Creċ la Muirceartaċ .h. Neill i feraiḃ Breġ, conustarraiḋ Gairbeiḋ .h. Caṫusaiġ, ri Breġ, i Cassan linne, 7 an muir lan ar a ċinn, co torċair Muirceartaċ ann, 7 alii multi. Carrṫaċ mac Soerbrethaig, ri Eoganachta Caisil, do loscad i tiġ ṫeined do hU Longarcan mac Duinncuan, cum multis nobilibus ustis. Caṫ etir Albanċu etarru fein i torċair Cronan ab Duine Caillenn.

Kl. Ianair. .iiii. f.; l. xx. Anno domini M.° xl.° vi.° Muiredaċ mac Flaiṫbertaiċ .h. Neill, ridamna Ailiġ, 7 Aiteiḋ .h. hAiteiḋ ri .h. nEchach Ulad, do loscaḋ i tiġ teneḋ la Coinulad mac Conġalaig, i n-Uachtair
Fol. 58bb. ṫire. Art .h. Ruairc, ri Connacht, do marbad do cenul Conaill. Ferġal .h. Ciarḋai, ri Cairpri, do marbad do .h. Flannacain, do riġ Tebṫa. Concobar .h. Loingsiċ, ri dal Araide, do marbad do mac Domnall .h. Loingsiċ, i Llaiġniḃ. Maelpatraic .h. Bileoce, aird ferleiginn aird Maċa, 7 sui crabaid 7 uaoiġi, in senectute bona quieuit. Dubdaleiṫi mac Maelmuire do gabail na firusa leiġinn.

Kl. Ianair. u. f.; l. i. Anno domini M.° xl.° uii.° Snechta mor isin bliadain si o ḟeil Muire (geiṁriḋ)

[1] *Ua Cetfadha.*—Nothing seems to be known regarding Domnall Ua Cetfadha, who is called "Head of the Dal-Cais" by the *Four Masters*, or as to the qualifications which obtained for him the title of ordan Muman, "glory of Munster"; not "Gubernator Momoniæ," as O'Conor renders the Irish.

[2] *Muirchertach.*—He was the son of Flaithbhertach Ua Neill, King of Ailech, whose obit is entered at the year 1036 *supra*.

[3] *Ua Cathasaigh.* — O'Casey. See note [3], p. 542 *supra*.

[4] *Cassan-linne.*—See note [12], p. 443 *supra*. O Conor renders *Cassan-linne*, which literally signifies the "path of the *linn* (or lake)" by "reditum æstus," and the original Irish for "the tide was full before him" by "mare plenum supra caput ejus."

[5] *Carthach.* — See note [15], p. 581 *supra*.

[6] *Donncuan.* — Brother of King Brian Borumha. The death of Donncuan is entered in the *Ann. Four Mast.* at the year 948 (=950), and in the *Chron. Scotorum* under A.D. 949.

[7] *Between.*—etarru, B. Not in A.

[8] *Dun-Caillen.*—Dunkeld, in Perthshire.

[9] *Flaithbertach.* — The remarkable man whose obit is recorded above at

Domnall Ua Cetfadha,[1] the glory of Munster, died. The herenagh of Leithglenn was killed in the church door. A predatory expedition by Muirchertach[2] Ua Neill to the men of Bregha. But Gairbhedh Ua Cathasaigh,[3] King of Bregha, overtook him at Cassan-linne[4] when the tide was full before him; and Muirchertach[2] and many others fell there. Carthach,[5] son of Saerbrethach, King of Eoghanacht-Caisil, was burned in a house set on fire by the grandson of Longarcan son of Donncuan,[6] together with many nobles. A battle amongst the men of Alba between[7] themselves, in which Cronan, abbot of Dun-Caillen,[8] was killed.

Kal. Jan. Wednesd.; m. 20. A.D. 1046. Muiredach, son of Flaithbertach[9] Ua Neill, royal-heir of Ailech, and Aiteidh Ua hAiteidh, King of Ui-Echach-Ulad were burned in a house set on fire, by Cu-Ulad, son of Congalach, in Uachtar-tire.[10] Art Ua Ruairc, King of Connaught, was killed by the Cinel-Conaill. Ferghal Ua Ciardhai, King of Cairpri, was killed by Ua Flannacain, King of Tebhtha. Conchobar Ua Loingsigh, King of Dal-Araidhe, was killed by the son of Domnall Ua Loingsigh, in Leinster.[11] Maelpatraic Ua Bileoice, chief lector of Ard-Macha, and a paragon of piety and chastity, died at a good old age. Dubhdaleithe, son of Maelmuire, assumed the lectorship. [1046.]

Kal. Jan. Thursd.; m. 1. A.D. 1047. Great snow in this year, from the festival of Mary (in winter[12]) to the [1047.]

---

the year 1036. See note [9], p. 489 *supra*.

[10] *Uachtar-tire*; lit. "Upper (part) of the land." See Reeves's *Down and Connor*, p. 351, where *Uachtar-tire* (or *Watertiry*) is stated to be chiefly represented by certain townlands of the parish of Kilmegan, which are included in the barony of Lecale, co. Down.

[11] *Leinster*. — In the *Ann. Four Mast.* the place where Domnall Ua Loingsigh was killed is described as in Ui-Buidhe, a territory nearly co-extensive with the present barony of Ballyadams, in the Queen's county. See *Leabhar na g-ceart* (ed. O'Donovan), p. 214.

[12] *Winter*.—Added in a later hand in A. Not in B. The "festival of Mary" (or Lady-day) in winter falls on the 8th of December.

co feil Patraic, do na friṫ samail, co ro la ar n-daine 7 innile 7 fiaḋmil in ṁara 7 en. Natiuitas Domnaill mic Amalgaḋa .i. comarba Patraic. Muirchertaċ mac mic Moṫaḋan, ri .h. mBresail, do marbad i n-Ard maċa do Mataḋan .h. Ceilecan per dolum. Lann ingen mic Selbaċan, comarba Brigte, in pace quieuit. Niall .h. Ruairc do marbad la .h. Concobair. Creċsluaiġeḋ la Niall mac Mailseċlainn i mBreġu, co ro marḃ .h. nIffernan.

b. Kl. Ianair. ui. f.; l. xii. Anno domini M.° xl.° uiii.° Dunlang mac Dungail a fratribus suis occisus est. Fergal .h. Maelmuaiḋ ri fer Cell, Gillacolaim .h. hEigniġ airdriġ Airgiall, Cennfaelad .h. Cuill airdḟili Muman, Maelfaballl .h. hEiḋinn ri .h. Fiacraċ Aiḋne, mortui sunt. Cloṫna airchinnech imleċa Iḃair, Ferdomnaċ .h. Innascaiḋ comarba Finnen, Dunchad .h. Ceileċair comarba Ciarain Saiġri, in pace quieuerunt. Comarba Petair 7 da fer dec da aes graiḋ do eibiltin imaille fris, iar n-ol neime do rat doiḃ in comarba ro h-innarbanaḋ as reiṁe.

Kl. Ianair. i. f.; l. xx. iii. Anno domini M.° xl.° ix.° Amalġaiḋ comarba Patraic, xx. ix. annis transactis

[1] *Domnall.*—His appointment to the abbotship (or bishopric) of Armagh, in succession to his brother Maelisa, is noticed at the year 1091 *infra*. See Ware's *Works* (Harris's ed.), Vol. 1, pp. 50–1.

[2] *Matadhan Ua Ceilechain.*—The only person so named mentioned in these Annals is the Matadhan Ua Ceilechain, vice-abbot (or "prior," according to the *Four Masters*), whose obit is entered at A.D. 1063 *infra*. See note [7], p. 573, *supra*.

[3] *Successor of Brigit*; i.e. abbess of Kildare. The name of Lann does not appear in Archdall's very imperfect list of the abbots and abbesses of Kildare.

[4] *Ua Conchobair.*—Aedh Ua Conchobair (Aedh "of the gapped spear"), King of Connaught.

[5] *Ua h-Iffernain.* — This name, which is not uncommon in Meath, is now written Heffernan. But the Heffernans of Meath and Kildare are to be distinguished from the Heffernans of Limerick and Clare, who come of a different stock.

[6] *Dunlang.* — He is described as "Lord of Ui-Briuin-Cualann," and

festival of Patrick, for which no equal was found, which caused a great destruction of people and cattle, and of wild sea animals and birds. Birth of Domnall[1] son of Amalgaidh, *i.e.*, successor of Patrick. Muirchertach, grandson of Matadhan, King of the Ui-Bresail, was killed in Ard-Macha by Matadhan Ua Ceilechain,[2] through treachery. Lann, daughter of Mac Selbhachain successor of Brigit,[3] rested in peace. Niall Ua Ruairc was killed by Ua Conchobair.[4] A predatory expedition by Niall, son of Maelsechlainn, into Bregha, when he killed Ua h-Iffernain.[5]

Kal. Jan. Frid.; m. 21. A.D. 1048. Dunlang,[6] son [1048] BIS.
of Dungal, was slain by his brothers Ferghal Ua Maelmhuaidh, King of Fera-Cell; Gillacoluim Ua hEighnigh, chief King of Airghialla; Cennfaeladh Ua Cuill,[7] chief poet of Munster, [and] Maelfabhaill Ua hEidhinn, King of Ui-Fiachrach-Aidhne, died. Clothna, herenagh of Imlech-Ibhair;[8] Ferdomnach Ua Innascaigh, comarb of Finnen,[9] [and] Dunchad Ua Ceilechair, comarb of Ciaran of Saighir, rested in peace. The comarb of Peter,[10] and twelve of his companions along with him, died after drinking poison which the comarb who had been previously expelled had given them.

Kal. Jan. Sund., m. 23. A.D. 1049. Amalghaidh[11] [1049.]
comarb of Patrick, having spent twenty-nine years in

---

the "glory of the east of Ireland," in the *Ann. Four M.*

[7] *Ua Cuill.* — O'Quill (or Quill without the O'). The compositions of this poet have not survived. O'Reilly (*Irish Writers*, p. lxxiv.) mentions one poem of 160 verses.

[8] *Imlech-Ibhair.*—See note [4], p. 42, *supra*.

[9] *Comarb of Finnen;* i.e. successor of Finnian, Finnia, or Finnen, founder of the monastery of Clonard, co. Meath.

[10] *Comarb of Peter.*—The 'comarb' (or successor) of Peter here referred to was apparently Pope Damasus II., who was enthroned on the 17th of July, 1048, in succession to Benedict IXth, and died on the 8th of August following.

[11] *Amalghaidh.* — Some lines of poetry in praise of this prelate are added in the lower margin of fol. 58*b* in A. But they are not worth printing.

in principatu, penitens in Christo quieuit. Mael-
Fol. 59aa. cainniġ .h. Taiċliġ comarb Daiminnsi, Tuaṫal .h. Uail airchinnech Boiṫi conais, in pace quieuerunt. Ḟlaiṫbertaċ .h. Loingsiġ do marbad la mac Concobair .h. Loingsiġ. Muircertaċ mac Maelseċlainn do marbad la Concobar .h. Maelseċlainn, dar airṫeċ De 7 daine. Concobar .h. Cinnḟaelad, ri .h. Conaill Gabra, Iṁar .h. Beice ri .h. Meiṫ, occisi sunt. Dubdaleiṫi do ġabail n h-apdaine ar a firus leiginn in eodem die quo mortuus est Aṁalgaiḋ. Aeḋ .h. Forreiḋ do ġabail na firusa leiginn. In hoc anno natus est [F]laiṫ[bert]aċ .h. Laiḋ[g]nen, ri Fer[n]-muigi.

Kl. Ianair. ii. f.; l. iiii. Anno domini M.° L.° dominice incarnacionis. Maelruanaiḋ mac Conċoirne, ri Eile, Donnchad mac Gillaḟaelain ri .h. Failġi, occisi sunt. Ceall dara co na daimliag do loscaḋ. Maelan ferleiginn Cenannsa, sapientissimus omnium Hibernensium, Dubṫaċ mac Mileḋa comarba Cainniġ, hUa Scula airchinnech innsi Caṫaiġ, Maelduin .h. hEicertaiġ airchinnech Lotra, Cleirċen .h. Muineóc, tuir crabaid na hErenn, in pace quieuerunt. Diarmaid .h. Cele airchinnech Telċa Fortcern, Maelsechlainn mac Cinnḟaelad, mortui sunt. Scanner etir ḟiru Muiġi Iṫa 7 Airġiallu, i torċair Eochaid

---

[1] *Ua Taichligh.* — According to O'Donovan (*Four Mast.*, A.D. 1049, note *d*), this name is anglicised Tully and Tilly.

[2] *Both-Conais.*—See note [15], p. 361, *supra.*

[3] *Ua Cinnfaeladh.* — Now anglicised Kenealy (or Kennelly), without the O'. The name is still common in the counties of Kerry, Cork, and Limerick.

[4] *Ui-Conaill-Gabhra.*—Now represented by the baronies of Upper and Lower Connello, in the county of Limerick.

[5] *Ua Beice.*—O'Donovan states that this name has been made Beck and Peck. But it would be more likely to assume the form "Beaky," as consisting of two syllables.

[6] *Dubhdaleithe.*—See note [3], p. 478, *supra.*

[7] *Aedh Ua Forreidh.*—The *Four Masters*, in giving his obit at A.D.

the government, rested penitently in Christ. Maelcainnigh Ua Taichligh,[1] comarb of Daimhinis, Tuathal Ua Uail, herenagh of Both-Conais,[2] rested in peace. Flaithbertach Ua Loingsigh was slain by the son of Conchobar Ua Loingsigh. Muirchertach son of Maelsechlainn was killed by Conchobar Ua Maelsechlainn, against the will of God and men. Conchobar Ua Cinnfaeladh,[3] King of Ui-Conaill-Gabhra,[4] [and] Imhar Ua Beice,[5] King of Ui-Meith, were slain. Dubhdaleithe[6] assumed the abbotship, from his lectorship, on the same day in which Amhalghaidh died, Aedh Ua Forreidh[7] assumed the lectorship. In this year was born Flaithbertach[8] Ua Laidhgnen, King of Fernmhagh.

Kal. Jan. Mond.; m. 4. A.D. 1050, of the Incarnation[9] of the Lord. Maelruanaidh son of Cucoirne, King of Eli, Donnchad son of Gillafaelain, King of Ui-Failghi, were slain. Cill-dara, with its cathedral, was burned. Maelan, lector of Cenannas, the most learned of all Irishmen; Dubthach son of Milidh, comarb of Cainnech;[10] Ua Scula, herenagh of Inis-Cathaigh;[11] Maelduin Ua hEicertaigh, herenagh of Lothra;[12] [and] Cleirchen Ua Muineoc, tower of piety of Ireland, rested in peace. Diarmait Ua Cele, herenagh of Tulach-Fortchern,[13] [and] Maelsechlainn, son of Cennfaeladh, died. A conflict between the men of Magh-Itha and the Airghialla, in [1050.]

1056, incorrectly style him "bishop of Armagh."

[8] *Flaithbertach.*—This entry, which is added in the margin in MS. B., in the original hand, is not printed in O'Conor's version. The obit of Flaithbertach is entered at the year 1119 *infra.*

[9] *Incarnation.*—The words "Dominice incarnacionis," though not in MS. B., are found in the MS. Clar. 49, alleged by O'Donovan to be a translation of B.

[10] *Comarb of Cainnech*; i.e., successor of St. Canice, founder of the monastery of Aghaboe, in the Queen's county.

[11] *Inis-Cathaigh.*—Scattery Island, in the River Shannon.

[12] *Lothra.* — See note [6], p. 348, *supra.*

[13] *Tulach-Fortchern.* — Otherwise written Tulach-Ua-Felmedha. Tullow, in the barony of Rathvilly, co. Carlow.

.h. hOissein. Duḃdaleiṫi for cuairt ceniuil Eogain, co tuc tri ced do buaiḃ. Cluain mic Nois d'argain fo tri isind oen raiṫi, feacht o ṡil Anmchada, 7 fa dó o Calraiġib corna Sinnċaiḃ.

Kl. Ianair .iii. f.; l. xu. Anno domini M.° l.° i.° Muirchertaċ mac Bric, ri na nDese Muman, do lorcad do hUib Faelan. Mac Buatan mac Bric do marbad i n-damliac Lis moir do Maelsechlainn .h. Bric. Amalgaid mac Caṫail, ri iarthair Conacht, do ḋallad la hAeḋ .h. Concobair. Laiḋgnen mac Maelain, ri Gaileng, cum sua regina .i. ingen in Guit, do dul dia ailiṫri do Roim, 7 a ec. Mac Loċlainn do innarbad a riġi Telċa og, 7 Aeḋ .h. Ferġail do riġaḋ.

b. Fol. 59ab. Kl. Ianair .iiii. f.; l. xx. ui. Anno domini M.° l.° ii.°

---

[1] *Cows.*—Ecclesiastical dues were, of course, paid in kind at the time.

[2] *Cluain-mic-Nois.* — This entry, which is added in a later hand in A., is not in B., although it is given in English in the MS. Clar. 49, which has been supposed to be a 'translation' of MS. B.

[3] *Sil-Anmchadha.*—The tribe-name of the O'Maddens, who occupied the district now represented by the barony of Longford, co. Galway.

[4] *Calraighi.*—There were several tribes named Calraighi, one distinguished from the other by some word indicating local situation. See the Index to O'Donovan's ed. of the *Four Masters.* The Calraighe above referred to were of the sept called *Calraighi-an-chala*, whose name is still remembered, and applied (in the form Calry) to the parish of Ballyloughloe, in the barony of Clonlonan, county of Westmeath. Down to the 17th century this territory was the patrimony of the Magawleys; but the name of Magawley (Mac Amhalghaidh) is seldom met there now. See O'Donovan's ed. of *O'Dugan*, note [46].

[5] *Sinnachs* (pron. *Shinnaughs*).—This was an offensive name (*sinnach* meaning 'fox') given to the family of O'Catharnaigh (or, as the name would be now written, O'Kearney), from the tradition that they were the murderers of the poet Cuan Ua Lochain. See note [1], p. 554 *supra*, and the *Chron. Scot.* (ed. Hennessy), note [3], p. 264. The author of the version in Clar. 49 has "Cuan O'Lochain, Archpoet of Ireland, killed treacherously by the men of Tehva, ancestors of the Foxes. They stunk afterwards, whereby they go the name of Foxes."

[6] *M[oon]* 15.—The age of the moon is set down as xx. in A., but this is wrong. B. has xv,, which is correct.

[7] *Son of Buatan.*—The *Ann. of Tigernach*, and the *Four Mast.*, have "Faelan, son of Bratan." The author of the version in Clar. 49 has "Maelbruadar mac Brick," which seems corrupt.

which Eochaidh Ua hOssein fell. Dubhdaleithe on a visitation of Cinel-Eoghain, when he brought away 300 cows.[1] Cluain-mic-Nois[2] was plundered thrice in the same quarter [of a year],—once by the Sil-Anmchadha,[3] and twice by the Calraighi,[4] with the Sinnachs.[5]

Kal. Jan. Tuesd.; m. 15°. A.D. 1051. Muirchertach, [1051.]
son of Brec, King of the Desi-Mumhan, was burned by the Ui-Faelain. The son of Buatan,[7] son of Brec, was killed in the 'daimliac' of Lis-mor by Maelsechlainn,[8] grandson of Brec. Amalgaidh son of Cathal, King of the West of Connaught, was blinded by Aedh Ua Conchobair. Laidhgnen son of Maelan,[9] King of Gailenga, with his queen, *i.e.*, the daughter of the Got,[10] went to Rome in pilgrimage, and died.[11] Mac Lochlainn was expelled from the kingship of Telach-og, and Aedh Ua Ferghail was made king.

Kal. Jan. Wednesd.; m. 26. A.D. 1052.[12] Domnall [1052.] BIS.

---

[8] *Maelsechlainn.* — Called "Maelsechlainn, son of Muirchertach, son of Brec," in the *Ann. Four Mast.*

[9] *Maelan;* i.e. Maelan Ua Leochain. See note [2], p. 542 *supra.*

[10] *The Got.*—See note [5], p. 562 *supra.*

[11] *Died.*—The translator in Clar. 49 states that the pilgrims "died by the way." In the Annals of *Tigernach* it is stated that Laidhgnen died "in the east, after coming from Rome." But the *Four Masters* represent Laidhgnen and his wife as having died on their return journey.

[12] *A.D.* 1052.—A note in an old hand in B., in the space between the last entry for 1051 and the first entry for 1052, has is e fa ri Ulad anno 1052 Niall mac nEochoda, qui venit isto anno go hOssraiġe. Ri Gall .i. Echmarcach mac Ragnaill ar na innarba o ri[g] Laigen .i. Diarmaid mac Mail na m-bo, 7 in riġe do fein de sin. "The King of Ulidia in 1052 was Niall, son of Eochaidh, who came in the same year to Ossory. The King of the Foreigners, i.e. Echmarcach, son of Ragnall, was expelled by the King of Leinster, i.e., Diarmaid, son of Mael-na-mbo, who had the kingship [of Dublin] thereby." See Todd's *Cogadh Gaedhel,* &c., p. 291, note ([22]). The learned author does not seem to have been acquainted with the entry just given, which is not in the Clar. 49 version of this Chronicle, or in Dr. O'Conor's edition of MS. B., although it seems of sufficient interest to be reproduced. The record of the expulsion from Dublin of the Danish King Echmarcach, as it appears in the *Ann. of Tigernach* and the *Four Masters,* would represent him merely as going on a voyage "over the sea."

Domnall ban .h. Briain do marbad do Connachtaiḃ. Domnall mac Gillachrist mic Concual[n]ge occisus est o riġ fer Rois. Broen mac Maelmorḋai, ri Laigen, do ec i Colanea. Macraiṫ .h. Donnchaḋa, ri Eoganachta Caisil, do ec. Echtigern .h. hAġrain, comarba Ciaran 7 Coman, Muiredaċ .h. Sinaċan, maer Muman, in pace dormierunt. Gillapatraic mac Domnaill, secnap aird Maċa, do marbad do mac Arċon .h. Ceilecan a mebail.

Kl. Ianair. ui. f., l. uii. Anno domini M.° l.° iii.° Mac na h-aiḋċi .h. Ruairc, ridomna Connacht, a marbad do Diarmait .h. Cuinn a n-innsi Loċa arbaċ. Muiredaċ mac Diarmata, airchinnech Rois cre, hUa Ruadrach airchinnech Termoinn ḟeicin, Flaiṫbertaċ .h. Maelḟaḃaill ri Cairce Bracaiḋe, Doilgen uasal ṡacart ard Maċa, Domnall .h. Cele airchinnech Slane, Murchad .h. Beollan airchinnech Droma cliaḃ, omnes in pace dormierunt. Creċ la mac Loċlainn 7 la firu Muiġe Iṫa for cenel mBinniġ Loċa droċait, co rucsat tri .c. bo, 7 co ro marbsat Dubemna mac Cinaeḋa, secnap Cluana fiacna, 7 Cumaċa mac Claircen, moer Dail cais. Maelcron

[1] *Domnall Ban Ua Briain.*—Domnall O'Brien "the Fair." The third son of Donogh, son of Brian Borumha, according to Dr. O'Brien. See Vallancey's *Collect. de Rebus Hibernicis*, Vol. I., p. 552.

[2] *Colanea.*—Cologne, on the Rhine. The history of the famous Irish monastery of Cologne has not been sufficiently examined. See Colgan's *Acta SS.*, p. 107; O'Conor's *Rer. Hib. Script.*, vol. 4, p. 327, and Lanigan's *Eccl. Hist.*, vol. 3, p. 406.

[3] *Steward.* — The *Four Masters* say "Patrick's steward" (maor Patraic).

[4] *Mac-na-haidche.*—This is a nickname, not a Christian name, and means "son of the night," applied to him, probably, in allusion to his having been frequently engaged in nocturnal forays.

[5] *Loch-Arbhach.*—Lough Arrow, on the borders of the counties of Sligo and Roscommon.

[6] *Herenagh.*—In the *Annals of the F. M.* (A.D. 1052), Muiredach is called *comarba* (or successor) of Cronan, founder of Ros-cré.

[7] *Termon-Fecin.* — Termonfeckin, co. Louth.

[8] *Carraic-Brachaidhe.* — See note [16], p. 369 *supra*.

[9] *Magh-Itha.*—"Plain of Ith"; a

Ban Ua Briain[1] was slain by Connaughtmen. Domnall, son of Gillachrist, son of Cucual[n]ge, was killed by the King of Fera-Rois. Braen son of Maelmordha, King of Leinster, died in Colanea.[2] Macraith, grandson of Donnchad, King of Eoghanacht-Caisil, died. Echtigern Ua h-Aghrain, comarb of Ciaran and Coman, Muiredach Ua Sinachan, steward[3] of Munster, 'fell asleep' in peace. Gillapatraic son of Domnall, vice-abbot of Ard-Macha, was killed by the son of Archu Ua Celechain, in treachery.

Kal. Jan. Frid., m. 7. A.D. 1053. Mac-na-haidche[4] Ua Ruairc, royal-heir of Connaught, was killed by Diarmait Ua Cuinn, in an island of Loch-arbhach.[5] Muiredach son of Diarmait, herenagh[6] of Ros-cre; Ua Ruadrach, herenagh of Termon-Fecin;[7] Flaithbertach Ua Maelfabhaill, King of Carraic-Brachaidhe;[8] Doilgen, noble priest of Ard-Macha; Domnall Ua Cele, herenagh of Slane, [and] Murchadh Ua Beollain, herenagh of Druim-cliabh—all 'fell asleep' in peace. A depredation [was committed] by MacLochlainn and the men of Magh-Itha[9] on the Cinel-Binnigh of Loch-Drochait,[10] when they carried off 300 cows, and killed Dubhemna son of Cinaedh, vice-abbot of Cluain-Fiachna,[11] and Cu-Macha son of Clairchen, steward of Dal-Cais.[12] Mael- [1053.]

district corresponding to the southern half of the present barony of Raphoe, co. Donegal. See Reeves's ed. of *Colton's Visitation*, p. 69, note [a], and other references given in the Index to that work, under *Magh-Itha*.

[10] *Cinel-Binnigh of Loch-Drochait.*—There were at least four distinct families of the Cinel-Binnigh (descendants of Eochaidh Binnech, son of Eoghan, son of Niall Nine-hostager), each of which was distinguished by its 'local habitation.' The territory occupied by the several branches of the Cinel-Binnigh is supposed to have comprised the northern part of the present barony of Loughinsholin, co. Londonderry. See Reeves's *Colton's Visitation*, pp. 73-4. But the mention of Cluain-Fiachna (Clonfeakle, barony of Dungannon, co. Tyrone) in connection with this raid would seem to indicate that the territory of the Cinel-Binnigh extended further south.

[11] *Cluain-Fiachna.*—See last note.

[12] *Steward of Dal-Cais.* — Dal-Cais was the tribe-name of the O'Briens of Thomond and their correlatives. The Translator in Clar. 49, renders moeṗ by "serjeant." It is not easy to conceive what could

mac Caṫail, ri Breġ, a marbad do U Riacain. Donnchad .h. Ceallaċain, ridomna Caisil, do marbad d'Osraiġiḃ. Niall .h. Eigniġ, ri fer Manaċ, do marbad do feraib Luirg. Coċlan ri Delmna a suis per dolum occissus est.

Kl. Ianair .iiii. f.; l. x.iiii. Anno domini m.° l.° iiii.° Imar mac Arailt, ri Gall, do ecaiḃ. Aeḋ .h. Fergail, ri Telċa og, 7 mac Arċon .h. Ceilecain, ri .h. mBresail, do marbad do feraiḃ Fernmuiġi. Dubgal .h. hEdacain, ri .h. Niallan, do marbad do U Laiṫein. Maidm Finnmuiġi for Uib Meiṫ 7 for Uachtar tire, ria nUib Eachach, du itorcair in Croibderg ridomna Uachtair tire. Aeḋ mac
Fol. 59*ba*. Cenneitiġ mic Duinnċuain, muire clainne Tairrdelbaig, do marbad do Connachtaiḃ. Caṫ etir firu Alban 7 Saxanu, i torcradar tri mile do feraiḃ Alban, 7 mile co leṫ do Saxanaiḃ im Dolfinn mac Finntuir. Loċ suiḋe Odrain i sleiḃ Guaire do eluḋ

---

have brought the steward or "serjeant" of Dal-Cais into the heart of Ulster, at a time when the O'Briens of the south and the MacLochlainns of the north were on very unfriendly terms.

[1] *Donnchadh Ua Cellachain*, i.e. Donnchadh, descendant of Cellachan Caisil, King Cashel [or Munster], whose obit is given at the year 953 *supra*.

[2] *Fera-Luirg.*—"Men of Lurg." See notes [10], p. 447, and [14], p. 575, *supra*.

[3] *Cochlan.*—This entry, which is added by a later hand in A., is not in B. The Cochlan here mentioned was the progenitor from whom the MacCoghlans, of Delvin MacCoghlan (now represented by the barony of Garrycastle, King's county), derived their name.

[4] *Telach-og.*—See note [7], p. 429, *supra*.

[5] *Ua Celechain.*—See note [7], p. 573, *supra*.

[6] *Finnmagh.* — O'Donovan alleges this place to be the same as "Finvoy, in the county of Down." (*Four Mast.*, A.D. 1054, note r). But there seems to be no place called Finvoy in the co. Down; though there are a townland and parish of the name in the barony of Kilconway, co. Antrim.

[7] *Uachtar-tirè.*—For the situation of this territory, and the meaning of the name, see Reeves's *Down and Connor*, p. 351, note w.

[8] *Donnchuan.* — This Donnchuan (ob. 948, *Four Mast.*), was the eldest brother of King Brian Borumha. His

cron son of Cathal, King of Bregha, was killed by Ua Riacain. Donnchad Ua Cellachain,[1] royal heir of Caisel, was killed by the Osraighi. Niall Ua hEignigh, King of Fera-Manach, was killed by the Fera-Luirg.[2] Cochlan,[3] King of Delmna, was treacherously slain by his own people.

Kal. Jan. Saturd.; m. 18. A.D. 1054. Imhar son of Aralt, King of the Foreigners, died. Aedh Ua Ferghail, King of Telach-og,[4] and the son of Archu Ua Celechain,[5] King of the Ui-Bresail, were slain by the men of Fernmhagh. Dubhgal Ua hEdacain, King of Ui-Niallain, was killed by Ua Laithein. The victory of Finnmagh[6] over the Ui-Meith and Uachtar-tirè,[7] by the Ui-Echach, where the Croibderg, royal heir of Uachtar-tire, was slain. Aedh, son of Cennedigh, son of Donnchuan,[8] steward of Clann-Tairdelbaigh,[9] was killed by Connaughtmen. A battle between the men of Alba and the Saxons, in which there were slain 3,000 of the men of Alba, and 1,500 of the Saxons, including Dolfinn son of Finntur. The lake of Suidhe-Odhrain[10] in Sliabh- [1054.]

grandson Aedh, whose death is above recorded, is described as muirn 7 ordan (the "delight and glory") of the Dal-Cais (*Four Mast.* 1054). O'Conor translates the term maire ("steward") of this chronicle "Maritimus dux;" probably thinking that maire was the same as muir, the Irish word for "sea" (Lat. *mare*).

[9] *Clann-Tairdelbaigh*; i.e. the family of Tairdelbach (Torlogh, or Terence), son of Tadbg (sl. 1023, *supra*), son of Brian Borumha. He was the progenitor of the principal branch of the O'Brien race. Tairdelbach, who was King of Munster (and "of the greater part of Ireland," according to some authorities), died in 1086. In giving his obit at that year *infra*, this Chronicle describes him as King of Ireland, as he is also described in the *Ann Loch-Cé*. But in the *Chron. Scotorum* (1082=1086), Tairdelbach is called King of the "greater part" (*urmoir*) of Ireland; while the *Four Masters* term him King of Ireland co fressabra ("with opposition").

[10] *Suidhe-Odhrain.* — The name of this lake is now represented by that of the townland of Seeoran, in the parish of Knockbride, barony of Clankee, co. Cavan, (where there is no trace of a lake). This is one of the *mirabilia Hiberniæ*. See Todd's *Irish Nennius*, p. 213.

a n-dereḋ aidċe ḟeile Miċeil, co n-dechaid isin Fabaill, quod non auditum est ab antiquis.

Kl. Ianair .i. f.; l. xx. ix. Anno domini M.° l.° u.° Domnall ruaḋ .h. Briain do marbad la .h. nEiḋinn. Maelmartain mac Assida, comarba Comġaill, Coluim .h. Caṫail airchinnech Ruis ailiṫir, Oḋor .h. Muireḋaiġ airchinnech Lusca, Gillapatraic ri Ossaiġi, Fiaċra .h. Corcrain, omnes in domino dormierunt. Maidm ria Tairrdelbach .h. mBriain for Murchad .h. mBriain, i torcradar .iiii. cet im .u. toisiuċa dec. Caṫ Martartaiġi, ria Duḃdaleiṫi comarba Patraic, for mac Loingsiġ .h. Maelseċlainn .i. comarba Finnein 7 Coluim cille, du i torcradar ili.

Kl. Ianair .ii. f.; l. x. Anno domini M.° l.° ui.° Caṫusaċ mac Sirrgarḃain, comarba Cainniġ i Cianacht, Cetfaid cenn cleireċ Muman, quieuerunt. Aeḋ .h. Forreiḋ, ard ferleiginn Aird Maċa, in .lxx. u. aetatis sue anno, in pace quieuit.

Ro tect roneiḃ cein ro mar,
Aeḋ .h. Forreiḋ in sui sean;
hi .xiiii. calend Iuil,
Luiḋ int escop ciuin ar ceul.

Gormgal, prim anmcara innsi Darcairgrenn, plenus

[1] *Fabhall*— O'Donovan thought that this is the name of a stream "which discharges itself into the Boyne"; the name of which is obsolete. (*Four Mast.*, A.D. 1054, note a.)

[2] *Ua hEidhin.*—He was King of Ui-Fiachrach-Aidhne (according to the *Four Masters*); which territory seems to have been co-extensive with the diocese of Kilmacduagh, in the south of the county of Galway. See O'Donovan's ed. of O'Dubhagain's *Topogr. Poem*, note 356. The family name Ua hEidhin, represented as "O'Heyn" in Clar. 49, is now generally anglicised "Hynes."

[3] *Comarb of Comghall;* i.e. successor of Comghall (or abbot of Bangor, co. Down). His name does not appear in Archdall's very imperfect list of the abbots of that important establishment.

[4] *Ros-ailithir.* — Now known as Rosscarbery, in the county of Cork.

[5] *Tairdelbach Ua Briain.* — Or Torlogh O'Brien. See note [u], p. 595.

[6] *Murchadh.*—He was the son of Donogh, son of Brian Borumha, and first cousin of Torlogh, who was the son of Tadhg the brother of Donogh.

[7] *Martartech;* lit. "relic house." This entry is not given by the *Four*

Guaire stole away in the end of the night of the festival of Michael, and went into the Fabhall,[1] a thing that had not been heard of from ancient times.

Kal. Jan. Sund.; m. 29. A.D. 1055. Domnall Ruadh Ua Briain was killed by Ua hEidhin.[2] Maelmartain son of Assidh, comarb of Comghall;[3] Colum Ua Cathail, herenagh of Ros-ailithir;[4] Odhor Ua Muiredaigh, herenagh of Lusca; Gillapatraic, King of Osraighi, [and] Fiachra Ua Corcrain—all 'fell asleep' in the Lord. A victory by Tairdelbach Ua Briain[5] over Murchad[6] Ua Briain, in which 400 men were slain, along with fifteen chieftains. The battle of Martartech,[7] by Dubhdaleithe, comarb of Patrick, over the son[8] of Loingsech Ua Maelsechlainn, *i.e.* the comarb of Finnen[9] and Colum-Cille,[9] in which many were slain. [1055.]

Kal. Jan. Mond.; m. 10. A.D. 1056. Cathasach son of Gerrgarbhain, comarb of Cainnech in Cianachta,[10] and Cetfaidh, head of the clerics of Munster, rested. Aedh Ua Forreidh, chief lector of Ard-Macha, in the 75th year of his age rested in peace. [1056.]

He obtained[11] great fame whilst he lived—
Aedh Ua Forreidh, the old sage—;
On the fourteenth of the Kalends of July
The mild bishop went to heaven.

Gormgal, chief soul-friend, of the Island of Darciargrenn,[12]

Masters. See *Ann. Loch-Cé* (ed. Hennessy), note [3] *ad an.*

[8] *Son.* — His name is given as "Murchadh" in the *Ann. of Tigernach.*

[9] *Comarb of Finnen and Coluim-Cille;* i.e. abbot of Clonard and Kells, in the county of Meath.

[10] *Comarb of Cainnech in Cianachta;* i.e. successor of St. Canice, or abbot of Dromachose (or Termonkenny) in the barony of Keenaght, co. Londonderry. See note [7], p. 510, *supra.*

[11] *Obtained.*—The original of this stanza, which is not in B., is added in the lower margin of fol. 59*b* in A., with a mark of reference to the place where it might be introduced into the text.

[12] *Darcairgrenn.*—This is probably the genit. form of Darcairgriu. But no island of that name is known to the Editor; nor does the name appear in any of the other Irish chronicles. See under the year 1018 *supra*, where the obit is given of a "Gormghal of Aird-ailen, chief soul-friend of Ireland," and the note regarding "Ard-ailen" (or "High Island"), p. 541, note [11].

dierum in penitentia pausauit. Taḋg mac in cleiriġ .h. Concobair do marbad do Uib Maine. Etrú mac Lobraḋa, toisech Manaċ, tuir ordain Ulad, in penitentia mortuus est. Creċ la Niall mac Maelsechlainn for Dal n-Araide, co tuc .xx. c. do buaiḃ 7 tri .xx. duine do ḃrait. Gillamura mac Ocan, rechtaire Telċa og, mortuus est. Flann mainistreċ, aird ferleiġinn 7 sui senċusa Erenn, in uita eterna requiescit. Tene gelain do ṫiachtain co ro marb triar ic Disiurt Tola, 7 mac leiġinn oc Surd, 7 co ro brisin bile. Creċ do ċuaiḋ Eochaiḋ .h. Flaiṫen aiḋce nodlaic mór, i maig nIṫa, co tuc .u. cet bo coruici

Fol. 59bb. uissin .i. co h-oḃuinn muiġi hUaṫa, 7 forascsat na bu isin obainn, 7 ro baete oċtur ar .xl. diḃ, im Cuilennan mac Dergain.

---

[1] *The Clerech*; i e. the Cleric.

[2] *Manachs*.—In the *Ann. Four Mast.* (*id. an.*) the name of the sept is written "Monachs" which seems the more correct form. See O'Donovan's *Four Masters*, A D. 1171, note x, and the authorities there cited.

[3] *Gillamura* — See this person mentioned above at the year 1024.

[4] *Telach-og*.—See note [6], p. 526 *supra*.

[5] *Flann Mainistrech*; i.e. "Flann of the Monastery" [Monasterboice, co. Louth]. Flann was Lector of the Monastery (not Abbot, as O'Reilly says, *Ir. Writers*, p. lxxv., *q. v.*) See O'Curry's *Manners and Customs*, Vol. II., pp. 149–169.

[6] *Disert-Tola*.—The "desert" (or retreat) of Tola. Now Dysart, in the parish of Killulagh, barony of Delvin, co. Westmeath.

[7] *Tree*.—bile. Meaning a sacred tree. Written indile (for in bile, "the tree"), in *Ann. Loch Cé* at A.D. 1056, where see note (in Hennessy's

full of days, rested in penitence. Tadhg, son of the 'Clerech'[1] Ua Conchobair, was killed by the Ui-Maine. Etru son of Lobraidh, chief of the Manachs,[2] pillar of the glory of Ulidia, died in penitence. A predatory expedition by Niall, son af Maelsechlainn, against the Dal-Araidhe, when he brought away 2,000 cows, and sixty persons as prisoners. Gillamura,[3] son of Ocan, steward of Telach-og,[4] died. Flann Mainistrech,[5] the chief lector and historical sage of Ireland, rested in eternal life. Lightning came and killed three persons at Disert-Tola,[6] and a student at Sord, and broke down the tree.[7] Eochaidh Ua Flaithen went on a predatory expedition on Christmas night into Magh-Itha, when he brought 500 cows to a water, *i.e.*, to the river of Magh-Uatha;[8] and they[9] left the cows in the river;[10] and forty-eight of them were drowned, along with Cuilennan son of Dergan.

---

ed.) In MS. B. the words are ın mıle (which O'Conor prints *in inile*, and translates "et confregit arcem"). The original reading of MS. A. was also ın mıle; but the old scribe added a "punctum delens" under the letter m, and substituted a b, to correct the text to ın bıle.

[8] *Magh-Uatha.*—O'Donovan states that the name of this river is written abainn Maiġe nIthа (i.e. the River of the Magh-Itha), "in the Annals of Ulster. (*Four Mast.*, A.D. 1056, note n.) But he must have been misled by the version in Clar. 49, which has "River of Magh-Itha," as the name is *Muighi* [genit. of *Magh-*]*h Uatha* in A., and *M-Ua·ha* in B. Regarding Magh-Itha, see O'Donovan's ed. of the *Ann. Four Mast.*, A.D. 1177, note o.

[9] *They;* i.e. the cow stealers.

[10] *In the river.*—:ſın obuınd, B.

END OF VOL. I.